A Century for Debate

1789-1914

Problems in the Interpretation of European History

EDITED BY
PETER N. STEARNS
Rutgers, The State University

Dodd, Mead & Company
NEW YORK 1969 TORONTO

Library of Congress Catalog Card Number: 69-18466

Printed in the United States of America

Introduction

THE nineteenth century has a somewhat special place in the literature of historical controversy. Any period of the past produces debate. It may be that the nineteenth century, extended to include the French Revolution and the years before World War I, has given rise to more argument than most centuries, because the issues are close enough to our own age to seem particularly important and are, by the same token, difficult to interpret. But the sheer number of debates is not the main point. More interesting is the combination of distance and involvement that characterizes so many of the controversies. The values and problems of the nineteenth century are related to our own, but they are not the same. Historical treatment of many issues has evolved within the last few decades to a rather detached and analytical approach, or so it seems. Yet varieties of partisanship are seldom absent, for the nineteenth century remains too close. It is still possible to capture the spirit of disagreement in the century itself, which develops a vital flavor in many accounts while preventing uniformity of view. Many historians also feel a need to use the nineteenth century to show where our own century has gone wrong, though they disagree widely in their focus. Our proximity to the nineteenth century has, most basically, prevented a consensus on what the character of the century was, even of the sort that provides a clear target for dissenters. Most historians of the century as a whole or of major developments within it feel that their subject had a fundamental direction, because so many people during the century assumed that there was a purpose in their history and because we know to some extent how the leading themes turned out. Few historians can translate this sense of direction into a clear statement, and fewer still agree on what the statement should be.

A selection of fifteen topics of historical controversy is necessarily incomplete for an age so rich in debate. There has been some bias toward the later part of the century and toward social history, on grounds of more important or more recent and novel discussion. But the selection is, hopefully, representative in several senses. At least one debate in each major national history is included, and at least one in each of the leading topical approaches to modern history, such as intellectual or diplomatic history.

More important, a number of different types of issue are presented. The most obvious and precise focus for discussion is an outstanding event, such as the Reform Bill of 1832 in England or the emancipation of the serfs in Russia. Around such events are the classic ingredients for controversy: a sufficiently narrow subject for the disputes over facts to be clear, yet a wide field for speculation over causes and impact, particularly when the results are seen to have ongoing historical importance.

Important historical debates have occurred over the evolution of leading institutions and even nations in the nineteenth century, apart from any single event. Where, for example, was Germany heading? To what extent was the character of twentieth-century Germany formed in the previous period? Some historians work above all to show the links between past and present, and may be inclined to believe in an almost inevitable movement to the known result. Others rebel against such a rigorous approach because they have studied a particular period in its own terms or perhaps because they are uncomfortable with any framework that does not allow some freedom of choice. Arguments over the direction of nineteenth-century historical developments are prevalent because historians are unusually tempted to try to explain their own age by their studies of the past. Yet historians disagree on the possibility of such direct applications of their discipline, and some feel that a preoccupation with the present distorts historical treatment. And there is always conflict over what vision of the present is applied to the past. Echoes of this great issue in historical method are evident in many of the controversies on specific topics in the nineteenth century.

Finally, an important category of debate concerns the definition of widely used terms and concepts in the nineteenth century. Terms such as "middle class" or "liberalism" are current in all sorts of historical literature. Rather recently, in some cases, historians have begun to investigate the meaning of such terms, sometimes challenging their utility. In certain instances the result has been a very specific and interesting argument, focusing on a particular historical instance of the term in question; in other cases the literature remains more diffuse, with controversy stemming from the very different standpoints from which historians have approached their topic. In issues of this sort especially, a full debate has yet to be organized, and existing controversies point up the need for further study.

The fifteen topics in this book interweave three or four major themes which dominate the nineteenth century. The impact of the French Revolution is discussed in Chapter 1, but the problem of the working out of French revolutionary principles emerges in several subsequent sections, particularly those on the revolution of 1848 and on liberalism. The nature and results of industrialization—the greatest single development of the nineteenth century—are treated in many discussions of social and political developments. The challenge to rationalism is specifically raised in the discussion of romanticism, but continuing manifestations of this challenge can be seen in several later chapters. Finally, sections on Germany, Austria-Hungary, and Russia raise a basic question of the relationship of central and eastern Europe to developments in the west, for in all three states the problem of merging distinctive social and intellectual traditions with modernization in western terms was felt in many ways.

The historians represented in each of the chapters have a variety of backgrounds. They should be assessed in light of the period in which they wrote, their nationality, and their political views. Similar backgrounds in these various senses may reveal important continuities in historical approach even on quite different topics. Most of the discussions also mix "professional" historians with writers from other disciplines. Here, too, evaluation is necessary. Do professional historians emerge as generally more precise but also more timid than other historical writers? In all the discussions historians have been chosen who provide an important view of the topic, and not simply because they disagree radically with a standard approach. There is, for example, no effort to include a Marxist interpretation of every topic simply because it is Marxist. The result is, sometimes, a more subtle controversy than a clash of general ideologies would produce, but a more significant one by the same token. Insofar as possible, snippets have been eschewed in favor of reasonably extended and coherent discussions. Footnote references have been removed from most selections, but interested students are encouraged to refer to the original works for further suggestions for reading.

I am deeply grateful to Mr. Marvin Ciporen for his assistance in preparing this book. Professor Gordon Wright has given valuable advice at several stages, and his own book on the twentieth century, *The Age of Controversy,* provides the model for the present work.

I wish to thank the many individuals and firms who have granted permission to publish the selections in this volume.

PETER N. STEARNS

Contents

Chapter I.

THE IMPACT OF THE FRENCH REVOLUTION

THE FRENCH REVOLUTION has, understandably, given rise to a passionate historiography. Since the publication of Edmund Burke's *Reflections on the Revolution in France* (1790), a conservative school has bitterly attacked the whole basis of the revolution. To this group, the revolution's impact was wholly destructive, for it stemmed from a falsely abstract political ideology. In the short run, the revolution meant above all terror and dictatorship, inevitable results of the presumptuous destruction of the traditions and institutions that held society together. To later generations of conservative historians, the legacy of the revolution was not only this example, which should teach the folly of political rationalism and consequent disorder, but also the tragic implantation of false principles, such as equality of rights and democracy, into actual political systems.

A second historical school was also based on political preconceptions; it, too, saw the motivating force of the revolution in a set of political ideals. But to the liberals, these ideals were basically good and fruitful. The liberals admit the revolutionary excesses and they detest the Terror. They find the core of the revolution, however, in the principles of 1789 and in the later Girondist period. The thrust of the revolution was a general attack on the privileged aristocracy and its ally, the Church. Out of this attack developed political institutions that carry through the nineteenth and into the twentieth century, institutions that are good and progressive: democratic and parliamentary government, legal equality, and freedom for economic advance.

Marxist historians cannot view the revolutionaries as a single force. They agree with the liberals about the obvious political achievements of the revolution, but see these as expressing the triumph of the middle class alone. Their interest lies primarily in pointing to the rebellion of the common people, in town and country alike. The rebellion failed, at least in the towns; even Robespierre is seen as a bourgeois spokesman, vaulted to power by the agitation of the masses but opposed to their demands for economic protection. To the Marxists the legacy of the revolution was twofold, the emergence of political and economic dominance of the middle class and the establishment of a vital precedent for protest against this dominance.

The three principal ideological approaches, though philosophical in orientation, do not lead merely to different interpretations of the revolution as a whole. They have produced major differences in what aspects of the revolution are studied, and by what methods.

The conservative school has produced vivid portraits of the revolutionary leaders and of leading revolutionary events. The chief liberal contributions have been political analyses of the first four years of the revolution, with attention to the diffusion of Enlightenment ideas. The Marxists, after a brief fling at glorifying the radical phase of the revolution, have turned chiefly to social analysis, particularly to studies of the common people. All three of these approaches continue to find their advocates, though broadly Marxist assumptions have dominated most recent French studies. Certainly, the historiography of the revolution provides a fascinating example of the interaction between a momentous event and its later study. All the major rifts created during the revolution itself are mirrored in the leading schools of interpretation. Even scholars outside France, though capable of taking a somewhat more detached and synthetic view, have been drawn into the debate largely on ideological terms. American interpretations, for example, have generally upheld the liberal view, though they usually express a willingness to recognize the validity of some aspects of the Marxists' social analysis.

Until relatively recently, a presentation of the major ideological approaches to the revolution would have adequately summed up the principal issues of historical debate. A few important studies did not fit neatly into this framework, most notably Alexis de Tocqueville's *L'Ancien régime et la révolution* [Paris, 1856]; and certainly there were important differences of quality and approach within the major schools. Since World War II, however, several new issues have been raised that only partly fit the distinctions set forth by ideological views. Significantly, scholars outside France have played an important role in formulating the new problems.

One issue concerns the geographical dimensions of the revolution. Obviously, events in France had a major impact on much of the rest of Europe and even on the New World. It has been customary to see this impact simply as a result of some imitation and much imposition by French armies; the distinctiveness of events in France has been upheld. But it is possible to take another view, which does not deny unique aspects of French developments, but which also sees the revolution as part of a larger upheaval in both Europe and the Americas. This view stems from the liberal school, for it stresses the generality of the political ideas that stemmed from the Enlightenment. Whatever its derivation, it clearly raises new issues and forces a reassessment both of the heritage of the revolution outside France and of the causes of revolution within.[1]

Yet another new approach raises the question, what changed? This view, without denying important political developments, sees the essence of revolution in its social effects. But it denies that the social basis of the revolution was in any way simple. The lower classes were not united; indeed, disputes within their ranks often overwhelmed any concern with upper-class dominance. And most important, the middle class was not united. What the revolution did, in France, was to solidify the power of conservative elements of society at all levels. Without doubt, the formal principles of the revolution were revolutionary, but ironically, they may have had a more dynamic effect outside France than within. It remains unclear what future this line of analysis will have, partly because it so thoroughly defies the traditional framework of argument about the revolution. Marxists have contributed to the view, by their increasingly subtle statements of the fuzziness of class structure during the revolution; but they probably cannot accept this view because of their more sweeping notions of what a "bourgeois" revolution must mean. In addition the view rests on

1. See R. R. Palmer, *The Age of Democratic Revolution,* 2 vols. (Princeton: Princeton University Press, 1959–64).

assumptions about nineteenth-century French society that are beyond the competence of many students of the revolution itself.

None of the students of the French Revolution would deny its massive importance for nineteenth-century history. Few would question that, in essence, the revolution opened the nineteenth century, setting up basic lines of ideological debate, political dispute, and, to some extent at least, social conflict. But, in assessing the heritage of the revolution, the differences in basic approach emerge quite clearly. Even scholars who agree on what happened during the revolution and substantially concur about what caused it, may differ widely on what resulted; for this is the most difficult as well as the most important question of all. From the major ideological disputes come, first of all, a judgment of whether the revolution was good or bad; and then, if good, what was good about it. Ideology also affects the choice of whether to view the impact of the revolution in primarily political or social terms; in both cases, ideology can lead to vigorous expressions of faith, in either a political theory or a segment of society. Ideology is not the only cause of differences in interpretation, as has been indicated. And certainly variations in what aspects of the revolution are studied and in the methods used in the study supplement purely ideological factors; some of the most recent debate over the revolution's impact stems from new efforts at objectivity. But the depth and diversity of interpretations reflect more than calm, scholarly argument. For what is involved is an assessment of one of the monumental events of modern times, and, through this, of the quality of modern life itself.

1. THOMAS CARLYLE: The French Revolution: A History *

Thomas Carlyle (1795–1881), the British historian and critic, was a bitter opponent of many of the major trends of the nineteenth century. Through intuition, even passion, he sought to remedy the deficiencies of rationalism and materialism, and his histories were a major weapon in his struggle. His account of the French Revolution was both a bitter denunciation of its brutality and folly and a Romantic effort to capture its essential energy. This is not, of course, a calm or detailed narrative. A far more elaborate presentation of the conservative interpretation can be found in Hippolyte Taine, *Origines de la France contemporaine* (1876–93). Still, Carlyle vividly conveys the beast which conservative historians have always found in the revolution. His attention to the blind force of the revolutionary process deserves serious consideration; one need not be conservative to feel that he portrays a reality that escapes more sober historians.

What then is this Thing, called *La Révolution,* which, like an Angel of Death, hangs over France, noyading, fusillading, fighting, gun-boring, tanning human skins? *La Révolution* is but so many Alphabetic Letters; a thing nowhere to be laid hands on, to be clapped under lock and key: where is it? what is it? It is the Madness that dwells in the hearts of men. In this man it is, and in that man; as a rage or as a terror, it is in all men. Invisible, impalpable;

* From Thomas Carlyle, *The French Revolution: A History* (New York: Random House, Inc., Modern Library edition), pp. 669–70, 713–14.

and yet no black Azrael, with wings spread over half a continent, with sword sweeping from sea to sea, could be a truer Reality.

To explain, what is called explaining, the march of this Revolutionary Government, be no task of ours. Man cannot explain it. A paralytic Couthon, asking in the Jacobins, "What hast thou done to be hanged if Counter-Revolution should arrive?" a sombre Saint-Just, not yet six-and-twenty, declaring that "for Revolutionists there is no rest but in the tomb"; a seagreen Robespierre converted into vinegar and gall; much more an Amar and Vadier, a Collot and Billaud: to inquire what thoughts, predetermination or prevision, might be in the head of these men! Record of their thought remains not; Death and Darkness have swept it out utterly. Nay, if we even had their thought, all that they could have articulately spoken to us, how insignificant a fraction were that of the Thing which realized itself, which decreed itself, on signal given by them! As has been said more than once, this Revolutionary Government is not a self-conscious but a blind fatal one. Each man, enveloped in his ambient-atmosphere of revolutionary fanatic Madness, rushes on, impelled and impelling; and has become a blind brute Force; no rest for him but in the grave! Darkness and the mystery of horrid cruelty cover it for us, in History; as they did in Nature. The chaotic Thunder-cloud, with its pitchy black, and its tumult of dazzling jagged fire, in a world all electric: thou wilt not undertake to show how that comported itself,—what the secrets of its dark womb were; from what sources, with what specialties, the lightning it held did, in confused brightness of terror, strike forth, destructive and self-destructive, till it ended? Like a Blackness naturally of Erebus, which by will of Providence had for once mounted itself into dominion and the Azure: is not this properly the nature of Sansculottism consummating itself? Of which Erebus Blackness be it enough to discern that this and the other dazzling fire-bolt, dazzling fire-torrent, does by small Volition and great Necessity, verily issue,—in such and such succession; destructive so and so, self-destructive so and so: till it end.

What Parliament that ever sat under the Moon had such a series of destinies as this National Convention of France? It came together to make the Constitution; and instead of that, it has had to make nothing but destruction and confusion: to burn up Catholicisms, Aristocratisms; to worship Reason and dig Saltpetre; to fight Titanically with itself and with the whole world. A Convention decimated by the Guillotine; above the tenth man has bowed his neck to the axe. Which has seen Carmagnoles danced before it, and patriotic strophes sung amid Church-spoils; the wounded of the Tenth of August defile in hand-barrows; and, in the Pandemonial Midnight, Égalité's dames in tricolor drink lemonade, and spectrum of Sieyes mount, saying, *Death sans phrase*. A Convention which has effervesced, and which has congealed; which has been red with rage, and also pale with rage; sitting with pistols in its pocket, drawing sword (in a moment of effervescence): now storming to the four winds, through a Danton-voice, Awake, O France, and smite the tyrants; now frozen mute under its Robespierre, and answering his dirge-voice by a dubious gasp. Assassinated, decimated; stabbed at, shot at, in baths, on streets and staircases;

which has been the nucleus of Chaos. Has it not heard the chimes at midnight? It has deliberated, beset by a Hundred-thousand armed men with artillery-furnaces and provision-carts. It has been betocsined, bestormed; overflooded by black deluges of Sansculottism; and has heard the shrill cry, *Bread and Soap*. For, as we say, it was the nucleus of Chaos: it sat as the centre of Sansculottism; and had spread its pavilion on the waste Deep, where is neither path nor landmark, neither bottom nor shore. In intrinsic valour, ingenuity, fidelity, and general force and manhood, it has perhaps not far surpassed the average of Parliaments; but in frankness of purpose, in singularity of position, it seeks its fellow. One other Sansculottic submersion, or at most two, and this wearied vessel of a Convention reaches land.

2. CRANE BRINTON: A Decade of Revolution, 1789–1799 *

The French Revolution captured the attention of the first large generation of American historians interested in Europe, those trained during the 1920's and 1930's. Most of them followed the liberal tradition of interpretation, owing to the influence of Alphonse Aulard † and to a sense of the congruence between revolutionary liberalism and the American political heritage. Professor Crane Brinton, of Harvard, is among the most eminent American students of the revolution. His summary of the revolutionary achievement raises many important questions. His stress on the role of ideas and basic mental attitudes resulting from the revolution is noteworthy; so is, of course, his focus on political changes, with social and economic developments following from these. Beyond this, his sense of the coherence of the revolutionary heritage must be assessed. It is no slight to Professor Brinton—indeed, it may reflect his most important contribution—to note the confidence with which he portrays the legacy of the revolution and the great importance he assigns to it in shaping the modern world.

France in 1789 had no elected assembly. In 1799 she had had the recent experience of four more or less representative assemblies, and was about to try another. The Revolution had given France for the first time, not a constitution —for to anyone but a most determined quibbler the France of the old régime had had a constitution—but what can be loosely called parliamentary government. That government, reduced to mere form under Napoleon, was revived under the *Charte* of 1814, and has persisted to the present day. Now, though the electoral qualification has varied, did vary in these ten years, between universal manhood suffrage and a more or less high property qualification, the fact is that since 1789 the ordinary French middle-class man has had the vote, that France has been a political democracy in the nineteenth-century sense of the term. Such a democracy has not achieved the Utopian results once hoped for by earnest theorists, but it has been a very different thing from the closed govern-

* From Crane Brinton, *A Decade of Revolution, 1789–1799*, abridgment of pp. 274–79, 285–88. Copyright 1934 by Harper & Brothers; renewed 1962 by Crane Brinton. Reprinted by permission of Harper & Row, Publishers.

† See his *The French Revolution, a Political History*, 4 vols. (New York, 1910).

ment of Versailles. Ultimate political decisions have not been made by a small council of royal advisers, but by the agreement of hundreds of thousands, even millions, of Frenchmen. French democracy has not always behaved politically the way Anglo-Saxon theorists thought their own democracy behaved, but only the very doctrinaire will deny that modern France has a democratic tradition. The government of France since 1789 has been a government by discussion: and that has involved parliaments, parties, the press, political stereotypes, pressure groups, mass contagions—all the phenomena so familiar today, so unknown to the Frenchman of 1788.

The régime begun in 1789 has proved a much more efficiently centralized governmental machine than the one it replaced. De Tocqueville was perhaps the first important historian to point out that the Revolution really achieved what the Capetians had striven for in vain, the concentration of power in the central government. By the end of the Revolution the old conflicting political jurisdictions, *province, généralité, baillage, gouvernement, sénéchaussée, seigneurie,* and many others, had given place to the unified hierarchical system of *commune, arrondissement, département;* the tangled jurisdictions of *seigneurs, haute, moyenne,* and *basse justice, parlements, présidiaux,* and the numerous special courts had all been united into one system of justice, with a *Cour de Cassation* as supreme court of appeal; the special fiscal privileges of nobles, priests, and corporations had been swept away; internal tariffs, salt taxes, *taille, capitation, vingtième, don gratuit, grosses fermes,* feudal dues—all the hodgepodge of taxation under the old régime—had given place to a simple, unified financial system; the bewildering variety of weights and measures had been supplanted by the metric system; the old customary law of the North and the written law of the South had been united in a new code; the medieval guilds had been abolished; and the church had been stripped of the special privileges which had made it an *imperium in imperio.* Even in 1799 the foundation had been laid for that modern hierarchy of *fonctionnaires* (civil servants) which was never to escape control from Paris as completely as the *intendants* had escaped control from Versailles. Aided by modern transportation and by universal education, the new régime was able to reduce French provincialism to a mere sentiment cultivated largely for the tourist trade, to make France perhaps the most completely unified great nation in the world today.

Obviously, to the ordinary Frenchman these political changes meant a great deal. They meant that he had acquired certain civil rights—the right to trial by jury in many cases, in all to trial in a court which recognized no social and political privileges; the right, if he possessed a certain income, to vote; the right, whether he were Catholic, Protestant, Jew, or Deist, to worship in public with his fellows; the right, subject to property laws on the whole determined in the interests of the landed classes, to pursue any occupation he pleased—and could afford; the right to hold a commission in army or navy; the right, subject to a censorship never again quite as arbitrary as, if sometimes even more effective than, the censorship of the old régime, to form and discuss opinions in the press and on the platform. Such rights, formulated in a hundred Bills of Rights in Europe and America, have never in practice proved quite as absolute as they are declared to be on paper. But their very formulation leaves a tremendous gap between the world of Louis XIV and the modern world.

Again, the new régime made certain kinds of economic activity easier than they had been under the old régime. Here—as, indeed, throughout this summary—the change must not be understood to have been catastrophic. The Revolution matured, rather than initiated, really important changes. The career of John Law had shown that money could be made with great rapidity—and lost also—under the old régime. But on the whole the France of 1799 was a very much more favorable country for the business man than the France of 1789 had been. Political changes, and especially the new system of taxation, made the conduct of business on a national scale much easier. To take a very simple example: it was almost impossible under the old régime to manufacture and market bushel measures from a single center when the definition of a bushel varied from town to town; under the metric system, grain measures could be made on a large scale and sold all over France. A single code of commercial law was equally indispensable for modern business, and the Revolution provided one. The abolition of guilds gave the entrepreneur a freer labor market, and supplanted fixed standards for goods with the modern adage of "caveat emptor." Complete laissez-faire was never to rule in France, but when the government interfered with business, as in imposing tariffs on imports, or in providing subsidies to certain manufacturers, or in improving commercial or agricultural standards by education, research, prizes, expositions, it usually interfered to the benefit of the entrepreneur. Even more important, perhaps, than any specific institutional change was the social change which made business wholly honorable, which set a premium upon the acquisition of wealth, which accustomed men to innovation and the career open to talents.

In agricultural life, still the backbone of all French life, the Revolution was decisive. The long process, begun in feudal times, of making France a land of small independent peasant proprietors and free tenants was virtually completed by the Revolution. After 1789, even where the peasant was a tenant, he held on a strictly commercial basis, and exploited his holding as his own enterprise. The Revolution did not so much eliminate an agricultural proletariat as strengthen an agricultural middle class. Thus the agricultural laborer commonly had rather the status of the American "hired man" than that of the English agricultural laborer or that of the Eastern European semi-serf. Great farms worked wholly by paid labor hardly existed. The typical farm was owned by a peasant who exploited it with the aid of his family and, if the scale of the holding permitted, a few hired men. Social distinctions between owner and laborer were never very rigid, and in spite of the scarcity of land the laborer might rise to ownership. The forbidding of entail and the other restrictions on the free testamentary disposal of land made by the revolutionary, or Napoleonic, code have further operated to maintain in France, at least until the "economic miracle" of the 1950's, a class of small or middling and very conservative peasants with a low birth rate. . . .

But for those two centuries, the great French Revolution paradoxically helped to perpetuate in France a *relatively* small-scale industry and a *relatively* stationary and balanced rural economy which was little more than the later manorial system liberalized and adopted to a money economy. When in addition one reflects on de Tocqueville's conclusion that administratively the Revolution did but perfect the work of the old régime, one is tempted to the final paradox that, in spite of the melodramatic horrors of events in France, the French Revolution has *in the long run* proved even more revolutionary in its effects on other countries than in its effects on France. For abroad the ideas of 1789, adopted by a rising middle class, helped remake Germany and Italy, helped reconcile the new industrial England to the old England; adopted by the working classes in the industrial countries and altered to suit their needs, these ideas helped stiffen their resistance to what they considered exploitation by a new set of feudal overlords. In France the tradition of the Revolution remained, but only as a tradition and a consolation; the realities of French life, in spite of surface changes in governmental forms, were sober, pedestrian, and, in a century so ridden with change as the last, relatively unchanging.

Again, the ordinary Frenchman of 1799 found himself in a world the educational possibilities of which were far different from those of 1789. Democracy had definitely set before itself the goal of universal education. Illiteracy had become a stigma instead of an ordinary accompaniment of humble life. And what is more, education had ceased to be the monopoly of religious orders, and was acquiring more and more of a secular cast. Universal education, like Bills of Rights, has not yet, and certainly had not in 1799, quite lived up to its paper promises. But the lad who passes through the discipline of the little schools so touchingly inscribed with the revolutionary trinity of "Liberty, Equality, Fraternity" is a very different lad from the illiterate peasant of the old régime, or even from the more privileged lad who had learned to read, write, and obey God and king in dame schools and church schools.

Another revolutionary institution which by 1799 had become inescapably a part of the life of the ordinary Frenchman was universal military service—an institution which during the next century spread to most parts of the civilized world. Universal military service has not had in manuals of democratic historians quite the attention given universal suffrage, universal education, and other benign universalities, but the origins and development of them all are inescapably the same. Neither in medieval nor in early modern times was fighting the occupation of the common man. In the Middle Ages a military caste, in early modern times mercenary armies officered by gentlemen, fought pretty continuously, but on a rather small scale. Since the famous mobilization of French men and money in 1793, modern wars have been somewhat more discontinuous, but they have directly touched every citizen.

The social structure of France was no less directly affected by the Revolution than the political structure. Broadly speaking, one may say that in spite of the ups and downs of Empire and Restoration, France has been since the great Revolution almost as fully a social democracy as the United States. . . .

The real changes in ideas marked by the French Revolution are not quite what the textbooks of the Third Republic make them out to be. The Revolution did not bring freedom of thought—the *philosophes* had long enjoyed an inefficient censorship far more favorable to the dispersal of ideas than an indifferent freedom. The Revolution did not immediately encourage political experimentation—its general European influence lay precisely in the other direction, and put a stop to a good deal of the work of the enlightened despots. The Revolution was no burgeoning of the human spirit, delighted with its emancipation, into the heights of artistic achievement—in general, it was a period of artistic conformity. The real significance of the Revolution for intellectual history is that it made necessary a new series of value-judgments to orientate the triumphant bourgeois among the ruins left by the *philosophes*. Some attempt has been made above to describe the theological aspect of these new value-judgments. To go much further would be to trespass on later volumes in this series. But it must be pointed out that even in 1799, the outlines of nineteenth-century intellectual—or if you prefer, spiritual—values are pretty well blocked out. The typical nineteenth-century conformist built his safe universe partly with the aid of the French Revolution. This universe still exists, though it seems now a trifle unsafe. Briefly, the "higher" life of the nineteenth-century middle-class European comprised more or less active participation in the religious life of some Christian sect, and a complete misunderstanding of traditional Christianity; patriotism, not infrequently allied with Christian reminiscences, so that God, who had once been Jehovah, became especially and exclusively disposed in favor of Englishmen, or Frenchmen, or Germans, according to need; a moral code in its more general passages close enough to the traditional code of European Christianity, but with an emphasis on thrift, labor, solvency, solid rather than luxurious living, sobriety, and female chastity which stems from Protestant capitalism as well as from the French Revolution; a set of abstractions varying somewhat according to the nationality and social position of their owner, but all involving some equivalent of "progress," and nearly all some equivalent of "Liberty, Equality, Fraternity"; a robust faith in economic individualism, an absolute assurance that government interference in business will always prove harmful; adherence to some form of parliamentary government, assumed to be the sole reasonable form of government, and transcending the old-fashioned divisions of monarchy, aristocracy, democracy; aesthetic standards tending generally towards the picturesque, the violent, the improbable, the pathetic, the unattainably perfect—in short, towards the romantic; a conviction that, however much order is necessary in moral and political life, anarchy is the natural condition of aesthetic life. This is the compromise made by the nineteenth century with the Utopian hopes of 1789.

The French Revolution was, however, an act of rebellion. If by 1799 there had begun to emerge from it the somewhat troubled bourgeois synthesis typical of the nineteenth century, there was also formed in this decade a tradition of rebellion which has sometimes adapted itself to certain aspects of bourgeois order, but which is none the less a pretty clear tradition in its own right. You may call it, if you like, the tradition of '93, as opposed to the tradition of '89. In its purest form it inspired Continental radicals throughout the century, and is even discernible in England in men like Charles Bradlaugh. Certain elements of it were taken over by the working-class movement, and helped to make up the socialist tradition. Both these forms must be briefly analyzed.

The pure radical tradition is a pretty faithful reproduction of the aims of Robespierre. This Jacobin legend sets up a republican form of government, based upon universal manhood suffrage (but usually hostile to female suffrage, fearing clerical influence); universal compulsory education wholly in the hands of lay authority; theoretical religious freedom, based upon a firm conviction that religious freedom will mean the end of the Roman Catholic Church; in practice, certain restrictive measures such as dissolution of religious orders and closing of church schools, calculated to hasten the extinction of superstition; an economic order based on private property and private enterprise, but so regulated by taxation and other forms of state action as to prevent the accumulation of large fortunes; a unified nation-state impatient of regional differences within itself, regulating its relations with other independent nation-states by open diplomacy based on the universal principles of morality; a patriotism in theory tolerant of other patriotisms, in practice quite easily converted into an aggressive nationalism; an industrious population untempted by luxury, virtuous, its artistic life untouched by aristocratic decadence; in short, the greengrocer's paradise of Robespierre. . . .

The socialists took over from the Jacobins their hostility to the Roman Catholic Church, or to the more privileged Protestant churches like the Anglican and the Lutheran, their republicanism, and, what is more important, their tradition of direct action. Jacobin political tactics—the organization of pressure groups, ceaseless propaganda, street manifestations and other forms of violence, use of ritual and other religious practices to maintain the cohesion of the group, belief in the necessity of a temporary "dictatorship" of the elect—all this was a valuable school for European socialism. It is significant that Marx, Jaurès, and other socialist leaders were careful students of the first French Revolution. . . .

In practice the French Revolution destroyed a social and political hierarchy buttressed by the Christian tradition (as an economic hierarchy this older hierarchy had already been undermined, which, briefly, is why the French Revolution was a success). In place of the older hierarchy it set up a new middle-class one, hastily buttressed by the curious amalgamation of old traditions and new ambitions which served the nineteenth century as an authority. But this buttress was weak in a fundamental point: it necessarily incorporated the egalitarian ideas with which the bourgeoisie had appealed to the lower classes for aid. It asserted in outright print the "self-evident truth" that all men are created equal. It was founded on the romantic faith in indefinite progress, in a "natural" order hostile to fixed hierarchies, in the virtues of rebellion and unrest. Its very faith in universal education made inevitable the spread of these ideas to the very lowest classes. Hitherto, at least, this process has not stopped, and through socialism the French Revolution is still at work in the modern world.

3. GEORGES LEFEBVRE: The French Revolution from 1793–1799 *

Georges Lefebvre, until his recent death the holder of the chair of French revolutionary history at the Sorbonne, has written the most authoritative general survey of the revolution as well as a number of detailed and penetrating monographs on more specialized subjects, including the long-neglected topic of peasant activities during the period. His approach was generally Marxist, but in no narrow sense; he worked constantly toward creating a portrait of the varied social composition of the revolution, without denying the fundamentally middle-class victory that resulted. Lefebvre's use of the terminology of social class to assess the effects of the revolution may at times conceal the subtlety of his analysis; one may ask, for example, whether he always means the same thing when he cites the "bourgeoisie." Lefebvre's view of the pervasive effects of the revolution, particularly in changing French society, also deserves careful attention. How different does the focus ultimately seem from that of a liberal historian such as Brinton?

It must be noted, however, that in this destruction of the corporate society the clergy and nobility were not (contrary to what one might tend to believe) the only ones involved. The bourgeoisie of the Old Regime were seriously affected as well. More than one of their members, possessing personal nobility or about to obtain it, saw this pleasing prospect (always exciting to the newly rich) vanish. Some, including representatives of the people, possessed fiefs, fragmentary manorial rights (*banalités,* for example), or even an entire manor. Others, yielding to vanity or self-interest (because manorial rents were redeemable only with the lessor's consent), had made use of the formulas of feudal lawyers in settling land rents, and had anticipated such items as the quitrents (*cens*). The law of July 17, 1793, dispossessed them of these.

Many officeholders were commoners; hence the redemption of their posts, and the suppression of the organized bodies on which their social rank and part of their income depended, hurt them as it did the others. The notaries became functionaries—recourse to attorneys was henceforth optional. Many bailiffs lost the employment derived from institutions that had disappeared. Even the other liberal professions that were not venal experienced some loss. With the lawyers dissolved as a body, the role of "public defender" was open to all. Physicians ceased to be an organized group. Beginning in 1791 the artists, under the leadership of David, vigorously challenged the monopoly maintained by the academicians over the Salon, and the authority they exerted over the School of

* From Georges Lefebvre, *The French Revolution from 1793–1799* (New York: Columbia University Press, 1964), pp. 265–68, 269–70, 303–4, 309–15. Reprinted by permission of Columbia University Press.

Rome. Finally, on August 8, 1793, the Convention, by suppressing the academies and universities, deprived some of the artists, scientists, men of letters, and professors of their claim to status.

During the Montagnard period the commercial middle class in turn found its future compromised. On August 24, 1793, the Convention eliminated the joint-stock companies, the most advanced form of capitalism. This was affected (far more than by the disappearance of the East India Company) by the disestablishment of the Discount Bank, which had acted as a national bank of issue and a "superbank." The advent of the controlled economy, taxation, and requisitioning slowed the rise of capitalism even more abruptly by regimenting business activity and limiting profits.

Nor did the "people"—the artisans, retail merchants, and employees—emerge unscathed. Many persons of small means had to seek new ways of making a living when the collection of indirect taxes ceased, especially the salt tax (*gabelle*), *octrois,* internal customs and duties, the tithe, and the field rent (*champart*). On February 16, 1791, the Constituent Assembly suppressed the craft guilds. Such action seemed democratic, at least to the extent that the technical conditions of the time permitted wage earners to profit thereby through opening their own shops. Nonetheless it deprived masters of their monopoly. Besides harming their interests, it wounded their pride, for they had been jealous of their special privileges and their carefully controlled authority. This was specially true of surgeons, booksellers, goldsmiths, and wigmakers.

Finally, the private life of the Third Estate was affected. The inheritance laws applied to commoners as well as to nobles, and occasionally ruined their legacies. Nor should it be forgotten that many bourgeois emigrated, that in the invaded areas a host of persons from all classes left France when the Carmagnoles reappeared, and that the great majority of those harmed by terrorist repression were neither priests nor nobles. It was essential, however, for the revolutionaries to loosen the bonds that subjected child and wife to the discretionary power of the paterfamilias under the Old Regime; and this applied to the Third Estate as much as to the aristocracy. It was particularly for this reason that limitations were placed on the right to make wills. The claim was made from the rostrum of the Assemblies that heads of families should be prevented from disinheriting next of kin who were favourable to the Revolution.

Paternal authority was greatly diminished. Henceforth the family court, instituted on August 16, 1790, shared disciplinary authority with the father. At age twenty-one (or eighteen in cases of emancipation) children were "liberated" and regained control of their property. No longer need a wife fear imprisonment by means of *lettres de cachet;* her consent was required for the marriage of her children, and like her husband, she could seek a divorce. The Convention had facilitated this last by its decrees of 8 Nivôse and 4 Floréal, Year II (December 28, 1793, and April 23, 1794). The rehabilitation of "natural" children heralded a still more formidable disruption of family solidarity. Every social revolution tends to carry its attack to the point where it seems fitting that individuals (particularly the young) be released from traditional conformity, so that, whatever the risks, they may adapt themselves to the new order because restraints have been removed. Once the goal is attained, however, discipline must be re-established within the remodelled society.

To stop here would be to leave an inadequate impression of the social upheaval. No less far-reaching were the effects of inflation, which, despite the return to metallic currency, continued its ravages until 18 Brumaire. The Directory flooded the market with its bonds, its warrants for payment (backed by insufficient funds), and its requisition certificates. Inflation was devastating to acquired wealth. In the Year III the depreciation of assignats brought a rush of debtors, hastening to pay, at low rates, not only for public taxes or national property, but also for landed rents which were redeemable by paying the capital. But the bourgeoisie willingly invested their savings in mortgage loans, of which these rents constituted the interest. On 25 Messidor, Year III (July 13, 1795), it was necessary to forbid the repayment of funds advanced before January 1, 1792, and to pay off the rest in advance.

Throughout the greater part of France land was cultivated on a share-crop basis. At the termination of his lease (normally of a year's duration) the tenant farmer returned the outlay made by the landowner; or if that was impossible, he paid a sum agreed upon as the value of the original loan. Beginning with the Year II, however, tenants hastened to sell, at the highest prices, whatever was exempt from the Maximum (chiefly livestock), so that they could make their payments in depreciated paper. On 2 Thermidor, Year II (July 20, 1794), the Committee of Public Safety forbade this practice so far as cattle leases were concerned, and on 13 Fructidor (August 30) for other items (*garniture morte*), but without success. The decree of 15 Germinal, Year III (April 4, 1795), repeated the prohibitions, and innumerable petitions have preserved the complaints of desperate lessors. Farmers also gained at the expense of landowners, since the former paid their debts in paper. On 3 Messidor, Year III (June 21, 1795), they were ordered to pay at the rate of six for one, and on 2 Thermidor (July 20, 1795) they were directed to pay half their farm rents and their taxes in grain. Still, they retained the right to plead that their harvests were inadequate.

During the entire period of the Directory the Councils considered methods of reconciling the opposing interests. Their concern with restoring acquired wealth (which has not been recovered to this day) is one more proof that the Thermidorians were able to re-establish the pre-eminence of the bourgeoisie in their ranks. In such cases, however, the losses to the property owners could not be restored in their entirety. Building property fared even worse. For example, the decree of 3 Messidor, Year III (June 21, 1795), which brought help to landed proprietors, maintained the payment of rents in assignats at par. Then a severe housing shortage developed, especially in Paris, and at the end of the Directory the value of real estate was still declining. Finally, the bourgeoisie held the greatest part of the public debt. Thus it bore the brunt of Cambon's readjustment of perpetual and life annuities, of Ramel's liquidation of the public debt, of the continued decline of income under the Directory, and of the payment of dividends in worthless notes.

The number of these changes, and the infinite variety of their repercussions, greatly influenced men's thinking. They alienated the aristocracy from modern society, rallied some members of the bourgeoisie of the Old Regime to counterrevolution, and caused others to desire a conservative reaction. This reaction, suitable for restoring stability, was perceptible as early as 9 Thermidor; but it was still far from complete by 18 Brumaire. Only those who speculated on the purchase of national property and provisions recovered their losses; but the principal benefits of these operations did not go to the bourgeoisie of the Old Regime. As is usually the case, the war and the monetary disorder produced *nouveaux riches,* whose intrusion into the ranks of the impoverished bourgeoisie added to the social upheaval a quality that had not been anticipated.

THE STATE

At the end of the Old Regime the state, embodied in a divine-right monarch, still retained a personal character. Since the seventeenth century, however, a centralized administration had been tending to make its bureaucratic regulations prevail, and it was making the state bourgeois by rationalizing it. This trend ran afoul of provincial and urban concern with autonomy and the chaotic diversity of an expanded kingdom, governed empirically as historical circumstances permitted, but far more often according to the wishes of the corporate hierarchy. The class which dominates a society always regards the state, created to ensure respect for the positive law and to maintain order, as the bulwark of its prerogatives. The rivalry between royal power and the interests of the aristocracy engendered the Revolution, and the bourgeoisie put an end to the contradiction by seizing the state themselves.

They abolished the privileges of the provinces and the towns, as well as those of the aristocracy, and proclaimed the equality of all Frenchmen before the law. The intermediate bodies, which Montesquieu had regarded as the only means of curbing the absolutism of the state, disappeared. Traditional institutions were swept away, and national unity was achieved through administrative uniformity. It seemed henceforth that the will of the state would encounter no obstacles other than distance and the technical difficulties of communication. In this sense Tocqueville was able to say that the members of the Constituent Assembly crowned the work carried on over the centuries by the Capetian dynasty.

But this was only part of their work. In proclaiming the rights of man, with liberty foremost, the bourgeoisie intended to protect them against the state; so they transformed the latter. Substituting popular sovereignty for that of the prince, they destroyed personal power. From an attribute of a proprietary monarchy, the state was transformed into an agent of the governed, and its authority was subordinated to the rules of a constitution. Monarchy was not abolished, but Louis XVI became the first of the "functionaries," that is, of the representatives for the nation. Heretofore his commands had been carried out through the administrative machinery. Hence the wishes of his subjects were voiced not only on behalf of liberty but equally against centralization. They desired to make themselves masters of local administration even more than of the central authority. The popular revolution drove out the royal agents, whose place was taken by elected councils established by the Constituent Assembly. This autonomy responded to a human inclination naturally antagonistic to centralization, even when the latter works to the advantage of the representatives of the people. Undoubtedly this is because bureaucracy occasionally abuses centralization or brings it into disrepute through stupid and routine sluggishness, or even negligence; also because uniformity irritates individual independence, and runs counter to the infinite variety of interests and peculiar habits of each of the small communities that comprise the nation.

Thus the Revolution of 1789 did not reinforce the power of the state. On the contrary, it weakened it by associating the elected representatives of the nation with the king, by requiring them to respect individual rights, and by diluting authority through decentralization extended as far as the localizing of tax collection and the maintenance of public order. Many citizens went further still. In the name of popular sovereignty and of Article 6 of the Declaration of the Rights of Man (which did not prohibit direct democracy) they claimed the right to subject the decisions of their representatives to review, and even to authorize their revocation. This tendency toward libertarian anarchy appeared as much among the counter-revolutionaries and moderates as it did among the sans-culottes. Its conflict with the indispensable predominance of a central authority thus reveals one of the eternal contradictions of every society—that of freedom and authority, the individual and the state.

THE NEW SOCIETY

Compared with the old, one obvious feature of the new society on the eve of 18 Brumaire derived from the disappearance of the Catholic clergy. Until about this time they had been numerous, honoured, rich, and supported by the secular arm; now they were decimated, poor and in part errant, treated as suspects, even as enemies, by the Directory, and reduced by the secularized state to a purely spiritual authority recognized by the piety of the faithful.

For the moment the fate of the nobility seemed no better. Yet apart from the prestige that birth and invalidated titles retained clandestinely, the aristocrats had not been despoiled of the material sources of their influence to the same extent. More often than is believed families (such as that of the Marquis de Ferrières) lived peacefully among their former tenants and under their tacit protection; or, at worst, they suffered only imprisonment and passing difficulties that left their landed property intact. Wives of émigrés even saved their dowries or widow's portions through fictitious divorces. Some returning émigrés, amnestied or not, had already enjoyed a degree of success during the White Terror in forcing purchasers of national property to make restoration. More numerous still were those who repurchased such lands through intermediaries. Finally, many nobles remained in the service of the Republic.

It goes without saying that the Revolution benefited the bourgeoisie, but not all to the same extent. Those who formerly had boasted of "living nobly from their own property" had been humbled. The time was coming when they would be satisfied with the title of *rentier,* or landowner, which corresponded more precisely with their origins and with the new principles of social classification. Some Old Regime bourgeois, hostile to the Revolution or the men of 1789 who had remained monarchists, had eventually been treated as nobles. Of those who survived, some emigrated, lost their property, and compromised their relatives; after 18 Fructidor others remained suspect to those of their kind who had become republicans. The fortunes of those whose prudence had kept them in the background were ruined by the abolition of corporate bodies and by revolutionary taxes, forced loans, and inflation. . . .

ECONOMIC FREEDOM AND EQUAL RIGHTS

Thus there proves to be greater continuity than might be believed from a logical analysis (based on pure speculation) of the principles proclaimed by the Constituent Assembly. Ultimately the progress of capitalist concentration altered the social structure, while the technical innovations of experimental science increased individual independence by transforming the material conditions of life. As a consequence, economic freedom appears as a basic feature of the new order; businessmen subordinated all others to it.

By the end of the eighteenth century, however, the most daring minds had not calculated its scope, and its immediate effects had not even gained general acceptance. Undeniably, it did attract the French in one respect. Each man was satisfied that henceforth he might try his luck if he secured the necessary means to go into business; and the wage earner clung to the right to sell his services where and when he pleased. It goes without saying that the Revolution did not engender these ambitions—they are inherent in human existence—but it did legitimatize them by liberating them. In this way economic freedom became inseparable from the other freedoms; indeed it was the most precious and symbolic.

Opinion proved less favourable towards technical innovations, which were now free of all hindrance. Out of caution, routine, pride, or lack of capital, artisans appeared no more disposed than before to adopt them without serious consideration. Dislike changed to hostility when the adoption of new processes, especially machines and steam, obviously were leading to capitalist concentration. The craftsman was afraid of being transformed into a wage earner; the worker knew that mechanization began by spreading unemployment; and the peasant foresaw that, with his collective rights suppressed, he would have to abandon the land. As for agricultural methods, the bourgeoisie desired their improvement, since landed wealth remained the most highly valued, and agricultural production supplied the bulk of national revenue.

Such was not the case, however, where industrial capitalism was concerned. The bourgeoisie of the liberal professions, indoctrinated by the economists and Encyclopedists, valued large-scale enterprise, because it associated science with production and offered the advantage of absorbing some of the indigent. Nevertheless its expansion worried them. They saw in it the hand of the financiers (whom the bourgeoisie continued to defy), an appeal to rapid enrichment (which was not in keeping with their tradition), and an eventual dominance over the economy (which would weaken the role of the spiritual life that they cherished) and over politics (in which they claimed a monopoly). Even among businessmen initiative remained limited, and the inadequacy of the banking structure attests their timidity. Nothing better demonstrates the lack of the spirit of industrial enterprise than the virtually universal prejudice of the nation against the English economy, and the conviction that the latter, based on credit and committed by machines to overproduction that only exports could absorb, would collapse if Europe were closed to it.

The psychological shock of the Revolution would have expanded these horizons if France had possessed the abundant coal of Great Britain, or at least if the introduction of British machinery and technicians had been accelerated. The war, however, interrupted the impact of foreign developments. It resumed slowly towards the end of the Directory, but cotton spinning was almost the only industry to benefit from it. Steam was not yet employed, and even water power was often lacking. Such was the case in Paris, which long remained the most important centre.

Taking possession of nationalized buildings, and employing a wretched labour force (notably foundlings brought together by public relief), several great capitalist entrepreneurs now became prominent—Richard and Lenoir in Paris, Bauwens in Paris and Ghent, and Boyer-Fonfrède in Toulouse. As in England, they were far from being strictly specialized, and they continued the tradition of commercial capitalism (Ternaux, for example), directing cottage workers and a rural labour force in addition to their factories, at the same time engaging in trade, commissions, transport, and banking as well. Contrary to the impression that their very real success has made on more than one historian, they did not let it be forgotten that manufacturing enterprise remained on a small scale and widely dispersed, that the artisans alone held sway in the greater part of the country, and that France still remained primarily agricultural.

The stagnation of farming technique also attests particularly the weakness in the rise of capitalism. Whatever their sympathies for British methods, the revolutionary assemblies dared not resort to enclosure, which would have permitted improvements to spread. To lessen popular hostility, the Constituent Assembly did authorize enclosure, but stipulated that the landowners (who would be exempt from common pasture), would forego sending their cattle elsewhere. It decided that artificial meadows would remain intact, without need of enclosure; and it discontinued all crop controls, thereby doing away with "compulsory fallow"—required crop rotation—without which common pasturing was no longer possible except on common lands.

Without arbitrary land redistribution, however, the effect of these provisions became apparent so slowly that contemporaries scarcely noticed them. When the Convention permitted the division of common lands, the sole result was an increase in small holdings. Poverty encouraged the raising of potatoes, chicory, and oil-bearing plants, just as the disappearance of the *aides* stimulated a considerable expansion of vineyards. These changes did not break the continuity of habit, however, and they by no means signified the advent of modern agriculture.

The progress of capitalism, then, was not accelerated during the decade; on the contrary, circumstances rather diminished it. Large-scale enterprise continued to disturb artisans and peasants, but there is no evidence that it caused them any more harm than heretofore. Nor did it concentrate the labour force or bring forth a strictly proletarian class. In any case, the distinction between the host of small employers and their workmen remained hazy in the minds of the men of the time.

The eventual contradictions between economic freedom and equal rights had not yet become fully apparent. The bourgeoisie saw none at all, because in their eyes equality meant simply that henceforth the law was the same for all. Yet by proclaiming this principle in order to eliminate the privileges of noble birth, it brought into the open the conflict of interests among the different social categories within the Third Estate; and it particularly accentuated the disintegration of the rural community. In other words, inequality came to the fore. Thus even in July, 1789, as it was expressing satisfaction at the popular revolution that saved the National Assembly, the bourgeoisie harboured the fear that the "people" and the "populace" always inspired in them. Even before the Declaration of the Rights of Man proclaimed the right of every citizen to participate in the making of laws, the Constituent Assembly followed Sieyes by making the franchise, and above all, eligibility for public office, dependent on the qualities associated with wealth.

Since a regime based on the ownership of property gave the bourgeoisie control over the state, they resolved to give priority to the problem of equal rights. Political democracy seemed to provide the answer, but from the outset some democrats went much further. They denounced the omnipotence of the "haves" over the wage earners, and their virulent criticisms were a prelude to those of future socialist theoreticians. They showed the emptiness of equal rights, and even of freedom, to those who lacked the ability to enjoy them.

Still, their thought remained overshadowed by the traditional opposition between rich and poor. They pleaded the cause of the "indigent" skilfully, but they never defined it precisely. Their analysis (the weakness of which is explained by the persistence of the old economy) did not extend to an emphasis on private appropriation of the means of production and on their technical development; and under pressure of food shortages they abandoned generalities. This led them, on one hand, to defend the consumer against the producer—actually the town dweller against the peasant—and on the other, to claim ownership of the soil for the people—not to remove it from the cultivator, but to legitimatize the nationalization of produce, that is, requisition.

It is characteristic that Momoro, supporting this thesis in September, 1792, should have added that industrial and commercial property, on the contrary, continued to be guaranteed by the nation. This, along with the all-powerful influence of circumstances, testifies to the essentially agricultural nature of the economy of the time. Finally, the Montagnards meant to impose arbitration by the democratic Republic on the "haves" and the wage earners. They protected the former by pronouncing the death penalty against partisans of the "agrarian law," but attempted to limit their wealth by inheritance laws. They placed public education at the disposal of the latter, and offered the most disinherited a rudimentary form of security. This social democracy constituted a second solution of the problem of equal rights, the memory of which was not lost, but which the bourgeoisie long and uncompromisingly countered with their own.

Nevertheless it is evident that the Montagnards contested neither the principle of hereditary property, as Saint-Simon was soon to do, nor economic freedom, for they accepted the Maximum only as a war expedient. The artisans and retail merchants were of the same opinion: they did not like the rich, but because of a basic contradiction, they did not abhor the idea of raising themselves to the same height. Countless petitioners among the peasants complained that not even a part of the national property was being reserved for them; they wished only to acquire property.

True, the sans-culottes attached more importance to regulation than did the Montagnards, but their immediate needs, aggravated by high prices and unemployment, counted for far more in the popular movements than ideological views and projects for the future. It even seems probable that the remedies they imposed lost prestige when put to the test, because scarcity and the annoyances of bureaucratic rationing came to be associated with them. Besides, the proletariat rebelled against the Maximum on wages; and for this reason those whom the liberal order favoured the least rallied to it involuntarily.

Whether political or social, democracy had already expired when Babeuf and Buonarroti proposed communism as the indispensable condition for equal rights. Yet their preaching bore the mark of the age. Advocating the "agrarian law," they proposed in effect to divide up the land among those who cultivated it. They had no thought of establishing collective production. Their communism was limited to socializing produce, which amounted to a generalizing of the controlled economy of the Year II. For the moment they remained the only advocates of this third solution.

Already, however, the Jacobin experiment had sufficed to alienate the greater part of the bourgeoisie from the fraternity that charity, based on "feeling" and optimism, had enjoined before 1789 and that the necessary solidarity of the Third Estate had counselled in the first months of the Revolution. The "notables" had taken fright, and they did not forget. Nine Thermidor inaugurated a long period of political and social reaction. The Constitution of the Year III reestablished the regime based on the ownership of property, and it was careful to define equality and property as the bourgeoisie conceived them. Under the Directory the greatest part of what remained of the national property fell into their hands. When, on 14 Ventôse, Year VII (March 4, 1799), the Republic surrendered to their holders the estates pledged by the monarchy—without charge or for a modest price—it was the bourgeoisie who once more profited the most. They would also have found advantages in reviving the law of July 17, 1793, in order to recover land rents that had been voided when the contract contained expressions borrowed from feudal vocabulary. The matter was considered, but they dared take no action. At least the obligation of redemption (*rachat*) was reimposed on the Breton tenants at will (*domaines congéables*), and it is significant that the new law on precarious tenure (*tenure convenancière*) was voted by the Council of Five Hundred before, and by the Elders after, 18 Fructidor.

In such matters the bourgeoisie were again of one mind. Once more the peasants found their collective rights contested (at least in the forests), and the division of common lands suspended. The judicial reform was altered: the family courts disappeared; arbitration proceedings were reduced in scope; and court clerks' fees were revived. The family also attracted attention: voices were raised against divorce, and the laws of the Year II that facilitated it were abrogated. Cambacérès explained that paternity suits had been authorized in 1793 only for the past, and his project for a code to some degree restored paternal and marital authority, at the same time that it reduced the rights of natural children. Nonetheless the reaction did not go very far, because, in spite of everything, the "notables" remained divided. Those who lamented the Old Regime did not forgive the others. The champions of the Revolution of 1789 who had remained monarchists disapproved of the republicans and execrated the regicides. The men of the Directory feared the neo-Jacobins. The aggressive anti-clericalism common to so many revolutionaries further increased the confusion.

4. ALFRED COBBAN: The Myth of the French Revolution *

Professor Alfred Cobban, of the University of London, has long been a student of France and the French Revolution. During recent years he has turned increasingly to a reassessment of the revolution's impact on society; † he raises numerous questions, which have already stirred extensive debate. How valid is an evaluation of the revolution in purely social terms? Regardless of whether Professor Cobban's evaluation is correct, can any such effort convey the principal impact of the revolution? And is his evaluation correct? Is Professor Cobban able to disprove or modify traditional terms and judgments by new empirical tests? Finally, how novel is the assessment? It must of course be compared with Lefebvre's views; a careful comparison with the Brinton selection will also be revealing.

History, said Napoleon, is a myth that men agree to believe. I would rather say that it is this so long as it is something which it is important to them to believe or not. While the past lives it remains a myth, and naturally like all

* From Alfred Cobban, *The Myth of the French Revolution* (London: University College, 1955), pp. 6, 8–11, 11–16, 18–19, 20–21. Reprinted by permission of University College, London.

† See his *The Social Interpretation of the French Revolution* (London, 1964).

things living, it changes. The history of the French Revolution, whether garbed in the apocalyptic vision of a Carlyle or the profound scholarship of a Lefebvre, has continued to live and to change because it has continued to be bound up with the beliefs and aspirations of mankind.

I am tempted to suggest that in another sense also the French Revolution might be called a myth. At first, I must confess, I thought of entitling this lecture, "Was there a French Revolution?" However, it seemed that to inaugurate this chair by eliminating the Revolution would be rather awkward; and it would certainly have been tactless to invite our French friends here and begin by abolishing their Revolution for them. I am therefore asking a safer question: "What was the French Revolution?" We used to think that it began in 1789. Now we know it began at least in 1787. It ended when? In 1815? Thiers and Aulard conclude their histories of the Revolution in 1799, Mathiez and Thompson in 1794, Guérin begins the reaction in 1793, Salvermini ends his history in 1792, and for some it has never ended. To each terminal date corresponds a different interpretation. Worse still follows. The Revolution has ceased to be a revolution and become a series of revolutions—the last Fronde of the nobles and the *parlements:* the revolution of the *tiers état,* the peasant rising, the republican insurrection, the revolt of the *sans-culottes,* the *neuf thermidor* and the various *coups d'état* under the Directory ending in that of *18 brumaire.* The French Revolution is in fact a name we give to a long series of events. What it means depends on the light in which we see the connection between these events. In this sense the French Revolution, if not a myth, is a theory, or rather a number of rival theories. . . .

To pass from the general to the particular, in the French Revolution, it is commonly said, the feudal order passed away and the rule of the bourgeoisie took its place. This is, put simply, the myth which has dominated serious research on the history of the French Revolution during the present century. It is often treated as an exemplification of a scientific law derived from the facts of history. If I am calling it a myth, this is in no derogatory sense but in a Platonic way of speaking, which may, of course, be worse. The fact that it has come to be taken for granted is my reason for re-examining it. Simplifying, but then this is essentially a *conte de fées,* the outline of the story is that there was once a social order called feudalism. This was a terrible ogre and lived in a castle; but for centuries a bourgeois Jack the Giant-killer climbed the beanstalk of economic progress, until finally in the French Revolution he liquidated the old order and put in its place something called alternatively bourgeois society or capitalism. The only divergence from the traditional story is that he did not live happily ever after. I think it would be fair to say that this is the generally accepted myth or theory of the French Revolution, and of course both the factors in it are themselves theories. I propose to discuss them in turn.

The first is feudalism. This is a term that was invented to describe the social organization that prevailed in the Middle Ages. By the time of the French Revolution, as a system of government based on the ownership of land it had long come to an end in France. Not only had the feudal aristocracy ceased to govern the country, it had even ceased to own a large part of the land. A rough estimate is that one-third of the land had passed into the possession of the peasantry, and a fair proportion of the remainder was forest or waste. The so-called feudalism of the eighteenth century consisted in the survival of antiquated dues and services owed to the descendants of the former feudal seigneurs, or to those who had purchased their *seigneuries*. A considerable body of *feudistes* lived out of the continual law-suits that these claims, registered in *terriers,* involved. In the years before 1789 an attempt was made by the possessors of feudal rights—and possibly in particular by their new possessors, though this is a matter that requires investigation—to revive old ones that had long fallen into disuse and to enforce surviving ones more rigorously. In spite of this, they remained a peculiarly functionless survival, the relics of an atrophied organ, which only a very adventurous social biologist could use to justify a classification with some fossil feudal order of the past. In the words of a legal historian, the fief, in the eighteenth century, was *une forme bizarre de propriété foncière*. The jurists of the time admitted that the *"seigneur utile,"* that is to say the *tenancier,* was the real proprietor, though his property involved certain obligations, which they described in legal terminology as a *"servitude au profit du seigneur foncier."*

How little the so-called feudal dues deserved their title was to be proved in the course of the attempt to apply the decrees of 4–11 August 1789, by which the Constituent Assembly proposed to abolish those dues that were feudal in origin, while at the same time maintaining those payments or services which were of the nature of economic rent. It proved impossible to make the distinction in practice and after years of legal struggle the attempt was abandoned and all dues which qualified ownership disappeared. This was just what the Constituent Assembly had feared and tried to avoid, for to suggest that the members of the Assembly wanted to abolish dues which many of them had acquired themselves would be a mistake. On the contrary, their disappearance was an unlooked-for and unwanted by-product of the Revolution. The night of the Fourth of August was not quite the spontaneous and generous gesture it has been made to seem. The men of property who sat in the Constituent Assembly, as Professor Lefebvre has pointed out, could not approve of confiscatory methods of dealing with property, especially when some of it was their own. The countryside took matters into its own hands when it broke out in the last jacquerie, under the stimulus of economic distress, the excitement of the drawing up of the *cahiers* and the election of the *tiers état,* and the general break-down of authority resulting from the *révolte nobiliaire*. The unrest in the spring and summer of 1789 was so widespread that a major military operation would have been necessary to suppress it. The night of the Fourth of August was an attempt by throwing overboard some of the dues to salvage the rest. In the age of Reason, feudal went with such terms of abuse as Gothic and medieval. If the property rights that were sacrificed were called feudal, this was at least in part to prevent the episode from becoming a precedent in respect of other property rights. It was necessary to give the dog a bad name in order to justify his having been hanged. But the peasantry did not draw such subtle legal distinctions. They simply ceased to pay their dues, whatever their nature, and no subsequent government had the strength to make them resume payment. In the words of Lefebvre, "they liberated themselves, and the successive Assemblies only sanctioned what they had accomplished." If the system of seigneurial rights can be identified with the medieval social order called feudal; and if the reluctant acceptance of a *fait accompli* by the Constituent Assembly can be called abolishing feudalism, then, I suppose, the first part of the prevailing myth of the Revolution can hold good. The qualifications seem to me so extensive as to make the statement practically meaningless.

What of the other factor in the theory, the revolt of the bourgeoisie? It is unnecessary nowadays to labour the point that the Revolution began as an aristocratic rising; the Counter-revolution, as it subsequently became, in fact preceded the Revolution by at least two years. . . .

In Great Britain we commonly think of the rise of the bourgeoisie as the rise of that class which was primarily concerned with the control of trade, industry and finance, as composed therefore of merchants, bankers, industrialists and capitalists, great and small. The accepted theory of the French Revolution is that it came when the new form of property which such men represented replaced the older form represented by the feudal landowners. Is this a correct analysis? I must begin by premising that if it was a revolt of the "monied men," to use Burke's term, it was certainly not provoked by economic grievances. The fine eighteenth-century quarters of French provincial towns are standing evidence of the wealth of the men who built them, as well as of the standards of taste that dictated their elegance. However, it is hardly necessary to discuss the reasons they might, or might not, have had for making a revolution until we are quite sure that they made it. Now, in fact, the men who made the Revolution of 1789 were the members of the Constituent Assembly; little of what had been achieved by 1791 was to be lost, and most of what was done subsequently was to be undone. The essential first question to ask, then, is who formed the *tiers état* of 1789?

Were they the representatives of a rising industrial capitalist class? To imagine that this was even possible would be to antedate such industrial revolution as France was to experience by more than half a century. Some kind of clue to their importance in society will be provided if we ask how many manufacturers there were among those elected in 1789. Those who actually sat in the Assembly, either as deputies or *suppléants,* in the *tiers état,* numbered 648. Among these there were just eight who are described as manufacturers or *maîtres de forges*. Perhaps, however, the bourgeois were the merchants? Some 76 of the *tiers* are described as *marchands* or *négociants*. Only about 20 of these came from places of any commercial importance; the remainder should perhaps be regarded primarily as local notables. Very few of them seem to have played any prominent part in the Revolution. The world of finance produced one solitary banker, though one merchant also described himself as a banker. Together, merchants, manufacturers and financiers amount to 85, or 13 per cent of the whole number.

If they were not merchants or manufacturers, then, what were the *tiers état* of 1789? The category of those concerned with trade and industry is easy to identify. The social status or function of the others is apt to be more difficult to distinguish, sometimes for lack of sufficient indication—"*bourgeois vivant noblement*" is fairly easy to place, as is even "*citoyen*"; but what is the significance of "*bourgeois fils aîné*"? Sometimes there appears also that great handicap which the modern historian suffers from as compared with the historian of medieval or ancient times, too much information. How is one to classify a member (of the Convention) described as "landowner, leather manufacturer, lawyer and professor of mathematics and physics"? My figures are, therefore, all approximate, but I do not think that a variation of a few either way would do much to alter the general picture that emerges of the kind of men who composed the *tiers état* of 1789.

It is usually said that the majority were lawyers. This is undoubtedly true, but it is not as illuminating a statement as might be supposed. True, we can make out an impressive list of well over 400 lawyers in the Constituent Assembly, but this description tells as little about their actual social status or functions. It is as useful as would be a contemporary social classification based on the possession of a university degree.

Fortunately we know something more about most of the members. Those who are described as lawyers (*avocats* or *notaires*) without any further qualification number 166, just about a quarter, and it might be held that this was quite enough for the health of the Assembly. The remainder of the huge legal contingent falls into a different category. It includes members of the *ministère public,* notaries royal, local judges, municipal officers, and above all *lieutenants généraux* of *bailliages* and *sénéchaussées*. It may be observed in passing that there was an extraordinary number of officers of *bailliage* and *sénéchaussée* among those elected, which is perhaps not unconnected with the fact that these areas formed the constituencies. Add to these the various officials of the state services—25—and the total of 278 is reached, that is some 43 per cent of the whole membership.

To describe these men simply as lawyers is to ignore one of the essential features of the *ancien régime*. It would be almost as justifiable as a social analysis which classified the Justices of the Peace in England primarily as lawyers, for as late as the eighteenth century administration and justice were inextricably mixed up in most countries. The great majority of the so-called lawyers were in fact juridico-administrative officers, holding *charges* in municipality or *bailliage* or one of the state services. These were nearly always venal posts, which went therefore to those with a sufficient competence to pay the purchase price, unless they were lucky enough to inherit them from a relation. Thus in 1789 the office of notary could cost as much as 300 or 400,000 *livres* in Paris; in the provinces it might be worth much less.

An office or *charge* was an investment, a status and a job. Those who bought them were not spending their money for nothing; they drew in return a commensurate income from fees. How much work they had to do for it must remain a matter of doubt: the number of office-holders is evidence of the financial needs of the Crown, rather than of the administrative needs of the country. One little *bourg* of 3,000 inhabitants in the seventeenth century rejoiced in a *bailli,* a *prévot,* a *lieutenant,* a *procureur fiscal,* six notaries, four *sergents,* twelve *procureurs,* and four *greffiers*. Doubtless they also served the surrounding countryside, but it seems a lot. It is difficult not to suspect that, whatever their fees, they were overpaid for their services. They could reply, of course, that having bought their jobs they were entitled to a return on their investment.

The presence of such a large proportion of venal officers in the Constituent Assembly is at first sight difficult to reconcile with the holocaust of their offices effected by the Assembly itself, apparently with little protest. One can understand that they were ready to sacrifice the privileges of the *noblesse* and the clergy, but that an important part of their own income should have gone the same way appears at first sight to indicate a spirit of self-sacrifice and idealism rarely to be predicated of the average political man. We need not, however, in this case hypothesize any superhuman virtue. The venal offices were abolished, it is true, but not without compensation. Admittedly, the compensation was in *assignats:* but no one as yet knew, or dreamed of, the depths to which the *assignat* was to fall. Those who clung to their paper money long enough doubtless lost it all; but it is permissible to suppose that many rapidly reinvested their compensation. It would be interesting to know to what extent the payment for the venal offices was used for the purchase of the nationalized lands of the Church. Certainly the coincidence by which the venal officers, who formed such an important element in the Constituent Assembly, obtained a large supply of free capital, just at the time when an unprecedented opportunity for its investment in land was opened to them, was a very happy one.

It need not be assumed that there were no other motives, of a more disinterested nature, involved in the treatment of the venal offices. But though the demands of a more efficient administration called for their abolition, the venal officers had no occasion to feel that their posts were contrary to social morality. They were all, in a sense, living on the state; but if they looked higher up the social scale they could see plenty who held places and pensions by favour of the Court, without having had to pay for them, or having to do any work in them at all. In their monopoly of the positions combining the maximum of remuneration with the minimum of duties the privileged orders had something more valuable than a mere decorative social superiority and the bourgeois a substantial grievance.

Thiers, who was close to the Revolution and knew many of its participants, held that if the Crown had established some equality in official appointments and given some guarantees, the major source of discontent would have been eliminated. De Tocqueville, a little later, put forward a similar view of the revolution of 1848. "If many of the conservatives," he wrote, "only defended the Ministry with the aim of keeping their salaries and jobs, I must say that many of the opposition only appeared to me to be attacking it in order to get jobs for themselves. The truth, a deplorable truth, is that the taste for official jobs and the desire to live on the taxes is not with us the peculiar malady of a particular party, it is the great and permanent infirmity of the nation itself. . . ."

Returning to the analysis of the revolutionary bourgeoisie, it may be said that the Revolution did not end with the Constituent Assembly, and that its subsequent developments brought, in the Convention, another set of men into power. An analysis of the membership of the Convention gives results which naturally vary from those for the Constituent Assembly. The financial, mercantile and manufacturing section is even smaller—83 out of 891, some 9 per cent. Lawyers are present in about the same proportion of one-fourth. Office holders are down from 43 to 25 per cent, though as the venal offices were now a thing of the past, it is unlikely that this figure represents all those who had held such positions under the *ancien régime*. A tiny group of *petits bourgeois* and ordinary soldiers appears, to offset which we have rather more nobles and colonial proprietors. There are more clergy, of course, now that they have no Order of their own. The most notable development is the appearance of a substantial group of what one might call professional men in addition to the lawyers: 32 professors or teachers, some of them also clerics; 58 doctors, surgeons or pharmacists; some lower officers of the army, the navy and merchant marine; a few writers and actors. Altogether this category has risen from about 5 per cent to 17 per cent.

Like the *Constituante,* the Convention is still almost exclusively a bourgeois assembly, and in 1792, as in 1789, bourgeois has to be interpreted in the sense of a class of *fonctionnaires* and professional men. Admittedly, its actions were not the same as those of the *Constituante*. Under pressure from the popular movement in Paris, and amid the storm and stress of counter revolution and war, policies were accepted by a purged Convention which, as is the way of revolutions, after the purgers had themselves been purged, it was to repudiate. These surface storms of the Revolution are not my subject. When they had died down, and under Napoleon it was possible to make some calculation as to who had emerged in triumph, it could be seen that the smaller fry had mostly continued to inhabit the shallows, while the officials and the professional men of the *ancien régime,* mixed with a fair number of former nobles and a few able men from the ranks, had emerged as the governing class of the new régime.

Once again figures tell the story better than words. Of the members of the Constituent Assembly and the Convention, 111 held high office, and 518 lower offices, under Napoleon, and of these over one-third had held office before 1789. Both Assemblies contained many obscure men who subsequently sank back into the obscurity from which they had emerged. They contained more than a few who, republican by principle, refused to accept the Empire and the share in the fruits of office which they might otherwise have had. There were also the liquidations, the method by which revolutions solve the problem of too many people pursuing too few jobs. But in the end it may have been that a fair proportion of those who had given up their venal offices for compensation at the beginning of the Revolution obtained new ones that were free from the stigma of venality at the end. It may at least be suggested as an hypothesis worthy of investigation that the essence of government in France after the Revolution remained where it had been before, in the great and now renewed bureaucratic *cadres*. . . .

If I have put forward the view that the interpretation of the Revolution as the substitution of a capitalist bourgeois order for feudalism is a myth, this is not to suggest that the Revolution itself is mythical and that nothing of significance happened in France at this time. The revolutionaries drew a line at the end of the *ancien régime,* subtracted the negative factors from the past, and added up the sum of what was positive, to be carried forward on the next page. A class of officials and professional men moved up from the minor to the major posts in government and dispossessed the minions of an effete Court: this was what the bourgeois revolution meant. The peasants relieved themselves of their seigneurial dues: this was the meaning of the abolition of feudalism. But even taken together these two developments hardly constitute the abolition of one social order and the substitution of another for it, and if the accepted theory is not quite a myth, it seems singularly like one.

Did the Revolution effect no more fundamental change than this? In French economy it might be considered that it held back rather than encouraged changes which were to come much later and are still very incomplete. Politically it replaced the divine right of the King by the divine right of the people. In theory this was to substitute an absolute power for one limited by its nature, and to eliminate the rights of the people as against a government which was henceforth theoretically themselves. The war dictatorship of the Committee of Public Safety, and the Napoleonic Empire, were the historical if not the logical sequel to the assertion of the sovereignty of the people. But this aspect of the Revolution has perhaps been unduly emphasized of late. Sovereignty remained sovereignty, whether exercised in the name of God or the people, even though the Revolution changed both the possessors and the nature of power in the state.

I implied, earlier in this lecture, that the Revolution was not one but many. One of the greatest of its aspects I have so far neglected. Men have ideas, whatever those historians who have tried to decerebrate history may say, and these ideas are not to be treated merely as the expression of material interests. The explanation of the causation of the Revolution simply in terms of the ideas of the eighteenth century has long been discarded from serious history, but this is not to say that the revolutionaries were mere economic animals to be summed up in terms of the stud book and the bank balance, or reduced to a number of holes punched in an index card. The members of the French revolutionary assemblies had been bred on the ideas of the Enlightenment. Reforms such as the abolition of torture in legal proceedings and many other legal changes, or the removal of the disabilities of Protestants and Jews, are not to be explained in terms of material interests. But here again, though the Revolution may have accelerated some of these reforms it perhaps put back others. Here also the historian has to admit not only that these reforms were the children of the ideas of the eighteenth century but that their implementation had already begun before 1789. The reign of Louis XVI was an age of reform, which the Revolution continued. The armies of the Revolution and Napoleon, it has been said, spread the humanitarian ideals of the eighteenth century to the rest of Europe, strange missionaries though they were. There is some truth in this, though if we consider the development of subsequent history we may be tempted to think that the seeds of the Enlightenment, east of the Rhine and south of the Alps and the Pyrenees, fell on very stony ground. The main point I want to make, however, is that whether we analyse the Revolutionary age in terms of social forces or of ideas, it appears more and more clearly as the child of the eighteenth century and only to be understood in terms of the society out of which it emerged. To interpret the Revolution we must look back as well as forward, and forget if possible that 1789 has ever seemed a date from which to begin.

5. GEORGE RUDÉ: Revolutionary Europe, 1783–1815 *

Much of the recent research on the French Revolution has dealt with the urban lower classes and their role in the massive upheaval. Professor George Rudé, of the University of Adelaide, has significantly contributed to this study by examining the nature and purposes of revolutionary crowds. In the following selection, he stresses the uniqueness of the French Revolution, a uniqueness that lay in the participation of the masses and the experience they gained from it; and in this he finds also one of the chief legacies of the revolution to the nineteenth century.

So we return to the wider question posed at the beginning of the last chapter. Are we dealing here with an essentially *French* revolution with its offshoots in other western countries; or are Professors Godechot and Palmer correct in suggesting that all these revolutions, the French and the American included, are merely "phases" of a more general "democratic" revolution of the West? There might perhaps be some point in attaching a general label of this kind to all the revolutions taking place in Europe and America from, say, 1550 to 1850—covering not only the American and the French, but the Dutch of the sixteenth, the English of the seventeenth, and various South American and European revolutions of the early nineteenth century. All of these raise, in one form or another, common problems relating to feudalism and capitalism, democracy and national sovereignty. In this wider context, the American Revolution of the 1760's and seventies may appear to be as closely linked with

* From George Rudé, *Revolutionary Europe, 1783–1815* (Cleveland: Meridian Books, The World Publishing Company, 1964), pp. 220–22. Copyright by George Rudé, 1964. Reprinted by permission of The World Publishing Company.

the English Revolution of 120 years before as with the French of twenty years after; and the German and Italian revolutions are seen in full flood rather than at their earliest beginnings. But if one chooses merely to consider the revolutions of the eighteenth century, one is struck rather by differences than similarities and by the small number that can claim to be revolutions in their own right. In Europe, the only "democratic" (or, more accurately, "liberal") revolutions taking place at this time in any way independent of the French were those in Liège, Brussels and Geneva; but the first two of these had been defeated by 1790 and only revived as the result of French military occupation. Revolutionary movements were also germinating, inspired by the French example, in the Rhineland, Piedmont and parts of Switzerland; but they only came to a head on the approach of France's armies. Elsewhere in Western Europe, revolutions, though owing something to local "patriots" and local conditions, were largely imposed by the French. In fact, of 29 constitutions adopted in European countries other than France between 1791 and 1802, all except three (two Genevan and one Polish) were the outcome of French intervention. So strictly speaking, outside America, and perhaps the tiny state of Geneva, the only revolution in its own right was the French.

Even more important perhaps is the fact that the revolution in France went much further than elsewhere—not only in the sense that it was more violent, more radical, more democratic and more protracted, but that it posed problems and aroused classes that other European revolutions (and the American, for that matter) left largely untouched. This was partly due to a different historical development in these countries from that in France and partly to the fact that the French after July 1794 (when they began to impose their ideas on their neighbours) were no longer interested in promoting the democratic ideals of 1793—and ruthlessly crushed the Piedmontese when they attempted to do so. If we are only concerned with the spread of the ideas of the Enlightenment, the permanent legislation of the revolutionary assemblies and the liberal "principles of 1789," then the similarities between the revolutions in France and in these other countries are strikingly close: all went, with greater or lesser thoroughness, through a common bourgeois revolution, which destroyed the old feudal institutions and obligations, expropriated the estates of the Church, abolished serfdom, legal inequalities and the privileged orders, and declared careers to be "open to talent"; and this process continued, though in a muted form, in Germany and Poland under the Empire. Important as this is, it leaves out an essential element of the French Revolution: the active participation of the common people from 1789 onwards and all the consequences that flowed from it. John Adams, it may be remembered, criticized the Dutch Patriots of 1787 for having been "too inattentive to the sense of the common people"; and they continued to be so. And this was by no means a failure peculiar to the Dutch: Belgian, Roman and Neapolitan "Jacobins" were equally divorced from the people and made little serious effort to bridge the gap. In some of these countries, it is true, there were temporary movements in which both "patriots" and peasants or urban poor took part and in which the latter classes voiced the slogans and ideas of their bourgeois allies; but these were exceptional and short-lived. In France alone, owing to the particular circumstances in which the revolution developed and broke out (and certainly not to any innate Gallic quality!), the "Fourth Estate" became the indispensable ally of the Third, exacted its reward, and even built up a distinctive political movement of its own. So in France we have such phenomena as the peasant "revolution," the *sans-culotte* movement of 1793, the Jacobin Dictatorship, the *levée en masse* and *armées révolutionnaires,* and the social experiments and Republic of the Year II. These factors reappeared, often in more advanced forms, in the European revolutions of the nineteenth century; but, with minor exceptions, they did not in those of the 1790's—and still less so under the Consulate and Empire. In this sense, the revolution in France, though casting its shadow all over Europe, remained quite peculiar and unique.

Chapter II.

THE NATURE OF ROMANTICISM

TO DEFINE a broad intellectual and cultural movement is one of the most difficult tasks the historian faces. It is hard, first of all, to date such a movement. Intellectual changes are not signaled by an event. There are always forerunners of any new style or philosophical orientation, and certainly the influence of an intellectual or cultural current may continue into later periods. The diversity of intellectual endeavor poses another problem for definition. Without doubt, there are fads and fashions, and many intellectuals are content to imitate; but the creative thinker is very consciously trying to find a new and different path. Further, each form of cultural activity has its own requirements and traditions. Can a cultural historian find patterns in music and philosophy which are sufficiently common to allow him to speak of a general cultural movement? And what of the historian's own taste? Intellectual history poses the problem of value judgment in an obvious way. The historian who finds an approach stylistically and philosophically appealing may seek to magnify its historical importance, whereas one who personally rejects the same approach may belittle it or attribute dire consequences to it.

An assessment of romanticism raises all these problems, some in an acute form. The romantic period for philosophy and the arts is usually seen as running from about 1780 to about 1840. But there are clear expressions of romantic styles and themes quite early in the eighteenth century, and the movement has had definite influence on some major cultural trends through the nineteenth century and into the twentieth. To assign a date to the movement is, to some extent, to assess its impact. Romanticism can be seen as the key to modern culture, in which case it is difficult to assign an end point to it; or it may be relegated to the specific styles of one or two generations of artists and thinkers, which makes periodization easier but may obscure the relationship of romanticism and later movements.

Romanticism is easiest to define in literature and painting. It is possible to find a romantic approach in philosophy, but what does it have in common with romanticism in the arts? And there were areas of thought, notably political theory, about which romantics did not agree at all. What can the historian say about a presumably general intellectual movement in which some romantics are extreme conservatives and others extreme radicals? For the facts are undeniable. Some historians explain the divergences by positing two different generations of romantics, the first conservative, the next radical. Others see a unity underlying the political differences. Still others claim that romanticism does not relate to political theory.

Romanticism, as all its interpreters quickly note, sought diversity and individuality in every field. Romantics were suspicious of fixed standards and categories. But then how can the historian find common themes on which to base any useful definition? The problem is certainly greater for romanticism than for the preceding intellectual current, the Enlightenment. For Enlightenment thinkers sought clear, fixed rules and, though they might disagree on exactly what these rules were, they at least had the effort in common. Romantics rebelled against this effort. On their rebellion, too, there can be general agreement, if only because the romantics themselves said so, and often. But can one say more? One of the keys to an assessment of the interpretations of romanticism is simply to ask: Is the historian finding any unity in romanticism other than its diversity and intellectual rebelliousness? Is this enough to define a whole cultural period?

Was romanticism a European movement? Without doubt, romantics existed in all countries, but were their efforts comparable and was their impact the same? One historian has noted romanticism as Germany's great contribution to the nineteenth century, an intellectual revolution as important as France's in politics and Britain's in industry. But to what extent did the German spirit penetrate elsewhere? Did romanticism seriously affect French philosophy, or merely French artistic styles? Here is another aspect of the problem of generalization about romanticism.

It is possible to dislike romanticism intensely. Romanticism can mean beauty or idealism, but it has also been used to mean puerility, hopeless unrealism, shallowness, immorality, and even fascism. One historian, betraying his own preferences, viewed partisans of romanticism and of the Enlightment as different personality types comparable to cat and dog fanciers: romantic values, like dogs, are for the multitudes who favor sentiment, whereas cats appeal to the smaller number who look for qualities of the mind. Is it better to entrust the interpretation of dogs to cat lovers or to dog lovers? Certainly, partisans of romanticism must deal with the criticisms leveled against the movement for its lack of clear standards, its devotion to irrational causes, and its shallow estheticism.

Finally, should romanticism be assessed in purely cultural or intellectual terms? Most of its students, obviously, have been intellectual historians and have tended to apply criteria in their own fields. But can roots of romanticism be discerned also in the social and political structure of the period? The question has been asked, if not yet elaborately explored. It is an important question, for it bears on the vital problem of assessing the impact of romanticism outside the intellectual sphere.

The problems of interpretation, then, are great, and the diversity of evaluations is accordingly considerable. No one seeking to understand the nineteenth century can avoid the issues. If romanticism is seen as a new world view, it becomes one of the central topics of modern history. Even if a more limited approach is taken, which confines the movement to the last two decades of the eighteenth and the first half of the nineteenth century, the subject remains important. There is no doubt that a new and rather consciously rebellious style developed in philosophy and the arts around the turn of the century. Nor is there any doubt that questions were raised about the validity of rationalism—questions that continue today—though perhaps in different forms. Any assessment of romanticism must ask how important these questions were and how widely they spread. It can be suggested that the very continuance of the debate over the issues the romantics raised, issues such as the extent of man's power to reason, represents the greatest difficulty in interpreting the movement itself. We must know if the romantics were right about the nature of man, about the movement of history, about the importance of art, about the relationship of the individual to some larger whole. We must know, in order to form our own set of values. We must also search for ways to combine this sort of interest in romanticism with a historical interpretation.

1. FREDERICK COPLESTON: *A History of Philosophy* *

Frederick Copleston, an English historian now at the Gregorian University in Rome and member of the Society of Jesus, finds a number of coherent and general features in romanticism. He stresses the philosophical aspects of the movement, though noting the esthetic impulse, and refers mainly to German thinkers. This circumscription may contribute to his ability to offer a reasonably elaborate definition of romanticism. He offers no direct judgments on the validity of the movement but approaches it sympathetically. Like many Catholics in the romantic period itself, he is particularly interested in the romantic striving for the infinite and its kinship to religion.

The romantic spirit is notoriously difficult to define. Nor indeed should one expect to be able to define it. But one can, of course, mention some of its characteristic traits. For example, as against the Enlightenment's concentration on the critical, analytic and scientific understanding the romantics exalted the power of the creative imagination and the role of feeling and intuition. The artistic genius took the place of *le philosophe*. But the emphasis which was laid on the creative imagination and on artistic genius formed part of a general emphasis on the free and full development of the human personality, on man's creative powers and on enjoyment of the wealth of possible human experience. In other words, stress was laid on the originality of each human person rather than on what is common to all men. And this insistence on the creative personality was sometimes associated with a tendency to ethical subjectivism. That is to say, there was a tendency to depreciate fixed universal moral laws or rules in favour of the free development of the self in accordance with values rooted in and corresponding to the individual personality. I do not mean to imply by this that the romantics had no concern for morality and moral values. But there was a tendency, with F. Schlegel for example, to emphasize the free pursuit by the individual of his own moral ideal (the fulfilment of his own "Idea") rather than obedience to universal laws dictated by the impersonal practical reason. . . .

Emphasis on the creative self was, however, only one aspect of romanticism. Another important aspect was the romantics' conception of Nature. Instead of conceiving Nature simply as a mechanical system, so that they would be forced to make a sharp contrast (as in Cartesianism) between man and Nature, the romantics tended to look on Nature as a living organic whole which is in some way akin to spirit and which is clothed in beauty and mystery. And some of them showed a marked sympathy with Spinoza, that is, a romanticized Spinoza.

* From Frederick Copleston, S. J., *A History of Philosophy,* Vol. 7 (Maryland: Newman Press). From the Image Books edition, 1965, pp. 30, 31–32, 32–33, 33–35.

This view of Nature as an organic totality akin to spirit again links the romantics with Schelling. The philosopher's idea of Nature below man as slumbering spirit and the human spirit as the organ of Nature's consciousness of herself was thoroughly romantic in tone. . . .

The romantics' attachment to the idea of Nature as an organic living totality does not mean, however, that they emphasized Nature to the detriment, so to speak, of man. We have seen that they also stressed the free creative personality. In the human spirit Nature reaches, as it were, its culmination. Hence the romantic idea of Nature could be and was allied with a marked appreciation of the continuity of historical and cultural development and of the significance of past cultural periods for the unfolding of the potentialities of the human spirit. Hölderlin, for example, had a romantic enthusiasm for the genius of ancient Greece, an enthusiasm which was shared by Hegel in his student days. But special attention can be drawn here to the reawakened interest in the Middle Ages. The man of the Enlightenment had tended to see in the mediaeval period a dark night which preceded the dawn of the Renaissance and the subsequent emergence of *les philosophes*. But for Novalis the Middle Ages represented, even if imperfectly, an ideal of the organic unity of faith and culture, an ideal which should be recovered. Further, the romantics showed a strong attachment to the idea of the spirit of a people (*Volksgeist*) and an interest in the cultural manifestation of this spirit, such as language. In this respect they continued the thought of Herder and other predecessors. . . .

Above all perhaps romanticism was characterized by a feeling for and longing for the infinite. And the ideas of Nature and of human history were brought together in the conception of them as manifestations of one infinite Life, as aspects of a kind of divine poem. Thus the notion of infinite Life served as a unifying factor in the romantic world-outlook. At first sight perhaps the romantics' attachment to the idea of the *Volksgeist* may appear to be at variance with their emphasis on the free development of the individual personality. But there was really no radical incompatibility. For the infinite totality was conceived, generally speaking, as infinite Life which manifested itself in and through finite beings but not as annihilating them or as reducing them to mere mechanical instruments. And the spirits of peoples were conceived as manifestations of the same infinite Life, as relative totalities which required for their full development the free expression of the individual personalities which were the bearers, so to speak, of these spirits. And the same can be said of the State, considered as the political embodiment of the spirit of a people.

The typical romantic was inclined to conceive the infinite totality aesthetically, as an organic whole with which man felt himself to be one, the means of apprehending this unity being intuition and feeling rather than conceptual thought. For conceptual thought tends to fix and perpetuate defined limits and boundaries, whereas romanticism tends to dissolve limits and boundaries in the infinite flow of Life. In other words, romantic feeling for the infinite was not infrequently a feeling for the indefinite. And this trait can be seen as well in the tendency to obscure the boundary between the infinite and the finite as in the tendency to confuse philosophy with poetry or, within the artistic sphere itself, to intermingle the arts.

Partly, of course, it was a question of seeing affinities and of synthesizing different types of human experience. Thus F. Schlegel regarded philosophy as akin to religion on the ground that both are concerned with the infinite and that every relation of man to the infinite can be said to belong to religion. Indeed art too is religious in character, for the creative artist sees the infinite in the finite, in the form of beauty. At the same time the romantics' repugnance to definite limits and clear-cut form was one of the reasons which led Goethe to make his famous statement that the classical is the healthy and the romantic the diseased. For the matter of that, some of the romantics themselves came to feel the need for giving definite shape to their intuitive and rather hazy visions of life and reality and for combining the nostalgia for the infinite and for the free expression of the individual personality with a recognition of definite limits. And certain representatives of the movement, such as F. Schlegel, found in Catholicism a fulfilment of this need.

2. GEORGE L. MOSSE: The Culture of Western Europe *

Here is another effort at a general definition of romanticism, drawn again from a general intellectual history. Professor Mosse, a historian at the University of Wisconsin, has frequently written on the culture of the nineteenth and twentieth centuries. His portrait of romanticism should be closely compared with that of Father Copleston. The two accounts are by no means totally different. But Professor Mosse sees less unity in romanticism and attempts to go beyond romantic philosophy to discuss its impulse in art and political theory as well, and not only in Germany. One may ask whether Professor Mosse finds enough unity in romanticism as a whole to justify the use of the term to denote an intellectual movement—is a "mood" sufficient common ground? Note also the periodization implied by a discussion which can range from the early nineteenth century to Benjamin Disraeli.

The romanticism which became all pervasive in modern European culture was a "mood" which escaped any rigid scheme of classification. That was part of the strength of the movement, for it could change from person to person and combine with various political and social ideals. Romanticism did have one explicit ideological base, however—it accorded the greatest importance to the emotions and to the imagination. The emotions of the heart, however irrational, were considered more valid than the thoughts of the head. The enemy was that cold reason which Charles Dickens had symbolized in Scrooge and which had provided the essence of the Enlightenment's hope for a better world. The rationalism of the eighteenth century had not been cold or selfish,

* From George L. Mosse, *The Culture of Western Europe* (Chicago: Rand McNally & Co., 1961), pp. 13–14; 16; 39–41. Reprinted by permission of Rand McNally & Co.

but the Romantics made no distinction between a Scrooge and those who believed that progress was possible only because of man's rational nature. For Romantics, human nature was best described through man's "soul" which contained his emotions and which furthered his imagination. All else was abstract "intellectualizing," typical of men who lacked true emotion and therefore a true soul.

Because the feelings of man became all-important in this romantic mood, the Romantics concentrated upon the intensity of the emotions. If feeling was the test of true virtue, of the possession of a soul, the story of a person who exemplified feeling was especially interesting, but of still greater importance was that moment when an emotion was at its height. To the Romantic the true nature of the world and life was more clearly revealed by emotion and vision than by the dry and comprehensive power of analysis. . . .

Yet such a heroine should not disguise the lasting impact of the movement. It formed a habit of mind which was hostile to rationalism—and which thought of man in terms of his soul rather than his reason. Focusing on the inner workings of human nature, it claimed that they alone were "genuine" and "true." Not only reason but also reality was held to be superficial, merely an "outward" thing not directly related to man's soul. The romantic mood thus capitalized on the dissatisfactions engendered by rationalism's disavowal of the emotions, particularly man's need for a security which discounted external reality by escaping into a contemplation of the inner man. No doubt the change of Europe from a rural to an industrial and urban civilization enhanced the attractiveness of this habit of mind. It gave men a feeling of importance, of stability in terms of their own souls amid rapid and uncomprehensible changes. . . .

"Action was all in antiquity and character played not the same role as in modern times." The greatness of the Romantics came from elevating character above action. These moderns avoided artificiality of action. Placing character in the foreground, they centered their attention upon honor, love, and bravery—in short, upon the internal condition of men rather than upon those external forces the ancients thought guided man's destiny. This meant the primacy of "emotion" and "sentiment," since the character of man must be detached from his environment and analyzed in terms of his own emotions. External events were mere superficialities when compared with man's true self. Reality was rejected as a determinant of man's action or of his nature. The distinction between outward phenomena and the real essence of things was thus present from the very beginning of romanticism, a part of its original definition. The tone was set for German idealism, indeed for a mood widely spread throughout Europe during the last century and a half. This distinction will be one of the principal themes running throughout this analysis of modern European culture. . . .

This substitution of Germanism for Christianity or art or nature as the only basis for true sentiment was already beginning when Chateaubriand and Schleiermacher wrote their works. It led into the link between romanticism and politics, a connection which existed on this more subtle level rather than on the association of Romantics with one or the other political movements of the times. Romantics were found in all political parties.

Some patterns do emerge, however, from the relationship between romanticism and politics. In France after the Revolution and during the first years of the Bourbon restoration, romanticism was closely tied to monarchism and the Catholic Church. This was hardly surprising, for the Revolution stood for that rationalism and scepticism which Romantics abhorred, while king and Pope fitted in with the romantic vision of the Middle Ages. Chateaubriand was at first an enthusiastic supporter of the Restoration, and Conservatives like De Maistre built their theories upon medieval foundations closely related to romanticism. Victor Hugo wrote, in 1824, that the new literature was an expression of a monarchical and religious society. But this society spurned the Romantics. Louis XVIII (1815–24) furthered the classicism which he remembered from pre-Revolutionary days, and the French Academy issued a proclamation against the "romantic sect." Moreover, the regime of Charles X (1824–30) seemed to further a schematic and sterile monarchism in the name of order. Both Lamennais and Chateaubriand suffered persecution—the romantic mood had too many revolutionary implications. To be sure, such implications were directed primarily against literary styles and social conventions, but they might branch out from this and endanger order.

The result of the restored monarchy's opposition to romanticism was the development of precisely those revolutionary implications it had feared—revolutionary inasmuch as they came to be directed against the existing political as well as literary order. French Romantics continued to repudiate the French Revolution but they now also repudiated the *ancien régime*. Chateaubriand worked for a revolution which came about in 1830 and Lamennais began to write about the necessity of disentangling Catholicism from the restored monarchy. Hugo, who had praised the Catholic and monarchical regime in 1824 now wrote in his preface to *Hernani*: "Romanticism is Liberalism in Literature. Literary Liberalism is not less popular than political Liberalism. Liberty in Art and freedom in society are identical goals. . . ." By 1827 the Romantics had broken their ties with the Bourbons and allied themselves with the liberal camp. The Greek war of liberation from the Turks (1832) stirred the Romantics in France as it did those of England. For Chateaubriand a defense of the Greeks meant at the same time a defense of freedom and Christianity, though unlike Lord Byron he did not rush into a personal involvement with the cause. What happened in France is a good example of romanticism pushing men in a liberal direction. Men like Hugo and Lamennais remained consistent voices for liberalism in the Europe of their age.

But the conservative impetus also continued. In England it was to lead a conservatism which was less rigid than that of De Maistre or De Bonald (1754–1840). The "Tory Democracy" of Benjamin Disraeli (1804–81) and his revitalized Conservative party showed a real concern for the social welfare of the people. Here also a vision of the Middle Ages predominated—a romanticized picture of the relationship of rulers and ruled. The nobility must once more take upon itself the role of leadership in order to improve the lot of the common man. The paternalism of the Lord of the Manor toward his tenants was to be generalized into a social consciousness for political leadership. Social reform, however, should never blur class lines or the necessary aristocratic leadership principle. "The people are not strong, the people can never be strong," Disraeli wrote at a time when the Chartist movement seemed to have failed.

This view of the people, however, was based not so much on any immediate cause as upon a nostalgic vision of the past—the medieval Arcadia of the Romantics. Tory democracy did not stand still in the new age; it tried to apply the vision of the past to the problems of industrial England. Social reform, within definite limits, and the knights of Sir Walter Scott transformed into an active aristocracy—these were Disraeli's goals. After all, the knights of old had not only been charitable toward the weak; they had protected them as well, and Tory leadership must imitate their example in modern politics. It is no wonder that Disraeli's attitudes toward representative government were ambivalent. Romanticism, in so far as it was linked to conservatism, tended to further ideas of government which stood outside the tradition of parliaments. It pointed backwards to what was considered the "harmonious" state of the Middle Ages where no shoddy politics and venal political parties divided the people. Thus Conservatives on the Continent took up the example of the medieval guilds where both masters and journeymen as well as apprentices had been a part of a harmonious whole. From this they envisioned a nation made up of professional and industrial guilds, all regulating themselves and all based on the cooperation of the people within them, whether employers or employees. . . .

If this concept of corporatism was one of the most important contributions of romanticism to politics, there was another. Romanticism gave great impetus to nationalism. In this guise it could penetrate the politics of many divergent political parties. The connection between romanticism and nationalism is best illustrated in Germany where it was to dominate both politics and thought. It produced a type of romantic thought quite different from that which came about in France at the same time. The Frenchman Lamennais, who called himself an anti-materialist, placed the soul above the body of man and the soul of peoples above their material organization. With that, the Germans would have agreed. But from these premises Lamennais pleaded not for an exclusive national "soul" nor for return to the vistas of a bygone age; instead, the superiority of the soul of a people meant to him the freedom of the individual spirit, the equality of the rights of man, and the general fraternity of all peoples. Lamennais wrote in the tradition of Rousseau and of the Jacobins; there was no tradition which could lead to such thought in Germany. The stress on individual freedom which was inherent in romantic expression found an outlet in France and England which were both territorially united nations.

But neither German Liberals nor German Romantics could ignore the national problem which their people faced. Germany had to be concerned with her own unity and independence, and those interested in German politics had little time to fight for the independence of others.

3. ARTHUR O. LOVEJOY: On the Discrimination of Romanticisms *

Arthur Lovejoy, long a professor of philosophy at Johns Hopkins University, whose study of *The Great Chain of Being* is a landmark in intellectual history, here offers an explicitly skeptical view of the term "romanticism," and an alternative to its conventional use. He implies that his concern for a more accurate term is philosophical, to clear up the ambiguities for philosophic discourse; but his procedure is eminently historical in attempting to discriminate by chronology in order to find real unities of ideas. His eschewal of moral judgments of romanticism is also worth noting; he clearly feels that we must have a much more definite notion of what the various strains of the movement were before we can evaluate them. The questions he raises are obvious: Is it necessary, in contrast to other historical views, to break romanticism down into quite different movements? If so, how? Professor Lovejoy uses units limited in time and geography: German romanticism at the end of the eighteenth century, English in the mid-eighteenth century, and so on; but he emerges dissatisfied with the coherence even of these. Yet if these are broken down still further, can intellectual history be much more than a listing of one thinker after another?

The word "romantic" has come to mean so many things that, by itself, it means nothing. It has ceased to perform the function of a verbal sign. When a man is asked, as I have had the honor of being asked, to discuss Romanticism, it is impossible to know what ideas or tendencies he is to talk about, when they are supposed to have flourished, or in whom they are supposed to be chiefly exemplified. Perhaps there are some who think the rich ambiguity of the word not regrettable. In 1824, as Victor Hugo then testified, there were those who preferred to leave—*à ce mot de romantique un certain vague fantastique et indéfinissable qui en redouble l'horreur,* and it may be that the taste is not extinct. But for one of the philosopher's trade, at least, the situation is embarrassing and exasperating; for philosophers, in spite of a popular belief to the contrary, are persons who suffer from a morbid solicitude to know what they are talking about. . . .

What, then, can be done to clear up, or to diminish, this confusion of terminology and of thought which has for a century been the scandal of literary history and criticism, and is still, as it would not be difficult to show, copiously productive of historical errors and of dangerously undiscriminating diagnoses of the moral and aesthetic maladies of our age? The one really radical remedy

*From Arthur O. Lovejoy, "On the Discrimination of Romanticisms" from *Essays in the History of Ideas* (Baltimore: Johns Hopkins Press, 1948), pp. 232, 234–36, 237, 251–53. Reprinted by permission of the Johns Hopkins Press.

—namely, that we should all cease talking about Romanticism—is, I fear, certain not to be adopted. It would probably be equally futile to attempt to prevail upon scholars and critics to restrict their use of the term to a single and reasonably well-defined sense. Such a proposal would only be the starting-point of a new controversy. Men, and especially philologists, will doubtless go on using words as they like, however much annoyance they cause philosophers by this unchartered freedom. There are, however, two possible historical inquiries which, if carried out more thoroughly and carefully than has yet been done, would, I think, do much to rectify the present muddle, and would at the same time promote a clearer understanding of the general movement of ideas, the logical and psychological relations between the chief episodes and transitions, in modern thought and taste.

One of these measures would be somewhat analogous to the procedure of contemporary psychopathologists in the treatment of certain types of disorder. It has, we are told, been found that some mental disturbances can be cured or alleviated by making the patient explicitly aware of the genesis of his troublesome "complex," i.e., by enabling him to reconstruct those processes of association of ideas through which it was formed. Similarly in the present case, I think, it would be useful to trace the associative processes through which the word "romantic" has attained its present amazing diversity, and consequent uncertainty, of connotation and denotation; in other words, to carry out an adequate semasiological study of the term. For one of the few things certain about Romanticism is that the name of it offers one of the most complicated, fascinating, and instructive of all problems in semantics. It is, in short, a part of the task of the historian of ideas, when he applies himself to the study of the thing or things called Romanticism, to render it, if possible, psychologically intelligible how such manifold and discrepant phenomena have all come to receive one name. Such an analysis would, I am convinced, show us a large mass of purely verbal confusions operative as actual factors in the movement of thought in the past century and a quarter; and it would, by making these confusions explicit, make it easier to avoid them.

But this inquiry would in practice, for the most part, be inseparable from a second, which is the remedy that I wish, on this occasion, especially to recommend. The first step in this second mode of treatment of the disorder is that we should learn to use the word "Romanticism" in the plural. This, of course, is already the practice of the more cautious and observant literary historians, in so far as they recognize that the "Romanticism" of one country may have little in common with that of another, and at all events ought to be defined in distinctive terms. But the discrimination of the Romanticisms which I have in mind is not solely or chiefly a division upon lines of nationality or language. What is needed is that any study of the subject should begin with a recognition of a *prima-facie* plurality of Romanticisms, of possibly quite distinct thought-complexes, a number of which may appear in one country. There is no hope of clear thinking on the part of the student of modern literature, if—as, alas! has been repeatedly done by eminent writers—he vaguely hypostatizes the term, and starts with the presumption that "Romanticism" is the heaven-appointed designation of some single real entity, or type of entities, to be found in nature. He must set out from the simple and obvious fact that there are various historic episodes or movements to which different historians of our own or other periods have, for one reason or another, given the name. There is a movement which began in Germany in the seventeen-nineties—the only one which has an indisputable title to be called Romanticism, since it invented the term for its own use. There is another movement which began pretty definitely in England in the seventeen-forties. There is a movement which began in France in 1801. There is another movement which began in France in the second decade of the century, is linked with the German movement, and took over the German name. There is the rich and incongruous collection of ideas to be found in Rousseau. There are numerous other things called Romanticism by various writers whom I cited at the outset. The fact that the same name has been given by different scholars to all of these episodes is no evidence, and scarcely even establishes a presumption, that they are identical in essentials. There may be some common denominator of them all; but if so, it has never yet been clearly exhibited, and its presence is not to be assumed *a priori*. In any case, each of these so-called Romanticisms was a highly complex and usually an exceedingly unstable intellectual compound; each, in other words, was made up of various unit-ideas linked together, for the most part, not by any indissoluble bonds of logical necessity, but by alogical associative processes, greatly facilitated and partly caused, in the case of the Romanticisms which grew up after the appellation "Romantic" was invented, by the congenital and acquired ambiguities of the word. And when certain of these Romanticisms have in truth significant elements in common, they are not necessarily the same elements in any two cases. . . .

But the essential of the second remedy is that each of these Romanticisms—after they are first thus roughly discriminated with respect to their representatives or their dates—should be resolved, by a more thorough and discerning analysis than is yet customary, into its elements—into the several ideas and aesthetic susceptibilities of which it is composed. Only after these fundamental thought-factors or emotive strains in it are clearly discriminated and fairly exhaustively enumerated, shall we be in a position to judge of the degree of its affinity with other complexes to which the same name has been applied, to see precisely what tacit preconceptions or controlling motives or explicit contentions were common to any two or more of them, and wherein they manifested distinct and divergent tendencies. . . .

We have, then, observed and compared—very far from exhaustively, of course, yet in some of their most fundamental and determinative ideas—three "Romanticisms." In the first and second we have found certain common elements, but still more significant oppositions; in the second and third we have found certain other common elements, but likewise significant oppositions. But between the first and third the common elements are very scanty; such as there are, it could, I think, be shown, are not the same as those subsisting between either the first and second or the second and third; and in their ethical preconceptions and implications and the crucial articles of their literary creeds, the opposition between them is almost absolute.

All three of these historic episodes, it is true, are far more complex than I have time to show. I am attempting only to illustrate the nature of a certain procedure in the study of what is called Romanticism, to suggest its importance, and to present one or two specific results of the use of it. A complete analysis would qualify, without invalidating, these results, in several ways. It would (for one thing) bring out certain important connections between the revolt against the neo-classical aesthetics (common to two of the episodes mentioned) and other aspects of eighteenth-century thought. It would, again, exhibit fully certain *internal* oppositions in at least two of the Romanticisms considered. For example, in German Romanticism between 1797 and 1800 there grew up, and mainly from a single root, *both* an "apotheosis of the future" and a tendency to retrospection—a retrospection directed, not, indeed, towards classical antiquity or towards the primitive, but towards the medieval. A belief in progress and a spirit of reaction were, paradoxically, joint offspring of the same idea, and were nurtured for a time in the same minds. But it is just these internal incongruities which make it most of all evident, as it seems to me, that any attempt at a *general* appraisal even of a single chronologically determinate Romanticism—still more, of "Romanticism" as a whole—is a fatuity. When a Romanticism has been analyzed into the distinct "strains" or ideas which compose it, the true philosophic affinities and the eventual practical influence in life and art of these several strains will usually be found to be exceedingly diverse and often conflicting. It will, no doubt, remain abstractly possible to raise the question whether the preponderant effect, moral or aesthetic, of one or another large movement which has been called by the name was good or bad. But that ambitious inquiry cannot even be legitimately begun until a prior task of analysis and detailed comparison—of the sort that I have attempted here to indicate—has been accomplished. And when this has been done, I doubt whether the larger question will seem to have much importance or meaning. What will then appear historically significant and philosophically instructive will be the way in which *each* of these distinguishable strains has worked itself out, what its elective affinities for other ideas, and its historic consequences, have shown themselves to be. The categories which it has become customary to use in distinguishing and classifying "movements" in literature or philosophy and in describing the nature of the significant transitions which have taken place in taste and in opinion, are far too rough, crude, undiscriminating—and none of them so hopelessly so as the category "Romantic." It is not any large *complexes* of ideas, such as that term has almost always been employed to designate, but rather certain simpler, diversely combinable, intellectual and emotional components of such complexes, that are the true elemental and dynamic factors in the history of thought and of art; and it is with the genesis, the vicissitudes, the manifold and often dramatic interactions of these, that it is the task of the historian of ideas in literature to become acquainted.

4. JACQUES BARZUN: Classic, Romantic, and Modern *

Jacques Barzun, professor of history and former Provost of Columbia University, is an unabashed partisan of romanticism. He finds it a truly realistic approach to man and his universe. Professor Barzun's partisanship leaves him open to a number of questions. Is the movement which he designates "romantic" historically assessable? He assigns a definite period to it, but also treats it as a permanent or recurrent intellectual orientation. Is he right about what values romanticism cherished and about their coherence, and is he right that these are good? Is he correct in exonerating romanticism from some of the results that have been attributed to it, while maintaining its continued influence in other respects? Professor Barzun, like any intelligent advocate, lends a stimulating vitality to his subject; but for the same reason one must evaluate his views and general approach with unusual care.

Historic romanticism can be defined as comprising those Euopeans whose birth falls between 1770 and 1815, and who achieved distinction in philosophy, statecraft, and the arts during the first half of the nineteenth century. Some of course were born outside these arbitrary limits of time, like Goethe. There are others whose fame came after the terminal date, like Blake. A few more resist classification with the main body. So long as they are few these irregularities will not disturb anyone who remembers that we are dealing with an historical grouping. History does not arrange its products in bunches; it is man who seeks to put order into the disarray of history. Hence the ragged edges, but they are the edges of something central and solid.

We have then a group of men known as romanticists and living as contemporaries between 1770 and 1850. What, besides time, binds them together? It is at this point that we pass from *historic* romanticism to what may be called *intrinsic* romanticism. I have suggested that if an attitude becomes noticeable or dominant in a given period, its elements must be latent in human beings, or in certain human beings, all the time. In individual instances we call it this or that kind of temperament. For example, it is probable that there are Puritans at all times and places; but when a great many occur at the same time and place, then we have a Puritan period. In the same manner there are heroic ages and ages of luxury, ages of classicism, of rationalism, of renaissance, of decadence—and of romanticism. Not that each of these represents a fixed type; rather it is a combination of human traits which for one reason or another happens to be stressed, valued, cultivated at a given historical moment. Why one attitude is preferred to another is something for the cultural historian to

* From Jacques Barzun, *Classic, Romantic, and Modern,* pp. 8–9, 14–15, 58–60, 137. Copyright 1943, 1961 by Jacques Barzun. Reprinted by permission of Little, Brown and Company, publishers.

explain after the event, but *that* it is preferred is the reason for our being able to speak of a romantic period.

This distinction between *permanent* elements in human nature and their periodic emphasis in history is the first of the devices by which we can make more exact and serviceable our use of the name "romantic." If, for instance, we hear William James called a romantic, we are entitled to say: "James was not contemporary with Byron; what precisely have you in mind when you classify them under the same head?" If, as is likely, the answer given is: "I call him romantic because of his irrationalism," the field is then open to argument over the correctness of the description and over the propriety of making one belief or opinion taken at random symptomatic of a whole temperament or philosophy. The libraries are full of books, usually written in wartime, and which show that from Luther to Hitler, or from Fichte to Mussolini, or from Rousseau to Stalin "one increasing purpose runs." The demonstration is made by stringing together on one line of development all thinkers who "believe in the will" or "believe in hero worship" or "believe in the divine right of the people." In these works the intention of human ideas is disregarded for the sake of finding a collection of scapegoats. . . .

In other words, what we want as a definition of intrinsic romanticism is the thing that gave rise to—and that incidentally explains—all the other attitudes I have enumerated. Why did some romanticists attack Reason, why did some turn catholic, why were some liberal, others reactionary? Why did some praise the Middle Ages and others adore the Greeks? Clearly, the one thing that unifies men in a given age is not their individual philosophies but the dominant problem that these philosophies are designed to solve. In the romantic period, as will appear, this problem was to create a new world on the ruins of the old. The French Revolution and Napoleon had made a clean sweep. Even before the Revolution, which may be taken as the outward sign of an inward decay, it was no longer possible to think, act, write, or paint as if the old forms still had life. The critical philosophers of the eighteenth century had destroyed their own dwelling place. The next generation must build or perish. Whence we conclude that romanticism is first of all constructive and creative; it is what may be called a solving epoch, as against the *dis*solving eighteenth century.

Because the problem of reconstruction was visible to many men does not mean that they all proposed the same solution, or saw all its aspects in the same way. The divergences were due to differences of temperament, geographical situation, and special interest. A poet such as Wordsworth or Victor Hugo saw the emptiness of eighteenth-century diction and the need of creating a new vocabulary for poetry; a philosopher such as Schopenhauer saw the illusoriness of eighteenth-century hopes of progress and the need of recharting moral reality, with suggestions for better enduring it; a political theorist like Burke, who apprehended the wholesale destruction of the social order, had to propose an alternative means of change; a thinker like Hegel, who was at once philosopher, political theorist, and esthetician, saw creation as the result of conflict in history and in the mind, and proposed nothing less than a new logic to explain the nature of change. He then showed how to use it for rebuilding on more lasting premises.

These men clearly cannot be made into a romantic *school*, but they equally clearly partake of a romanticist *temper*. More than that, they share certain broad predilections in common, such as the admiration for energy, moral enthusiasm, and original genius. It is because an era faces one dominant problem in varying ways that certain human traits come to be held in greater esteem than they were before. The task of reconstruction manifestly does demand energy, morality, and genius, so that the new passion for them was thus not a whimsical or useless trait in the romantics, but a necessity of their position.

By the same logic, one is led to see that romanticism was far from being an escape from reality on the part of feeble spirits who could not stand it. The truth is that these spirits wanted to change the portions of reality that they did not like, and at least record their ideals when the particular piece of reality would not yield—both these being indispensable steps toward reconstruction. Our modern use of the term "escape" is unfortunately vitiated by smugness and double meanings, and one should refuse to argue its application with anyone who will not first answer this question: "Suppose a primitive man, caught in a rainstorm, who has for the first time the idea of taking shelter in a cave: is he facing reality or escaping it?" The whole history of civilization is wrapped up in this example, and a universal test for distinguishing creation from escape can be deduced from it. The mere fact that a man is seen making for a cave or heard declaring his intention to build a hut is not enough; what is he going to do *then*? What is the relation of that single act to his whole scheme of life? Applying this test to romanticism, we shall see that on the whole it was infinitely more constructive than escapist. . . .

What I am concerned with here is to show that what the romanticists of the period 1790 to 1850 sought and found was not a dream world into which to escape, but a real world in which to live. The exploration of reality was the fundamental intention of romantic art.

Before we come to particulars, the general setting may be put in a few words: classicism perished from an excess of abstraction and generality. This was most visibly true in the several arts, and nothing shows more clearly the romanticists' realistic purpose than their refusal to go on imitating forms whose contents had evaporated. Seeing this refusal, we believe too readily in the miscalled "romantic revolt." We imagine a sudden and irresponsible rebellion of brash young men against the wisdom and experience of their elders. It was nothing of the kind. The breaking away was reluctant, painful, and deliberate. After much soul-searching and abortive efforts to continue in traditional ways, a whole generation of talents came to see that to write or paint in the manner of Pye, Gottsched, and Delille, of David and Reynolds, was no longer possible.

There was no choice but to begin afresh. The romanticist was in the position of a primitive with the seven arts to create out of nothing. At the same time, he labored under the handicap of having "inimitable" classical masterpieces held up to him to imitate, even though the substance of these great works had already been rendered threadbare by repetition and refinement. The romantic revolt consisted solely in refusing to do the undoable.

Having perforce given up conventional abstractions, clichés, poetic diction, and classical rules, what did the romanticists turn to? The answer can be generalized: for substance they turned to the world about and within them; they tried to meet the claims of every existing reality, both internal and external. For form, they relied on earlier romantic periods and on their own inventive genius.

The characteristics of romanticism which the textbooks list as if they were arbitrary choices by eccentric artists are merely the embodiment of what I have just said. As against poetic diction and "noble" words, the romanticists admitted all words; as against the exclusive use of a selected Graeco-Roman mythology, they took in the Celtic and Germanic; as against the uniform setting and tone of classical tragedy, they studied and reproduced the observable diversities known as "local color." As against the antique subjects and the set scale of pictorial merits prescribed by the Academy, they took in the whole world, seen and unseen, and the whole range of colors. As against the academic rules prohibiting the use of certain chords, tonalities, and modulations, they sought to use and give shape to all manageable combinations of sound. As against the assumption that no civilization had existed since the fall of Rome, they rediscovered the Middle Ages and the sixteenth century and made history their dominant avocation. As against the provincial belief that Paris and London were the sole centers of human culture, they traveled to such remote places as America and the Near East and earned the name of "exotic" for their pains. As against the idea that the products of cosmopolitan sophistication afford the only subjects worth treating, they began to treasure folk literature and folk music and to draw the matter of their art from every class and condition of men. As against the materialistic view that only the tangible exists, they made room in their notion of reality for the world of dreams, the ineffable in man and nature, and the supernatural. . . .

But youth is also the time of melancholy and the first realization of death, so we should not wonder that Shelley, Keats, Poe, Beddoes, and Büchner, return to this theme. Yet even in their song it is possible to discern more notes than we generally hear. Poe is not always macabre. He is a great critic and writer of "scientific" stories; Keats's letters are not indited to "easeful death," they are boisterous and gay; Büchner is a revolutionist and a satirist; Beddoes a critic and a creator of grotesques, as well as a politician and medical man. The pace and variety of romantic life may be too fast for us, or we may be overimpressed by what is striking; but the truth remains that the romantic artist has often modulated to a new and different experience while we are still complaining of his "constant" addiction to a previous one.

The seeker after experience loves variety because the world is various, because life is made up of contrasts, because opposites help destroy the temptations of provincialism. Hence the romanticist travels. Foreign lands and customs and literatures truly exist, and not only one's own. Nothing, therefore, could be more inappropriate than the term "exotic" applied to romantic tastes, for exoticism implies the classic belief that one is at the center of the universe and that everything else is *ex*-otic to it.

This cultural relativism does not contradict the general report that the romanticists were also nationalists. But the label "nationalist" has considerably changed its meaning since the romantic period. The men of that time seldom, if ever, used the word to describe themselves, and if we must use it about them, it must be with the modifier *cultural* in front of it. The romantics' nationalism is culture nationalism. They spoke less of nations than of "peoples," whom they considered the creators and repositories of distinct cultures. The romantics could hardly have overlooked popular cultures and remained good historians, or even good critics. But they went further and maintained that each human group, being a unique product of history, was worth preserving in its integrity. They compared Europe to a bouquet, each flower growing in its appointed soil, a simile which only slowly degenerated into the racial absolutism of blood and fatherland.

The romantics indeed repudiated the classical effort to impose a common speech and art on all of Europe. Whether we turn to Herder's *Thoughts on History,* where he rejects "those ignoble words, 'the races of men,'" whether we read Wordsworth's full exposition of romantic nationalism in his pamphlet on the *Convention of Cintra,* or whether we follow Victor Hugo's wanderings in *The Rhine,* we find this same nonaggressive cultural nationalism, which cherishes diverse folkways for what they are.

Modern critics of romanticism are prone to assert that out of this doctrine grew present-day mysticisms about nation and *Volk*. This outcome, they add, was all the more natural because the romantics preached the struggle for life—an idea, they go on, which is not only included in the Faustian myth but is a part of the biological view of man which twice in our century German imperialism has exploited.

This implication of descent is plausible but not true. By hurrying over the points of contact between one idea and the next it shows as inevitable and universal what was in fact only local and possible. We saw earlier how the peculiar condition of Germany under the Napoleonic tyranny put a premium upon aggressive energy. This energy developed around the idea of the state and was re-enforced by that of a nation united through its common culture. At this stage it was indeed cultural nationalism militant—but militant in defense. Even so, it was not a unanimous feeling. Many felt as Goethe did in looking back upon this period: "How could I take up arms without hatred? And how could I hate without youth? I have never shammed. I have never given utterance to what I have not experienced. I have only composed love-songs when I have loved. How could I write hate-songs without hatred? And between ourselves, I did not hate the French, though I thanked God when we were free of them. How could I, to whom culture and barbarism are alone of importance, hate a nation which is among the most cultivated on earth, and to which I owe so great a part of my acquirements?"

Out of his younger fellow poets' hatred grew, without question, the mood of 1870 and 1940. It was a progressive shift from defense to offense, about which I shall have more to say in the next chapter. But its setting and purpose have nothing specifically romantic. As for the idea of struggle, Goethe's oft-quoted text says *streben,* that is to say "strive," a word which can be filled with any contents, and which it is sheer demagogy to interpret as necessarily meaning human fighting.

Striving, to be sure, implies resistance, opposition, and ultimate victory or defeat. But these are metaphors that apply to exploring the Antarctic or building a tunnel as well as to winning battles. The romantic view of life did rejoice in risk, adventure, and heroism. It said that these things *were* life, and it still remains to be proved that life can be maintained individually or collectively without them. When the Western world as a whole adopts the creed of passivity, rewards those who decline adventure, and cherishes the lotus-eater above the doer, it will be time to scorn the romantic apostles of Faustian striving. . . .

The romantic era in Europe produced two generations of men who attempted, between 1780 and 1850, a feat of cultural renovation. The classical order, dying of overabstraction and false generality, had been devoured by its own children, the Enlightened philosophers. Political revolution and Napoleonic dictatorship buried the past and leveled the ground. The romanticists had the task of reconstruction. The vast horizons opened up by war and social upheaval gave romanticism its scope: it was inclusive, impatient of barriers, eager for diversity. It treasured fact and respected the individual as a source of fact. Accordingly, its political philosophy was an attempt to reconcile personal freedom with the inescapable need of collective action. Rousseau, Burke, Kant, Hegel, agreeing on the nature of the problem, differed only in lesser particulars. They were not anarchists or imperialists, but theorists of equilibrium in motion.

Alive to diversity, romanticism bound up patriotism with the life of peoples and gave form to a cultural nationalism compatible with international amity. Observant and imaginative, it rediscovered history and gave an impulse to the arts which has not yet died out. True to its inclusive purpose, romantic art was simultaneously idealistic, realistic, and symbolic; impressionist, expressionist, and surrealist. It produced forms and amassed contents only now nearing exhaustion, after furnishing the models for the movements which we enumerate through the past century as Realism, Symbolism, Impressionism, Naturalism, and Post-Impressionism.

break from the classical. Recognizing that there was form in everything, beauty everywhere. That the near past and present was as deserving of analyses and form as was the ancient times of Greece and Rome.

5. BENEDETTO CROCE: History of Europe in the Nineteenth Century *

Benedetto Croce (1866–1952) was one of the leading Italian historians, philosophers, and political theorists of modern times. His essay on the nineteenth century, an elaboration of lectures given in 1931, attempts a general assessment of the major developments in the century. Croce's views on romanticism almost completely contradict those of Barzun. Barzun sees romanticism as a continuation of vital elements of the Western cultural tradition; Croce sees it as a tragic departure from this tradition. Croce attributes to romanticism precisely those catastrophic results in the later nineteenth century from which Barzun sought to exculpate it. There are issues raised here beyond the crucial question of which man is right. As with Barzun, Croce's definition of romanticism must be carefully weighed, for it is very broad and confident.

Contemporary with the rise and growth of idealism and liberalism, and often in the same individuals, was the birth and expansion of romanticism; a simultaneity that is not a mere juxtaposition, but a relation or a multiplicity of relations, as it will be advisable to make clear and to keep in mind.

To this end it is necessary, first of all, to emphasize a distinction that has almost always been lost sight of by those (and they have been of late years and still are many) who talk of romanticism and write histories of it. Without this distinction it is inevitable that certain spiritual manifestations of a positive character fall, as it were, under a cloud of disapproval, and others of a negative character are illumined in a favourable light, so that the history one sets out to write comes forth contradictory and confused. The distinction is between romanticism in the theoretic and speculative sense and romanticism in the practical, sentimental, and moral field: these are two diverse and even opposite things to one who does not wish to limit himself to the surface and to appearances.

Theoretic and speculative romanticism is the revolt, the criticism, and the attack against literary academicism and philosophic intellectualism, which had dominated in the illuminist age. It awakened the feeling for genuine and great poetry, and set forth the doctrine thereof in the new science of the imagination called aesthetics. It realized the great importance of spontaneity, passion, individuality, and gave them their place in ethics. It knew and made known the right of what exists and operates in all its varieties according to time and place, and founded modern historiography, interpreting it no longer as mockery and derision of past ages, but as understanding of these as parts of the present and of the future. And it reintegrated and retouched all the aspects of history, civil and political history no less than religious, speculative, and artistic. It thrust back into their natural limits the natural and mathematical sci-

* From Benedetto Croce, *History of Europe in the Nineteenth Century* (New York: Harcourt, Brace & World, Inc., 1963), pp. 42–54. Reprinted by permission of Agenzia Litteraria Internazionale, Milan, Italy.

ences and their correlative mental form, showing that, outside of their own field, they were impotent to resolve the antinomies with which the mind came into conflict no less than those which had to remain in abstractions and separations. It grasped life in its active and combative sense, and thus prepared the theoretical premises of liberalism. Even in its irrationalistic concepts, as in the primacy sometimes allotted to emotion and mystic ecstasy, there was a justified polemic against abstract intellectualism, and, in irrational and provisional form, a nucleus of rational truth. Even in its mistaken attempts, as in those of a philosophy of history over and above all histories and of a philosophy of nature over and above all the natural sciences, there was visible the activity of the profound necessities of a history that should be at the same time a philosophy and of a nature understood both as such and as development and historicity, and recognized again as such either beyond or at the bottom of the classifications and the conventions with which and on which the scientists properly so called is obliged to work. In short, this romanticism is not only in no wise in disagreement with modern philosophy, whether you choose to call that idealism or absolute spiritualism, but it is that philosophy itself, or certain particular doctrines of that philosophy, and therefore a duplicate appellative with its correlative double meanings and verbal paradoxes, as when the philosophy that goes from Kant to Hegel is called the "philosophy of romanticism" and then "classic idealism"—therefore at the same time "romantic" and "classic."

But the romanticism that is spoken of in the practical, sentimental, and moral field is something quite different, belongs to quite a diverse sphere. And if speculative romanticism is resplendent with truth, if the attempts to refute it have always been and always are vain, if it has indeed at various times been judged to be extreme and audacious and yet at the same time never been debased to infirmity, feebleness, and insanity, the other, on the contrary, at once assumed this unhealthy aspect and has always been the object of ethical reproval, more or less stressed, now indulgent and pitying, now severe and satirical, and the necessity has always been felt of treating it and bringing about its cure. The greatest liberators from the chains of intellectualism, the greatest fathers of idealism and romanticism in critical and speculative concepts, Goethe and Hegel, considered moral romanticism in this fashion, and shrank from it and blamed it, pronouncing it pathological and shameful. Most certainly the praises that later were spent on romanticism, defining it as "protestantism in philosophy" or "liberalism in literature," did not belong to it. The divergence between the two concepts, the one positive and the other negative, becomes apparent again in the distinction, which has become customary among historians, between the "first" and the "second" romantic generation, between romanticism's period of splendour and its period of unrest and decadence; but in truth the real distinction is not, or not exclusively, one of persons or chronology, but ideal and intrinsic. And still less clearly is the difference visible in the common contraposition of Latin healthiness and German morbidity; for if among the Germans there might be noted some of the first and more pronounced manifestations of that moral ailing, it was also among the Germans that arose the proclaimers of the thought and the ethics which alone were able to cure it; and so this thought and the ethics conjoined to it as well as the malady had their precursors and followers outside of Germany. For these phenomena corresponded to mental creations and psychic conditions that belonged to the modern age and were to be found or might have been found in any people. And in fact the malady received the name, which fitted the truth better, of *"mal du siècle."*

Romanticism was not, as it has so often been interpreted and represented, an effect of the departure from the hereditary and traditional faith, which had yielded certainty and tranquillity of feeling and will; because when an old faith is followed by a new one, the warmth and enthusiasm of the latter covers and makes almost imperceptible the pain and melancholy over the separation and severance from the former. In the eighteenth century society had become widely dechristianized in its intellectual and ruling classes, without any resultant formation of a divided or morbid state of mind, such as romanticism was, and the process even developed with a certain gaiety and cheerfulness. Even the violent rebels against the law, the customs, and the ideas of existing society, the *Stürmer und Dränger,* who for such aspects are considered as proto-romantics, in the achievement of their negations and their rage of destruction gave signs of disordered force rather than of confusion and weakness. But moral romanticism, romanticism as a malady, the *"mal du siècle,"* possessed neither the old nor the new faith, neither the authoritative one of the past nor the clear one of the present, and showed precisely that it was a lack of faith, travailing in eagerness to create one and impotent to do so, or to obtain satisfaction from those which in turn it proclaimed, or to stick to them as principles of thinking and living. For faith is born spontaneously and necessarily from the truth that obliges us to listen to it in the depths of our consciousness, and can never be found by going in search of it with the restless combinations of desire and imagination.

Rather than to the separation from the traditional faith, this malady was related to the difficulty of truly appropriating and living the new, which required, if it were to be lived and carried out, courage and manliness, and the renunciation of certain outworn motives now grown impossible, flattering and comfortable though they might be. To be understood and grasped by reason, and defended, it demanded experience and culture and a trained mind. This might be not impossible for robust intellects and characters, who followed its genetic process without allowing themselves to be entangled in it and, passing through their inner storms, reached the haven; and in another way it was possible for clear and simple minds and straightforward hearts who at once learned and adopted its conclusions and put them into practice, conquered and held by the light of their goodness and good. But it was beyond the powers of feminine souls, impressionable, sentimental, incoherent, and voluble, who stimulated and excited in themselves doubts and difficulties that they were not able to master, who loved and courted the dangers in which they perished. Unable to find their way back to the natural centre that they had questioned, they wandered here and there, clinging now to one point and now to another that could not possibly become a centre. They had severed the connections of the finite with the infinite, of the senses with the ideal, and now in despair they identified the infinite with this or that finite, the ideal with this or that phenomenon. They had lost the true God, and now they moulded idols, which they themselves soon unmade or which dissolved of themselves, because the part cannot stand for the whole, nor a phantom woven by wild fancy or caprice for the solid concept, which is light and strength.

And so these feminine souls, these "romantics," dreamed of returning to religious transcendence and the peace that it seemed to promise, to the cessation, in silence and in renunciation, of the doubts and anxieties of thought, to the norm accepted because of its very character as a norm that imposes itself and exonerates from all independent solution of the battles waged within the conscience. And as the highest expression of this sort of transcendence and of this imperative ruling was the Catholic faith; not only those who belonged to Catholic peoples and had been brought up from childhood in Catholicism, but also Protestants, Lutherans, or those of other confessions, or even men come from the most distant religions or from no religion at all, became Catholics again or for the first time and even were converted with the due rites, and yet none the less never became intimately or genuinely Catholics, and assumed an ambiguous aspect in the eyes of real Catholics. For this Catholicism of theirs was too rich in sensuousness and imagination, was too eager for colours, music, singing, ancient cathedrals, figures of Madonnas and saints, cradled itself too fondly in the pleasures of sin, in penitence and tears; in regard to dogma it did, in truth, give itself ultra-Catholic airs, but was not equally obedient and faithful to the Roman pontiff and to his decrees and his policy. They called themselves or believed themselves anti-Protestant, but in such a way that they could not refrain from frequent allusions to the necessity for a new form or for a reform that should be fundamentally Catholic, but should resolve within itself the dissonances of Protestantism and Catholicism. Others, or the same ones, would at times be seized by rage against Catholicism, or even against Christianity, and turn to championing a restored paganism, opposing to the figure of the Holy Virgin that of the goddess Venus, now the Hellenic one, now the Germanic-mediaeval. Others, attracted by the studies, initiated at this time, of Oriental languages and literature, borrowed from them ideas of ancient rites, or compounded eclectically new and bizarre ones, or recurred to the practice of magic. Others, last of all, flung themselves into a sort of pantheism, adoring Nature, losing themselves in the sensations that she seemed to provide them, and returning, as they liked to say, to the primitive religion of the Germanic peoples.

Those who were more metaphysically or sacerdotally disposed were followed, and often joined, by those who enjoyed a more erotic tone, who sought for redemption in love and for divinity in the beloved lady, not so much with a revival of motifs that had belonged to the *stil nuovo* of the thirteenth century and to the Platonism of the Renaissance, as with a refinement and sublimation of sensuality, which is the kernel of the romantic religion of love. The resulting figure was no longer that of the woman who is strong in her virtue and her chastity, who repels and chastens and educates the man who loves her and obliges him to purify his passion of every low and earthly desire and elevates him, thus purified, with herself to the Highest Beauty and the Highest Goodness, which is God; but a creature equally susceptible and loving, made to suffer and to die of love, a creature adored and sometimes deified, emanating a charm such as alone could lend warmth and meaning to human life. At times, this creature of love would rise with solemn gesture like a priestess of her God and celebrate acts of initiation and worship. There was pathos in the series of expectations, ecstasies, inebriations and disappointments and despair, from which, however, would always arise the idea of this form of love and of this feminine figure, which would descend from time to time to crown with a heavenly nimbus the blond or dark head of this or that earthly woman, encountered on the earthly path.

In other spirits, or at other moments, the bent of the imagination was preponderantly ethical and political—"political fantasy" because "romantic politics," that is, a politics of the romantic malady, is a contradiction in terms—and in this case belief and happiness were sought for in social modes of living differing from the present ones and particularly in the restoration of past ages. And as the immediate past, that of the *ancien régime,* was still too clearly remembered, was too precise in its limits, and did not easily lend itself to idealization and sacred sublimation, their desire was transferred to the remoter past. Meanwhile learning had re-established the continuity of historical development, and investigated and better understood the Middle Ages, and so they turned to the mediaeval period, in which they saw or thought they saw shadows as solid figures, marvels of fidelity, loyalty, purity, generosity, discipline and lack of discipline at the same time, and what was constant alternating with what was unexpected, simplicity of life in a small and peaceful circle with the charm of adventures throughout the vast unknown world that was full of surprises. To this religion of the Middle Ages we owe the more or less academic restorations of old castles and old cathedrals, the false Gothic that raged everywhere in Europe, the false poetry that in dilettante fashion set itself to imitating the mediaeval forms of epic, lyric, and miracle plays, romances telling of knights and tourneys, chatelaines and enamoured pages, minstrels and clowns, romantic masquerades. And we owe to this the aspect given here and there to some of the ancient monarchies of the restoration, which sometimes beheld themselves grotesquely attired with emblems and costumes fished out of the antiquaries' shops, and the spirit that pervaded the Prince of Prussia, later Frederick William IV, and, with moderation, Louis I of Bavaria.

But if the religion of the Middle Ages was the main one and the most widely spread, it was not the only one; and next to it, and sharing the honours with it, there rose and towered the religion of the race and the nation, of that nation which, because of scanty information and historic reflection, was considered the creative and dominant race of the Middle Ages, the Germanic, whose courage was now being sought for and discovered and celebrated in every part of Europe—where, historically speaking, should rather have been found, as a common foundation, the Romanic peoples, which for the first time gave it unity and consciousness. And it was exalted as an element of youth and purity, which had produced the histories of Spain and Italy no less than those of France and England, and even now, weakened or bastardized in those countries, still preserved itself youthful and strong, and ready to regenerate the world, in the Germanic race, in modern Germany.

Less fortunate were the other pure races or self-styled pure races that, instigated by this example, also raised their voices, the Latin, the Celtic, the Iberian, and the Slavic. Other religions of an ethical and political tendency also had their more or less numerous devotees, such as that idyllic return to nature and the country and the simple peasant's garb in which there breathed the inspiration of one of its principal precursors, Rousseau; and, opposed to it, the tendency to the stormy, the enraged, the titanic, in which persisted instead the impulse of *Sturm und Drang*. But above all worthy of notice, because of its capacity for proselytizing and the various offshoots that it sent out, was the aestheticizing conception, of life to be lived as passion and imagination, beauty and poetry. This was in fact the contrary of life, for life demands the distinction and with it the harmony of all its forms, and does not admit the pathological superposition and supremacy of one single form over all the others, which are equally necessary, each for its own task. And it was also the opposite of poetry, which is the conquest of action in cosmic contemplation, a pause imposed on practical activity, even if that is also the preparation for new activity. Therefore romanticism, corrupting life, also corrupted to greater or less extent the poetic form, reducing it to something practical, to an immediate and violent expression of passionate reality, to a cry, a shriek, a delirium.

All these, considered in their source, were perversions, inasmuch as they substituted the particular for the universal, the contingent for the eternal, the creature for the creator. But into such diverse and complicated and intricate sentiments there crept also those which are more appropriately called perversions, that is, not only exaggerations and usurpations but somersaults of values: lust and sensuality set in the place of ideality, the cruel and the horrible savoured with voluptuousness, the taste for incest, sadism, Satanism, and other like delights, at the same time monstrous and stupid; as can be seen or divined in poets and men of letters even of the very highest class, such as Chateaubriand, Byron, Shelley, in whom, fortunately, there is not only this, and even this exists as a rule in incidental or evanescent fashion.

Here we do not mean to pause and portray in its varied combinations and gradations, which run to infinity, the *"mal du siècle,"* which moreover has often been portrayed, with more or less skill, by others; for all that was needed was merely to explain its genesis in relation to the philosophy and the religion of liberty. This genesis, as we have seen, lay in its impotence to appropriate to itself this philosophy and religion, although at the same time it took from it a few elements, which promptly corrupted it, and falsified historicity by sentimentalizing over the past and by leanings towards restoration, nationality by the fanaticism of race, liberty by egoarchy and anarchy, and the value of poetry to life by poetry-life and life-poetry. But we must not, on the other hand, ignore all—and it was much—that the liberal faith was able to influence in this romanticism, nor the way in which, according to the various cases, it transcended it or hemmed it in or subdued it to itself in varying degrees. This sentimental malady was a danger to every form of ideal and of pure sense of religion, and not only to liberalism but also to its very anthitheses and oppositions, all of which it would have dissolved if it had prevailed, just as it would have weakened and spoiled all strength of thought and will in sensuality, in disordered desires, in untrammelled passions, in flabby fancies, in restless caprices. This danger was bound to grow all the greater, the smaller became the forces of resistance capable of defying it; a danger that, in its moral essence, belongs to all times, but which in modern society assumes a particular consistency and with this society's greatness and complexity dilates, and with the growth of its contrasts, or with the diminution of their nobility, puts on a more malign nature. Later, in fact, it spread in art, thought, feelings, customs, in national and international politics; and when it had grown more evident and more monstrous, it received, and often acknowledged with pride, the name of "decadence," which is after all nothing but the old moral romanticism, exasperated and grown uglier, whose fundamental motifs it repeats, applying them to less distinguished matter and behaving in a less distinguished manner.

But in the first decades of the nineteenth century, the religion of liberty was fresh with youthful enthusiasm, and the very oppositions against which it fought—the traditional religion, the traditional monarchy, the democratic school of natural law—wore an air of majesty and respectability that was lacking in the opposition which arose later. Moral romanticism operated in the midst of a growth of generous hopes, intentions, and works that confined it, tempered it, and often turned it towards the good. Superior spirits, taking part as they did in the drama of their time, did indeed suffer from this malady, but as from a growing-sickness, from which they recovered and from which they drew fruits of experience, powers of discipline, a capacity for a wider human understanding. And from their midst emerged the keenest judges and the severest critics of romanticism, such as Goethe, whom we have mentioned before, who defined romantic poetry as "hospital poetry" and manifested his aversion to the "sentimental people" who, when they are put to the test, always fail and show themselves to be little and bad, and Hegel, whom we also mentioned, who uttered the most caustic satire and the most varied analysis of romantic fatuity and vanity, up to which he held, so that they might gaze upon themselves as in a magic mirror, the good and savoury prose of real life with its unwearying activity, its physiological pains and physiological joys.

To be sure, not a few romantics, those who could never succeed either in overcoming and calming the uproar they had excited in their own breasts or in eliminating it by forgetting it and resuming their modest everyday lives, went to rack and ruin. Some of them ended in madness and physical suicide, others in moral suicide, in debauches or the insincere practice of a religion that was not serious and not felt. The greater part of them, in inactivity and groaning in solitude and ennui, were like Byron's Manfred, who spoke of himself as "averse from life" and who might have been (says someone who watched him) a noble creature and was instead

> an awful chaos—light and darkness—
> And mind and dust—and passions and pure thought
> Mix'd, and contending without end or order.

Yet there were some who, although unable either to triumph over the enemy or to forget him, did not wish thus to end their lives or drag them out ignominiously, and practially, in action or in the moment of deciding upon action, clung to that ideal of liberty which theoretically they could not defend and assimilate consciously, but which alone, because of its pure, radiant beauty, had power over their souls. And so some of them, pessimists because they had not been able to disentangle the tangle of their ideas, or desperate because of betrayed or hopeless love, or unable to support inactivity and ennui, went out to fight and to die for the cause of oppressed peoples; and others alternated romantic follies and depression with patriotic and civil ardour. In general, the romantic features are very strongly marked in all the men of that age, as can be seen in their letters and biographies, and even, almost, by merely looking at their portraits, with the characteristic look, the hairdress, the pose, and the cut of the garments. And if in some countries where the feeling and the activity for liberty did not stand in the forefront, the romantics (who politically were nothing, because they were simply nerve-sick and fancy-sick) were able, by their words of consent or dissent, by the manifestations of their humour or ill-humour, to pass as conservatives and reactionaries among the peoples whose hearts beat with a quicker rhythm, in whom the idea and the flower of the intellectuals were liberal, yet their name soon became synonymous with "liberal," and priests and police suspected and kept an eye on romantic youth. The sorrow of the world, the mystery of the universe, the impetus towards the sublimity of love and heroism, the desolation and the despair over desired and unattainable beatitude, the walks under the friendly moon, the Hamlet-like visits to cemeteries, the romantic beards and curls, the romantic style, these and other like things furnished evidence of unruly spirits, of whom it was to be expected and feared that they might conspire in the factions and rise in arms as soon as occasion presented itself.

6. ERNST FISCHER: The Necessity of Art, a Marxist Approach *

Ernst Fischer, an Austrian Socialist politician and dramatist, views romanticism from a Marxist viewpoint, as first a bourgeois protest against aristocratic

* From Ernst Fischer, *The Necessity of Art, a Marxist Approach,* translated by Anna Bostock (Baltimore: Penguin Books, 1963), pp. 52–58. Reprinted by permission.

classicism and next as a petty bourgeois protest against the capitalist world. His approach inevitably seems strange after so many intellectual approaches to the phenomenon; and one can wonder at the logic of seeing the same movement serve two opposed segments of a social class or at the utility of condemning it for not associating itself with the rising class of workers. Yet the effort deserves attention. Cultural movements are not important merely in the abstract or from the viewpoint of creative intellectuals alone; they have a constituency, a public, or they are not important at all. This public must be assessed and its influence on cultural creativity described. There is, in fact, much evidence to indicate a middle-class preference for products of romanticism in music and literature. Does an approach which takes this dimension into account add to the understanding of romanticism or aid in its definition?

Romanticism was a movement of protest—of passionate and contradictory protest against the bourgeois capitalist world, the world of "lost illusions," against the harsh prose of business and profit. The harsh criticism by Novalis, the German Romantic, of Goethe's *Wilhelm Meister* was characteristic of this attitude (although Friedrich Schlegel, another Romantic, was full of praise for the great novel). In *Wilhelm Meister,* Goethe presents bourgeois values in a positive spirit and traces the path from aestheticism to an active life within the prosaic bourgeois world. Novalis would have none of this.

Adventurers, comedians, courtesans, shopkeepers and philistines are the ingredients of this novel. Whoever takes it properly to heart will never read another.

From Rousseau's *Discourses* until *The Communist Manifesto* of Marx and Engels, Romanticism was the dominant attitude of European art and literature. Romanticism, in terms of the petty-bourgeois consciousness, is the most complete reflection in philosophy, literature, and art of the contradictions of developing capitalist society. Only with Marx and Engels did it become possible to recognize the nature and origin of those contradictions, to understand the dialectic of social development, and to realize that the working class was the only force which could surmount them. The Romantic attitude could not be other than confused, for the petty bourgeoisie was the very embodiment of social contradiction, hopeful of sharing in the general enrichment yet fearful of being crushed to death in the process, dreaming of new possibilities yet clinging to the old security of rank and order, its eyes turned towards the new times yet often also, nostalgically, towards the "good old" ones.

To begin with, Romanticism was a petty-bourgeois revolt against the Classicism of the nobility, against rules and standards, against aristocratic form, and against a content from which all "common" issues were excluded. For these Romantic rebels there were no privileged themes: everything was a fit subject for art.

The extremes and excrescences [Goethe, the admirer of Stendhal and Mérimée, said as an old man on 14 March 1830] will gradually disappear; but at last this great advantage will remain—besides a freer form, richer and more diversified subjects will have been attained, and no object of the broadest world and the most manifold life will be any longer excluded as unpoetical.

Opposed though he was to everything that Goethe stood for, Novalis, too, saw that Romanticism encouraged the poetic treatment of hitherto forbidden themes. "Romanticizing," he wrote, "means giving a lofty significance to that which is common, a mysterious appearance to the ordinary, and the dignity of the unknown to the familiar." Shelley wrote in *The Defence of Poetry:* "Poetry . . . makes familiar objects appear as if they were not familiar." Romanticism led out of the well-tended park of Classicism into the wilderness of the wide world.

Yet Romanticism opposed not only Classicism but also the Enlightenment. In many cases it was not a total opposition but one directed only against mechanistic ideas and optimistic simplifications. It is true that Chateaubriand, Burke, Coleridge, Schlegel, and many others—especially among the German Romantic school—solemnly dismissed the Enlightenment; but Shelley, Byron, Stendhal, and Heine, whose insight into the contradictions of social development was more profound, carried on the Enlightenment's work.

One of the basic experiences of Romanticism was that of the individual emerging alone and incomplete from the ever-increasing division of labour and specialization and the consequent fragmentation of life. Under the old order, a man's rank had been a kind of intermediary in his relations with other men and with society at large. In the capitalist world the individual faced society alone, without an intermediary, as a stranger among strangers, as a single "I" opposed to the immense "not-I." This situation stimulated powerful self-awareness and proud subjectivism, but also a sense of bewilderment and abandon. It encouraged the Napoleonic "I" and at the same time an "I" whimpering at the feet of holy effigies, an "I" ready to conquer the world yet overcome by the terror of loneliness. The writer's and artist's "I," isolated and turned back upon itself, struggling for existence by selling itself in the market-place, yet challenging the bourgeois world as a "genius," dreamed of a lost unity and yearned for a collective imaginatively projected either into the past or into the future. The dialectic triad—*thesis* (unity of origin), *antithesis* (alienation, isolation, fragmentation), and *synthesis* (removal of contradictions, reconciliation with reality, identity of subject and object, paradise regained)—was the very core of Romanticism.

All the contradictions inherent in Romanticism were carried to their extreme by the revolutionary upheaval of which the American War of Independence was the prologue and Waterloo the final act. The revolution and the attitudes adopted to it as a whole and to its separate phases are a key-subject of the Romantic movement. Again and again, at each turning-point of events, the movement split up into progressive and reactionary trends. Each time the petty bourgeoisie proved itself to be, as Marx wrote to Schweitzer, "contradiction incarnate."

What all the Romantics had in common was an antipathy to capitalism (some viewing it from an aristocratic angle, others from a plebeian), a Faustian or Byronic belief in the insatiability of the individual, and the acceptance of "passion in its own right" (Stendhal). In proportion as material production was officially regarded more and more as the quintessence of all that was praiseworthy, and as a crust of respectability formed round the dirty core of business, artists and writers attempted more and more intensively to reveal the heart of man and to hurl the dynamite of passion in the face of the apparently well-ordered bourgeois world. And as the relativity of all values was made increasingly clear by capitalist production methods, so passion—intensity of experience—became increasingly an absolute value. Keats said that he believed in nothing so much as in the "heart's affection." In the preface to *The Cenci,* Shelley wrote: "Imagination is as the immortal God made flesh for the redemption of mortal passion." Géricault, "extreme in all things" as Delacroix said of him, wrote in an essay of the "fever of exultation which overthrows and overwhelms everything," and of the "fire of a volcano which must irrepressibly break though to the light of day."

Romanticism was indeed a gigantic breakthrough. It led to the wild and the exotic, to limitless horizons: but it also led back to one's own people, one's own past, one's own specific nature. The greatest of the Romantics all admired Napoleon, the "cosmic self," the unbounded personality; yet at the same time the Romantic revolt merged with the national liberation struggles. Foscolo greeted Napoleon with an ode entitled *A Bonaparte Liberatore.* In 1802 he pleaded with Napoleon to proclaim the independence of the Cisalpine Republic, i.e. of Italy. In the end he turned, full of loathing, against Napoleon the conqueror. Leopardi, similarly embittered and disillusioned by the French liberator's failure to set his country free, exclaimed in the *Canzoni:*

> . . . l'armi, qua l'armi! io solo
> Combatteró, procomberó sol io.
> Dammi, o ciel, che sia foco
> Agli italici petti il sangue mio.

Arms, bring arms! I alone shall fight, I alone shall fall. Heaven provide that my blood be an inspiration to Italian hearts.

And in Eastern Europe, where capitalism had not yet triumphed and where the people were still labouring under the yoke of a decaying medievalism, Romanticism meant rebellion pure and simple, a trumpet call to the people to rise against foreign and home-bred oppressors, an appeal to national consciousness, a struggle against feudalism, absolutism, and foreign rule. Byron carried these countries by storm. The Romantic idealization of folk lore and folk art became a weapon for stirring up the people against degrading conditions, Romantic individualism a means of freeing the human personality from medieval bondage. The bourgeois–democratic revolution, as yet unaccomplished in the East, flashed like distant lightning through the works of the Romantic artists of Russia, Hungary, and Poland.

But for all these differences in its manifestation in various countries, Romanticism everywhere had certain features in common: a sense of spiritual discomfort in a world with which the artist could not identify himself, a sense of instability and isolation out of which grew the longing for a new social unity, a preoccupation with the people and their songs and legends ("the people" being endowed with an almost mystical unity in the artists' minds), and the celebration of the individual's absolute uniqueness, the unbounded Byronic subjectivism. The "free" writer rejecting all ties, setting himself up as an opponent of the bourgeois world, and at the same time, though himself unaware of this, recognizing the bourgeois principle of production for the market, made his first appearance at the time of Romanticism. In their Romantic protest against bourgeois values and in their emancipation which ultimately forced them into the role of Bohemians, such writers made of their works precisely what they wanted to denounce: a market commodity. Despite its invocation of the Middle Ages, Romanticism was an eminently bourgeois movement, and all the problems regarded as modern today were already implicit in it.

Because of Germany's central position between the capitalist world of the West and the feudal world of the East and because of the "German wretchedness," *die deutsche Misere,* which was the result of disastrous historical developments, German Romanticism was the most contradictory of all the Romantic movements. The capitalist "disenchantment in the arts" had set in before the bourgeois-democratic revolution had spread to Germany; illusions were lost before they had been properly accepted; and so, in its disgust with the capitalist aftermath of revolutionary upheavals, German Romanticism turned against those upheavals themselves and their postulates and ideas. Heine recognized here the element of anti-capitalist protest.

> Perhaps it was distaste with the money cult of today [he wrote] and disgust with the ugly face of egoism which they saw lurking everywhere, that first led some poets of the Romantic school in Germany, whose intentions were honest, to seek refuge from the present in the past and to call for the return to the Middle Ages.

The German Romantics said "No" to the developing social reality of their day. Bare negation can never be a permanent artistic attitude; to be productive, such an attitude must point to a "yes" as a shadow points to the object which casts it. But this "yes" cannot, in the last analysis, be anything other than affirmation of a social class in which the future is embodied. In Western countries, the working class was beginning to rise behind the bourgeoisie. In the East, the entire people—peasants, workers, bourgeois, and intellectuals—opposed the ruling system. But the German Romantics, already seeing the bourgeois businessman as a repellent figure, could not yet detect in the wretched German working class any force capable of building a future, and therefore tried to escape into an idealized feudal past. In doing so they were able to set certain positive features of that past against corresponding negative features of capitalism, e.g. the producer's, artisan's, or artist's close bond with the consumer, the greater directness of social relationships, the stronger collective sense, the greater unity of the human personality due to a more stable and less narrow division of labour. But these elements were taken out of their context, idealized, and turned into a fetish, before they were opposed to the justly criticized horrors of capitalism. The romantics, yearning for a "totality" of life, were unable to see through the real totality of social processes. In this respect they were true children of the capitalist bourgeois world. They did not understand that precisely by wiping out all social stability, destroying all fundamental human relationships, and atomizing society, capitalism was in fact preparing the way for the possibility of a fresh unity—whilst itself being utterly incapable of forming a new whole out of the fragments.

Chapter III.

THE ENGLISH REFORM BILL OF 1832

THE REFORM BILL of 1832 offers a number of excellent ingredients for historical controversy, and debate over the meaning of the bill has indeed loomed large in studies of nineteenth-century Britain. The most obvious basis for argument about the bill is simple partisanship. One can approve of the bill or not, with the usual gradations in between. Historians of relatively recent vintage have criticized the bill from a conservative standpoint, believing that the measure itself was too radical or, more commonly, that it opened the door to further reforms that created an objectionable democratic society. In another view, held by most socialist historians and others as well, the bill was inadequate precisely because it failed to be democratic; it represented the betrayal of the working classes by the liberal middle class. Historians sympathetic to the bill usually see it not only as a decisive break with the old order and the forerunner of further reforms, but also—and equally importantly—as a product of a peculiar British political genius for compromise and evolutionary change, in which revolutionary demands are placated or thwarted without the best features of the existing order being destroyed.

As with many issues in the nineteenth century, purely partisan arguments no longer dominate historical controversy. The passions of advocacy and opposition have, inevitably, declined, though partisan sentiments still influence the points of view taken on the major issues that are currently discussed.

Who or what was responsible for the bill? Historians have cited a number of factors. Some have posited a nearly revolutionary situation in which the influence of the 1830 uprisings on the Continent helped spur the development of an uneasy combination of middle-class radicals and working-class agitators—a picture that can easily raise the difficult and fascinating question of why England had no nineteenth-century revolution. According to some historians, the Reform Bill is a key part of the answer to this question. Without disagreeing completely with this judgment, labor historians have stressed the role of workers and have typically attributed a high degree of political consciousness to their agitation; this belief helps justify the view that the bill was a betrayal of its leading supporters and that its main consequence was to further working-class radicalism and discontent. Still other historians look to the importance of aristocratic compromise, in the House of Lords for example, and to the support given to reform by rural gentry. They play down the notion of a revolutionary threat and see the Reform Bill more a result of doctrines of reform within Parliament and a pragmatic step to improve the workings of Parliament itself. Recently, Asa Briggs has called attention to the diversity of support for reform in different areas of the country and the great variations in the motives for it.[1]

Finally, did the Reform Bill signify a decisive change in British politics? This is not a new question, but recent studies have given it a new importance. There are a number of reasons for stressing the significance of the bill. Partisans of the bill, in the Whig tradition of British historical writing, feel that it was a crucial step in the destruction of the rule of privilege and led, inevitably if calmly, to further reform. Historians who look at British history in a European context are also inclined to view the bill as essentially revolutionary—for it was in many ways more radical than measures introduced by revolutionary regimes on the continent in the same period. But the partisans of labor cannot see the bill itself as decisive, except in its effects on the working classes. Much recent historical investigation has questioned whether the bill really led to major changes in the personnel of government, in the alignment of political groups and parties, or even in the government's openness to other types of reform.

As the controversy implies, it is quite difficult to pin down either the environment or the impact of any legislative measure. A change on paper may not bring corresponding changes in the way politics actually works, much less in the broader structure of society. Yet the process of picking away at traditional assessments of importance may go too far. If the Reform Bill ended a threat of revolution (did it?), it must have had great symbolic importance if nothing else. Did the bill produce changes significant in the terms of the 1830's, if not in terms of our own time? Here the relevance of comparisons with continental Europe must be evaluated. Finally, how long a period should be considered in assessing impact? Here one must decide what, if anything, the Reform Bill had to do with later changes in British politics.

1. GEORGE M. TREVELYAN: British History in the Nineteenth Century and After, 1782–1919 *

George M. Trevelyan (1876–1962) was a grandnephew of the great Whig historian and politician Thomas Macaulay, and his work reflects the same sort of liberal view that Macaulay helped introduce into British historical writing. Much of Trevelyan's voluminous historical writing focused on the reform period in England. He viewed the Reform Bill as a demonstration of British political genius for moderate but significant change and as the product of pressure by enlightened groups on a recalcitrant aristocracy.

The genius of the English people for politics was faced by new problems arising out of those which it had solved of old. The age of the Tudors had seen the destruction of the mediaeval privileges of Church and Baronage, that had prevented the unity and progress of the nation; in their place the full sovereignty of the Crown in Parliament had been established. Under the Stuarts, Parliament had won the supremacy in its partnership with the Crown, while

1. Asa Briggs, *The Age of Improvement* (London, 1959).

* From George M. Trevelyan, *British History in the Nineteenth Century and After, 1782–1919* (New York: David McKay Company, Inc., 1937), pp. 224–28, 230–31, 235–39. Reprinted by permission of David McKay Company, Inc. and Longmans, Green & Company, Ltd.

the principle of local government had been preserved against despotic encroachment. In the eighteenth century, Parliament had acquired executive efficiency through the Cabinet system. These institutions were England's unique and native heritage. But they were administered by a privileged group of borough owners, magistrates and members of close corporations, roughly identified in sympathy with the country gentlemen, but not co-extensive even with that class. This group had by long possession come to regard their own monopoly as synonymous with the Constitution itself. To speak ill of the rotten boroughs and close corporations was to utter "seditious" words against our "matchless Constitution." But in spite of Lord Eldon and those who thought with him, Parliament, Cabinet and local government had been created by England's practical imagination in the past, and had now by a fresh creative process to be adapted to the needs of a new type of society born of the Industrial Revolution. . . .

To the Whigs between 1830 and 1835 belongs the credit of destroying the monopoly, reinterpreting the Constitution, and harnessing public opinion to the machine of government. Whatever some of the Whigs might say about the "finality" of their Bill, this new principle, when once admitted, could brook no limitation until complete democracy had been realised under old English forms. On the other hand the belief of the anti-Reform Tories that the Reform Bill would lead at once to the overthrow of Crown and Lords, Church and property, was the exact reverse of the truth. It was due to the Bill that England was not involved in the vicious circle of continental revolution and reaction, and that our political life kept its Anglo-Saxon moorings.

Both the Liberal-Tories in Canning's day, and the Whig followers of Grey and Althorp, were acting under the direct inspiration of middle-class opinion, and under compelling fear of working-class revolt.

The movement of Parliamentary Reform was revived in the nineteenth century first of all by the working-men, because their economic misery was the most acute. The middle classes had been divided or indifferent during the radical agitation of the Peterloo time. The Whigs, meanwhile, to prevent division in their own ranks, waited on the middle-class lead, Lord Grey always abiding by his declaration of 1810 that he would again move for Reform when, but only when, the English people had taken it up "seriously and affectionately." In the year 1830 he saw his condition fulfilled. The middle classes, in whom he read public opinion, took up Reform "seriously and affectionately"; whereupon, greatly to the surprise of friends and foes, the old nobleman was as good as his word.

There were many reasons why the middle classes moved rapidly towards Parliamentary Reform in the three years following Canning's death. The removal of the statesman whom so many had begun to regard as the national leader, threw them back into their former attitude of opposition to Government, and the reversal of his foreign policy by Wellington was a sharp reminder that only Parliamentary Reform could secure that national affairs should be continuously guided on popular lines.

Meanwhile any avenue of escape through "bit by bit" reform was closed by the action of the Parliamentary Tories in 1828, when they refused to allow the seats of certain boroughs disfranchised for peculiarly gross corruption to be given to the unrepresented cities of Manchester and Birmingham. It was on that issue that Huskisson, Palmerston and Melbourne had left Wellington's Ministry, and the event made a deep impression on public opinion.

In January 1830 Thomas Attwood founded the Birmingham Political Union, to agitate for a large but undefined measure of Parliamentary Reform. It was, professedly and actually, a union of middle and working classes; it was the first step towards their co-operation in Radical politics which marked the Victorian era. In other industrial centres, such as Manchester, it was more difficult for employers and workmen to co-operate, though both were now avowed enemies of the "borough-mongers."

Bad trade and hard times had returned. Common economic misery sharpened the sense of common political wrongs, and predisposed the whole nation to unite in the demand for Reform. In 1830 Cobbett enjoyed a second period of great popular influence, which he used as he had used his popularity in 1817, to turn all streams of discontent into the one channel of Parliamentary Reform. But whereas in 1817 he had been the leader of the working class alone, he found in 1830 that even the farmers thronged to hear him speak, as he rode on his cob from one market-town to another. Radicalism had become for the moment almost a national creed.

There were differences of opinion as to the economic cure for the distress of the time. Some, like Attwood, saw it in currency reform; more, like Cobbett, in retrenchment; others in Free Trade; others in Factory Acts or in Socialism. But all were agreed that reform of Parliament was the necessary first step before anything effective could be done.

The greatest danger to the cause of Reform arose from dissension as to what the new franchise ought to be. Some claimed household suffrage, others desired government by "the solid and respectable part of the community." But the rallying cry of "Down with the rotten boroughs" served to harmonise these discords. Every class that was hoping to exert greater influence over Parliament was enraged that more than half the House of Commons owed their seats to individual peers or commoners. The borough owners, who for generations back had pulled the strings of ministerial favour and lived on the fat of patronage—they and their kinsmen and their servants—suddenly found themselves objects of universal execration, and the "borough property" which they had inherited or purchased denounced as having been stolen from the nation. The cry against the "borough-mongers" rose on every side. Capitalists, clerks, shopkeepers, besides that great majority of the inhabitants who were comprised under the two categories of working-men and Dissenters, all were talking against "Old Corruption." The very ostlers and publicans entered into the spirit of the hour. Even country gentlemen who did not happen to have an "interest" in a borough, began to think that they would like to see a fairer proportion of county members in the House, honestly chosen by themselves and their farmers. The only class that remained solid for the old system was the Church clergy, who were so conscious of unpopularity that they believed Reform would lead to the destruction of the Establishment.

Into the midst of a society thus agitated came the news of the Paris revolution of 1830, the "glorious days of July." Charles X and his minister Polignac had provoked their own downfall by illegally suspending the Constitution. Although the fighting on the barricades had been done by the workmen, the movement was not permitted to turn "red," but solidified round Lafayette, the National Guard and the *bourgeois* King, Louis Philippe. The *noblesse* and the Clericals had fallen once more, but property was safe. These events could not, like the French Revolutions of 1792 and 1848, and the Commune of 1871, be used as a warning against change over here. The year 1830, still stands as the one occasion when the French set a political example that influenced us otherwise than by repulsion.

The first effect of the inspiring news from France was to increase the number of open seats carried by the Opposition in the General Election that August. A new Parliament had to be elected, on account of the death of George and the accession of William IV, the popular sailor king. It was the House of Commons chosen in these circumstances that turned out Wellington and carried the Reform Bill by one vote. Brougham, the interpreter between the official Whigs and the national movement for Reform, was sent up as a member for Yorkshire, amid the rejoicings of the whole country. He never again touched such a height of popular influence.

But the French Revolution of 1830 did more than affect the elections. It gave Englishmen the sense of living in a new era, when great changes could safely be made. To act boldly on behalf of the people, it was seen, did not produce anarchy as the Tories had argued ever since 1789. Rather, it was half-measures that were dangerous, and resistance to the people that was fatal. Our middle class saw the *bourgeoisie* governing France, and blushed that in England they themselves were still subject to an aristocracy. The working-men heard that the *ouvriers* had defeated the Army in fair fight, and the word went round that what Frenchmen had done Englishmen could do at need. Pamphlets on the technique of street-fighting had a suggestive popularity. The knowledge that Englishmen were so thinking, and that Frenchmen had so acted, gravely affected the politics of the propertied class as a whole, and not a few of the borough owners themselves, persuading them to make concessions they would never have dreamt of two years before. . . .

All autumn the agitation in the country was deeper than political. Economic misery, pauperism, starvation and class injustice had brought society to the verge of dissolution. Rick-burning, under the orders of "Captain Swing," that dark abstraction of the vengeance of the ruined peasantry, kept the rural south in terror. In the industrial north the workmen were drilling and preparing for social war. The middle classes clamoured for Reform, equally to pacify the revolutionary spirit below, and to secure their own rights against an aristocracy they had ceased to trust.

In the first fortnight of November, when Wellington met the recently elected Parliament, came the most important political crisis of the century. Everyone was looking to the new House of Commons to save the country, yet no one knew what it would do, even in making its choice between Wellington and Grey. The group system still prevailed, and many of the groups had no defined political allegiance. As late as November the First, there were three future Prime Ministers waiting to find out whether they were Whig or Tory; for the Canningites under Lords Melbourne and Palmerston, and the independent group led by Edward Stanley, "the Rupert of Debate," came up pledged to moderate Reform and looking to see whether Wellington or Grey would give them what they wanted. If the Duke had made a declaration promising a peaceful and liberal policy towards France and Belgium, and a small measure of Parliamentary Reform, he could have rallied these men round him and stayed in office. It is indeed unlikely that a Tory Reform Bill would have been large enough to pacify the country. But in any case the experiment was not destined to be tried.

The King's speech mentioned the Belgian revolution with ominous disapproval, and when Lord Grey called attention to the absence of any promise of Reform, the Duke replied that "the system of representation possessed the full and entire confidence of the country."

The Duke had challenged the nation, and the nation took up the challenge. The excitement inside Parliament was a feeble reflection of the feeling outside; yet never were the lobbies and clubs more busy, or busy to better purpose. In a week the basis had been laid of the Whig-Liberal party that was to dominate the next generation. The Canningites and moderate reformers all enlisted under Grey's banner, and were prepared to join a Whig Government on the programme of "Peace, Retrenchment and Reform." With the help of a few High Tories who were still so anxious to be revenged on the Duke for Catholic Emancipation that they cared not what happened afterwards, the Government was beaten in the Commons on the Civil List. Wellington resigned, and the King sent for Lord Grey. . . .

At the very moment of the change of Ministry, the labourers of the southern counties, driven by famine, were marching through the countryside demanding a living wage of half a crown a day. They were cruelly punished at the assizes, when 450 of the rioters were torn from their families and transported to Australia, besides three unjustly executed. The new Whig Ministers, in a panic lest the propertied classes should confound "Reform" with "Jacobinism and disorder," would not mitigate these sentences. In connection with the same riots they prosecuted Richard Carlile and Cobbett for articles in the Press. Cobbett at his trial in the following July, made the Whigs look as foolish before a British jury as the Tories of old. His acquittal effectually discouraged a revival of that spirit of coercion which Peel as Home Secretary had so wisely abandoned.

The Whigs had made a bad start. But when on March 1, 1831, Lord John Russell introduced the Reform Bill into the Commons, and revealed the well-kept secret that all the "nomination" boroughs were to be abolished without compensation to the borough-owners, Ministers sprang to the summit of popularity at a single bound. The Tories were dumfounded. They had confidently expected a weak measure, buying up a few of the rotten borough seats to give them to a few great cities; such a Bill would have left the nation cold and the reformers divided; lacking support from outside, it could pass the Houses only by agreement, after being further whittled down; finally the Whigs would be turned out as incompetent sciolists and power would revert to its long-tried possessors. But instead of lending themselves to this plan, Ministers had summoned the whole nation to their support, to overawe the recusants at Westminster. The bold appeal was not merely a winning move in the political game, but it established the fundamental principle of the "new constitution," namely, that in the last resort the opinion of the nation was to count for more than the opinion of the legislators. . . .

A defeat in Committee soon narrowed the issue to a choice between a new Ministry with a much modified Bill, or a General Election to save Bill and Ministry together. In such circumstances a modern Prime Minister could claim a dissolution of Parliament as of right. But under George III and his sons dissolution was, in custom as well as in law, a personal prerogative of the king. Would William dissolve at Grey's request? The decisive crisis in the fortunes of the Bill had come, and the choice lay with a retired admiral of no great brains or experience in affairs of State, but with an instinct of personal loyalty to his Ministers which sharply distinguished him from his father and brother before him.

In January 1831, while the Draft Bill had been a secret between William and his confidential servants, Grey had persuaded his master to allow him to introduce it—a permission necessary under the custom of the Constitution as George III had defined it. Grey had persuaded the King that the Bill was an "aristocratical" measure, designed to save the Constitution from more revolutionary changes. And so it was in Grey's mind. Its "democratical" implications only began to be apparent to William after it had become public, when the joy of the Radicals of whom he lived in terror, and the rage of the Tories with whom he lived in intimacy, gradually made him realise what he had done. In April he had to decide whether he would accept Grey's resignation or his advice to dissolve. The straw that weighed down the balance in his mind was the fact that there had been a majority of one for the second reading. With many misgivings he granted Grey his dissolution.

The General Election was almost as onesided and enthusiastic, so far as popular opinion was concerned, as the elections for the Restoration Parliament. The Reformers carried almost all the open constituencies, including seventy-four English county seats out of eighty. But no amount of popular intimidation could shake the hold of the proprietors on the nomination seats. In their last Parliament the rotten borough members voted two to one against the Bill, in much the same numbers as before the election.

But there was now a majority of 136 for the Bill. It passed through the Commons that summer under Lord Althorp's patient management in Committee, and went up to the Lords, where it was thrown out on second reading by a majority of forty-one votes. . . .

A single false step by the Ministers might have precipitated anarchy. The Army, smaller than at any other period in our modern annals, was insufficient to keep order in England and Scotland, in addition to its usual task in Ireland. Peel's police as yet only existed in London. It was impossible to raise volunteer forces to put down Reform mobs. The workmen in the North were drilling and arming to fight the Lords. In the South the ricks were blazing night after night. Unemployment and starvation urged desperate deeds. The first visitation of cholera added to the gloom and terror of the winter of 1831–2.

Employers and City men clamoured more loudly every week for a creation of peers to pass the Bill and save social order. The working classes, if it came to blows, would fight not for this Bill of the Ten Pound householders, but for a Bill that enfranchised their own class, and for much else besides. Civil strife, if it came, might easily degenerate into a war between "haves" and "have-nots." The Bill seemed the sheet-anchor of society. Even the burning of the central part of Bristol by Radical ruffians failed to cause a serious reaction, each side drawing its own moral from the event.

Grey kept his head. He neither resigned nor, as the King urged, whittled down the Bill. On the other hand he refused, in spite of the remonstrance of the leading members of his Cabinet, to force the King to a premature decision about peer-making, before the time came when circumstances would be too strong for William's reluctance.

Before Christmas a new Bill was introduced, modified in detail to meet some reasonable criticisms and so save the face of the "waverers" among the peers, but not weakened as a democratic measure. It quickly passed the Commons, and was accepted by nine votes on the second reading in the Lords.

The final crisis, known as the "Days of May," was provoked by an attempt of the Lords to take the Bill out of the hands of the Ministers in charge, and amend it in their own way. This was countered by the resignation of the Cabinet. Resignation in the previous autumn, when the Lords had thrown the Bill right out, would have produced anarchy. Now it secured and hastened the last stages of a journey of which the goal was already in sight. In October 1831 the country, taken by surprise by the Lords' action, was not properly organised, as the riots had shown. But in May 1832, the Political Unions had the situation in hand. Grey's resignation was not followed by violence or rioting, but by a silent and formidable preparation for ultimate resistance in case he did not speedily return. The English genius for local self-government, voluntary combination and self-help, which had little or no expression in the close municipalities, found its outlet in these unofficial Political Unions of citizens determined alike on order and on freedom.[1] These organisations, improvised by the British

1. They had been formed in most towns. The model of Attwood's Birmingham Union, presided over by middle-class leaders, but including all classes, prevailed in the midlands and west. In the industrial north there were "low Political Unions" of working-men only. In some towns there were both kinds of Political Union formed side by side.

people, constituted the strongest proof of its fitness to work self-governing institutions of a more official character. Abhorred by the King and Tories who clamoured for their suppression, the Unions were tolerated by the Whig Ministers on the condition of their ceasing to arm and drill.

Grey had resigned because the King refused to create peers. But William was now prepared to do anything short of that to get the Bill through intact. He appealed to Wellington to form a Tory Ministry for the purpose of carrying "the Bill, the whole Bill and nothing but the Bill" through the House of Lords—on the precedent of Catholic Emancipation three years before. The most fearless, if not always the wisest, of public servants accepted this extraordinary commission, the nature of which was not understood in the country, where people naturally supposed that the victor of Waterloo, who had pronounced against all Reform, was coming back to rule them by the sword. If Wellington had succeeded in forming a Ministry, the Political Unions would have led resistance, with what result it is impossible to say. But the actual cause of the Duke's abandoning the task was not his fear of popular resistance, but the refusal of Peel and the Tories in the House of Commons to take part in a scheme so absurd and dangerous, no longer with a hope of modifying the Bill, but solely to save the face of the Lords. The King was obliged to come to terms with Grey, and could only get him back by a written promise to create any number of peers necessary to carry the Bill. The threat when known in the Upper House sufficed, and the Reform Bill became law.

2. O. F. CHRISTIE: The Transition from Aristocracy, 1832–1837 *

O. F. Christie (1867–1953) was a lawyer and businessman who turned to historical writing late in life. Writing in the 1920's and 1930's, he was perhaps influenced by the problems of his own age; in any case, he clearly regretted the trends which the Reform Bill helped usher in. His conservatism impelled him to stress, even more than did the liberal historians, the importance of the bill and the agitation that surrounded it. His bias may also allow him to characterize the resistance to reform more accurately than other types of historian can; or it may lead him to exaggerate it.

"But you might have heard a pin drop as Duncannon read the numbers. Then again the shouts broke out, and many of us shed tears. I could scarcely refrain. And the jaw of Peel fell; and the face of Twiss was as the face of a damned soul; and Herries looked like Judas taking his necktie off for the last operation." So wrote Macaulay to Ellis of the division of 22nd March 1831, when the Second Reading of the Reform Bill was carried by a majority of one; but it was not till 7th June of the following year that the Bill, twice altered, became law. The last scene in the House of Lords, when it received the Royal assent, was in utter contrast with that described by Macaulay. In Samuel Rey-

* From O. F. Christie, *The Transition from Aristocracy, 1832–1837* (New York: G. P. Putnam's Sons, 1927), pp. 35–36, 42–45, 57–62.

nolds's painting the Government benches are full, the Tory benches are empty; almost alone on the left of the Throne stands the Duke of Sussex, the Whig son of George the Third. One has an impression of the calm and gloom that are appropriate to "The Tapestry." Between these two dates the hopes and fears of the Bill's champions and opposers had risen and fallen. In the country there had been terrible riots, in London incessant intrigue; but the Zenobias of Mayfair had exerted themselves in vain. The King had wavered; Earl Grey had resigned; the Duke had been obliged to advise his recall. During eleven fateful days of May 1832 England had been on the brink of revolution.

Macaulay, in likening one Tory to a devil and another to Judas, gives proof—if proof were needed—of the violent political passions of the day and of how ardently he himself entertained them. Party feeling poisoned even his kindly temperament, and (what was less excusable) his literary criticism. Not content with hating Croker as a political opponent, he virulently attacked him as a man of letters. It was in September 1831, in the very height of the Reform struggle, that his criticism of Croker's Boswell appeared in *The Edinburgh Review:* "A dog of the House of Montague moves me. . . . I will take the wall of any man or maid of Montague's." But Macaulay did not exaggerate the consternation in the Tory ranks. And yet, perhaps, it is necessary for us to call to mind what the Tories stood to lose, in order fully to understand, and indeed to sympathize, with their apprehensions. . . .

The Tories fought against Reform, firstly for selfish and personal reasons, because it affected their fortunes and careers; and yet this latter fear—the fear of the loss of an honourable career—was by no means an ignoble motive. But there was another thing they feared, which no man may blame them for fearing, and that was Revolution, "The dark, unbottom'd, infinite abyss"/which they believed to be yawning in front of them. It was the unknown future that they apprehended, of an England with a new kind of government that would represent forces incalculable and immeasurable. They feared, in fact, the destruction of Monarchy, House of Lords, and Church, and all the ancient preservative institutions of the country.

These fears of some terrible cataclysm had been felt long before Reform had come within the range of practical politics. In 1809 (we read in Creevey) "Charles Warren the lawyer predicts the present reign will end quietly from the popularity of the King, but that when it ends, the profligacy and unpopularity of the Princes with the situation of the country as to financial difficulties, and the rapidly and widely extended growth of Methodism, will produce a storm." In 1812 Creevey himself writes: "The more one sees of the conduct of this most singular man (the Prince Regent), the more one becomes convinced he is doomed, from his personal character, to shake his throne." Greville . . . was moved by the condition of the poor in Sunderland and Rotherhithe, and by revelations made at an Old Bailey trial, to the gloomiest prognostications. And we may take it as certain that since the French Revolution, which (according to Burke) had affected one-fifth of the population with subversive ideas, vague apprehensions had been endemic. These fears now centred round the Reform agitation. Some were alarmed at the prospect, if the Bill should pass; some, if it should be rejected. Macaulay claimed "that the question, whether the change in itself be good or bad, has become a question of secondary importance; that, good or bad, the thing must be done; that a law as strong as the laws of attraction and motion has decreed it" (House of Commons, 10th November 1831). Whether the Bill were passed or rejected, it seemed as if terrible results were to be expected.

In the great towns the "Mob"—the unknown or little-known *residuum* of the population—had always been a formidable monster. In London it had shown its power in the Sacheverell riots and the Wilkes riots; at the Gordon Riots it had poured out of its fastnesses—the Minories, the Dials, the Mint, and the purlieus of the Fleet—and for a time held the City at its mercy. But these riots had been urban, and had been occasioned by political and religious rather than by social grievances; there had been no real *jacquerie* in England since the Peasants' Revolt of 1377. In the winter of 1830–1831 many counties in England did experience something very like a *jacquerie*. "This part of the country," wrote Mrs. Edward Bulwer (on 5th December 1830), from Heydon in Norfolk, "like every other, has been in a terrible state of disturbance. Meetings of five or six hundred desperadoes in every village. About ten days ago there was a meeting of this sort at a place called Reepham, which all the noblemen and gentlemen in the county went to try and put down, by telling the people that their wrongs should be redressed, their wages raised, and employment given to them. Upon which the mob shouted: 'It is very well to try and talk us over, but we will have blood for our suppers!' They then began pelting the magistrates and gentlemen with large stones. . . . The burnings are dreadful, but every house in this part of the world is in a state of defence, and all the farmers, shopkeepers, servants, etc., etc., sworn in special constables." By the middle of December incendiary fires were burning in thirteen counties, and the Government appointed a special Commission to try the incendiaries. Of the Rotundanists, so called from their place of weekly assembly in Blackfriars Bridge Road, Place himself said: "Among these men were some who were perfectly atrocious, whose purpose was riot, as providing an opportunity for plundering." At Bristol the Bishop's Palace, public buildings and many private houses were burnt to the ground. At Nottingham the Castle and several factories were burnt. In Darlington a lady driving beside Lord Tankerville was nearly killed by a paving stone that was hurled at her. The house of Mrs. Musters in Nottinghamshire was burnt; she had to pass the night out of doors in the damp and died of exposure. There was said to exist a scheme to seize the families of certain peers and hold them for hostages. . . .

Thanks to Reform the danger of civil war was averted. And yet, although this prime object was attained, and although everywhere there was great public rejoicing, it is easy to understand the apprehensions with which the great event of 1832 was regarded by all who had a "stake" in the country. In 1688 Divine Right was discredited, and the King who claimed it was driven into exile. "What we did at the Revolution," said Johnson in his old age, "was necessary, but it broke our Constitution." Burke maintained, on the contrary, that it cured a "peccant" part of our Constitution which was thereby brought to a state of perfection; and the Tories of 1832, whatever they still thought of 1688, had become Burkeites in this sense—that they believed that any change at all would now be for the worse. "If I had imposed on me the duty of framing a legislature for any country," said the Duke of Wellington in the House of Lords (2nd November 1830), "I do not mean to assert that I could form such a legislature as you possess now, for the nature of man is incapable of recasting such excellence at once, but my great endeavour would be to form some description of legislature which would produce the same results." So of 1832 the Duke and his high Tory followers would have said what Johnson said of 1688—that what was done then was necessary, but that it "broke our Constitution." The nation was moving from the known to the unknown. A venerable lady who died quite recently, and yet could remember those days, has written: "The floodgates were opened in 1832, and never since has the current stopped." This was the favourite metaphor of Sir Leicester Dedlock, whom Dickens presented as the type of the stupid reactionary Tory; but can anyone now say whither the current is carrying us? It is true that the fears which Macaulay had ridiculed were duly falsified. No Marats, no Santerres appeared in the House of Commons; it has been reserved for our own day to see therein members who openly advocate a violent revolution. By 1835 even the high Tory Gladstone could take a sanguine view of the situation: "To think that notwithstanding the Ten-Pound Clause a moderate Parliament may be returned; in fine, to believe that we have now *some* prospect of surviving the *Reform* Bill without a bloody revolution, is to me as surprising as delightful; it seems to me the greatest and most providential mercy with which a nation was ever visited." Nevertheless, since 1832, wise and thoughtful Englishmen have been continually obsessed by forebodings as to the stability of our social order. If France has never had a stable Government since 1789, England has never been free from political uneasiness since 1832. In 1842 armed mobs destroyed factories; Stockport was plundered and part of Manchester destroyed; Peel requisitioned arms to protect his country house. In 1846 Croker (writing to Brougham) prophesies that, after a period of anarchy, "we shall have a federal republic after the American fashion." It was Gladstone's opinion that there would have been a revolution if the Corn Laws had not been repealed. In 1848 Matthew Arnold writes from London: "It will be *rioting* here, only; still, the hour of the hereditary peerage and eldest sonship and immense properties has, I am convinced, as Lamartine would say, struck. . . . Carlyle gives our institutions, as they are called, aristocracy, Church, etc., five years, I heard last night." In this year houses in the West End of London were put in a state of fortification. In 1850 Stanley writes to Croker, with reference to the next General Election: "If this or any Free Trade Government *then* acquire a majority, the game is up; and I firmly believe we shall be in a rapid progress towards a republic in name as well as reality. . . . We are falling into the fatal sleep which precedes mortification and death." Henry Drummond to Croker (1853): "I say that Bright is right, and we are on the eve of becoming a Republic." Carlyle (*Journal*, 1866): "Sometimes I think the tug of revolution struggle may be even *near* for poor England, much nearer than I once judged—very questionable to me whether England won't go quite to *smash* under it." Shaftesbury to Granville (1868): "Be assured, my dear friend, that no merely human skill will save the British Empire from utter shipwreck." I will conclude with a wail from Beaconsfield, who so rarely desponded, in a letter written to Lord John Manners in December 1880: "And yet I see no prospect of salvation, and really believe that you, at least, will live long enough to see the crown fall from our gracious Sovereign's head."

I could quote, if it were necessary, sad vaticinations to which many other personages have given utterance since 1832, men so diverse as Harrowby, Hobhouse, Wellington, Greville, Salisbury, Dr. Arnold, Bagehot, Lowe and Peel. The fear common to all of them arises from a deep-seated conviction that government can only be properly carried on by the few and not by the many. But this is a doctrine which, since Reform, could not be preached from a platform by any politician who valued his career. It has been more and more necessary for anyone who aspires to political success to pay compliments to democracy, and no doubt many of these compliments have been sincere. Yet the most sincere believers have become disillusioned. Lord Morley, towards the close of his long life, asked: "As for progress, what signs of it are there now? And all the Victorians believed in it from the Utilitarians onwards."

At least we may say that the fears of a cataclysm have not yet been fulfilled. Our social order still stands unbroken, and we have much that may hearten us to look the doubtful future in the face. In writing of a period of transition one may also remark that the men whose gloomy prophecies I have quoted, and who were not fools, were nearly all survivors from the previous age—an age which was so far from taking the virtues of representative government for granted that it regarded "democracy" as almost certainly connoting revolution. Democracy was associated with the excesses of the French Revolution, and that revolution was almost as near to the men of 1830–1832 as Queen Victoria's first Jubilee is to ourselves. "A perfect democracy," wrote Burke, "is the most shameless thing in the world"—because it is absolute and unrestrained. Croker continued of the same opinion in 1845: "The *facilis descensus Averni*—that is Democracy." To the progressive Whig or Liberal, it is true, Croker stood for reaction and blind pessimism. But Macaulay himself, who detested Croker, said of purely democratic institutions that "they must sooner or later destroy liberty or civilization or both." We have lately heard a cant phrase about "making the world safe *for* Democracy." Our great-grandfathers were preoccupied in making the world safe *from* Democracy. As late as 1865 Disraeli was hoping that the House of Commons would "sanction no step that has a tendency to democracy." Now the Reform Bill was inspired by the same democratic ideal as had inspired the French Revolution. The vote was a Right, one of the Rights of Man, a Right that should be claimed by all, and not (as Disraeli used to argue) a privilege that should be granted only to those who proved they deserved it. Though the Bill enfranchised only 220,000 voters, it recognized the democratic principle of an individual's right to a vote, and that Parliament should be in this sense "representative." But this theory of representation, also, was clean contrary to the doctrine of Burke. "When," he asked, "did you hear in Great Britain of any province suffering from the inequality of its representation; what district from having no representation at all? Not only our monarchy and our peerage secure the equality on which our unity depends, but it is the spirit of the House of Commons itself . . . Cornwall elects as many members as all Scotland, but is Cornwall better taken care of than Scotland? Few trouble their heads about any of your bases, out of some giddy clubs." In 1794 the Attorney-General, prosecuting Thomas Hardy for high treason, described representative government as "The direct contrary of the government which is established here. There was a Tory view held in that day that men should first decide what sort of persons would be their best representatives and then, second, what sort of persons would be most likely to elect them. There may be something to be said for this old-fashioned notion; but it is only necessary here to bear in mind how it contrasts with the later doctrine—that the more numerous the electors the wiser will be the representative."

The Reform Movement in England, says Mr. G. M. Trevelyan, began with the Yorkshire freeholders, afterwards received support from the philosophic Dissenters, and still later from the working classes. Was it also in the end inspired by ideas even more subversive than those of Paine and Hardy?

3. CRANE BRINTON: English Political Thought in the Nineteenth Century *

Crane Brinton † outlines his reasons for viewing the Reform Bill as essentially revolutionary. His approach reflects his familiarity with French history, in which most of his historical writing has been done, and provides a comparative dimension that must be assessed. His focus is on political thought, and it might be suggested that the historian of ideas sees more decisive changes than many political historians do, because intellectuals are more articulate about their desire to cause change; but how relevant were formal ideas to the Reform Bill?

There is hardly a better example of the imprecision of sociological terms than the word revolution. To apply it to the inventions of Watt and Cartwright, to the summoning of the Estates General in 1789, to the first performance of *Hernani,* to the flight of Charles X., and to the latest South American *coup d'état* is almost to deprive it of meaning. In a narrower and purely political sense, it does denote an extra-legal and usually violent change in the existing government. But even here the word revolution, as contrasted with *coup d'état,* implies a change affecting the lives of quite ordinary citizens. Now England

* From Crane Brinton, *English Political Thought in the Nineteenth Century* (London: Ernest Benn Limited), pp. 11–14. Reprinted by permission of Ernest Benn Limited.

† See Chapter 1, on the impact of the French Revolution.

underwent in the first third of the nineteenth century industrial and artistic changes which all are agreed in calling revolutionary. A justifiable pride in the fact that the political changes of the time—the repeal of the Test Act, Catholic Emancipation, the Reform Bill of 1832—were achieved without violence, and a less justifiable desire to emphasize that Englishmen are not as Frenchmen are, have prevented our applying the word revolutionary to these political changes. Yet if revolution means in politics, as it does in art, morals, and industry, a real and only comparatively rapid alteration of our fundamental ways of doing things, the term should be used of the transfer of power symbolized in the Act of 1832.

Englishmen of the time were certainly aware of that sense of crisis which is one of the signs of revolutionary change. The ageing Wordsworth declared that, if the Bill were passed, he would retire to a safe and conservative country like Austria. Indeed, the parallel between the French Revolution of 1830 and the Reform Bill crisis is surprisingly close. How real the threat of violence was in England need not be recalled to readers familiar with Mr. Graham Wallas's *Life of Francis Place*. To alter the constituencies and the franchise by what was obviously something close to Rousseau's general will seemed to alter in its fundamentals a constitution certainly as well established as had been the constitution of Richelieu and Louis XIV. in 1789. To yield to the demands of men like Cobbett seemed almost like yielding to Wat Tyler.

The generation of thinkers with whom we are now concerned were quite conscious that a new England was in the making, and that theirs was the task of seeing that this new England should be a good one for Englishmen. Some such notion, indeed, runs through all English political thought in the nineteenth century, and is as strong as ever to-day. It is no doubt possible to exaggerate the uniqueness of our modern acceptance of the fact of change. Even Tennyson's Cathay was probably less stationary than he liked to think. But how much we are all inured to discontent and hope in earthly matters is startlingly evident if one recalls that after all what Herbert Spencer was trying to do was to construct a modern *Summa*. How different from the Thomist acquiescence in the will of God is Spencer's petulant dislike for conditions which could hardly be other than the inevitable product of his law of evolution! Not even the absolutist position in metaphysics, as witness the work of T.H. Green, could in nineteenth-century England accept the highly logical Leibnitzian best of all possible worlds.

The year 1832 is then at best a mere halting-place for convenience in a century which was always seeking to remake itself according to a better pattern. The generation which fought the struggle over the Reform Bill has, however, a certain unity. In the first place, as the text-books unfailingly point out, the French Revolution and the war with Napoleon did put a stop to any kind of political agitation, even to any kind of political thinking. Godwin's *Political Justice* ends rather than begins a period of fruitful discussion. For nearly twenty years, until the publication of Wordsworth's *Tract on the Convention of Cintra* in 1809 (a pamphlet, moreover, which was hardly noticed at the time) there was produced but one work of importance in the history of English political thought. And even Malthus's great work was the product of a closet philosopher, and at first taken to be the best possible bulwark of the old order. The mature Bentham, Brougham, Owen, Cobbett, Coleridge and the rest were starting afresh.

In the second place, the long tenure of the Liverpool Cabinet and its patent failure to produce even a policy, let alone a programme, led to a situation curiously like that of France under Louis XVI., where the intellect was definitely in opposition. You cannot find a competent apologist for things as they are in the England of the time. The ablest political minds—Canning, Huskisson—on the Government side are all boring from within in the direction of reform. What may be called eternally Conservative ideas and temperaments indeed there are—a Cobbett or a Coleridge—but they are not on the side of the Government. To study the ideas of the complete standpatter between 1800 and 1832 would be to study the ideas of Eldon or Croker, to study the *Quarterly Review*—not, on the whole, a profitable proceeding.

Finally, there is the commonplace that 1832 marks the accession of the middle class to political power. The phrase "middle class" had complete currency at the time, and, if it hardly received rigorous definition, it was pretty generally understood to correspond to a political and economic reality. This is not the place to inquire too deeply into the question as to where to draw the lines between upper, middle, and working classes. From Defoe onwards the English trading people, from "City" bankers to small retailers, had been growing aware of the fact that they had virtues and tastes not shared by the nobility. From the beginnings of the commercial revolution they had been gaining in wealth and numbers. From the industrial revolution on they had been reminded, often forcibly, that their new wealth had created (some indeed suspected had in a measure been created by) an altogether new urban proletariat. This proletariat, it was clear, was not adequately cared for under existing conditions. Lancashire, within the memory of man, had changed so much, done so much, and Dorset had done so little! Was it unreasonable to suppose that the men who made such excellent and such abundant cotton cloth could also make an excellent England? Into the passing of the Reform Bill there went many and conflicting desires, as we shall see, but chiefly there went the confidence of the children of the industrial revolution that theirs was a better world in the making.

4. G. D. H. COLE: A Short History of the British Working Class Movement, 1789–1927 *

G. D. H. Cole (1889–1959) taught political theory at Oxford, wrote widely in the field of labor history, and was active in British socialist politics. His approach to the Reform Bill naturally stresses the role of workers and the

* From G. D. H. Cole, *A Short History of the British Working Class Movement, 1789–1927* (London: George Allen & Unwin Ltd.), pp. 94–101. Reprinted by permission of George Allen & Unwin Ltd.

disappointment that the bill was to them. Is this an adequate focus? Is the stress too great? Were the political concerns of workers as deep as Cole implies?

Meanwhile the movement for the reform of Parliament was speedily gathering force. The House of Commons up to 1832 not only made no pretence of being a democratic body, but was hardly, in any ordinary sense of the word, a representative assembly. The most that could be claimed for it was that it "virtually represented" the classes which had a stake in the country—in other words, that it represented property rather than persons. The distribution of seats bore no proportion either to population or even to the number of electors. In 1780, the ninety-two members for the counties were returned by 130,000 voters—the county freeholders; whereas the 421 members who sat for towns and universities were returned by only 84,000 electors. Moreover, whereas the county elections did, in most cases, give at least the gentry some opportunity of expressing their views, the majority of the borough elections were pure farce. . . .

The Reform Movement, which arose between 1769 and 1780, was crushed by the terrors aroused by the Revolution in France. Thenceforth all proposals for reform were denounced as Jacobinism—the first steps towards a complete destruction of British institutions, which would inevitably end in the tearing-up of all property rights and the triumph of Republicanism and Revolution. The Reform agitation, recovering slowly during the later years of the Napoleonic wars, only came to command widespread support in the troublous period which followed the Peace. Thereafter it gradually gathered force until it came to a head in the decisive struggle which issued in the Reform Act of 1832.

We are concerned with this struggle here only in so far as it enters into the history of the Working-class Movement. The workers were by no means the only class which had reason to object to the unreformed Parliament. While the rich merchant or financier could find a seat in the House of Commons and climb into the governing class—this openness of the English aristocracy to the infusion of mercantile elements had been for centuries the greatest source of its strength—the growing body of industrial employers and tradesmen found itself, for the most part, excluded and unrecognised. The rapidly increasing middle-classes had no share in political power; the great towns in which they lived were grossly under-represented, or not represented at all, in the House of Commons. The tenant farmers had no share in the county franchise. And all this body of middle opinion, strongly imbued with the idea of its own growing importance, was becoming more and more critical of corruption and inefficiency in high places. The small employer who, by scraping and saving, raised himself to affluence, keenly resented the spendthrift habits of the older rich, and their little way of helping themselves, by pensions, and sinecures, out of the public purse. The sharp rise in the taxes, due largely to war spending and the War Debt, roused a vigorous demand for economy and "business government."

At the same time, the demand for Universal Suffrage, as one of the "Rights of Man," had by no means spent the force acquired under the influence of revolutionary thought. Bentham and his followers, indeed, pooh-poohed the rights of man, and argued for Universal Suffrage on utilitarian grounds of common sense; but Major Cartwright's agitation, and the continued popularity of Paine's writings, kept the doctrine alive in its more revolutionary form. Cartwright, and still more Paine, doubtless appealed chiefly to the working class; but both Cartwright and Cobbett had also a large following among the smaller middle class, while Cobbett had, in addition, great influence with many of the farmers as well as with the labourers and artisans.

The Reform Movement from 1815 to 1832 was, indeed, essentially a popular movement in which the main body of the working class found itself in temporary alliance with the rising middle classes of the industrial towns. Naturally the latter, who had already some parliamentary influence, tended, in the main, to assume the leadership. Cobbett and Hunt, the outstanding men with influence among the workers, were both countrymen and farmers, not artisans. Gast, Lovett, Benbow, Doherty, and the other working-class leaders occupied only a secondary position. In Parliament the leader of the extreme Radicals was the millionaire Sir Francis Burdett. But none of these men really controlled the strategy of the Reform Movement. From the time when the Whig Party took up the question, the movement passed into the hands of those middle-class elements which were prepared to accept Whig leadership. Henry Brougham counted for more than Burdett in Parliament; and most of the local Reform Associations and Political Unions were mainly dominated by middle-class men of substance. Their attitude, even when it was Radical, was far more influenced by Benthamism than by the Rights of Man.

But these different groups of Reformers, however varying their real aims might be, were at least united in desiring a reform of Parliament. They tended, therefore, especially in the earlier stages of the campaign, to work together without too close a scrutiny of one another's principles. They could all demand Reform without defining too particularly what they meant. And they could all seize occasions for putting the opponents of Reform in an awkward predicament. The political importance of the famous case of Queen Caroline lay largely in this, that the defence of the Queen against the King could be turned into an attack on George IV and his anti-Reform Ministers. Brougham and Denman, on the one hand, and Cobbett, on the other, were equally enthusiastic in the Queen's defence. The same bodies as passed republican resolutions one day sent "loyal addresses" to the Queen the next. Loyalty to the Queen became a form of disloyalty to the King and Constitution.

The Queen Caroline case is mentioned here because it was an important factor in giving the Reform movement a popular backing. Organised by Cobbett, a great working-class agitation sprang up in the Queen's support; and this, when the case was over, swung itself into the Reform Movement. The creation by Daniel O'Connell and his friends of the Catholic Association in Ireland (1823) was another great encouragement to the Reformers, and Irish oppression was used as a stick to beat the Government. Irishmen were active in every section of the Radical Movement in Great Britain, and especially in the working-class societies in the older towns. The struggle which led to the Catholic Emancipation Act of 1829 did a great deal to dissolve the solidity of the Tories and to prepare the way for the return of the Whig Party to power, under conditions which made parliamentary reform inevitable.

Events abroad also influenced the growth of the movement. The Spanish Revolution of 1820 and the Greek Revolution of 1821 aroused widespread sympathy, while the French and Belgian Revolutions of 1830 were among the chief causes which precipitated the crisis of 1830–1832.

In 1830 the Whigs came back to power, and their leader, Grey, at once announced that parliamentary reform would be the chief item in their policy. But what sort of reform? The Whig leaders were by temperament fully as aristocratic as the Tories, and had certainly no intention of using their power to institute a democratic system. The Reform Bill which they introduced actually went further than most people had expected, sweeping away the whole system of rotten boroughs, redistributing seats more in accordance with population, and extending the franchise to practically the whole of the middle class. But it left the manual workers almost wholly voteless, and even took away the votes they had possessed in a few boroughs having an exceptionally wide suffrage. At once the advocates of Universal Suffrage, and especially the working-class bodies which had been pressing for reform, had to decide upon their attitude to the Whig measure. Should they support it as a blow at the old order, and at least a step towards the new? Or should they oppose it as merely an attempt to substitute for the domination of the landowning aristocracy the even more hostile rule of the industrial capitalists?

In 1830 this issue was being debated in every Radical society in which the workers formed an important element. Generally, following Cobbett's lead, the main body of the workers backed the Bill, while declaring their distrust of the Whigs and reiterating their demand for a really democratic measure. But there was a left wing which denounced the Whig Bill, and refused to play any part in supporting a measure of "treason to the working class." Henry Hunt, who had been elected to Parliament in 1830 as Member for Preston, though he voted for the Bill, roundly denounced it in the House and moved many Radical amendments, which were, of course, overwhelmingly defeated.

The first Reform Bill was beaten in Committee in the House of Commons. An excited General Election followed, and gave the Reformers a big majority. A second Bill passed the Commons, only to be beaten in the House of Lords.

The excitement was by this time tremendous; and the working-class Radicals were swung into the agitation, which had clearly become a national trial of strength. Great meetings were held all over the country; the Political Unions threatened to withhold all taxes until the Bill was passed. At Bristol rioters held the city for several days, sacking the gaols, the Mansion House, and the Bishop's Palace. Derby gaol was sacked, the Nottingham Castle burnt down. In London the King was hustled, and the windows of noted anti-Reformers were broken. A third Reform Bill passed the Commons, and was thrown out by the Lords. Grey asked the King for power to create peers, and was refused. He resigned, and the Duke of Wellington tried to form a ministry, with the object of passing, against his own convictions, a Reform Bill going just far enough to divide the Reformers. The Duke failed, and Grey was recalled to power. At the close of a year of unprecedented excitement, the Lords gave way and passed the Bill. At the beginning of 1832 it received the Royal Assent and became law.

It had been impossible for the working-class bodies, in face of the opposition encountered by the Whig Bill, to press their own claim for a more far-reaching measure. They could only join in the popular cry for "the whole Bill and nothing but the Bill," and prevent it from being whittled down by further compromise with the opponents of Reform. Thus the identity of the working-class groups appeared for the time to be submerged in the general agitation. But the struggle was, none the less, a big factor in rousing the political consciousness of the workers and preparing the way for the independent working-class political programme of the Chartists.

We can see this independent political movement beginning to develop during the years of agitation. In 1828 the London Irish had organised an Association for Civil and Political Liberty, and in 1829 this had developed into a Society for Radical Reform, supported by most of the advanced working-class Radicals in London. This in turn became, in 1830, the National Union of the Working Classes, the body which chiefly preserved left-wing Radical opinion during the critical years of the Reform struggle, and survived long enough to be the direct ancestor of working-class Chartism. In the provinces, the workers were mostly attached to the Political Unions, which were largely under middle-class leadership; but the N.U.W.C. was in close touch with the more Radical elements in these Unions, and, when the National Political Union was formed in 1831 to unite the local bodies, the working-class elements were strong enough to secure half the seats on its Council.

The Reform Act was carried chiefly by working-class agitation, and by the threat of a revolution in which the workers would have played the leading part. But it left the workers voteless and detached from them the main body of middle-class support on which they had previously relied. The middle classes obtained, in 1832, their share in political power. They had only to use their opportunities in order to ensure in the long run that their interests should dominate national policy. The vast majority of the middle class accordingly dropped out of Radical agitation, and the temporary alliance of middle and working classes was broken. . . . Attempts were made to revive it later, and in the end a new alliance was made in the Liberal-Labour compromise of the mid-Victorian period. But for the time the "betrayal" of 1832—as it was widely regarded—left the workers angry and disillusioned. They had won the battle, they felt, and yet they had none of the fruits of victory. They were left in a mood to try what they could do by their unaided efforts against a combination of the old and new ruling classes. We shall find them . . . turning to industrial action in their mood of political disillusionment. And then we shall see them, having met defeat in the industrial field, turning back to politics, there to meet with a no less crushing disaster. For the new governing class created in 1832 was far stronger, and rested on a far broader national basis, than the old. After 1832 the leading poachers turned gamekeepers. Cobbett, elected to the Reformed Parliament, found himself fighting the new power as fiercely as ever he had fought the old.

5. D. C. MOORE: The Other Face of Reform *

D. C. Moore, who now teaches at the University of California, Los Angeles, has closely studied the electoral basis for the Reform Bill; he challenges the notion that the measure was primarily a concession to radical pressures. He sees important support for the bill in the conservative countryside and, relatedly, notes the benefits that the rural gentry gained in the bill. From this point of view, how important was the reform?

In most of nineteenth-century Europe the growth of political democracy was essentially revolutionary. It has therefore been understood in terms of the class antagonisms which are said to have caused the Continental revolutions. In Britain, on the other hand, political democracy was established by parliamentary vote, not by revolution, by deliberation among members of the established ruling classes, not by decree of popular tribunal. The British experience would therefore seem to require a separate interpretative framework. This historians have not provided. While in England Reform Acts take the place of revolution, they are fitted to the general revolutionary pattern.

The equation of reform and revolution has held the field since the early nineteenth century. It is not unreasonable. It derives from much contemporary evidence and involves well-established social theory. Obviously, reform can not be isolated from the general context of economic and social change. Obviously, too, before the cycles of reform began, many members of the industrial middle classes were deeply annoyed at the lack of correspondence between their increasing economic strength and their continuing representational weakness in Parliament. Again, the passage of each of the three major Reform Acts was attended with considerable public disorder. And still again, following each Act the newly enfranchised classes were the beneficiaries of considerable legislative attention. In these circumstances, historians have tended to introduce the protagonists of reform almost solely against the background of increasing industrialization; they have tended to attribute the occurrence of reform almost solely to the activities of the various industrial classes, or to men who are regarded as their advocates; they have tended to find the meaning of reform almost solely in the needs of these new classes. Considering that each successive Reform Act was passed by an unreformed Parliament this view of the total process carries its own interpretational imperative—that each Act was a concession by which the established ruling classes managed to prevent the outbreak of revolution.

Yet for several reasons, if we take the first Reform Act as an example, this concession theory is not altogether satisfactory. In the first place, it prematurely

* From D. C. Moore, "The Other Face of Reform," *Victorian Studies V* (Bloomington: Indiana University Press, 1961–62), pp. 7–12, 17, 31–34. Reprinted by permission of *Victorian Studies*.

sets the stage for an urban middle-class drama. As recent studies have increasingly tended to show, the first Reform Act did not mark a clear break in English political life. Least of all did it mark the arrival of the urban middle class to political power. In the second place, it tends to assume an unwarranted modernity in early nineteenth-century electoral behavior. And finally, it tends to distort the reform calendar.

The standard chronology of the first Reform Act posits two essential penultimate events, the death of George IV and the July Revolution in Paris. The latter bears the burden of reawakening reformist sentiments which had lain dormant for many years, the former of transmitting these sentiments to Parliament. Because George's death required that elections take place within six months it is used as the occasion when many persons, inspired by the example of Paris, entered Parliament. However, as Professor Gash has shown, many English elections were already well under way before news of the Revolution arrived. Indeed, reform emerged from its hibernation not in the summer of 1830 but a year earlier. In the summer of 1829 it appealed neither to the aristocratic Whigs nor the urban Liberals. Apart from the Radicals, its perennial advocates, reform appealed to many Ultra-Tories, or, to use a more generic term, to many members of the Country Party. It showed the extent of their hostility towards Wellington.

It is true that the demand for political reform had long been associated with the Foxite Whigs, Liberals, and Radicals. Yet in the immediate pre-reform years it was largely monopolized by the Country Party. While it may be an exaggeration to designate as a Party the heterogeneous group of active opponents to Wellington's Government in 1829 and 1830, their opposition, as well as their demands for political, fiscal, and tariff reforms, were major phenomena of these years and important factors in the elections of 1830. As will be seen, however, by the spring of 1831 the exigencies of parliamentary politics tended to induce an historical amnesia. The efforts of the administrative Tories to reconstitute a Party after their defeat the previous November were hardly compatible with the memory that numerous Tories had played major roles in defeating them. Furthermore, because the possibility of Country Party parentage could lead to expectations that the reform progeny would take after its parents by showing a tendency towards inflation or a renewal of protection, Liberals, Radicals, and many Whigs found it essential to deny this possibility outright and to claim the baby for their own. Their plea, which the administrative Tories did their best to support, was contained in two assertions: first, that reform was a Whig-Liberal-Radical monopoly, and second, that the issue of reform was fundamentally social.

Because these assertions won the day, most historians have ignored the Country Party's demands for reform, or, like Halévy have deprecated them on two grounds: that they "lacked the support of the Whig or Liberal party leaders," and that they "lacked the support of the masses." The first of these arguments is tied to the notion that the Reform Ministry was a Whig Ministry, a notion which Professor Aspinall has recently tried to correct. The other is tied to the notion that the course of history in both the long and short term is defined by popular desires. While it must be allowed that this latter notion has some pertinence today, when means for transforming such desires into law have been highly developed, when social communities are extremely fluid, and when leaders are more often made than born, to apply it to the early nineteenth century without reservation is a distinct anachronism.

Yet inevitably the concession theory presupposes that in the early nineteenth century "the support of the masses" had specific electoral effectiveness—at least in certain constituencies. Towards this end it makes a sharp distinction between close constituencies, the corrupt and nomination boroughs, and open constituencies, best exemplified by the English counties.

Granted the social assumptions of the concession theory, the further assumption that these two types of constituency differed from each other basically is an efficient means of explaining the votes of many M.P.'s. The majority of Members for the close constituencies voted against the second Bill on its crucial second reading. Of the eighty-two English county Members only four did so. According to the concession theory this striking disagreement may be attributed, on the one hand, to the entrenched powers of the established ruling classes in the close constituencies, which prevented the free expression of public opinion, and, on the other, to the freedom of the 40s. county freeholders. To balance the bad reputation of the former constituencies historians have endowed the latter with essentially democratic attributes.

Two questions are basic: What determined the electoral behavior of English county voters in 1830 and 1831? And how did the English counties, the open constituencies *par excellence,* differ from the corrupt and nomination boroughs?

To date, these questions—particularly the former—have been accorded but little attention. Yet the poll books, a sadly neglected source for the study of English political and social history, are readily at hand and might suggest answers.

Until 1872, when the Ballot Act separated the voter's name from the vote he cast, voting in England was a public act. After each contested election one or another local political group generally published a list of the local voters, these being identified by their places of residence or of electoral qualification. The electoral choices of each voter were entered in these lists against his name.

The purpose of publishing poll books is clear. So too is their value to historians. By providing a record of electoral behavior poll books allowed the wielders of influence, or their agents, to make sure their influences were not violated. For the historian, who can never know intimately the complexities of influence, poll books measure its effectiveness inadequately.[1] Yet in spite of their inade-

1. Complete accuracy in measuring the effects of influence would require that each wielder of influence and each of his dependents be identified in positive fashion. Poll books, however, merely indicate the voter's name, and address—county poll books show his village of residence, or qualification, or both, sometimes his occupation, and his votes. They do not specify the referent of his possible dependence. When used in conjunction with local guide books [that] will help give fairly precise indications of local landownership, county poll books provide much circumstantial evidence

quacies county poll books do reflect the existence, and to some degree at least, the effectiveness, of influence. They do so in two ways: by showing the degree of electoral agreement on the village level, a level often congruent with the boundaries of an estate, and by showing the intense localism of changes of electoral sentiment. Whenever the overall polls of a county show a change from one election to another, the change is not homogeneous throughout the county. Rather, it is a sum of local changes. Within a locality changes were generally unanimous; from one locality to another such changes were often contradictory.

In circumstances where each voter is free to express his own opinions at the polls—where the modern concept of public opinion is valid—the electoral map of a large geographical constituency will normally consist of shadings from a region where one political group is dominant to another region where another group is dominant. Within these different regions a fair amount of political disagreement will usually exist. No region will be entirely white or entirely black. The differences which define them will consist of shadings of grey.

In the nineteenth century, however, the electoral maps of the English counties were very often spotted, black and white. The Northamptonshire poll book of 1831, for example, shows that all the voters in the village of Lowick polled for the anti-Bill candidates; all the voters in the village of Aldwinkle, directly adjacent to Lowick to the east, polled for the pro-Bill candidates; with two exceptions, all the voters in the village of Brigstock, directly adjacent to Lowick to the northwest, also polled for the pro-Bill candidates. Circumstances suggest that the influences of the dominant local landowners were the major factors both in creating these local communities, and in conditioning the residents' electoral behavior.

Several considerations reinforce this interpretation. Since each elector could cast two votes at each election, he could cast many possible combinations of votes at successive elections. Yet in any particular election local agreement was the general rule. It was so in spite of the utter lack of clearly defined parties, to which, had they existed, such local agreements might possibly be attributed.

of influence. Yet this evidence will inevitably fail to reflect the full effectiveness of influence. It will fail to reflect influence in those instances where it only affected one of an elector's two votes, where it derived from other sources than local landownership, where the individual voter did not reside in the same locale as the other men who responded to the same influence, and where the geographical units listed in the poll books were the foci of two or more separate influences. Often this use of poll books in conjunction with local guide books will help not at all with respect to the outvoters, those who lived outside the county; its value with respect to the residents of the larger towns is doubtful. Frequently, poll books do not specify the outvoters' local geographical connections; outvoters are often lumped together under a separate heading of their own. Often, too, the voters in the larger towns were by no means politically agreed. While the size of the community might tend to make the individual resident at least somewhat anonymous, it is questionable whether the frequent lack of internal agreement in the larger towns should be taken to mean that all the voters in these towns had full individual control of their votes. Since local political agreement is found most often where landownership was concentrated in the hands of a single individual it is not surprising that diversity of local political expression should be found most often in those communities, among which most of the larger towns must be included, where several interests were focused. These considerations will explain why the use of borough poll books for a study analogous to the present one could hardly be contemplated.

But such parties, as distinct from factions, simply did not exist. This is evident both from the large number of plumped votes cast for one candidate who agreed politically with another standing in the same constituency, and also from the large number of split votes between candidates of opposing political views. Even in May 1831 when all of electoral England is supposed to have been divided on the Bill, a large proportion of pro-Bill candidates stood as individuals and were supported as individuals. In Oxfordshire, the two pro-Bill candidates went out of their ways to deny all "coalition." At the polls each enjoyed a few plumped votes and a larger number of split votes with the anti-Bill candidate, although understandably, in 1831, such a-political cross-voting was less frequent than usual. In Buckinghamshire, as *The Times* of 10 May 1831 complained, some two hundred voters whom they described as "Smith votes" —the name of a local squire—plumped for one of the two pro-Bill candidates instead of polling for both. As a result of Smith's instructions to his voters, and the instructions of others similarly inclined, the county returned one pro- and one anti-Bill Member. . . .

Thus, a distinction must be made between the return of a vast majority of pro-Bill Members to Parliament from the English counties in 1830 and 1831, and the popularity of reform among the English "masses." To a large degree the return of these Members must be attributed to the attitudes and activities of relatively small groups of men, many of them members of the aristocracy, gentry, and urban magnate class, whose composite influences were electorally decisive. . . .

A detailed analysis of the ways in which the first Reform Act effectively restored the political powers of the landed interest is beyond the scope of this paper. However, these points may be noted: the Act withdrew certain constituencies from the control of the Government; it withdrew others from the control, or significant influence, of urban leaders.

By disfranchising or reducing the representation of the smallest boroughs, those from which Wellington's power had largely derived, the Grey Ministry gained a redistribution fund of over one hundred and forty seats. Of these, they assigned sixty-four seats to new English boroughs, primarily in the industrial north. However, the social significance of the Act tends to be distorted unless these new borough seats are balanced against the political redefinition of the English counties and the assignment to them of sixty-two new seats.

Two important aspects of the elections of 1830 and 1831 were the growth and decline of reform sentiment among the aristocracy and gentry, and the emergence of urban leaders in the arena of county politics. In 1831 urban leaders played prominent parts in returning the majority of the eighty-two English county members. The basis of their doing so lay in the relative electoral weights of the urban areas of the counties. In large measure the Act destroyed these relative weights. Thus, while urban leaders retained control of the majority of the sixty-odd seats for open boroughs which existed before 1832, and gained control of the majority of the sixty-four new borough seats, rural leaders were restored to predominant control in the majority of the eighty-two pre-reform

English county seats and provided with an additional sixty-two new county seats. Unless Wellington's assertion be allowed—which, after the legislation of the previous years, many peers and more squires would hardly have done—that the nomination boroughs were the true defenders of the landed interest, on balance the landed interest came out ahead.

The Grey Ministry made no secret of their intentions regarding the English counties. In introducing the first Bill, Russell declared that the counties should be isolated from the towns so that these might not "interfere with the representation of the counties." In part this isolation was achieved by means of new electoral qualifications, in part by enfranchising new boroughs.

Before 1832, urban interference in the counties was primarily the result of most urban freeholders' being qualified as county electors. As has been seen, before 1832 many counties were electorally urban. After 1832, in most counties, the rural balance was significantly increased. This was achieved in large measure by two complementary procedures. First, the urban elements in the county electorates were reduced by enacting new borough qualifications, by providing that a freehold property in a borough should not convey a county franchise if it conveyed a borough franchise, and by granting new borough status to many of the larger towns. Second, the rural elements in the county electorates were increased by enfranchising certain copyholders and leaseholders, and by accepting the Chandos clause, which extended the right to vote to tenants at will.

The rural and aristocratic nature of the counties was still further enhanced by the means adopted of increasing their overall representation in Parliament. The Ministers suggested that most of the counties be cut into two divisions, each to return two members, and that a third member be given to all but a few of the others. As far as the Ministers were concerned, such divisions, besides increasing the number of county Members, would also increase the localism of county politics. It was Althorp's boast that this localism would weaken the tendency of certain counties to return persons on the basis of their "mere popularity."

The provisions of the measure which sought to reduce the expense of county elections involved a number of technical points of electioneering practice which are too complicated to examine in the present paper. However, they too were conceived as a means of increasing the effective powers of local oligarchs.

The similarity of intent is clear between these various provisions of the Act and the earlier suggestions of the Marquis of Blandford and articles in *Blackwood's Edinburgh Magazine*. This is not to suggest that the committee which drew up the ministerial plan took their cue from the Tories. It is to suggest that the polemical arguments which conceived of reform in social terms were largely irrelevant.

This paper does not tell the whole story of the Bill. Even less does it tell the whole story of reform. It does, however, suggest aspects of these phenomena which historians have tended to ignore: that they are far too complex to be satisfactorily described within a simplified revolutionary framework. Not only did the Bill provide an enlarged number of constituencies for representatives of the urban middle classes, it also clarified the political powers of the landed classes, the aristocracy and gentry. As their own regroupment progressed these classes settled back to a half century during which their control was absolute in the majority of the remaining small boroughs, and in all English county divisions except those in which significant urban populations lacked borough representation of their own. In practical terms, the first Reform Act was far less a blow against the powers in the State of the aristocracy and gentry than it was against the powers of the Ministers.

This realization caused dismay to some Whigs, and to many Liberals and Radicals when, as early as 1835, certain traits of the child they had claimed as their own became apparent. Their dismay is not to be wondered at. They were the disillusioned victims of one of the first of the numerous propaganda wars of the nineteenth century.

Yet while these men had not gained what they sought, they had not entirely lost. To enhance the independence of members of Parliament from Ministerial control was not to transfer power away from the ruling oligarchies. Rather, it was to transfer power from Whitehall to the constituencies. There it resided during the middle years of the century until the development of centralized political parties brought it back. But the transfer of power effected by the Act provided that whenever local control changed hands, or local leaders changed their attitudes, such changes would be reflected in Parliament.

In view of the use to which Ministerial power had been put in the years before 1832—to emancipate Catholics, to liberalize the Corn Laws, and in view, also, of the Radicals' subsequent impatience with Parliament, the question arises of the relationship between the Reform Act and later "bourgeois" legislation. As observers after 1832 were not slow to notice, legislation became increasingly responsive to changes of public opinion. Such changes, however, are far slower, far more cumbersome, than those initiated by the spark of an idea within a fairly intimate group of fairly intelligent men.

The fondness of the Benthamites for Wellington and Peel in 1829 and 1830 may, indeed, be extremely significant. If history followed a logical progression (which it never does), it might be argued that the first Reform Act did more to delay such measures as the repeal of the Corn Laws than it did to accelerate them.

6. NORMAN GASH: Reaction and Reconstruction in English Politics *

Norman Gash is professor of History at St. Salvator's College, St. Andrews University, and has written extensively on political history in the reform period. His work, like Moore's, shows the results of detailed research on the practical workings of early nineteenth-century politics. Without denying changes that the Reform Bill may have set in motion in the long run, he is

* From Norman Gash, *Reaction and Reconstruction in English Politics* (Oxford: The Clarendon Press), pp. 1–2, 3, 30–34, 157–58. Reprinted by permission of The Clarendon Press.

primarily concerned with pointing to many areas in which change seemed to occur but really did not.

"This," said the *Edinburgh Review* in 1831, "is the age of reform." Yet John Stuart Mill, looking back on his early manhood among the Philosophic Radicals of the 1830's, reflected that "their lot was cast in the ten years of inevitable reaction" after the Reform Act and the "few legislative improvements which the public really called for" had been effected. The sententious truism of the *Review* is a commonplace; Mill's observation has been less often repeated. Yet there is an undeniable truth in what he said. The truth, moreover, is considerably broadened if we interpret reaction not merely in the political sense of negative opposition but also in the physical sense: the response of men and institutions who were not eager for innovation but who under pressure were politic enough to accept and even initiate reforms of a select and modified kind. There is even a third category: men who started as reformers but were either disappointed at the results of reform or disturbed at the lengths to which others wished to carry it.

It is a melancholy thought that as soon as reforms are put into practice, disillusionment enters the political scene. The great initial reforms of the 1820's, designed to pacify and heal, seemed only to exacerbate feeling. The return to gold in 1821 and the attempts to revise the Corn Laws between 1822 and 1828 created the unease among agriculturists which flared up so memorably in 1846. The repeal of the Test and Corporations Acts in 1828 was followed by twenty years of greater bitterness between Church and Dissent than had been known since Queen Anne's reign. The passage of Catholic Emancipation was followed by twenty years of growing fear and dislike of Roman Catholicism. The Reform Act of 1832 was followed by the political alienation of the working classes, the progressive disillusionment of many of the middle classes, the decline of parliamentary radicalism, and the emergence of the two greatest extra-parliamentary political movements of the century; while the Crown and the House of Lords were more active in the succeeding five years—and more active against reform—than in the preceding twenty-five. The domestic history of the 1832–52 period can be largely construed in terms of those who wished to press forward, those who wished to compound with, and those who wished to resist "the Movement" (in the phrase borrowed from continental politics) which had won its first successes in the great organic changes of 1828–32. By themselves those changes decided very little; they were facilitating rather than operative measures. The crucial issue was what religious equality and parliamentary reform would mean in the language of practical legislation and exercise of power. In a sense, it was only after the Reform Act had passed that the real crisis began: the post-Reform crisis of adjustment between what had been done and what men thought should be the consequences of what had been done. Many of the subsequent reforms are important; but equally significant is the phenomenon of reforms attempted and defeated, and those deflected or transformed. . . .

Much was done; a great deal abandoned as impracticable. The exaggerated hopes and fears of the reform era gave way to a more sober appraisement of the realities of social and political life; and in the end the moderate men were left in possession of the field.

An analysis of post-Reform Act politics from this standpoint may conveniently begin with the obvious and relatively simple problem of the monarchy. When men spoke, in the conventional constitutional vocabulary of the day, of the destruction by the Reform Act of the balance of the constitution, they were not entirely unreasonable or unrealistic. If the Act enhanced the power of the Commons, it inevitably diminished that of the other two branches of the legislature: the Crown and the House of Lords. Yet the power of the Crown in this context largely meant its ability to influence the House of Commons; and this power had been declining for the previous half-century. The Reform Act added to the decline in a physical sense by diminishing the number of close constituencies. But the ability of the Crown to "make a House" had disappeared before 1832. The general election of 1830 did not see, in any modern sense, the defeat of the Government; yet the resignation of the Wellington Ministry in November, through lack of support in the Commons, and so soon after a general election, was a clear sign of the weakness of executive influence. Any technical effect the Reform Act had in increasing this weakness operated mainly in one narrow but important sphere: the inability of a new Ministry even to be sure of getting its official House of Commons men re-elected on taking office, for sheer lack of enough safe seats in which to stow them. . . .

In one sense the most revolutionary aspect of the Reform crisis of 1831–2 was not the Reform Bill itself but the coercion of the House of Lords. The blow to the independence of the Upper House seemed a more serious because a more immediate derangement of the theoretical balance of power in the constitution than any consequential limitation of Crown influence. In the period after Waterloo two things had characterized the activities of the House of Lords: the generally good relations between them and the Government, and the generally good-humoured acceptance of their rejections and amendments by the Commons. Though far from liberal, the Upper House had never degenerated into a reactionary chamber; and it was peculiarly amenable to executive influence. If the peers under Eldon's leadership massacred the legal reforms put up by Mackintosh's committee in 1820, they gave an easy passage under Lord Tenterden's auspices to Peel's criminal legislation between 1822 and 1830. They accepted the currency reforms; they accepted the emergency corn measure of 1826. Wellington upset Canning's Corn Bill in 1827, but this was largely due to a genuine misunderstanding between himself and Huskisson. Even in the volcanic field of religion the peers passed with only minor emendations the repeal of the Test and Corporations Acts in 1828. It was true that over Catholic Emancipation the House of Lords twice (in 1821 and 1825) rejected Bills sent up to them from the Commons; but the important fact here was that the Bills were not Government measures and that they were opposed by the Prime Minister and most of his Cabinet colleagues in the Upper House. Even so, after

1825 Liverpool thought it impossible that the peers could much longer resist the repeated sense of the Commons. When in 1829 for the first time an Emancipation Bill came before the Lords with the recommendation of the Government, they passed it. In the decade preceding the Reform Act the Lords might fairly have claimed that they were equal but not unreasonable partners in the business of legislation.

The shock of coercion was therefore great, because it concerned a reality of political power: the semi-independent function of the Upper House. Moreover, unlike the Reform Bill which was the occasion for the collision, the coercive tactic of the Government was the unpremeditated and desperate measure of a Cabinet which had gone too far not to go further. The language of the Ministers themselves is sufficient. "It is a question then which goes to the absolute destruction of the House of Lords," wrote Grey to Burdett in November 1831, "an event which I certainly did not contemplate in endeavouring to reform the House of Commons"; and to Althorp in March 1832 he described a large peerage creation as "a measure of extreme violence; there is no precedent for it in our history, the case of Queen Anne's peers not being in point; it is a certain evil, dangerous itself as a precedent." Campbell, the Whig Lord Chancellor, looking back at the issue across the reflective gap of ten years, put it down as his considered opinion that "a numerous creation of peers to carry a particular measure against the opinion of the existing House, cannot in my opinion be considered a constitutional proceeding, and can only be defended as a *coup d'état* to ward off greater evils." The traumatic effect of the 1832 operation was therefore felt as keenly by the surgeons as by the patients. Whatever else was to be done, it was humanly improbable that the members of the Reform Cabinet would expose themselves to such an experience again. Seven years later, when rejecting any suggestion that the Whigs should support the Corn Law repeal agitation, Melbourne observed that even if the movement were strong in itself, "we shall still only carry it by the same means as we carried the Reform Bill, and I am not for being the instrument . . . of another similar performance." Ten years later still, in 1849, Palmerston told Russell that his parliamentary reform proposals, unless very moderate, would "meet with much opposition in the Commons and certain defeat in the Lords, and I doubt whether public opinion would support us in re-enacting in these times, and in this matter, the scenes of the Reform Bill conflict." It is not surprising that with these scarred memories the general attitude of Whig Cabinets in the 1830's towards obstruction in the Lords was one of scriptural patience relieved by occasional mutters of resignation.

Yet, after all, the crisis of the House of Lords had been psychological rather than physical. There had been in fact no mass creation of new peers, and the House of Lords remained after the Reform Act much as it had been before. In the eyes of Radicals and Radical-Whigs, the Upper House was still a reactionary Pittite chamber, and its conduct during the crisis had only put it more evidently in need of reform. At the start of the struggle Whigs of advanced views and little responsibility could talk in aggressive terms of doing something about the peers. Colonel Torrens, in September 1831, spoke of putting the House of Lords in Schedule A if they persisted in rejecting reform. Charles Western, another M.P., privately argued with Graham on the even greater need to reform the Upper House than the Lower, and declared that no Whig or Liberal Ministry could stand unless after sixty years of Tory creations there was an infusion of fresh blood into the peerage. For a brief interval after the collapse of resistance in the Lords, there was room for optimistic hope among Radical politicians that the morale of the peers had been broken. At the start of the first session of the reformed Parliament, Robert Ingham (M.P. for South Shields and, according to James Wortley, "a frightened Whig") said that when he spoke to the wild men of the Reform majority on the danger of opposition to Government Church reforms in the House of Lords, they merely laughed and said, "Let them! Lord Grey settled that for us last year." But Lord Grey had not settled it, and three months later he was being warned by Brougham, now sitting among their lordships, how much they had recovered their courage and how ready they were for mischief. The Government's Irish Church Bill provided an admirable vantage ground for a move to unseat the Ministry, and by July 1833 it seemed as if Wellington (himself wavering on the issue) was losing control of the Opposition peers. Cumberland and Buckingham were running in effect a separatist group, holding private meetings of ultra-Tory supporters; and even ex-Ministers like Ellenborough and Lyndhurst leaned towards a rejection of the Bill on the second reading. In the end the tactical restraint of the Duke of Wellington, aided by the private influence of the Crown, carried the day. Nevertheless, the Government was beaten on the clause for suspending moribund benefices and for a time seriously considered resignation. By the end of the 1833 session it was clear that the hostile and potentially obstructive majority in the Lords, combined with the instability of Government support in the Commons, already made the continuation of a Reform Ministry a doubtful proposition. Though Grey was not disinclined to a token creation of five or six peers as a demonstration of royal confidence, any notion of creating enough peers to counterbalance the hostile majority was put out of the question by the Cabinet. Everything depended therefore on the self-restraint of the peers, or conceivably on the mobilization of a strong public opinion against them. . . .

"I always thought," wrote Lord John Russell in 1839, "that the Whig party, as a party, would be destroyed by the Reform Bill." That, with retrospective wisdom, was perhaps ultimately true. It could equally well be argued, however, that the Reform Bill gave the Whigs a new lease of life. In the 1820's they had come near to extinction as a party, and only Canning's death, and the failure of Wellington to form a second coalition, enabled Grey to reunite them as the preponderant element in a new Government and to endow them in the Reform Bill with a store of political credit on which they lived for another generation. But parliamentary reform was for many Whigs an eleventh-hour conversion; and whether the overriding motive was a genuine conviction that the political state of the country required such a drastic remedy or a party calculation that the Whigs could only retain office if they reformed Parliament, the passage of the Act in 1832 raised—not immediately but in the long run inevitably—the dividing question: was the Reform Bill to be a terminus or a point of departure. So long as Grey remained in office, his Ministry retained its fundamentally conservative character, and the legislation of 1833–4 contained little that could not have been brought forward by Peel, or for that matter by Canning or Liverpool.

Chapter IV.

THE WORKING CLASS IN THE EARLY INDUSTRIAL REVOLUTION

NO SOCIAL grouping in the nineteenth century has been more fully studied than the workers. The source of interest is obvious: factory labor was the most novel social product of industrialization. The conditions of work and of urban life were new, as were the grievances which ultimately resulted from these conditions. Labor grievances, as channeled through various types of unions, gradually changed the face of industrial life. And as workers learned to express their demands politically, again in various movements beginning most clearly with English Chartism, they helped create some of the basic issues of modern politics: how to distribute income, how to control the economy, how to deal with collective protest that is at least in part within the law.

Most historians of the working class have been deeply sympathetic to the cause of labor; many have been Marxists of one sort or another. The resulting possibilities of bias have been great, but so have the opportunities for insight into the needs and demands of workers themselves. For all the vital work done by the partisans of labor, however, the basic issues of working-class history revolve around their partisanship: How real were the horrors of working-class life? By what standards are these horrors judged? What was the relation between worker attitudes and the ideologies of Socialist theorists and labor movements? And (with increasing insistence), how inclusive and how unified was the working class itself? Beyond the specific questions rests the broad issue of the relationship between labor history, usually treated as a separate theme of the nineteenth century, and the more conventional topics of modern history. Some labor historians view the workers as a bitterly isolated element of nineteenth-century society; others tend to exaggerate the general influence of their subject. Broader political or economic surveys often relegate the working class to self-contained chapters which are not integrated with their general themes.

What conditions or ideas, if any, unified the working class and when? Few spokesmen emerged from its ranks during the early industrial period. There are no vigorous statements of common values, such as middle-class publicists penned at the same time. No organizations united the majority of the class. Perhaps Chartism provided common bonds in England, but only fleetingly; and the diversity of the various types of Chartism limited its unifying influence. On the Continent, and in

England after 1848, no large-scale working-class movements developed until late in the century. But a class consciousness may well have preceded such formal activities, a sense born of the common conditions of industrial life.

The problem of evaluating working-class attitudes, including any sense of class, is immensely complicated by the number of self-appointed labor spokesmen that arose early in any industrial revolution. Radicals and Socialists, of whatever type, believed they knew what workers needed and could appeal in their name; to varying degrees, they also sought directly to win worker converts. It is relatively easy for the historian to know what they said and even to prove that they had a certain amount of influence among groups of workers. And from this, it becomes possible to talk about a labor movement quite early in the nineteenth century. Questions remain, however: How widely shared were the radical opinions? How much of working-class life can be described in terms of a labor movement?

Historians now disagree widely on the boundaries of the working class. Marxists, following the example of Marx himself, have generally sought to include as many types of manual labor as possible. Insofar as Marxism as a political movement does the same, this can be an important way to approach the labor movement, at least from the late nineteenth century onward. Certainly a good case can be made that workers in the domestic putting-out system, artisans, as well as factory laborers were subjected to an increasingly capitalist economy and a loss of much personal independence. Moreover, there was undoubtedly much movement from one group to another, as domestic workers and artisans were often forced or attracted into the factories. From other viewpoints, however, historians have seen decisive differences among various groups. Studies of the revolutions of 1848, particularly in Germany, have increasingly revealed the difficulties of talking about a broad working class, for factory labor stayed out of the agitation for the most part, whereas artisans participated vigorously and for specifically artisanal goals. Similar distinctions have to be made in any examination of the British union movement after 1850; but was the exclusiveness of skilled workers new, a betrayal of a broader working class, or did it follow logically from earlier differences?

A huge debate has raged over the relative quality of conditions of early working-class life, echoes of which must appear in any discussion of the class in general. Defenders and opponents of capitalism have argued the beneficence or maleficence of its early industrial form. No one claims that working conditions were good; the question is whether they represented improvement or deterioration in comparison with preindustrial conditions. The debate is important, if not primarily to bear out moral judgments of economic systems. If workers were doing better than their traditional values led them to expect, this might explain their frequent slowness to develop protest movements. If worse, the vigor of some early protest and the ultimate tension of class conflict within industry can be understood. And no simple answer need be given. It may vary from country to country within Europe. It will probably vary with the type of workers under consideration, which again raises the question of the definition of the class. And it will vary with the conditions stressed in any general examination, for the historian must try to decide what was essential in working-class life.

All of these issues repeat a basic problem: Why study workers at all, in the early industrial period? The obvious answer to this question, and the real motivation for many studies, is that the workers came to be politically important later and that their problems were sensed by some influential people even at the time. But although these facts may properly motivate a study, they can lead to the application of inappropriate standards and interests. No student of the process of industrialization can ignore some aspects of the labor force, but workers were more than economic men. Some historians argue the interest of studying a social group, particularly a largely inarticulate one, for its own sake, and certainly the study poses unusual challenges. So far, however, this remains an aspect of modern history in which the criteria and justifications are not fully worked out and are open to vigorous dispute.

1. JÜRGEN KUCZYNSKI: Labor Conditions in Western Europe, 1920–1935 *

Jürgen Kuczynski has devoted several decades to the study of the impact of industrialization on working-class conditions in Europe and the United States. He works mainly with wage statistics, but he also assesses other aspects of the quality of worker life. A German Marxist, he is bent on showing the general deterioration of conditions under industrial capitalism. His theoretical framework already tells him what the basic trends were and why. But he does note periods of exception; and his preconceptions, common among many labor historians, may be accepted even by people who reject other aspects of Marxism. For a direct contrast in the judgment of industrial conditions in Germany, the reader is urged to refer to the selection from Theodore Hamerow in Chapter 6, on the revolutions of 1848.

Labour conditions in Germany developed in a way very similar to that in England. If one keeps in mind two facts: that industrialization started later and was slower in the beginning in Germany than in England, and that German imperialism did not develop with the same rapidity, until much later, and on a much smaller scale than in England, then almost all the differences in the development in England and Germany explain themselves very easily.

If we look at the development of wages we observe at first a decline of real wages just as in England. But while in England this decline lasted only up to the end of the 'forties, in Germany real wages declined until far into the 'fifties. And while in England this decline was not so great that the former peak could not be reached quickly again, in Germany real wages did not attain the peak of 1830–39 before the end of the 'seventies.

The low point of real wages was reached in England at the end of the 'forties—taking losses through unemployment, etc., into account. At the end of the 'forties labour conditions in England had reached the end of one line of development. Real wages could not be lowered any further and hours of work could not be lengthened any more. The same situation we find in Germany about a decade later, around the middle of the 'fifties.

Not much is known of labour conditions in Germany about the middle of the century. While in England royal commissions and sincere friends of labour

* From Juergen Kuczynski, *Labour Conditions in Western Europe, 1920–1935* (New York: International Publishers), pp. 83–86, 110–12. Reprinted by permission of International Publishers Co., Inc.

revealed the terrible plight of the English worker, German labour had not many such friends, and only few could give voice to their findings and opinions.

But the few data available indicate a degree of pauperization very similar to that in England, and in many respects worse. German labour probably was housed a little better than English labour and many of the evils of city congestion were not so pronounced in Germany, but other evils, especially those due to a greater degree of industrial feudalism, made labour conditions at least as difficult to endure as in England.

Already in 1828 Lieutenant-General von Horn drew the attention of the authorities to the fact that the extent of child labour and the conditions under which children had to work endangered the physical standing of the army, and that the physical deterioration of the population in the Rhenish industrial districts had reached such a point that the material from which recruits were drawn for the army, was growing worse and worse.

Another indication of the low standard of German labour is that English manufacturers again and again referred to the low standard of German labour, and to the competitive superiority of the German manufacturer because of these working conditions—if labour conditions in England should be improved. In answering these arguments of English employers, Macaulay could not refute the contention that labour conditions in Germany were even worse than in England, but answered as follows:

> You try to frighten us by telling us that, in some German factories, the young work seventeen hours in the twenty-four, that they work so hard that among thousands there is not one who grows to such a stature that he can be admitted into the army; and you ask whether, if we pass this bill, we can possibly hold our own against such competition as this? Sir, I laugh at the thought of such competition. If we ever are forced to yield the foremost place among commercial nations, we shall yield it, not to a race of degenerate dwarfs, but to some people pre-eminently vigorous in body and in mind.

And yet, after the failure of the revolution of 1848, labour conditions had become still worse and during the following years labour conditions had grown so bad that only a race of degenerate dwarfs unable to produce or to defend the interests of the governing class in a war, could continue to live under them.

Just as in England it became absolutely necessary to change the venue of exploitation. Just as in England, only about ten years later, it became necessary to increase real wages and to improve labour conditions in many other ways, if an increasing rate of surplus value was to be taken from the worker. Consequently real wages were raised, hours of work were shortened, child-labour was restricted—and as a result of these measures the intensity of work could be and was increased very considerably.

From the middle of the 'fifties to the end of the 'seventies real wages undoubtedly increased considerably and reached again their former peak. At the end of the 'seventies real wages were again about as high as during the peak years of the 'thirties. Hours of work were lower. Child work did not play so great a rôle any more. On the other side labour conditions had worsened in many respects. While, during the first half of the century, a very considerable number of workers still had some kind of agricultural income the importance of this income had declined greatly up to the end of the 'seventies. During the 'sixties, and especially during the 'seventies, urbanization in Germany began to increase at a somewhat quicker pace than before. Many of the ill-effects of city congestion, especially of worsening housing conditions, began to take effect upon an increasing part of the German working class. And, of course, the intensity of work, the chief reason for the improvement in certain aspects of the worker's life, had increased very much.

During the 'eighties and 'nineties real wages continued to increase and reached a new peak at the end of the century. During these twenty years urbanization took full effect upon labour conditions. Housing conditions became as bad as in England, the agricultural resources of the industrial working class dried up almost completely. The shortening of working hours slowed up. And the intensity of work increased at a rapid pace.

At the same time, German capitalism began to invest heavily abroad. Foreign labour employed by German capital in Russia, in Turkey, in South America, in the Balkan countries, and in Austria-Hungary, subsequently in Africa too and in China, began to make extra profits for German capitalism.

These extra profits on the one side, and the increasing pressure from organized labour on the other side, lead to a situation of the labour class which perhaps might be called stabilized. During the 'eighties and the 'nineties labour conditions in general did probably not deteriorate in Germany just as in England the 'seventies and 'eighties probably were years of stabilization.

If in Germany, on the one hand, labour conditions suffered increasingly more from the growing effects of urbanization, while in England these ill-effects could barely be further increased at this time, in Germany, on the other hand, social insurance was introduced on a larger scale than in England.

On the whole one may assume that labour conditions in Germany did probably not deteriorate during the last decades of the nineteenth century.

But, just as in England the turn of the century meant a turn in the development of labour conditions, so also in Germany. Real wages remained about stable until the World War with a slight tendency to decline. Hours of work remained about stable with a slight tendency to be shortened. Urbanization and its ill-effects developed at a very rapid pace. Intensity of work increased quickly. . . .

It is only possible to write this chapter under this heading ["Labour Conditions in Western Europe"] because labour conditions changed so very similarly in England, Germany, and France.

There are only two other small industrial countries whose labour conditions we have not investigated: Belgium and Luxembourg. Spain is mainly agricultural, the same holds true, for most of the time under review, of Holland; and the number of agricultural wage earners in these two countries is small.

In Belgium, labour conditions as far as we can find out from the data available, moved very similar to those in France and the same holds true of labour conditions in Luxembourg.

But even if labour conditions in Luxembourg and Belgium had developed differently, the number of workers in England, Germany and France is so great as compared with that of these two countries, that a different development of wages in these two countries, and also in Spain and Holland would not have affected considerably the movement of average labour conditions in the whole of Western Europe.

Since Western Europe is the cradle of modern industrial capitalism, the survey of wages and labour conditions in Western Europe is at the same time a review of the history of labour conditions in the beginning of industrial capitalism.

Common to all three countries in the beginning of the spread of industrial capitalism over a preponderantly agricultural and commercial area is a period during which the physical deterioration of the working class increases quickly and spreads rapidly.

Long hours of work, increasingly long hours per day, low wages, increasingly deficient purchasing power undermine the health and the working capacity of the working class.

Since the aim of capitalist society is the appropriation of surplus value by the capitalists, and since this appropriation found at the end of this period its natural limit in the physical "deficiencies" of the human body which "unfortunately" needs a certain minimum amount of food and rest, capitalist society had to change its methods of appropriation of surplus value.

This change of methods brought for the workers better food and fewer hours of work. It meant at the same time increasing intensity of work per hour. The body of the worker was not spared during this period, which stretches from the 'fifties to the end of the last century. It only was handled more carefully in order to be able to do a much more strenuous job: producing goods at a rate and at an intensity unforeseen in the previous period.

During this second period extensive exploitation of foreign labour, of labour outside of Western Europe was added to the activities of Western capitalism. In consequence of this enormous broadening of the field of exploitation gigantic extra profits were made. These gigantic extra profits allowed the ruling class in Western Europe the luxury of giving for a short period some of the extra profits to the workers at home, chiefly in order to ensure industrial peace which was threatened more and more through better organization and more militant tactics of labour. Another reason for letting the workers share a little in these extra profits was to get the help of the workers in the finishing struggle with the landed interests.

In consequence of this temporary sharing of the workers in the extra profits, made from the exploitation of workers employed abroad, labour conditions during the second half of the nineteenth century partly improved absolutely or remained stable, that is, they at least ceased to deteriorate in the "mother countries." This improvement or stabilization of labour conditions in England, Germany and France, during the second half of the nineteenth century must, however, not cloud the issue. Western capitalism continued also in the second half of the nineteenth century to increase the exploitation of labour, and if we would be able to compute average wages and an index of average labour conditions of all labour employed by English, or French, or German capitalism, whether this labour be employed abroad or at home, then we would see that labour conditions of all workers combined, those employed at home and abroad, continued to deteriorate also during the second half of the nineteenth century, and probably deteriorated more quickly than during the first half of the nineteenth century.

During the twentieth century, when the rate of extra profits (but not the mass of extra profits) began to decline, labour conditions deteriorated also in the home countries, real wages declined, even taking into account the benefits from social insurance, and misery and pauperism in England, Germany and France were on the increase again.

To-day, labour conditions in England, in Germany, and in France, are undoubtedly and considerably worse than they were forty years ago. The purchasing power of the worker is smaller and the intensity of work is very much higher.

A process has set in, very similar to that in the beginning of the history of industrial capitalism. The worker is less and less able physically to stand the pace of production, to keep up the intensity of work.

But while about eighty years ago capitalism was able to change its methods of exploitation because of increasing extra profits from labour employed abroad, the situation to-day is quite different. The exploitation of labour abroad is still growing in intensity and extension—but the world market begins to shrink relatively, new markets are not being opened up, the realization of profits is becoming more and more difficult.

A world in which imperialism, in which industrial monopolism predominates, a world of which one-sixth is closed to exploitation by Western capitalism through the erection of a workers' republic, a world shaken again and again by economic crises and wars, a world in which labour increases in strength through better organization and better strategy makes it impossible for Western capitalism to return to the former methods of increasing the exploitation of labour.

As far as the future of labour conditions under Western capitalism is concerned, one can only expect a further decline of the purchasing power of the worker and probably a slow lengthening of the hours of work per day while at the same time unemployment and short-time will show a tendency to grow. As long as Western capitalism still holds the sceptre a rapid deterioration of labour conditions is to be expected.

2. T. S. ASHTON: A Revisionist View *

Thomas S. Ashton, a professor first at Manchester and then at the University of London, is the most recent and important revisionist contributor to a classic debate on working conditions in Britain in the early industrial period. He believes that, on balance, conditions improved over those of the preindustrial era. His approach involves several important elements: a plea for objective consideration of economic history rather than moral judgment; a re-evaluation of existing evidence plus consideration of some neglected aspects of worker life; and an effort to complete a comparative statement by urging more attention to conditions before industrialization. The first selection that follows indicates the general orientation; the second, drawn from an outstanding summary of the industrial revolution, indicates more precise conclusions on some features of industrial life.

To occupy a chair of economic history in the University of London means that, instead of being able to give one's vacation to the refreshment of body and spirit or the pursuit of knowledge, one is forced to spend much of it in reading examination scripts produced not only by one's own students but also by several hundred young men and women in all parts of Britain and, indeed, in the uttermost parts of the earth. This situation is unenviable. But at least it enables one to speak with assurance about the ideas held about the economic past by those who, in a short time, will be holding positions of authority in industry, commerce, journalism, politics, and administration and will therefore be influential in forming what we call "public opinion."

It is a truism that men's political and economic ideas depend as much on the experiences of the preceding generation as on the needs of their own. Asked by Lionel Robbins what they considered to be the outstanding problem of today, the majority of a class of students at the School of Economics answered unhesitatingly, "To maintain full employment." After a decade of full, or overfull, employment in England, the shadow of the 1930's hides from large numbers the real problems of postwar England. There is, however, a deeper shadow that obscures reality and darkens counsels. It is cast by the grievances—real or alleged—of workingmen who lived and died a century ago. According to a a large number of scripts which it has been my lot to read, the course of English history since about the year 1760 to the setting-up of the welfare state in 1945 was marked by little but toil and sweat and oppression. Economic forces, it would appear, are by nature malevolent. Every labor-saving device has led to a decline of skill and to an increase of unemployment. Is it not well known that, when prices rise, wages lag behind, and the standard of life of the workers falls? But what if prices fall? Is it not equally well known that this must result

* (1) From F. A. Hayek, ed., *Capitalism and the Historians,* pp. 33–43, 50–54. Copyright 1954 by the University of Chicago Press and reprinted with their permission. (2) From T. S. Ashton, *The Industrial Revolution, 1760–1830* (London: The Oxford University Press, 1948; rev. ed., 1962), pp. 115–18, 120–21. Reprinted by permission of The Oxford University Press.

in a depression of trade and industry, a fall of wages and unemployment, so that, once more, the standard of life of the workers falls?

Modern youth is prone to melancholy; like Rachel, it refuses to be comforted. Yet I think it is something more than adolescent pessimism that is responsible for this climate of opinion. Students attend lectures and read textbooks, and it is a matter of common prudence to pay some heed to what they have heard and read. A good deal—indeed, far too much—of what appears in the scripts is literal reproduction of the spoken or written word. Much the greater part of the responsibility must lie with the professional economic historian.

The student of English economic history is fortunate in having at his disposal the reports of a long series of Royal Commissions and Committees of Inquiry beginning in the eighteenth century but reaching full stream in the 1830's, 1840's, and 1850's. These reports are one of the glories of the early Victorian age. They signalized a quickening of social conscience, a sensitiveness to distress, that had not been evident in any other period or in any other country. Scores of massive folios provided statistical and verbal evidence that all was not well with large numbers of the people of England and called the attention of legislators and the reading public to the need for reform. The economic historians of the succeeding generations could do no other than draw on their findings; and scholarship, no less than society, benefited. There was, however, loss as well as gain. A picture of the economic system constructed from Blue Books dealing with social grievances, and not with the normal processes of economic development, was bound to be one-sided. It is such a picture of early Victorian society that has become fixed in the minds of popular writers and is reproduced in my scripts. A careful reading of the reports would, indeed, lead to the conclusion that much that was wrong was the result of laws, customs, habits, and forms of organization that belonged to earlier periods and were rapidly becoming obsolete. It would have brought home to the mind that it was not among the factory employees but among the domestic workers, whose traditions and methods were those of the eighteenth century, that earnings were at their lowest. It would have provided evidence that it was not in the large establishments making use of steam power but in the garret or cellar workshops that conditions of employment were at their worst. It would have led to the conclusion that it was not in the growing manufacturing towns or the developing coal fields but in remote villages and the countryside that restrictions on personal freedom and the evils of truck were most marked. But few had the patience to go carefully through these massive volumes. It was so much easier to pick out the more sensational evidences of distress and work them into a dramatic story of exploitation. The result has been that a generation that had the enterprise and industry to assemble the facts, the honesty to reveal them, and the energy to set about the task of reform has been held up to obloquy as the author, not of the Blue Books, but of the evils themselves. Conditions in the mills and the factory town were so bad, it seemed, that there must have been deterioration; and, since the supposed deterioration had taken place at a time when machinery had increased, the machines, and those who owned them, must have been responsible.

At the same time the romantic revival in literature led to an idyllic view of the life of the present. The idea that agriculture is the only natural and healthy activity for human beings has persisted, and indeed spread, as more of us have escaped from the curse of Adam—or, as the tedious phrase goes, "become divorced from the soil." A year ago an examinee remarked profoundly that "in earlier centuries agriculture was widespread in England" but added sorrowfully, "Today it is confined to the rural areas." There was a similar idealization of the condition of the domestic worker, who had taken only the first step in the proceedings for divorce. Bear with me while I read some passages with which Friedrich Engels (who is usually acclaimed a realist) opens his account of *The Condition of the Working Classes in England in 1844*. It is, of course, based on the writings of the Reverend Philip Gaskell, whose earnestness and honesty are not in doubt, but whose mind had not been confused by any study of history. Engels' book opens with the declaration that "the history of the proletariat in England begins with the invention of the steam-engine and of machinery for working cotton." Before their time, he continues,

> the workers vegetated throughout a passably comfortable existence, leading a righteous and peaceful life in all piety and probity; and their material condition was far better than that of their successors. They did not need to overwork; they did no more than they chose to do, and yet earned what they needed. They had leisure for healthful work in garden or field, work which, in itself, was recreation for them, and they could take part beside in the recreation and games of their neighbours, and all these games—bowling, cricket, football, etc., contributed to their physical health and vigour. They were, for the most part, strong, well-built people, in whose physique little or no difference from that of their peasant neighbours was discoverable. Their children grew up in fresh country air, and, if they could help their parents at work, it was only occasionally; while of eight or twelve hours work for them there was no question.[1]

It is difficult to say whether this or the lurid picture of the lives of the grandchildren of these people presented in later pages of the book is more completely at variance with the facts. Engels had no doubt whatsoever as to the cause of the deterioration in the condition of labor. "The proletariat," he repeats, "was called into existence by the introduction of machinery." "The consequences of improvement in machinery under our present social conditions," he asserts, "are, for the working-man, solely injurious, and often in the highest degree oppressive. Every new advance brings with it loss of employment, want and suffering."

Engels had had many disciples, even among those who do not accept the historical materialism of Marx, with which such views are generally connected. Hostility to the machine is associated with hostility to its products and, indeed,

1. London, 1892. Engels continues: "They were 'respectable' people, good husbands and fathers, led moral lives because they had no temptation to be immoral, there being no groggeries or low houses in their vicinity, and because the host, at whose inn they now and then quenched their thirst, was also a respectable man, usually a large tenant farmer who took pride in his good order, good beer, and early hours. They had their children the whole day at home, and brought them up in obedience and the fear of God. . . . The young people grew up in idyllic simplicity and intimacy with their playmates until they married, etc."

to all innovation in consumption. One of the outstanding accomplishments of the new industrial age is to be seen in the greatly increased supply and variety of fabrics offered on the market. Yet the changes in dress are taken as evidence of growing poverty: "The clothing of the working-people in a majority of cases," Engels declares, "is in a very bad condition. The material used for it is not of the best adapted. Wool and linen have almost vanished from the wardrobes of both sexes, and cotton has taken their place. Skirts are made of bleached or coloured cotton goods, and woollen petticoats are rarely to be seen on the wash-line." The truth is that they never had been greatly displayed on the wash line, for woolen goods are liable to shrink. The workers of earlier periods had to make their garments last (second or third hand as many of these were), and soap and water were inimical to the life of clothing. The new, cheap textiles may not have been as hard-wearing as broadcloth, but they were more abundant; and the fact that they could be washed without suffering harm had a bearing, if not on their own life, at least on the lives of those who wore them.

The same hostility is shown to innovation in food and drink. Generations of writers have followed William Cobbett in his hatred of tea. One would have thought that the enormous increase in consumption between the beginning of the eighteenth and the middle of the nineteenth century was one element in a rising standard of comfort; but only a few years ago Professor Parkinson asserted that it was "growing poverty" that made tea increasingly essential to the lower classes as ale was put beyond their means." (This, I may add, unfortunately meant that they were forced to consume sugar, and one must suppose that this practice also led to a fall in the standard of living.) Similarly, Dr. Salaman has recently assured us that the introduction of the potato into the diet of the workers at this time was a factor detrimental to health and that it enabled the employers to force down the level of wages—which, it is well known, is always determined by the minimum of food required for subsistence.

Very gradually those who held to these pessimistic views of the effects of industrial change have been forced to yield ground. The painstaking researches of Bowley and Wood have shown that over most of this period, and later, the course of real wages was upward. The proof is not at all easy, for it is clear that there were sections of the working classes of whom it was emphatically not true. In the first half of the nineteenth century the population of England was growing, partly because of natural increase, partly as the result of the influx of Irish. For those endowed with little or no skill, marginal productivity, and hence earnings, remained low. A large part of their incomes was spent on commodities (mainly food, drink, and housing), the cost of which had hardly been affected by technical development. That it why so many of the economists, like McCulloch and Mill, were themselves dubious about the beneficial nature of the industrial system. There were, however, large and growing sections of skilled and better-paid workers whose money incomes were rising and who had a substantial margin to spend on the products of the machine, the costs of which were falling progressively. The controversy really rests on which of the groups was increasing most. Generally it is now agreed that for the majority the gain in real wages was substantial.

But this does not dispose of the controversy. Real earnings might have risen, it was said, but it was the quality of life and not the quantity of goods consumed that mattered. In particular, it was the evil conditions of housing and the insanitary conditions of the towns that were called as evidence that the circumstances of labor had worsened. "Everything which here arouses horror and indignation," wrote Engels of Manchester in 1844, "is of recent origin, belongs to the industrial epoch"—and the reader is left to infer that the equally repulsive features of cities like Dublin and Edinburgh, which were scarcely touched by the new industry, were, somehow or other, also the product of the machine.

This is the legend that has spread round the world and has determined the attitude of millions of men and women to labor-saving devices and to those who own them. Indians and Chinese, Egyptians and Negroes, to whose fellow-countrymen today the dwellings of the English of the mid-nineteenth century would be wealth indeed, solemnly declare, in the scripts I have to read, that the English workers were living in conditions unworthy of beasts. They write with indignation about the inefficiency of the sanitation and the absence of civic amenities—the very nature of which is still unknown to the urban workers of a large part of the earth.

Now, no one who has read the reports of the Committee on the Sanitary Condition of the Working Classes of 1842 or that of the Commission on the Health of Towns of 1844 can doubt that the state of affairs was, from the point of view of modern Western civilization, deplorable. But, equally, no one who has read Dorothy George's account of living conditions in London in the eighteenth century can be sure that they had deteriorated. Dr. George herself believes that they had improved, and Clapham declared that the English towns of the mid-century were "less crowded than the great towns of other countries and not, universally, more insanitary." The question I wish to raise, however, is that of responsibility. Engels, as we have seen, attributed the evils to the machine; others are no less emphatic in attributing them to the Industrial Revolution, which comes to much the same thing. No historian, as far as I know, has looked at the problem through the eyes of those who had the task of building and maintaining the towns. . . .

In the years that followed the long war, then, the builders had the task of making up arrears of housing and of meeting the needs of a rapidly growing population. They were handicapped by costs, a large part of which arose from fiscal exactions. The expenses of occupying a house were loaded with heavy local burdens, and so the net rent that most workingmen could afford to pay was reduced. In these circumstances, if the relatively poor were to be housed at all, the buildings were bound to be smaller, less substantial, and less well provided with amenities than could be desired. It was emphatically not the machine, not the Industrial Revolution, not even the speculative bricklayer or carpenter that was at fault. Few builders seem to have made fortunes, and the incidence of bankruptcy was high. The fundamental problem was the shortage of houses. Those who blame the jerry-builder remind one of the parson, referred to by Edwin Cannan, who used to upbraid the assembled worshippers for the poor attendance at church.

Stress has rightly been laid by many writers on the inadequacy of the provisions for safeguarding the public against overcrowding of houses on limited sites. But London, Manchester, and other large towns had had their Building Acts for generations, and no one who has looked at the *Builders' Price Books* can possibly believe that Londoners suffered from a deficiency of regulations. Mr. John Summerson, indeed, has suggested that the depressing monotony of the newer streets of the capital were the direct result, not, as is often assumed, of free enterprise, but of the provisions of what the builders called the Black Act of 1774—a measure that runs to about thirty-five thousand words. It is true that what was uppermost in the minds of those who framed this act was the avoidance of fire. But some writers like the Webbs (as Redford has shown) have done less than justice to the work of the early organs of local government in such matters as the paving, lighting, and cleaning of streets. If more was not done, the fault did not rest on the builders. Thomas Cubitt told the House of Commons that he would not allow a house to be built anywhere unless it could be shown that there was a good drainage and a good way to get rid of water. "I think there should be a public officer paid at the public expense, who should be responsible for that." If the towns were ridden with disease, some at least of the responsibility lay with legislators who, by taxing windows, put a price on light and air and, by taxing bricks and tiles, discouraged the construction of drains and sewers. Those who dwell on the horrors that arose from the fact that the products of the sewers often got mixed up with the drinking water, and attribute this, as all other horrors, to the Industrial Revolution, should be reminded of the obvious fact that without the iron pipe, which was one of the products of that revolution, the problem of enabling people to live a healthy life together in towns could never have been solved.

If my first complaint against commonly accepted views of the economic developments of the nineteenth century is concerned with their pessimism, my second is that they are not informed by any glimmering of economic sense. In the generation of Adam Smith and his immediate successors many treatises appeared dealing with the history of commerce, industry, coinage, public revenue, population, and pauperism. Those who wrote them—men like Anderson, Macpherson, Chalmers, Colquhoun, Lord Liverpool, Sinclair, Eden, Malthus, and Tooke—were either themselves economists or at least were interested in the things that were the concern of Adam Smith, Ricardo, and Mill. There were, it is true, many rebels, on both the right and the left, against the doctrines propounded by the economists; but few of these, it so happened, were historically minded. There was, therefore, no sharply defined cleavage between history and theory. In the second half of the nineteenth century, however, a wide breach appeared. How far it was due to the direct influence of the writings of Marx and Engels, how far to the rise of the Historical School of economists in Germany, and how far to the fact that the English economic historians, following Toynbee, were primarily social reformers, I must not stay to discuss. There can be no doubt, however, that the tendency was to write the story in other than economic terms.

The Industrial Revolution

In spite of a widespread impression to the contrary, the period 1760–1830 saw an increased concern for human unhappiness, and especially for that of the young—even on the part of the cotton men. It was Peel who, stimulated by a Manchester physician, Thomas Percival, pressed on Parliament the need for regulation of the factories. His Act of 1802—the Health and Morals of Apprentices act—limited hours of work and prescribed minimum standards of hygiene and education. It is true that it was passed only when the worst was over, and that neither it nor Peel's second Act of 1819 (which applied to all children, pauper or "free") went very far. But at least the basis was laid for that code of legislation which is one of the corner-stones of modern industrial society.

Not all who worked in the country factories were parish apprentices. At Arkwright's three mills in Derbyshire, in 1789, about two-thirds of the 1,150 workers were children, but at other establishments, a few years later, the proportion was somewhat lower. For the adults it was necessary to put up houses, shops, and places of worship, and so there arose small communities in which, as time went on, men and women were able, in some measure, to direct their own lives. As the children grew up and had families of their own the practice of drawing on the overseers declined, and the factories came to be staffed by free labour.

The women and children who had spun on the jenny in their own homes found it difficult to compete with the power-driven machines, and, from the early 'nineties, many began to learn from their menfolk how to weave the calicoes, muslins, and cambrics that were now demanded. At the same time the steam engine and the mule were being applied to the spinning of cotton. The first made it possible to set up factories in the towns, where labour was more plentiful, and the second created a need for a new type of labour in spinning. The mule called for both strength and skill beyond that of a child, and many of the weavers now handed over their looms to their wives and took to factory employment. The occupations of the sexes were reversed, but the family economy remained intact.

As places of work the town factories were no more eligible than those of the country. There was the same dearth of managers and overlookers, and many of the women and children were hired and directed by the male spinners. But the proportion of the very young employed in them was lower than that in the water-driven mills of the older pattern. In 1816 at the country factory of Samuel Greg, of a total of 252 workers, 17 per cent. were under ten, and not quite 30 per cent. above eighteen, years of age. A few miles away in Manchester,

M'Connel and Kennedy were giving employment to 1,020 people, of whom only 3 per cent. were under ten, and 52 per cent. were above eighteen. Even in the town factory, however, it is clear that a large part of the labour consisted of young people. The reliance on workers of tender years was partly the result of technological change and partly of the fact that (as Dr. Ure put it) it was "nearly impossible to convert persons past the age of puberty, whether drawn from rural or from handicraft occupations, into useful factory hands."

In the early decades of the nineteenth century weaving began to follow spinning and became a factory process. But whereas the water-twist and mule-spinning factories had sprung up almost overnight, the power-operated weaving mills came very slowly. This was due partly to imperfections in the power-loom itself, partly to the long war with France (which, by raising the rate of interest, discouraged investment in plant), and partly to the reluctance of the weavers, many of them women, to leave their homes. With peace and the falling rates of interest of the 'twenties, many master spinners came to attach weaving sheds to their mills; but it was not until after 1834, when the austerity of the new Poor Law was brought to bear on the semi-starved weavers, that the full triumph of the factory was assured. As the power-looms increased in number the demand for domestic weavers declined; but the supply of these was maintained by an influx of Irish who, content with low standards of living, were even less patient than the English of the discipline of the factory. It is sometimes suggested that the "evils" of the industrial revolution were due to the rapidity with which it proceeded: the case of the domestic textile workers suggests the exact opposite. If there had been in weaving a man of the type of Arkwright, if rates of interest had remained low, if there had been no immigration and no Poor Law allowance, the transfer to the factory might have been effected quickly and with less suffering. As it was, large numbers of hand workers continued, for more than a generation, to fight a losing battle against the power of steam. In 1814 the price paid for weaving a piece of calico by hand had been *6s. 6d.;* by 1829 it had fallen to *1s. 2d.*

The plight of overworked apprentices and underemployed domestic weavers does not constitute the full story of the revolution in textiles. It is not necessary to accept as evidence the picture drawn by the egregious Dr. Ure of the "lively elves" whose work in the factory "seemed to resemble a sport," in order to believe that, all in all, the effect of the inventions was to lighten labour. Most of the factory operatives were engaged at rates of pay which raised family incomes above those of any earlier generation. As women and girls became less dependent on their menfolk they gained in self-respect and in public esteem. As the factories moved to the towns, or towns grew up about the factories, the practice of the long pay gave way to weekly or fortnightly disbursements, and truck and the indebtedness of workers to employers declined. Since the operatives were no longer isolated cottagers it was easier for them to form unions to defend their standards of hours and wages; and it became possible to enlist in the fight against abuses, the force of a public opinion which, through the medium of church and chapel and the Press, was becoming increasingly vocal. . . .

It is sometimes suggested that the presence of women in an industry has a humanizing effect on the men who work in it; but one would need to take a very optimistic view of the nature of man to believe that this was true of coal-mining. The evils brought to light in the reports of the early 'forties have sometimes been laid at the door of the industrial revolution, but, like so many other abuses, they went back to a more primitive stage of production, and were, in fact, tending to disappear.

The improvements in spinning, weaving, and mining were broadly of a labour-saving character: they enabled a few workers to achieve results that had previously required many, and children to perform tasks that had formerly been set to men or women. But output was so much enlarged that, in spite of this, the earnings of most of the adults were increased. There were other industries in which progress followed a different course. In engineering (civil and mechanical) and in the manufacture of iron, chemicals, and pottery the problem was that, not of finding semi-skilled labour to tend machines, but of training up men in the new techniques. Much of the time of the inventors themselves was taken up in this way. Brindley had been obliged to begin his task with the aid of miners and common labourers, but in the process of constructing his canals he created new classes of tunnellers and navvies of high skill. In his early days Watt had to make shift with the millwrights—men who could turn from one job to another and were willing to work alike in wood, metal, or stone, but were hide-bound by tradition: before he died there had come into being specialized fitters, turners, pattern-makers, and other grades of engineers. The first generation of cotton-spinners had themselves employed "clock-makers" to construct and repair their frames and mules; but gradually these were replaced by highly trained textile machinists and maintenance men. Cort's innovations meant that the craftsmanship of the finers and hammermen was no longer required, but they demanded a dexterity no less great from the puddlers and rollermen whom he himself trained. If Wedgwood split up the manufacture of pottery into a score of separate processes, each of these required its own special aptitude, and some a high degree of artistic talent. Nor was this access of skill at the expense of the handicrafts that remained outside the field of large-scale industry. The building of the factories called for proficiency from bricklayers, masons, and carpenters, and their equipment for the craftsmanship of spindle-makers, filesmiths, and a host of others who worked individually or in small concerns. The statement, sometimes made, that the industrial revolution was destructive of skill is not only untrue, but the exact reverse of the truth.

3. E. J. HOBSBAWM: The British Standard of Living *

Professor Eric Hobsbawm, of the University of London, here undertakes a direct refutation of Ashton's optimistic position, based on a detailed examina-

* From E. J. Hobsbawm, "The British Standard of Living," *The Economic History Review*, Second Series, X, No. 1 (1957), pp. 46–49, 51–53, 57–61. Reprinted by permission of *The Economic History Review* and the author.

tion of varied statistical sources. His article helped reverse the trend to "revisionism," and now the pessimistic judgment seems to be carrying the day; * but the debate is not over. Hobsbawm claims objectivity and imputes a lack of it to the optimists; is he right? His general historical approach is Marxist, which does not prevent objectivity but which should be considered in assessing it. More important, are his facts conclusive, and do they adequately cover the main features of worker life? He does not mention some of the points raised by Ashton. Do the trends he cites outweigh them even without a direct comparison? Are they talking about the same types of worker?

The debate about the standard of living under early industrialism has now continued for some thirty years. Among academic historians, in Britain at any rate, the pendulum has swung away from the classical view, held by enquirers and historians of all political views until the appearance of Clapham's *Economic History of Modern Britain*. It is today heterodox to believe that early industrialisation was a catastrophe for the labouring poor of this or other countries, let alone that their standard of living declined. This article proposes to show that the currently accepted view is based on insufficient evidence, and that there is some weighty evidence in favour of the old view. So far as possible, I propose to refrain from using the type of evidence (Royal Commissions, observers' accounts) which has been criticised as biased and unrepresentative. I do not in fact believe it to be unreliable. It is dangerous to reject the consensus of informed and intelligent contemporaries, a majority of whom, as even critics admit, took the dark view. It is illegitimate to assume that even reformers who mobilise public support by drawing attention to dramatic examples of a general evil, are not in fact attacking a general evil. But the classical case can be based, to some extent, on quantitative evidence, and, in order to avoid irrelevant argument, I shall rely mainly on it. For the sake of convenience the classical (Ricardo-Malthus-Marx-Toynbee-Hammond) view will be called the *pessimistic,* the modern (Clapham-Ashton-Hayek) view the *optimistic* school.

An initial observation is perhaps worth making. There is no *a priori* reason why the standard of living should rise markedly under early industrialism. An initial rise must almost certainly take place, on demographic grounds, but it may be very slight indeed and need not be lasting once the new rhythm of population increase has been set up. It should be remembered that the decrease in mortality which is probably primarily responsible for the sharp rise in population need be due not to an *increase* in per capita consumption per year, but to a *greater regularity of supply; i.e.* to the abolition of the periodic shortages and famines which plagued pre-industrial economies and decimated their populations. It is quite possible for the industrial citizen to be worse fed in a normal year than his predecessor, so long as he is more regularly fed.

This is not to deny that the increase in production, which greatly exceeded that of population, in the long run brought about an absolute improvement in

* See also E. P. Thompson, *The Making of the English Working Class* (New York: Alfred A. Knopf, Inc., 1963).

material living standards. Whatever we may think of the relative position of labourers compared to other classes, and whatever our theory, no serious student denies that the bulk of people in Northwestern Europe were materially better off in 1900 than in 1800. But there is no reason why living standards should improve at all times. Whether they do, depends on the distribution of the additional resources produced among the population. But we know that under early industrialism (a) there was no effective mechanism for making the distribution of the national income more equal and several for making it less so, and (b) that industrialisation under then prevailing conditions almost certainly required a more burdensome diversion of resources from consumption than is theoretically necessary, because the investment mechanism was inefficient. A large proportion of accumulated savings were not directly invested in industrialisation at all, thus throwing a much greater burden of savings on the rest of the community. In countries with an acute shortage of capital a depression of popular living standards was almost inevitable. In countries such as Britain, where plenty of capital was theoretically available, it was likely, simply because much of what was available was not in fact pressed into the most useful investment. At best, therefore, we should expect improvements in the standard of living to be much slower than they might have been, at worst we should not be surprised to find deterioration.

There is no reason to assume that in countries with a rapidly rising population and a large reserve of rural or immigrant labour, shortage as such is likely to push up real wages for more than limited groups of workers.

It may be argued that industrialisation and urbanisation automatically improve living-standards in any case, because industrial wages normally tend to be higher than non-industrial or rural ones, and urban consumption standards than village ones. But (a) we are not merely concerned with the incomes of one section of the labouring poor, but of all. We must not isolate any group of the labouring poor, whether better or worse off, unless it forms a majority of the population. Moreover (b) the argument is not always correct. Thus while in many continental countries social indices, like mortality and literacy, improve faster in town than country, in Britain this was not always so. Lastly (c) we must beware of interpreting the qualitative differences between urban and rural, industrial and pre-industrial life *automatically* as differences between "better" and "worse." Unless we bring imponderables into the argument, townsmen are not necessarily better off than countrymen; and as the Hammonds showed, imponderables can also be thrown on the pessimistic side of the scale.

One final point must be made. Optimists often tend to exonerate capitalism from blame for such bad conditions as they admit to have existed. They argue that these were due to insufficient private enterprise, to hangovers from the pre-industrial past or to similar factors. I do not propose to enter into such metaphysical arguments. This paper is concerned primarily with fact, and not with accusation, exculpation or justification. What would have happened if all citizens in Europe in 1800 had behaved as textbooks of economics told them to, and if there had been no obstacles or frictions, is not a question for historians. They are, in the first instance, concerned with what did happen. Whether it might have happened differently, is a question which belongs to another argument. We may now consider the views of the "optimistic" school. Its founder, Clapham, relied primarily on calculations of real wages which showed them to rise in the period 1790 to 1850 at times when contemporaries, and the historians who followed them, assumed that the poor were getting poorer. On the money side these calculations depended mainly on the well-known collections of wage-data by Bowley and Wood. On the cost-of-living side they depended almost wholly on Silberling's index. It is not too much to say that Clapham's version of the optimistic view stood or fell by Silberling.

It is now generally realised that the statistical basis of Clapham's conclusions is too weak to bear its weight; especially as the argument for the period 1815–1840 odd turns largely on the question whether the curve of the cost-of-living sloped downwards more steeply than that of money-wages, it being admitted that both tended to fall. Clearly in extreme cases, e.g. when prices fall and wages rise or the other way round, even a thin index may be reliable. In this case, however, the possibilities of error are much greater.

Now our figures for money-wages are chiefly time-rates for skilled artisans (Tucker, Bowley). About piece-workers we know very little. Since we also know little about the incidence of unemployment, short-time etc., our figures cannot be regarded as a reliable reflection of actual earnings. (Clapham, by the way, makes no attempt to discover the extent of unemployment, though mentioning the absence of data about it. His index to vol. I does not even contain the word). For large sections of the "labouring poor"—the unskilled, those whose income cannot be clearly expressed in terms of regular money-wages, we are almost completely in the dark. We therefore possess nothing which would be regarded as an adequate index of money-wages today. The weakness of the cost-of-living figures is equally great. Silberling has been criticised by Cole, by Judges, and most recently by Ashton, the most eminent of the "optimists." For practical purposes it is no longer safe to generalise about the working-class cost-of-living on this basis. Indeed, practical, as distinct from methodological, doubt has been thrown on such attempts to construct real wage indices for the first half of the nineteenth century. Thus Ashton's figures for retail prices in some Lancashire towns 1790–1830 show nothing like the post-war fall which Silberling would lead one to expect. Tucker's index of London artisan real wages shows the major improvement in their position in the period 1810–1843 to have occurred in 1813–22. But, as we shall see, these were years of stagnant or falling per capita consumption of meat in London, and of sugar and tobacco nationally; facts which hardly support the assumption of rising real wages.

In defence of Clapham it ought to be said that he was more cautious in his conclusion than some of the optimistic vulgarisers have been. Thus Silberling's index itself shows living-costs to have remained fairly steady for about twenty years after 1822, rising and falling about a level trend. Not until after 1843 did they drop below the 1822 level. Tucker's, a later index, shows that between 1822 and 1842 the real wages of London artisans rose above the 1822 level in only four years, the average improvement for the whole period, even for them, being only about 5 or 6 per cent. The two decades of, at best, relative stagnation of real wages—which R. C. O. Matthews confirms for the 1830's—are significant, though often omitted from the argument. In fact, one is bound to conclude that Clapham has had a surprisingly easy passage, thanks largely to the extreme feebleness of the reply of his chief opponent, J. L. Hammond, who virtually accepted Clapham's statistics and shifted the argument entirely onto moral and other non-material territories.

However, today, the deficiencies of Clapham's argument have been admitted and the most serious of the optimists, Professor Ashton, has in fact abandoned it, though this fact has not always been realised. Instead, he relies on arguments or assumptions of three types. First, on various theoretical arguments designed to prove that a rise in real wages must have taken place. Second, on factual evidence of rising material prosperity—such as improvements in housing, food, clothing etc. Third, on the—so far as one can judge—unsupported assumption that the part of the labouring population whose real wages improved must have been larger than the part whose real wages did not. It is admitted that conditions for part of the working population did not improve. I do not propose to discuss the first lot of arguments, since, if there is evidence that the standard of living did not improve significantly or at all at the relevant periods, they automatically fall to the ground. . . .

We may consider three types of evidence in favour of the pessimistic view: those bearing on (a) mortality and health, (b) unemployment and (c) consumption. In view of the weaknesses of wage and price-data, discussed above, it is best not to consider them here; in any case actual consumption figures shed a more reliable light on real wages. However, we know too little about the actual structure of the population to isolate the movements of working-class indices from the rest of the "labouring poor" and of other classes. But this would be troublesome only if the indices showed a fairly marked rise, which they do not. Since the "labouring poor" clearly formed the majority of the population, a general index showing stability or deterioration is hardly compatible with a significant improvement of their situation, though it does not exclude improvement among a minority of them.

A. SOCIAL INDICES

Our best indices are mortality rates (average expectation of life, infantile, TB mortality etc.), morbidity rates and anthropometric data. Unfortunately in Britain we lack any reliable anthropometric data such as the French, and any index of health such as the percentage of rejected recruits. Nor have we any useful morbidity figures. The Friendly Societies, whose actuarial advisers made some useful calculations about sickness rates, cannot be regarded as representative samples, since it is agreed that they included mainly the more prosperous or stably-employed workers; and in any case, as Farr (1839) demonstrates, there is little enough evidence from them before that date. It is possible that work on hospital records may allow us to find out more about sickness trends, but too little is available at present for judgment.

We must therefore rely on mortality rates. These have their limitations, though it has been plausibly argued that even the crudest of them—general mortality below the age of 50—is a sensitive indicator of living standards. Still, a high or rising mortality rate, a low expectation of life, are not to be neglected. We need not be too much troubled by the known imperfections of the figures, at any rate where trends emerge over periods of time. In any case, the worst imperfection, the fact that births are less completely registered than deaths—thus swelling earlier figures for infant mortality—helps to correct a pessimistic bias. For as registration improves, recorded mortality rates also drop automatically on paper, though in fact they may change much less in reality.

The general movement of mortality rates is fairly well known. On theoretical grounds, such as those discussed by McKeown and Brown, it is almost inconceivable that there was not a real fall in mortality rates due to improvements in living standards at the beginning of industrialisation, at least for a while. General mortality rates fell markedly from the 1780's to the 1810's and thereafter rose until the 1840's. This "coincided with a change in the age-distribution favourable to a low death-rate, namely an increase in the proportion of those in healthy middle life." The figures therefore understate the real rise in mortality rates, assuming the same age-composition throughout the period. The rise is said to have been due chiefly to higher infantile and youth mortality, especially in the towns, but figures for Glasgow 1821–35 suggest that there it was due primarily to a marked increase in the mortality of men of working age, greatest in the age-groups from 30 to 60. Social conditions are the accepted explanation for this. Edmonds, who discusses the Glasgow figures, observed (1835) that "this is just what might be expected to occur, on the supposition of the rising adult population possessing a lower degree of vitality than their immediate predecessors." On the other hand we must not forget that mortality rates did not improve drastically until very much later—say, until the 1870's or 1880's—and may therefore be less relevant to the movement of living standards than is sometimes supposed. (Alternatively, that living standards improved much more slowly after the 1840's than is often supposed). Nevertheless, the rise in mortality rates in the period 1811–41 is clearly of *some* weight for the pessimistic case, all the more as modern work, especially the studies of Holland during and after World War II, tend to link such rates much more directly to the amount of income and food consumption than to other social conditions.

B. UNEMPLOYMENT

There is room for much further work on this subject, whose neglect is rather inexplicable. Here I merely wish to draw attention to some scattered pieces of information which support a pessimistic rather than a rosy view.

Little as we know about the period before the middle 1840's, most students would agree that the real sense of improvement among the labouring classes thereafter was due less to a rise in wage-rates, which often remained surprisingly stable for years, or to an improvement in social conditions, but to the upgrading of labourers from very poorly to less poorly paid jobs, and above all to a decline in unemployment or a greater regularity of employment. In fact, unemployment in the earlier period had been heavy. Let us consider certain components and aspects of it.

We may first consider *pauperism,* the permanent core of poverty, fluctuating relatively little with cyclical changes—even in 1840–2. The trends of pauperism are difficult to determine, owing to the fundamental changes brought about by the New Poor Law, but its extent is sufficiently indicated by the fact that in the early 1840's something like 10 per cent of the total population were probably paupers. They were not necessarily worse off than the rest, for Tufnell, in the Second Annual Report of the Poor Law Commissioners, estimated that farm-labourers ate less than paupers; perhaps 30 per cent less in crude weight of foodstuffs. This was also the case in depressed towns. . . .

C. CONSUMPTION FIGURES

As Britain was not a bureaucratic state, we lack official national data, except for wholly imported articles. Nevertheless, we can get a good deal more information than has hitherto been brought into the discussion. This shows that, from the later 1790's until the early 1840's, there is no evidence of any major rise in the per capita consumption of several foodstuffs, and in some instances evidence of a temporary fall which had not yet been completely made good by the middle 1840's. If the case for deterioration in this period can be established firmly, I suggest that it will be done on the basis of consumption data.

Tea, sugar and tobacco, being wholly imported, furnish national consumption figures which may be divided by the estimated population to give a crude index of per capita consumption. However, we note that Clapham, though an optimist and aware of the figures, wisely refused to use them as an argument in his favour since absolute per capita consumption in this period was low, and such increases as occurred were disappointingly small. Indeed, the contrast between the curve before and after the middle 1840's when it begins to rise sharply, is one of the strongest arguments on the pessimistic side. All three series show a slowly rising trend and after the 1840's a much sharper rise, though tobacco consumption fell (probably owing to increased duties) in the 1810's. The tobacco series includes Irish consumption after the middle 1820's and is thus difficult to use. The tea series is also hard to interpret, since it reflects not merely the capacity to buy, but also the secular trend to abandon older beverages for a new one. The significance of tea-drinking was much debated by contemporaries, who were far from considering it an automatic sign of improving living standards. At all events it only shows four periods of decline—1815–6, 1818–9, a dramatically sharp fall in 1836–7 after a sharp rise, and a slighter fall in 1839–40. Tea seems to have been immune to the slumps of 1826 and, more surprisingly, 1841–2, which makes it suspect as an index of living-standards. Tobacco does not reflect the slump of 1836–7, but does reflect the others, though not much. Anyway, this article shows virtually stable consumption. Sugar is the most sensitive indicator though—owing to various outside factors—it does not always reflect trade-cycle movements. It shows the slumps of 1839–40 and 1841–2 well. Broadly speaking there is no tendency for sugar consumption to rise above the Napoleonic peak until well into the 1840's. There is a sharp post-war decline, a sharp rise to rather lower levels after 1818, a slow rise—almost a plateau—until 1831, and then an equally slow decline or stagnation until 1843 or 44. Tea, sugar and tobacco indicate no marked rise in the standards of living, but beyond this little can be deduced from the crude series.

The case of *meat* is different. Here we possess at least two indices, the Smithfield figures for London for the entire period, and the yield of the excise on hides and skins for the period up to 1825. The Smithfield figures show that, while London's population index rose from 100 in 1801 to 202 in 1841, the number of beef cattle slaughtered rose only to 146, of sheep to 176 in the same period. The following table five gives the figures by decades:

DECENNIAL PERCENTAGE INCREASE IN LONDON POPULATION, BEEF AND SHEEP AT SMITHFIELD, 1801–51

Date	*Animals*	*Index figure*			*Decennial increase*		
Population	*ave. of*	*Population*	*Beef*	*Sheep*	*Population*	*Beef*	*Sheep*
1801	1800–4	100	100	100			
1811	1810–12	119	105	119	+19	+ 5	+19
1821	1819–22	144	113	135	+25	+ 8	+16
1831	1830–34	173	127	152	+29	+14	+17
1841	1840–43	203	146	176	+30	+19	+24
1851	1850–52 *	246	198	193	+43	+42	+17

* The choice of base-dates for the animals cannot be rigid. Thus 1800–4 is chosen, because say 1800–2 would give abnormally high figures, thus understating the rise in the following decade. For sheep 1840–2 has been taken as a base-date, because the exceptionally high figure for 1843 would overstate the decennial rise. The choice of different dates would change the results slightly, but not substantially.

It will be seen that the increase in beef lagged behind that in population in all decades until the 1840's. Mutton also lagged—though less—except in the first decade. On the whole a per capita decline in London meat consumption up to the 1840's is thus almost certain.

The Excise on hides and leather yields somewhat cruder figures. . . . The following table summarises what little we can get from them:

YIELD OF EXCISE ON HIDES AND SKINS IN LONDON AND REST OF COUNTRY, 1801 (1800–1 FOR EXCISE) = 100

Date	*Population*	*Country yield*	*London yield*
1801	100	100	100
1811	114.5	122	107
1821	136	106	113
1825	150	135	150

Without going further into the somewhat complex discussion of the sources, it seems clear that the figures do not indicate a major rise in per capita meat consumption.

About *cereals and potatoes,* the staple of the poor man's diet, we can also find out some things. The fundamental fact is that, as contemporaries already knew, wheat production and imports did not keep pace with the growth of population so that the amount of wheat available per capita fell steadily from the late eighteenth century until the 1850's, the amount of potatoes available rising at about the same rate. It follows that, whatever the literary evidence, somebody *must* during this period have shifted away from wheat; presumably to potatoes. The simplest view would be that the major change from brown to white bread had already taken place by, say, the 1790's, and that the drift from wheat took place thereafter; but this would not explain the almost certain later drift from brown to white bread in the North and West. But this may have been "paid for" by a decline of per capita consumption elsewhere. This is technically possible. The mean consumption of bread-stuffs among farm-labourers in 1862 was about 14½ lb per week. Twelve counties consumed less than this—from 10¼ to 11¾ lbs, six more than 13 lb, fourteen about the average. Where per capita consumption varied so widely—between 10¼ and 15¼, not to mention the 18¾ of Anglesey, there is scope for both an earlier decline in per capita consumption in some places and for considerable "compensation" between counties. However, it is not my purpose to suggest explanations. All we can say is, that a rise in the per capita consumption of white bread in this period *at nobody's expense* is out of the question. Wheat consumption may have fallen with or without additional potato consumption, or some areas may have seen it rise at the expense of others (with or without a rise in potatoes).

We have no general statistics about the consumption of other common foodstuffs. It is difficult to see anything but a decline of *milk,* because cow-keeping must have declined with urbanisation (though it probably continued in towns on a larger scale than is sometimes admitted) and because of the decline of the traditional rural diet which relied heavily on "white meats." It survived longer in the North and West. Even in 1862 some fortunate groups of poor workers stuck to it, doubtless much to their benefit: the Macclesfield silk weavers consumed 41.5 fluid oz per head per week, as against the 11 oz of the Coventry weavers, the 7.6 oz of the Spitalfields weavers and 1.6 oz of Bethnal Green. But all the evidence points to a decline in milk consumption. Not so with *butter,* which was evidently—and naturally, since bread formed so large a part of the labourer's diet—considered a greater necessity than meat. In Dukinfield and Manchester (1836) outlays on it were comparable to those on meat, and comparison with 1841 shows that they were rather inelastic. The few comparable budgets from Eden show a similar pattern of expenditure, though perhaps a rather smaller outlay on butter than on meat. The poor man thus ate butter; only the destitute man might be unable to. It is not impossible that butter consumption rose during urbanisation, for other things to spread on bread—e.g. lard or dripping—must have been harder to come by when people kept fewer pigs and meat-consumption was low and erratic. *Cheese* consumption seems to have declined, for many urban workers seem not to have had or to have developed the fashion of substituting it for meat. In Dukinfield and Manchester they spent much less on cheese than butter, and the 1862 farm-labourers ate much more of it, even allowing for their slightly better position, than the "urban poor." *Eggs* seem to have been of small importance. Per capita consumption can hardly have risen.

The evidence is thus not at all favourable to the "optimistic" view. Though it does not necessarily or firmly establish the "pessimistic" one, it rather points towards it. The growth of *adulteration* slightly strengthens the pessimistic case. Even if we assume that late eighteenth-century urban shopkeepers were no less dishonest than nineteenth-century ones, it must have affected more people, since a greater number and proportion had to rely on them. The *Lancet* enquiry in the 1850's brings the following points out very clearly: (i) *all* bread tested in two separate samples was adulterated; (ii) over half of oatmeal was adulterated; (iii) *all* but the highest-quality teas were invariably adulterated; (iv) a little under half the milk and (v) *all* butter was watered. Over half the jam and preserves included deleterious matter, but this may have been due simply to bad production. The only commodity of common use not largely adulterated was sugar, almost 90 per cent of which seems to have been straight, though often filthy.

The discussion of food consumption thus throws considerable doubt on the optimistic view. However, it should be pointed out that this does *not* mean that early nineteenth-century Britons had an "Asiatic" standard of living. This is nonsense, and such loose statements have caused much confusion. Britain was almost certainly better fed than all but the most prosperous peasant areas, or the more comfortable classes, in continental countries; but then it had been so, as Drummond and Wilbraham pointed out long before the Industrial Revolution. The point at issue is not whether we fell as low as other countries, but whether, by our own standards, we improved or deteriorated, and in either case, how much.

There is thus no strong basis for the optimistic view, at any rate for the period from c.1790 or 1800 on until the middle 1840's. The plausibility of, and the evidence for, deterioration are not to be lightly dismissed. It is not the purpose of this paper to discuss the evolution of living standards in the eighteenth century, since the major discussion on living standards has been about the period between the end of the Napoleonic Wars and "some unspecified date between the end of Chartism and the Great Exhibition." It is altogether likely that living-standards improved over much of the eighteenth century. It is not improbable that, sometime soon after the onset of the Industrial Revolution—which is perhaps better placed in the 1780's than in the 1760's—they ceased to improve and declined. Perhaps the middle 1790's, the period of Speenhamland and shortage, mark the turning-point. At the other end, the middle 1840's certainly mark a turning-point.

We may therefore sum up as follows. The classical view has been put in

Sidney Webb's words: "If the Chartists in 1837 had called for a comparison of their time with 1787, and had obtained a fair account of the actual social life of the working-man at the two periods, it is almost certain that they would have recorded a positive decline in the standard of life of large classes of the population." This view has not been so far made untenable. It may be that further evidence will discredit it; but it will have to be vastly stronger evidence than has so far been adduced.

4. EDOUARD DOLLÉANS AND GÉRARD DEHOVE: History of Labor in France *

Two students of French labor here offer a general approach to a detailed survey of the nineteenth century. Both have written a number of books on the French labor movement; Edouard Dolléans' main work, *Histoire du mouvement ouvrier* (3 vols., Paris 1953) remains the most comprehensive survey available. The following selection raises a number of questions. The recurrent issue of worker conditions appears, and the effort to get beyond purely material conditions should be noted. What "working class" is being discussed? Are the authors consistent in their focus? The answer to these questions may explain the judgment both of conditions of work and of the activity of the labor movement; it may also, when compared with British material, reflect distinctive features of French labor. The authors have tried to take a long-range view of the implications of industrial labor. This view must be assessed in its application to the early working class and the early labor movement. If, indeed, the authors are right about ultimate trends, how helpful is this knowledge in understanding the labor movement in the mid-nineteenth century?

If, in the history of a society, the role of the common people is destined to grow, it is because singular and strong personalities appear among them in each generation. They are strengthened and defined by several significant characteristics: a desire for education, a tenacious ardor in intention, a heroic patience in action. It is curious to note that the appearance of these obscure militants, in the second third of the 19th century, coincided with an increased rigor in the conditions of worker life, in the shop and at home; they gained their learning in spite of days of 14, 15, and 16 hours of work. These obscure men brought to their difficult and halting advance a concern for quality which, in their trade, allowed them to obtain a polished final product. Their constant contact with material things gave them an almost physical sense of balance and a harmonious view of the whole.

These militants were the animators of masses which, after being passive for centuries, became active. What were the reasons for this new dynamism? The most important reason, without doubt, was this desire for learning which characterized the three working class generations from 1795 to 1833, generations

* From Edouard Dolléans and Gérard Dehove, *Histoire du travail en France; mouvement ouvrier et législation sociale,* Vol. I (Paris: Editions Montchrestien), pp. 21–23, 24–25, 33–35. Reprinted by permission of Editions Montchrestien and Madame Georges Monier. Translated by the editor.

which educated themselves, in the absence of any organization of elementary instruction, and at the time when the days of work were at their peak length. The worker elite had gained a real culture, which was the demanding and persevering rigor in their self-discipline.

The influence of these elites, which obscure men incessantly produced, is incontestable. It is not contradicted by more recent developments or by the influence of the newly-active masses on the destinies of the world. *It is the coexistence of these two powerful factors that gives the twentieth century its singular character.*

This second new factor, the eruption of the masses, broke with tradition with a brutality disconcerting to those who trusted too much in the patterns of history and did not suspect the potential of these neglected forces.

The formation of the masses was the result of industrial and urban civilization, because the conditions of life in the industrial centers resulted in a physical and nervous disequilibrium. Engulfed in the urban multitudes, the individual felt more isolated than amid the plains and the fields. And this feeling of isolation coincided with a weakening of religious and traditional beliefs. Lost in the crowd, the individual sought support outside himself, a remedy for his solitude. He found this in precisely that crowd of human beings that first seemed foreign to his sentiments. He gradually understood that his suffering was theirs too. He saw them subjected to the same labors and the same problems, the same enthusiasms and the same disappointments. Most particularly, he realized that he shared their dependence on a common fate. This feeling of a common fate first grouped these men, until then lost in their solitude.

Thus the masses, united by their common feelings, were so to speak "resoldered." They became ultra-receptive, ready to welcome magic formulas of hope, ready to participate in any enthusiasm that inspired them by raising their thoughts above daily cares. They sought reasons to believe.

The crowd is a passing formation, most often the result of pure chance. Precisely because an external event unites them, crowds dissipate as rapidly as they assemble; they have no permanence. The mass, on the contrary, which is a completely modern phenomenon, possesses a permanent existence which it owes, first, to a community of durable sentiments, because the source of these sentiments is internal. The masses have an armature which rests on a community of destiny. But one must distinguish between passive masses and active masses.

The passive mass is formed by all individuals who, no matter how withdrawn they are from each other, are capable of feeling similar impressions and reactions, in the presence of certain influences intentionally destined to exert an action on the masses. These masses are formed because, in the modern world, each of us is, even in spite of himself, like many other individuals, exposed to definite suggestive influences. The essential element is the subconscious element which is thus at work, in whatever fashion. The formation of these passive masses is due to the development of industrial capitalism. Capitalist industry can increase its production to the maximum, thanks to mechanization and standardization. This industrial civilization, carried away by its own impetus, sought to apply its technical procedures to the formation of a more and more extensive clientele, more and more open to the suggestions of advertising. And to this end it applied, in the domain of opinions and thoughts, some methods which were effective in the manufacture of products. Even at the beginning of the industrial era, one of the first great capitalists, the philanthropic employer Robert Owen, already spoke of manufacturing characters. This standardization of thoughts and opinions, this manufacture of tastes and sentiments, was part of the logic of industrial capitalism. . . .

As to the active masses, these are more self-conscious communities, in which the durable emotional forces tend to create organized communities, effective or ready for action. They are based on the convergence of wills, even when their members remain scattered. For it is not their assembling which gives them their original character, but the convergence of emotions, of desires, and of aspirations. The active masses are characterized by the community of will and of emotions, but also by the fact that, being receptive, they are the object of suggestions from without.

The constant theme of the classical economists was personal interest, the active element and the motive force of society. But this idea is contrary to historical reality. Men are not moved only by personal interest, understood materially, but more often by emotional motives. Even within the economy, it is rare to encounter a material interest in a pure state. Almost always it is an alloy, in which emotional motives combine with personal interest.

The evolution of the influence of the masses in the modern world is a new fact. The collective existence and action of the masses, spurred essentially by emotional motives, had never been felt so directly as it was throughout the 19th century. It was these motives of passion which troubled the harmonious order, the natural order of society, announced by the philosophers and economists of the 18th century. This brusque eruption of these passionate motives in modern history singularly decreased the influence of individual personal motives, but not of personalities; for, at certain times and at certain moments, the influence of personalities made itself felt even so.

The influence of the masses in contemporary history proves that economic motives no more govern modern societies than they did ancient societies. Beside the economic factors, an objective analysis includes all the political, institutional, juridical, technical, psychological factors. There is an interdependence and a reciprocal interaction among all these aspects. The facts contradict the ideal descriptions that the economists traced of the natural order of society. Economic laws are not alone in play; their action is incessantly limited by the influence of factors of another order, which people try in vain to escape, when indeed they do not rush forth to meet them. . . . We witness, in *the first two thirds of the nineteenth century,* the first social push, timid and at first badly understood, but irresistible none the less, in spite of its failure. Labor is henceforward implicitly "oriented" by the vague but profound needs for emancipation of the laboring masses. Already at this time worker legislation, protecting the employee, was born.

To understand this, we must refer to themes already evoked. Work is like a loom, essential, beneficent in certain respects, on which man weaves his existence; by it and in it he intuitively tries each day to balance joy and effort. But since the beginnings of the century, work took new forms; in this complex, pain and joy, of which work is composed, pain brutally overbalanced the elements of personal satisfaction, for machines gradually displaced the artisan from his trade, which is the basic reason for his existence. Feeling himself dispossessed, the worker was constrained to seek support outside his work.

From the end of the eighteenth century, the revolution of technology presaged the arrival of big industry, which developed during the Restoration and the July Monarchy. The market expanded and sales outlets were extended. Mechanization developed, which implied the possession of important monetary capital. The size of enterprises reflected this, and those who had the desire or means to adapt found it impossible to continue to live on such a modest basis as that of artisans in former times. They were obliged to use outside capital and to appeal systematically to an outside labor force. The factors of production, capital and labor, thus ceased to be principally supplied by a single individual. They were henceforward supplied by economic agents different from the man expected to put them to work. This fact had many consequences, from our point of view, for one can say that from that moment dates what we are accustomed to call (rather inappropriately) "industrial relations," which would be much more accurately called "professional relations."

In effect, as long as the master artisan put his own hands to work, among his several journeymen, social distinctions remained relatively unimportant. The similarity of styles of life and the frequency of shared contacts contributed to reduce them further. But from the moment when the entrepreneur withdrew from the work of material execution, corresponding to the work of production understood in its most physical sense, to limit himself to tasks of direction, organization, and administration, the distance between him and his collaborators, who were increasingly numerous, grew greater. A gap was created which the rising price of the means of production, resulting from the introduction of mechanization, only increased.

Technology became more powerful, and at the same time more demanding. It grouped men in compact masses, around the machine. And these masses, without whom such progress could not have continued, felt that they lacked the human place in the social structure which was their due. Their suffering, amplified by economic crises, led them to unite, to organize. Thus the common life of the shops, and then machine labor itself, aroused the sense of community of interests on the part of workers who shared the same tasks.

With the freedom of enterprise, mechanization, and the psychology of profit, the need for labor constantly increased. The mirage of industrial work provided an influx of country people to the urban agglomerations, which developed rapidly. This led to an excess of labor supply which in turn provoked unemployment. And this was aggravated by the introduction of machines and the recourse to female and child labor. The days of work were long: up to sixteen and seventeen hours; wages were still low. Thus worker misery was great:

there were no measures of hygiene either in the shops or in the working class quarters of the cities, which were overpopulated.

Attracted in greater and greater numbers from the countryside toward the nascent great industrial cities, crowded into slums, grouped by work into common locations, the labor force gradually became conscious of its misery, of the community of its interests and of its political power. Social distinctions became more precise and social antagonisms more bitter as a result. Thus arose the problem of relations between entrepreneurs and their employees.

Thus *technology,* by engendering a new *psychology* and supported by new *economic* forces, led to a transformation of the *doctrinal* and *political* atmosphere. *This general environment explains the birth of the modern labor movement.*

After 1830 the republican party tried to recruit among working class groups. Roused by the same interest in propaganda, social reformers, who were particularly numerous in the period, were roused to seek a worker clientele which had been so clearly useful during the 1830 riots in leading to the change in dynasty. At the same time, an elite of worker militants steadily emerged from the still backward mass of workers. From this moment, political emancipation became the first objective of a working class which, gradually, became conscious of itself.

5. PETER N. STEARNS: Patterns of Industrial Strike Activity in France During the July Monarchy *

This article, without being in any sense a direct response to the Dolléans-Dehove approach, offers obvious contrasts in its assessment of French labor in the same mid-nineteenth-century period. Yet, though both the tone and the material are quite different, would the article destroy the idea that the period saw the formation of a modern working-class movement? Part of the judgment must, again, rest on what the boundaries of the working class are. Finally, what might the low level of factory-worker protest mean about labor conditions in the period? Did workers refrain from rebelling because conditions seemed good or because they were demoralized by unusual misery?

During the Restoration and July Monarchy, factory workers and artisans formed fairly distinct groups. Their methods and places of work differed, obviously. Instead of the small shops and manually operated tools of the artisan, relatively large plants with relatively complex machinery surrounded the factory worker. More important, artisans, particularly in the cities, had far firmer traditions, including many traditions of mutual organization and protection, than did the factory workers. There were, to be sure, many artisans of peasant origin filling expanding cities such as Paris, but even the newcomers encountered a large nucleus of established artisans, accustomed to the city and to the work, who helped educate them in the ways of their new life. In contrast,

* From Peter N. Stearns, "Patterns of Industrial Strike Activity in France During the July Monarchy," *American Historical Review,* Vol. LXX, No. 2 (Jan., 1965), pp. 371–94. Reprinted by permission of the *American Historical Review* and the author.

factory workers for the most part had no traditions and no traditional elements to direct them when they entered a new plant, often fresh from the countryside. Their standards of living might differ little from those of urban artisans, but their behavior necessarily differed considerably. Among the many areas of activity where such differences prevailed was that of agitation and strikes. The simple fact was that most of the strike activity of the period, both in quantity and quality, was conducted by urban artisans. For very good reasons, most factory workers protested their lot collectively far less often and, usually, in different ways than did their brethren in the crafts. It is, then, misleading to discuss "the workers" in a study of labor movements in the early years of French industrialization. Such a discussion obscures the bases of the agitation that did take place, and, equally important, it prevents an understanding of the conditions that would later allow the development of strike activity among factory workers. This essay concentrates on sectors of manufacturing labor directly affected by mechanization. By implication it shows many of the factors separating these workers from the urban artisans. It does not, however, discuss the labor movement as a whole because such a single movement really did not exist. The experience of artisans was, at this time, largely irrelevant to factory workers. Only by separating the two classes can the activities of either be properly understood.

Any student of the factory worker in the first decades of French industrialization is struck by an obvious if superficial anomaly. In the midst of conditions of such misery that extreme and frequent protest might be expected, the French industrial worker was almost totally quiescent. Certainly the factors favorable to strikes and other forms of industrial agitation were numerous. In the first place, challenges to the social order had a clear precedent in the traditions of the Great Revolution and even in the events of 1830. Furthermore, the increase in numbers of industrial workers provided a greater quantitative opportunity for strikes to occur; in some fields, such as mining, the labor force actually doubled in the period, though usually the increase was not so great. Growing concentration of industry around certain urban centers also facilitated contacts among workers and was a potential spur to organization. Most important, the workers had ample cause for complaint. In a period when the wealth of the middle classes was increasing noticeably, the lot of most factory labor remained stagnant and depressing. In the plant, the worker was kept under the discipline of both machine and foreman for thirteen hours or more a day. The rewards of this labor were meager. Some workers, in fact, did not earn enough to subsist without charity. The majority could pay for bread, a few clothes, and a tiny apartment, but little or nothing remained after these were provided. Illness, and industrial crisis, or even old age might lower this minimal standard of living still further. Yet, in this period, when industrial conditions were at their worst, protests by factory labor were almost nonexistent.

This is not to say, of course, that there was no strike activity by industrial workers. Jean-Pierre Aguet, in his description of strikes during the July Monarchy, has counted 98 strikes by workers who might be called industrial. Actually, consideration of local reports of agitation reveals a number of strikes not recorded in Aguet's count; at least 40 additional cases can be added to the list as a result of this information, and quite possibly that many more could yet be found by diligent searching. Nevertheless, even a total count of 130 or 150 industrial strikes results in an average of only 7 or 8 a year. And analysis of what is usually included in the category "industrial" detracts even further from the impact of the figures. Aguet, for example, quite sensibly includes in his category mining, metallurgy, machine building, and textiles—all industries affected by the new mechanical methods and organized in part at least in a factory system of production. Of the industries in the group, however, textiles provided the largest number of strikes (82 in Aguet's count). But the textile industry was incompletely transformed by modern industrial methods and systems. To be sure, cotton and wool spinning were vastly altered, but weaving was still largely done by hand, and whole areas of production, such as silk and ribbons, were untouched either by power machinery or by factories. Such industries, particularly the silk manufacturing of Lyons, were among the most productive of strikes; furthermore, their strikes were unusually forceful and well organized. Even aside from such well-known cases, a high percentage of textile strikes were conducted by workers, particularly weavers, who produced either at home or in very small shops. In fact, of the 128 industrial strikes that I have been able to count, 51 of them were conducted by domestic or small shop labor. Actual factory labor was engaging in merely 4 or 5 strikes a year on the average. This paucity is particularly startling because labor as a whole, including artisans, was definitely increasing its activity during the July Monarchy. Aguet has counted 284 strikes by artisans and construction workers, virtually three times the number produced by the industrial categories. To be sure, artisans outnumbered industrial workers, even broadly construed, possibly by as much as two to one; nevertheless, it is clear that industrial labor was not keeping pace with its brethren in the crafts. Both on the basis of absolute numbers of strikes and of relative activity, the sluggishness of industrial labor is clear.

The nature of most industrial strikes, moreover, demonstrates still further the ineffectiveness of factory workers at the time. In the first place, few strikes boasted any real organization or planning; they were usually spontaneous responses to an immediate subject of discontent. Often they were conceived in a tavern the evening before, or even on the same morning as they took place. There was no real leadership, no funds to support the effort. As a result, it was rare for a strike to last more than a single day. In Lille, for example, during the crisis year 1837, workers on short time had the habit of attending band concerts in the late afternoon; one afternoon they replaced the concert with a riot—and that was the extent of Lille's labor agitation that year. In 1838 the thread piecers in Cateau-Cambrésis were incited by some spinners not to work on Ash Wednesday; they spent all day in a bar and then rioted around closing time. Strikes of this sort served mainly to vent a complaint for the satisfaction of the strikers themselves. They could not be the vehicles of a prolonged or intensive effort. In addition, they could not hope to attract large numbers. Without planning or organization, many strikes did not go beyond a single plant. Usually strikers in one plant would attempt to arouse their colleagues in neighboring factories, and sometimes they would succeed. But even in a major industrial city such as Lille, worker demonstrations never boasted more than three or four hundred participants; most strikes affected only a few dozen workers. The average strike was brief, small, disorganized, and lacked formal leadership.

It is obvious that workers were in no position to sustain any elaborate links with their fellows in other places. To be sure, workers in Thann sometimes imitated riots by workers in Mulhouse; workers in Bédarieux had even more active contacts with their neighbors in Lodève. And there were reports of some general awareness of the major riots in Lyons and Paris. But seldom did any action result, and almost never was any coherent contact maintained. What initiative there was came from the individual town or city, often even from the individual factory.

Methods employed by strikers naturally reflected the lack of planning and real strength. Labor protests usually took one of two courses. The first was an appeal to the authorities, usually the local government but sometimes the employer himself. A group of workers would abandon the plant, march to city hall, and present a verbal petition. A soothing speech from the mayor, urging patience and resignation, would calm all passions, and the workers would disperse in an orderly manner. This was the pattern of most labor agitation in Tourcoing during the depression year 1847. Workers there, and often elsewhere, were simply too resigned to do more than briefly demonstrate in the hope that some higher power would solve their problems. When the higher power refused, they had no other recourse. Often, however, workers went beyond the humble petition or did not attempt it at all. In such cases, a strike usually involved considerable violence against property. Frequently the windows of the employer's home or of the factory would bear the brunt of the anger. In Elbeuf in 1846, employees of a man who had introduced a new wool-cleaning machine massed around his home, shouting threats and breaking windows; troops were required to break up the riot. But the attack could focus on machines or on bakers' shops as well. No matter what the target, the pattern was usually the same: an hour or two of intense violence, and then the strike would be over. Again, there was no possibility of constructive or prolonged strike action. At best, it could be hoped that a show of wrath would induce concessions out of fear. But usually the thinking of strikers did not seem to go this far. The strike, with its violence, was an expression of pent-up emotion and hostility; it was not a tool to achieve lasting improvements in conditions. Once passions found expression in an hour or two of howling riot, and were perhaps calmed by a certain amount of fatigue, there was nothing left of the strike.

Seldom did striking factory workers have any long-range goals in mind. Here again, the basic weakness and inadequacy of industrial agitation in the period were reflected. Workers generally struck for a single purpose only; they could not formulate a series of demands. More important, they were seldom capable of envisaging long-range improvement in their conditions. As a result, most industrial strikes were protests against some immediate change in the workers' situation. In most cases, strikes were called solely to protest a lowering of pay, and all that was usually demanded was a return to the previous level. A reduction of wages provided a definite issue and a definite purpose. Further, the announcement of reduction was the sort of clear-cut, single event against which grievance could be most easily directed, particularly since the announcement usually found workers assembled or assembling for work. Most strikes, then, took place immediately upon workers' hearing the news of a pay cut, or within the next twenty-four hours, after a night of rising excitement and hasty planning. Characteristically, spinners in Dornach in 1830 walked out as a result of an announcement of salary reduction, which was made in particularly unsympathetic terms; in 1847, wool spinners of the Ménage plant in Elbeuf struck the day after a similar announcement.

In a smaller number of cases, other changes provided the goals for some strikes. Often, agitation focused on a rise in food prices, the introduction of machines, or rising unemployment. Sometimes even changes in systems of work that had no particularly adverse effect on workers would give rise to strike. Again, change was the only phenomenon clear enough to rouse factory labor, however rarely, from its lethargy. Industrial strikes were overwhelmingly designed simply to defend the *status quo* against deterioration. Hence most industrial strikes took place during business slumps. Then alone was change sufficiently drastic to goad apathetic workers into brief protest. In many cases the workers who struck were simply expressing the abysmal misery of unemployment and hunger. Tragically, however, a strike or riot during a crisis period was almost doomed to failure because employers had neither desire nor need to improve conditions of labor when their own profits were often being reduced or even eliminated. Only a strike in prosperous times had a real chance of effecting permanent improvements in conditions. But in prosperity industrial workers were incapable of formulating demands because there was no adverse change to provide the goal for action. In contrast, strikes of artisans increased in number during prosperous years, for many artisans could plan and organize for the future and could understand something of the economic forces under which they operated. During the boom months from September 1833 to April 1834, for example, Aguet counted fifty strikes by artisans, only nine by industrial labor—far above the ratio for the period as a whole. For factory workers, protest during relatively good times was years in the future. During the July Monarchy, they remained quiet unless given an obvious stimulus in the form of some alteration of their lot. And even then, the vast majority of pay reductions and dismissals passed by without a hint of protest from their victims.

Factory labor, lacking the ability to act except under the stimulus of immediate deterioration of conditions, was not in a position to be stirred by doctrinal influences. In contrast, leaders of artisan movements, especially in Paris and Lyons, often had a definite, if hazy, ideological bent; as a result their approach was more diversified and even stronger, in the sense that it did not depend so heavily on specific economic changes. There were, of course, a number of active socialist propagandists who tried occasionally to make contact with factory workers, but they were almost always completely unsuccessful. The workers were neither ready nor able to be roused by any talk of rights or justice. What industrial protest there was lacked any support from general ideas or programs.

The confused quality of the sporadic industrial agitation was reflected, finally, in the lack of any consistent object of attack. Most commonly, to be sure, grievances were directed against employers. But there were several other directions that protest could take. In cases where rising prices competed with falling wages for workers' attention, bakery shops and their owners were as likely to be attacked as were the plant and its director. The only real agitation in the whole period on the part of Troyes cotton workers focused on bakers alone. There were several instances, also, of attacks on machines as the cause of misery; it was felt that destruction of machines would result in an improvement of conditions for workers generally. Hence in 1830 Lille thread twisters expressed their discontent at the unemployment and low pay that were part of the industrial crisis of that year by demonstrating against machines. Finally, there were a number of riots against other workers, particularly foreigners—another possible scapegoat for unsatisfactory conditions. In sum, the protests of factory labor in this period expressed much bitterness and generalized unhappiness. But there was no clear focus for this intense feeling, and no clear conception of what improvements could be brought about and by what methods.

Chapter V.

THE MIDDLE CLASS

FEW SURVEYS of any major topic in nineteenth-century history avoid some use of the term and concept "middle class." Contemporary observers, whether Socialist, Liberal, or Conservative, talked of the middle class, either as a menace or as the mainstay of a progressive society. Publicists who addressed themselves to businessmen and professional people sensed the middle class as a distinctive social grouping, remote from the idleness of the aristocracy and the apathy or immorality of the masses of poor. And certainly, historians of industrialization, liberalism, and even culture and demography have found the middle class a vital element of their studies.

Most commonly, the middle class is seen as an economic unit, dominated by businessmen. Characteristic class attitudes of hard work, thrift, and ambition can be praised as motive forces for the economic transformation of the nineteenth century. Equally characteristic attitudes of selfishness, moralism, and harsh individualism can be damned as responsible for much of the suffering which this transformation brought; and socialist historians are not alone in adopting this interpretation. The relevance of middle-class interests to politics seems obvious. Members of the middle class developed increasing political awareness along with their new wealth. They sought to compete actively with the aristocracy for political place, while attempting to keep the lower orders in their place; for this effort, the doctrines of liberalism were evidently appropriate. The economic and family values of the class dictated self-restraint and limitation of the birth rate, which ultimately helped shape the demographic trends of the century. The class extended its influence to formal culture. Middle-class people demanded educational systems useful to their technological and business interests; they demanded a literature and art which would promote good morals and help establish social status. And the class had a missionary zeal. Its members sought, with some success, to convert upper and lower social elements to their values. By this effort as well as by direct gains in wealth and political position, the middle class came to dominate the nineteenth century.

These generalizations probably seem familiar enough. Like most such generalizations, they are correct in many ways. They have, however, only rarely been subjected to close historical examination. The term middle class has been a catch-all for historians. Its validity is usually assumed, rather than tested. Yet the importance of the class cries out for detailed study. In recent years, a variety of new studies have been undertaken, accompanied, understandably, by a wide range of questioning and debate.

The difficulty of finding and selecting sources for the study of the middle class has retarded careful research and facilities controversy. The class was not an institution; it left no well-defined records. Individual members, particularly politicians and formal intellectuals, were articulate, and it is tempting to use their views as representative of the whole. But is this valid? Recent work has increasingly opened up business archives, family papers, and records of wills and marriage settlements, but the problem of finding comprehensive information has not been fully solved.

Many of the interpretive problems of dealing with the middle class in the nineteenth century can be easily stated, if not simply solved. The class has been cited and, to varying degrees, studied for most areas of Europe. But how similar was it from nation to nation or, indeed, from city to city? Few careful studies have sought, in fact, to transcend the boundaries of a city or a small region. Generalizations about national middle-class characteristics abound: the cautious French, the politically apathetic German, the culturally philistine English. But the stereotypes are seldom based on intensive comparative analysis; and if they are correct, they severely modify the general applicability of the term middle class.

Chronological variations are no less troubling. Some of the most clearly defining features of the middle class, features that some historians have deemed inseparable from the class, prove on examination to have been rather short-lived. Even the assertive confidence of the class reached a peak around mid-century which waned, or at least became more complicated, thereafter.

Problems of asking where and when, with regard to any historical concept, are reasonably familiar. For the middle class, historians have recently been asking the more penetrating question of whether. Was there a middle class at all? How can it be defined? Should we rather say middle classes? Was it, or were they, conscious of itself, or themselves? For what aspects of social activity was the grouping relevant? [1]

On all sorts of major issues close examination reveals scant coherence within the middle class. There was seldom a common political view, even within a single country, because in fact the political needs of various groups within the class differed widely. Economic and social attitudes of businessmen (not to mention other professions) varied. Some businessmen met the conventional criteria of self-denial and unbounded ambition, but others were devoted to tradition, some self-indulgence, and stability. Harshness toward workers and suspicion of aristocrats varied in degree and changed over time. There are constant problems of defining the limits of the class. The line between middle class and aristocracy is not as neat as a simple statement "absence of title" might imply, partly because—even in nineteenth century—titles could often be acquired. Was a master artisan a member of the middle class? By convention, he usually was in Germany but often was not in France; probably the personal views of the master played a major role in either case. And what is to be done with professional people, distinctive by their education at the very least, and with bureaucrats? Are they the representatives of businessmen (unless they are noble)?

In sum, what criteria can be realistically applied to this vital segment of nineteenth-century society, and will they yield a definable middle class at all? Do we measure by wealth, profession, political stance? Or should more subjective standards

1. For a recent challenge to the concept of the middle class, written in specific rebuttal to Professor O'Boyle's article, see Alfred Cobban, "The 'Middle Class' in France, 1816–1848," *French Historical Studies* (1967), 42–51.

be used: key attitudes, which could be adopted even by peasants or workers, depending on individual psychology; or, relatedly, family habits—who married whom, and with what plans for the family in mind?

The study of the middle class is one of the open subjects of nineteenth-century history. Current doubts about every feature of the class history, including its existence, may conceivably prevail; or they may prove a way station toward a more subtle, vastly more detailed, interpretation. At present, there is a great gap between the confident commonplaces about the middle class, which have been genuinely serviceable in various aspects of nineteenth-century history, and the new detailed research. For the future, the questions remain: Will the conventions be displaced or merely modified? If the former, what will happen to all the related generalizations of economic and political history?

1. E. J. HOBSBAWM: The Age of Revolution, 1789–1848 *

Eric Hobsbawm has produced some of the most varied and stimulating work in social history of any scholar in recent years. His approach is, broadly speaking, Marxist. In this survey of the early nineteenth century, Professor Hobsbawm treats the middle class sweepingly and somewhat critically. He finds it possible to describe a number of key middle-class attitudes, some of which came to characterize the whole society; most basically, he sees a definite class consciousness, defined principally against the aristocracy. Some of the confidence of Professor Hobsbawm's generalizations may be due to his focus on only the manufacturers and only in Britain, though he clearly believes the generalization can be extended.

The effect of the Industrial Revolution on the structure of bourgeois society was superficially less drastic, but in fact far more profound. For it created new *blocs* of bourgeois which coexisted with the official society, too large to be absorbed by it except by a little assimilation at the very top, and too self-confident and dynamic to wish for absorption except on their own terms. In 1820 these great armies of solid businessmen were as yet hardly visible from Westminster, where peers and their relatives still dominated the unreformed Parliament, or from Hyde Park, where wholly unpuritan ladies like Harriete Wilson (unpuritan even in her refusal to pretend to being a broken blossom) drove their phaetons surrounded by dashing admirers from the armed forces, diplomacy, and the peerage, not excluding the Iron and unbourgeois Duke of Wellington himself. The merchants, bankers, and even the industrialists, of the eighteenth century had been few enough to be assimilated into official society; indeed the first generation of cotton millionaires, headed by Sir Robert Peel the elder, whose son was being trained for premiership, were fairly solidly Tory, though of a moderate kind. However, the iron plough of industrialization multiplied its hard-faced crops of businessmen under the rainy clouds of the

* From E. J. Hobsbawm, *The Age of Revolution, 1789–1848* (New York: The World Publishing Co., 1968), pp. 221–26.

North. Manchester no longer came to terms with London. Under the battle-cry "What Manchester thinks today London will think tomorrow" it prepared to impose terms on the capital.

The new men from the provinces were a formidable army, all the more so as they became increasingly conscious of themselves as a *class* rather than a "middle rank" bridging the gap between the upper and lower orders. (The actual term "middle class" first appears around 1812.) By 1834 John Stuart Mill could already complain that social commentators "revolved in their eternal circle of landlords, capitalists, and labourers, until they seemed to think of the distinction of society into these three classes as though it were one of God's ordinances." Moreover, they were not merely a class, but a class army of combat, organized at first in conjunction with the "labouring poor" (who must, they assumed, follow their lead) against the aristocratic society, and later against both proletariat and landlords, most notably in that most class-conscious body the Anti-Corn-Law League. They were self-made men, or at least men of modest origins who owed little to birth, family, or formal higher education. (Like Mr Bounderby in Dickens' *Hard Times,* they were not reluctant to advertise the fact.) They were rich and getting richer by the year. They were above all imbued with the ferocious and dynamic self-confidence of those whose own careers prove to them that divine providence, science, and history have combined to present the earth to them on a platter.

"Political economy," translated into a few simple dogmatic propositions by self-made journalist-publishers who hymned the virtues of capitalism—Edward Baines of the *Leeds Mercury* (1774–1848), John Edward Taylor of the *Manchester Guardian* (1791–1844), Archibald Prentice of the *Manchester Times* (1792–1857), Samuel Smiles (1812–1904)—gave them intellectual certainty. Protestant dissent of the hard Independent, Unitarian, Baptist, and Quaker rather than the emotional Methodist type gave them spiritual certainty and a contempt for useless aristocrats. Neither fear, anger, nor even pity moved the employer who told his workers:

> The God of Nature has established a just and equitable law which man has no right to disturb; when he ventures to do so it is always certain that he, sooner or later, meets with corresponding punishment. . . . Thus when masters audaciously combine that by an union of power they may more effectually oppress their servants, by such an act, they insult the majesty of Heaven, and bring down the curse of God upon themselves, while on the other hand, when servants unite to extort from their employers that share of the profit which of right belongs to the master, they equally violate the laws of equity.

There was an order in the universe, but it was no longer the order of the past. There was only one God, whose name was steam and spoke in the voice of Malthus, McCulloch, and anyone who employed machinery.

The fringe of agnostic eighteenth-century intellectuals and self-made scholars and writers who spoke for them should not obscure the fact that most of them were far too busy making money to bother about anything unconnected with this pursuit. They appreciated their intellectuals, even when, like Richard Cobden (1804–1865), they were not particularly successful businessmen, so long as they avoided unpractical and excessively sophisticated ideas, for they were practical men whose own lack of education made them suspect anything that went much beyond empiricism. Charles Babbage the scientist (1792–1871) proposed his scientific methods to them in vain. Sir Henry Cole, the pioneer of industrial design, technical education, and transport rationalization, gave them (with the inestimable help of the German Prince Consort) the most brilliant monument of their endeavours, the Great Exhibition of 1851. But he was forced out of public life nevertheless as a meddling busybody with a taste for bureaucracy, which, like all government interference, they detested, when it did not directly assist their profits. George Stephenson, the self-made colliery mechanic, dominated the new railways, imposing the gauge of the old horse and cart on them—he had never thought of anything else—rather than the imaginative, sophisticated and daring engineer Isambard Kingdom Brunel, who has no monument in the pantheon of engineers constructed by Samuel Smiles, except the damning phrase: "measured by practical and profitable results the Stephensons were unquestionably the safer men to follow." The philosophic radicals did their best to construct a network of "Mechanics' Institutes" —purged of the politically disastrous errors which the operatives insisted, against nature, on hearing in such places—in order to train the technicians of the new and scientifically based industries. By 1848 most of them were moribund, for want of any general recognition that such technological education could teach the Englishman (as distinct from the German or Frenchman) anything useful. There were intelligent, experimentally minded, and even cultured manufacturers in plenty, thronging to the meetings of the new British Association for the Advancement of Science, but it would be an error to suppose that they represented the norm of their class.

A generation of such men grew up in the years between Trafalgar and the Great Exhibition. Their predecessors, brought up in the social framework of cultured and rationalist provincial merchants and dissenting ministers and the intellectual framework of the Whig century, were perhaps a less barbarous lot: Josiah Wedgwood the potter (1730–1795) was an FRS, a Fellow of the Society of Antiquaries, and a member of the Lunar Society with Matthew Boulton, his partner James Watt, and the chemist and revolutionary Priestley. (His son Thomas experimented with photography, published scientific papers, and subsidized the poet Coleridge.) The manufacturer of the eighteenth century naturally built his factories to the design of Georgian builders' books. Their successors, if not more cultured, were at least more prodigal, for by the 1840s they had made enough money to spend freely on pseudo-baronial residences, pseudo-gothic and pseudo-renaissance town halls, and to rebuild their modest and utilitarian or classic chapels in the perpendicular style. But between the Georgian and the Victorian era there came what has been rightly called the bleak age of the bourgeoisie as well as of the working classes, whose lineaments Charles Dickens has forever caught in his *Hard Times*.

A pietistic Protestantism, rigid, self-righteous, unintellectual, obsessed with puritan morality to the point where hypocrisy was its automatic companion, dominated this desolate epoch. "Virtue," as G. M. Young said, "advanced on a broad invincible front," and it trod the unvirtuous, the weak, the sinful (i.e., those who neither made money nor controlled their emotional or financial expenditures) into the mud where they so plainly belonged, deserving at best only of their betters' charity. There was some capitalist economic sense in this. Small entrepreneurs had to plough back much of their profits into the business if they were to become big entrepreneurs. The masses of new proletarians had to be broken into the industrial rhythm of labour by the most draconic labour discipline, or left to rot if they would not accept it. And yet even today the heart contracts at the sight of the landscape constructed by that generation:

> You saw nothing in Coketown but what was severely workful. If the members of a religious persuasion built a chapel there—as the members of eighteen religious persuasions had done—they made it a pious warehouse of red brick, with sometimes (but this only in highly ornamented examples) a bell in a bird-cage on the top of it. . . . All the public inscriptions in the town were painted alike, in severe characters of black and white. The jail might have been the infirmary, the infirmary might have been the jail, the town hall might have been either, or both, or anything else, for anything that appeared to the contrary in the graces of their construction. Fact, fact, fact, everywhere in the material aspect of the town; fact, fact, fact, everywhere in the immaterial. . . . Everything was fact between the lying-in hospital and the cemetery, and what you couldn't state in figures, or show to be purchaseable in the cheapest market and saleable in the dearest, was not and never should be, world without end, Amen.

This gaunt devotion to bourgeois utilitarianism, which the evangelicals and puritans shared with the agnostic eighteenth-century "philosophic radicals" who put it into logical words for them, produced its own functional beauty in railway lines, bridges, and warehouses, and its romantic horror in the smoke-drenched endless grey-black or reddish files of small houses overlooked by the fortresses of the mills. Outside it the new bourgeoisie lived (if it had accumulated enough money to move), dispensing command, moral education and assistance to missionary endeavour among the black heathen abroad. Its men personified the money which proved their right to rule the world; its women, deprived by their husbands' money even of the satisfaction of actually doing household work, personified the virtue of their class: stupid ("be good sweet maid, and let who will be clever"), uneducated, impractical, theoretically unsexual, propertyless, and protected. They were the only luxury which the age of thrift and self-help allowed itself.

The British manufacturing bourgeoisie was the most extreme example of its class, but all over the Continent there were smaller groups of the same kind: Catholic in the textile districts of the French North or Catalonia, Calvinist in Alsace, Lutheran pietist in the Rhineland, Jewish all over Central and Eastern Europe. They were rarely quite as hard as in Britain, for they were rarely quite as divorced from older traditions of urban life and paternalism. Léon Faucher was painfully struck, in spite of his doctrinaire liberalism, by the sight of Manchester in the 1840s, as which Continental observer was not? But they shared with the English the confidence which came from steady enrichment—between 1830 and 1856 the marriage portions of the Dansette family in Lille increased from 15,000 to 50,000 francs—the absolute faith in economic liberalism, and the rejection of non-economic activities. The spinners' dynasties of Lille maintained their total contempt for the career of arms until the first world war. The Dollfus of Mulhouse dissuaded their young Frédéric Engels from entering the famous Polytechnique, because they feared it might lead him into a military rather than a business career. Aristocracy and its pedigrees did not to begin with tempt them excessively: like Napoleon's marshals they were themselves ancestors.

2. LENORE O'BOYLE: The Middle Class in Western Europe *

Professor Lenore O'Boyle, of Connecticut College, is primarily interested in German history, but here undertakes a major survey of the early nineteenth-century middle class in western Europe generally. She believes that the class existed, but also finds a need for definition and proof that Hobsbawm largely ignored; and in her treatment the middle class, although comparable across national boundaries and forming an ultimate social whole, must be broken down into professional segments for actual study. Professor O'Boyle's basic interest in the middle class is political, an assessment of the class's rise to power and the impact this had on the political process. It might be suggested that this is the most difficult of all aspects of a social class to assess because of the diversity of ideas, regional situations, even of political rights involved.

About twenty years ago David Thomson wrote of the middle class as "this peculiarly self-raising class" and noted that "To explain broad historical development by the 'rise of the middle classes' has become an overworked device of historians."[1] Today there seems to be growing dissatisfaction with the abstraction "middle class," a feeling that the concept does not adequately express what historians know about events. Alfred Cobban has recently expressed this dissatisfaction in a learned and stimulating study, *The Social Interpretation of the French Revolution*.[2] David Pinkney is engaged in an interesting re-examination of the bourgeoisie in the French Revolution of 1830.[3]

Cobban argues that the theory of the Revolution as the overthrow of feudalism by the bourgeoisie is a historical myth. Merchants, financiers, and manufac-

* From Lenore O'Boyle "The Middle Class in Western Europe," *American Historical Review*, Vol. LXXI (April, 1966), pp. 827–32; 835–36; 844–45.

1. David Thomson, *Democracy in France: The Third and Fourth Republics* (2d ed., London, 1952), 53.

2. Alfred Cobban, *The Social Interpretation of the French Revolution* (Cambridge, Eng., 1964).

3. D. H. Pinkney, "The Myth of the French Revolution of 1830," in *A Festschrift for Frederick B. Artz*, ed. *id.* and Theodore Ropp (Durham, N.C., 1964), 52–71.

turers did not lead the Revolution, and the Revolution did not result in the kind of legislation that would have best expressed business views and interests. The Revolution was prepared and led by the professional and official classes. Far from being a movement for capitalism, it was largely the means by which the peasant proprietors, lawyers, *rentiers,* and men of property in the towns successfully resisted the encroachments of early capitalism into French society. The result of the Revolution, Cobban concludes, was the consolidation of power in the hands of a new aristocracy of landowners.

Pinkney examines changes in the personnel of state in 1830 and finds that the *grande bourgeoisie* did not gain any significantly increased hold on public office. From this fact he argues that the Revolution did not represent, as is usually said, the accession of the *grande bourgeoisie* to power. A major purge of government personnel did take place, but the effect of this was to give office to a different group of individuals, not to a new class. "After the Revolution the landed proprietors, the official class, and the professional men continued to predominate in the key offices of state as they had under the Empire and the Bourbon Restoration. Here the Revolution had introduced no new regime of the *grande bourgeoisie.*"[4]

Cobban's study raises very complex problems. Here it can only be suggested that what seems to trouble him is a too close identification of bourgeoisie or middle class with the businessmen; it is as if every time middle-class victory were mentioned this had to be taken to mean a victory for the business interests, or capitalists. Yet does not the concept of the middle class just as often, and as properly, refer to the middling ranks of society, those intermediate between the laboring class and the aristocratic landowners? R. R. Palmer in *The Age of the Democratic Revolution* uses the term in that way and includes the businessmen as only one element in the middle class.[5] Indeed without such a usage it is hard to see how historians could generalize about the period from 1750 to 1850. It appears undeniable that basic changes in European society did take place during that time and that these changes were bound up very closely with the growth in power and importance of those who were neither laborers nor members of the traditional privileged groups. To describe such long-term changes, as Palmer does, the term "middle class" can be justified as economical and accurate. The question probably reduces itself to a matter of time perspective. It is when shorter periods of time are involved that "middle class" becomes, not wrong, but simply unhelpful, because it obscures the complex relations among the various groups within the middle class. Cobban, for example, seems to have had the direction of his work largely determined by his initial realization of how large a part was played in the French Revolution by professional men and state officials. No one has drawn attention more effectively to the role of the lawyers in the Revolution,[6] and in 1956 he wrote, "The class that is omitted in

4. *Ibid.,* 71.
5. R. R. Palmer, *The Age of the Democratic Revolution: A Political History of Europe and America, 1760–1800* (2 vols., Princeton, N.J., 1959, 1964).
6. Alfred Cobban, *The Myth of the French Revolution* (London, 1955).

most interpretations of social history, the official class, may be one of the most important classes of all. . . ."[7] His work is most valuable to the degree that he suggests, not that the term "middle class" is meaningless and should be abandoned, but that it needs fuller study in terms of its main components, the businessmen, the free professions, and the state officials.

One would expect historians to find this question of the interrelationship among the elements of the middle class an interesting one, but there has been surprisingly little attempt to think about the problem in any systematic way. There is a considerable amount of scattered observation about the behavior of professions and officials at particular times and places, and a certain amount of speculation, much of it desultory and offhand. The attempt to formulate generalizations about the way in which these three middle-class elements interacted, however, has seldom been made. Were the three elements of equal importance, or did one dominate? Through what means did one group succeed in determining the actions of the other two? What common aims held the three together? Conversely, how did their interests differ, how much, and with what results for themselves and the greater society? Was one of the elements more exposed than the other two to the pressure of the greater society? The following discussion represents an attempt to take some of the findings of contemporary scholarship that seem relevant and to see if they can be pieced together to yield some general framework in which the West European middle class in the period 1815–1848 can be explained.[8]

The initially striking fact about the businessmen is their apparent lack of interest in political power; their immediate aims were profit and status. It was the realization that to achieve these goals they needed a certain type of society that led the businessmen to consider the acquisition of political power, but only so much as was necessary to achieve social equality and the right to the unre-

7. *Id.*, "The Vocabulary of Social History," *Political Science Quarterly*, LXXI (Mar. 1956), 10.

8. Class is, of course, an economic category, and Karl Marx was correct, at least for the early nineteenth century, in seeing relationship to the means of production as decisive. What the members of the middle class had in common was capital, in the form of either money or skill. Marx was chiefly interested in money capital used in industry; it is probably from his emphasis that the tendency has come to identify the middle class with the businessmen and to neglect the intellectuals whose capital was their acquired specialized abilities. Max Weber's definition of class as a group who share a common chance in the market is perhaps more satisfactory. In the following discussion businessmen are defined as all those whose main occupation was manufacturing, commerce, or banking. The professions are likewise defined by enumeration; they were the lawyers, doctors, teachers, journalists, engineers, and so forth. It is usual to distinguish these as the "free professions," in contrast to the state officials. The category of state officials can be used in a broad sense to include all those whose chief occupation was the management of state affairs. It is common usage, however, to distinguish between elected officials—"politicians"—and career officials—"bureaucrats." The many minor state employees are not as a rule considered state officials, but rather professional men. Occupation is the decisive factor in classification. For example, a lawyer may be also a state official, or a state employee, or a politician; his chief occupation decides to which group he is assigned. Source of income is not considered crucial. A man whose chief occupation was the management of public affairs but who drew his income mainly from land would be considered a state official; a man whose career was teaching but who drew his income largely from business investments would be classified as a teacher. It will be immediately obvious that the landed interest is omitted as a chief component of the middle class. The omission will be discussed in the body of the article in relation to France.

strained search for profit. What evidence there is does not indicate that the ordinary man of business wanted to exercise political power directly and to form part of the political elite of paid officeholders and elected officials. Presumably the members of the business group had neither time nor aptitude to involve themselves in the full-time process of decision making. They did identify with the movement for representative government, but even this demand was to some extent forced upon them by the unwillingness of existing governments to provide institutions suitable for the new economy. Eighteenth-century French businessmen did not, after all, start from constitutional demands but from the desire for social and administrative reforms; it was the weakness of the monarchy and the pretensions of the nobility that pushed the reform movement in a political direction. In the same period English manufacturers and merchants showed little interest in agitation for parliamentary reform, and some apparently felt resentment at the attempt to involve them in politics. They acted promptly enough when they felt their interests threatened; William Pitt's initial condescension and lack of consideration toward the manufacturers changed in time to respect and cooperation.[9]

In the first half of the nineteenth century it was in England, if anywhere, that one would have expected the businessmen to claim predominant control in government. Instead there was a basic class harmony built largely on the businessmen's willingness to leave extensive political power in the hands of the landed interest.[10] In France businessmen did not predominate even in the so-called bourgeois governments of Louis Philippe.[11] Certainly they did not in the governments of the German states before 1848.[12] Even the political theory of

9. Witt Bowden, *Industrial Society in England towards the End of the Eighteenth Century* (New York, 1925), 162 ff.; Simon Maccoby, *English Radicalism 1762–1785: The Origins* (London, 1955), 441. Palmer, *Democratic Revolution,* II, 24–26, judges that throughout Europe in the years just before 1800 the businessmen seldom took any initiative in bringing on revolution, but once revolution was an accepted fact they very commonly supported it and benefited from it.

10. It was not until 1885 that commercial men and manufacturers outnumbered landowners in the House of Commons. (F. M. L. Thompson, *English Landed Society in the Nineteenth Century* [London, 1963], 276–79.) Some studies of the personnel of the House of Commons in the nineteenth century are J. A. Thomas, "The House of Commons," *Economica,* V (Mar. 1925), 49–61; S. F. Wooley, "The Personnel of the Parliament of 1833," *English Historical Review,* LIII (Apr. 1938), 240–62. W. O. Aydelotte's forthcoming study of Parliament in the 1840's should be of outstanding importance. Among his already published articles may be mentioned "The House of Commons in the 1840's," *History,* XXXIX (Oct. 1954), 249–62, "Voting Patterns in the British House of Commons in the 1840's," *Comparative Studies in Society and History,* V (Jan. 1963), 134–63, "On the Business Interests of the Gentry in the Parliament of 1841–47," appendix in G. Kitson Clark, *The Making of Victorian England* (Cambridge, Mass., 1962), 200–305.

11. Ch.-H. Pouthas, "Les ministres de Louis-Philippe," *Revue d'histoire moderne et contemporaine,* I (Apr.–June 1954), 102–30. In regard to elected assemblies, one notes a franchise heavily weighted in favor of the landowners and the importance of the official element among the deputies. On the franchise, see Sherman Kent, *Electoral Procedure under Louis-Philippe* (New Haven, Conn., 1937); on the composition of the Chamber, see S. Charlety, "La Restauration (1815–1830)," in *Histoire de France contemporaine depuis la Révolution jusqu'à la paix de 1919,* ed. Ernst Lavisse (10 vols., Paris, 1920–22), IV, 91, 196, 331, and "La monarchie de Juillet (1830–1848)," *ibid.,* V, 161, 300, 347.

12. Jacques Droz, *Les révolutions allemandes de 1848* (Paris, 1957), 33 ff.

Western liberal parties reflected this unwillingness to assume the sole burden of political decision. In France theorists like François Guizot and Pierre Royer-Collard, quintessentially bourgeois in mentality, expounded the doctrine of the sovereignty of reason and warned against locating sovereign power in any one group of men.[13] Exponents of German liberalism assumed a division of sovereignty between a ruler and a representative assembly who were to cooperate in establishing the rule of law.[14] This refusal to accept the responsibilities of power could even be used as a basis for moral censure of the nineteenth-century middle class, and was so used by Karl Marx.[15]

If business did not choose to rule directly, how then did it exert influence? That it did exert influence seems indisputable; there is no other explanation for the restructuring of Western European society in this period to suit the convenience of business interests. In the nature of the case, the indirect exertion of power is hard to see clearly. Here it is suggested that the problem can be approached in at least three different but complementary ways: first, study of the types and functioning of business organizations; second, investigation of the personnel of government; third, analysis of the interaction of society and culture.

As for business organizations, it is obvious enough that businessmen developed a variety of pressure groups, techniques of lobbying, and methods of influencing public opinion through the press. In representative systems they helped to organize and finance political parties. Beyond such general knowledge, however, comparatively little detailed work is known to me, and, without a basis of specialized studies, significant generalization about the functioning of business organizations as a common European phenomenon in this period cannot be expected.[16]

More can be said about the study of government personnel; here the crucial fact is certainly the predominance of professional men, lawyers above all. These were the men who accomplished business' purposes. Jean Lhomme, in his excellent study *La grande bourgeoisie au pouvoir (1830–1880)*, has developed the useful idea of clientage.

Sans qu'il soit nécessaire de remonter jusqu'aux clientèles romaines, on sait que des liens unissent très souvent telles personnes à telle autre, plus puissante, par exemple plus riche. Ce sont des liens *individuels,* créés par la dépendance. Ils sont récip-

13. Gabriel Rémond, *Royer-Collard: Son essai d'un système politique* (Paris, 1933); Douglas W. Johnson, *Guizot: Aspects of French History, 1787–1874* (London, 1963); Lothar Gall, *Benjamin Constant: Seine politische Ideenwelt und der deutsche Vormärz* (Wiesbaden, 1963).

14. E. R. Huber, *Deutsche Verfassungsgeschichte seit 1789* (2 vols., Stuttgart, 1957–60), II, 309–23, 371–90.

15. For an interesting contemporary restatement of Marx's indictment, see Hannah Arendt, *The Origins of Totalitarianism* (2d ed., Cleveland, 1958), Pt. I.

16. Much more may have been done in this direction than I know. French historians in particular have recently shown great interest in special economic studies; one need only mention names such as Georges Duveau, Bertrand Gille, and Paul Leuilliot.

roques, mais asymétriques, ce qui correspond bien à l'idée d'un pouvoir. Le supérieur exerce, par définition, son pouvoir sur l'inférieur; mais, en même temps, le supérieur n'est pas sans dépendre, d'une manière quelconque, de son inférieur.[17]

The value of this particular concept lies in its applicability to a wide range of relationships whose essential similarity is not immediately obvious. The businessman and the professional in our period could be linked in a variety of ways, more or less direct, more or less obvious. At one extreme would be the very marked dependence of the lawyer directly employed by a chamber of commerce or the journalist editing a newspaper owned by a banker. More complex and problematical would be the case of an elected representative in England or France. He might have gained his seat by direct purchase of votes, with the purchase money coming from a rich patron, in which case his debts would be clear. He might, however, have owed a variety of obligations to party backers, press owners, and accommodating bankers; his dependency, being thus diffuse, would be masked and might lack almost any element of personal subordination. Career officials in the bureaucracy would seem to have been comparatively removed from any dependent relationship, but even they could have been subjected to pressure through promises or threats regarding promotion, and by way of direct or indirect financial aid.[18]

17. "Without having to go back to Roman clientage, we know that there were often bonds between some people and another person, more powerful, possibly richer. These are *individual* bonds created by dependence. They are reciprocal but unequal, which fits the idea of a government. The superior exercises, by definition, his power over the inferior; but, at the same time, the superior is not without some sort of dependence on his inferior." [Ed.] Jean Lhomme, *La grande bourgeoisie au pouvoir (1830–1880): Essai sur l'histoire sociale de la France* (Paris, 1960), 254–55.

18. Lhomme's approach seems fully congruent with René Rémond's interesting analysis in *La droite en France de 1815 à nos jours* (Paris, 1954). Rémond reviews the July Monarchy as a government of elites, the notables of birth, fortune, and intelligence; he notes the high proportion of men who rose only through talent and intelligence. As for England, for an interesting picture of the symbiotic relationship between the landlord and his various retainers, see Thompson, *English Landed Society,* 95, 151. In England patronage and purchase were the chief methods of selecting public officials until 1870. Some prominent critics of the liberals in the eighteenth and nineteenth centuries showed a measure of condescension or contempt for the professional. Edmund Burke charged that the lawyers worked for revolution to further their private ends, seeking the "innumerable lucrative jobs which follow in the train of all great convulsions and revolutions in the state. . . ." He saw the worst elements in the nobility betraying their fellow nobles so that in the "spoil and humiliation of their own order these individuals would possess a sure fund for the pay of their new followers." (Edmund Burke, "Reflections on the Revolution in France," in *The Works of the Right Honorable Edmund Burke* [12 vols., Boston, 1899], III, 287, 292.) Henri Saint-Simon denounced lawyers and metaphysicians as bastard classes who sold their services to the highest bidder. (F. E. Manuel, *The New World of Henri Saint-Simon* [Cambridge, Mass., 1956], 266–67.) Baron Heinrich vom Stein planned representative assemblies composed of nobles, landowners, and peasants, but wanted to exclude lawyers and the usual men of letters. (Fritz Valjavec, *Die Entstehung der politischen Strömungen in Deutschland, 1770–1815* [Munich, 1951], 387.) Marx and Engels wrote in general of the professionals as "the *ideological* representatives and spokesmen of the above classes [i.e., bourgeoisie and peasantry], their savants, lawyers, doctors, etc., in a word: their so-called *talents.*" (Karl Marx, "The Class Struggles in France, 1848–1850," in *Selected Works,* ed. V. V. Adoratsky and C. P. Dutt [2 vols., New York, 1933], II, 194.) Marx himself might, at least at one point, have been classified as one of "their . . . *talents*" since he served as editor of the *Rheinische Zeitung,* a paper founded in 1842 primarily to express the viewpoint of a group of leading business and professional men in Cologne. (Josef Hansen,

Thirdly, understanding of the interaction of society and culture can clarify the ways in which business interests determined nineteenth-century society. In any society the importance of those who control the means of production is obvious. Direct pressure on government is hardly needed to ensure that every consideration be given to the economic elite. Such consideration, moreover, is in the main accepted as proper, not only by the wealthy but by all classes. The values of the economic elite become the common values. It is surely in this sense that Marx is to be understood when he speaks of a society's culture as the superstructure built on the material base, and the state as the executive committee of the ruling class. A bureaucracy is composed of men reared to accept the prevailing values of their society; their spontaneous tendency will be to preserve the existing society and its hierarchy. Revolutionaries do not become state officials, or, if they do, they soon cease to be revolutionaries or cease to be officials. In early nineteenth-century Europe the bureaucrat was himself in most cases a member of the middle or noble class and the product of a higher education built on dominant social attitudes and values. There was then really no paradox in the fact that governments whose personnel was never composed mainly or even largely of businessmen followed policies that were essentially more favorable to business than to other interests of society.[19] . . .

In politics the professionals had obvious grounds for cooperation with both business and officials. All three groups were egalitarian in so far as that meant the career open to talent and an end to aristocratic privilege. They shared a bias in favor of policies determined by purely rational considerations rather than tradition. Each of the three stood to benefit from any growth in the size and complexity of society since such growth meant a corresponding increase in the demands for goods and professional services. These common values and aspirations made for a degree of unity in action among the three groups that justifies use of the term "middle class." The term should not, however, be used in such a way as to obscure the differences and tensions among businessmen, professionals, and officials. Professional men could not approve the putative materialism of businessmen and some of the social consequences of business activity. Tensions also arose from the disparity in economic rewards and social prestige enjoyed by businessmen and the professions. The most important differences, however, arose between business and professional men on the one hand and state officials on the other. Businessmen and the professionals distrusted the

Gustav von Mevissen [2 vols., Berlin, 1906], I, 245–62.) The theme of patronage appears frequently in nineteenth-century novels. It is prominent in all of Honoré de Balzac and Stendhal. In England one may note especially Maria Edgeworth's *Patronage* (1814), Jane Austen's *Mansfield Park* (1814), George Eliot's *Middlemarch* (1871–72), Anthony Trollope's *Phineas Finn* (1869). Interesting analyses of the dependent character of the professional men in the later nineteenth century in Russia and the United States are George Fischer, *Russian Liberalism: From Gentry to Intelligentsia* (Cambridge, Mass., 1958), and Richard Hofstadter, *The Age of Reform: From Bryan to F.D.R.* (New York, 1955), 135–55.

19. See notes 10, 11, 12, above. A work like Emmanuel Beau de Loménie, *Les responsabilités des dynasties bourgeoises* (2 vols., Paris, 1943–47), offers strong evidence in support of the argument that France from the time of the Revolution was in actuality governed by a number of great business families.

state, resented its direction of their activities, and increasingly demanded more personal and economic freedom; state officials quite naturally tended to enlarge the sphere of state action and to judge any opposition to themselves as a reflection of group self-interest.

The role of the state officials is probably the most difficult to analyze. They were professional men, inasmuch as they had special intellectual skills and lived by the sale of them. There was, however, an ambivalence toward the dominant economic groups built into their role. On the one hand the official's chief professional obligation was to preserve the stability and well-being of the state, and accordingly he had no choice but to pay attention to the economic elite on whose functioning so much of the country's strength depended. On the other hand, since the welfare of the total society is never perfectly coincident with the interests of any one group no matter how important economically, the state official in the exercise of his profession found himself forced to override any class interest that he judged inimical to the social welfare.

While the official necessarily had an ambivalent attitude toward the dominant economic interests, he in turn was more or less distrusted and opposed by them. In representative systems this tension was even institutionalized in the relationship between career officials and elected representatives, the career official identifying with the state, the elected official identifying with a specific social group and as a rule expressing resentment and distrust of bureaucratic regulation.[20] In both representative and nonrepresentative systems, however, this clash between official and nonofficial was always mitigated by common class membership, for the state official was by background and education, or by choice, almost always a member of the upper class that disputed control of the state.

In conclusion, it may be suggested that the above analysis has a bearing on problems of social stability and social change in this period.

Businessmen, professionals, and state officials helped to preserve a stable society because each group worked for the same ends and each profited from the success of the others. The businessmen used and rewarded the intellectuals to perform those functions for which business direction was unsuited. In return the intellectuals worked toward the creation of a type of society in which the economically dominant groups could function securely: the bureaucrat ran the political machinery; the teacher and journalist propagated appropriate values; the lawyer was the indispensable middleman between business and the state. The universities formed the bureaucrat; in turn the bureaucrat determined how the universities were to function. All in all, each relationship among the different middle-class groups confirmed adherence to a common set of values, strengthened the unity of the middle class, and made possible the emergence of middle-class, nineteenth-century society.

At the same time, the existence of a measure of independence in the functioning of the bureaucracy and the professions was apparent; it was in this way that necessary social change could be translated into political and moral terms. The

20. This point is developed by Thomson, *Democracy in France,* 58–64.

crucial factor was the way in which professional interest cut across class affiliation. This is not to be explained in terms of the supposed disinterestedness of the professions as contrasted with the selfish search for profit on the part of businessmen or landowners.[21] The professional man wanted success and economic rewards just as the businessman did. It was rather that the professional person worked against his own success if he neglected professional considerations, and thus he found himself at some points required to act in ways that might not directly satisfy the economically dominant groups. The bureaucrat provided the clearest example of this conflict; he could not be totally subservient to the ruling class without harming the state, which it was his professional obligation to safeguard. Similarly, the teacher's obligation was not only to indoctrinate students with prevailing values but also to help them to think objectively and critically, activity as apt to subvert as to consolidate. A successful journalist had to maintain some standards of objectivity. Even the lawyer, who was doubtless tied most closely to the economic elite, had to work within a framework of existing law that was not subject to endless manipulation in his client's interest.

Those who paid for the intellectuals' services may not always have been pleased with what the intellectuals did. Their acceptance of what was done must have involved a belief that it was necessary for the attainment of larger purposes; there was no getting around the fact that without social stability there would be neither private profit nor social status. Moreover, a profession by definition involves esoteric knowledge and special skills; thus outsiders are for the most part incapable of intelligent supervision. The late eighteenth and early nineteenth centuries witnessed a great expansion of the professions, and a striking feature of this growth was the way in which the professions succeeded in becoming largely self-regulating. They developed a high degree of control over the admission of new members, the setting of standards of competence, and the definition of operating procedures. In the case of the state official the acquisition of tenure gave considerable security against interference from both politicians and the public. Clearly this marked an enormous advance in independence against even the most economically powerful.

The hypothesis may be considered that where this professionalism did not develop, government became dangerously identified with one social interest. Class considerations then outweighed the sense of professional responsibility. This seems to have been the case in France before 1848.

3. PETER STEARNS: European Society in Upheaval *

This description of the mid-nineteenth century middle class raises several questions about the coherence or even the existence of the class. The selection

21. See Talcott Parsons' now classic essay, "The Professions and Social Structure," in *Essays in Sociological Theory Pure and Applied* (Glencoe, Ill., 1949), 185–200.

* From Peter Stearns, *European Society in Upheaval* (New York: The Macmillan Company, 1967), pp. 158–62. Reprinted by permission of The Macmillan Company.

does assume that a middle class existed, marked off from lower classes and from the aristocracy by economic differences above all. Unlike Professor O'Boyle, however, the author finds it impossible to define a "middle class politics" that applied to more than a few of the constituent groups in the class. Does this render the concept of a middle class useless, or are there features of the class more comprehensive than political attitudes? The definition of independently coherent subgroups in the class requires assessment, particularly as they do not complement each other as they do in Professor O'Boyle's interpretation. Should a lower middle class be considered apart from the other elements, as a separate class? What of the relationship between professional people and businessmen? Here the two groups fit together most uneasily; their relationship has clearly become a major problem in the historiography of the middle class.

The shopkeeping elements grew to almost half the whole middle class by 1850; but despite the many new opportunities in cities and towns alike, the small size of most shops limited average earnings. About 15 per cent of the group was in a really marginal position with earnings little above those of artisans; some shopkeepers intermarried with artisans and sent their sons into the crafts. Such tiny shopkeepers hovered near the brink of ruin and had little beyond the bare necessities. The average shopkeeper was considerably more affluent; in Paris or London he possessed at least twenty times as much capital as the 80 per cent of the population not in the middle or upper classes. His standard of living was comfortable but not luxurious. He could keep a servant and send his sons at least to primary school. This was a group solidly in the middle class.

Most members of the lower middle class had a fairly firm sense of status in the period. They felt keenly that property ownership, relative wealth, and avoidance of manual labor separated them from lower elements. Hence they usually married within their own group; in Paris approximately 80 per cent of the daughters of shopkeepers married shopkeepers during the period 1820–1848.

At the same time the economic position of this group tended to stagnate. Those who rose into the ranks of shopkeepers usually improved their economic position, but the group itself made no major gains in average wealth. In a city like Paris the average shopkeeper was no better off in 1848 than his counterpart in 1820. And this was in a period when other business groups were gaining rapidly in wealth. The relative economic standing of shopkeepers was slipping, yet it became increasingly difficult to rise into the groups with greater earning power. Some economic operations of the merchants and industrialists competed with those of the lower middle class. In the textile industry small entrepreneurs who in the early years of the industrial revolution had bought a few looms or spinning machines often struggled for years in great hardship, but ultimately had to yield to the greater efficiency of larger competitors. Most retail transactions still took place in small shops, but shopkeepers in big cities did face some competition from new commercial outlets such as department stores.

The lower middle class often suffered burdensome political restrictions not applied to wealthier business or professional men. In France during the July Monarchy the upper-middle class alone could vote; property qualifications limited the suffrage to approximately 250,000 males. Later in the century property qualifications and class voting systems deprived all but the upper-middle class of effective political participation in Italy, where only 2 per cent could vote, and in Prussia. The lower middle class gained the vote in Austria only in the 1880s. The lower-middle class tended to be more radical politically than other elements of the middle class because of its political and economic disadvantages. In France, the group became republican in the late 1840s. After the hardships of the siege of Paris in 1870 shopkeepers joined artisans to form the revolutionary Commune. There was substantial democratic sentiment among shopkeepers in Germany in 1848. Only in Britain, where shopkeepers received the vote along with other elements of the middle class in 1832, was this sort of political division avoided. Generally, the lower middle class proved unable to take full advantage of the opportunity of industrialization and political reform. Its isolation within the middle class increased.

The professional group was distinguished in the middle class by its level of education. In western Europe it represented about 10 percent of the whole middle class. In the east, particularly in Russia, a new professional group was arising by midcentury, largely for government service; until the 1890s it represented the greater part of the middle class.

The growth of the professional group was based on an extension of educational opportunities at the upper levels. Governments everywhere expanded higher educational facilities in the first part of the nineteenth century, largely to support their growing need for bureaucrats. Not only lawyers but also doctors and writers were trained as a result. Between 1809 and 1842 attendance at French *lycées* doubled. Russian university attendance rose from 1,700 in 1825 to 4,600 in 1848.

For the most part jobs kept pace with the increased production of professionals in this period, but in western Europe there was a decline in the relative status of professionals. The prestige of professional work, including government service, declined as industry rose, and the group did not share in the growing wealth of the business elements. There were a few very wealthy, but many poor professionals; average incomes did not rise sharply. The political role of professionals was often threatened. Factory owners sought control of municipal governments, which lawyers had often controlled before, and some national administrative posts were being offered to the masters of industry. Factory owners partially displaced professional people as the leaders of local social groups. Professionals in local artistic and philanthropic societies had to pay increasing deference to the power and wealth of businessmen. Professionals sensed the challenge to their status and often tried to compensate by new forms of political activity.

In eastern Europe there was no business group to rival the professional element, yet professionals had grievances which they often tried to redress through political activities. These people, who had been trained for administrative efficiency, resented the backwardness of their governments. Suppressions of liberty, of the press, and of teaching were matters of immediate importance to the professional group. By midcentury Russian middle-class professionals were taking an increasing role in the intelligentsia. And whereas gentry intellectuals had spoken mainly in liberal terms, the new professionals were often more radical. Nowhere else in Europe did educated professionals feel themselves so distinctive and isolated as in Russia. Nowhere else did so many turn so radical. But everywhere an unusually intense political activism pervaded the professional element in the nineteenth century.

Everywhere professionals were distinguished by their advanced education and receptivity to new ideas. Universities were a principal center of political agitation in western Europe in the early nineteenth century and in Russia by the 1860s; student riots could assume considerable importance. Even outside the university professionals remained the most self-consciously political element of the middle class. Lawyers particularly espoused political causes, but professors and doctors also played a role. Businessmen, of course, had a political interest and often acted as a pressure group to win governmental economic assistance. For the most part, though, their politics were more occasional and more limited to the economic sphere than were those of professional elements. Much of what is termed middle-class politics was the activism of professionals. Politics of various sorts constituted a channel for the energies and goals of professionals during the century. Through politics jobs might be found, ideals expressed and new status achieved.

The majority of the members of political societies such as the Carbonari were from the professional element, and middle-class revolutions were led by professional people. Journalists directed the French revolution of 1830. Professors led the delegation to urge reforms on the king of Prussia in 1848, and lawyers took the major role in the activities of the Frankfurt assembly. As parliamentary regimes spread, professional people again took a leading role as middle-class representatives. In all these activities the professional group worked for interests that the business elements also supported; but it continued to be the most politically conscious segment of the middle class.

A few professional men were unusually interested in social reform, although they often sought business support for their efforts. British doctors like Edwin Chadwick and several doctors and teachers in French cities were among the earliest advocates of labor reform. Many of the most active and articulate critics of business life came from the professional group. They were not representative, but their professional position was directly relevant to their reformist and revolutionary efforts. Most of the initial socialist leadership was derived from the professional class. Early Russian socialists, both Marxist and agrarian, were drawn from the professional intelligentsia.

Leadership within the middle class rested with the larger merchants and industrialists. Within this group there was a fairly clear upper element, for a segment of the economic middle class possessed extraordinary and increasing wealth. In Paris during the July Monarchy 1 per cent of the middle class controlled 30 per cent of the wealth of the class. In 1848 there were only 712 really large merchants in Berlin out of a population of 400,000. Members of this upper middle class had a truly luxurious standard of living. They alone could maintain private mansions in major cities such as London and Paris. They alone could rival the style of life of the wealthy aristocracy. Toward the end of the century, in fact, they increasingly intermarried with the aristocracy, though this was not common before 1850. The economic interests of this group were diverse. Some men started out as industrialists or bankers or large merchants, but most members of the upper middle class steadily diversified their interests, acquiring holdings in industry and commerce and often in banking as well. Most owned some landed property too. The wealth of the group brought it great political power. In many cases this was almost the only middle-class group that could vote, as in Italy after 1861 or France during the July Monarchy. Even in more democratic systems the group had disproportionate political influence. Generally, the upper middle class was the most conservative segment of the bourgeoisie. It had the greatest stake and power in the established order and tried most actively to preserve that order.

Most industrialists and merchants were considerably less wealthy than the upper group. Owners of medium-sized factories, particularly in the textile industry, managers of plants in heavy industry, and many others could afford a high but not luxurious standard of living. They had large apartments or, particularly in factory cities, private homes. Some had country houses as well. The average businessman owned furniture worth half the entire capital of the average shopkeeper. Such businessmen had several servants and a private carriage, but usually not a coachman. They could afford good education for their children. However, many business families went through a period in which they had to restrict their spending in order to build up capital. Often it took almost a generation for successful industrialists to enter a period of substantial expenditure on private consumption. The business group, like the middle class generally, valued material comfort and did not glory in self-denial. As soon as they could, businessmen did increase their spending, particularly on housing. Their diet and clothing were from the first superior to those of the lower classes, and their health was correspondingly much better. However, spending was not unrestrained; the highest levels of luxury were inaccessible to most of the business element.

4. ADÉLINE DAUMARD: The Parisian Bourgeoisie *

Mlle Daumard's book, from which the following selection is drawn, is one of the most detailed studies ever undertaken of a particular middle class.† She

* From Adéline Daumard, *La bourgeoisie parisienne* (Paris: published 1963 by Section VI of the École pratique des Hautes Études, 54 rue de Varenne, Paris, 7e). Reprinted by permission of the École des Hautes Études and the author. Translated by the editor.

† Most French scholars dealing with the nineteenth century use the term "bourgeoisie" in preference to "middle class." It should be noted, however, that the terms may not always mean the same thing, in English or in French; in the eighteenth century, certainly, the bourgeoisie was a legal category far narrower than the "middle class" (if there was one). On the terms themselves, then, there is important debate and, perhaps, significant difference in connotation.

relies extensively on records of marriage contracts and wills to develop an elaborate picture of the diverse economic levels within the class. This selection from her final conclusion cannot, of course, do justice to the richness of the monograph. But it is worth noting that, following such an exhaustive effort, Mlle Daumard finds it both possible and useful to talk about a middle class and portrays it in terms that in many ways seem to confirm the conventional view of the class. Obviously, it should be compared to Cobban's interpretation of the same period. If her approach is accurate, it indicates that the defining characteristics of the middle class consisted of common attitudes more than of precise economic or political position. It is very hard to know the attitudes of a large group, however; it may be that values were the most important attribute of the whole middle class but that historians will always have to rely on incomplete evidence, interpreted as carefully as possible, in order to know what attitudes were shared, and how widely.

Bourgeois society was hierarchical, with great contrasts between the groups at either extreme, with a subtly-graded structure, because of the proliferation of intermediary situations and the multitude of professional activities. The study of these structures has allowed us to suggest a terminology to designate the different social levels. The upper bourgeoisie, headed by the financial aristocracy, dominated a middle group composed of two rather different categories, in terms of levels of wealth and especially of occupations and styles of life: the solid bourgeoisie and the middle bourgeoisie; beneath this, was a level of popular bourgeoisie, which was numerically important. The bulk of our study confirmed this initial classification. It also made it more precise, notably by showing how the upper bourgeoisie can be combined with the national notables and by placing a great number of the representatives of the solid bourgeoisie among the notables of city districts. This hierarchy, however, was neither rigorous nor absolute; the gradations were numerous, and many individuals could belong to several groups, depending on whether one considered their position, their antecedents, or their participation in public life. . . .

Social preeminence was based both on fortune and on position, that is, on material bases and on values which implied a deference to traditions of culture, of prestige, and of influence. But with some few individual exceptions apart, the Parisians in each of the categories that we have enumerated were rich or were destined tc become rich, by the end of their career, through inheritance, marriage, and profit. Not only were they rich, but also they strove to become richer, by expanding the capital which they held. However, as soon as their position was established, they tried to set up a reserve and not to risk heedlessly the capital that assured their rank and their influence in society. Capital was one of the bases of bourgeois society but for contemporaries, wealth, which lost part of its power anyway when it was held by men who lacked a position equal to their riches, was only a symbol of ability and merit for the man who had succeeded in acquiring it or preserving it. To appreciate the full importance of this belief, one must consider the age: Parisian society and economy were undergoing a full transformation and the birth of a new social and economic order cast many established positions into doubt. The importance the Parisian bourgeois attributed, in this period, to the fortune and position acquired by individuals reflected one of the fundamental characteristics of the Parisian bourgeoisie: it rested on a love of risk, on a spirit of enterprise. But the bourgeois took calculated risks; they were not gamblers, they were workers and not speculators; they tried to foresee the future in order to control it and to attain the place in society which they desired. . . .

Effective renewal or, more precisely, the possibility of social advancement was one of the characteristic elements of bourgeois society. The Parisian bourgeois was a man athirst for social prestige. He wished to improve his own lot or that of his children, by trying to acquire a higher position. Wealth, the exercise of a profession or of honorific functions usually brought tangible advantages, but they were also signs of success. In contrast to the aristocrat whose superiority rested on birth, who based his pride on his name and his ancestors, the bourgeois always had to prove his worth to himself and others and needed the approval of society.

The possibilities of renewal in the Parisian bourgeoisie were limited, however. Nothing was organized to facilitate social advancement. The organization of teaching and the conditions of credit, for example, in no way favored ambitious men without fortune or family, whatever their gifts or abilities. . . . To characterize the Parisian bourgeoisie, especially in the last ten years of the reign of Louis-Philippe, during which acquired positions were being consolidated, we must define it not as a mobile society but rather as a setting for expansion. Prosperity was thus an indispensable factor for the equilibrium of bourgeois society.

The numerical importance of the petty bourgeoisie and of the middle groups could increase almost indefinitely, but there were limits to the expansion of the upper groups. At the end of the reign of Louis-Philippe, all the intermediary levels between the petty and upper bourgeoisie remained, no category was clearly set apart, but a bourgeois aristocracy was beginning to arise, separated from the rest of the Parisian bourgeoisie not only by its wealth and power in economic life and in the state, but also by its increasing exclusiveness in recruitment and by some of its reactions, which were more and more becoming distinctive in matters such as politics. The development of this bourgeois aristocracy risked giving a fixed quality to Parisian society, in opposition to the dogma of mobility which was central to bourgeois psychology. This intensified social distinctions, this threatened the unity of the Parisian bourgeoisie. . . .

In spite of these divergences, in spite of the contrast of wealth, positions, and reactions, the bourgeoisie was a single class, for even when they behaved differently, all Parisian bourgeois obeyed the same imperative, they had the same soul.

The Parisian bourgeois were free men. This point is so fundamental that it is almost a characteristic in itself, but we must specify that this freedom was a psychological need before becoming an economic and social reality. In effect, many professions implied varying degrees of dependence. Even apart from those who lived on a salary, many apparently independent bourgeois lacked complete autonomy; heads of businesses, for example, had always been at the mercy of the reliability of their debtors and the demands of their creditors, but the development of credit, of discount, and especially of joint stock operations, in short, the beginning of industrial and commercial associations ultimately reduced the role of strictly individual initiative. However, the tendency toward concentration was barely begun; the only true limit to economic liberty was set by import tariffs, but the principle of State protection was not incompatible with liberalism. Liberty, likewise, was easily reconciled to the constraint of laws. The love of liberty was one aspect of the individualism of Parisian bourgeois. They sought to be independent. To attain a specific objective, to succeed in an enterprise or a career, they might be led to compromise, but all, rich or poor, powerful or insignificant had the ideal of becoming the masters of their own destiny.

Control and direction involve choice and the exercise of foresight. The bourgeois was above all a man of choice and the option among several possibilities was one of the forms of his liberty, an aspect of his individualism. In their private life members of the bourgeoisie had possibilities of choice, when they were to choose a career, in most circumstances of their professional life, even when they planned to retire from active life to live on their investments. Certainly, the pressure of events was felt more within the lower levels, but the opportunity to make decisions remained a characteristic trait of the bourgeois, who did not live from day to day but who could and had to envisage a longer period, under penalty of failure. Likewise the bourgeoisie had responsibilities to take in its public life, for example as voters, national guardsmen, or jurors. As citizens or private individuals, the bourgeoisie was sustained by traditions and customs, by a whole civilization that was impressed strongly on its mind and conscience, although it was only incompletely expressed. But the class obeyed no absolute imperatives. Each individual created his own rules for life. Proud of the possibilities open to human intelligence, the members of the bourgeoisie organized their private life and their personal future. A supplementary stage was passed when the class turned to the destinies of the whole society. Laws still affected only a part of human activity, but bourgeois civilization is based on a faith in reason and planning is its logical result.

Foresight and liberty are reconcilable only with difficulty. This caused the weakness of the bourgeoisie, for the organization established by the men of 1830 left little place for the weak; the popular masses for example were not excluded from society like laborers by aristocrats or slaves by the citizens of antiquity, but, left to themselves, overwhelmed by their weakness, they had little chance ever to escape their low condition, save by violence. But the conflict between organization and free choice also constituted the strength of the Parisian bourgeoisie, in the period of Louis Philippe. Satisfied with living in a system which seemed the best possible to them, they had a good conscience and, aside from individual difficulties, they were happy men. They accepted the laws and decisions which organized the future, for they knew that in them were guarantees for the exercise of their free choice. Their greatness lay in refusing to accept orders and directives. They wished to govern themselves in their public as in their private life, willing only to delegate their political sovereignty to representatives from whom they demanded an accounting. To sum it all up, the members of the Parisian bourgeoisie were adults and conscious and proud of being so. . . .

It remains to state the situation of the lower classes in relation to the bourgeoisie. In spite of the doctrine of social mobility, in spite of the renewal of bourgeois groups by continuous tapping of the lower classes, in spite of the existence of a massive popular bourgeoisie, the common people were excluded from bourgeois society. Bourgeois civilization excluded the weak, whom it relegated to an inferior position; it was made for the strong, for those who could succeed in imposing their will. . . .

Thus it seemed absolutely impossible for the conditions of the bourgeoisie to characterize a whole people. The bourgeois was a privileged person, but one who earned and preserved his privilege by steady effort. Certainly inheritance played a role, acquired positions favored those who held them, sometimes in a decisive way. Inheritance and commercial or industrial profit were basic to the domination of the bourgeoisie in the first half of the 19th century. But other periods or other countries could have a bourgeoisie while repudiating these bases. The existence of a bourgeoisie corresponds to a phase of the social evolution of any civilization. It develops when men make themselves judges of the traditions and beliefs among which they live, when they repudiate both dogmas unchecked by reason, and the absolute and exclusive authority of leaders, and the determining influence of the masses. Bourgeois men are men who wish to know, to understand, and to choose, and whose whole social life is organized around these imperatives. But knowledge, understanding, and choice imply the renunciation of certain enjoyments, they demand strength, work, intelligence, a certain insensibility and even hardness to pass from a dream to reality. These qualities and these faults cannot belong to the masses. Any bourgeoisie is based on a selection by talent, it believes in the strength of reason and progress, but its power and prosperity are rooted in the grinding down of the masses and the creation of a new aristocracy which degenerates when it breaks with the traditions of its original class.

5. DAVID LANDES: French Entrepreneurship in the Nineteenth Century *

Professor David Landes, an economic historian at Harvard University, has contributed many studies of entrepreneurial behavior in western Europe, particularly France. In this essay he describes a predominant business mentality in France which many observers have found persisting into the twentieth century.

* From David Landes, "French Entrepreneurship in the Nineteenth Century," *Journal of Economic History,* Vol. IX (1949), pp. 47–49, 52–53, 54–56. Reprinted by permission of the *Journal of Economic History* and the author.

Not everyone would agree with Professor Landes' assessment. Some, for example, look more to deficiencies in French natural resources than to a lack of entrepreneurial vigor to explain France's slow economic advance in the nineteenth century; others find somewhat similar timidity in businessmen elsewhere in Europe. Obviously, Professor Landes is not talking of the whole French middle class. His concentration on a single segment of it may explain the differences between his conclusions and those of historians attempting to define a whole social class. It is not unknown, in historical writing, for concepts or generalizations to be applied to unrealistically narrow areas or time periods and on this basis proved inexact and misleading in detail; yet, sometimes, the value of the generalization may remain on a larger scale. This is a real problem of historical orientation, by no means confined to the assessment of the middle class. Still, the contrast between Landes' picture of entrepreneurial goals and other views of middle-class values is striking. Perhaps France's middle class was different from the venturesome middle class of, say, Great Britain. If so, how can the apparent contrasts between Daumard and Landes be accounted for? Perhaps Paris was different from the provinces (to which Landes largely refers, in dealing with French manufacturing); if so, the geography of the middle class becomes quite complex. Landes also suggests unusual complexity in defining the balance of business and professional elements within the French middle class, and casts doubt on the clarity of the boundary between middle class and aristocracy. Here are a number of important challenges to other interpretations of the middle class.

What, then, was the French entrepreneur of the industrial revolution like? Here a word of caution is in order. As one writer put it: France is diversity. It is astonishing to note the geological, climatic, ethnographic, cultural, and other variety found in an area smaller than the state of Texas. In one sense, therefore, there is no such thing as *the* French businessman. On the other hand, the development of a single, conscious nation with its implications for economic, social, and spiritual unity has inevitably shaped the individual more or less to the common mold. In spite of nuances and exceptions, there are definitely certain characteristics of entrepreneurship during this period generalized enough to constitute a type.

To begin with, the average French entrepreneur was a small businessman acting for himself or at most on behalf of a handful of partners. This was especially true in 1815. To take the two most important industries, in textiles he was still at that time the "undertaker," the little capitalist who furnished the raw material to scattered spinners and weavers and then collected the finished goods for market, and in metallurgy he was the isolated *maître de forges,* with his furnace built along some country stream in the neighborhood of iron deposits and forests. Transportation in those days was provided by a multitude of *maîtres de poste,* haulers, boatmen, and, especially for local shipments, peasants exploiting their livestock in the quiet season. Foreign trade was in the hands of small commission and shipping firms, some of them with perhaps one or two coasting vessels, others with as many as half a dozen ocean-going sailers, while retail trade continued in the small, cluttered shops of the eighteenth century.

Finally, such credit as was available came from private lenders or from small local banks, many of them built on profits made in commerce and industry and most of them restricting their clientele to an intimate circle of trusted friends and relatives. The corporation, to all intents and purposes, did not exist.

Naturally, the years that followed changed this picture in many important respects. Certain districts, notably Alsace, the Nord, and Normandy, saw the rise of impressively large cotton factories. If the woolen industry, owing to slower mechanical progress, cannot show developments of comparable magnitude, companies like Paturle-Seydoux at Câteau-Cambrésis and Holden at Reims nevertheless represented important concentrations of capital and labor. In the manufacture of iron and steel, where a more important outlay of capital was required, the Schneider plant at Le Creusot and the De Wendel mills at Hayange and Stiring were only the best known of the larger units. During these years, the railroad, which necessitated an unprecedented accumulation of private capital, completely transformed land transport. Foreign trade was similarly affected, though to a lesser degree, by the steamship. It was during this period also that retail commerce made its first significant departure from the tradition of centuries with the introduction of fixed prices and the creation under the Second Empire of the first successful department stores and branch outlets. As for finance, it required the boom psychology of the 1850's and 1860's to launch the first corporative investment and deposit banks.

Nevertheless, a survey of French business in 1870 quite clearly shows that these new concentrations of economic strength were still the exception. In land transport the change was complete; the very nature of the new technique imposed regional monopolies and large corporations. But in the other primary economic sectors, the small entrepreneur remained the norm, even in those areas where the factory system had come to prevail.

In the second place, the French businessman was a fundamentally conservative man, with a firm distaste for the new and unknown. Security was his first concern, and it was generally felt that the quickest road to success was the slow but sure one. The main thing was to watch the sous; the francs would take care of themselves. Thus enterprise was generally characterized on the one hand by a high rate of book amortization—also intended incidentally to conceal the size of profits—and on the other by slow turnover of equipment. The average French producer was reluctant to buy machines to begin with; when he bought them, he wanted them to last. How much this emphasis on caution and thrift was due to the influence of the peasant mentality it is hard to say. Suffice it to point out that even today the visitor to France is struck by the passion for conservation of the most trivial objects, even *la ficelle* of Maupassant.

A third major characteristic of the French entrepreneur was his independence: the typical firm was pretty much self-sufficient. Since the cost of expansion usually came out of company revenues and, if necessary, the pockets of the owner or his relatives and friends, the goal of enterprise was the highest possible *rate* of profit. Naturally, all were not equally successful in this endeavor, but the fact remains that most French industrial growth in this period was financed precisely in this manner. To choose merely one striking example among many, the unusually prolific and prosperous Motte textile interests of Roubaix, who were said to purchase or build a new mill every time a Motte was born, never found it necessary to request outside credit or funds of any sort.

It is fairly obvious, however, that cautious management, obsolescent plants, and high profits are not a combination designed to flourish in a world of cutthroat competition. As stated above, the French entrepreneur prized security above all, and a secure market meant one well protected from foreign inroads. For all but the last few years of this period, therefore, French industry and commerce were protected by a series of impassable duties and prohibitions, which for most businessmen came to represent as much a permanent element of the environment as the ground on which their factories stood.

Nevertheless, the elimination of foreign competition was not in itself sufficient to guarantee the prosperity of any and all producers. This was, after all, a period of technological change, and certain firms inevitably fell behind in capacity and efficiency. Theoretically, the competion between these marginal units and the more progressive firms should have been enough in itself to eliminate the laggards and hasten modernization. In many cases it did have this effect. Yet the fact remains that backward forms of production and distribution remained widespread in France for a surprisingly long period side by side with far more efficient techniques. In part, of course, this was due to the cost of transportation, which made it difficult, especially in the heavy industries, to compete far from the base of operations. But there are far too many cases where this explanation will not suffice, and there it would seem that the usual mechanism of competition was not operative. It is not easy to find concrete examples owing to the inaccessibility of records of business costs and prices, but the data available in the many government tariff inquiries and similar sources would seem to show quite definitely that the more efficient French producer was not inclined to push his advantage. . . .

With rare exceptions, French enterprise was organized on a family basis and the entrepreneur conceived of his business, whatever its nature, not as a mechanism for the production or distribution of goods nor a means to indefinite wealth and power but as a sort of fief that maintained and enhanced the position of the family, just as the produce of the manor and the men-at-arms it could muster were the *material* basis of medieval status. If the family was inclined to remain in business, there was always room for future generations. Thus some firms, like the Japy hardware and watchmaking company, had careful rules regulating the right of each partner to introduce a son or son-in-law into the organization. And if, as was only too often the case, the family was looking forward to "higher" things, a good business was always a steppingstone to a career in the government service, possibly even to ennoblement or marriage into the aristocracy. In either case, the *affaire* was never an end in itself, but the means to an end. The obsession of the entrepreneur with the enterprise as such, which Sombart finds so common in America and Germany, to all intents and purposes did not exist in France. . . .

Furthermore, a family firm is necessarily a cautious firm. It is easy to speculate with the money of others; it is sometimes even easy to gamble with one's own funds. But it is somewhat harder to take chances when every question must be approved by a keenly critical circle of relatives primarily interested in the conservation of the patrimony. And in France at least as much attention has always been given to the preservation as to the creation of wealth. . . .

In the French social structure the businessman had always held an inferior place. Three major forces conduced to this result. In the first place, he was detested from the start by the nobility, which rightly saw in him a subversive element. The aristocracy, its military and administrative functions slowly but surely ossifying in a new world of gunpowder and mercenaries, centralization and bureaucracy, turned at bay on its bourgeois adversaries and wreaked revenge with the strongest weapon it had left, prestige. Unable to compete with the driving spirit of these ambitious newcomers, unable to defeat them on their chosen ground of business with their chosen weapon, money, the nobility deliberately turned its back and tilted its nose. Against the practical, materialistic values of the businessman it set the consciously impractical, unmaterialistic values of the gentleman. Against the restless ambition of the parvenu, it placed the prestige of birth; against the mercurial efficacy of money, the solid stability of land; against the virtues of diligence and austerity, the dignity of leisure and the splendor of pomp and circumstance.

If anything, the revolutions of 1789 and 1830 strengthened this attitude. Those few nobles who under the old regime had been active as ironmasters, glass manufacturers, and so on, or had followed the Colbertist tradition of encouragement of and investment in industry, were now for the most part impoverished. To be sure, many of the new generation, especially those whose titles were of recent vintage, were to lend their names and prestige to entrepreneurial efforts and place their capital in railroads, insurance, and other corporative enterprises. But the aristocracy as a group had hardened its heart. The early years of the July Monarchy saw a marked reaction against the new way and the consecration of the myth of noble superiority, social, spiritual, and even physical. One has only to read the flood of scornful literature that followed the Revolution of 1830 to feel the bitterness approaching revulsion on the part of the dispossessed toward anything smacking of bourgeois business and money.

That the entrepreneur was considerably influenced by the prestige of this "superior" group is obvious from his continued efforts to rise into its ranks, either directly or through marriage. For the same reasons, the businessman was rare who did not acquire sooner or later a landed estate, considered the safest of investments and an important criterion of social status. Obviously, most of these new gentry were simply absentee landlords. In some districts like Bordeaux the practice was just about unanimous, and there shippers and merchants were at least as well known for their vineyards and vintages as for their commercial activities. It is impossible to say with any precision how much of the national wealth was diverted from business enterprise on this account, but most writers are agreed that, whether made as a form of conspicuous consumption or for more serious reasons, such investments by businessmen and nonbusinessmen were a significant obstacle to industrialization.

The hostility of the aristocracy would not have been enough in itself, however, had it not been for the acceptance of this concept by the nonbusiness elements of the *bourgeoisie*. This heterogeneous group, which is more easily defined negatively than positively since it includes almost everyone not falling into the small category of nobility or the large mass of the people, had developed in the course of centuries of slow ascension a scale of status heavily weighted with the prejudices of an aristocratic society. Of the multitude of professional groups that composed the *bourgeoisie,* the businessmen were generally relegated to the bottom of the ladder, other things being equal. In the last analysis, this social inferiority was what made possible the system of *charges* under the old regime, which by conferring on the *nouveaux riches* the prestige, security, and sometimes ennoblement of public office further depreciated the entrepreneurial classes and intensified their efforts to rise up and out of their "sordid" occupations.

These prejudices by no means died with the Revolution. Instead, the older *bourgeoisie,* dominated by civil servants and the liberal professions, tended to stress their prestige in the face of rising capitalist elements. In this they were, generally speaking, quite successful, and the invidious distinction between the two groups has continued right up to the present, though with considerably less force since the economic and monetary disasters due to World War I. Considerations of status, moreover, were strengthened by such factors as the security of official or professional positions and the character of the French educational system, a primary force for social conservatism. For these reasons, the best talents in France almost invariably turned to the traditional honorific careers such as law, medicine, or government. This was true even of the children of businessmen.

6. ERNST KOHN-BRAMSTEDT: Aristocracy and the Middle Classes in Germany *

Dr. Kohn-Bramstedt's book, initially written as a Ph.D. thesis for the University of London, attempted to apply some of the techniques of German sociology, from the schools of Max Weber and Karl Mannheim, to German literature. The first question it raises is the adequacy of literary evidence. Dr. Kohn-Bramstedt is able to draw a coherent picture of middle-class values, but it depends on the representative quality of statements in the novels and magazines of the period. Beyond this, the selection must be evaluated with problems of geography and chronology in mind. Was there a middle-class culture common at least to western and central Europe? And, as Dr. Kohn-Bramstedt vividly suggests, how do the problems of dealing with the later evolution of the class affect its use as a historical category?

It is striking to see how strongly every section of the nineteenth-century German middle-class stressed the idea of the family. The individualism of the

* From Ernst Kohn Bramstedt, *Aristocracy and the Middle Classes in Germany* (London: P. S. King and Sons, copyright 1937), pp. 202–204, 205–206, 208–209. Reprinted by permission of the University of Chicago Press.

economic struggle was counterbalanced by the social collectivism of the family. Whilst literature of the classical and romantic periods sharply underlines the contrast between genius and philistine, between the aristocracy of culture and the conventional respectability of the family, both the higher and lower literature of poetical realism after 1830 emphasize unceasingly the virtues of the middle-class family. The conservative sociologist, W. H. Riehl, affirmed at that time with much satisfaction the actuality of the family in literature and science. The new science of the family was for him an instrument for its preservation.

How completely different [he said] is the attitude of science now towards the home, from what it was 100 years ago! The family has earned an infinitely deeper recognition from science, and at the same time it has become once again a matter of public interest in our nation. Recognition is already half an improvement.

The concentration of the middle-class periodical on the family meant in practice a specific selection in its contents. All its articles laid stress on the moral aspect of things; if social realities were not completely concealed, good care was taken not to probe them too thoroughly. The discussion of sexual problems was completely taboo. Divorces and suicides did not exist. Since wives and daughters formed the major contingent of its readers, and since their interests were concentrated mainly on the family or on the rearing of families in the future, the family-journal had to adapt itself to their mentality. The result is to be seen in the story-pages of the family journal.

The stories printed therein catered for the average woman-reader whose mental capabilities had not been over-developed in the girls' high-schools and who, in accordance with prevailing custom, rarely took up a professional career. They were written for the most part by women, for women. They were discussed in family circles and amongst the ladies, and formed just as much an intimate bond between the authoress and her feminine readers as did the political article between its author and the male readers.

We shall now attempt to present the attitude assumed in the family-journal novel towards the aristocracy and middle-class; and for this purpose have chosen the *Gartenlaube* and *Daheim,* two periodicals of opposed political tendencies. We therefore have to distinguish between the novel of liberal protest and the conservative novel of loyalty.

THE "GARTENLAUBE" AND THE CHANGE IN MIDDLE-CLASS POLITICAL OPINION

The most widely-spread and most representative family-journal of the liberal bourgeoisie between 1850 and 1900 was the *Gartenlaube*. Its contents, taken as a whole, reflect characteristically the intellectual and political changes within this class. The political and social ideologies of a broad stratum of merchants, officials, artisans, teachers, in short of the non-professional middle-class are just as faithfully reflected in it as is the attitude of the Prussian national-liberal university intelligentsia in the *Preussiche Jahrbücher*. The *Gartenlaube* is a gold-mine for research into the thoughts and feelings of the so-called middle-class. Its founder, Ernst Keil, was a self-taught man, and he embodied the self-reliant, industrious, German merchant who was able to recognize and skilfully exploit in the middle of the century the new possibilities offered by technical progress and improved communications. He was born in a small town of central Germany, the son of a petty official, became first a bookseller, and firmly favoured both the writings of the Young Germans and a democratic policy. Later on he founded several periodicals which all fell foul of the censor, before and after 1848, and then in 1853 he started the *Gartenlaube* which, as we have already seen, soon achieved an extraordinary success. Keil's intention was to produce a popular journal whose chief aim should be to popularize the achievements of science. In other words, the periodical wanted to be the organ of a middle-class, liberal enlightenment. Its readers were to be informed about the human body and its functions, as well as about the significance of a liberal middle-class in a united Fatherland. The paper fought against superstition of all shape and form, against the political pressure of feudalism as well as against the intellectual pressure of tyrannical clericalism. It combined at one and the same time two tendencies that were later to prove mutually exclusive; for it advocated on the one hand an enlightened humanitarianism, and on the other, a nationalism in the sense of an integration of a rent and torn Germany under the leadership of the middle-class. Its watchwords were "Down with German reaction!" and "Up with German unity!"

But the attitude of this middle-class organ underwent an astonishing change in the period between 1866 and 1880. We can best realize the extent of this change if we examine and compare the contents of different volumes. For this purpose we shall take those for 1866, the year of the German civil-war, for 1871, the year of the unification of Germany, and for 1887, the year which saw the ninetieth birthday of William I. . . .

The increasing pride of the burgher, which we have already found on a higher literary plane in Freytag, is proclaimed with similar high-sounding phrases. The harm caused by the feudal régime and the arbitrariness of princes is denounced in essays like "Fr. Chr. Daniel Schubart. A victim of the arbitrariness of German princes," or "Heinrich the 72nd Prince of Reuss-Lobenstein-Ebersdorf, ruler of a petty state." On the other hand, inventors and entrepreneurs are lauded as representatives of middle-class efficiency and solidarity. Thus an essay entitled "Prussia's Military Luther" praises Dreyse, the inventor of the needle-gun, and an idyllistic account of this ennobled arms-manufacture, who supplied weapons to all the German states, declares with satisfaction that in spite of his social and economic success he has still remained a simple man of the people. The work of Krupp, the cannon-king, is treated in the same way; and acknowledgment is given to the importance of the Prussian bank, as "the greatest business-house of Prussia," for the development of trade and industry. The support of capitalist development does not preclude the democrats from an interest in the social problem. Schulze-Delitzsch, the well-known founder of the German co-operative associations (*Genossenschaften*), analyses the serious social consequences of the division of labour. . . .

The volume for 1888 reflects with astonishing clarity how large sections of the middle-class have accepted their due place within the social order of the imperialistic Reich. Both upper- and lower-class feel themselves to be an indispensable component of the Empire and now express an admiration for the court circle, Emperor and royal family. The celebration of the ninetieth birthday of Kaiser Wilhelm I takes up considerable space in this volume: a large picture shows the Kaiser riding over the battlefield of Sedan, and accounts of his childhood and of the birthday celebrations in Berlin follow. Prince Wilhelm's bear-hunting expeditions are reported and illustrated, and also the summer holiday of Moltke. Previously it had been exceptional to have aristocratic contributors, but now a whole string of aristocratic writers were able to make their appearance in the pages of this middle-class periodical. Aristocratic titles no longer sounded degrading in middle-class ears, but flattering. The accounts written by aristocrats gave readers the illusion of knowing the feudal places of amusement and the court world still closed to them. The antipathy towards flunkeyism that the once very independent and democratic middle-class had, has disappeared. The same stratum that twenty years before had read with keen approval the descriptions of princely arbitrariness and democratic courage, now submitted under a changed sky to a bombastic servility such as is expressed in an article entitled "In the Marble Palace of Potsdam." The author of this, Georg von Amyntor, was allowed to inscribe a congratulatory poem of ostentatious devotion on the occasion of the birth of an heir to the later Kaiser Wilhelm II, and his wife Victoria "in the autograph book of the high lady."

Chapter VI.

THE REVOLUTIONS OF 1848: GERMANY

THE REVOLUTIONS of 1848 quickly extended across most of western and central Europe, becoming the most widespread protest movement in European history. Most historians, however, have concentrated on individual national revolutions, leaving general treatment of the whole movement to the textbook or the survey. The few studies that purport to deal with the revolutions in general really consist of separate essays on the national risings. The first question that must be asked of the historiography of 1848 is, then, whether the national focus is necessary. Did the revolutions share only such general elements, on which most historians would agree, as a preceding economic crisis and the impact of liberal and nationalist ideologies? Were the goals and results of the national revolts so different that they preclude a more systematic study of the whole movement?

Of the major revolutions, it is generally agreed that the German revolt was the most important. Revolution in Italy led more directly to Italian unification than revolution in Germany did to German, but Italy has played a less decisive role in modern European history. The rising in Paris seems so much a part of the series of French revolutions that it has commanded less attention from historians outside France; because it was part of a series, it changed France less than the revolution in Germany intended to do. The year 1848 was as decisive for the history of the Hapsburg monarchy as it was for Germany, but again, the Hapsburg monarchy is less important for the history of the nineteenth century as a whole. The attention given to the German revolution, then, reflects a sense of the importance of Germany in modern history generally as well as a feeling that the revolution played a decisive role in shaping modern Germany. It is this latter sense that has determined the approach most historians have taken to the revolution: they have been less interested in the revolution itself or its direct results than in its more subtle, long-range impact on German character and German politics.

Germany's only significant effort at revolution in the nineteenth century occurred in 1848. It involved many of the same doctrines and social groups that frequently shook such countries as France or Italy. There is a natural tendency to compare the German and French revolutionary movements; certainly, the German seems pale by comparison, not only because there were fewer revolutions, but because the rising of 1848 itself was so short-lived and abortive. Most historical treatments of 1848 in Germany must be examined to gauge the extent to which they measure the German experience by some more general, French-derived standard of what revolutions should be. Such a standard may be appropriate, but it must be tested for its relevance to the German situation.

Three major questions, which can apply to any revolution, dominate the treatment of Germany in 1848: Was it a revolution at all? To what extent did it fail, and why? What did its consequences have to do with what happened in Germany later?

Historians who question that 1848 was a revolution stress the lack of revolutionary sentiment among the men who led the revolt and their timidity in action. This approach is important, not as an exercise in the interpretation of the word "revolution," but as an effort to determine the essential character of the movement. But one must note also that the leaders of the French Revolution in 1789 were not revolutionaries in initial sentiment. The determination of motives and degree of fervor is difficult, and there is always the possibility that the initial impulse of the German revolution has been judged by the results of the revolution alone.

Most historians agree that the revolution failed. But again, there is increasing question about the success of "successful" revolutions. The 1848 revolution produced some important changes in German political and social structure directly, and within two decades many of the revolutionary goals had been achieved, though admittedly not by revolutionary means.

The more common question about the failure of the 1848 revolution concerns its cause. The inadequacy and abstractness of the revolutionary ideologies, the rapid development of social rifts within revolutionary ranks, and the distraction and impediment of nationalism are most often cited, but there is pointed disagreement about the balance of these factors. The question of why the revolution failed is related to one that must be posed for any revolution: Who participated in it? All historians agree that various groups were involved, but they do not agree on what the groups were or about what role they played. Most focus on the middle class and attribute to it much of the failure of the revolution. But this focus can be challenged to some extent, and there is always the problem of defining the middle class itself. Quite soon after the revolution, Marx and Engels stressed the role of the lower classes, and recent historians have re-examined this role, in contrast both to the Marxist method and to the more conventional focus of intellectual and political historians.

Most twentieth-century historians of 1848 have been dominated by the belief that, somewhere, somehow, Germany went wrong in the nineteenth century, and they have seen much of the error in 1848. From 1848 came the amoral, tough-minded character of German politics and nationalism and the weakness of German liberalism. But here, too, questions abound. Did 1848 cause these developments or merely express pre-existing features of German political life or, perhaps, of a "German character" more generally? Were the effects of 1848 so enduring? If, for example, it is admitted that the failure of the revolution led to a decline of liberalism in the 1850's, can one go on to say that the revived liberalism of the 1860's was marred by a fatal flaw resulting from the revolution? Was Germany more affected by the revolution than Italy or Austria? Cannot one talk of failures of liberalism there as well? If so, what was distinctive about Germany? Here again, the problem of dealing with only one national experience is apparent. And, most basically, is German history in the nineteenth century, including 1848, best interpreted by a constant foreboding about what happened in the twentieth century? Stated simply, what has 1848 to do with Germany's role in World War I and with nazism? Most recent historians have suggested some connection, but they disagree about how strong this connection is and how greatly it should be stressed.

In sum, the problem of 1848 in Germany is wrapped up in the problem of modern German history more generally. Historians have been preoccupied with explaining the tragedy of modern Germany. This orientation is fully understandable; it has accounted for much fruitful attention to German history. But it is an orientation derived from recent developments, not from historical events in themselves. Its utility must be tested when it is applied to any specific historical material.

1. PRISCILLA ROBERTSON: Revolutions of 1848 *

Priscilla Robertson's book, the *Revolutions of 1848,* deals with all the major revolutions and finds in them a common pattern of failure. This brief selection, from the conclusion, stresses social and psychological explanations for this general failure and states the vital roles the failure played in shaping a tragic later history.

When hostility that has been repressed is first released into consciousness, there is a moment, for individuals at least, and perhaps also for nations, when it appears to be of uncontrollable violence. Perhaps this is because there exist, at first, no habitual or institutional skills for dealing with it overtly. Thus violence erupted among the lower classes as they began to dare to ask for more equal conditions, a violence which came in good part from the release of their old resentments. At the same time the upper classes, who were just beginning to dare to give more equality, found that this process simultaneously brought to the surface in themselves the fears which they had long kept hidden of the results of lower class resentment.

The great advantage which America had was that its social arrangements to a large measure prevented these hatreds from forming; not completely, but enough to make a startling contrast with Europe in those days.

Another psychological factor took the men of 1848 by surprise. It was noted by Massimo d'Azeglio, although its explanation had to wait for a hundred years—and that was the distinct ambivalence in the human soul toward freedom. It was not only the unexpected violence that shocked people, it was that freedom itself terrified them. This ambivalence has been expounded psychoanalytically by Erich Fromm, in *Escape from Freedom.* He shows that from the time of the Reformation freedom has been a burden, and indeed a threat, for men who are not prepared to accept its responsibilities—and there are many. This quality made every demand for a revolution two-faced, so that men were always retreating as well as moving forward, in spite of themselves. Or, as Massimo d'Azeglio perceived it: "The gift of liberty is like that of a horse, handsome, strong, and high-spirited. In some it arouses a wish to ride; in many others, on the contrary, it increases the desire to walk." A great many people felt more like walking as the year 1848 passed,—all the French who voted for Napoleon, on the ground that he would restore "order," all the Prussians who paid their taxes after their parliament had been dissolved in the very act of

* From Priscilla Robertson, *Revolutions of 1848* (Princeton: Princeton University Press, 1952), pp. 414–15, 419. Reprinted by permission of Princeton University Press.

telling the citizens not to pay them, all the Hapsburg subjects who in 1849 did not have a chance either to vote for anybody or to support a constitution. All these were people who found that the effort of doing something for themselves was not so rewarding as letting somebody on top do it—especially when it came to the task of overcoming the violence of the lower classes.

When the moderates took fright at the contemplation of their danger, they accused the radicals of trying to destroy order and property. To the radical intellectuals, this was ill-will and insult. They loved order and property and class conciliation as much as anybody, but being somewhat closer to the people than the other leaders they realized that they would not be satisfied with constitutions but would require some social reforms. None of the radicals had a chance to show how far he would go before he was stopped. He was lucky if he was stopped by foreign arms, as Mazzini was, so that his dream could go on. To be halted by civil war such as the June Days of Paris seemed to prove that the radical case was hopeless, or that, as Frederick William put it, soldiers are the only cure for democrats.

After the middle classes had won most of what they wanted, they often voluntarily gave up some of their new privileges so that the lower classes would not have to be given liberties too. They were like the man in the story who was asked what he would like best in the world, provided his worst enemy could have the same thing in double measure—and he answered, *one blind eye*. There was practically no one to say that the cure for democracy was more democracy.

. . .

Was nothing gained by all the year of revolution, either from the violence or from the quiet talk? The answer is very little. Some revolutions shake up society so that when the pieces fall together again they are in a new pattern which permits growth in a new direction. In 1848 that hardly happened. The Austrian serfs were freed, but did this make up for the extra repression on all other Austrian subjects? Italy made a new start toward greater freedom, but Germany was disillusioned about freedom. Some old illusions were destroyed, but the new myths created by men like Marx and Bismarck were as one-sided as the ones they supplanted and failed equally to represent a synthesis of values. The test of whether a revolution is successful is not whether some power with a new name exercises the same essential restraints as before (which happened to Europe in 1870), but whether some important group has won some important new freedom—economic, political, social, or religious.

Out of 1848 and its struggles no important new freedom was wrested. Instead men lost confidence in freedom and imagined they had made a great advance in sophistication by turning from idealism to cynicism. After 1848 classes and nations played power politics, each unashamed to get what it could each for itself with very little thought for the common welfare of society. This was not realism, though it was called *Realpolitik*. In 1870 this policy brought a new chance to win many of the specific demands of the 1848 revolutionaries, yet no one can say that the basic questions of justice and cooperation among classes and nations were settled at that time. For these problems failure was worse than mere failure, for no new chance arose. In 1914, at the time of the next continental explosion, many of the powers that had been half rotten in 1848 disappeared for good, but with them disappeared a good part of the class and nation structure itself. For the appeal of totalitarianism comes partly from its indifference to these problems which had seemed so unyielding to solution. Today millions of classless, stateless people crowd the continent in hatred and despair—and in a way they are the end product of the futility and ruthlessness of the 1848 revolutions.

2. LEWIS NAMIER: 1848: The Revolution of the Intellectuals *

Sir Lewis Namier (1888–1960), long Professor of Modern History at the University of Manchester, was one of the most versatile historians of recent generations. His major work dealt with British politics in the eighteenth century, but he also wrote on central European history. In his 1944 lecture on the German revolution of 1848, from which this selection is drawn, he stressed two essential themes: that ideology was the central force in shaping the revolution, and that nationalism clearly overshadowed liberalism in this ideology. The inevitable result was failure, for nations are not created by ideas, and the failure changed the face of Europe. Aside from drawing comparisons between this approach and others, Namier's definitions of the national and constitutional impulses must be examined, as well as his generalizations about the continent as a whole.

The European Continent responded to the impulses and trends of the revolution with a remarkable uniformity, despite the differences of language and race, and in the political, social, and economic level of the countries concerned; but then the common denominator was ideological, and even literary, and there was a basic unity and cohesion in the intellectual world of the European Continent, such as usually asserts itself in the peak periods of its spiritual development. 1848 came not as an aftermath of war and defeat (as so many revolutions in the following century), but was the outcome of thirty-three creative years of European peace carefully preserved on a consciously counter-revolutionary basis. The revolution was born at least as much of hopes as of discontents. Odilon Barrot, under the July Monarchy one of the leaders of the Dynastic Opposition, writes: "Never have nobler passions moved the civilized world, never has a more universal impulse of souls and hearts pervaded Europe from end to end: and yet all this was to result in failure. . . ." And Lamartine, another of the makers and shipwrecks of 1848, describes it as "the product of a moral idea, of reason, logic, sentiment, and of a desire . . . for a better order in government and society." The sequence and emphasis of his enumeration are significant. 1848 was primarily the revolution of the intellectuals—*la révolution des clercs*.

* From Lewis Namier, *1848: The Revolution of the Intellectuals* (New York: Oxford University Press, 1946), pp. 3–6, 23–24, 31–33. Reprinted by permission of the Oxford University Press.

There was undoubtedly also an economic and social background to the revolution. Lean harvests in 1846 and 1847, and the potato disease, were causing intense misery in most parts of the Continent. Agrarian riots occurred in France where 1847 was long remembered as "l'année du pain cher"; there was a "potato revolution" in Berlin (complete with barricades), bread-riots in Stuttgart and Ulm, labour troubles in Vienna and in Bohemia, rank starvation in Silesia, &c. Count Galen, the Prussian Minister, wrote from Kassel on 20 January 1847: "The old year ended in scarcity, the new one opens with starvation. Misery, spiritual and physical, traverses Europe in ghastly shapes—the one without God, the other without bread. Woe if they join hands!" Against this background, economic or social conflicts were assuming a bitter, acute character. In most parts of the Austrian Empire, but more especially in Hungary and in Galicia, a final adjustment between big landowners and peasants was overdue: seignorial jurisdictions, *corvées,* and other remnants of serfdom had to be cleared away, and the title of the peasant to the land which he worked on his own, had to be established. Even in south-western Germany, on the confines of France and Switzerland, feudal survivals were fomenting agrarian revolt. All over Europe independent artisans were fighting their drawn-out losing battle against modern industry, especially desperate in the case of hand-spinners and weavers, or of carriers and bargees facing the competition of railways, and steamboats: hence the attacks against modern machinery and means of transport at the outbreak of the revolution. On the other hand, the new class of factory workmen was starting its fight for a human existence. And when in 1847–8 a severe financial crisis set in, widespread unemployment ensued both among artisans and workmen, and among the large numbers of unskilled labour engaged on railway construction. Here was plenty of inflammable matter in ramshackle buildings. But was there a social-revolutionary movement at work, pursuing a feasible aim?

The French Revolution of 1789 and the Russian of 1917 were made and sustained by the converging action of the two greatest revolutionary forces: the people of the capital, effective through concentration at the very centre of government, and the peasant masses, invincible through their numbers, their dispersion, and the primitive, practical character of their demands (they never seek by revolt to establish new and higher forms of production, but to free themselves of burdens, or seize more land in order to cultivate it in their traditional inadequate manner). In 1848 it was the proletariat of the quickly growing modern capitals which brought the widespread discontents to a head: and "accidents" and "misunderstandings," epidemic in character—the "fusillade" of the Boulevard des Capucins on 23 February, the salvo before the Vienna Landhaus on 13 March, and the "two shots" fired in front of the Royal Palace in Berlin on the 18th—converted revolts into risings. For lack of support from other sections of the population, and of faith in themselves, the monarchical Governments collapsed under the impact of the working-class revolution.

. . .

The proletariat was defeated in Paris, the peasants were bought off in the

Habsburg Monarchy. The social forces behind the revolution of 1848, disjointed and insufficient from the very outset, were thus practically eliminated. What remained was the middle classes led by intellectuals, and their modern ideology with which they confronted the old established powers and interests. Foremost in that ideology was their demand for a share in the government of States to be remodelled in accordance with the national principle.

The basic conflict of 1848 was between two principles—of dynastic property in countries, and of national sovereignty: the one feudal in origin, historic in its growth and survival, deeply rooted, but difficult to defend in argument; the other grounded in reason and ideas, simple and convincing, but as unsuited to living organisms as chemically pure water. To the men of 1848 the dynastic principle stood for arbitrary rule and autocracy, that of popular sovereignty for human rights and national self-government: by a crude over-simplification the conflict presented itself to them as a fight between reason and unreason, between freedom and unfreedom. The British system of representative and responsible government, carried on through parliamentary institutions, seemed to them to secure in practice the basic maxims of the French Revolution; and they did not realize how deeply ingrained the proprietary principle is in the public life of this country, where even abuses tend to become freeholds with redeemable value, where to this day heredity enters into the choice of parliamentary representatives, and no basic distinction exists between private and public law. The proprietary claim of dynasties centres in the land, and works through it; popular sovereignty is primarily the claim of men considered apart from the land. The title of "roi de France" stressed the territorial principle; "roi des Français" transferred the emphasis to the human element, and paid tribute to the sovereignty of the people. The growth of urban agglomerations and of an urban civilization stimulates the rise of a non-territorial ideology, but unless there be a complete return to the conditions of the horde, the basic element of territory cannot be eliminated: there is no escape from the interplay between groups of men and tracts of land, which forms the essence of history. . . .

In the interplay between constitutional and national movements on the European Continent, which opens in 1848, it is the latter that win: and they cut across into the international arena. A constitutional régime is secure when its ways have become engrained in the habits and instinctive reactions—*dans les mœurs*—of the political nation: it safeguards civilized life, but it presupposes agreement and stability as much as it secures them; and it can hardly be expected to build up, recast, or dissect the body in which it resides. (Hence the talk about "missed opportunities" of uniting Germany by "Parliamentary action" lacks substance.) States are not created or destroyed, and frontiers redrawn or obliterated, by argument and majority votes; nations are freed, united, or broken by blood and iron, and not by a generous application of liberty and tomato-sauce; violence is the instrument of national movements. Mass violence takes two forms, denoted as revolution and war; and there is close interaction between the two—they shatter political structures, and open the way for each other. In 1848 the subversive social forces were not equal to the task, and war had to come first: hence the bellicose ardours of the social revolutionaries, and the prudent pacifism of the Conservatives—for once both sides understood their business (better, indeed, than many historians who have written about it since). The national revolutionaries, recruited mainly from the middle classes or the petty gentry, and, most of all, from the intellectuals, could not become effective except by laying hold of governments and armies: as in Piedmont and Hungary. But these were small States, the one hampered by hesitations and the other beset with difficulties, which still further reduced their strength, while Prussia's action in Slesvig-Holstein was less than half-hearted. Throughout 1848 the ultimate control of the state-machine, and still more of the armies of the Great Powers on the European Continent, remained with the Conservatives; and it is this which preserved peace in Europe. The "Revolution of the Intellectuals" exhausted itself without achieving concrete results: it left its imprint only in the realm of ideas.

In its initial stage it looked to Britain and her parliamentary Government for patterns; and Englishmen, conscious of the excellence of their constitutional system and ascribing to it universal applicability, responded by taking a benevolent, fatherly, interest in these endeavours. They also sympathized with national aspirations, if respectable and "legitimate"; but few there were who would have dissented from Palmerston's pronouncement that peace was "the first object, to the attainment of which the efforts of enlightened statesmen ought to be directed." As yet the conflict between constitutional development and national movements was not patent: and its unfolding in 1848 could be written in terms of British disillusionment and disgust. Lord Minto had a foretaste of it when in 1847 he went out to Italy with a roving commission, and set to work to teach rulers how to carry on constitutional government, and liberal leaders how to conduct an opposition; failing in either task, he bitterly concluded that "rogues and fools and cowards form the whole stock-in-trade of this country in the article of public men." And after the *annus mirabilis* had run its course, early in 1849, Lord Brougham wrote in his magniloquent manner: "I must . . . lift up my voice against that new speculation in the rights of independent States, the security of neighbouring governments, and indeed the happiness of all nations . . . termed 'Nationality,' adopted as a kind of rule for the distribution of dominion." While rebutting some of Brougham's indictments of the revolution, John Stuart Mill sadly reflected on the feelings which make men indifferent to the rights and interests "of any portion of the human species, save that which is called by the same name and speaks the same language as themselves. These feelings are characteristic of barbarians." Now it was seen "that in the backward parts of Europe and even (where better things might have been expected) in Germany, the sentiment of nationality so far outweighs the love of liberty that the people are willing to abet their rulers in crushing the liberty and independence of any people not of their race and language." Lastly, W. N. Senior, in 1850: "This barbarous feeling of nationality . . . has become the curse of Europe."

Thus in the *Völkerfrühling,* "nationality," the passionate creed of the intellectuals, invades the politics of central and east-central Europe, and with 1848 starts the Great European War of every nation against its neighbours. But this is a theme so massive in its core and so vast in its ramifications that not even a summary can be attempted in this paper. I shall limit myself to certain international developments during the first months of the revolution, and to the early manifestations of aggressive nationalisms, especially of German nationalism which derives from the much belauded Frankfort Parliament rather than from Bismarck and "Prussianism"; and in examining the relation of these German "Liberals," in reality forerunners of Hitler, to the Poles and Czechs, and also of the Poles to the other Slavs, I shall be discussing problems which ninety years later, in 1938–9, were to become once more a touchstone of German mentality, and a decisive element in East-European politics.

3. THEODORE S. HAMEROW: Restoration, Revolution, Reaction: Economics and Politics in Germany, 1815–1871 *

Theodore S. Hamerow, professor of History at the University of Wisconsin, has produced one of the leading American contributions to the study of nineteenth-century Germany. His approach to 1848 is distinctive in three respects. First, in contrast to Namier and others, he sees the essential features of the revolution and its failure in social conflicts, admitted by most historians but often placed in the background. Second, he defines the social conflicts not in terms of a factory proletariat against the middle class, terms which many historians besides the Marxists have assumed, but as clashes between artisanry and the middle class, and peasantry and middle class. Finally, he seeks to look at the revolution, or revolutions, largely in the terms of the time; there is no quick effort to associate revolutionary failure with the nature of twentieth-century Germany. Does this caution produce a more valid view of the significance of the revolution?

The great depression of the Forties enabled the various groups in opposition to the Restoration, groups disparate in social composition and economic objective, to overcome their differences and form a single political force. For the masses it came as the climax of a long series of disasters extending over thirty years, intensifying the disruptive effects of capitalism in industry and agriculture, accelerating the decline of the master handicraftsman and the independent peasant, and driving the proletariat of Germany from Europe to America in a great wave of emigration. To the middle class it brought new courage and new resourcefulness, providing constitutionalism with a mass following ready to use violence for the overthrow of the old order. Some of the liberals even came to feel that a civilized revolution, a revolution of maximum enthusiasm and minimum bloodshed, might compel the government to share its power with the bourgeoisie without inviting the danger of mob rule. The economic crisis thus

* From Theodore S. Hamerow, *Restoration, Revolution, Reaction: Economics and Politics in Germany, 1815–1871* (Princeton: Princeton University Press, 1958), pp. 75, 78–80, 124–25, 138–39, 153–56, 160–62. Reprinted by permission of the Princeton University Press.

prepared the way for the spring uprising of 1848 by endowing the political opposition with popular support and forcing it to adopt more radical tactics. . . .

For the time being, however, the depression drove the proletariat into a partnership with bourgeois liberalism and thus made possible the overthrow of the old order. It intensified all the ills which had plagued German society since the beginning of the century, exposing the artisan to new dangers and forcing the small rural proprietor closer to bankruptcy. Under its pressure the vague restlessness of the masses turned into revolutionary enthusiasm, discontent developed into sedition. By the late Forties the popular literature dealing with social problems was becoming increasingly acrimonious, even ominous in tone. There were shrewd observers of the political scene who realized that an insurrection of the lower classes was a distinct possibility, for signs of widespread disaffection were there for all to see. The countryman sinking into debt ever since the promulgation of land reform now faced total disaster, as mortgage obligations increased so rapidly that in states like Württemberg they almost doubled in value during the economic crisis. Failure to meet tax and commutation payments became a common occurrence in the overcrowded lands of the west, and foreclosures and public sales of the holdings of insolvent farmers multiplied. Critical conditions in the country drove countless agricultural workers to the city, where they joined the ranks of the unemployed to swell still further the heavy labor surplus. Governments which hoped to win popular approval by the promulgation of new commutation laws discovered that the villager who did not have enough money for clothing and shelter was not interested in schemes of rural reform. They found, therefore, solace in the reflection that since mass privation was the natural outcome of overpopulation, the misery of the lower classes was only the price of their incontinence.

The peasantry, close to the soil and familiar with husbandry, could usually scrape up enough food to keep body and soul together. For the artisan masses of the city, however, there was no relief from hunger. After 1845 thousands of journeymen and apprentices were thrown out of work, as their masters sought to ward off bankruptcy by curtailing expenditures. Even those fortunate enough to find employment worked as much as fourteen hours a day to earn a meager subsistence for their families. Silesian weavers unable to make ends meet were forced to sell their looms and then rent them back during the brief periods when work was available. The Thuringian guildsman, swallowing his self-respect, was ready to offer himself as a mere hand on a road gang. Throughout Germany the proud artisan was sinking into a bottomless sea of unskilled day labor.

The true proletarian of the Forties was the handicraftsman. As for the industrial worker, he too had to endure the long working day, the reduced income, even unemployment, but after a decade of prosperity he was in a better position to face economic misfortune than the long-suffering artisan. Since during the depression mechanical production did not contract as rapidly as the output of the handicraft system, the demand for trained factory labor remained on the whole stable. Wages paid by industrial enterprises were consistently higher than those which the guild shop could offer, and while a linen weaver in Westphalia was earning barely one mark for a week's work, an unskilled hand in a textile mill could get twice as much and more. Hence the spirit of insurrection throve among the artisan masses who soon became the shock troops of revolution, whereas the employees of iron foundries and locomotive works were as a rule only interested by-standers in the great events of 1848. . . .

Chosen in a manner predisposing it in favor of the enlightened bourgeoisie, the Frankfurt Parliament could not reflect the multiplicity of interests of the German people. It was not the inept professorial parliament of the conservative myth, but neither was it an assembly of selfless patriots completely dedicated to shining ideals of liberty and brotherhood. It was the creation of a liberal middle class resolved to make its dominant position secure in a new system of government. Its members did not march in St. Paul's Church from the academician's ivory tower or the martyr's prison cell. They came from the government bureau, from the newspaper room, from the landed estate, from the business office, from the bank, from the shop, and even from the pulpit. There were indeed 49 university professors among them, but the parliamentarians par excellence of 1848 were jurists, who numbered more than 200 in the Frankfurt Parliament. They were joined by 40 school principals and teachers, 35 writers and journalists, 30 merchants and industrialists, 26 clergymen, and 12 physicians. Far from being the parliamentary freak which peers out of the pages of a thousand histories, the national assembly bore a family likeness to other European legislative bodies which throughout the nineteenth century attempted to govern the universe in accordance with the imperatives of the bourgeois ethic. And it suffered from an excess rather than lack of narrow practicality, for in its exclusive concern with the interests of a single class it lost sight of the broad masses on whose backs it had climbed to power.

In the world outside St. Paul's Church the clamor for industrial regulation and rural reform was growing louder, but within all was dignity and decorum. Four handicraftsmen and one lonely peasant sat in awed silence, while their polished colleagues prepared blueprints of a New Jerusalem. . . .

Yet the thesis that the Revolution was talked to death by petty lawyers and absent-minded professors raises more questions than it purports to answer. The debate in St. Paul's Church was certainly crucial, but as deliberations of parliamentary conventions go, it was not excessive. As far as Germany is concerned, the national assembly of 1848 could not match the accomplishments of the national assembly of 1919 which drafted a constitution in six months, but it acted with greater dispatch than the Italian national assembly of 1946 which was in session eighteen months, or the French national assembly of 1789 which continued to meet for two years. It was not the passage of time which destroyed revolutionary fervor, but the failure to satisfy the needs which had inspired it. The Frankfurt Parliament, far from being the do-nothing gathering of garrulous politicians portrayed by a fraudulent tradition, displayed considerable ingenuity in dealing with the political and economic problems of Central Europe.

It asserted its views clearly and boldly, and it acted with decision and promptness. The causes of its defeat are not to be found in vapid mentality or ineffectual artlessness.

They must rather be sought in the policies followed by liberalism which disrupted the united front of bourgeois and proletarian forged during the March days. Once the common foe fell, the common purpose vanished, and the victorious alliance disintegrated into its component elements. During the spring uprising of 1848 the middle class was able to enlist the aid of the worker and the peasant; during the spring uprising of 1849 it could command only its own slender resources. In the course of one year it had squandered its popular following, and by ignoring the wishes of the lower classes it destroyed the one force which might have perpetuated its domination of the state.

Only with the masses of declassed masters and unemployed journeymen behind it could a political party achieve power during the Revolution. The first to discover this truth were the radical socialists of the Rhineland. In vain did Karl Marx, Friedrich Engels, Andreas Gottschalk, Karl Schapper, and Fritz Anneke seek to awaken the spirit of insurrection among factory workers, the bearers of the revolutionary tradition in France and England. In Central Europe their arguments fell on deaf ears. The *Neue Rheinische Zeitung,* struggling to win the attention of the world, was read by at most six thousand subscribers. Attempts to form an alliance between the socialists and the democrats collapsed, when neither side could overcome its distaste for the principles and tactics of the other. And the mill hand himself remained indifferent to shibboleths of class conflict and economic justice. He wanted only a higher wage and a shorter working day, not the good society of dialectical materialism. . . .

A conflict between bourgeois and proletarian was unavoidable, because the differences in their social philosophies and economic interests were too profound to be adjusted. Their friendship had suffered the first rude shock when liberalism suppressed the spring uprising of the urban masses. It received a further blow after the artisan discovered during the summer that the new order had no intention of supporting him in the struggle against industrial capitalism. It reached the breaking point in the autumn, as the national assembly prepared to write economic freedom into the constitution.

Paragraphs 133 and 158 of the Fundamental Rights of the German People gave the citizen the authority to establish his domicile wherever he liked, to acquire full residence privileges, to purchase any property, and to pursue every occupation. An industrial code promulgated by the federal government was to determine the conditions under which these rights could be exercised, but in view of the economic outlook of parliamentarianism it was obvious that the new order would not hesitate to overthrow the guild system. Had not Justin von Linde announced from the floor of St. Paul's Church that "there is not the slightest doubt in the assembly that the people of Germany must obtain freedom of movement and freedom of industry?"

The Frankfurt Parliament proved true to its colors. On July 21 the task of preparing an industrial code was assigned to the economic committee, but by February, when its report was completed, the national assembly was already engaged in the bitter party struggle which ended in dissolution, and one more ambitious project was left to molder in the Frankfurt archives. Yet a small corner of the curtain had been lifted, and Germany caught a glimpse of stage-hands changing the scenery and moving the properties for the grand constitutional spectacle. It saw the wishes of artisan meetings and guild petitions ignored in a state paper urging the removal of government controls over manufacture, the abolition of the coercive powers of trade corporations, and the freeing of admission to handicraft occupations. For the urban proletariat there could no longer be any doubt about the economic intentions of the middle class. Liberalism was a more zealous champion of the factory and the bank than conservatism in its heyday had dared to be.

With the publication of the economic committee's report on an industrial code the last links in the great coalition of social classes forged in the March days broke. Moderates preached that competition was a necessary stimulus to progress, radicals criticized corporate guilds as survivals of the authoritarian age, and socialists sneered at "small tradesmen, whose entire manufacturing system is a mere relic of the Middle Ages." The artisan masses therefore turned in the one direction still open to them. During the year which followed the spring uprising they completed the circle from conservatism back to conservatism again. They offered their support to the crown on terms of social stability and economic regulation, the same terms which they had presented to liberalism. Once the bargain was concluded, they ended where they had begun, loyal to king and hostile to revolution.

The Revolution was all things to all men. To the bourgeois liberal it meant the establishment of a new nation of parliamentary government and material prosperity. To the guild master it meant the restoration of corporate control over industrial production. To the peasant it meant above all the abolition of manorialism and the redistribution of landed property. Each fought for his own cause, and therefore their common victory destroyed their common purpose. Once the Restoration fell, the new order began to dissipate its energies in a futile strife of social classes and political factions which made possible the ultimate triumph of the reaction.

By its devotion to economic freedom the middle class alienated the country no less than the city. During the spring uprising the peasantry had collaborated with the proletariat and the bourgeoisie in the struggle against absolutism, and as long as the liberals could count on the support of the village, they had nothing to fear from aristocratic agitation. But something happened between the defeat of conservatism in 1848 and its victory in 1849 to destroy the spirit of insurrection among the rural masses. The same rustic who had forced constitutionalism on the princes of Germany during the March days remained indifferent to its repudiation twelve months later. And his defection from the new order doomed the Revolution. . . .

The peasant wanted first and last emancipation from economic bondage, and the classic revolutionaries would have lived up to the occasion. Robespierre was too sober a statesman to rely on slogans of liberty, equality, and fraternity for the conversion of the village, nor did Lenin preach dialectical materialism to illiterate muzhiks. Their alliance with the countryside was based not on doctrinal agreement but economic interest. They expropriated the aristocracy and divided its possessions among the rural masses, bartering fields and flocks for votes and soldiers. Once the hungry farmer accepted their gift, he became their partner in crime. The French republic of virtue and the Russian soviet state were saved by peasants in uniform who valued a few acres of land more than the teachings of political theory.

The leaders of German liberalism, however, were neither Jacobins nor Bolsheviks. They were only industrious bourgeois politicians, conscientious and sincere enough, but completely incapable of opportunistic audacity. They feared bloodshed and insurrection, because once the mob broke the chains of habitual obedience, there was no telling where it would stop. The Revolution had provided them with an opportunity to translate their theories into practice, yet they were always a little ashamed of the illegitimate origin of their authority. They sought to maintain a spurious respectability through the fiction that the new order was only the legal extension of the old. Hence they left the princes on their thrones, hence they convoked the national assembly by the authority of the Diet of the Confederation, hence they paid constitutional homage to the particularism of the past. But the lot of the parvenu was not easy. To the masses they became snobs too good to hobnob with former friends, to the patriciate they remained climbers eager to rise above their station. At the end they earned the contempt of all.

In approaching the agrarian problem the Frankfurt Parliament resolved to walk the tightrope of dogmatic rectitude. Yet Anton von Schmerling, the suave Austrian aristocrat who became minister of the interior in the provisional central government, warned the new order of the need to appease the countryside: "The self-interest of all German governments demands that the broad masses of the German people receive as soon as possible the material relief which they are entitled to expect as a result of the March revolution. It demands that the agricultural population of Germany be entirely freed from the burdens which have oppressed it for centuries, and that it be brought to realize through direct benefit . . . that the peaceful and legal course adopted by the German national assembly has not been without advantage for it." The democratic physician from Kalbe Wilhelm Löwe was more vivid in his appeal: "If there is any cause at all to fear the proletariat, then it is of the agricultural proletariat that we must especially beware. . . . It has aroused the most frightful passions in the heart of man, and it has bred a barbarism which may carry all the achievements of civilization to the grave. Let us therefore rather carry the Middle Ages to the grave." And his party colleague, the Silesian schoolteacher Adolf Rösler, combined radical predilections with a gymnasial Latinity in his address to St. Paul's Church: "I speak to you in behalf of tranquillity and German unity. Grant legally what will otherwise happen anyway illegally. The peasant war stands without the gate. *Hannibal ante portas*. Think about that, gentlemen."

The liberals were at a loss. Had they fought against royal authority only to prepare the way for anarchic democracy? In endorsing the Revolution they had hoped to establish the inalienable human rights to life and property on a firm legal basis. And now they were being asked to destroy the only moral justification of the March days by promulgating laws more arbitrary than any which absolutism had sanctioned. They had to refuse. Before the peasant could become a loyal citizen of the state, he would have to learn that ownership is inviolable, that social inequality is decreed by nature, and that Providence itself divides mankind into the rich and the poor.

4. VEIT VALENTIN: 1848: Chapters in German History*

Few German historians have been able to take as harsh a view of the revolution of 1848 as most outside observers have. They stress the validity of the national goals of the revolution, the sincerity of the revolutionary ideals, and the humane procedures of the revolution itself. Veit Valentin, a devoted German liberal, goes further than this. Though ousted by the Nazis from his academic posts, he believed in the continuing liberal legacy of 1848. His glowing assessment of the Frankfurt revolutionaries deserves careful attention, for it may come closer to the spirit of the time than the interpretations of historians who are preoccupied with the results of revolutionary failure. The importance given to radical minorities and their social base invites comparison with Professor Hamerow's view.

The German Revolution was over, but its spirit was not dead. Revolution had already laid latent in the preparatory era, as Counter-Revolution in the Revolution itself, and in Counter-Revolution again the later period of reform lay latent, which was to lead to the foundation of the Empire in 1871. But this was not all; the victory of the Counter-Revolution in Germany was also a victory of the party of constitutional reform over parliamentary and social-revolutionary democrats; the communists, who had warned against half-measures, above all against trustfulness, were shown to have been in the right. The moderates sank wounded and fainting into impotence; the extremists confronted one another in bitterest enmity, dictatorial authority, with its militarist-capitalistic idea of a Great Power—and Marxism.

The victory of the Counter-Revolution in Germany bankrupted the previous revolutionary methods and ideas. Politics became materialistic, intellect, and culture too. The active revolution had been imbued with ideas. The reaction was avowedly exactly the reverse. The naïve pleonasm *Realpolitik* was born at this time. Authoritative power policy, natural-scientific over-assertion of self and Marxian socialism equalled each other in materialism. Nothing proves more saliently the actual importance of the idea in history than the embitterment with which it was opposed and the often unconscious hypocrisy with which it was used as an excuse.

* From Veit Valentin, *1848: Chapters in German History* (New York: Archon Books, 1965), pp. 426–27, 431–33, 446–50, 456–58. Reprinted by permission.

Many observers of the German Revolution of 1848–49 have refused to permit the name of revolution to be applied to it. Certainly, Latin and Slavonic revolutions have exhausted the last possibility of revolutionary action; the English revolution of the seventeenth century was full of stronger tension, although it had one curious characteristic in common with the German revolution, which was, to return to a new legitimacy as rapidly as possible. Every nation makes revolution in accordance with its inner nature. War and foreign policy produce an absolute measure of the best super-national achievement: revolutions are an individual revelation of a people's soul. Revolutions that are choked down are apt to be indigestible; the Revolution of 1848–49 was not able to develop itself to the full, and the German people are still suffering for it today. The Counter-Revolution has shaped German destiny all the more energetically since. The attempt at revolution had been made, with its apparent successes. Since then, all German princes and statesmen have reckoned with revolution and taken countermeasures against it. The fissure had opened, innocence was no more. Experience raised a strident voice. One might say that it took the Counter-Revolution in Germany to demonstrate the full historical existence of the Revolution. . . .

Bruno Bauer called the Revolution of 1848–49 "the bourgeois revolution" and thus helped to found a conception which, although completely erroneous, has prevailed to this day.

The designation "bourgeois" has been commonly used for the Revolution of 1848–49 in opposition to "proletarian" or "socialistic." Certainly the urban middle-class, though in process of decay, stood in the forefront of the movement and its main objective was the reform of the Constitution. But the fate of the population was decided by auxiliary factors, working beside and behind the scenes—the agrarian revolts, the associations of artisans and workmen, the striving after new forms and conditions of social intercourse in Germany, often with a strong undercurrent of philosophic principles, a sharply critical tendency, a revolutionary inspiration. The battle for a new Constitution was in itself by no means hopeless, and would perhaps have met with success had it not been for the radical minorities whose existence rendered it easier for the forces of counter-revolution to split up and weaken the bourgeoisie. Apart from the sociological development which sought, not to consolidate, but to separate and build up anew—the intellectual spirit of the popular movement was as determinedly bourgeois in the one camp as it was deliberately revolutionary in the other. It is these contrasting and conflicting forces which make the aspect of the time so contradictory. Counter-revolutionaries pointed mockingly to many philistine and puritan elements among the new forces; but far more marked was the spirit of youthful enthusiasm which informed the movement to the last. The young were glad to be young, they were proud of their youth; they called things fearlessly by their right names and the very boldness and uncompromising spirit of their youth awakened confidence and won them followers from among the simple hearts of the lower classes who did not want to be pedantically instructed, but led with enthusiasm. Sometimes a little foolishness is both subtle and more fruitful than too much wisdom; the rising classes were all for emotion and sentiment; their strongest feature was a blind natural urge and they sought passion in which they could take fire. They believed because they wished to believe and had need of sacrifice, often the sacrifice of their very lives. It has rightly been said that revolutions bring about outbreaks of both sensual and religious emotion. Something absolute arose and masks were laid aside. Nature demanded her eternal rights. It was the task of the leaders to find an ethical and reasonable justification in opposition to everything conventional. Everything in reason was supposed to be attainable. No doubt the last great battle for the Constitution was beset by stupidities; nothing is easier than to prove this; but it is quite unimportant. The new, free, strong, just Germany was sought after with passionate heroism by the blinded, excited, newly-awakened combatants; they, too, wished for better times; why not, indeed? Every true fighter battles for himself and for his cause at the same time. The two things should not be separated. In any case it was anything but bourgeois to possess so much imagination, such a capacity for sacrifice. It was these qualities which made the conquered of 1849 into prisoners for the eternal revolution of humanity.

Naturally there were fanatics and quacks in this German revolution, as in every other. The masses were too enraptured by what was new for its own sake to distinguish the charlatan and the profiteer at first sight. This condition of things most bitterly affected the old guard of 1848; their seriousness and experienced knowledge was suddenly challenged and overwhelmed by unbalanced hysteria; disgusted, the former opposition either retired altogether from the scene or sought alliance with the older powers, being usually unable to discern the element of strength in the new, young oppositional spirit.

This procedure meant something decisive in German social history and in the later development of the German party system. Before 1848 there were many signs that a new lower-class might be formed in Germany on a broad basis, consisting of artisans, employees, servants, working-men, peasant-farmers, and small shopkeepers; a class that would have been democratic in the widest sense of the word; that is, national, parliamentary, and social, and which would not have been disinclined to acknowledge a democratic emperor. The Counter-Revolution prevented the development of this class and thus the evolution of such a party. The very name of "democratic" vanished for a time. In South Germany, it was replaced by "People's Party" (Volkspartei). The name and conception "social-democratic," which we have seen appearing in Baden, Saxony, and Electoral Hesse, was destined to a splendid career later. . . .

Comparison with all other revolutions in modern history shows the German Revolution of 1848–49 to have had the smallest percentage of deeds of violence, also of crimes against property. During his revolt, Friedrich Hecker ran along the ranks, urging his men to take nothing without paying for it on the nail, since the villagers were already lamenting as if a band of robbers were approaching. When, during the Berlin March Revolution, certain people threatened to take a fancy to the silver vessels in the Jerusalemer Church, Wolff the sculptor, who had marched to revolution in his dressing-gown, girt with a sabre and crowned with a flapping broad-brimmed hat, pretended to be seized with revolutionary fury, bore the vessels off and secreted them in his house until things quieted down. There was no organized revolutionary terror; a couple of isolated acts such as the tearing down of the Dresden opera house were mere individual excesses. But there is much evidence that the soldiers beat their prisoners, and the treatment of political prisoners in convict prisons was often purposely harsh.

The German Revolution of 1848 erected no guillotines and held no extraordinary courts of a purely political nature. No one except Prince Metternich was banished; there was no confiscation of fortunes, no holding-up of salaries, no refusal of pensions. No one in Germany thought that in order to combat the past, its representatives must be made personally defenceless and economically impotent. Outwardly it was nothing more than a purely political reversal, borne aloft by representatives of pure humanitarianism; a humane revolution is necessarily a semi-revolution. This was probably the deepest error of the men of 1848. Revolution is battle and carries the principle of force into the formation of the State. The princes had always made their wars ruthlessly without regard either to other peoples or to their own. The German democratic movement of 1848 wished to achieve a gentle victory. No historian will reproach the leaders with shedding too little blood; there are other ways of removing opponents. The Revolution of 1848 did not perceive them or took no note of them. The leaders must have known their opponents well enough, but did nothing to cripple their activity or to replace them in their posts by followers of the new order. The Frankfort central power could have chosen people in whom they could have confidence; the old particularistic bureaucratic machine continued to rattle untroubled on its way. There were martyrs enough from the Revolution of 1830 and the Wars of Liberation. Certainly they were elected to the Frankfort Parliament—Ernst Moritz Arndt, Jahn, Uhland, Eisenmann, Sylvester Jordan—but they had very little voice in affairs. The young revolutionaries suffered from the German fault of overtrustfulness. They took no revenge; the patriotic and liberty-loving citizens saw the principal danger in the Jacobins, Social-Revolutionaries, and Communists.

Naturally, there was much malicious joy over the fall of the mighty; the lack of talent for quick, sharp action was compensated for by a tremendous gift for scolding: grumbling, criticism, speculations as to how it could have been better done, frittered away the urge to action. Curiously enough, this quarrelsome criticism rapidly turned from the old to expend its force against the new leaders. The new men may have had their weaknesses; but they were mercilessly exposed. The moment anyone rose to the top, he was attacked with embittered jealousy; Welcker, Heinrich von Gagern, Robert Blum, Friedrich Hecker—the same fate overtook them all. This was the reverse side of the medal of the conscientious revolution of 1848; it destroyed its own children. The Revolution had practically talked itself to death by the time the Counter-Revolution was on the march. The people's leaders had only a momentary authority; they had continually to fight for it; their weaknesses were those of the people themselves and therefore unforgivable. Public opinion was particularly resentful if the new men profited economically from their work. Anyone who accepted a government position with a fixed income, like Karl Mathy or Wilhelm Jordan, was already half a traitor. Heinrich von Gagern was so sensitive on this point that it was necessary absolutely to force upon him the salary accompanying the post of President of the Frankfort Parliament by passing a law that there could be no refusal of this salary. A healthy desire to see clean hands in public affairs was thus so exaggerated as to lead to pure absurdity. For the bureaucratic apparatus remained, just for this reason, practically unchanged.

Thus the humanitarian State, as the March movement dreamed of it, could not come into being. Men longed for action and feared it at the same time. When the big speeches were over, there was remarkable modesty in deeds and also a certain hesitation. The old layer of officialdom presented a very solid front in comparison. It did not glitter, it did not trifle, it was something in itself and had no need to become anything different. When these people accused the democratic leaders of wanting to snatch office, of vanity and who knows what else, there was scarcely anyone who thought to rebuff the questioner by asking where these noblemen, these property-owners, these manufacturers had come by their fortunes. Most of the new people were poor and suffered from poverty; they therefore hesitated between shyness and excited claims; they had talent, good sense, patriotism, a feeling for what was right, they turned everything into debate, believed they could convince the majority and carried motions; they thought they could alter German realities by a new Constitution, by new laws. It was an honourable undertaking, but unfortunately the mass of the public soon grew tired of it. There was not enough going on, it was not rapid, not dramatic, not wild enough. The loud-mouthedness which sprang up by the side of the noble pioneers of a new justice, awakened in the mass of the public a respect for what had been; pity and sympathy for fallen greatness is also a good trait of the German nature; only a clever twisting of contemporary events was necessary to weld a new loyalty, in exercising which the people thought themselves mighty fine fellows and true as steel. It was just those who had always been despised and ill-treated by the old powers who now made use of the opportunity to get a little nearer to the throne, without running any great danger and so to gain social and economic advantages. The nobles had always had a certain independence; unquestioning devotion was to be the characteristic of this new class of citizen.

The Reform movement had tried to be just to everyone, a political point of view must never anticipate the judgment of history. Will to righteousness made these men self-righteous. This roused their political opponents to absolute hatred. The Republicans, the Social-Revolutionaries, the Communists had the active courage to be unjust; but only minorities followed their lead.

The Counter-Revolution certainly had more courage to be unjust. There was no question of asking whether blood might be shed or property destroyed; there was no need to seize the means of power; the Counter-Revolution had all that was necessary. If the popular movement in North Germany, except in Berlin, seemed somewhat lacking in temperament, the Counter-Revolution was undoubtedly more emotional. Religion, patriotism, morality, loyalty to the traditional ruling house proceeded to the attack. The Revolution had branded only Metternich as a criminal; the Counter-Revolution branded a whole social class as rogues and vagabonds. When the vanquished marched out of Rastatt, the Prince of Prussia turned away. He did not want to see "such people." The Revolution had built up a legend of its own pre-history; the Counter-Revolution now wrote the legend of the nature of this democratic movement and thus exercised a decisive influence upon two German generations. The Revolution had taken care to make no martyrs; the Counter-Revolution had no such scruples. Ordinary courts competed with courts-martial. The feeling of justice, so sensitive at this time, was once more deeply wounded by a whole series of political trials.

Jacob Burckhardt said power was an evil thing. There is something worse than power. Power is, above all, fickle. It must be won and manifested afresh from day to day. Only use can keep it bright and keen. It serves only those who grasp it firmly. Woe to them who possess it and do not use it, for it will turn against them. This was the experience of the German citizen of 1848; the measure of logical retribution which he had not in himself, was visited upon him with interest by the Counter-Revolution. The humanitarian, the decent citizen, the cosmopolitan dialectician, had no more to say. The world had shown that it was not beautiful and pure as the classic form, nor joyous and brightly-coloured like an intellectual romantic play. A dashing age usurped the scene, impudent and coarse, unashamed, inclined to mockery and brutality. Certainly no political movement could be suppressed entirely by police and the courts; there were more subtle measures and these had a decisive effect. The "people," it was said, had proved themselves to be insolent, avaricious, rough, and treacherous; they needed control and they should have it. Arrogance and contempt of mankind, the ancient vices of ruling classes, now went disguised as the art of protective government. . . .

The new never entirely destroyed the old. The German is not good at destruction. Even after the founding of Bismarck's empire, German unity was a foreign political and economic reality, but not a spiritual experience of the people as a whole. This is still more true of the political forms of the Weimar republic period. The demands arising from them will always lead us back to 1848. He who is not certain what to do will certainly not find that history informs him. But he whose will is clearly set to certain aims ahead can search the past and find an answer there. Every century since the sixteenth has brought severe civil struggles in Germany. The old German lust of battle found vent in wars between the individual states every time a quarrel arose. Not until the German Confederation of 1815 was there any peacefulness, at the cost of freedom. When the people of 1848 arose, everyone once more fought against everyone else; but the struggle did not come fully to a head. To this extent the year 1866 represents the late realization of everything that had been neglected or could not be achieved by the better way of understanding. The year 1866 is a secular epoch—it was thrust into the background by the brilliance and fulfilment of the year 1870–71, but historically speaking, it weighed almost more heavily.

Nations have the primeval right to throw off foreign oppression. They also have the primeval right so to shape the State that it is ruled by a class of leaders so fitted for the task that the working people are taught to be contented. A great deal of force has been used in Germany—formerly it was mostly the slaves, peasants, citizens, working-men, who bore the brunt. The peace-loving cosmopolitan, too, may be turned into a world-revolutionary by the narrow-minded opposition of those in power. Revolution is not a sin. With the year 1848, a new era of revolutions began, which is not yet at an end. Fichte already sought the Revolution which Napoleon had ruined. Just as Bismarck in 1866 asked an indemnity from the Prussian people's representatives, so should the whole military-bureaucratic epoch of Imperial Germany have begged a timely indemnity from the idea of the free democratic State. The right to revolution finds its only limitations in the degree of talent available to carry it through and create a new State. Formerly revolutions and wars were strictly divided. The danger of revolution was parried by declaring war, and lost wars usually ended in revolution. Today pointing of war and revolution is seen as an identical threat, pointing in different directions, achieved by the same means. Every revolution, too, is a technical fighting problem. In 1848, fighting was done simultaneously with antiquated weapons, such as the barricade system and the volunteer principle, and with very modern weapons, such as the utilization of means of transport and the organization of news. Wars and revolutions seem to be growing more and more to resemble one another; the revolutions have learned from the wars the idea of universal arming of the people, as was repeatedly done in 1848. War learnt terrorism from revolution. We know that the reform of the Prussian Army in the 'sixties can be traced back to the attitude of the Prussian Landwehr or reserve troops, in 1848–49, which, in many places, felt themselves as militia rather than as tools of authority.

The popular movement of 1848, the strongest motive in which was the national urge, ended with the conviction that nationalism and internationalism are contrary poles. But always, ever since the days of feudalism, Europe has been a unit. Have not Kant and Goethe influenced England; Hegel, France; Nietzsche, Italy; Marx and Engels, Russia, to the greatest extent? There is no isolation. Today we see very plainly that a fruitful and peaceful international life is only possible between democratic nations, ripened, grown peaceful, nationally satisfied. The history of Germany as a nation and as a form of State and society is not yet complete. It may be carried on by fresh revolutions, but not necessarily. There is no danger of revolution which cannot be banned by reforms and wise statesmanship. The Revolution of 1848, trodden underfoot by the Counter-Revolution, was not dead. It sat in the Eternal Paulskirche of Greater Germanism and waited for the hour of re-birth. Doubtless it is still sitting there to this day. The old cannot and will not return. But the patriotism of 1848, in its purity and its resolve, is the immortal ally in all future struggles of the German nation.

5. A. J. P TAYLOR: The Course of German History*

A. J. P. Taylor, of Oxford University, is a prolific writer on modern European history who delights in controversy. His specialty is diplomatic history, and much of his work on national histories stresses the political-diplomatic causes and results of major events. He is no lover of Germany, and he sees in 1848 perhaps more a symptom than a major cause of Germany's modern character. Taylor's account accords with Namier's and Hamerow's in certain respects, but even the similar judgments may have a different tone; and they are certainly put in a different specific framework, for Taylor believes that there was no real revolution at all.

1848 was the decisive year of German, and so of European, history: it recapitulated Germany's past and anticipated Germany's future. Echoes of the Holy Roman Empire merged into a prelude of the Nazi "New Order"; the doctrines of Rousseau and the doctrines of Marx, the shade of Luther and the shadow of Hitler, jostled each other in bewildering succession. Never has there been a revolution so inspired by a limitless faith in the power of ideas; never has a revolution so discredited the power of ideas in its result. The success of the revolution discredited conservative ideas; the failure of the revolution discredited liberal ideas. After it, nothing remained but the idea of Force, and this idea stood at the helm of German history from then on. For the first time since 1521, the German people stepped on to the centre of the German stage only to miss their cues once more. German history reached its turning-point and failed to turn. This was the fateful essence of 1848. . . .

The revolution of 1848 was not the explosion of new forces, but the belated triumph of the *Burschenschaft,* the students of the war of liberation who were now men in their fifties. Arndt, the writer of patriotic poems against Napoleon, and even "gymnastic father" Jahn were as much the symbols of 1848 as they had been of 1813; but now their voices quavered as they sang of their youthful energy and their muscles creaked as they displayed their youthful energy in Swedish drill.

The liberals who occupied the forefront of 1848 were the men of 1813, now sobered by the long empty years. They had learnt to be cautious, to be moderate, learnt, as they thought, worldly wisdom. They had sat in the parliaments of the lesser states and had come to believe that everything could be achieved by discussion and by peaceful persuasion. Themselves dependent on the princes for their salaries or pensions as civil servants, they put belief in the good faith of princes as the first article of their policy, and genuinely supposed that they could achieve their aims by converting their rulers. Behind them were the radicals, men of unknown names and without experience: members of the

* From A. J. P. Taylor, *The Course of German History,* pp. 68–73; 77. Capricorn Edition.

same intellectual middle class, but of a younger generation—the product of the Romantic Movement, the contemporaries of Liszt, of Paganini, and of Hoffmann. These radicals were not interested in practical results. For them revolution was an end in itself, and violence the only method of politics. Yet, though they appealed constantly to force, they possessed none. The radical attempts of 1848—Hecker's proclamation of the German republic in April and Struve's rising in September—were not even damp squibs, merely bad theatre. The radicals appealed constantly to the people, and demanded universal suffrage and a People's Republic. But they had no connection with the people of Germany, no mass support, no contact with the masses, no understanding of their needs. Thus the revolution was played out on a carefully restricted stage: on the one side the ruling princes, on the other the educated middle class in its two aspects, liberal and radical. In the end the peasant masses cleared the stage; but these peasants were disciplined conscripts in the Prussian army.

Yet the unpropertied uneducated masses were discontented and restless both in town and country; and there was in 1848 an unconscious mass revolution as well as a conscious liberal one. The inexorable increase of population made the peasants of eastern Germany land-hungry and drove the peasants of western Germany into the grip of the moneylender. The intellectual talk of revolution filtered down to the peasants, just as the intellectual ferment of the Reformation had filtered down to them in the sixteenth century. In the early months of 1848 central Europe experienced a sporadic peasant stirring, pale image of the Peasants' Revolt of 1525. In the east peasants refused their services, even attacked castles, proclaimed their freedom by appearing with clean-shaven chins; in the west they expected the community of goods and assembled in the village market places to await the general division of all property. This universal movement was altogether ignored by the middle-class liberals, and even the most extreme radicals averted their eyes. The peasants were left leaderless and unorganized. Often they turned back to their "natural leaders," the landowners. Elsewhere they accepted the directions of "authority." But everywhere the revolutionary impulse was lost. The revolution of 1848 had no agrarian programme.

The revolutionary leaders lived in the towns and therefore could not ignore so completely the movement of the urban masses. But they had no social programme, or, at best, one produced shamefacedly and *ad hoc*. The handicraft workers were being ruined by the competition of cheap mass-produced English goods; and in the winter of 1847 to 1848 the first general economic crisis devastated the larger German towns. The revolution of March 13th in Vienna and the revolution of March 18th in Berlin, which together cleared the way for the German revolution, were both glorified unemployed riots. Yet there was no connection between the political leaders and this movement of the unemployed. The town workers were given soup kitchens and relief on task work but not as part of a deliberate social policy. The liberals yielded against their economic principles in order to still the social disorder; the radicals seconded the demands of the masses not from conviction but in order to capture the masses for what they regarded as the real revolutionary aims—universal suffrage, trial by jury, election of army officers, cancelling of pensions to state officials and so on. The liberals used the mass unrest to extract concessions from the princes. The National Guard, that universal liberal expedient, for instance, was everywhere advocated as the defender of social order. The radicals, more daring, whipped up the masses in order to frighten the princes still more. But not even the few extreme radicals such as Marx, who called themselves Socialists, had any real concern for the masses or any contact with them. In their eyes the masses were the cannon fodder of the revolution; and they had no words too harsh for the masses when they wearied of filling this role. Nothing could exceed Marx's horror and disgust when his friend Engels actually took an Irish factory girl as his mistress; and Marx's attitude was symbolical of the German revolutionaries.

This divorce between the revolutionaries and the people determined the happenings of 1848. The revolution had officers but no rank and file. The old forces, on which the system of 1815 rested, succumbed to their own weakness and confusion; but no new forces took their place. There followed instead the rule of ideas, and this rule ended as soon as the old forces recovered their nerve. The German Confederation of 1815 had depended not on its own strength, but on the triangular balance of France, Austria, and Prussia. In the early months of 1848 this balance was overthrown by the revolutions in Paris, Vienna, and Berlin. The citizens of Germany—quite literally the established inhabitants of the towns—suddenly found themselves free without effort of their own. The prison walls fell, the gaolers disappeared. The Germany of intellectual conception suddenly became the Germany of established fact. For this transformation the three revolutions on the circumference were all essential. Had a single centre of power remained the German revolution would never have taken place. To consider the causes of the failure of the German revolution is thus a barren speculation. The successful revolutions were in Paris, Vienna, and Berlin. There was no successful revolution in Germany; and therefore nothing to fail. There was merely a vacuum in which the liberals postured until the vacuum was filled. . . .

The Prussian monarchy had none of the diseases which it needs a revolution to cure. Its administration was efficient, its finances in good order, the discipline of its army firm and the self-confidence of the army officers unshaken. The atmosphere of 1848 was certain to produce riots in Berlin. But according to all reasonable expectation the Prussian army was strong enough to restore order and to maintain absolutism. And so it did when the riots flared up into street fighting on March 18th. The rioters were pressed back, the streets cleared, the army was within sight of controlling all Berlin. The abnormal factor was the character of Frederick William IV. Disliking the army and hating the military traditions of his house, bewildered and depressed by the failure of his romantic ideas during the meeting of the United Diet, he could not go through with the conquest of his capital. Even on March 18th he had coupled force with exhortations. On the next day he lost his nerve altogether: promised first to withdraw the troops if the barricades were removed, and at length ordered the troops to withdraw unconditionally. By March 21st Berlin was, outwardly, in the hands of the revolution. A burgher guard patrolled the streets; the King drove through the streets wearing the revolutionary colours of national Germany; and ostensibly he embraced the revolutionary cause in the most famous of all his many phrases—"Prussia merges into Germany."

The victory of the Berlin revolution determined the course of events in Germany. Where the Prussian army had failed no prince could hope to succeed. The way was open for the liberal middle classes to put into practice their programme of a Germany united by consent. Radicalism, even if it had possessed more driving power, seemed unnecessary. After all, no one would choose the way of the barricades if the meeting of committees could achieve the same result. But the Berlin victory was illusory—hence all the disasters of the future. The Prussian army was not defeated: it was resentful, humiliated, but still confident. The army leaders were determined somehow to win back the King and to renew the struggle broken off on March 19th. Nor was Frederick William IV a convert to the liberal cause. His nerve had failed. He complained to Bismarck that he had been unable to sleep for worry. Bismarck replied roughly: "A king must be able to sleep." Short of going out of his mind (which did not happen until 1858) Frederick William would have a good night sooner or later; and thereupon Prussian policy would begin to recover its strength. Moreover Frederick William at his most distraught had all the cunning of the mentally unstable. Forced to agree to the meeting of a Prussian parliament, he tried to turn his surrender to advantage by suggesting that all Germany should send representatives to the Prussian parliament and so achieve German unification *ipso facto.* His readiness to sink Prussia in Germany was fraudulent, and the Germans were asked to entrust themselves to Frederick William's erratic impulses. . . .

The Frankfort liberals were not actuated, as is sometimes supposed, by class interest. They were not capitalists or property owners; they were lawyers and professors. Disorder and revolution offended their principles and threatened their high ideal of creating a united Germany by consent. Nothing good, they believed, could come of the intrusion of the masses into politics; and they regarded the repressive activities of the armed forces as essential to the security of the liberal cause.

The refusal of Frankfort to go with the masses, the failure to offer a social programme, was a decisive element in the failure of the German liberals. This refusal and this failure are the theme of *Germany: Revolution and Counter-Revolution,* the pamphlet which Engels wrote for Marx and which is still the best analysis of the events of 1848. But there was another, and even more important cause of failure, a disastrous mistake which Marx, Engels, and most German radicals shared. The National Assembly had come into being when the armed power of Austria and Prussia collapsed; and its prestige waned as Austrian and Prussian armed power revived. These armies won new confidence, no doubt, in the repression of internal disorder. But the prime purpose of armies is foreign war, and it was in foreign war of a sort that Austrian and Prussian absolutism were reborn. Not the social conflict, but the conflict on the national frontiers—in Bohemia, in Poland, and in Slesvig and Holstein—determined the fate of German liberalism. In the struggle against the Czechs, against the Poles, against the Danes, the German liberals unhesitatingly supported the cause of the Prussian and Austrian armies and were then surprised when these weapons were turned against themselves. Liberalism was sacrificed to the national cause.

6. HANS ROTHFELS: 1848—One Hundred Years After*

Here is a last effort to put 1848 in proper historical perspective. Hans Rothfels taught in German universities until he was forced out by the Nazis; he then taught in England and the United States before returning to the University of Tübingen. His interpretation of the revolution in some senses returns to the liberal view of historians like Valentin; certainly he cannot see a fatal corruption of German character resulting from 1848. Particularly interesting is his effort to place the revolution in a contemporary, comparative framework, showing its close correspondence to presumably praiseworthy movements in other countries.

Within the crucial year, this seems to be more or less accepted as the crucial question: Would not a success of the German revolution, i.e., a timely "Westernization" and democratization of Germany, have helped to turn history in a more promising direction?

In fact, social and international conditions were far from auguring well for such a perspective. But this is not a sufficient answer. Undoubtedly some specific problems of German history are involved in the failure; or, as some observers are inclined to state, the failure indicates a characteristic German deficiency. According to this view it is one of the blameworthy things in the general development of this nation that it never carried out a successful revolution. On the basis of either inborn qualities or acquired habits the Germans are simply not made of revolutionary stuff.

It can readily be admitted that the German revolution of 1848 (just like that of 1918) had a certain predilection for "orderly" procedures (incidentally one approved by Americans in 1848) and showed many philistine traits. The Berlin tailor who after the events painted the Prussian eagle over the door of his shop and wrote underneath, "I can peacefully press under the shadow of thy wings," was no isolated case. And the "freedom to smoke" (even in the *Tiergarten*) may have appeared to many good burghers more important than other achievements of the revolution. It is also undoubtedly true that the German people were still largely parochial, that multiple authority, parceled out as it was among thirty-nine states, and allegiance to small and even tiny entities did not exactly further self-reliance. Even the popular upheavals themselves sometimes resulted in what has been called *gemütliche* anarchy; they were not free of

* From Hans Rothfels, "1848: One Hundred Years After," *Journal of Modern History* (Chicago, 1948), pp. 305–307. Reprinted by permission of the *Journal of Modern History* and the author.

naïve and melodramatic elements which combined strangely with shocking outrages committed by both sides.

On the other hand, it would be unjust to minimize the courage and resoluteness displayed in the actual fighting. The Frenchman Adolphe Circourt, who witnessed the engagements in Paris as well as in Berlin, found that the men of March 18 fought more fiercely than the Parisians had done on February 24. But quite apart from some biases which have clouded these facts (in German as well as in non-German books), there seems to exist, behind the condemnation of German "legalism" and "loyalism," a certain dogmatic assumption which is popular in French and American rather than in English thought and which holds that revolution is good per se. One can easily understand the background of this tradition and the preference for a manifestation of manliness and of an unconditional love of freedom. It was strikingly displayed, for example, in liberal sympathies for the heroic figure of Louis Kossuth, though he was fighting for feudal privileges and against the rights of oppressed nationalities struggling under the Magyar yoke. At any rate, the historian cannot overlook the fact that revolutions are conducive to evil as well as to good and that there are differences between those which may more aptly be called "wars of liberation" and those in which classes or ideologies fight, or try to eliminate, one another in the fashion of religious wars. Moreover, with recent as well as with present experiences in mind, one may wonder whether the somewhat abstract and platonic sympathy with revolutions as such is still so strong in the Western world. Now that the specter of a threat to the traditional way of life and a potential split within national societies has come uncomfortably close, it is perhaps easier to render justice to the men of 1848 and to their sense of crisis.

This is not meant to be an apology for the social shortsightedness which many German liberals of 1848 showed or for their bourgeois instincts. They wore the blinkers of their own time. But in principle history has confirmed their view that the deification of the masses is no sounder political tenet than the deification of the state and that liberty can be threatened from two sides. Certainly, a man of the moral stature of the historian F. C. Dahlmann who in his previous career had given sufficient evidence of civil courage, could claim with good conscience that it was strength rather than weakness to be moderate and not to advocate an abstract ideal of national unity and freedom, which involved the elimination of all dynasties and required other concessions to popular emotions. He spoke of a "noble resistance" to the temptation of power.

But there are the voices of those who doubt the genuineness of such convictions. To them Frankfort stands as a "byword for unreality and phrasemongering"; in their view the majority, i.e., the deputies of the modern groups, thought that "by talking about human liberty they could conceal their shameful weakness." In fact, it is believed, they sacrificed all principles of freedom and a real social reform to their "dreams of world conquest" and to their national aggressiveness. In sum they proved that they were true representatives of a "destructive people" (Taylor) whose history finds nothing but its natural climax in Hitler.

While the more obvious points of excess and the propaganda slogans in this interpretation can be left aside, the historian, nonetheless, is faced with the striking fact that judgment of the German Forty-eighters and of Frankfort in some respects has gone the full circle. The attitude of contempt and disparagement which Marx and Engels had taken toward the typically liberal trends of the revolution was followed by a sort of lukewarm appraisal in the period of Bismarck (an appraisal tempered by *Realpolitik*). Then evaluation extended to the democratic trends; it became more emphatic particularly after 1918; and in the German celebrations of the centenary, however little there was to celebrate actually, serious efforts have been made to salvage and revive the positive and idealistic elements in the tradition of 1848. At the same time, however, not only has the Marxist view regained credit (even among people who would shudder at the idea of this ancestry), but this has been accompanied by a debunking tendency, by a neorealism, a "surrealism," which tries to discover the "dreams" and the subconscious mentality underlying a surface idealism and which consequently distorts many historic features. This interpretation concentrates on the nationalist aspects of 1848 and of the German revolution in particular.

Chapter VII.

LIBERALISM

FEW TOPICS are as elusive, or as important, as the "isms" of the nineteenth century. Liberalism is a case in point. For the century as a whole, this was clearly the most important new political force at work in western and central Europe. Most of the revolutions of the century can be properly termed liberal to some extent. Most political systems evolved toward some degree of liberalism, however compromised. Major liberal parties existed in most countries, after mid-century at least.

Yet there have been very few efforts to assess liberalism as a whole. Historians refer to it constantly, whether dealing with some large characterization of the century or with a limited topic in intellectual, political, or economic history. Its existence is, then, usually assumed. There are several barriers to its study, however. First, there is the recurrent problem of national boundaries and differences. Liberal ideas and political impulses spread widely across Europe, but it is easiest to study them within a particular national framework. And, as soon as this approach is adopted, it becomes clear that each national liberal movement had peculiarities of its own. The scholar is discouraged, then, from making remarks about liberalism in general. Yet here is an anomaly: the scholar who points out the weakness or statist orientation of German liberalism, or the unusual anticlericalism of French liberalism, is implicity using some more general (probably Anglo-Saxon) standard of measurement; surely this standard requires separate study and comment.

Aside from national distinctions, liberalism resists easy definition because it cannot be neatly categorized as "ideological" or "political" or "economic." Liberal political theory existed, of course, and like most formal systems of ideas it is open to reasonably clear characterizations, though there are major disagreements even here. But liberalism in politics did not necessarily correspond nicely to liberal ideas. Like members of any political movement, liberals sought to attract various kinds of support and were often tempted to compromise their ideals. And even to begin with, many liberal politicians had interests that failed to coincide with liberal theory. Many, for example, were bureaucrats who were at least as anxious to rationalize and expand the operations of the state as to protect individuals from the state. Others were businessmen who certainly sought to limit governmental action that hampered economic growth, but who sought positive government support with equal vigor. Similar difficulties arise for economic liberalism. The economic theory of classical liberals is definable, but most businessmen of liberal learnings failed to apply liberal principles consistently.

The historian of liberalism must ask, then, what strand of liberalism is most important. Many have been tempted to choose liberal ideas, because they are the easiest to get at and because they convey something of the liberal impulse in general. But are not other aspects of liberalism slighted or distorted by the ideological approach? If liberalism existed at all, as opposed to separate categories of liberal endeavor such as political theory, there must be some essence to it; but how can one describe it?

Finally, there is the inevitable problem of chronology. Liberalism did not stand still, either ideologically or politically. Thus, its definition depends greatly on the period chosen. Liberalism before 1848 can be seen as a revolutionary movement, but not afterward. Liberals progressively abandoned some of their opposition to state activity, particularly in the realms of education and economic reform. Is it possible to select some criteria to fit liberalism of any period, and would such criteria be historically useful? And relatedly, at what point, if at all, does liberalism become so altered that it is no longer liberal?

Following from these general problems of orientation, a number of more specific issues arise in the treatment of liberalism. How exclusive is the term to be? It is certainly possible to separate liberalism, as an ideal and, sometimes, as an organized movement, from democracy or nationalism or capitalism, and even to see essential oppositions between liberalism and these other forces. It is equally possible to view these forces, or aspects of them, as outgrowths or associates of the liberal impulse. Disagreements here might be largely chronological in origin, resulting from disputes over the period in which essential liberalism can be defined. Or they might reflect a more basic difference concerning the essence of liberalism: whether it is a spirit which can pervade many different movements (possibly even socialism) or an ideological or political movement in its own right.

The most obvious difficulty in treating liberalism is that of personal commitment. However weakened or altered, liberalism is not dead in the twentieth century. The issues it raises still stir debate. One of the basic motives for the study of nineteenth-century liberalism has been a desire to show the power and beauty of its principles. This approach can bring a subtlety of understanding and a vigor of presentation impossible to the uncommitted. But it also leads to overpersonal interpretations and to judgments that reflect what the author wishes liberalism to be in the twentieth century, rather than to valid interpretations of what it was in the nineteenth. This approach almost inevitably stresses the ideological elements of liberalism, its most permanent and pure features. A study of liberalism can, equally, be undertaken in opposition, to show its inadequacy or villainy. This approach will usually focus on the practical effects of liberalism, particularly in the economy. Of course, in terms of accuracy or objectivity, it promises no necessary improvement over the sympathic approach.

The assessment of the histories of liberalism involves, then, a number of factors, ranging from an evaluation of partisanship to a determination of the time and place, if any, to which a history has reference. All students of the subject grant its importance, its vital role in shaping the nineteenth century. Yet this importance in itself guarantees controversy, and not merely because of continuing political passions. A basic force such as liberalism leaves no neat, easily catalogued records. Of course, the historian can look to the statements of politicians or the writings of political theorists; but liberalism did not end there. It was, to some extent, a mood that had wide popular currency. Such a spirit, however, is hard for historians to treat (though they are forced to deal with it in texts and lectures) precisely because the source material is so diffuse. Hence, most efforts to capture the nature of nineteenth-century liberalism have come from philosophers rather than historians. The latter prefer to work on more modest topics within the general framework, such as the evolution of a particular liberal party or the ideology of a generation of liberal theorists in a single country. One final question to raise in an assessment of the historiography of liberalism is whether the phenomenon (as a whole) admits of historical treatment at all. There may be very real impulses or tendencies, which can be assessed historically only in some specific manifestations. Perhaps, by default, this is what most historians believe.

1. L. T. HOBHOUSE: Liberalism*

Professor Leonard Hobhouse (1884–1929) taught at Oxford and later served as editor of the *Manchester Guardian*. He was early aroused by the liberal writings of John Stuart Mill and remained a devoted liberal throughout his life; he wrote *Liberalism,* one of his many books, in 1911. His effort at a definition of liberalism, portions of which follow, is a mixture of a partisan statement—called the best modern defense of liberalism—and a historical view. The attempt to show the evolution of liberalism must be assessed both for its historical accuracy for the later nineteenth century and for its treatment of the continuity between this brand of liberalism and the earlier one.

I cannot here attempt so much as a sketch of the historical progress of the Liberalizing movement. I would call attention only to the main points at which it assailed the old order, and to the fundamental ideas directing its advance.

Both logically and historically the first point of attack is arbitrary government, and the first liberty to be secured is the right to be dealt with in accordance with law. . . .

To put the same point from another side, the first condition of free government is government not by the arbitrary determination of the ruler, but by fixed rules of law, to which the ruler himself is subject. We draw the important inference that there is no essential antithesis between liberty and law. On the contrary, law is essential to liberty. Law, of course, restrains the individual; it is therefore opposed to his liberty at a given moment and in a given direction. But, equally, law restrains others from doing with him as they will. It liberates him from the fear of arbitrary aggression or coercion, and this is the only way, indeed, the only sense, in which liberty *for an entire community* is attainable. . . .

There is one point tacitly postulated in this argument which should not be overlooked. In assuming that the reign of law guarantees liberty to the whole community, we are assuming that it is impartial. If there is one law for the Government and another for its subjects, one for noble and another for commoner, one for rich and another for poor, the law does not guarantee liberty for all. Liberty in this respect implies equality. Hence the demand of Liberalism for such a procedure as will ensure the impartial application of law. Hence the demand for the independence of the judiciary to secure equality as between the Government and its subjects. Hence the demand for cheap procedure and

* From L. T. Hobhouse, *Liberalism* (London: Oxford University Press, 1964), pp. 16–18, 22–23, 28–29. Reprinted by permission of the Oxford University Press.

accessible courts. Hence the abolition of privileges of class. Hence will come in time the demand for the abolition of the power of money to purchase skilled advocacy. . . .

Fiscal liberty raises more searching questions than juristic liberty. It is not enough that taxes should be fixed by a law applying universally and impartially, for taxes vary from year to year in accordance with public needs, and while other laws may remain stable and unchanged for an indefinite period, taxation must, in the nature of the case, be adjustable. It is a matter, properly considered, for the Executive rather than the Legislature. Hence the liberty of the subject in fiscal matters means the restraint of the Executive, not merely by established and written laws, but by a more direct and constant supervision. It means, in a word, responsible government, and that is why we have more often heard the cry, "No taxation without representation," than the cry, "No legislation without representation." Hence, from the seventeenth century onwards, fiscal liberty was seen to involve what is called political liberty. . . .

Apart from monopolies, industry was shackled in the earlier part of the modern period by restrictive legislation in various forms, by navigation laws, and by tariffs. In particular, the tariff was not merely an obstruction to free enterprise, but a source of inequality as between trade and trade. Its fundamental effect is to transfer capital and labour from the objects on which they can be most profitably employed in a given locality, to objects on which they are less profitably employed, by endowing certain industries to the disadvantage of the general consumer. Here, again, the Liberal movement is at once an attack on an obstruction and on an inequality. In most countries the attack has succeeded in breaking down local tariffs and establishing relatively large Free Trade units. It is only in England, and only owing to our early manufacturing supremacy, that it has fully succeeded in overcoming the Protective principle, and even in England the Protectionist reaction would undoubtedly have gained at least a temporary victory but for our dependence on foreign countries for food and the materials of industry. The most striking victory of Liberal ideas is one of the most precarious. At the same time, the battle is one which Liberalism is always prepared to fight over again. It has led to no back stroke, no counter-movement within the Liberal ranks themselves.

It is otherwise with organized restrictions upon industry. The old regulations, which were quite unsuited to the conditions of the time, either fell into desuetude during the eighteenth century, or were formally abolished during the earlier years of the industrial revolution. For a while it seemed as though wholly unrestricted industrial enterprise was to be the progressive watchword, and the echoes of that time still linger. But the old restrictions had not been formally withdrawn before a new process of regulation began. The conditions produced by the new factory system shocked the public conscience; and as early as 1802 we find the first of a long series of laws, out of which has grown an industrial code that year by year follows the life of the operative, in his relations with his employer, into more minute detail. The first stages of this movement were contemplated with doubt and distrust by many men of Liberal sympathies. The intention was, doubtless, to protect the weaker party, but the method was that of interference with freedom of contract. Now the freedom of the sane adult individual—even such strong individualists as Cobden recognized that the case of children stood apart—carried with it the right of concluding such agreements as seemed best to suit his own interests, and involved both the right and the duty of determining the lines of his life for himself. Free contract and personal responsibility lay close to the heart of the whole Liberal movement. Hence the doubts felt by so many Liberals as to the regulation of industry by law. None the less, as time has gone on, men of the keenest Liberal sympathies have come not merely to accept but eagerly to advance the extension of public control in the industrial sphere, and of collective responsibility in the matter of the education and even the feeding of children, the housing of the industrial population, the care of the sick and aged, the provision of the means of regular employment. On this side Liberalism seems definitely to have retraced its steps, and we shall have to inquire closely into the question whether the reversal is a change of principle or of application.

Closely connected with freedom of contract is freedom of association. . . . Men may make any agreement with one another in their mutual interest so long as they do not injure a third party. . . .

We have now passed the main phases of the Liberal movement in very summary review, and we have noted, first, that it is co-extensive with life. It is concerned with the individual, the family, the State. It touches industry, law, religion, ethics. It would not be difficult, if space allowed, to illustrate its influence in literature and art, to describe the war with convention, insincerity, and patronage, and the struggle for free self-expression, for reality, for the artist's soul. Liberalism is an all-penetrating element of the life-structure of the modern world. Secondly, it is an effective historical force. If its work is nowhere complete, it is almost everywhere in progress. The modern State as we see it in Europe outside Russia, in the British colonies, in North and South America, as we begin to see it in the Russian empire and throughout the vast continent of Asia, is the old authoritarian society modified in greater or less degree by the absorption of Liberal principles. Turning, thirdly to those principles themselves, we have recognized Liberalism in every department as a movement fairly denoted by the name—a movement of liberation, a clearance of obstructions, an opening of channels for the flow of free spontaneous vital activity. Fourthly, we have seen that in a large number of cases what is under one aspect a movement for liberty is on another side a movement towards equality, and the habitual association of these principles is so far confirmed.

2. GUIDO DE RUGGIERO: A History of European Liberalism*

Here is another statement about liberalism by a twentieth-century partisan. Guido de Ruggiero has undertaken the most ambitious effort to date to assess

* From Guido de Ruggiero, *A History of European Liberalism,* R. G. Collingwood, trans. (Boston: Beacon Press, 1959), pp. 357–63. Reprinted by permission of the Clarendon Press, Oxford.

European liberalism historically. His interest lies mainly in liberal theory, and his definition differs from that of Hobhouse by being less directly political; his notion of the possible dissociation of liberalism as a spirit from liberal political parties is particularly interesting. Does this belief in a liberal spirit, however admirable, produce a sufficiently coherent historical criterion?

Various definitions of Liberalism have been given. It has been called a method, a party, an art of government, a form of State organization. These descriptions are complementary rather than exclusive, since each expresses a particular aspect of the Liberal spirit. One might endeavour to arrange them in a progressive order of complexity.

(*a*) First and foremost, Liberalism appears as the recognition of a fact, the fact of liberty. Every mental habit, every method, every art, presupposes this single act, which is the first organic element of Liberal experience. Now, only one who is himself free can recognize the freedom of others. Only the man who has experienced in himself the value of intelligent and autonomous personality is in a position to understand another's right to assert himself as a person. This understanding or recognition does not imply a merely theoretical observation; it also signifies a respect for that which it observes, a personal moral adhesion. *Homo homini res sacra,* said the ancient writer, and this mutual reverence can be established only through a profound sense of human identity, originating within us before it can arise between us.

(*b*) But the individual act, the isolated recognition, is not sufficient; as we have already seen, it may be deluded, it may let itself be deceived by appearances and attribute freedom to that which does not possess it, or deny it to that which does. Such acts must occur habitually, and thus form a watchful and discriminating experience. Liberalism has rightly been called a method, that is, a capacity to reconstruct within oneself the spiritual processes of others, and to estimate their purposes and results. Not all the manifestations of freedom have the same value and deserve the same respect: these values belong only to the moral and genuinely free personality, and can only be indirectly ascribed to the personality as yet in process of formation, as the capacity and ability to pursue a moral end, the hope of future goodness. The Liberal method begins with the presupposition that this capacity belongs to every man as man, and is not the privilege of a few. Every man must therefore have his opportunities, through the removal, so far as possible, of obstacles to his development, yet without the substitution of another's work for his own. The Liberal method is equally hostile to the solicitude of an impatient moralism claiming to shape everything after its own image, and the arrogance of an enlightened despotism which would create human progress by its own *fiat.*

Liberalism is conscious that the formation of human individualities is the work of freedom. No demand of the higher life can be effectually made, unless it is made spontaneously by the spirit; no progress will be enduringly achieved, unless it is a conscious development from within. To raise to our own level those who are living a lower life, we cannot either by grace or by force excuse them from the labour and pains that are the price of human progress, or from the necessity of traversing step by step the distance which divides them from us.

This freedom is therefore no privilege, but rather a task which the spirit imposes as the price of the benefits it confers: no one can obtain them freely; any one can obtain them by application, toil, and sacrifice. Hence the error of the authoritarians and the moralists, who arrogate to themselves the functions of a providence.

More modest, but far more difficult, is the task which a man may reasonably take upon himself in relation to other men. It begins with a conviction of the autonomy of every spiritual process, and proceeds by the rare art of arousing within himself, as a demand of his own, that which he would impart to others, and thus in causing these others to impose upon themselves those principles which he wishes to impose upon them.

(*c*) In the world of politics, this method has for partisans the so-called Liberal parties, social groups peculiarly interested in the free play of individual forces because, from their own experience, they understand their vital importance and energizing power. The function of these parties is especially critical and polemical: it consists in removing all artificial and harmful impediments to the expansion of individual energies, in refuting the sophisms of a degrading authoritarianism, and in leaving men so far as possible to act for themselves. But the end to which these Liberal means are directed is nothing but freedom; if freedom is the means, freedom in a higher and more organic form is the end. The conviction that liberty arouses energy, trust, and consent, and creates a spontaneous spirit of association and co-operation, is characteristic of all Liberal parties worthy of the name.

Those tasks proper to the State which authoritarianism discharges with immense toil and waste of energy, through ignoring or repressing the voluntary consent and co-operation of individuals, are therefore discharged by Liberalism more speedily and efficaciously. For the older Liberals, this self-government of freedom was to serve the purpose of reducing legislative and governmental functions to a minimum; but since their time experience has shown that to extend the benefits and responsibilities of freedom to all citizens and to interest them effectually in a great common task, it is necessary to embark upon new and more complex legislation and a watchful governmental activity, in order to guarantee the free development of all energies and to support them without replacing them. Thus has come about not only an enlargement of the State's action, but also its intellectual and moral advancement, since these new functions demand a power of psychological penetration and moral judgement concerning the needs of citizens, which despotic governments were not called upon to possess.

But Liberalism is only in part identical with a Liberal party; to a great extent the two may be divergent and even opposed. The critical and polemical zeal which inspires a party on the eve of its rise to power is commonly destined to languish and decay when power has been attained. It is easier to criticize others than to criticize oneself; the habit of government becomes inveterate, leads to action where none is required; administrative routine blunts quickness of perception; and the tendency to erect freedom into a monopoly for oneself, a privilege of some at the expense of others, after having demanded it for everybody, is inevitable. Thus by degrees the Liberal spirit deserts the Liberal party; and at times it appears equally in opposing or competing parties which affirm their own right to exist and to destroy the privileges of those in power.

There is also a danger, inherent in every Liberal party, of creating a fanaticism of liberty, an intolerence in the name of respect for the autonomy of the human conscience. The sectarian bigotry of the partisans of free thought is notorious; but it is not an isolated case; it often happens that the very energy with which Liberals defend their own cause destroys their calm estimation of difficulties and makes them unjust towards their adversaries and therefore, in the last resort, dogmatic and illiberal.

These limitations and distortions are accidental; but there are more essential reasons why Liberal parties cannot enclose within themselves the whole of the Liberal spirit. They start with the presupposition that the life of individuals, whether men or peoples, develop through competition; that it constantly renews itself by overcoming the inertia and passivity of habit, tradition, and servile obedience. There is here the implicit assumption of a hostile resistance, something immovable which opposes motion, but nevertheless is its necessary condition. Now a Liberal party, as a part or division of a whole, cannot contain within itself, in its limited programme of action, the ideal motives of its opponent: if it recognized the necessity of the thing against which it was fighting, this recognition would end by paralysing its activity. Its strength, but also its weakness, lies in being partial. A more comprehensive Liberalism would recognize the dialectical ground of the antithesis and would see resistance and movement, conservation and progress, justified and validated in a higher synthesis which is political life in its concreteness. And from this point of view, the development of the struggle between Conservatives and Liberals, and their alternation in power, represent not an alternation of freedom and unfreedom, light and darkness, but the rhythm of an uninterrupted movement. But no Liberal, in his capacity as a party man, could ever consider the defeat of his party a triumph of Liberalism.

There is another aspect of this party conflict, which has been acutely analysed by Silvio Spaventa. The spirit of modern progress and of the political renewal of the European peoples, he says, is rooted in the principle that the world is reconstructed by thought and through thought. But this principle, the instrument by which the face of Europe has been changed, is essentially Radical, and stronger in criticism and demolition than in reconstruction. This is because reconstruction is the work not of the thought of one man or of one generation, but of every one's thought, present and past generations alike. Now a respect for this work and the moral interests enshrined in it is a spirit not of innovation but of conservation, not a Radical spirit but an historical spirit.

This consideration helps us to grasp the ideal value of the principle which lies at the root of Conservatism and nourishes the dialectical antithesis of the Liberal thesis. It confirms our view that Liberalism, as a synthetic reality, rises above the terms of the conflict, and justifies them both. In this wider form, it embodies itself in the activity forming the focus upon which the action of all parties converges, and the resultant of all their conflicting energies: the activity of government.

(*d*) Liberalism has been defined, with profound insight, as an art of government. To govern, said Bismarck, is to find the diagonal of the parallelogram of forces. A Liberal government, in this task, always depends upon the spontaneous and sometimes involuntary co-operation of the public. It allows the conflicting opinions and interests to check and balance each other, the forces of Society to reach a state of equilibrium; and thus, working with a material already of itself reduced to equilibrium, without the intervention of the government, it imparts movement to the whole with a minimum expenditure of energy on the part of the State. And when we think of the immense complexity of modern societies as compared with ancient, we can easily understand why modern societies have given rise to Liberal governments. To rule them by force, to control and direct them from outside, would be an impossibility, an absurdity.

The function of government has a synthetic character. A government, even if derived from one party, governs for all and has in view the interests of all. It is obliged, as a party is not obliged, to consider fairly the motives of its late opponents and to reconcile these with its own. Care for the interests of the minority is the most strictly liberal of its tasks.

As an art of government, Liberalism consists of a capacity to unite the principle of conservation with that of progress, Radical initiative with historical tradition. To distinguish what is feasible from what is chimerical, that for which the mind of the people is ripe from that which must be postponed; but at the same time to permit the discussion of all opinions, and indeed to keep alive in the social organism the active spirit of inquiry, the love of the new, the trust in initiative, upon which the spiritual wealth of the government of to-morrow will be based; all this goes to make proficiency in this art. "Trust the people" has been the motto of the most sincerely Liberal governments, the governments which have set before themselves, as the ideal goal of their action, the self-government of the people.

This Liberalism cannot be the exclusive property of this or that type of government. It comes into being in the continual exercise and impartial discipline of governing, in the alternate rule of parties each of which learns that in this activity there is something that a mere party can never know: the mutual criticism of parties and of the currents of public opinion; the legal, administrative, and financial skill which the act of governing calls into existence. Thus it comes about that governments pass away; widely differing political views follow one another on the stage of public life; but through all these fluctuations something remains unchanged, and asserts itself by degrees with a prestige and an authority which nothing contingent and transitory can impair. This is the Liberal State, a being which in its inmost essence is sanctioned by no law, no statute, but is an historical growth to which all generations of politicians have contributed, on which all governments have left the traces of their activity, and which is different from every one of these because it is the work of them all.

3. HAROLD J. LASKI: The Rise of European Liberalism*

Harold J. Laski (1893–1950) was long a professor of political science at the London School of Economics and a prominent member of the Fabian Society and of the Labour party. His lack of sympathy with liberalism is clear. He associates it with the middle class strictly and refuses to attribute to it the degree of flexibility that both Hobhouse and Ruggiero imply. He, too, sees a philosophy as the essence of liberalism, but looks to an earlier period for its definition and sees it as a relatively complete political theory, tied to the interests of capitalism, rather than as an evolving and independent spirit.

This new philosophy was liberalism; and it is the purpose of these pages to trace, in general outline, the history of the forces by which it was shaped into a coherent doctrine. The evolution, of course, was never direct and rarely conscious. The pedigree of ideas is never straightforward. Into the development of liberalism there have entered winds of doctrine so diverse in their origin as to make clarity difficult, and precision perhaps unattainable. To the evolution of liberalism have gone contributions of the first importance from men unacquainted with, often hostile to, its aims; from Machiavelli and Calvin, from Luther and Copernicus, from Henry VIII and Thomas More, in one century; from Richelieu and Louis XIV, from Hobbes and Jurieu, from Pascal and Bacon in another. The unconscious impact of events was at least as responsible as the deliberate effort of thinkers in shaping the mental climate which made it possible. The geographical discoveries, the new cosmology, technological invention, a renewed and secular metaphysic, above all, new forms of economic life, all made their contributions to the formation of its motivating ideas. It could not have become what it was without the theological revolution we call the Reformation; and this, in its turn, received much of its character from all that is implied in the revival of learning. Much of its character has been shaped by the fact that the breakdown of the medieval *respublica Christiana* divided Europe into a congeries of separate sovereign states each with its own special problems to solve and its unique experience to offer. Nor was its birth an easy one. Revolution and war presided over its emergence from the womb; and it is not beyond the mark to say that there was hardly a period until 1848 when its growth was not arrested by the challenge of violent reaction. Men fight passionately to retain those wonted habits in which their privileges are involved; and liberalism was nothing so much as a challenge to vested interests rendered sacred by the traditions of half a thousand years.

The change it effected was, on any showing, an immeasurable one. A society in which social position was usually definite, the market predominantly local,

* From Harold J. Laski, *The Rise of European Liberalism* (London: George Allen & Unwin Ltd., 1962), pp. 11–15, 154, 155, 156–57, 167–69. Reprinted by permission of George Allen & Unwin Ltd.

learning and science rather in society than of its essential texture, change usually unconscious, and as a general rule resented, habits dominated by religious precepts which few doubted at all and none successfully, in which there was little capital accumulation and production was dominated by the needs of a market for local use, slowly broke down. With the triumph of the new order in the nineteenth century, the church had given birth to the state as the institutional arbiter of human destiny. The claims of birth had been succeeded by the claims of property. The invention of invention had made change, instead of stability, the supreme characteristic of the social scene. A world-market had come into being, and capital had accumulated upon so immense a scale that its search for profit affected the lives and fortunes of societies to which European civilization had previously been without meaning. If learning and science were still the handmaids of property, their significance was appreciated by every class in society. If religious precepts still counted, their power to dominate the habits even of their votaries had disappeared.

Not, indeed, that liberalism, even in its triumph, was a clear-cut body of either doctrine or practice. It sought to establish a world-market; but the logic of that effort was frustrated by the political implications of the nationalism which surrounded its birth and flourished with its growth. It sought to vindicate the right of the individual to shape his own destiny, regardless of any authority which might seek to limit his possibilities; yet it found that, inherent in that claim, there was an inevitable challenge from the community to the sovereignty of the individual. It sought relief from all the trammels law might impose upon the right to accumulate property; and it found that the vindication of this right involved the emergence of a proletariat prepared to attack its implications. No sooner, in a word, had it achieved its end than it was compelled to meet a defiance of its postulates which seems certain to change the order it had brought into being.

What, then, is the liberalism we have here to discuss? It is not easy to describe, much less to define, for it is hardly less a habit of mind than a body of doctrine. As the latter, no doubt, it is directly related to freedom; for it came as the foe of privilege conferred upon any class in the community by virtue of birth or creed. But the freedom it sought had no title to universality, since its practice was limited to men who had property to defend. It has sought, almost from the outset of its history, to limit the ambit of political authority, to confine the business of government within the framework of constitutional principle: and it has tried, therefore, fairly consistently to discover a system of fundamental rights which the state is not entitled to invade. But, once more, in its operation of those rights, it has been more urgent and more ingenious in exerting them to defend the interests of property than to protect as claimant to their benefit the man who had nothing but his labour-power to sell. It has attempted, where it could, to respect the claims of conscience, and to urge upon governments the duty to proceed by rule rather than by discretion in their operations; but the scope of the conscience it has respected has been narrowed by its regard for property, and its zeal for the rule of law has been tempered by a discretion in the breadth of its application.

Liberalism has usually, by reason of its origins, been hostile to the claims of churches. It has tended, less perhaps to the Erastianism of Hobbes, than to view religious bodies as associations like any other within the community, entitled to tolerance so long as they do not threaten the existing social order. It has been favourable to representative self-government even when this has involved admitting the principle of universal suffrage. It has, in general, supported the idea of national self-determination. As a rule, though by no means universally, it has been tender to the claims of minority-groups, and to the right of free association. It has been suspicious of the control of thought and, indeed, of any effort, by government authority, to impede the free activity of the individual. I do not mean that its history is a conscious and persistent search for these ends. It is more accurate, I think, to say that these were the ends its more ultimate purposes caused it to serve; and I shall seek later to bring out the implications of this difference.

But liberalism, as I have urged, is hardly less a mood than a doctrine. Its tendency has been sceptical; it has always taken a negative attitude to social action. By reason of its origins, it has always regarded tradition as on the defensive; and, for the same reason, also, it has always preferred to bless individual innovation than to sanction the uniformities sought for by political power. It has always, that is, seen in both tradition and uniformity an attack upon the right of the individual to make of his own affirmations and insights a universal rule made binding not because authority accepts it, but because its inherent validity secures for it the free consent of others. There is, therefore, a flavour of romanticism about the liberal temper the importance of which is great. It tends to be subjective and anarchist, to be eager for the change which comes from individual initiative, to be insistent that this initiative contains within itself some necessary seed of social good. It has, accordingly, always tended to make an antithesis (as a rule an unconscious one) between liberty and equality. It has seen in the first that emphasis upon individual action for which it is always zealous; it has seen in the second the outcome of authoritarian intervention of which the result, in its view, is a cramping of individual personality. The outcome of this is important. For it has meant that liberalism, though it has expressed itself always as a universal, has, in its institutional result, inevitably been more narrow in its benefit than the society it sought to guide. For though it has refused to recognize any limit in theory, whether of class or creed, or even race, to its application, the historic conditions within which it has operated effected a limitation despite itself. It is the meaning of this limitation which is the key to the understanding of the liberal idea. Without it, we cannot explain either the triumphs or the failures in its record.

For what produced liberalism was the emergence of a new economic society at the end of the Middle Ages. As a doctrine, it was shaped by the needs of that new society; and, like all social philosophies, it could not transcend the medium in which it was born. Like all social philosophies, therefore, it contained in its birth the conditions of its own destruction. In its living principle, it was the idea by which the new middle class rose to a position of political dominance. Its instrument was the discovery of what may be called the contractual state. To make that state, it sought to limit political intervention to the narrowest area compatible with the maintenance of public order. It never understood, or was never able fully to admit, that freedom of contract is never genuinely free until the parties thereto have equal bargaining power. This, of necessity, is a function of equal material conditions. The individual liberalism has sought to protect is always, so to say, free to purchase his freedom in the society it made; but the number of those with the means of purchase at their disposal has always been a minority of mankind. The idea of liberalism, in short, is historically connected, in an inescapable way, with the ownership of property. The ends it serves are always the ends of men in this position. Outside that narrow circle, the individual for whose rights it has been zealous has always been an abstraction upon whom its benefits could not, in fact, be fully conferred. Because its purposes were shaped by owners of property, the margins between its claims and its performance have always been wide. . . .

The nineteenth century is the epoch of liberal triumph; from Waterloo until the outbreak of the Great War no other doctrine spoke with the same authority or exercised the same widespread influence. Its triumph, no doubt, was a complex phenomenon; complex if only because, as in its rise, many of those who rendered it the most profound service conceived themselves to be worshipping at a different altar. Its conquests are so vast that the world it created in those hundred years would have seemed well-nigh unthinkable even to men who, like Adam Smith, were the principal doctrinal architects of its advent. It was the prophet of industrialism; and it transformed Great Britain into the workshop of the world. It was the exponent of free trade; and it created a world-market which has broken down the isolation even of the most distant peoples. It was the advocate of religious toleration; and it both broke the temporal power of Rome and ended the right of religion to define the boundaries of citizenship. It insisted that statehood should be in general coterminous with the boundaries of states; and, under its aegis, Italy and Greece, Hungary and Bulgaria, realized a new consciousness of self. It established universal suffrage and parliamentarianism almost as principles of natural law; and those who, in Western Europe opposed their advent, always on the defensive. There is a sense, indeed, in which American civilization of the last hundred years may not illegitimately be regarded as the fulfilment of the liberal ideal. America, and the awakening of the ancient East, are nothing so much as a tribute to its world-wide empire. . . .

The essential attack on the liberal idea in the nineteenth century was that of socialism. It is not a movement the summary of which is simple. There go to its making ideas derived from the most disparate sources. But it is not, I think, an inaccurate emphasis to say that the essence of its attack derived from the realization that the liberal ideal secured to the middle-class its full share of privilege, while it left the proletariat in their chains. The effort of socialism was towards the correction of this inadequacy. In its vital formulation by Marx and Engels, it was an insistence that the bourgeois revolution merely transferred effective political power from the owners of land to the owners of industrial property. The state, in their view, was not a neutral organ seeking as best it could the well-being of the whole community, but a coercive power enforcing upon the working class that social discipline required by the owners of property in their search for profit. They denied that a just society was attainable in these terms. They argued that precisely as the middle class had overthrown the feudal aristocracy, so the working class would be compelled to overthow its masters in order to obtain possession of the state for its own benefit. . . .

After 1848, for something like half a century again, the liberal idea seemed to have entered amply into its kingdom. The immense wealth it produced made possible concessions to the masses which, if they did not arrest the progress of socialism, at least blunted the edge of its revolutionary fervour in most states in which political democracy had obtained an effective foothold. Liberalism did not abandon its belief in the validity of the private ownership of the means of production; its conquests were too spectacular, not least in the United States, for that to be practicable. But it was at least taught by the pressure of trade unions, on the one hand, and by thinkers like Green and Matthew Arnold, in England, by Tocqueville in France, by the socialists of the chair in Germany, that it must adopt a positive conception of the state. The conception of progressive taxation in the interest of the masses then became an essential part of the liberal idea. The revolutionary challenge was to be evaded by the gospel, as Mr Chamberlain termed it, of "ransom," a gospel which, in essence, was the notion that wealth must justify its possessors by paying for reasonable amenities for the poor. Hence the emergence after, roughly, the seventies of the last century of the social service state. Its fundamental principle was twofold. While it affirmed that, as a general rule, the private ownership of the means of production was to be maintained, it was prepared to regulate the consequences of that ownership in the general interest of those who could not afford, out of their wages, to purchase those amenities which had come to be regarded as part of a reasonable standard of life.

Until, at least, the war of 1914 this phase of the liberal idea dominated the mind of all Europe save those who were infected by the Marxian philosophy. How dominating it was can be seen, above all, by the failure of Marxism in this period to obtain any serious hold of the English mind. The typical English socialism was Fabian, a body of doctrine upon which the emphasis of John Stuart Mill's ideas was far more profound than that of Marx. Fabianism assumed that revolution as a method of social change was outworn, and it did so for two reasons. Born in the serene self-confidence of Victorian England, it was profoundly rationalist in temper; and it therefore believed that the straightforward capture of Parliament by the conversion of an electoral majority to socialism would enable the machinery of constitutional democracy to be used for the peaceful transformation of a capitalist, into a socialist, state. Accepting, in the second place, the fundamental economic postulates of liberal capitalism, it saw no reason to anticipate that collapse of the postwar years which would not only set definite limits to taxable capacity under a system based upon the predominant motive of profit-making, but would also, once the making of profits was in jeopardy, persuade, as in Italy and Germany, the owners of economic power to overthrow the democratic foundations of society in the interest of their right to make profit. Neither Fabians nor advanced liberals had seen that the success of parliamentary government was dependent upon two conditions. It required, first, the sense of security that came from the ability to go on making profit, that enabled it, from its surplus wealth, to continue the distribution of amenities to the masses. It required, in the second place, an agreement among parties in politics to all matters of fundamental social constitution in order that each might succeed the other as the government of the day without a sense of outrage. Without the ability to operate these conditions, parliamentary government was powerless to settle differences in terms of reason. The political forms of liberalism, in a word, were dependent upon a conjuncture of economic circumstances the permanence of which could alone guarantee their effective functioning. . . .

As a doctrine, [liberalism] was, effectively, a by-product of the effort of the middle class to win its place in the sun. As it achieved its emancipation, it forgot not less completely than its predecessors that the claims of social justice were not exhausted by its victory. The crisis it has encountered is no new thing. It has, writes Signor de Ruggiero, "long been concealed by the survival of outward forms and historical institutions created by freedom, veiling an internal decay beneath an unbroken surface, and its whole gravity only appeared when finally the evil reached the surface and destroyed or decomposed certain parts of this also." But that internal decay goes back to the foundations of the doctrine. For, as I have here sought to show, the liberals of the epochs before the French Revolution had only a negative theory of the state; to them, for quite intelligible reasons, it was a tyranny from which they sought an escape. After their victory, they saw it either as a means of protecting themselves from invasion from below, or as, somewhat later, a technique for distributing such concessions to those who challenged their supremacy as might enable them to maintain it unchanged in its larger outlines. To the demand for justice they replied by the offer of charity.

This, no doubt, is an unfair description of the more generous minds amongst them, of, for example, T. H. Green, or Tocqueville, or Hobhouse. But it is not unfair as an account of the evolution of the doctrine as a whole, and, particularly, of its expression as a social environment, on the one hand, and a body of legislation, on the other. Liberalism has always been affected by its tendency to regard the poor as men who have failed through their own fault. It has always suffered from its inability to realize that great possessions mean power over men and women as well as over things. It has always refused to see how little meaning there is in freedom of contract when it is divorced from equality of bargaining power. It has never sought in any full measure to realize the consequences of the depersonalization of industry, the transformation—the phrase is a significant one—of the worker into a "hand." Particularly notable has been its effect on the agrarian situation. There, for the most part, it set itself out to break up the great estates without seeing that, thereby, it was calling into existence a class of peasant proprietors without the means of effective economic independence, and without the coherence or the leisure to take an elevated view of public questions. Its whole philosophy was so much the outcome of its concentration upon the powers and the possibilities of the free entrepreneur with whom its rise is associated, that his needs exercised an altogether excessive influence in the making of its principles. Its purposes, no doubt, were always expressed in universal terms; but they were, in practical operation, so much the servant of a single class in the community that it was his wants which predominated in the making of the liberal state.

That state, in fact, by reason of the interests which went to its making, had purposes more limited than the general well-being of the community. Its fundamental aim was to serve the owners of property. It extended, no doubt, the idea of ownership in such fashion as to confer rights in law upon all who exercised effective demand. It destroyed the claims of birth to specialize rights to itself. It prevented the owners of land from claiming any special privilege in the state. But its fundamental horizons did not extend beyond that achievement. That is shown by its attitude to the poor. It is shown by its attitude to the rise of trade unionism. It is shown by the long struggle which was necessary—a struggle still far from ended—to establish decent standards of education, of health, of housing and labour protection. For, given the nature of the liberal state, all questions had ultimately to be referred to the essential motive upon which the liberal state was built—the motive of profit-making. . . . As an organized society, the liberal state, at bottom, had no defined objective save the making of wealth, no measurable criterion of function and status save ability to acquire it.

4. THOMAS P. NEILL: The Rise and Decline of Liberalism*

Mr. Neill's detailed effort to define liberalism is to an extent an amalgam of the approaches seen thus far, with the important addition of the author's Catholic viewpoint. He shares the view that liberalism was constantly linked to the middle class and that it ultimately proved inadequate. Yet he sees a number of stages to liberalism in the nineteenth century, each one differing considerably from the other, and each demonstrating considerable adaptability. Finally, his distinction between a liberal spirit and liberal politics might help reconcile some common divergences in interpretation. Unlike the previous efforts, Mr. Neill's assessment is strictly limited in time; he is not seeking a definition that will fit either earlier political theory or some sort of ongoing political movement. He is sufficiently sure of his definition to assert that significant liberalism has a clear beginning and a clear end.

Throughout modern history, then, and especially throughout the nineteenth century with which we are concerned in this book, Liberalism has been associated with the middle class. It has therefore taken on typical bourgeois charac-

* From Thomas P. Neill, *The Rise and Decline of Liberalism* (Milwaukee: Bruce Publishing Co., 1953), pp. 22–30, 312. Reprinted by permission of The Bruce Publishing Co.

teristics. It has found its strongest expression in dissenter ranks; it has stressed the rationality and the inherent goodness of man; it has adopted an empirical, scientific approach to social problems. It has held property sacred, but at the same time it has favored change in the name of progress and has therefore backed reform movements in church, state, and social custom.

Little toward clarifying the meaning of Liberalism has been accomplished by the descriptions of Liberalism so far offered, and the discussion of which features are only occasionally and which are constantly associated with the term. But these definitions and descriptions have suggested that Liberalism is used today in two main senses. This has been the basic cause of confusion on what the term means. It has divided men who agree basically on almost everything into *pro* and *contra* camps relative to Liberalism. For the term means something essentially different to the two groups, and its meaning is the result of historical associations. Thus we find Americans with a Latin background using the term in a more specific, limited sense than those with an Anglo-Saxon heritage or no recent European heritage at all. Catholics, again, because of their struggles against certain kinds of antireligious and anticlerical Liberalisms in the Latin countries, tend to use the word in a derogatory sense.

It therefore seems proper and useful to distinguish between ecumenical Liberalism and sectarian. The former refers to that Liberalism which is identified with generosity of spirit or liberality of mind, the latter to a precisely defined and rigidly held body of doctrine, a secular religion. The former is a generally accepted thing; the latter is reserved to relatively few. Many of the descriptions of liberalism we have so far given obviously refer to the ecumenical kind, especially the definitions of contemporaries like Dorothy Thompson, and Herbert Hoover. This certainly is the liberalism Brotherston referred to as "one of those long-continued historical movements which have arisen from primal demands of human life. . . . Reflection soon reveals that Liberalism is the sum total of all movements in the history of man which have had their rise in the normal urgency of the human spirit. It has covered the whole field of life, practical and theoretic." It is the ecumenical brand that Ogden Mills had in mind when he asserted that "our American social philosophy can be expressed in the single term—liberalism." This is the type that John H. Hallowell, one of America's leading authorities on Liberalism, has in mind when he writes that "in the United States . . . practically everyone calls himself liberal and embodies in the term all that is congenial to his particular way of thinking."

Other descriptions we have employed obviously refer to sectarian Liberalism. This is the type Eugene Lyons had in mind when he wrote that Liberals "are notoriously illiberal," and that "Liberalism had become just another orthodoxy." Sarda y Salvany and Cardinal Billot were referring to the sectarian kind of Liberalism when they condemned the doctrine as sinful and satanic. Historically the term "Liberalism" has generally been used to refer to a sectarian doctrine rather than a certain attitude. It is still so used in most of Europe and in South America. But in England and especially in this country the ecumenical meaning has come in our time to be more generally accepted. The result is the confusion we referred to above, the sort of confusion of tongues that cause a scholar like Hallowell to say that Liberalism "should be more precisely defined than it is today or else it should be abandoned."

There is little likelihood that the term will be abandoned. The most we can hope for is an approach to greater precision by distinguishing various types of Liberalism. The ecumenical kind is at most a temper or a spirit or a habit of mind, a disposition or an attitude toward the problems of life. It is so defined by almost all Americans and Englishmen using the term nowadays. On this point there is general agreement. Professor Ramsay Muir described ecumenical liberalism well in these words:

> Liberalism is a habit of mind, a point of view, a way of looking at things, rather than a fixed and unchanging body of doctrine. Like all creeds it is a spirit not a formula. It gets expression from time to time in formulae and programmes of policy, but these are always and necessarily determined by the circumstances of the time in which they are framed; they can, therefore, have no permanent validity; they need to be continually revised and recast, or they become mere shackles on the spirit which they try to express.

In similar fashion Blease defined it as "not a policy, but a habit of mind," Cohen called it "an attitude rather than a set of dogmas," and Miss Thompson, as we have seen, considered it "a kind of spirit and a sort of behavior."

Liberals of this ecumenical school include at least half the human race. In America they number many more than half. Robert Bendiner went so far as to estimate in the *Nation*: "Out of some 140,000,000 people in the United States, at least 139,500,000 are liberals, to hear them tell it, 'liberal' having become a rough synonym for virtuous, decent, humane, and kind to animals. . . . Any American would sooner drop dead than proclaim himself a reactionary." We can dismiss this type of liberalism as being too general for profitable discussion —unless we were to attempt a full cultural and political history of modern times. Our concern is instead with the more definite body of doctrine which is sectarian Liberalism. In the following pages we shall therefore discuss something that has no direct reference to Dorothy Thompson or the Tennessee Valley Authority or adult education in the Great Books.

Our discussion is instead about the sectarian Liberalism of the nineteenth century, or, more properly, the period between the surrender of Napoleon in 1815 and the beginning of World War I in 1914. Let us therefore see if we can begin to isolate this term by seeing what attitudes remain constant in it—for even sectarian Liberalism will be forced by its very nature to change its creed according to the circumstances with which it is confronted. In doing this we must remember that the two kinds of Liberalism are not always mutually exclusive. There will consequently seem to be in the next few pages a certain amount of repetition of matter already considered. This is inevitable, however, if we are to approach a definition of our subject matter.

In the first place, sectarian Liberalism has consistently opposed the established government. When its political battle is won and its program comes to be worked into the law of the land, as happened in England after 1832, in France after 1830, and in this country after the Civil War, its champions become conservative. They hold the same doctrines, to be sure, but they are given another label. Thus Guizot was a sectarian Liberal of the Restoration period (1815–1830), but under Louis Philippe's bourgeois monarchy of 1830–1848, wherein his program was fully accepted and he governed as premier, he became the enemy of all further change. So it was with those Whigs who accepted the Victorian compromise as a final settlement. As opponents of further change they became conservative, and the mantle of sectarian Liberalism fell on others who were dissatisfied with the settlement of 1832. The former Liberals do not easily surrender the name, and even today many use the term "Liberalism" to refer to the doctrines and policies of those who were in power in the middle of the nineteenth century. Hence the confusion. But the label of sectarian Liberal is properly attached to those who oppose the established order.

In the second place, and a corollary of the first point, sectarian Liberalism has consistently inveighed against authority of any kind. Between authority and Liberalism there has always been strong antipathy. They can make peace, as we shall see, only by one or the other denying its own nature. For the essence of sectarian Liberalism has consistently been a throwing-off of restraint, a cutting loose from what seems to oppress the individual. Liberalism therefore demands that the government surrender its power to the Liberals. Historically it has stood for resistance to absolute, arbitrary government, and it has fought the good fight for responsible parliamentary rule. It has stood for resistance to undue interference with industry and trade. It has stood for the rejection of authority in both Church and State, for a repudiation of tradition, custom, convention. And in the struggle it has championed bad causes as well as good; it has rejected much that was evil and some that was good.

It therefore follows, in the third place, that the tendency of sectarian Liberalism has been toward anticlericalism, and toward an anarchism which it never reached but always approached. Tom Paine considered government at best a necessary evil—but an evil nonetheless; and Adam Smith adopted what has become the typical Liberal attitude toward that "insidious and crafty animal vulgarly called the statesman or politician." The evil of government was to be reduced to the minimum, the Liberal always hoped, and long before Marx sectarian Liberals prophesied the eventual withering away of the State. Spencer put this idea pithily when he asserted that "the ultimate man will be one whose private requirements coincide with public ones." For the aim of progress is to reach that condition where "the individual is everything and the State nothing." In the same way, Liberalism has been hostile to religious authority. "The religious mind," Spender has written, "is naturally repelled by Liberalism, which sets up humanity in place of God, the doctor or the psychologist in the place of the priest." Liberalism has tended to make the individual person absolute master and final judge of all things. It stands for the subjection to individual judgment of all claims—political, intellectual, and spiritual—and it therefore regards with hostility organized churches, party discipline, or philosophical systems.

Sectarian Liberalism is obviously bound to be forward-looking, always in favor of change from the existing order toward something new and, the Liberal feels sure, better. The doctrine of the sectarian Liberal therefore changes with each generation, unless the conservative element in a society is strongly enough entrenched in power to remain for successive generations. But though the Liberal's doctrine changes, his state of mind remains the same.

This state of mind, this attitude toward existing institutions is indeed the only constant element in sectarian Liberalism throughout its history. We shall see in later chapters that the sectarian Liberal of 1914 has essentially the same temper as his predecessor of 1815 or of 1865. The constant element even in sectarian Liberalism, then, is not a set of doctrines but a doctrinaire temper of mind. But it differs from ecumenical liberalism in having a definite fighting creed at each moment in history, in having a program and frequently an organization dedicated to putting that program into practice. It is the Liberal

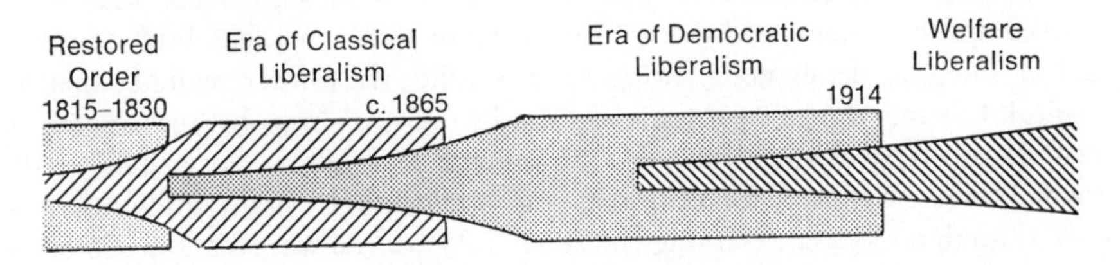

frame of mind, however, and not any consistent body of doctrine which justifies the use of word "Liberalism" to describe certain groups of thinkers and actors in modern history.

As a final word of introduction to our subject, let us take an overview of the way sectarian Liberalism has evolved through the nineteenth century. In 1815 sectarian Liberals, represented in the accompanying diagram by the light dotted area, were excluded from power, except in France where they had a precarious, partial grip on the government which was threatened by reactionary groups gathering around the restored Bourbon king, Louis XVIII. These Liberals . . . stemmed from the French Revolution on the continent and from the Industrial Revolution and its associated economic and political thought in England. (In America the case was quite different, because there was no "conservative" group entrenched in power. In many ways we started with a clean slate in America and for a while there was nothing to be "against" except perhaps sin or the memory of George III. As we shall see later, political parties soon formed, but not on the clear-cut issue of Conservatism versus Liberalism.)

Sectarian Liberals in this period before 1830 built up the doctrine of classical or integral liberalism, and with that program they came to power in England in 1832 and in France in 1830 and temporarily in other places in 1848. The period of classical Liberalism—called the Victorian compromise in England, the Bourgeois monarchy in France—lasted until about 1865. Within it, while the satisfied classical Liberals were growing conservative, there grew up a new sectarian Liberalism which held the same position and the same temper toward the classical Liberals that the latter had formerly held toward the restored order of 1815–1830. This new Liberalism of Gladstone and John Stuart Mill was democratic. Its program was the enfranchisement of all adult males and the extension of governmental protection over a severely restricted group of "legal infants," such as women and children working in the mines. In most other respects it did not differ from its predecessor type of Liberalism.

Democratic Liberalism was generally accepted by about 1885, and for the next thirty years it was in power in most of western Europe and in the United States—at least formally and on paper. But there had grown up in its midst a new sectarian Liberalism which urged a larger role upon the State, the positive role of guaranteeing minimum existence to all citizens and of protecting the people against the new tyrant of big business. Its opponents labeled this new brand of Liberalism "socialist." A better term would be "welfare Liberalism." It had won a number of victories in all European countries by the time World War I began in 1914, and there were many who believed that socialism of some kind or other would be generally realized at the end of the war.

Although this threefold division of doctrinaire sectarian Liberalism into classical or integral, democratic, and welfare is valid, we must remember that all classical Liberals did not conveniently die by 1865, or even by 1900. Some of them lived on, protesting the new movements and calling for a halt to the trend. Herbert Spencer, for example, was a classical Liberal, still writing in 1900; though no longer deserving the label "Liberal," he was still using it. So in our own generation Ogden Mills' *Liberalism Fights On* is an attack on the New Deal by a man who would have rightly been called Liberal in 1850 but not in 1936. The Liberals by this latter date were the New Dealers. . . .

Thus we can see that a man who holds the same doctrine in old age that he accepted in his youth will unlikely remain a Liberal in the sectarian sense—at least he would not in the nineteenth and twentieth centuries. A man born in 1806, as John Stuart Mill was, who was a sectarian Liberal in 1830 would be a conservative by 1850 and a reactionary by 1875, unless he consistently discarded one set of beliefs in favor of another more advanced set. John Stuart Mill actually did this, so that he remained consistently, though not always as confidently and stridently, Liberal down until his death in 1873, when he was a qualified and moderate socialist. . . .

By 1914 there simply was not enough agreement among Western men on basic values in life for Liberalism to survive. The world of the twentieth century was made possible by Liberalism because it performed so successfully its negative role of destroying the traditional framework of society and rejecting the old political and ecclesiastical authorities. Its role was chiefly a negative one, and it did its work thoroughly. But it did not of itself have substance and muscle enough to grapple with the new problems of the latter nineteenth and twentieth centuries. That is why the masses of men sought protection under various kinds of totalitarian rule. Dictators did not have to force themselves upon the people anywhere. They used guile and specious arguments, to be sure, but they were welcomed everywhere because men stood naked, alone, stripped bare by Liberalism of their old social, moral, and metaphysical protections. This was the principal historic role of bourgeois Liberalism.

There were some good elements in Liberalism, as we have indicated throughout this study, chiefly a dedication to liberty, a critical frame of mind, a constant probing for ever better social arrangements. These good things should not be rejected. But classical Liberalism is dead. Although there is no hope of resurrecting it intact, as some sociologists and politicians still try to do, it is nevertheless imperative to save everything of value from its wreckage. Human life is not worth living without liberty; indeed life without freedom is not human. Any new form of Liberalism which does not want to sign its own death warrant at the time of its inception must subscribe to a true and positive form of freedom such as was long postulated in the Christian tradition. A future Liberalism, if it is based on sound principles, can improve on the Christian past by realizing more fully in practice the ideals generally held but not well implemented in centuries gone by. If such a thing were to be achieved, classical Liberalism will be credited with the negative role of making it possible. For in the nineteenth century it dissolved the old society, but was itself incapable of creating an endurable new society in which persons could live a truly human existence.

5. BENEDETTO CROCE: History of Europe in the Nineteenth Century*

The final three selections deal with liberalism in specific periods of the nineteenth century; they invite comparison with the periodization that Neill suggests. In this selection, Benedetto Croce (1866–1952) evokes the variety of specific purposes, yet common idealistic fervor of early nineteenth-century liberalism. Croce himself found many affinities with the sort of liberalism he describes, including a revulsion against democracy; but for this reason the distinctions he draws must be assessed with care. Beyond this, if Croce describes an enthusiasm that certainly did characterize some early liberalism, one must ask if his picture can be applied to any specific liberal movement, and, if so, to how many. Does his description focus too much on the realm of ideas? Is it all reconcilable with the dry, calculating liberalism that has been portrayed for the same period?

Since the historical antecedents and the existing conditions, the spirit and the customs, of the various nations were diverse, these demands differed in the several countries, as to order of appearance, as to magnitude, as to details, and as to their general tone. In one country precedence was given to liberation from a foreign domination or to national unity, and in another to the change from absolutism in government to constitutionalism. Here it was simply a question of reform of the franchise and the extension of political power, while there it was a question of establishing a representative system for the first time, or on new foundations. In one country, which through the efforts of the preceding generations—especially during the French Revolution and the Empire—already

* From Benedetto Croce, *History of Europe in the Nineteenth Century* (New York: Harcourt, Brace & World, Inc., 1963), pp. 4–5, 18–19, 31–34. Reprinted by permission of Agenzia Litteraria Internazionale, Milan, Italy.

enjoyed civil equality and religious tolerance, the people began to call for the participation in government of new social strata. In another country it was necessary to delay first to battle with the political privileges of the feudal classes and persistent forms of servitude, and to shake off the yoke of ecclesiastical oppression. But though these demands were different in importance and in order of appearance, they were all linked in a single chain, and sooner or later one drew another along after itself, and brought to light still others that could be seen in the distance. And over all of them rose one word that summed them all up and expressed the spirit which had given them life—the word *liberty*. . . .

No longer did history appear destitute of spirituality and abandoned to blind forces, or sustained and constantly directed by alien forces. Now it was seen to be the work and the activity of the spirit, and so, since spirit is liberty, the work of liberty. It was all the work of liberty, its unique and eternal positive moment, which alone is made effective in the series of its forms and gives them their significance, and which alone explains and justifies the function fulfilled by the negative moment of subjection, with its constraints, its oppressions, its reactions, and its tyrannies, which (to quote Vico once more) seem to be "untoward events" and are really "opportunities."

Such was the thought, the philosophy, of the age that was at its beginning, a philosophy that was springing up everywhere, spreading everywhere, that was found on the lips of everyone, appearing in the stanzas of poetry and in the words of men of action no less than in the formulas of those who were philosophers by profession. . . .

Now he who gathers together and considers all these characteristics of the liberal ideal does not hesitate to call it what it was: a "religion." He calls it so, of course, because he looks for what is essential and intrinsic in every religion, which always lies in the concept of reality and an ethics that conforms to this concept. It excludes the mythological element, which constitutes only a secondary differentiation between religion and philosophy. The concept of reality and the conforming ethics of liberalism were generated, as has been shown, by modern thought, dialectical and historical. Nothing more was needed to give them a religious character, since personifications, myths, legends, dogmas, rites, propitiations, expiations, priestly classes, pontifical robes, and the like do not belong to the intrinsic, and are taken out from particular religions and set up as requirements for every religion with ill effect. Such a process is the origin of the somewhat numerous artificial religions ("religions of the future") that were devised in the eighteenth century; they all met ridicule, which they deserved, since they were counterfeits and caricatures. But the religion of liberalism showed itself to be essentially religious in its forms and institutions, and since it was born and not made, was no cold and deliberate device. Therefore at first its leaders even expected to be able to live in harmony with the old religions, and to bring them a companion, a complement, an aid. As a matter of fact, it set itself up against them, but at the same time summed them up in itself and went further. Beside philosophical motives it set the religious motives of the near and the remote past. Next to and above Socrates it set the human and divine

Redeemer Jesus. And it felt that it had undergone all the experiences of paganism and Christianity, of Catholicism, Augustinianism, Calvinism, and all the rest. It felt that it represented the highest demands, that it was the purifying, deepening, and power-giving agent of the religious life of mankind. Therefore it did not point to the chronological dates of its beginnings, nor to new eras that cut it off sharply from the past, as the Christian Church and then Islam had done, and as the National Convention, in imitation of them, had done by its decree expressing the abstract concept of liberty and reason—a concept that lived for a brief moment a life as abstract as itself, and was first forgotten and then abolished.

On every side rang out the cry of a new birth, of a "century that is being born again," like a salutation full of promise to the "third age," the age of the Spirit, which Gioacchino da Fiore had prophesied in the thirteenth century, and which now opened out before the human society that had prepared for it and waited for it. . . .

This is precisely, amidst all these resemblances, where the difference lay, because the democrats and the liberals considered the individual, equality, sovereignty, and the nation in entirely different fashions. For the first, individuals were centres of equal forces to which it was necessary to attribute an equal field or an equality, as they said, in fact; for the second, the individuals were persons, their equality only that of their humanity, and therefore ideal or legal, a liberty of movement or competition; and the people was not a sum of equal forces, but a differentiated organism, varying in its components and in their associations, complex in its unity, with governors and governed, with ruling classes—open, to be sure, and mobile, but ever necessary for this necessary function—and the sovereignty was that of the whole in its synthesis and not of the parts in their analyses. The democrats in their political ideal postulated a religion of quantity, of mechanics, of calculating reason or of nature, like that of the eighteenth century; the liberals, a religion of quality, of activity, of spirituality, such as that which had risen in the beginning of the nineteenth century: so that, even in this case, the conflict was one of religious faiths. That the one faith was the precursor and the parent of the other must be granted, in the general sense in which Catholic theocracy and absolute monarchy had been precursors of liberalism; and in a more particular and closer sense, that modern thought passed progressively and dialectically from naturalism and rationalism to idealism, and Galileo and Descartes had prepared the way for Kant and Hegel; and in the other sense that in every individual life there is usually a youthful radical phase, one of negation and affirmation that are equally abstract. But once the transition was made, the two faiths, the living and the surviving, stood and still stand face to face, staring at one another with eyes now friendly and now hostile. The philosophy of idealism rejected the philosophy of natural law, the contractualism, the social atomism, of Rousseau; his "general will," which ill represented the will of Providence and historical reason; the opposition of the individual to the state and of the state to the individual—for these are terms of a single and indissoluble relation.

In the more distinctly political field, liberalism had completed its separation from democracy, which in its extreme form of Jacobinism not only had destroyed by its mad and blind pursuit of its abstractions the living and physiological tissues of the social body, but also by confusing the people with one part and one aspect—the least civilized—of the people, with the inorganic howling and impulsive mob, and by exercising tyranny in the name of the people, had gone to the other extreme and had opened the way for an equal servitude and dictatorship instead of one for equality and liberty. The horror of revolution that made itself felt at this time and which runs through the entire nineteenth century, which was yet to carry out so many revolutions, was in reality the horror of democratic and Jacobin revolution with its spasmodic and bloody convulsions, with its sterile attempts to achieve the inachievable, and with its consequent collapse under despotism, which debases the intellect and destroys the will. The terror of the Terror became one of the fundamental social convictions; and in vain did some undertake the defence of that method, arguing its necessity, and maintaining that it alone had guaranteed the benefits of the French Revolution and that it alone could ensure those of the new revolutions that were brewing—in vain because other, more critical minds were not slow in discovering and revealing the sophistry of this argument.

If somewhat later the image of the French Revolution cast a shadow over its worst aspects and set in relief the admirable side of its passions and actions, thanks to the effect of distance and still more to biased and flattering histories, it was then too near, there were still too many eye-witnesses of what had happened, for the democratic ideal to derive any strength and glamour from it: and indeed this ideal had issued from it in badly damaged shape and was rejected generally, and by the most different parties. Several of the surviving actors in the Revolution and authors of the Terror, the least inept for active works amongst the old Jacobins or those who had corrected and educated their natural capacity through experience, had entered the service of Napoleon and later that of the absolutist régimes of the restoration, and were counted among their most unprejudiced followers and their most inexorable instruments in the war against democracy and liberty: in agreement with what the most serene of poets observed, that every fanatic should be nailed to the cross at thirty, because he who has been under an illusion, when he comes to his senses turns into a knave. Others, candid souls, had preserved their illusions and survived in a mist, vaguely reliving with regret the errors and the betrayals and the accidents that had prevented their pure and beautiful ideal of equality and popular sovereignty from reaching the goal that had been almost in sight, prevented the happy instant from tarrying forever, beatifying the human race. And though the word "republic," as we have shown, struck an unpleasant note at that time, now strident and now dull, some, even of the younger generation, still cherished a regard for the republic because of its venerable classical memories or because of a rationalistic and simplifying longing. But neither republicans nor democrats at this time figured among the major forces at play; and liberalism, which had surpassed them in philosophy and politics, and had even operated many conversions among them, could on the one hand make use of surviving democrats and republicans in certain alliances that were offered spontaneously, and on the other hand watch vigilantly to prevent them, at decisive moments and on the days of upheavals, from compromising the fruit of their efforts by excesses, by acts of madness and disorder, and from unconsciously and unintentionally preparing for the offensive and victorious return of clericalism and absolutism.

6. DAVID HARRIS: European Liberalism in the Nineteenth Century*

David Harris, professor emeritus at Stanford University, here treats liberalism as a practical political movement with some conflicting ideological impulses, mainly in the middle of the nineteenth century. Both the dates and the places under discussion are unusually clear in this selection, but this very precision raises questions. Do his references to Belgium, France, and Britain allow the formation of generalizations about liberalism beyond these countries? And what criteria are used to pin down the nature of liberalism? For example, Professor Harris seems to equate liberalism with the July Monarchy, at least for a time; but were not many opponents of the regime liberal as well? Finally, Professor Harris can be reasonably precise because he judges liberalism most significant as a practical movement, in or near power. This view should be contrasted both with the more diffuse efforts to define a liberal spirit and with Neill's belief that liberalism could remain true to itself only in opposition.

These political changes in France and Belgium and Britain between 1830 and 1832 charted the main direction of liberal hopes in other lands during the years that followed. Since they represented the program of a liberalism sufficiently victorious to give practical effect to its major objectives, they established the new benchmarks in the political terrain beyond the realms of princely grace.

With respect to the control of the state, there was at least a hint of a dilemma in the liberals' position. The old suspicions of the state which went back to Seneca and Augustine had found more than vindication at the hands of John Locke and his rationalist successors, and their children of the new generation were not without the family trait. On the other hand, there was a mundane consideration which also had an imposing history. Harrington had pointed it out back in the seventeenth century: that the possessors of economic power are not content until they gain political power commensurate with it. For all of the aura of dubiety about the state—indeed, on account of it—the state was a reality worth a great deal of effort to influence and to control.

None the less, the liberals of the first half of the nineteenth century did not desire to push forward to a complete mastery of the state: being moderates, they were prepared to leave old elements of privilege. Still, the share which they

* From David Harris, "European Liberalism in the Nineteenth Century," *American Historical Review,* Vol. 60 (1955), pp. 505–10, 515–17. Copyright *American Historical Review.* Reprinted by permission of the *American Historical Review* and the author.

demanded for the middle class was materially greater than that allowed by the charters handed down from sovereign thrones.

The first victorious act of the continental liberals, following the precedent of England, was to settle their case against the undue pretentions of royal authority—without destroying monarchy. In France King Louis Philippe had to proclaim his dependence on the national will,[1] and the constitution of Belgium was most precise in its theoretical and practical curbs on kingly power.[2]

The great positive achievement of the liberalism of these years was to build up the strength of the lower legislative house. Bicameralism remained, but the place of the nobility in the body politic suffered a new reverse. In Belgium an elected bourgeois senate, in France a house of peers in which nobility had a declining role, in Britain a house of lords under notice that it must bow to the will of the nation—in such developments was eloquent proof that the liberals were attacking the custom-grounded pre-eminence of the noble estate.

The dissatisfaction with which the middle rungs of the social ladder looked upward did not prevent their turning to look downward with even less friendly eyes. These men of the middle, and their fathers before them, had once read earnest lessons about people being born and remaining free and equal in rights. But now those days were gone. The memory of revolutionary experience, the more recent evidences of proletarian unrest, the disposition of the successful to see moral failure in a humble station in life—all these considerations afforded grounds enough to deny the lesser orders of mankind a share in the great prize of political power. The upshot was that liberalism pronounced against political democracy; control of the state remained the privilege of men of property.[3]

With respect to what the state should do, a movement dedicated by tradition and by conviction to liberty had naturally a marked prejudice, if not an entirely clear principle or program. And that was, manifestly, that the state should do nothing more than the minimum required by some vaguely defined social necessity.

1. Because of the delicacy of the crisis in July and August 1830, it was essential to proceed tactfully with the revision of the Charter. The declaration of the Chamber, adhered to by the peers, disposed of the theoretical issue of sovereignty in these words: "Selon le voeu et dans l'intérêt du people français, le préambule de la Charte constitutionelle est supprimé, comme blessant la dignité nationale en paraissant *octroyer* aux Français des droits qui leur appartiennent essentiellement" (Duvergier, XXX, 94–95). In his act of August 9 Louis Philippe said, "J'accepte, sans restrictions ni réserve, les clauses et engagements que renferme cette déclaration et le titre du Roi des Français qu'elle me confère, et je suis prêt à en jurer l'observation" (*ibid.*, XXX, 104).

2. Article 3 of the Declaration of the Rights of Man and Citizen in 1789 states, "Le principe de toute souveraineté réside essentiellement dans la nation." The Spanish constitution of 1812 took the sentence in this form: "La soberanía reside esencialmente en la nación" (Title I, chap. 1) and the Portuguese document of 1822 repeated it (Title II, art. xxvi). The declaration of the French chamber in 1830, as indicated in the preceding note, repeated the adverb *essentiellement*. The Belgian constitution-makers dropped the adverb as an unwarranted equivocation: "All powers emanate from the nation . . ." (Title III, art. xxv).

3. For the text of the French election law, April 19, 1831, see Duvergier, XXXI, 177–219. This law raised the number of voters from about 94,000 to about 188,000. In Belgium the more generous suffrage qualifications were determined variably from province to province. The Reform Bill of 1832 increased the number of British voters from about half a million to slightly more than 800,000.

To keep government within the bounds of common sense, the liberals pinned their hopes to two devices. The first was a scheme to make the machinery incapable of quick or efficient action. Recalling the old tyrannies of royal despotism and the later tyrannies of the mob spirit, these twice-bitten men wished, as the abbé Sieyès said, to quench the fires of Rousseau's popular sovereignty by the waters of Montesquieu's separation of powers. The European constitutions, following the American adoption of the old principle, effected therefore a distinction between the executive, legislative, and judicial branches. In their prescriptions of bicameralism they also hoped to insure a check on hasty legislation. None the less, while an independent judiciary retained its position, very shortly the newer principle of ministerial responsibility so undermined the old that the separation of powers as a part of the credo of European liberalism was gradually pushed off into limbo.[4]

The second, and far more important, device for restraining government was, of course, the confirmation and the amplification of the bill of individual rights which the restored sovereigns had already rescued from the wreckage of the French Revolution. By its prescriptions *all* men, in their persons and in their property, were to be secured against tyranny; *all* men were to be free to think and to believe and, within limits, to write as they wished.

When one moves on into the story of the role which these early liberals assigned to the state in relation to economic enterprise, one point stands out in all clarity: the protection of property from foreign aggression, from state encroachments, from the disorders of the mob, and from the tricks of rascality. Among these last, the refusal to honor a contract was of prime and horrifying significance, since contract made the difference, so thoughtful men believed, between order and chaos.

In such unquestioned necessities there was a large and, unhappily for the liberal, an expensive role for the state—that of the self-denying nightwatchman. In a positive work of facilitating economic enterprise, the stopping point of state action was not so readily established. For such things as a stable currency and the improvement of roads and harbors there was soon no serious opposition, but a fairly general liberal rejection of protective tariffs came slowly, and policy toward the new railways ranged from British private enterprise to Belgian state operation.

None the less, the prevalent theory, and increasingly the practice, left a wide latitude to the self-interest of economic man. Under its inspiration legislatures poured out a veritable stream of acts which removed qualifications from prop-

4. Benjamin Constant (Henri Benjamin Constant de Rebecque) offered an ingenious argument in support of a system of five powers (*Cours de politique constitutionnelle* [Paris, 1818–20], I, *passim*). François Pierre Guillaume Guizot, *Histoire des origines du gouvernement représentatif et des institutions politiques de l'Europe* (Paris, 1855), translated as *History of the Origin of Representative Government in Europe* (London, 1861): "Il faut qu'il y ait plusieurs pouvoirs égaux et indispensables l'un à l'autre, dans l'exercise de la souveraineté de fait, pour qu'aucun d'eux ne soit conduit à s'arroger la souveraineté de droit" (I, 122). Charles Edward Merriam, Jr., *History of The Theory of Sovereignty since Rousseau* (New York, 1900), chap. v. Jeremy Bentham launched an attack on the doctrine of separation of powers in *Fragment on Government* (1776) reprinted in *Works . . .* ed. Sir John Bowring (Edinburgh, 1838–43), I, part 1.

erty rights,[5] extended freedom of contract, and struck ancient shackles from commerce and industry and finance. Before the middle of the century, the social consequences of industrialization were beginning to creep from England to the Continent, there also to raise grim questions of policy; but the rank and file of the liberals, genuinely humanitarian though they were, found it hard to reconcile themselves to state regulation. Inescapably there had to be a great deal of confusion when Europe faced problems hitherto undreamed of, and, quite apart from a powerful economic theory, there could only have been much doubt as to the ability of state agencies, given their notoriously bad history, to do an effective social service.

The practical applications of this ideal of liberty, however, betrayed an inner contradiction, an inherent conflict of purposes. The constitutional and legislative enactments bestowed rights on all men without distinction of birth or fortune. Likewise the principles of the inviolability of private property, liberty of individual enterprise, and freedom of contract vouchsafed blessings to all men equally.

But, as these doctrines worked out in daily practice, they created disparities in wealth and position which boded ill for any morally rooted concept of freedom. The high regard for property rested on the old conviction that property was essential for the full achievement of the human personality. Something was wrong, therefore—as Thomas Jefferson saw[6]—when many men had no property. Something was wrong, too, for the prospects of human personality when freedom sent the penniless factory worker to negotiate single-handed a contract with an owner, or the landless peasant to deal with a great proprietor. These pregnant years of the first half of the century were demonstrating that seemingly inescapable paradox of man's finite destiny which decrees that a liberty which is not within hailing distance of equality is not really a human liberty. It is, rather, a citadel of privilege, something alien to the birthright of all men as envisaged in Jefferson's Declaration of Independence and in the French proclamation of the Rights of Man.

When political privilege was added to the economic, the citadel was complete.

The citadel, however, rested on precarious foundations. There was hardly any man so libertarian that he was prepared to deny a paramount claim of society. In the realm of economic enterprise and, too, in the realms of intellectual and spiritual enterprise, the ends of society could be achieved in one of two ways. The most direct was by means of social controls. The liberals rejected this alternative in favor of a wide latitude of individual freedom. But, caught in their commitment to social primacy, they could do so only on one logical condition: that, by some alchemy of the nature of things, there presided over free individual activities a benignant and harmonizing force which served the high claims of social justice. In a very literal sense, therefore, the liberalism of the

5. For a discussion of the increased freedom of property in England see Albert V. Dicey, *Law and Public Opinion in England during the Nineteenth Century* (London, 1905), pp. 200 ff.

6. Jefferson to the Rev. James Madison, Fontainebleau, Oct. 28, 1785, Julian P. Boyd, ed., *The Papers of Thomas Jefferson* (Princeton, 1950—), VII, 682.

first half of the century was nailing its case for freedom, for the full realization of the potentialities of the individual personality, to the future fortunes of capitalism. . . .

In 1848 there burst over Europe a new revolutionary fury. For a fleeting moment many a liberal glimpsed a day of new triumphs, but only for a fleeting moment. That frenzied year was compounded of a variety of suddenly unleashed forces and they served notice, at times in brutal language, that the future did not necessarily belong to liberalism. Yet, for all the power of upsurging competitors, and for all the triumphs of the old order, liberalism defied the current epitaphs and went on to the period of its greatest victories. If liberalism after 1848 was living on borrowed time, it made good use of the loan. Liberalism in the first half of the century had been more a state of mind, a set of impulses, than the doctrine of a single political party. Gradually parties took shape which claimed to act as the special custodians of the credo and their services to the cause were great. Theirs, however, were by no means the only services rendered. The whole work of the great day of liberalism was not a monopoly product of party spirit, but the effect rather of a pervasive flow of conviction. . . .

One of the great internal crises of later nineteenth-century liberalism has already been suggested: the debate on political democracy. The second was over the vexing question of what to do next. So much had been done within the old framework that the movement showed signs of reflecting John Bright's outlook, when, in 1873, he said that the great causes to which he had devoted his public life had been brought to fruition.[7] A revival of energy required a new liberal principle, and a new liberal principle depended on a new analysis of the relation between individual liberty and the state, that problem on which Mill and Spencer had produced nothing new.

The crucial decision had eventually to be made on whether something should be done by the state about the social consequences of industrialization, the old question first raised by nonliberal humanitarians earlier in the century. Some liberals had found in the iron law of wages an argument against intervention; some had been torn in mind and spirit over the issue; but the dominant voice of the movement had happily assured the anxious and the outraged that economic freedom would find the answer. The march of the years, however, did not deal gently with these responses. The logical plausibilities of the iron law of wages persuaded no one to reconcile himself to a marginal existence, and, worse still, the spread of free industry, for all of its miracles, showed no signs of binding the wounds of humanity. The meagerness of the life of the lower orders was revealing all too clearly that the old combination of certain rights for all men and special rights for certain men was not, after all, a harmonious and defensible synthesis. If liberalism was to maintain its concern for the universality of its principles, if it was to rise above the charge of being simply a pig philosophy, it was going to have to follow the nonliberals in a critical assessment of the laissez-faire state.

7. George Macaulay Trevelyan, *The Life of John Bright* (Boston, 1913), pp. 411–15.

Both in England and in France there was noteworthy thought which helped to clarify and to solve the problem of liberalism. Within its own arsenal there was a weapon that could be put to a new use, and that was Benthamite utility. Stripped of Bentham's own cumbersome rationalizations, the principle raised the simple but searching demand that every institution and every practice should be weighed in terms of a calculable social benefit. William Stanley Jevons invoked it in an important book published in 1882. Jevons proposed to go forward empirically with social questions, assessing the good and the bad of each suggestion as it arose without tenaciously holding onto the old presuppositions against state intervention.[8] About the same time, Thomas Hill Green approached the same set of problems from the point of view of an emerging school of British idealism. Green lodged the right and the necessity of positive state activity in its assistance to the moral self-realization of the individual.[9]

In France a wide variety of students gave their attention to this question. Out of their discussions came the doctrine of *solidarité* which, like that of Green, put its emphasis on the inherent dignity and worth of the individual human being. To serve the high purpose of moral individuality, these French thinkers were prepared to place restrictions on, without abolishing as a matter of dogmatic principle, the rights of private property.[10]

In so far as it rallied to such considerations, liberalism made a new affirmation of its concern for all men. After Gladstone was gone, the British liberal party became converted to the doctrine of the state as an engine of social betterment, and these same ideas were gaining ground on the Continent when the war came in 1914.[11] This reshaping of liberal thought, however, was not easily accomplished. The conception of a positive role of the state won out only at the expense of more divisions within the ranks of liberalism, as in the case of the move toward political democracy. The social group which, a generation and more earlier, had shown a high degree of cohesiveness, was beginning to break up.

This propensity for dissension appeared at the same time in another complex issue of state intervention. Disillusionment with the happy confidence of early

8. William Stanley Jevons, *The State in Relation to Labour* (3d ed., London, 1894).

9. Richard L. Nettleship, ed., *Works of Thomas Hill Green* (London, 1894–1900). "Lectures on the Principles of Political Obligation" may be found in Vol. II, and "Liberal Legislation and Freedom of Contract" in Vol. III. David G. Ritchie, *The Principles of State Interference* (2d ed., London, 1896), chap. IV; John MacCunn, *Six Radical Thinkers* (London, 1907), chap. VI.

10. Charles Gide and Charles Rist, *History of Economic Doctrines* (New York, n.d.), pp. 587–607; Francis W. Coker, *Recent Political Thought* (New York, 1934), pp. 410–15; Scott, pp. 157–86; Michel, *L'idée de l'état,* pp. 581–622.

11. The principle of the state as an agency of social reform must be distinguished from the proposition that the economically privileged classes should attempt through legislative benefactions to assuage the dissatisfactions of the less fortunate. This latter doctrine was articulated in a rough frankness when Joseph Chamberlain in 1884 and 1885 began to speak of the "ransom" which property would have to pay for its security. Charles W. Boyd, ed., *Mr. Chamberlain's Speeches* (London, 1914), I, 130–39; J. L. Garvin, *The Life of Joseph Chamberlain* (London, 1932–51), I, 541–43. A comparable thought appeared in France in the writings of Emile Littré, who wished to undermine the revolutionary nature of the proletariat by a policy of "social conciliation" (Scott, pp. 100–105).

liberalism was by no means limited to an acknowledgment of the poor fortunes of the proletariat. Time revealed, and especially the time after 1873, that all was not well with the fortunes of the middle possessing class.

In a period, accordingly, when the state loomed larger and larger as the ark of salvation, it was inescapable that uneasy entrepreneurs should also see in this erstwhile Moloch the instrument of their own redemption. Earlier, when Europe had lived under that regime of state intervention so inaccurately called mercantilism, the "sneaking arts" of the self-regarding pressure group had put an uncountable array of laws on the statute books. In the hard times of the 1870's and later, the growing practice of turning to the state offered an opportunity which industrialists and landowners could ill afford to overlook.

The whole story of Europe's abandonment of international free trade and its reversal of colonial policy cannot be told simply as the machinations of capitalists who had lost their nerve. At the same time, the work of the Central Union of German Manufacturers and comparable societies elsewhere leaves no doubt but that, in no small measure, the return to protection and imperialism was state intervention in economic enterprise for the direct benefit of the bourgeoisie.

The rising of these issues meant further splits and defections within the ranks of the liberal parties. In spite of the continued dedication of many liberals to the "sacred principle" of free trade, in spite of hesitations about imperial adventures, liberalism was perforce to some degree driven away from its older outlook, that outlook which had in it the vision of a peaceful world joined together by the bonds of unfettered trade.

While these internal crises were racking liberalism, the movement was suffering from a costly competition. In earlier times, the ancestral set of liberal ideas had engaged in what had been essentially a straight two-sided contest. When, however, the liberals began to search out their position after the French Revolution, they found that they no longer stood face to face with one antagonist; they were, rather, caught between two opponents, one to the left and one to the right. By the fourth quarter of the century, liberalism was beginning to feel keenly the disadvantageous consequences of its middle ground.

7. CARLTON J. H. HAYES: A Generation of Materialism*

Carlton J. H. Hayes (1882–1964), who taught at Columbia University until 1950, has been one of the most prolific American students of modern European history. In this general survey of the late nineteenth century Professor Hayes undertakes an evaluation of liberalism after 1870. Like other historians, he makes a distinction between a generalized and a specific liberalism; but his distinction is not the same as that of the others, not the same even as Neill's use of the same words. Can one make a case for an "ecumenical" liberalism, as

* From Carlton J. H. Hayes, *A Generation of Materialism, 1871–1900,* pp. 46–50. Copyright 1941 by Harper and Row, Publishers, Incorporated. Reprinted by permission of Harper and Row, Publishers.

Hayes defines it, this late in the nineteenth century, after all the previous changes in the movement? Is this the first significant emergence of what Hayes calls sectarian liberalism?

The "generation of materialism" began not only with war and heightening militarism. It began also with certain events which seemed to betoken the triumph of liberalism: the extinction of the pope's temporal power; the establishment of a "moderate" French Republic; Bismarck's acceptance of constitutional government; Gladstone's advent to the British premiership; the abolition of serfdom in Russia and of slavery in America; the heralded discovery, in Darwinism, of scientific proof of the liberating progress which would be universally assured by free competition. Such a multiplicity of omens could not fail to render old-fashioned the strenuous conflicts of previous decades between "liberals" and "conservatives"—between "revolutionaries" and "reactionaries." Liberalism, now so obviously a part of the evolutionary process, was no longer to be regarded as "revolutionary"; and most conservatives now felt constrained to disavow any sympathy with "reaction" and to concentrate on conserving those individual liberties which they held dearest. Thus, while liberals became a bit more conservative, conservatives were becoming a good deal more liberal. It was a tribute to contemporary pragmatism no less than to the comprehensiveness of liberal philosophy.

For liberalism by the 1870's was truly "ecumenical." It had become all things to all men. The one constant in it, throughout its whole development, had been, of course, a basic regard for the individual and for safeguarding his liberty against despotic authority. But "liberty" and "authority" were relative terms, signifying a wide range of objectives; and an attack upon a particular kind of authority had tended to bring forward a special set of liberties, which usually made way for a different set when the attack shifted to another kind of authority.

If one passes over the Protestant Reformation as of questionably liberal character and effect, one finds that the first successful campaigns of modern liberalism were waged against political despotism and resulted, on the one hand, in "bills of rights," guaranteeing the individual against arbitrary taxation, arrest, and imprisonment, and promising him liberties of speech, press, and association, and on the other hand, in "constitutional parliamentary government," putting an end to monarchical absolutism and vesting abridged powers of government in elective representatives of the nation. It was the political stage of liberalism which had been illumined by England's "Glorious Revolution" of 1689 and by the subsequent American and French Revolutions.

It appeared, however, that the French Revolution, at least in its Jacobin period, was a perversion of political liberalism; that it produced a mob tyranny as destructive of individual freedom as had been the previous tyranny of kings. Hence against the "excesses" of the French Revolution, many liberals reacted. These developed an almost pathological aversion to mobs.

The political stage of liberalism had further involved a reaction against the domination of one nation by another; and with the rise and diffusion of romanticism, it had become fashionable in liberal circles to favor the freeing of "oppressed" and "enslaved" peoples from alien and therefore "tyrannical" rule. In this way liberalism became an ally of nascent nationalism, without abandoning altogether its earlier attachment to the cosmopolitanism of the Enlightenment.

Presently the political stage of liberalism led into an economic stage. As industrialization took root in England and spread to the Continent, foreshadowing a material millennium in which Europe would no longer lack food and could have wealth and creature comforts in abundance, most liberals had become convinced that the one obstacle to the realization of such a pleasant prospect was the existing tyrannical regulation of trade and industry—fitting enough for medieval economy, but not at all compatible with the new need of large-scale capitalistic enterprise—and that steps should accordingly be taken to introduce freedom of trade and freedom of contract, freedom to buy and sell commodities and to employ and dismiss laborers with a minimum of restrictions by state, church, guilds, or trade-unions. This was the economic liberalism which stemmed doctrinally from the French Physiocrats, Adam Smith, and the Manchester School.

But certain liberals began to see a tyranny in capitalism itself and in the private ownership of the new industrial and commercial machinery; and, eager to free individual workingmen from "wage slavery," they furnished leaders to embryo socialism and anarchism. Thus the same fundamental concern with individual liberty which characterized economic liberalism entered into movements most critical of it.

Theoretically, all liberals were committed to religious toleration. But to some, the churches, and especially the Catholic Church, loomed as an "obscurantist" and peculiarly intransigent foe of individual liberty, and such liberals were impelled to move against the tyranny of "priestcraft" and "theocracy" as they had previously moved against divine-right monarchy, and at least to offer to the rising generation a secular schooling which would emancipate their minds. But it was also quite in the liberal spirit that still others should detect in anti-clerical legislation a threatening revival or extension of state despotism and should endeavor to protect individuals against it by invoking liberty of conscience and worship, and particularly liberty of religious education.

By the 1870's, therefore, there were many varieties of liberalism, affecting different persons in different ways. There was a political, an economic, an intellectual liberalism. There was a radical, an atheistic, a moderate, a conservative, a Christian liberalism. Wherefore such diverse groups as English Tories and French Radical Republicans, Italian followers of Mazzini or of Cavour, German admirers of Bismarck and German disciples of Karl Marx were all somewhere in the liberal tradition. They all adhered, in one way or another, to that "ecumenical liberalism" which had ever been actuated by a general and generous desire to free and dignify the individual and which drew support from every social class, from nobility and clergy, from bourgeoisie, peasantry, and proletariat.

Nevertheless, at the very time when such ecumenical liberalism was permeating all classes and parties and countries, something like a calamity befell it in the sudden upsurge of a special sect of liberals. These took to describing themselves as Liberals (with a capital letter) and anathematizing anyone who did not join their coterie and embrace their detailed and exacting creed. So seriously did they regard themselves that (following a not unusual human inclination) others accepted them at their own valuation and conceded to them the magical word "Liberal." In the long run, they were to discredit the name, and with it much of what was fine in the broad liberal tradition itself.

This fateful "sectarian liberalism" was grounded in peculiar developments of the 1860's and 1870's, particularly the speeding and spreading process of industrialization, the rising vogue of materialistic philosophy, and the stirring triumph, in international as well as in national affairs, of *Realpolitik*. Its main props were bourgeois promoters of big business: bankers, speculators, builders of railways and steamships, coal and iron magnates, proprietors of expanding foundries and factories. Supporting them, somewhat in the nature of a flying buttress, was an embellishing array of intellectuals: those scientists, engineers, physicians, lawyers, professors, and literary men who aspired to the utopia promised by Auguste Comte through the yoking of science with industry and who perceived the same axiomatic character in the "inexorable laws" of liberal political economy as in the physical law of gravitation. Both industrialists and their intellectual aides were urban people, and urban-mindedness was a conspicuous feature of the sectarians they mobilized and commanded among the petty bourgeoisie and the artisan class. Hence the newer Liberalism (with the capital letter) was much more narrowly urban and bourgeois than was the older and more general liberalism; and at least with its advocates among the *intelligentsia,* it was far more doctrinaire.

Its central stress was upon economic liberty, upon the paramount importance of encouraging individual initiative and private enterprise. Wherefore it demanded the lowering or entire removal of tariff barriers to trade, evinced hostility to labor associations in so far as they might interfere with freedom of contract, and vigorously opposed any governmental regulation of commerce or industry. As further means to its economic end, it appropriated and adapted much of historic political liberalism. The state, the Liberal doctrinaires explained, should be a "passive policeman" after the English model, with functions rigidly limited to the preservation of order, the protection of private property, the fostering of public education and necessary public works, and with a constitutional government in which the propertied classes would predominate and under which personal liberty would be large and public taxation small.

In international affairs the doctrinaires pursued what proved to be conflicting ideals. On the one hand, they realistically criticized war (in the abstract) as financially burdensome, as injurious to property and profitable trade, and as destructive of human life and liberty; and for the sake of thrift as well as of peace they sought to reduce expenditure for armaments. On the other hand, they were not averse individually to making profits from war loans and the munitions industry, and collectively they were quite patriotic and positively devoted to the belief that liberal nations must acquire and maintain leading positions in the world.

Finally, in the intellectual sphere, sectarian liberalism possessed a distinctive ethos. While in common with much of the older liberalism it postulated freedom of thought and liberty of press and speech, it placed novel emphasis upon the liberating blessings, ultimately, of technology, natural science, and "machine civilization," and immediately, of secularized popular education. Its horror of possible ecclesiastical dictation was prodigious. Religion it would concede to be a tolerable and probably temporary peccadillo of the individual's conscience, provided, of course, one's conscience was not too imperative.

Chapter VIII.

THE EMANCIPATION OF THE SERFS

THE EMANCIPATION of the serfs, in 1861, is the major event of nineteenth-century Russian history. Few acts of legislation have so quickly or so massively altered the life of a whole nation. Earlier abolitions of feudalism elsewhere in Europe had far more limited effects, either because they were more gradual, as in Germany, or because they eliminated a feudal structure already loose, as in France. The Russian feudal system embraced almost the whole population, and it was the harshest in Europe. Its rigor increased even in the late eighteenth and early nineteenth centuries. Russian feudalism was a system both political and economic. The landlord, whether an aristocrat or the state itself, was the effective ruler of his serfs. His courts tried most crimes; his punishments, which could extend to anything short of a death penalty, were those that affected most of the Russian people. Russian agriculture was clearly based on the feudal system. Landlords attempting to produce for the domestic market and for export relied on servile labor. Peasants constantly had to shape their economic efforts in light of their heavy obligations to their landlords, in work service or payments or both. Manufacturing was also partly involved in the feudal system, since many landlords encouraged their peasants to seek manufacturing work so that they would be able to fulfill their obligations. With minor exceptions, particularly in the cities, Russian society was sharply divided between serf and lord. There were important gradations in wealth and status among the lords, and there were some within the peasantry, but they never threatened the fundamental distinction between servile and free, between laborer and master.

Now feudalism was abolished. The effects of this on Russian politics and the economy were of course immense. Many traditional peasant ways were preserved, and the autocratic character of the government was only dented; but the emancipation cleared the way for the modernization of Russian agriculture and industry, even if progress in this direction was slow at first. Emancipation was undertaken partly in imitation of western Europe, and it was a precondition of other efforts at westernization. Peculiarly Russian qualifications were added to the process, however. The continued discouragement of individualistic farming and the maintenance of legal disabilities for the peasantry altered and probably delayed economic advance in western terms. The burdens placed upon the peasantry in the interests of the aristocracy were less unusual; even greater hardships were imposed in the abolitions of feudalism in Prussia, Rumania, and southern Europe. But these, too, complicated the situation and actually heightened peasant grievances.

The nature of the emancipation offers insight, then, into the basis of Russian politics and society and into the ambiguous relation of both to western European patterns. It is small wonder that such a complex event has caused significant historical controversy. Even to describe the nature of the emancipation legislation is no easy matter. The laws were extraordinarily detailed, and many provisions were unclear or contradictory. The great differences among the regions of Russia make simple or uniform interpretations of the causes and effects of emancipation impossible.

There have been a number of different assessments of the causes of emancipation. Some historians have viewed emancipation chiefly as a stage in Russian modernization, as a measure really compelled by Russia's backwardness in relation to the rest of Europe. Yet evidence to prove this as the major motive is scanty. The argument may be correct without such proof, for some of the most important statements about the basic direction of a historical process cannot be fully documented. But historians suspicious of such an overview and working more carefully from documentary evidence have looked to the motives of the tsar, the bureaucrats, and the nobles; and even here the evaluation is not uniform. The same elements are commonly mentioned: fear of unrest, the Crimean War, the pressures of liberals, and the desire to increase the power of the government and to improve the productivity of rural labor. But the balance of factors can be stated in various ways.

The interpretations of the causes of emancipation are related to the most important area of dispute: the effects of the whole process. Historians who explain emancipation mainly by the arguments of bureaucrats and liberals are likely to look primarily for legal and political effects. Historians who see the need for economic modernization as a cause usually look to this as an effect. Certainly, the range of evaluations of emancipation's impact is vast. There is, often, a basic value judgment: emancipation was a good thing or it was bad. The process can be viewed as one of the most generous in history or as an outright despoiling of the peasantry. There is the usual problem of determining the time period over which the effects of emancipation extended. If only the first decade is examined, the act seems clearly to have harmed the peasantry and probably to have benefited the landlords; but a longer view complicates this picture. Historians have often used different time periods to make different points, sometimes without being explicit about their procedure. Historians bent on condemning the political hold of the government over the peasantry may look particularly at the 1880's and 1890's, when local governments had been placed under strict controls; but this orientation distorts the emancipation measures themselves. To praise the emancipation, it is useful to take a long view and include the Stolypin reforms in the assessment; these reforms were different in character from the emancipation, although they admittedly were related to it. The problem of periodization, often linked to a basic preconception of the value of the emancipation, must be faced in dealing with differences of interpretation.

Two facts necessarily condition judgments of the emancipation. As Professor Geroid Robinson points out, there was only half a century between the abolition of feudalism and the revolutions of 1905 and 1917. No student can fail to ask what relationship existed between the emancipation and the revolutions, and most will be tempted to say that emancipation failed because, in its harshness to the peasantry, it furthered rather than prevented disorder. But should the emancipation be viewed with such explicit reference to the later upheavels in Russia?

More recent politics color interpretations as well. Liberalism was widespread among historians in Russia early in this century and could induce a largely political evaluation of the emancipation. Russian Marxists have dealt extensively with the subject, so vital to their own history, and have placed it primarily in an economic framework. There is some clumsiness in their efforts to apply Marx's industrially based concepts of social class to the ending of feudalism, but the Marxists can clearly show the hardships that resulted from emancipation and the revolutionary strain involved. Non-Russian scholars must, of course, deal with the Marxist view and must derive much of their information from Marxist sources. This can lead to substantial acceptance of the Marxist approach, but it can also encourage a reaction that might itself be excessive.

The emancipation stands open to judgment in the most basic terms. Did it free the serfs? Did it aid the peasant economy? Did it encourage better agricultural methods? What did it do to the aristocracy? What was its relationship to later revolution? Did it try to salvage too much of the old order, or was it too brash an innovation? The decisiveness of the act is clear, but in what direction did it point?

1. ALEXANDER KORNILOV: Modern Russian History*

Alexander Kornilov (1862–1925) was a professor at the Politechnicum of Peter the Great, in Petrograd (Leningrad); a liberal, his history was written before the revolution and is as interesting a comment on his own political views as it is on the emancipation. His focus is almost entirely political. Emancipation was a precondition for reforms in administration and local government; its effects are assessed largely in terms of the alteration of legal conditions. This approach must seem somewhat anachronistic today, when attention is largely devoted to economic conditions and peasant attitudes, and it is certainly incomplete. It calls attention, however, not simply to a distinctive historical approach but to a major element of the emancipation itself. It was, after all, a legal change, and it did form part of an important administrative reform movement in the 1860's; these aspects are perhaps now unduly neglected. Further, Kornilov's moderate liberalism resembles the political views of some of the contemporary advocates of reform and may allow him to convey the intentions of the reformers more adequately than later or more critical accounts can possibly do.

The chief significance of the Great Reform has been its *legal* aspect; in this respect the fall of bondage has been the most important event in all the modern history of Russia. Contemporaries and especially participators of the reform were fond of saying that by the Act of February 19 the people were for the first time brought on the historical arena in Russia. At any rate we may say that the whole status of the people has fundamentally changed with the introduction of the reform. Whatever the material consequences of the reform have been, one cannot deny the enormous importance of the fact that men were no longer permitted to sell other men or to transfer them from field work to house service, i.e., to a state of domestic slavery. The peasants got rid of the unlimited

* From Alexander Kornilov, *Modern Russian History,* Alexander S. Kaun, trans., Vol. II, pp. 46–48, 51–54. Copyright 1917 and renewed 1945 by Alfred A. Knopf, Inc. and reprinted with their permission.

interference in their life, which the landowners had exercised even to the extent of arranging marriages among them.

From the generally human point of view the legal significance of the reform has been colossal, but we must observe here that the abolition of serfdom, having freed the peasants from personal and legal subjection to the landowners, has not equalised the peasants with the landowners in their civil rights: the reform has transferred them from the class of bonded peasants *not into the class of fully able citizens, but into the class of the so-called tributary orders.* This vestige of the general binding of all orders, on which the Muscovite state had been based, has continued to exist. The legal position of the tributary orders consisted in their being taxed by the Government per capita, not according to their income; the tax had to be paid by the group as a whole, by *mutual guarantee,* which bound every one to the group in which he was registered, by the aid of a special *passport system.* Every tributary order was responsible for all its members, and for this reason the Government was obliged to allow such groups a certain authority over its members, the right to keep them forcibly within the group. As long as the "mutual guarantee" system and the per capita tax existed there could not be any full rights of separate classes in Russia, or actual equality of all citizens before the law; those under the burden of the tributary system had no freedom of movement or of profession, for in order to be transferred from one group into another one had to obtain a verdict of dismissal. One limitation logically resulted in another, and the traces of that bondage are still noticeable in Russia.

Another article in the General Act stated that during the first nine years after the publication of the Act the temporary Obligatory peasants could not refuse their allotment and had to perform obligations for it; their personal freedom was thus definitely limited. One should have in mind that the men who worked out the peasant-reform of 1861 did not profess the liberal views of the men of the end of the eighteenth or of the beginning of the nineteenth century, whose starting points were the rights of human personality, the ideology of the Declaration of Rights of Man and Citizen. The members of the Editing Commissions desired primarily the security of the welfare of the people and of the State. They undoubtedly were well disposed towards the peasants and sincerely wished to improve their life in a fundamental way, but since they acted for *welfare,* and not for *personal freedom* in the proper sense of the word, it is natural that at times questions of welfare prevailed against questions of personal liberation. As a result of that attitude came the beneficial part of the reform—the liberation of the peasants with land, but the same circumstance conditioned the element of guardianship which was considered necessary to introduce for the time of the organisation of the freed peasants.

The reasonable apprehension that the emancipated peasants might again fall under the power and even bondage of the landowners, resulted in the *administrative organisation* established for the peasants. The peasantry was organised in autonomous social units, of which the smallest was a village community. Economically the communities had considerable independence; in "communal" villages the taxation was determined by the peasants according to the size of individual allotments, which in their turn were determined by the general assembly of the village community. That general assembly could tax the members with dues for various spiritual, mental, or moral needs, and for social exigencies.

Originally it was intended that while the village-communities should have complete management of the economic part, the *volost* was to be another unit of the local administration, not connected hierarchically with the economic unit; but in the end the *volost* was placed above the village community in many administrative matters. The elected village functionaries, the Elders, had to submit in police questions to the *volost*-chiefs and the *volost*-boards, and together they were subordinate to various police and administration authorities of the district, whose orders they had to fulfil without dispute, under the fear of disciplinary penalties which could be inflicted by the Peace Mediator at his own initiative or upon complaints of various officials. In the end the persons elected by the village-autonomy became virtually petty agents of the district-police; although chosen by the village communities and *volosts* they were responsible not to their electors, but to the "authorities." This circumstance undermined the principle of self-government at its root.

We have seen that those defects in the administration were decisively attacked by the delegates of the first summons. The Editing Commissions, fearing the ferule of the landowners over the peasants, objected to having the *volost* represented by all classes and remaining independent from the district administration; but they fell into another extreme, and subjected the village communities to bureaucratic arbitrariness.

In the *economic* respect the Editing Commissions considerably deviated from the recommendations of the provincial committees, particularly in regard to the norms of the allotments, the norms of the peasants' obligations for those allotments, and the question of redemption and compensation. According to the Act, the peasants were to *retain approximately those allotments which they had been using in their bondage-state*. But the Commissions regarded the fact that in some places the landowners gave their peasants larger allotments than were needed (because in the industrial, non black-soil provinces land was of small value); while in other regions the landowners gave their peasants such small allotments that the peasants could neither subsist on them nor be able to eke out the assessed *obrok*. In view of this the Editing Commissions worked out special norms for the regulation of existing conditions. In every region there was to be a *maximal norm*; if peasants on a certain estate were in possession of more land than was limited by that norm, the landowner had the right to let them use the whole land for additional obligations or he could demand the cutting off of the surplus. On the other hand *minimal norms* in the measure of one-third of the maximal norms were established. Where the peasants' allotments were below that minimum, the landowner was obliged to add land for the completion of the norm.

In respect to the maximal norms, the size of which naturally determined the minimal norms, Russia was divided into three regions: the non black-soil, the black-soil, and the steppes. In the non black-soil region there were seven possible grades of norms, from three and a quarter to eight desiatins, so that there could be maximal allotments of three and a quarter, three and a half, four, five, six, seven, and eight desiatins. In the black-soil region were five grades: three, three and a quarter, three and a half, four, and four and a half desiatins; in the region of the steppes were four grades: six and a half, eight and a half, ten and a half, and twelve desiatins. In establishing these norms the Editing Commissions increased about twice the norms recommended by the provincial committees. In the course of the Commissions' work they had to take into account the considerations and protests of the delegates, and decrease many norms by one-quarter, one-half, and even by whole desiatins. Later the bargaining affair between Grand Duke Constantine and Panin further reduced the size of the norms. But after all the insufficiency of the peasants' allotment was due not so much to the diminution of the original norms recommended by the Editing Commissions, as to the fact that *in the best cases the peasants received those allotments that had been in their possession during the bondage state, and those allotments required only half of their labour, and could not therefore yield enough for their subsistence and for the fulfilment of the obligations.*

In respect to the *obligations* of the peasants, the Editing Commissions subdivided Russia into four regions: non black-soil, industrial (i.e., of the *obrok*-system); non black-soil (of the *barshchina*-system); black-soil (all of *barshchina*); and the steppe region. The maximal, or full, *obrok,* which corresponded to the maximum norm of the allotment, was in the non black-soil industrial region nine rubles per soul, and ten rubles in the more advantageous places, as those in the vicinity of the Capitals or in the province of Yaroslavl. In the other regions the norm was originally estimated to be eight rubles all over, but in view of the protests of the delegates and of some of the members of the Commissions, the *obrok* in the black-soil region had to be raised to nine rubles.

The "full" *obrok* could be levied only on maximum allotments in a given region; smaller allotments were assessed with lower *obroks,* but the diminution of the *obroks* was not made proportional to the diminution of the size of the allotment. A special *gradational system* was accepted for the estimation of additional desiatins, so that if a peasant had seven desiatins in a region of an eight desiatin-norm, his nine rubles *obrok* was diminished not by one-eighth, but only by fifty-six and two-thirds copecks. In regions where under the bondage-system the peasants had allotments below one-third of the maximal norm, additional allotments required *obroks* almost twice above the norm. For this reason the peasants preferred in such cases "beggarly" gratuitous allotments to additional land, where for one-third allotment they had to pay two-thirds *obrok*. There were many disturbances in places where landowners refused to yield to the peasants' demand for gratutitous "quarterly" allotments.

From the aforesaid we can see what were the allotments received by the peasants after the liquidation of the bondage, and what were their obligations.

Their allotments were equal approximately to one-half of the amount of their earning capacity, for in the best cases they received only that land which they possessed under bondage and which required only three days' work in a week, the rest of the time being given to *barshchina.* In order to utilise their labour power, the peasants had either to rent the other half of the land from the landowner, or to hire themselves to the landowner, or to look for some side work which would enable them to pay the taxes and the *obroks* and to buy such necessaries as their own property could not supply them with. With the growing density of the population the dearth of land was felt more and more, rent rose higher and higher, and the peasant grew poorer and poorer; for this reason *in the most fertile part of Russia the misery of the peasants is at the present time the greatest.* The peasants of the black-soil regions, particularly rich in soil, as in the provinces of Tula or Tambov, live in worse poverty than the peasants of the provinces of Tver or Yaroslavl, where the land yields little, but where they earn from industrial occupations.

By the Act of February 19 the peasants received the land in "perpetual," or as Panin insisted—in "permanent" utilisation. By *voluntary agreements* with the landowners they could eventually redeem their obligations, and receive the land in personal possession. Not the land but the obligations were redeemed. *Compulsory redemption* was rejected both by Alexander and Rostovtzev who consented only to redemption by mutual agreement. Yet, as one could have foreseen, the majority of the landowners *had* to seek redemption. In the non black-soil provinces they wished it themselves; in the black-soil provinces, especially in the *barshchina*-estates, the position of the landowners grew unbearable, for with the abolition of their authority over the peasants the latter performed their *barshchina* very inadequately and evasively, so that those estates deteriorated considerably. The landowners in the black-soil regions began to hope for redemption as the only way to settle with their bondmen. On the whole the redeeming operation was realised more rapidly than one could have expected, and it was delayed only in cases where the peasants were unwilling to meet the offers of the landowners.

Such was the economic side of the reform of February 19 for the peasants and for the landowners. For the gentry proper the results of the liquidation of bondage were not alike in all regions. In the black-soil provinces, after the hard *barshchina*-period, the landowners retained most of their land, were able to get cheap labour in view of the dense population and the absence of non-agricultural occupations. Besides, they received a compensation which they could employ either for the improvement of their estates or for the extinction of their debts. If they were not inclined to manage their estates, they could profitably rent their land, since the rentals were very high on account of the insufficient allotments of the peasants.

But in the non black-soil industrial region the landowners, having received their compensation, severed in most cases all connections with their former possessions; only a few remained on their estates, and endeavoured to continue agricultural pursuits. It was difficult to obtain labour hands from a population that catered to industrial occupations, and the majority of the landowners sold out their estates, and employed their capital for industrial purposes, if they did not waste it otherwise. Thus with the abolition of serfdom industry received new capital.

In conclusion let us say that the chief significance of the abolition of bondage has lain not only in the enormous economic consequences which it bore for the peasantry, gentry, and industry of the country, but still more in the fundamental change wrought by it in the legal conditions of the Empire. Only after the abolition of serfdom did all those great reforms that were promulgated during the Sixties become possible. Only then could the road for the judiciary reform be cleared. During the bondage-system the whole administration structure was based on class-principles, with the prevalence of the gentry; the landowner was the caretaker of everything on his estate, and the Central authority had confidence in the management of the "gratuitous chiefs-of-police" (Nicolas's expressed idea of the rôle of the nobles. Tr.). Now had the bureaucratic method been feasible, everything should have been rebuilt from top to bottom; but the bureaucracy did not possess sufficient power for such a grandiose transformation. Hence the abolition of serfdom resulted in the introduction of local self-government, in one way or another.

2. GEROID ROBINSON: Rural Russia under the Old Regime*

Geroid Robinson, long a professor of Russian history at Columbia University, made peasant conditions and attitudes the essential subject of his masterful study of rural Russia. Naturally, the emancipation process is evaluated primarily in these terms. And the process is evaluated unfavorably. Professor Robinson sees a direct link between emancipation and ultimate peasant revolt. He believes that the intent of the reformers and the factors that influenced them—including, possibly, peasant traditions and pressures themselves—are relatively academic matters compared with the results of the process. Along with the material hardships and legal disabilities emancipation involved, Professor Robinson notes the degree to which it solidified peasant communal traditions that quickly proved inappropriate to the demands of modern agriculture. Does this account overstress the role of emancipation in creating peasant grievance compared, for example, with population growth? Would peasants have accepted a reform that encouraged agricultural improvements more directly?

As life runs, the downfall of serfdom and the triumph of social revolution in Russia do not stand far separated: in 1926, nine years after the Revolution, the writer lived for some weeks in a provincial household where the soup and the samovar were brought in each day by a spry old *babushka* who had been a serf—the goose-girl on a neighboring estate. During the period of revolution and civil war, this town had been occupied and re-occupied by various groups

* From Geroid T. Robinson, *Rural Russia under the Old Regime* (New York: The Macmillan Company, 1957), pp. 64–66, 80–83. Reprinted by permission.

of Reds and Whites; some of its buildings were still in ruins, a Communist Club was quartered in the House of Nobles, and on one occasion the writer happened to see a goat looking out through the empty window of a neighboring mansion; but the old *babushka* lived on in another age: she still resented, and volubly disapproved of, any attempt of the mistress of the house to lend a hand in the kitchen—to those old eyes this was still a thing most unbecoming and unseemly.

But the Emancipation and the Revolution are joined by much more than mere proximity in time. One September day in the fateful year 1917, by a roadside in the south-central *step,* a man climbed a telephone pole, and cut the minute thread of communication which joined a manor-house on the northern horizon with the towns, the police-offices, and the barracks along the railway line to the southward. In one sense, this manor-house now stood quite alone; but not really so, for within sight of its groves there were several peasant villages. Thus the two elements—peasant and proprietorial, were left momentarily to react upon each other in isolation; and within a few hours the estate had been looted, the mansion was in flames, and somewhere within the fiery circle the master of the house lay dead.

From the day when the servile system was still in the making, fire had smouldered in the Russian village, and several times a hurricane of fire had raged through the country, never sweeping the manors clean, but never quite extinguished. On the eve of the Emancipation, the smell of smoke was strong enough to alarm the Tsar-Liberator himself, and the air was by no means cleared by his "Great Reform." In very much that it preserved, even in much that it created, the Emancipation of the 'sixties contributed powerfully to the making of the Revolution of 1917; the meaning of the Proclamation of 1861 did not become altogether clear until it was illuminated by the glare of that great conflagration.

If the reader will consider the peasant reforms of the 'sixties in terms not of law but of life—if he will think of an individual peasant in his long coat, his feet in plaited bark slippers and his legs wrapped to the knee with strips of linen; of his crowded log house, the whitewashed interior and the great brick stove, the cluster of outbuildings around the court, and the scattered strips of plow-land; of the village with its grass-grown street as wide as a field, where wheel-tracks wander in deliberate confusion and the peasant assembly forms its triple circle of bearded householders, grave-faced women, and scooting, tumbling children—if the reader will think in such terms as these, he will be impressed by the fact that very much of the old life survived the changes of the time.

The peasants on the lands of the State and of the Imperial family were made the subject of special legislation, but it was the bound people on the private estates who were most deeply affected by the reform. "The right of bondage over the peasants settled upon the landlords' estates, and over the courtyard people, is forever abolished"—so declared the first article of the General Statute of Emancipation. Among the private bondsmen, it will be convenient to deal first with the plowmen of the villages, and to leave the non-agricultural bondsmen for later consideration. The Statutes of 19 February 1861 provided not only for the emancipation of these millions, but for their endowment with land, and for their social-economic organization. These laws of 1861 were so verbose, so full of variables, so loaded down with qualifications and exceptions, and in general so astonishingly involved and complicated, that it is difficult to understand how any serf could ever by any possibility have known what rights might be hidden in this legislative haystack. As late as 1906, the Ministry of the Interior could still quite properly report to the Council of Ministers that the provisions of the peasant land-laws were "incomplete, inexact, and in some instances even contradictory." In certain respects, the regulations for the three Little Russian *guberniias* [administrative districts] of Chernigov, Poltava and Kharkov, and for the western *guberniias* from Kiev and Podolsk to Kovno and Vitebsk, differed from those about to be described. No attempt will be made here to deal with the peculiarities of the former Emancipation-settlement, but in the case of the more numerous western *guberniias* several important points of variation will be indicated hereafter.

Under the Statutes of Emancipation, the former serf was not simply offered an allotment; he was required to accept it, in one form or another, at least for the time being. Because of the obligations attaching to it, he might think his allotment a liability rather than an asset, and might therefore wish to renounce it outright; but it will presently be shown that there were serious obstacles to such a renunciation—obstacles which were quite often insuperable. If instead of wishing to "throw away" his allotment, the former serf desired rather to transfer it, and perhaps to receive some sort of compensation for his land-right and for his improvements, he was faced with difficulties which varied with the character of his tenure (either hereditary or repartitional), and will presently be discussed. The point to be made here is that there were important obstacles to the sale of the allotment—even to its being "thrown away"; and this fact is inseparably bound up not only with the subject of peasant organization under the reform, but also with the question (to be considered later) of the economics of the Emancipation.

The Great Reform did not effect a revolutionary change in the internal organization of the peasantry on the private estates: on the contrary, for the purpose in part of securing the payment of the excessive charges laid upon the emancipated serfs, the government shored up and strengthened with legal guarantees those basic institutions of peasant life—the household and the commune. Even a glance at the Statutes of Emancipation will show that they deal primarily in terms, not of individuals, but of groups and group-functions. . . .

But how is one to interpret the great official solicitude for the preservation of the household and the commune? Is it to be taken as a sign that the nobility (the group most influential in the government) were especially devoted to these institutions, in and for themselves? And as for the households and the communes—were they in need of such solicitude? Would the peasants have dissolved these bodies, if they had been entirely free to do so? A prerequisite to any attempt to answer such inquiries, is a study of the work which these institutions had now been set to do—above all, the work of guaranteeing the redemption of the peasant's allotment at a price so high that it in fact included a redemption of his person also. Under these circumstances, the household and the commune might usually be looked upon as burden-bearing groups; and so long as they maintained this character—so long as they were employed as engines of an over-priced redemption, the circumstances were hardly favorable for a peasant plebiscite upon their value. But whether it was official solicitude, or popular desire, that was chiefly responsible for the survival and strengthening of these institutions, in any case their existence drew out and developed, or gave expression to, a capacity for collective action—for doing things in common —which helped most powerfully to shape the course of a peasant history in the catastrophic time to come.

The serf of the manorial village did not become, under the terms of the Emancipation, a free-moving, landless man. It has been shown that he was far from free, but it still remains to inquire more closely into the conditions under which he was given—perhaps it would be better to say, required to accept—a plot of earth. In this connection, there are three matters of first and last importance: the social apparatus of allotment and redemption, the size and quality of the holding, and the weight of the redemption-payments. The functions of the household and of the commune as recipients and payors have previously been discussed, and it is now appropriate to ask what it was that the peasantry received, and at what cost.

The Statutes of Emancipation provided that the allotments were to be assigned on the basis of the number of "revision souls" found in each commune in 1858—that is, the number of males of all ages recorded in the census of that year. Throughout the greater part of the country, local maximal and minimal norms were established for the allotment per soul, the minimum amounting in each case to one-third of the maximum. In the extreme South, as well as in the Southeast, only one statutory norm was set up for each locality. The norms having been established, it was provided that the size of the allotments might be fixed by voluntary agreement between the landlord and his peasants, with this general restriction: that the old pre-reform allotments might not be diminished to less than half the maximal or statutory norm, and might not be reduced at all where they already stood below this level.

Where the landlord and the peasants did *not* reach an agreement, there were certain regulations which in a measure determined the size of the allotment. In the South, the peasants were supposed to receive allotments according to the statutory norm, but on the other hand, the landlord was free to retain one-half of the non-waste land of the estate no matter how much this might limit the area of the peasant lands. In the black soil and the forest, the landlord had the choice of cutting off from the former allotments any surplus *above* the maximal norm, or leaving the surplus in the hands of the peasants, if the terms they offered were sufficiently attractive. If, on the other hand, the former allotment fell *below* the statutory minimum, the landlord might make a proportionate reduction in the dues, or (if the peasants did not object) he might increase the amount of the land to the minimal norm. Where the old allotments fell *between* the norms, there was to be in general no change in their size, but special regulations deprived many of the peasants of the forests which they had been using. And finally (whatever effect this might have upon the realization of the other conditions just mentioned) each landlord of the black soil and the forest was free to reduce any and all allotments as far as the minimal norm, if this were necessary in order to enable him to keep in his own hands one-third of the non-waste land of his estate.

For nine years after the confirmation of the Statutes, or at any time when redemption was begun with State aid, an allotment already granted might be reduced by mutual agreement to a legal minimum fixed for the district—usually not to less than one-third of the maximal or statutory norm. Under certain conditions the peasants might redeem the house-and-garden plot, or *usadba,* separately from the remainder of the allotment, but if the landlord refused to come to terms in the matter of the price, there were special financial difficulties in the way of such a fractional redemption. If the peasant did redeem the *usadba* separately, he could, after 1870, refuse to hold any longer the remainder of the allotment, unless the landlord had in the meantime enforced a redemption. If the landlord exercised at any time his right to compel redemption, the peasants on their part might refuse to buy out more than the legal minimum. If, on the other hand, the landlord were willing to surrender all claims for dues, services, and redemption-payments, and to make an outright gift of an allotment equal to one-fourth of the maximal or statutory norm, and the peasants were willing on their part to accept such an allotment, a final settlement might be arranged on this basis; the grants offered under this provision, the "beggarly allotments," were accepted by about six per cent of the peasants as a means of avoiding the excessive charges on the larger plots. But among all these complications, the most impressive fact is that whenever during the first nine years a decision in respect to the size of the allotment was to be made not by mutual agreement but by a one-sided choice, the right to make that choice belonged to the peasants only in the case of enforced redemption; otherwise it belonged to the landlord, who would usually make his decision with an eye to the dues and services which the law would permit him to extract, in exchange for a given acreage assigned to the peasants.

The size of the allotment was not the only crucial point; its quality was also a matter of the first importance. In spite of the peasants' essential need for timber and fuel in this country of white winters, log-walled houses, and huge stoves, forest-lands were seldom included in the new allotments. The superior position and influence of the landlords, and in particular their right under the conditions already described to make "cut-offs" from the peasants' former holdings, and to demand a reallocation of the holdings in order to eliminate the intermixture of the peasants' lands with their own (the peasants on their side did not possess the latter right)—all this made it possible for the landlords to impose numerous inconveniences in the arrangement of the allotments, and even sometimes to leave the peasants without such essential elements of village economy as water-courses and meadow lands.

For an indeterminate period of "temporary obligation," the whole area of the estate was to continue to be the property of the landlord, while the peasants were to hold of him their revised and officially approved allotments, and to render in return such services or payments as were mutually agreed upon, or were prescribed by the Statutes of Emancipation when no agreement was arrived at. The peasants were given the option of passing from the system of labor-dues to that of money-payments or *obrok,* and—for reasons to be explained hereafter—the statutory rates for payments in this latter form affected profoundly the course and the outcome of the whole reform.

The two most conspicuous characteristics of the official rate-schedules were: first, that the charges usually exceeded the rental value of the allotments; and second, that this excess was not equitably distributed among the allotments of a given district, or among the districts of the country. For each district, the official schedule provided a maximal annual charge, to correspond with the maximal allotment per peasant soul; but in most of the districts the charge was not diminished in full proportion when the amount of land fell below the maximum, and where the allotment stood at the official minimum, the rate often amounted to double as much *per acre* as was assessed upon maximal allotments in the same locality. A second method of comparison, not between small and large allotments in the same district, but between different districts as a whole, makes it apparent that the official rates were often inversely proportional to the rental value of the land, and stood at higher levels for a given acreage in some of the clay-soiled central-industrial *guberniias,* than in the rich black-soil *guberniias* farther south. These apparent inconsistencies did not arise by chance; if the payments were disproportionately high when the allotments were small, it was because there went with the smallest allotment, as well as the largest, not only the house-yard but the person of the peasant; if the rates were at a maximum in the thin-soiled industrial *guberniias,* it was not because the land was here more valuable (actually it was less so), but because the person of the peasant had here a greater value, by reason of the greater development of side-earnings in the household crafts and in wage-work in the towns. For the time being, the peasant was really renting not only his land but his own person from his former master.

3. SERGE A. ZENKOVSKY: The Emancipation of the Serfs in Retrospect*

This overview of emancipation, written on the centennial of the measure by a professor of Slavic and Eastern studies at the University of Colorado, takes a

* From Serge A. Zenkovsky, "The Emancipation of the Serfs in Retrospect," *The Russian Review,* Vol. 20, no. 4 (October, 1961). Copyright *The Russian Review* and reprinted with their permission.

somewhat more sympathetic position toward that reform than that of Professor Robinson, though there is no major disagreement over the essential facts. The link to the later revolution is not stressed, while the radical character of the process is brought out. And Professor Zenkovsky notes that some peasants were ultimately able to do well under the terms of the emancipation.

A hundred years ago Russians of all classes eagerly listened to or read the words of Emperor Alexander II with which this autocratic ruler announced the termination of serfdom and the liberation of about one-third of his subjects from the arbitrary and often cruel power of the landlords. Indeed, this memorable Act of February 19, 1861, gave personal freedom to 23 million serfs, or 34.4 percent of the total population of Russia, promoting them to the status of "free rural inhabitants."

The mere fact that such a tremendous number of people were freed from the control and supervision of the nobility points up the particular importance of this law and made this reform one of the most remarkable events in Russian history. In no other country besides Russia and the United States (which only two years later, on January 1, 1863, likewise liberated the Negroes of this country from slavery) was the liberation of the rural manpower accomplished so swiftly and so radically, by one single legislative enactment. In most lands of Western Europe, as for instance England, France or Italy, the emancipation of the peasantry was a very slow process and its legal enactment often only confirmed the results of long-evident historical trends. Moreover, very rarely did the emancipated serf or slave automatically receive the lands on which he used to work and live. Even in the United States, the slaves liberated by Lincoln's promulgation did not receive the lands they had previously cultivated for the plantation owners.

Certainly it can be argued that in no other land did the emancipation of the rural manpower involve such a considerable part of the population as in Russia and that Russian reform was therefore bound to be more far-reaching. Since the number of slaves in the United States in the 1860's (some four or four and a half million) was considerably less than the number of Russian serfs, therefore the social implications of the reform were less grave for the nation as a whole than in the land of the Tsar. Still, in the South, where the majority of the Negro slaves was to be found, their proportion was 35–40 percent of the total local population, slightly greater than the corresponding percentage of peasants bound to the nobles in Russia. Throughout the entire territory of the United States, the percentage of Negro slaves in 1862 can be estimated at no less than 15 percent of the total number of inhabitants of this country at that time.

Therefore, keeping in mind that the Act of 1861 changed so drastically the legal status and the life of millions of people, it seems rather paradoxical that Russian emancipation became one of the most contested legal and political acts in history. To this day there are debates and discussions among Russian and Western historians as to the importance and consequences of Alexander II's manifesto. It would not be justifiable, however, to accuse the Russian rulers of the seventeenth and eighteenth centuries of negligence for not having emancipated the serfs. At that time Russian tsars were by no means in a position to do it, for both fiscal and political reasons. The first Romanov was obliged to the nobles for his election to the tsardom. Under Tsar Alexis (1645–1676) the nobles actually participated in the disturbance of 1647 which resulted in the Code of Law of 1649 (*Ulozhenie*) and the final legalization of perpetual serfdom. In the next century the nobles continued to command the destinies of the Russian rulers, putting four tsars of their choice on the throne and removing three others in 1741, 1762 and 1801, two of these last being killed during palace upheavals. Incidentally, in the dethroning of Paul I a factor of considerable weight was the nobility's indignation at Paul's decrees establishing a legal minimal allotment of land to the serfs by the landlords. Thus this concern of Paul I for the serfs was at least partially responsible for his murder. The end of the liberal policies characteristic of the early years of the reign of Catherine II was also brought about to a large extent by her fear of a new palace upheaval by the aristocratic guards. In view of the influence of the nobility on the throne, it is not astonishing that even the spectacular increase of Russian territory and consequently of arable lands failed to improve the lot of the peasant. Actually, the power of the nobility was not broken until the reign of Nicholas I, who was prompted by the Decembrist uprising to curb the influence of the nobles. Thus Nicholas became the first Tsar of Russia who could have freed the serfs, but even he, being educated in the spirit of eighteenth century absolutism, refrained from carrying out this radical reform, detrimental to the well-being of the nobility.

Still, by the second part of the eighteenth century serfdom had already developed into an unjust and senseless institution. Abolition of compulsory military service for the nobility in 1762 had deprived the serfdom of its only logical foundation. Now the peasant continued to serve the noble, but the noble no longer served the state. Of course, a large proportion of nobles continued their service in the army or administration, but this was no longer a compulsory service remunerated by serf labor, but rather a free choice of a salaried career.

One of the main paradoxes of Russian serfdom was its regional distribution: Serfdom was almost the exclusive and tragic privilege of the Russian peasantry —that is, the peasantry of Great Russia, White Russia, and Little Russia, or the Ukraine. Among the Finno-Ugric and Turkic nationalities of Siberia and the eastern provinces, serfdom was practically unknown. So, for instance, among the Tartars of the Volga there was hardly more than one percent of serfs. Among the Bashkirs, Chuvash and Finno-Ugric tribes there were actually no serfs, despite the fact that all of these peoples were incorporated into the Russian state during the era of the rise of serfdom. The Estonians and Latvians were liberated by the Russian government from dependence on the Baltic German Barons in 1816–1819. Among the Jews of southwestern Russia serfdom never existed. The Polish peasants were liberated from serfdom by Napoleon in 1807. It is, however, true that this emancipation deprived them of the lands on which they lived and which they cultivated, and that only in 1846 was their economic condition improved by the so-called "inventory rules," which limited the arbitrary actions of the Polish nobles. These rules also determined, at least partially, the rights and obligations of the peasants of the southwestern region of Russia, present-day western Ukraine. But the remainder of the Russian peasantry, especially the Great and White Russians, continued to live under serfdom. In the provinces of Tula and Smolensk, for instance, seventy percent of the population was comprised of serfs. In the provinces of Kaluga, Nizhni-Novgorod, Vladimir, Kostroma, Yaroslavl, Tver and Ryazan the proportion of serfs vacillated from fifty to sixty percent of the total population, although it was the same Russian population of these provinces which bore the brunt of the defense and build-up of the empire for centuries. Also very high was the proportion of serfs in the provinces of the Ukraine. From the national viewpoint, a paradoxical phenomenon consisted in the fact that in the Ukrainian provinces west of the Dnieper and in Belorussia, about six million Orthodox Ukrainians and Belorussians—who belonged to the "ruling" nationality of the Russian empire—were the serfs of Polish-Catholic landlords, who considered themselves victims of Russian imperialism.

Only by the late 1850's did it become evident to the government that the obsolete social organization of Russia was strongly handicapping the country's political, cultural, and economic growth and even endangering its very existence. The Crimean War of 1854–1856 clearly demonstrated the inefficiency and bankruptcy of the system of serfdom. Only fifty years prior to the Crimean War Russian industry had produced more iron than any other country in the world and the Russian army was better organized and equipped than that of Napoleon; but now, fifty years later, Russian economy and technology had become stagnant, and the industrial revolution, which entirely transformed the life of Western European countries, had hardly affected the land of the tsars. By the time of the Crimean War, Russia, together with Turkey, counted among the economically most backward countries of Europe. Serfdom paralyzed initiative, and was basically responsible for the Russian defeats of 1854–1856 and the considerable social tension which ensued. Alexander II in a speech on March 30, 1856, clearly pointed out that it would be to the interest of the Russian ruling classes to solve the problem of serfdom from above, before the peasants themselves tried to solve it from below.

Realizing that emancipation of the serfs had become inevitable, some ultraconservatives sought to limit the possible effects of emancipation. They hoped that it would be possible to grant personal freedom to the peasants without giving them any land. Emperor Alexander II was aware, however, that it would be extremely dangerous for the state to transform 23 million serfs into an army of landless and restless rural proletarians. Therefore, the struggle between leaders of the conservative nobility and the liberals became concentrated around the question: how much land should be given to the peasant?

Most of the nobility and especially its petty provincial representatives had very little influence on the Tsar and his policies. But along with these were others who were not numerous and not even necessarily members of the old traditional aristocratic families, but who were rich and close to the throne. According to the data of the tenth census, taken on the eve of the reform of 1861, it is possible to divide the whole body of landlords, of which there were some 103,000, into five major groups:

1. 43,000 had an average of 7.9 male serfs
2. 36,000 had an average of 49.9 male serfs
3. 20,000 had an average of 197.1 male serfs
4. 2,500 had an average of 649 male serfs
5. 1,700 had an average of 2,202 male serfs

Thus approximately some 99,000 landlords, who belonged to the lesser provincial nobility, had less than 200 male serfs each. In contrast, the last two groups of 4,200 wealthy and very wealthy aristocrats, which accounted together for only 4% of the total number of Russia's landlords, owned 44% of all the serfs or 4.7 million male peasants, the census covering only the male population of the empire. It is natural that from this rather narrow circle of big landlords came the leaders of the reactionary opposition to the reform. They comprised the court of the Tsar, and from their number were usually recruited the higher offices of the guard and the army, the leading administrators and diplomats, the members of the senate and often the upper bureaucracy. Due to their position they were particularly close to the Tsar and exercised considerable influence on government decisions. Minister of the Interior, S. S. Lanskoy, was well informed when he reported to Alexander II that "it is particularly sad that the main opponents to the desire of Your Majesty belong to the circle, which is particularly close to the throne . . . The discontent of the landlords is quite understandable. It is hard for them to give up their planters' privileges; being ashamed, however, to admit it, they attempt to explain their feelings as those of purely political opposition."

Lanskoy was certainly justified in expressing his apprehensions. The strongest voices against the reform came exactly from these upper four thousand, who were so well represented at the court. These voices claimed primarily to be inspired by their concern over the future of the country, rather than by embitterment at the prospect of giving up their hold over a part of their immense estates and thousands and thousands of peasants. "Finis Russiae," they would say, "the time of Pugachev once more is not far away . . . The folk change very little . . . The speeches of the peasants are gloomy . . . It is nothing other than the roots of a new Pugachev's rebellion . . . People say that in Penza the peasants are excited to the extreme and that the slightest pretext would suffice for them to start a massacre . . ."

These quotations, taken from the letters of Russian nobles written on the eve of the reform, reflect their thoughts and fears. Many of them felt that the emancipation should be postponed. "Before we begin with emancipation, we must first combat alcoholism among them and educate them," claimed some of them. Still others feared that emancipation would result in an economic catastrophe for the nobility, and they tried to sell their estates in order to invest their money in industrial enterprises in Russia and abroad. A Russian aristocrat living in France informed a friend that according to his information, in the first four months of 1857 alone over forty million rubles were transferred by his noble countrymen from Russia to foreign countries. Many others, fearing revolts by their serfs, preferred to go abroad. "There are so many Russians abroad," wrote Count N. Tolstoy in a letter, "that one must undertake foreign travel in order to see one's friends."

This conservative group of courtiers and wealthy landlords, a part of whom, fearing peasant disturbances, transferred their fortunes to France, Germany and England or took up residence in Paris and in German spas, finally succeeded in partially limiting the reform. At their insistence many ultra-conservatives were included in the committees set up to prepare the emancipation laws. The most influential among these reactionary bureaucrats and nobles were Prince B. Golitsyn, Prince P. Paskevich, Count V. Apraksin, and Count P. Shuvalov, as well as some representatives of the Polish magnates in Lithuania and Belorussia.

Fortunately there were among the Russian statesmen not only representatives of the reaction. Among the closest relatives of the Emperor were two staunch supporters of the liberation of the serfs—his brother, Grand Duke Constantine, and his aunt, Grand Duchess Helen. Also, many influential statesmen pointed to the inevitability of the reform, such as the Minister of the Interior, S. S. Lanskoy, Prince V. A. Cherkassky, Yurii Samarin, and the actual head of the supporters of emancipation in the secret committee, General J. Rostovtsev.

The struggle between the liberals and the reactionaries in the secret committee on the peasant reforms became reflected in the compromise formulation of the final emancipation enactment. The serfs received personal freedom. The government also decided that they should "basically" receive the lands which they were cultivating for their own purposes. The landlords were supposed to keep the lands which together with the income and crops from them, they traditionally called their own, despite the fact that these lands were also cultivated by the serfs. However, having taken as the basis for the division of land between serfs and landholders the actual use of the fields in 1861, the committee carried through a considerable number of stipulations to the benefit of the nobility. The committee considered that, in view of the loss of the non-paid labor force, the government should try to alleviate the economic situation of the landlord. Alexander II pointed out in speeches of September 4, 1857, and January 28, 1861, that he wanted to limit the losses and sacrifices of the nobility. The landlords were thus allowed the right to keep, in certain circumstances, up to one-half of the peasant's allotment provided that the peasant would be granted at least "the legal minimum of land." This "legal minimum" varied according to the soil and the economic conditions of the particular province. Moreover, the peasants had to pay the government for what land they did receive according to the law, while the government compensated the landlord directly for the price of the peasants' land.

Especially detrimental to the economic well-being of the peasants was the provision of the so-called "grant allotments." According to this provision the landlord and the peasant could "voluntarily" agree on a special grant allotment, considerably smaller than the average normal allotment decreed by law, but for which the peasant had to pay nothing. About half a million peasants, tempted by the prospect of debt-free land, concluded such agreements with the landlords and received lots which were hardly sufficient for their barest subsistence.

In view of often inexact and conflicting statistical data, it is not easy for a contemporary Western scholar to determine the exact extent of losses suffered by peasants during the reform. In any case, the available data do not confirm the tendentious claims of vociferous nineteenth-century leftist journalists and of some contemporary historians. Indeed, some of them, on the basis of the data from 27 *selected* provinces, insist that the peasants lost as much as 16 percent of their acreage. Professor G. T. Robinson, on the other hand, believes that these losses were of some 1.4 million *desiatins,* or only 1.2 percent. Perhaps more accurate is the data supplied by the Soviet historian S. Yushkov, who maintains that the reform cost the peasantry 5.2 million desiatins or 4.5 percent of their total pre-reform landholdings. Unfortunately, the recent and most authoritative Soviet investigator of the reform, P. A. Zaionchkovsky, shuns any exact conclusions, preferring to claim that even before the reform many landlords, had appropriated substantial parts of the fields of their serfs.

Equally unclear is the picture of the financial aspect of the reform, and particularly of the exact value of the land received by the peasants. A. E. Lossitsky, the oft-quoted authority in this field, considered that the former serfs overpaid for their masters' allotments about 219 million rubles, the official redemption price being 38.4 percent above the average market price at the time. Certainly it is possible that this average price of 27 rubles per desiatina, or $5 per acre of cultivated land, paid by the peasants to their former masters was really beyond the actual price before the reform. Still, keeping in mind that land value rose sharply in the following years and some forty or forty-five years later skyrocketed fourfold to 103–116 rubles for unimproved peasant land, it may be admitted that the prices paid were from the standpoint of money investment not too high, and that in any case the peasants could not lose money selling their allotments.

A study of the changes in the Russian rural landholdings in the late nineteenth and early twentieth centuries to a large extent equally refutes the well-known assumptions of the Russian radical writers that the nobles' landholdings actually dominated the picture of the pre-revolutionary countryside. After the reform of 1861, former serfs, "state" peasants, and the Cossacks became either collective or individual owners of 121.9 million desiatins, while in the hands of the nobility remained 73.2 millions. After that time the acreage of the estates of the nobility rapidly dwindled, dropping in 1905 to 52 million desiatins and in 1914 down to 39.5 million. Correspondingly, peasant and Cossak land tenure rose in 1905 to 153 million desiatins and in 1914 to 170. Adding to these 170 million desiatins some 21 million desiatins which were in the possession of Russian and native peasants of Asiatic Russia, it would seem reasonable to state that with its 190 million desiatins, peasant land tenure surpassed that of the nobility almost five times. It may be added that along with the peasantry and the nobility there was appearing a rapidly growing "third estate" consisting of the urban and rural capitalist or collective landowners, whose property by 1914 accounted for no less than 31 million desiatins. Hence, on the eve of World War I the Russian nobility owned hardly more than 15 percent of 263 million desiatins in private or communal ownership (not including the lands owned by the state and crown). In his writings Stalin indirectly admitted this fact when he indicated that in the pre-revolutionary era only 12 percent of the grain crops were harvested on the estates of the landlords.

The loss of the nobility of 10 million desiatins in the years 1907–1914 clearly proved the rapid decline of "noble" landholdings in the land of the tsars. The continuation of this process was unavoidable in view of heavy mortgages and the deplorable financial situation of a great part of the estates. On the other hand, it is true that a certain number of wealthy aristocrats managed to strengthen their economic position by turning their lands into prosperous agricultural enterprises of the capitalist type. By 1900 about 23 percent of all acreage in the hands of the nobility and about one-quarter of the entire income from agricultural enterprises, were concentrated in some 700 mammoth economies of this dynamic capitalist type, which were owned by some two or three hundred very wealthy families. Together with these, the estates of non-noble agricultural capitalists also flourished, such as those of the Ukrainian sugar-barons Tereshchenko and Kharitonenko, owners of dozens of large sugar beet plantations and sugar refineries. On the lower Dnieper and along the Black Sea were located 200,000 desiatins of farms and ranches owned by one Falz-Fein. In the Urals, especially in some districts of the Perm province, many lumber and mining "empires" averaged up to 280,000 desiatins (about 750,000 acres). On the other hand, many estates of nobles were hardly more than glorified farms. In some districts of Poltava, Chernigov, Minsk, Kovno, and other southern and western provinces the average size of a landlord's "estate" was around a hundred desiatins, often smaller than the farm of a prosperous and enterprising peasant. The total number of such "pocket-size" noble landowners and their slightly bigger neighbors was about 44,000–45,000 in 1900, but this number was steadily diminishing.

Despite all its shortcomings, the peasant reform of 1861 did not perpetuate the domination of rural Russia by the nobility, nor did it deprive the peasants of the opportunity for growth and development. Indeed the Russian allotment was not very large, and considerably smaller than an average American farm, but the Russian peasant's landholding was nevertheless rather substantial compared with peasant landholdings in Western Europe. In France, for instance, three-quarters of all landholdings were less than five acres or 2 desiatins, while the average size was 9 acres or 3.5 desiatins. In pre-revolutionary European Russia still only 15.7 percent of the peasants owned 4.0 desiatins (10.8 acres) or less; 73.8 percent of them had from 4.1 to 20 desiatins (10.9 to 54 acres) while the remaining 10.5 percent of rich peasants had over 20 desiatins (54 acres). These data, currently used by historians and economists, cover *only* the land held in communal tenure. The average size of the peasant holdings, including not only communal but also *privately owned lands,* was in 1914 slightly over 14.0 desiatins (37.8 acres) for European Russia, and considerably higher for Siberia. But the Russian peasant did not know how to produce as much as the Western European farmer, nor was he acquainted with modern market agriculture. A considerable number of peasants remained poor even in the early twentieth century, and many of them joined the restless army of dissatisfied and hungry rural proletarians. The primitive methods of cultivation, lack of means for land reclamation, the absence of machinery, and unimproved seeds and stock were primarily responsible for the peasants' low standard of living. The frustrating system of Russian communal land tenure further handicapped development of initiative and progress in the Russian village. While there was always a plentitude of advice at hand on how to seize the estates of the nobles, unfortunately for the Russian peasant too few of his advisers were concerned with helping him improve his methods of cultivation. However, after the abortive revolution of 1905 and Stolypin's reforms, many peasants liberated from the compulsion of village community bonds, altered their ways of farming. The spectacular rise of crops in European Russia alone from 13.6 billion puds in 1896–1900 to 18.5 billion puds for the five years 1909–1913 clearly demonstrates the technological and economic changes in the Russian village.

Historians like to consider Stolypin's reform a failure, pointing out that *only* one-fifth (actually just 24 percent) of all the peasant households preferred to change their communal landholdings to individual ones. It may be argued, however, that, on the contrary, it was remarkable that as *man*y as this number of households were able to decide to change their traditional method of landownership during the short seven-year period when this agrarian reform was sponsored by the government.

4. PETER I. LYASHCHENKO: History of the National Economy of Russia to the 1917 Revolution*

Peter I. Lyashchenko (1876–1955) was a professor in the Ethnological Faculty of the First Moscow State University and of the Institute of National Economy. He surveys Russian economic history and the emancipation in Marxist terms; he sees the emancipation as a crucial development in the transition between a feudal and a capitalist economy. The approach has subtlety. While Professor Lyashchenko stresses the encouragement emancipation gave to commercial agriculture, he notes important remnants of older ways; and the advocates of bourgeois or commercial principles were mainly larger landowners. Many of his comments on the effects of emancipation on the peasanty coincide with those of Zenkovsky and Robinson; one must be careful to distinguish between a novel terminology and really novel conclusions. Still, the approach toward motives for reform is simpler than that of Zenkovsky and in partial

* From Peter I. Lyashchenko, *History of the National Economy of Russia to the 1917 Revolution,* L. M. Herman, trans. (New York: The Macmillan Company, 1949), pp. 376–77, 392–93, 396–97.

disagreement as to the landowners' role. And his focus on broad economic change separates his assessment of results from that of Robinson. Both see a link between emancipation and later revolution, but Professor Lyashchenko finds the link in the decisive alteration of the character of the economy.

RAISING THE QUESTION OF THE REFORM

Looking through the controversial literature dealing with economic and agricultural questions during the last three pre-Reform years, that is, at a time when the problem of liquidating serfdom was largely decided and officially promulgated, we find it full of lively discussion of the Reform. The landowner, the sole arbiter of the fate of 20 million serf peasants, well understood that it was a matter of life and death for the serf economy as a whole. The other interested party, the serf peasant, was not represented in any of the various official commissions of the government and the nobility, and gave expression to its demand for emancipation by even more frequent outbreaks. In literature alone the struggle of the peasantry against serfdom was effectively mirrored in the articles of Chernyshevsky, Dobrolyubov, and others.

There was, indeed, still a third party, the emerging bourgeoisie, likewise concerned with the abolition of serfdom. During the period of the literary phase of the Reform discussion, the bourgeoisie expressed itself in favor of liquidating serfdom from the standpoint of its own interests (the well-known addresses of the broker Kokorev). But the proportional size of the bourgeoisie was small, its interest found no official recognition in the implementation of the Reform, and its voice went almost unheeded. In part the latter circumstance may be explained by the censorship applied against any comprehensive discussion of the Reform even at a time when the question of abolishing serfdom had already been officially raised. Therefore, in carrying out the Reform the problem was considered exclusively from the standpoint of the nobility's interests, and resulted in a type of liquidation that was most advantageous to the landowner.

In view of the steady development of a money economy throughout the country and the peasant household's constantly growing need for money, it became necessary to create such conditions for land allotment under which the peasant would still feel the same "economic compulsion" to surrender some of his surplus labor to the landowner as before, although in a somewhat different manner. The Reform, as we shall see later, did not accomplish the final "purging" of the nobility's land or the conditions of serfdom. Bourgeois relationships continued to develop, despite the fact that the Reform itself contained a number of elements retarding this development.

Within the landowner class the most avowed representatives of bourgeois tendencies in the capitalist development of agriculture were the landlords of the nonblack-soil provinces. In the words of Unkovsky (a deputy from Tver Province), who demanded the immediate emancipation of the peasants along with their redemption of the land and their persons, the landowners declared that "a grant of capital was vital to the support of their farms and the latters' adaptation to maintenance by hired labor." These protagonists of future capitalist development, however, in many cases had to yield to the interests of another group of serf-owning landowners, the so-called "planters," who endeavored to preserve as much as possible of the former relationships of serfdom. In the eventual execution of the Reform, the latter interests emerged predominant. . . .

TWO PATHS IN THE DEVELOPMENT OF CAPITALISM IN AGRICULTURE

Such were the land, financial, and payment settlements and the general results of the Reform of 1861, and of the subsequent acts of 1863–1866 implementing the main regulation and extending its effect over other categories of the peasantry and into other regions. The land settlement instituted for the landowners' peasants was, of course, of greatest importance to the new economic structure of the nation. By the Reform the landowners with great success expropriated a substantial part of the peasant lands, retaining large latifundia for themselves, appropriating a part of the peasant lands through various reductions, imposing, moreover, payments amounting to billions of rubles for the abolition of the peasants' feudal liabilities, and eventually retaining a form of semifeudal economic dependency through the peasants' "obligatory" services, labor dues, and so forth.

The collapse of serfdom and the bourgeois Land Reform, as prerequisites of the growing need for bourgeois development, assumed a special character by virtue of special historical conditions and the interplay of social forces, which for some time predetermined the entire future course of the development of capitalism.

In examining the general conditions of agrarian development in Russia after the Reform, Lenin notes that the very application of the Reform had objectively raised the question of those "two paths" of possible capitalist development in the village, which he calls the "Prussian" and "American." The struggle between the two was in process in 1861, served as the basis for the entire subsequent development of agrarian conditions, and eventually appeared very clearly in the Revolution of 1905. The Reform itself contained the objective causes of the circumstance that, in the post-Reform economic structure of the village as a whole, "the point of the struggle" of the peasantry was the serf estates "as the most conspicuous incarnation and the most solid supporter of the vestiges of serfdom in Russia." The development of commercial farming and capitalism once and for all put an end to these vestiges. In this respect only one course of bourgeois development lay open for Russia.

The forms of this development could, however, be twofold. The vestigial remains of feudalism could disappear either by the reorganization of the landowners' farms or by destruction of the large latifundia, that is, "by reform or by revolution." The first, or Prussian type, in which

> the landowners' feudal economy is slowly transformed into the bourgeois *Junker* variety of farming, condemned the peasantry to decades of agonizing expropriation

and indebtedness, while a small minority of *grossbauers* (wealthy peasants) make their appearance. In the second instance, no landowner agriculture exists or it is destroyed by a revolution which confiscates and distributes the feudal estates.

Of the two paths of development, "which in 1861 were barely outlined," and "in the Revolution of 1905 . . . developed, grew, and found expression in the movement of the *masses*," the Reform of 1861 had projected a development along the "Prussian" way of transforming landowner and peasant farming into bourgeois capitalist agriculture. The revolutionary "American" way of development, breaking up and destroying the owners' latifundia and developing a free capitalist and farmer-peasant economy, did not materialize in 1861. Therefore, irrespective of the rapid process of differentiation and commercialization in agriculture during the first decades following the Reform, survivals of semiserf conditions and "agonizing expropriation and indebtedness" of the peasantry continued long afterward, while the farms of the owners themselves "slowly grew into bourgeois *Junker* farms." . . .

GENERAL RESULTS OF THE REFORM

Thus, along with being emancipated from personal bondage to the landowner, the peasantry was also "emancipated" from a considerable and invariably better part of the land it held. For the portion of the land retained, the peasantry had to pay billions of rubles in redemption payments. Furthermore, in lieu of his former obligations in kind, the peasant now had to eke from his farming enough cash with which to pay his steeply rising money dues and taxes of all kinds. The general development of a commodity and money economy and the replacement of the former household trades by factory industry increased still further the peasant's need for money and resulted in a decline in the living standard of the erstwhile pastoral natural economy of the peasant. Yet, "the more such a peasant is impoverished, the more he is compelled to resort to the sale of his labor power, and the greater is the proportion of his (to be sure very meager) means of subsistence which he must seek to acquire in the market." The Reform thus furnished a strong impetus toward the accelerated development of a money economy, the expansion of the domestic market, and differentiation among the peasantry; that is, a development of capitalist conditions in agriculture.

In this new epoch, however, the beginning of a commercial economy and capitalist relationships among the peasantry coincided with the prevalence of poorly developed production forces within the economy, as well as the prevalence of extremely small landholdings. Hence arose the struggle for land by the peasantry so characteristic of the entire post-Reform period, the struggle against the feudal latifundia, and the search for land to produce an extra pood of grain. His own land was insufficient, and once again, as of old and exactly as under serfdom, partly for payment in money but largely for payment in kind on the basis of labor duties or sharecropping, the owners' fields began to be cultivated by the peasant with the peasant's implements and livestock. This was particularly true of the old serf regions in the central agricultural region, in the Volga area, and elsewhere.

In other regions the passing of the vestiges of serfdom, the differentiation among the peasantry, and the development of capitalist relationships proceeded more rapidly. In the southern and eastern steppe regions both the landowners and the wealthy peasants were successfully adapting capitalist methods of production, working with the aid of hired labor and machinery, and developing their commercial production intensively. Moreover, in the nonblack-soil belt peasant labor was steadily diverted from agriculture into the sphere of industry. All this increased the differentiation of the regions to a high degree, created a wide domestic market, an advance in commercial agriculture, and social stratification inside the village, and strengthened the industrial character of the nonblack-soil belt along with its demand for the products of southern agriculture, as well as the sale of its industrial products to the agricultural regions. If we add the fact that simultaneously with the Reform came the beginning of large-scale railroad construction, which likewise accelerated and invigorated the progress of commodity exchange, it becomes clear that the collapse of serfdom released the forces necessary for leading the national economy into new capitalist conditions at a rapid pace.

Finally, the bourgeois Land Reform of 1861 necessitated a reorganization of other parts of the state apparatus and social life along bourgeois lines: a rural reform (1864), a court reform (1864), a reform of the urban system of self-government (1870), and even a military reform (the introduction of universal military service in 1874).

However, the conditions under which the Peasant Reform was conducted were responsible for the fact that the vestiges of feudal economic relationships persisted in the Russian countryside for a long time. The income level of the landowners from the financial and agricultural exploitation of the peasant household was so high that, by comparison, there was at times little profit in maintaining the estate farm on a capitalist basis. Hence, in a considerable number of regions and localities—including primarily the old serf region of the central agricultural region—the landowners' farms were organized, even after the Reform, chiefly with a view to exploiting the peasant household as much as possible in connection with its land famine and by land usury. The "Prussian type" of agrarian development was solidly and permanently implanted in the very Reform of 1861, [and] "condemned the peasantry to decades of agonizing expropriation and indebtedness, while a small minority of *grossbauers* (wealthy peasants) make their appearance."

The ruling agricultural class, whose voice in the Reform was decisive, was able to conduct it in such a manner as to leave the peasant in a position in which he could be exploited most harshly through economic compulsion, even without the device of the "right" of serfdom. Lenin says in this connection:

The peasants of Russia were "emancipated" by the landowners themselves, and by the landowners' government of the autocratic tsar and his officials. And these "emancipators" so managed the affair that the peasants emerged "at liberty" as tattered beggars from slavery to the landowners and into financial bondage to the same landowners and their agents.

These conditions, inherent in the Reform itself, left their peculiar imprint on the entire post-Reform economic development for some time, and became one of the major causes of those peculiarities in the development of Russian industrial capitalism in Russia.

5. JEROME BLUM: Lord and Peasant in Russia*

Professor Blum is a historian at Princeton who has studied peasant history in Austria as well as in Russia. He offers an explicitly revisionist view of emancipation, and especially of its causes, which in many ways suggests the older, liberal approach. His criticism of a largely economic approach to the emancipation stands out clearly. Political and even ideological factors re-emerge. His assessment of results is broadly political too, with the stress on limitations on freedom rather than economic conditions. Interestingly also, Professor Blum's whole survey ends with this evaluation of emancipation, suggesting the radical break emancipation brought in lord-peasant relations rather than the decisive link to later revolution; yet the traditional quality of peasant history after 1861, even after 1917, is also noted.

The explanations for the abolition can be divided into five general causal categories. The first of these themes associates the emancipation with the process of economic development. Those who have emphasized this interpretation claim that the growth of an exchange economy, marked by the expansion of the market and an increase in the use of money, made serfdom obsolete. The old system, because of its inefficiency, low productivity, and restrictions on free movement, was an obstacle to the growth of towns, commerce, and industry, and so it was abolished. Modern Soviet historians have adopted this line of reasoning, but have put it into a dialectical setting. Following standard Soviet practice they usually begin with texts from the classics of Marxism-Leninism that declare that serfdom could exist only so long as a "natural economy" persisted. The "feudal" estate formed a self-sufficient closed entity, with only the weakest sort of connection with the rest of the world. When it began to produce for the market it doomed itself, for the "feudal" producers could not by their very nature adjust themselves to the market and become commercial producing units. Lack of capital, the low productivity of serf labor, and the nature of the structure of the entire "feudal" economy, blocked the introduction of technical improvements and efficient organization. For these reasons a crisis developed in agriculture in the last decades of serfdom that evidenced itself by violently fluctuating prices, an absolute decline in the number of serfs, increasing seignioral indebtedness, and a quickening in the tempo of peasant unrest.

* From Jerome Blum, *Lord and Peasant in Russia from the 9th to the 19th Century* (Princeton: Princeton University Press, 1961), pp. 612–18, 618–20. Reprinted by permission of Princeton University Press.

The agricultural crisis, in turn, was responsible for the political crisis of the mid-fifties. "The Sevastopol defeat and the oppressive peace terms that followed were a clear symptom of the collapse of the entire political and economic system of the old feudal order in Russia."

Another economic interpretation that is much less sweeping attributes the emancipation to the self-interest of the serfowners. According to this view, the interest of seigniors in production for market increased during the first half of the nineteenth century. They became convinced that serf labor was an insuperable barrier to the increased productivity of their properties. They believed that free hired labor would prove more profitable to them, and therefore they supported emancipation. They wanted to liberate the serfs without land so that they would become a rural proletariat whose only means of livelihood would be to work for their former masters. But these seigniors had to give up this part of their program because serfowners of the non-chernozem provinces, who drew their incomes from obrok payments, had no desire to keep all their land for themselves. The proprietors in the less fertile regions wanted to free their peasants with sizable allotments, and with a correspondingly high cost of redemption. The fear that a landless emancipation would bring on a storm of peasant violence also dissuaded serfowners from insisting on it.

The economic explanations of the emancipation won much acceptance among Russian historians before 1917, as well as after that time. The materialistic interpretation, as Lazar Volin pointed out, "had become intellectually fashionable long before it gained the monopolistic exclusiveness of a political orthodoxy after the Revolution." Attractive as these interpretations may have been, or still are, they ignore or glide over too many facts. Their most glaring deficiency is that they disregard the indisputable evidence that the overwhelming majority of the serfowners did not want to give up serfdom. Far from regarding it as wasteful and inefficient, most proprietors had a very high regard for serfdom as both a social and an economic institution. They tried to extend it to other parts of the empire, they resisted the attempts the government made to limit the system or to improve the status of the serf, they protested bitterly when the tsar told them to draw up plans for emancipation, and they procrastinated for as long as they could. There can be no question that most serfowners felt strongly that the emancipation was very much against their economic interests.

Moreover, it seems very likely that they knew what they were talking about. The available evidence does not support the arguments of the minority among the proprietors that free labor was more profitable to the landowner than the barshchina of serfs. In the Central Agriculture provinces, with their heavy concentration of serfs, hired farm labor was cheap because there was little demand for it. Peasants there who wanted to hire out as farmhands had to migrate southward. The proprietors of the Central Agricultural region were well satisfied with these conditions, as is evidenced by their great reluctance to have them changed. In the provinces of the Lower Volga and in New Russia, where the density of the serf population was much less, labor was in short supply, and so hired hands were more expensive than they were in the Central Agricultural guberniias. To reduce their labor costs the proprietors transferred or brought serfs from the Center. So they wanted to keep serfdom, too. Nor were the serfowners who drew their incomes from payments in cash and kind any less desirous of retaining the system. Indeed, data on the prices paid for land and serfs in the mid-nineteenth century indicate that these proprietors found serf ownership more profitable than did those who demanded labor services from their peasants.

The argument that serfdom had become anachronistic within the context of the growing Russian economy also has serious weaknesses. Factory industry was able to find the labor it needed among the serfs and state peasants who left their villages to find work elsewhere, and plants owned by nobles and manned by serfs continued to thrive up to the emancipation. Commerce, much of it conducted by serfs and state peasants, also expanded. The shortcomings of the transportation system, and the inadequacies and poor distribution of natural resources, and not serfdom, offered the greatest obstacles to Russian economic growth.

The belief that agriculture itself was engulfed in a crisis in the last decades of serfdom also seems ill-founded. The producers of the Central Agricultural provinces certainly felt some competitive pressure from the southern steppes. Possibly this may help in explaining why the proprietors in the Central Agricultural regions did not increase their production for market sale during the first half of the nineteenth century. The high cost of shipping grain from the south, however, served to protect a large share of the domestic market for them. The claim that the grain supply normally exceeded demand, and that this had much to do with creating a crisis situation, is also open to serious question.

P. B. Struve, in his critique of the argument that the internal development of serfdom led to its liquidation, presented an entirely original explanation for the emancipation. He insisted that serfdom was not obsolescent in the mid-nineteenth century. Instead, it reached the peak of its productivity in the decade of the fifties. Nonetheless, economic necessity demanded the liberation of the serfs. For, said Struve, the economic future in the form of the railroad had thrown its shadow across serfdom and had condemned it, despite its flourishing condition. The introduction of the railroad effected a revolution in economic relationships, and Russia would not have been able to endure the chains of an unfree labor system. It is difficult (to understate the matter) to do much with an historical interpretation that places the cause after the effect, except to observe that the evidence does not support the assumption that the men who urged abolition, or who drew up the emancipation legislation, were discounting the railroad.

The other major explanations that have been developed to explain the coming of the emancipation seem to me to have more validity that those that base themselves primarily upon supposed economic phenomena or motivations. One of these themes emphasizes the importance of humanitarian and liberal ideas. According to this view, liberal Russian intellectuals from Radishchev on had laid the foundations for the abolition of serfdom. The scholars among them had worked out the theoretical bases for liberation, and the publicists and novelists acted as apostles of freedom. Their work convinced enlightened people of the era, who were almost exclusively members of the nobility, that even though emancipation seemed against their self-interest they would benefit from it morally and spiritually. A conversation in *Anna Karenina* between the Levin brothers can serve to illustrate this attitude. Tolstoi has one brother say:

"Excuse me, self-interest did not induce us to work for the emancipation of the serfs, but we did work for it."

"No!" Constantine Levin broke in with still greater heat, "the emancipation of the serfs was a different matter. There self-interest did come in. One longed to throw off that yoke that crushed us, all devout people among us. . . ."

The fear of peasant revolt is another theme that is emphasized by nearly all historians. They point out that the never-ending current of unrest served to convince the rulers of the empire that emancipation was absolutely essential to preserve public order. Alexander II gave the classic formulation of this conviction when he said that serfdom had to be abolished from above before it destroyed itself from below. There were also serfowners who supported abolition because they feared peasant violence. But to judge from the reaction when Alexander announced his intention to free the serfs, a far larger number were certain that emancipation would engender still greater dangers to the social order. They warned that the freed peasants, lacking self-discipline and responsibility, would turn to idleness, drink, and trouble-making.

The Crimean War, too, nearly always is counted as one of the major factors in bringing on the emancipation. Some have assigned it primary importance, arguing that sweeping reforms are only possible after some great disaster from without reveals the weaknesses within a society. For even though people may have lost their faith in their old institutions, the *vis inertiae* of custom is so strong that radical change can only be made under the stern compulsion of military collapse. Most historians, however, consider the defeat in the war as a catalyst that speeded up the adoption of reforms certain to have been introduced in any event.

The final major interpretation sees the emancipation as the outcome of Alexander's decision that abolition was necessary for *raisons d'état.* The great authority of the sovereign allowed him to carry through social revolutions whenever he saw fit. Alexander II imposed his wishes upon the nobles without regard for their vested interests, and without heed to their outraged protests. Tsar Nicholas had already recognized the need for reform, but his repugnance for change made him temporize. The shock of the Crimean defeat compelled Alexander to take positive action.

There is much to be said, I think, for this last view. The arguments and writings of the humanitarians and liberals provided intellectual and technical preparation for the emancipation among educated men, and especially among some of the bureaucrats who played a key role in drafting the emancipation legislation. Similarly, the discontent of the peasantry made it clear that rural unrest jeopardized the security of the realm. Given the autocratic structure of the Russian state, however, emancipation or any other great change was impossible without the approval of the tsar. Alexander, convinced by the defeat in the Crimea that his state teetered on the edge of political collapse, had the will to introduce reforms, and the determination to carry them out.

The emancipation law wiped out the powers and privileges that the lord had for so long held over his peasants. He could no longer sell his peasants, or compel them to move from one place to another, or have them shipped off to Siberia, or to the army, and so on through the list of powers the seignior once had over his serfs. The age of "silent obedience" was forever abolished. With its disappearance Alexander's government was able to introduce a series of laws designed to reform the legal and administrative structure of his empire. These reforms had as their most significant result the replacement of class privileges and distinctions by legal equality.

Legal equality, that is, for everyone except the peasants. In his proclamation of emancipation the Tsar-Liberator (for so Alexander was called) had promised the peasants that "within the period fixed by the law" they would be allowed all the privileges of free men. There is every reason to believe that this was a sincere pledge. Alexander looked forward hopefully to the day when the freed peasants would enjoy the same civil rights as the rest of his subjects. But he and his counselors believed that the peasants were not ready for the privileges and the responsibilities of full citizenship. Besides, the state had advanced the freedmen money to buy their holdings from the lords, and the drafters of the emancipation statutes wanted to make sure that the peasants would pay back their debt. So they decided that the peasants must go through a transitional stage. The former serfs and state peasants were placed in a peculiar legal category in which they were recognized as free persons, yet were deprived of many of the civil rights that adhered to personal freedom. In most of the empire the individual peasant was not given the right of private landownership. Instead, the commune held title to all the land of a village and distributed it to its member households. Every peasant had to belong to a commune and to a household whether he wanted to or not, and every household had to accept a land allotment regardless of its own wishes. The peasant did not have the right to renounce his membership in his household and commune, and he retained his membership even if he left the village and spent his life elsewhere. All commune members were mutually responsible for taxes and other obligations. To make sure that no one would escape his share of these burdens, the commune and the head of the household concerned had to give their approval before a peasant could leave the village for a lengthy absence. The freed peasant did not have the right of free movement any more than he had it in the days before the emancipation.

All these limitations on personal liberty were supposed to fall away when the peasant completed his redemption payments to the state. That, at least, was the intention of the men who framed the emancipation law. But this intention was soon forgotten. Instead of being thought of as candidates for full citizenship, the peasantry came to be regarded as a unique class whose communal life contributed irreplaceable moral values to Russian society. It therefore had to be accorded special attention and protection. Peasant land was considered to be fundamentally different from other kinds of land, for its purpose was to guarantee the continued existence of the peasantry as a class, and therefore, it could not become the private property of those who tilled it. Nor could the members of the peasantry be permitted to leave that class and become workers, for the proletarianization of the rustic would lead to the moral decay of the Russian people. To implement these concepts a special body of law was created for the peasants that dealt not only with their property relationships, but with their other legal relationships as well. There were even separate provisions of the criminal law that applied only to peasants.

The change in attitude toward the peasantry evidenced itself within a few brief years of the emancipation, and became firmly entrenched in the reign of Alexander III (1881–1894). These views were not restricted to the ruling circles alone. They were shared by men from one end of the political spectrum to the other, from the blackest reactionaries to the wildest radicals. The leftist agrarian program that, in its broadest sense, was called Populism, was as Zaitsev pointed out "nothing other than a fined version of the attitude toward the rights of the peasants that had to a certain extent been brought to maturity by measures taken by the government, and that were firmly fixed in the text of the laws."

Then, after the revolutionary storm of 1905, the government instituted a dramatic reversal of its policy. A series of decrees abolished most of the restrictions upon the personal liberty of the peasant, allowed him to free himself from his subjugation to the commune and become the owner of his holding, replaced the joint family ownership of the peasant household with individual ownership, wiped out the remaining redemption payments, and set up credit facilities for the purchase of land by peasants. Still further measures were planned to close the gap between the status of the peasantry and that of the other classes of Russian society.

The freedom that had been promised in 1861 seemed at hand at long last. But the hopes for full civil equality for the peasantry were doomed by war and revolution. The new order that came to power in 1917 offered pledges of freedom, too, but its realities turned out to be worlds removed from the utopia promised by its leaders. Instead, "bullying and fawning, arrogant command and servile obedience," for so many centuries the lot of the Russian peasantry, became its fate once more.

Chapter IX.

PIUS IX AND THE DILEMMA OF NINETEENTH-CENTURY CATHOLICISM

THE DECLINE of religion, and particularly of Catholicism, was one of the key developments of nineteenth-century Europe. The most obvious feature of this decline was institutional, evident in the decrease of the political power and influence of the Church. The Church lost its independent territorial base, the Papal States, and also its traditional privileges in many Catholic countries. Accompanying this institutional decline was a loss of influence over many large segments of society, the working classes most clearly, and a continued conflict with many of the leading intellectual movements of the day.

In all these aspects, the pontificate of Pius IX, which lasted from 1846 to 1878, was crucial. Here was a pope who seemed to declare war on virtually every aspect of the modern world. He began his papacy as something of a favorite of moderate Italian liberals; he ended a self-styled prisoner with a moderately liberal Italian state, his papal lands gone and his relations with many other European governments poisoned by his unwillingness to grant or recognize political change.

The historical literature dealing with Pius IX raises a number of problems, not all of them obvious. First, there has not been a great deal of work done. Historians do tend to focus on successes, and Pius does not seem to have been one of those. Indeed, the history of Catholicism generally in the nineteenth century has received only spotty treatment from historians. Certainly, no one has lavished on the First Vatican Council even a fraction of the attention devoted to the councils of the Counter Reformation, and doubtless it was not as important. Yet one is left with an impression of undue neglect. Church history in the nineteenth century was dramatic in many ways. Its course affected millions of people—many more, during the century itself, than were touched by socialism. The structure of the Church and, ultimately, of its politics changed decisively. Yet the most detailed works on the Church were written during the period itself, often as a continuation of general studies of the Church through the centuries. Elaborate studies of the Vatican Council appeared during the 1870's, and most subsequent historians have relied on these for their facts and, often, many of their interpretations.

One result of the paucity of research on the pontificate of Pius IX is the ample opportunity afforded for factual disputes. Was the Pope neurotic and superstitious or courageous and enlightened? How was the Vatican Council run? Some historians have claimed that Pius deliberately rigged the affair, for example, by failing to summon many liberal prelates; others believe the Council fairly represented the sentiments of the hierarchy. Questions of this sort are influenced by more general interpretive bias, of course, but they are in part empirical. In assessing judgments of Pius IX, then, more than in dealing with most major topics, one must ask what facts were used, how they seem to have been selected, and how adequate they are.

The major source of dispute over Pius IX is the political and religious division among historians of the Church. Nineteenth-century Church history has perhaps drawn more obvious partisanship among historians than any other subject. Three principal positions have appeared. The first is non- or anti-Catholic, which sees the Church as inappropriate in the modern world if not downright evil. Pius IX is, of course, an ideal target for such views, for he himself proclaimed the gulf between Catholicism and modernity. At the other extreme is the conservative Catholic view, which can simply take the position that Pius was correct or can at least show the very good reasons for his actions or pronouncements. Then, uncomfortably in between, there is the liberal Catholic approach, which holds that Pius was wrong but also maintains that he can be understood, and that his enemies were wrong too.

Which of these approaches best represents the history of Pius IX's pontificate? The choice is difficult. Most of us will share, to some degree, one of the basic positions which have been applied to the history, for the issues involved are not dead. We may profess a desire to shake off partisanship, but it is hard to do so. If we sympathize with liberal Catholicism, for example, can we nonetheless maintain that Pius was right in terms of his own time? The argument is theoretically tenable, but difficult to apply in practice.

In addition to the problems of outright partisanship, the study of Pius IX raises one other general difficulty. Any biographical approach must be assessed in terms of the importance of its subject. Pius IX was, of course, a key individual; but how much of the history of the Church in mid-century can be conveyed through a focus on him? There were, as the following selections indicate, quite diverse views within the Church at this time. Pius overrode his opposition, but he did not eliminate it, and it rose again after his death. The evaluation of Pius' importance is partly factual: How much power did the pope have, and how enduring were the other currents in the Church? But such an evaluation also involves a more basic orientation to the importance of individuals in history, or at least nineteenth-century history.

Relatedly, could Pius have acted other than he did, and would it have made much difference if he had? Might the Church have developed the bases of cooperation with liberalism had Pius not pronounced against it? And could Pius have avoided such pronouncements? Historians of the Papacy have disagreed. Again, assessment demands not only a clear understanding of the facts, but, beyond this, some approach to the question of the freedom of individual action within the framework of historical causation.

Finally, how does Pius IX look from the perspective of what is now becoming the later twentieth century? Is his papacy as important as it had to seem to people caught up in the Church-State conflicts of the period? Did it set the Church on a course from which it could not escape? It is probable that, in the light of recent developments within Catholicism, Pius will seem something of an aberration, remote and hard to understand. In dealing with the mid-nineteenth century papacy, more than with most other topics from the same period, an exercise in historical imagination may be needed even to grasp the terms of the problem. Precisely because of this, the topic can be one of the most interesting in modern history, and one of the most revealing for an understanding of the nineteenth century.

1. ROBERT HAVARD DE LA MONTAGNE: History of Christian Democracy*

The conservative Catholic rejection of liberalism, which Pius IX himself came to represent, is not dead in Europe, and its advocates have developed a small but interesting historical effort. In this selection Robert Havard de la Montagne, a vigorously conservative writer who was linked to the rightist *Action française* movement between the world wars, views the *Syllabus of Errors* not just sympathetically, but with real approval. His purpose is clear; in this selection, and in his book as a whole, he seeks to discredit liberal Catholicism, which has gained increasingly in the French Church since World War II. Though this goal may seem a bit unusual, the basic effort to use history to illumine a contemporary situation is common, as we have often seen. And M. Havard de la Montagne's very predilections may assist a historical understanding of his subject precisely because they are at variance with most modern views. Worth particular note is his effort to set the discussion on the basis of Catholic tradition and to provide supportive materials from the period.

The following year Pius IX promulgated the Encyclical *Quanta Cura* and the *Syllabus* which . . . attacked a mass of errors some of which, without doubt, were spread by the liberal Catholics. As the bishop of Poitiers said to his clergy:

The act of December 8 (1864) has considerable significance. It is directed against our adversaries, against those outside, to be sure; but it is addressed still more, if that is possible, to those within. By means of affirmation more than of condemnation, it seeks to end our domestic quarrels, to regulate the belief and the language of those Catholics who are drifting from the doctrine and the spirit of the Church. Political naturalism, established as a dogma of modern times by a sincerely faithful group, but one which agrees in this with the deChristianized society within which it lives—this is the chief error which the Holy See wished to indicate and to which it wishes to oppose the true principles of Catholic belief.

What is political naturalism? Pius IX wrote: "There are many men who apply to civil society the impious and absurd principle of Naturalism, as they call it; they dare to teach that the perfection of government and civil progress absolutely demand that human society be constituted without regard to religion, as if religion did not exist, or, at least, without establishing any difference between the true religion and the false." The text did not say, as M. Charles

* From Robert Havard de la Montagne, *Histoire de la démocratie chrétienne de Lammenais à Georges Bidault* (Paris: Amiot-Dumont, Presse de la Cité, 1956), pp. 57–60. Reprinted by permission of Amiot-Dumont. Translated by the editor.

Maurras has remarked, that today, in the contemporary world, the secular government must be committed to the religious law and employ material constraint if necessary; but that it is absurd to believe that the perfection of society and the greatest political good can be found in a society indifferent to religion. The text states that it is absurd to say, in general, that the best government is that least disposed to place its physical strength in the service of religious strength; it warns us that concessions and tolerance granted to avoid a great evil do not constitute models of political structure; it affirms that such a model would consist of a society where the State would be ready to serve the Church.

The Encyclical attacks a false manner of thinking, and it is incontestable that the intellectual position of the liberal Catholics is incoherent, as Cardinal Billot has said; that it notably confuses tolerance with approval and that ultimately it relegates truth to a region of abstractions. To reason as they do, Father Le Floch observed, interpreting the *De Ecclesia* of the cardinal, would prove also that all precepts concerning the virtues should remain in a purely speculative domain, since the human condition cannot fulfill them perfectly; it would, further, show that mathematical knowledge cannot and should not be applied to the arts, because the ideal, exact, geometrical triangle does not exist in practice, or because the experimental effort always contradicts the rigorous purity of the calculation.

The Encyclical *Quanta Cura* introduced the Syllabus, a catalogue of eighty condemned propositions. These, for example:

The Church is not a true, perfect, and fully free society . . .
The government has the right to define what the rights of the Church are and the limits within which it can exercise them.
The Church does not have the right to use force; it has no temporal power, direct or indirect.
The Church should be separate from the State, and the State separate from the Church.
Political authority is nothing but the sum of numbers and of material forces.
The Roman Pontiff can and should be reconciled with progress, liberalism, and modern civilization.

From 1864 to our own days, the enemies of the Church have ceaselessly exploited the *Syllabus* against the Church, most of them without having read it. This reminds us of a session of the Chamber [of Deputies] in which a radical deputy, boasting of knowing it well, was urged to supply the proof. "Yes," he shouted, "The Pope declared: 'Anathema to any one who says. . . .' " But the word "anathema" does not appear once in the *Syllabus*. In the legislative elections of 1869, the last of the Second Empire, many quarters of Paris elected Jules Ferry with slogans of "Down with the Syllabus!" But we could swear the conscious and organized citizens of the capital did not know the *Syllabus* any better. The ironic aspect of this story is that the adversary of Jules Ferry, the candidate defeated by this grotesque slogan, was Augustin Cochin, the great friend and companion-in-arms of Montalembert, Broglie, and Fallou. These liberal Catholics could not deny the *Syllabus,* although its publication had been a crushing blow to them. But why were the unbelievers so exasperated? By condemning a false way of thinking, the Pope fulfilled a duty of his office, neither threatening nor constraining people, who, by repudiating his office, could continue to think as wrongly as they wished.

It is a fact that Catholic liberalism was the repeated object of the admonitions of Pius IX. Ten years after the Encyclical and the *Syllabus,* in a letter to a Catholic committee in Orléans, the diocese of Monseigneur Dupanloup, he spoke of "that equivocal doctrine which, while rejecting the extreme consequences of errors, obstinately retains and nourishes their first seed." In a letter to the faithful of Anjou, the diocese of Fallou, he complained of "the sweet and subtle speeches of those who sometimes treat this or that doctrine of the Church as inopportune, believing that they have found some middle ground onto which they can lead truth and error, which ceaselessly struggle, to a mutual embrace." The same lesson to the faithful of Quimper, condemning those who preserved and maintained "the hidden virus of liberal principles, on the pretext that it is not infected with obvious malice." Same lesson to foreign Catholics. To a religious circle of Milan, Pius IX stated that the tricks and violence of the children of the century "would be less successful if a great number of those who bear the name Catholic did not extend a friendly hand to them," did not try to establish an alliance between light and shadows by means of liberal Catholic doctrines. Finally, to the president of the Catholic Circles of Belgium, he wrote that, if liberal Catholics professed to love the Church and to devote their talents to it, "they nonetheless worked to pervert its spirit and its doctrine" and placed themselves in the service "either of Caesar or of those who invented the rights of a false liberty."

2. J. B. BURY: History of the Papacy in the 19th Century*

Here is the anticlerical view of Pius IX—indeed, of the whole modern Papacy—delivered quite succinctly. J. B. Bury (1861–1927) was Regius Professor of Modern History at Cambridge University and wrote widely on subjects in ancient as well as recent history. The lectures from which the following selection is drawn were delivered in 1908. Bury's premise is that the Papacy is incompatible with modern society; in dealing with a specific pope, such as Pius IX, he has only to show specific reasons for unusual foolishness. That Pius deliberately, if madly, intended to make war on the nineteenth century cannot be doubted, according to Bury.

When the temporal power of the Papacy was tottering to its fall, in consequence of the Liberal movement and the political ability of the Sardinian Government, Pius IX. flung down the gauntlet of challenge and defiance to Nineteenth Century civilisation. His immediate predecessors, in their conflict with liberalism, had issued Encyclical Letters condemning modern doctrines; but even the fulminations of Gregory XVI.'s *Mirari vos* were taken quietly and

* From J. B. Bury, *History of the Papacy in the 19th Century* (New York: Schocken Books, Inc., 1964), pp. 1–2, 51–54, 164–65. Reprinted by permission of Schocken Books.

rather as a matter of course. Not so the *Quanta Cura* of Pius IX. and the Syllabus of Errors which accompanied it. Appearing thirty-two years later than the *Mirari vos,* it struck with amazement a generation which was so much further away from the days of the Holy Alliance. With the majority of educated people in Europe, the liberal ideas which were winning their victory about 1830 had already become commonplaces, and they were astonished by a drastic and authoritative reminder that the Papacy was as mediaeval as ever in its attitude to modern society and civilisation, and uncompromisingly hostile to the ideas which commanded the assent of the most civilised sections of mankind. . . .

I may digress here to call attention to certain psychological traits in Pius IX. which predisposed him to co-operate vigorously in a development which was mainly guided by the Jesuits and extreme ultramontanists. He was exceedingly superstitious, in the common sense of the term, and credulous of legends and prophecies. In his youth, as Count Mastai, he had been cured of epilepsy by "water of Jesus of Nazareth" which was given him by a well-known prophetess of the day, Elizabeth Canori-Mora. Later, a more celebrated woman, Anna Maria Taigi, who was a great power in Rome, exercising influence over cardinals and prelates, honoured successively by Pius VII., Leo XII., and especially by Gregory XV., was known to Pius, and she foretold his pontificate and the definition of Infallibility. As Pope, he often spoke of her prophecies, and he raised her memory to the ecclesiastical rank of "honourable" in 1863. Rosa Columba Asdente also prophesied his pontificate, and Marie Lataste foretold the definition of the Immaculate Conception. Leonardo of Porto Maurigio was canonised by Pius; in his tomb were found parchments with prophecies of which one prognosticated the Immaculate Conception and declared it would abolish heresies and bring peace to the Church. In 1858 at Lourdes the Mother of God appeared and made a statement which to a profane ear seems meaningless: "I am the Immaculate Conception." Pius favoured the Lourdes cult; in 1876 he had the image crowned, and the bishops who were present referred to the epiphany of 1858 as confirming the proclamation of 1852.

In 1846 the Virgin appeared to two children at La Salette. She gave each of them a secret communication for Pius. He was very anxious to receive them and they reached him in 1851. He was highly pleased but did not communicate the secrets to anyone. The message of Melania, however, apparently contained a prediction of the definition of Infallibility, for in writing the secret which was to be transmitted to Rome she asked how to spell Infallibility and antichrist. Missionaries soon settled at La Salette; it became a place of pilgrimage and miracles; and the "Annales de Notre Dame de la Salette" were founded, to publish the wonder that occurred.

It is not an insignificant fact, in illustration of the Pope's mentality, that the letter containing Melania's secret reached the Pope's hands on July 18, 1851, and the dogma of Infallibility was declared on July 18, 1870. Archbishop Manning asserted that the Pope himself was not anxious for the definition of Infallibility; it mattered little to him, and he only acquiesced in the wishes of the Catholic world. This is simply false. Pius disavowed Manning's history of the Council, and sealed with his approval the history of Plantier. From it we learn that Pius recognised from the very beginning that Infallibility was to be one of the glorious tasks of his reign, and, convinced of this, he allowed nothing to deter him from carrying through the Council. He believed he had a special mission, and here we touch upon the point of contact between the Vatican Council and the miracles of La Salette. The destinies of the Church were affected by the visions and prophecies of neurotic women.

There grew up also something resembling a cult of the Pope himself, which was not surprising considering what he claimed to be. His claims were sometimes expressed by himself in a form which, if he were not a Pope, we should describe as megalomania. He said in 1866, "I am the way, the truth and the life." The *Civiltà Cattolica* said about the same time, "When he meditates, it is God who thinks in him," and compared the mystery of his vicariate to the mystery of the sacrament—an analogy of which you can easily see the implication.

His Pontificate will always be memorable for two things: for the movement which revived the ecclesiastical claims of the Middle Ages in a most extreme form, and for the fall of the temporal power. The significance of the abolition of the Pope's temporal sovranty, apart from what it meant for the unity, lay in the breach with the mediaeval side. Perhaps we are too close to it still to see fully its great historical importance. Mr. Gladstone was one of the few statesmen who comprehended that it was a change of vast importance—a change which, just because it meant a change in the realm of ideas, might be more profound and far-reaching than the political changes of great magnitude which had recently attracted far more attention. And not less than Prince Hohenlohe did he understand the significance of the *Syllabus* and the Vatican decrees, as he showed in the vehement pamphlet which he published on the subject—*The Vatican Decrees in their Bearing on Civil Allegiance*—in 1874, in which he described the Jesuits as the "deadliest foes that mental and moral liberty have ever known."

We have recently seen a continuation of the struggle in France and another victory for the modern State. The victory is not surprising. For the fact which gives us most cause for thought, and which I have endeavoured to bring out in these lectures, is that the Papacy, based as it is in mediaeval ideas, has maintained and in many ways increased its moral power and influence, in an atmosphere which is repugnant to it, in the midst of social and political institutions, tendencies, and ideas to which it is fundamentally opposed.

3. E. L. WOODWARD: Three Studies in European Conservatism*

On the whole, Professor Woodward manifests views similar to those of Professor Bury on the inadequacy of the Church in the modern world. However, rather than treating Pius IX primarily as a symptom of this inadequacy,

* From E. L. Woodward, *Three Studies in European Conservatism* (London: Frank Cass & Co. Ltd., 1963), pp. 321–22, 325–26, 342–43. Reprinted by permission of Frank Cass & Co. Ltd.

he assigns more importance to him as a cause of it. His approach thus lends itself to a different kind of assessment. Was the Church so thoroughly cut off from modernity by Pius' actions? Were liberal Catholics so completely ruined? And is the explanation for what would seem to be supreme folly provided or assumed?

The encyclical *Quanta cura* and the syllabus of errors were an ultimatum to the world; a last protest—to be reinforced five years later by the insistence upon the infallibility of their author—against any compromise with modern ideas; a final throw to keep that rule over a few square miles of land which seemed of more importance than the peace of mind of thousands of catholics. There was no sort of moderation. Socialism, communism, and Bible Societies were grouped together as plagues. The ideas upon which the best minds of modern Europe were attempting to build up a new society were "monstrosa opinionum portenta"; liberty of conscience and liberty of the press were dangerous errors; the pope could excommunicate any one who attacked the property of the church. Against the devastating effect of these false opinions the pope asked for the help of the Immaculate Virgin; Pius had long expected a miracle.

The encyclical summed up the ignorance of the papal court for a century and more. The separation of the church from the state was a damnable error; so was the belief that the papacy might well do without the temporal power; so was the belief that the pope could and should come to terms with "progress, liberty, and the new civilisation."

To liberal catholics the syllabus was the ruin of their hopes. Outside the morbid atmosphere of the curia no man could take this miserable catalogue with any seriousness; within the curia the words were scarcely understood. The pope knew nothing of the way of life he was condemning. He only saw the encroachment of Italian soldiers upon his diminished kingdom. In France liberal-minded bishops—notably Dupanloup of Orleans—tried to minimise the violence of the Roman anathemas. The pope's words had been taken out of their context; he was only dealing with general principles; the church would always tolerate these monstrous errors, and would adapt its theory to the practice of the day. Yet the pope gave only a guarded approval to Dupanloup's interpretation. Those who took the syllabus literally were not condemned; among them were the pope's own friends. The French government repudiated the most offensive clauses; but the devil's ally was thought of as outside the church. . . .

The history of the Vatican council is the epilogue to the history of the isolation of the papacy and the last renunciation of the intellectual standards of the world outside its gates. Two days before the publication of the encyclical *Quanta cura* the pope had mentioned in utmost secrecy to one of the congregations that he had long been thinking about calling an œcumenical council. Nineteen of the twenty-one cardinals of the Congregation of Rites agreed that a council was desirable; none was convinced of its necessity; only two opposed its convocation. In the course of the year 1865 the pope consulted a number of bishops (including Manning), and the nuncios appointed to the European capitals. In 1867, during the celebration of the eighteen-hundredth anniversary of the martyrdom of the apostles Peter and Paul, the pope announced to the assembled bishops that a council would be held.

What was the council to discuss? Pius wished for a recognition of his infallibility; the school of Jesuit theologians in Rome were ready to support him. But the most careful preparations were necessary. It was known that the leaders of liberal opinion among the bishops north of the Alps welcomed the council—if they welcomed it at all—only because it would give an occasion for the episcopate to assert itself against the ignorant tyranny of the curia. The pope and the papalists had therefore to take care not to lose control of the procedure of the council, and the subjects of its deliberations.

Twenty years earlier Pius had drifted into a disastrous experiment from no other motive than a vague desire to do good in a popular and easy manner. His facile optimism had failed to foresee the thousand little difficulties in the way of any great undertaking. In the twenty years of makeshift and failure which lay between the attempt to liberalise the papal government and the summoning of the Vatican council the pope had never learned the difference between a good intention and a good action; he had not understood what it meant to count the cost, to see the consequences of his acts. He never troubled himself about the opinions of the laity. His clerical advisers assured him that catholic opinion could only be his opinion, and recommended anathema as the right method of dealing with opponents. . . .

The popes had defended a kingdom of this world, a dominion and a title resting upon documents long proved false and the use of a time long past. They had reached the height of unreason when they put forward for their anathemas, their denials, and their negations the authority of the Voice of God. Their pretensions, their methods, their alliances had darkened the hopes of generous men far from the organisation of the curia, yet near enough in temperament and loyalty to the impetuous surrender of the Prince of the Apostles. The successors of the Roman bishops who tamed the fury of the Lombards had lost the power of bringing into their antique order the men who dreamed of a better time and thought more clearly upon the foundations of obedience and rule in civil society. Linked to the forces of the past and the unpitying complacency of the Neapolitan Bourbons or the house of Habsburg, the visible power of the church fell with these ignoble ruins. The denial of a new way of progress made the church powerless in a new world, powerless even for compassion in the evil days of Europe. In the interest of a vanished temporal authority the popes had sacrificed their claim to be heard. They might still embarrass statesmen; they could not dominate Europe.

4. E. E. Y. HALES: Pio Nono*

E. E. Y. Hales is an English Catholic who has written widely on the history of the modern Church. His study of Pius IX is clearly sympathetic. Without

* From E. E. Y. Hales, *Pio Nono* (New York: P. J. Kenedy & Sons, 1954), pp. 11, 13–15, 341–43, 347.

directly embracing Pius' political views, he tries to show their historical comprehensibility in terms of Church tradition and their justifiability in the terms of the time. Is the partisanship overdone, the attempt at understanding carried too far? Even if one accepts Hales's explanations for the Pope's actions, is the framework too narrow to convey the larger significance of Pius' pontificate for the Church in the modern world?

In an important sense Pio Nono was the central figure of the mid-nineteenth century. But we name epochs after their political arbiters, we talk of Metternich's Europe, and Bismarck's Europe, so that the period between the flight of Metternich in 1848 and the foundation of the German Empire in 1870 becomes Napoleon III's Europe—or Palmerston's. If, with Shakespeare, we were to choose for our title the suffering tragic hero, the symbolic central character, then the middle of the century would be called the age of Pio Nono—for the same reasons as Shakespeare called his plays *King Lear* or *Othello,* rather than Goneril or Iago. Those who were working for change, or for power, assailed the Pope's claims, and brushed him aside; but they could not prevent the eyes of a world-wide audience being fastened upon the stage of his misfortunes. Nor could they stop him from rekindling, in his old age, flames of fervour that have burnt ever since around the world. . . .

It is still slightly shocking to suggest that aught but obstinacy and ill-will towards his fellow human beings dictated the Pope's retention of his sovereignty at Rome and Bologna, his issue of the Syllabus of Errors, his support for Ultramontanism.

It is the argument of this study that there was a case for Pio Nono in his policies as Italian Prince, at the time of the Risorgimento, and that there was a case for him as Pope at the time of the Syllabus and the Vatican Council. But the most important point is that they were two aspects of the same case. English scholarship has tended to separate the two because we have come to distinguish sharply between the temporal and the spiritual power and to relegate the latter to the "foro interno," to conscience alone. But Pio Nono conceived of a much closer interdependence of politics and religion. To him his sovereignty over the Papal State was an aspect of his spiritual sovereignty; and he was profoundly concerned with the policies of governments all over the world—not merely with their attitude towards clerical appointments, or church property, but with their legislation concerning education, or compulsory military service, or matrimony.

His enemies took a like view. Mazzini saw the political problem as primarily religious; his political dreams were only the reflections of his religious visions. And Napoleon III, or Cavour, or Bismarck might talk about separating Church and State, but what they meant was subordinating Church to State. They knew well enough that the two were interdependent, and they meant to put the State in control. The theories that flitted fitfully through Napoleon's imaginative mind, the utilitarian aspirations of Cavour, the Erastian ambitions of Bismarck had as their starting-point a "settlement" with the Church, and by this they meant control over clerical appointments and clerical pronouncements, or closure of convents, or launching of *Kulturkampf*. Shall we call their aspirations political or religious? No doubt we shall call them political, and rightly so, as we shall rightly call the Pope's religious; but they could not advance their purposes without fighting in the field of religion, and the Pope could not defend the Church without fighting on the front of politics.

That is why the study of Pio Nono's eventful reign has to be undertaken as a study in politics and religion. Every move made by the Pope or by his enemies demonstrates this. The defeat of Mazzini's Roman Republic in 1849 was a check to the political aspirations of Mazzini and Garibaldi, but it was also a (temporary) victory for the Papacy over Mazzini's Religion of the People. Cavour's victory in closing the Piedmontese monasteries was the prelude to his assuming political sovereignty over the Papal State. Napoleon's planned withdrawal from defending Rome in 1864 provided the occasion for the issue of that notorious religious-political document, the Syllabus of Errors. The Errors of that Syllabus were largely Cavour's, Mazzini's and Napoleon's. The Vatican Council was in constant danger of political intervention from abroad. It was Bismarck's political success that led him to invade the religious field with his *Kulturkampf*.

To understand the Roman viewpoint in these struggles it is no doubt advantageous to be in communion with the See of Rome; but it is not necessary. The man who best understood Pio Nono's purposes, in his later years, was the Protestant Premier of France, Émile Ollivier. And the most effective critic of Papal policy, in the same period, was the Catholic Lord Acton, to whom communion with Rome always remained "dearer than life itself." Nor, to appreciate Pio Nono's policies, is it necessary to be conservative in outlook. He started as a political liberal and became a political conservative; but he fought, always and everywhere, for the Church, and for freedom for the Catholic life, and that meant utilizing whatever political assistance lay to hand, in fact it meant political opportunism. His real and permanent achievement was to give victory to the Ultramontanes, but Ultramontanism by its very cosmopolitan nature was often compelled to be anti-conservative, and even politically rebellious, since it was necessarily hostile to the Gallican claims of legitimist princes. In the 'thirties and 'forties, and even in the 'fifties, Ultramontanism was very generally in alliance with political liberalism. By the 'sixties it was generally anti-liberal, and so was Pio Nono, but even in that decade the most persuasive of all the Ultramontanes was Montalembert, and he remained passionately liberal till his death in 1870. Pio Nono never ceased to protest his own indifference as to "forms of government." States might be absolute monarchies or popular republics so long as they allowed the Church her rights and liberties—a Papal view which the Neapolitan Bourbons found distressing.

The victory of the mob at Rome, in October 1848, and the peculiar character of the Papal State turned Pio Nono into an absolutist prince. But he had toyed—rather rashly—with liberalism and, to the end, he retained an open mind as to the extent to which, given peaceful conditions, the enlightened propertied classes might properly be given some share in his government. It was an open question in the later eighteen-fifties whether he would broaden the basis of his government; that he did not do so was due partly to the irksome (and far from disinterested) pressure brought to bear upon him from Piedmont and from France, and partly to the absence of a class of man in the Papal State to whom political power could possibly be safely entrusted. But all this is of small consequence. It is not as a petty Italian prince that Pio Nono will stand to be judged by history. He will have to be considered in his role as the most important opponent of the extravagant claims, political and ideological, of the nineteenth-century progressives, as the most obstinate and influential of those who denied the infallibility of progress, the moral authority of majorities, and the omnipotence of the State. By refusing, in the name of eternal truths, to accept the passionate enthusiasms of the men of Progress he earned for the Papacy much hatred in his own day. But he restored to it an authority within the Church and an influence without such as it had not enjoyed since the time of the Council of Trent.

He was, in short, the creator of the Modern Papacy. . . .

In the pontificate of Pio Nono the Church, vis-à-vis Society, was on the defensive. In their various ways Rationalists, Nationalists, Liberals and the rest were laying claims to men's allegiance that were new and the Pope—most notably in the Syllabus of Errors—was condemning these claims in the sense that he was rejecting the notion that their doctrines offered an alternative means of salvation to that offered by the Church. Within the framework of the Church's teaching the new ideas might have validity; on the political plane they might be useful; but in antithesis to the Church's teaching, and offered as a philosophical alternative, they were anathema. In so far as men like Mazzini, or Proudhon, or Bakunin (operating on a wide front in Italy), or Marx, or Treitschke, or, on the political plane, Napoleon, Cavour, or Bismarck represented "modern society"—and in the accepted sense they did—the Pope was prepared to say that he would not be reconciled with modern society; nor would he be reconciled with Progress or Liberalism as those ideas were manifesting themselves around him, whether in the risorgimento, or in Germany, or in the anti-clericalism of the republicans in France. So, in an important sense, he did throw down the gage to modern civilisation; but he threw it down in the Syllabus of Errors, not at the Vatican Council which was irrelevant to the issue; and he threw it down against movements and tendencies which may have had good in them, but which were showing themselves in so hostile and arrogant a light during the last years of his life, after 1870, that he felt no occasion, in his closing years, to withdraw, but rather to emphasise afresh his strictures.

So, as the end approached, it seemed to Pio Nono that the darkness was dark, indeed, and was growing darker and spreading more widely. But he had lit a bright light in the Church. He had recalled men to a truer vision of her universality, and of her unity, he had reasserted, in contradiction to the current emphasis upon the "autonomous man" or the "autonomous state" the existence of the divine law and the role of the Church as its interpreter. He had imparted a new emphasis to prayer, to devotion, to sacrifice, to personal purity; and he had recalled Catholics to the traditional faith of the Church in the merits, as intercessor, of the Blessed Virgin Mary. At the end of his life he stimulated the devotion to the Sacred Heart, contributing 50,000 francs, in the penury of his last years, to the new cathedral dedicated to that name which Parisians, in expiation of the crimes of the Commune, were beginning to raise high on the hill of Montmartre.

"When the history of the Pontificate of Pius IX shall be written," said Manning, "it will be found to have been one of the most resplendent, majestic, and powerful—one that has reached over the whole extent of the church with greater power than that of any other Pope in the whole succession." Now that Professor Aubert, of Malines, has written a balanced and authoritative history of the Church under Pio Nono, considered scholarship has, in an important sense, endorsed Manning's bold prediction. No achievement of mere administrative centralisation was Pio Nono's; nor was it just an excitement of the human emotions of affection and devotion towards the Papacy. He made the Church, as Professor Aubert puts it, *sensiblement plus "Réligieuse."*

What more can be asked of a Pope?

This, perhaps, that he should have a profound understanding (or at least that his entourage should) of the intellectual tendencies of his times; that he should understand, too, social and economic trends and tendencies and how they must affect society and the Church. Pio Nono cannot be acquitted of a certain ignorance and indifference towards the great writers and thinkers of his age; he was far from being a scholar, with the result that the Curia was below that level of intellectual eminence that was desirable. And he cannot be acquitted of some responsibility for what was the greatest tragedy of his pontificate; namely the failure of the Church, as a whole, to win the affection and respect of the new proletariat in the rapidly growing towns. Some of her leaders—and notably Manning—saw the problem and strove heroically to meet it; but it was more obvious in London than in Rome, and Pio Nono and his Curia, though prodigal in private charity, scarcely perceived that firm teaching was needed, especially by employers, in the principles of social justice. It was left to Leo XIII to provide the necessary guidance, in his Encyclical *Rerum Novarum*. But by the time this was issued Marx and Bakunin had had a long start. . . .

It was Pio Nono's fate, after travelling, with sympathy, in his earlier years, more than half way to meet the Revolution, to be compelled, though not naturally a fighter, to turn and withstand its pretensions. It was his glory that "he confronted the tempest without flinching, and was faithful to the end." He died a hero to his followers; to the world, apparently, a failure. Few thoughtful men, in 1900, thought he had been right. It was necessary to find excuses for the Syllabus—better, even, to forget it. But we, today, who have met the children and the grandchildren of European Liberalism and the Revolution, who have seen Mazzini turn into Mussolini, Herder into Hitler, and the idealistic early socialists into the intransigent communists are able from a new vantage ground to consider once more whether Pio Nono, or the optimistic believers in an infallible progress, like his cultured friend Pasolini, will have, in the eyes of eternity, the better of the argument.

5. JOSEPH N. MOODY: Church and Society*

Father Joseph Moody, of the Catholic University of America, writes his essay on the papacy from a broadly liberal Catholic point of view. He, too, sees clear and understandable reasons for Pius' stance, but they are not so elaborate or compelling as those in Hales's account. Father Moody is more impressed by Pius' failure and implies the existence of alternatives which the Pope simply did not grasp. Is this approach historically valid, or is it, for the period involved, wishful thinking?

So patent was the failure of Gregory XVI that it took only the unusually short time of two days for the conclave of 1846 to elect a man who seemed to embody the very tendencies which his predecessor had combatted. Cardinal Mastai Ferretti, who became Pius IX, was known as a nationalist and a liberal—a patriotic Italian who believed in far-reaching reform. Liberals everywhere greeted his election with intense enthusiasm, and Italian nationalists rejoiced that an active sympathizer now occupied the Papal Throne.

Only to a limited extent was this expectancy justified. The new Pope was an earnest partisan of Italian independence. He had read the leading literature of the *Risorgimento*. He was critical of the past administration of the Papal States and was determined to grant the concessions most loudly demanded by public opinion. But there were two limiting factors which were to have important bearing on his reactions to the events of 1848:

1. The Pope, deeply religious, was very conscious of his pastoral obligations to all Catholics. Though opposed to Austrian rule in the peninsula, he had no intention of leading a holy war against his other Catholic subjects in Austria for the sake of Italian independence.

2. Though critical of all regimes which would not make concessions, he had no intention of surrendering his Temporal Power, which he sincerely believed was essential for the spiritual interests of the Church. His reforms would be extensive but would not affect his sovereignty. Actually, they were not to go beyond the demands of the representatives of the Great Powers of 21 May 1831. Nor did he accept the neo-Guelf thesis: he had no desire to enlarge the Temporal Power.

It is these limitations which explain his action in the decisive year, 1848. His allocution of the 29th of April came as a shock to the nationalists, who could not appreciate his refusal to join the war against Austria. The Pope maintained that he was the Vicar of a Christ Who was the Author of peace and charity and that he was thus bound to embrace all nations with the same paternal love. *This decision, correct though it was, was the key to all the Pontiff's future troubles.* That it was correct is clear: in a Europe of mounting

* From Joseph N. Moody, ed., *Church and Society* (New York: Arts, Inc., 1953), pp. 36–40. Reprinted by permission of Arts, Inc., and the author.

nationalism, no tragedy would be greater than for the Papacy to become a national institution. In March, the Pope had granted a parliamentary Constitution to his subjects. In mid-September he appointed the liberal, Pellegrino Rossi, as his chief minister. Rossi, laboring energetically to make the new constitution work, was assassinated on the 15th of November in disorders that threatened the safety of Pius himself. The Pope, despairing of achieving any result by reform, fled in disguise to Gaëta in the Kingdom of Naples. On the 4th of December, he appealed to the Christian Powers, invoking the international guarantees of the Congress of Vienna. The reforming phase of Pope Pius's pontificate was concluded, and the Temporal Power had become an international issue.

From Gaëta, Pius IX watched the Constituent Assembly at Rome declare the end of the Temporal Power and the establishment of a Republic for all Italy. He was now convinced that liberal reforms were incompatible with papal rule and would only lead to further disturbance. The European Powers were agreed on a restoration, but Austrian-French rivalry and British suspicions of French intentions made a solution difficult. Pius would have preferred Austrian intervention on the model of 1831. The issue became critical when a French expeditionary force landed at Civitavecchia on 24 April, 1849. The Pope was not well disposed to a restoration by the cynically irreligious and nationalistic President of the French, nor were the other Powers gratified by the dominant role France was assuming in Italian affairs. But all bowed before the *fait accompli*. Pius was back in his capital on 12 April, 1850. It was evident at once that he was no longer the bold political innovator of 1846. He resented the suggestions that a modified constitutional government be re-established, on the ground that such a government would impede his spiritual freedom.

From 1849 until 1870, the question of the Temporal Power retained the twofold feature of the Gaëta interlude. First, it remained an international issue, dependent for its solution on the action of the Powers. Thus, the Austrian defeat in 1859 prepared the way for the loss of all the papal territories save those around Rome; and even these latter in turn had to be surrendered when the withdrawal of the French sealed their doom in 1870. Second, the Pope remained adamant against all substantial concessions both to his subjects and to the encroaching power of Italian nationalism, now incarnate in the House of Savoy. His interpretation of the Piedmontese legislation of 1855 made him even more unyielding, and he saw each advance of the House of Savoy as an extension of godlessness in Italy. Indeed, the fundamental dilemma lay unresolved: for the Italian nationalist, there could be no Italy without Rome; for the Vatican, there could be no Catholicism without the territorial independence of the Papacy. On this latter assumption, Pius remained irreconcilable until the end. A more politically minded Pope might have sought an arrangement; Pius actually went to his death believing that the fate of the Church was linked to this issue.

After 1870, the Roman question entered a new phase, with the Pope accepting voluntary imprisonment in the Vatican. He cut off all official ties with the Italian State. He rejected the Law of Guarantees, which was in fact a tissue of compromises that contained concessions tó the Italian Left. To Pius IX, it was totally unacceptable because it was a unilateral grant that could be amended or abrogated by any subsequent Italian government. To him it seemed the most fragile sort of protection for papal independence. In 1876, the formation of the actively anti-clerical Depretis government ended for the time the possibility of compromise.

Two points in the *Dissidio* need to be noted:

1. The King of United Italy, Victor Emmanuel II, was sincerely Catholic, as were most of his ministers. It is ironic that "the Roman Question was created by a government of Catholics and settled by a government largely composed of agnostics."

2. A serious divison existed among Italian Catholics on the wisdom of the *Dissidio*. The considerable body of Catholic opinion that supported the nationalist cause provided an important bridge between the Vatican and the government. Earlier, the neo-Guelfs had made it possible to reconcile the Catholic cause with nationalist feeling; now, clerical and episcopal dissent from the official papal position diminished the danger of serious popular repercussions. In the North and in the South, most Catholics were friendly to a united Italy. The bishops, generally, remained silent out of respect for the Pope, but many were known to be sympathetic to the nationalist position. This internal division helps to explain why Italian anti-clericalism never attained the success achieved by the French. No one can deny the seriousness of the anti-Catholic feeling of the convinced opponents of the Church. But they never won the masses, and in rural Italy were almost without influence. As a consequence, the Church-State conflict in Italy had some of the atmosphere of those scenes in Verdi's operas where the singing soldiers shout defiance to the accompaniment of the drums and the brandishing of wooden spears, only to retire into the wings to chat amiably till the next entrance.

These divisions among Catholics saddened the Pope, but they did not dissuade him. His pontificate was a prolonged personal tragedy. The longest since Peter, it spanned one of the most decisive periods of European history. It witnessed the forging of an industrial society, the triumph of the principle of nationalism, the creation of a new balance of power in Europe with the unification of Bismarck's Germany, the elaboration of the social theory of Marx, and the emergence of a new intellectual mood that has been summarized under the title, *A Generation of Materialism*. Distracted by his Italian troubles, Pius IX watched these aforementioned changes with deep anxiety. Personally, he was refined, affable, spiritual, and anxious for popular approval; yet, in Italy and in Europe generally, he was driven by his convictions into an intractable position that he maintained without reference to consequences.

Politically, his pontificate was an almost unrelieved record of failure. Before the unification of Germany, he was involved in disputes with several German states; after 1871, he sustained the shock of Bismarck's Kulturkampf. Relations with Switzerland were generally unhappy. He managed to negotiate a Russian concordat, but it was not put into effect; and the Catholic subjects of the Czar, especially the Poles, continued to suffer persecution. His concordat with Austria was subsequently abrogated. There were conflicts with governments in the Iberian peninsula and in several Latin American countries. At his death, only four states continued to send representatives to the Holy See, and the international position of the Papacy reached its nadir. His pronouncements on contemporary issues, especially *Quanta Cura* and the *Syllabus of Errors,* created intense antipathy among non-Catholics and considerable uneasiness among many Catholics.

The clear antithesis between his political views before and after 1848 suggests that they were influenced by the collapse of his hopes for moderate reform in the Papal States. Before the murder of Rossi, he had criticized regimes "which attempted to rule by force instead of charity." Thereafter, his optimism vanished. He was not impressed by the arguments for the separation of Church and State. The contention that they could be divorced, or, in the words of T. S. Eliot, that the "public affairs of this world and those of the next have nothing to do with each other. . . . ," and that "in a perfect world those who like golf could play golf and those who liked religion could go to Church," appeared to him as nonsense. Either a regime would be benevolent, in which case it would publicly proclaim its protection of religion, or it would be hostile. The neutrality of the state in religious or economic matters, which so appealed to his contemporaries, was for him a myth.

Nor was he impressed by claims to complete liberty of opinion and worship. Total liberty, he felt, was a mirage. No state would permit dissent were its existence threatened, nor would any civilized nation carry religious tolerance to the point where it would recognize a creed which proclaimed human sacrifice or polygamy. Hence, professions of full liberty were hypocritical. He invoked the principle: error may not claim the same rights as truth.

These objections were vigorously presented. But when one examines the many declarations of this Pontiff, one is struck by their predominantly negative character. Certainly his pontificate was a "Time of Resistance." He condemned many contemporary movements of thought and action, but he did not provide well-constructed alternatives. This was particularly true in regard to the social question, which had become acute in Europe during his time in the Vatican. He did denounce Socialism and Communism in terms which many in our time would accept. But there was no examination of the new social conditions and no positive proposals. The most profound of modern movements was scarcely reflected in papal declarations up until 1878.

6. JOSEF ALTHOLZ: The Churches in the Nineteenth Century*

This recent survey, by Josef Altholz, a historian at the University of Minnesota, was undertaken in a spirit "neither Catholic nor Protestant, nor even

* From Josef Altholz, *The Churches in the Nineteenth Century* (Indianapolis: The Bobbs-Merrill Company, Inc., 1967), pp. 81–84, 88–89. Reprinted by permission of The Bobbs-Merrill Company.

distinctively Christian, but simply historical." * Is such an approach really possible in religious history? Does it produce results significantly different from those of partisans? There is an interesting effort, certainly, to explain the apparent extravagance of Pius IX's phrasing and to note the successful aspects of his papacy.

Pius IX denounced those who had despoiled him and excommunicated Victor Emmanuel. Cavour, whose motto was "a free Church in a free State," made overtures to reconcile the Papacy to the kingdom of Italy, but his reputation for anti-clericalism discouraged trust in him, and in June, 1861, he suddenly died. He had unified Italy but had not stabilized the new regime. His successors were restrained from seizing Rome only by the presence of a French army. Pius, however, could not rely on his French protector. Napoleon III, anxious to disengage himself from his Italian entanglements, actually agreed in 1864 to evacuate his troops from Rome, but a Garibaldian attack on the city in 1867 brought them back. For the defense of his temporal sovereignty, the Pope was dependent upon foreign arms.

The "Roman question," the issue of the temporal power of the Papacy, became the dominant issue in the history of the Church for over a decade. The ideal solution, no doubt, would have been the cession of the temporal power—an embarrassment rather than a source of strength to the Pope—in return for an effective guarantee of the independence of the Papacy, such as was arranged in 1929. However, Pius IX could not accept such a solution, partly because of the past history of Sardinian aggression, but also because he felt himself personally obligated to maintain unimpaired the heritage of the Church which he had received. The ideal of the "free Church in a free State" was a liberal ideal with apparently secularistic connotations; and behind liberalism Pius saw the spectre of revolution led by still more radical elements. He determined upon a course of intransigence, drawing Catholicism in upon itself and presenting a solid front of resistance to a hostile world. The Roman Catholic Church came to regard itself as in a "state of siege," and it adopted the hard, militant mentality appropriate to that condition. It is in this period that the word "Ultramontanism" came to have its ultimate meaning of thoroughgoing resistance to the dominant tendencies of the modern world.

A by-product of this state of tension among Catholics was the final defeat of the Liberal Catholic movement. The Ultramontane outlook, stressing dependence on Roman and suspicion of modern ideas, dominated both the hierarchy and the Catholic masses. Its advocates were led in France by Veuillot, in Ireland by Paul Cullen, Archbishop of Dublin, and in England by the converts W. G. Ward, editor of the *Dublin Review,* Frederick Faber, a noted hymnologist, and Henry Edward Manning, who became Archbishop of Westminster in 1865. Men such as Montalembert, Döllinger, and Acton came under increasing suspicion and, in turn, tended toward more liberal positions which further alienated them from the sympathies of most Catholics. In 1863, Montalembert,

* *Ibid.,* vi.

addressing the Belgian Catholics at Malines, espoused the ideal of a "free Church in a free State" and demanded liberty of conscience. The Jesuit editor of the Roman journal *Civiltà Cattolica* attempted to justify Montalembert's speech by drawing a distinction between the "thesis," the full claims of the Church, and the "hypothesis," the practical adjustment to the necessities of the actual situation. Pope Pius, much disturbed by this, expressed his displeasure privately. In the same year, Döllinger, presiding over a congress of German scholars at Munich, demanded the replacement of scholasticism by historical research conducted with perfect freedom. He was rebuked by a Papal letter to the Archbishop of Munich, early in 1864, which insisted that scholarly research must be subordinated to ecclesiastical authority. The condemnation of freedom of scholarship was so clear that Acton in England felt obliged to put an end to his periodical, the *Home and Foreign Review*.

The reign of Pius IX saw the fullest exposition and exercise of the authority of the Pope and was more prolific of doctrinal statements and condemnations than any since the Counter-Reformation. The various condemnations of "the principal errors of our times" issued by Pius were gathered together in one document, the famous *Syllabus of Errors,* appended to the encyclical *Quanta cura* in 1864. The encyclical condemned the idea that society should be governed without regard to religion and censured the Liberal Catholic doctrine that assent may be withheld from those Papal decisions which did not deal with dogmas of faith or morals. The *Syllabus* was a list of eighty propositions which had been condemned in previous Papal utterances. While many of the condemned propositions were obviously anti-Christian, the *Syllabus* attracted attention by its condemnation of liberal doctrines concerning the political rights of the Church, civil marriage, the separation of Church and State, liberty of thought and religion, and the position of the Pope. It concluded by condemning the proposition that "the Roman Pontiff can and ought to reconcile himself and come to terms with progress, liberalism and modern civilization."

To most readers, unacquainted with the technical language of Roman documents,[1] it seemed as if the Pope had declared war on the nineteenth century. The position of the Liberal Catholics, who had hoped for a reconciliation of Roman Catholicism with liberal society, was clearly untenable; and even many moderates were stunned by the sweeping condemnations, while the extreme Ultramontanes rejoiced. Balance was restored to the situation by a brilliant

1. The *Syllabus,* designed for the use of bishops, was drawn up in technical theological language and was unsuited for public dissemination. It consists of a list, compiled by Cardinal Antonelli as Secretary of State, of eighty condemned propositions, to each of which is appended a citation of the Papal document in which it was condemned. Thus the condemnations cannot be understood by themselves, without reference to the original sources (encyclicals, allocutions, and letters) from which they derive whatever force they possess. In their original form they were generally of specific and limited application. Thus the final proposition, so extreme when quoted by itself, is taken from the allocution *Jamdudum cernimus* (1861) which, criticizing political liberalism as manifested in Italy, denied that "the Roman Pontiff should reconcile himself and come to terms with *what they call* progress, Liberalism, and recent civilization." Much of the apparent harshness of Papal documents results from the process by which statements such as this are reduced to abstract propositions asserted or condemned in universal terms.

pamphlet published by the liberal Bishop Dupanloup of Orléans, who "minimized" the offense given by the *Syllabus* by placing the condemned propositions in their proper context. Dupanloup made use of the distinction between thesis and hypothesis, pointing out that the *Syllabus* dealt with absolute propositions, while the Church often allowed practical adjustments to the actual state of society. Dupanloup's interpretation was generally accepted among Catholics. However, no amount of minimization could disguise the fact that the *Syllabus* was, if not a complete condemnation of modern society, certainly a sign of unchanged opposition to the trend of liberalism on the Continent. . . .

Chapter X.

GERMAN UNIFICATION

CONTROVERSY SURROUNDING the assessment of the unification of Germany has centered on several related key questions: How much did the process flow from and confirm German political and social structure? How extensively did the methods of unification alter the character of European diplomacy? Were the institutions and ideas enshrined in the new Germany good or bad? An element of moral judgment of the methods and achievements of German unification seems almost inescapable in any evaluation, and the morality is not abstract. We know, after all, what happened to Germany later. As has already been apparent in the discussion of the revolutions of 1848, no recent historian of nineteenth-century Germany has been free from a preoccupation with the sources of the catastrophic development of Germany in this century. A. J. P. Taylor states his interest, and his conclusion, quite simply: his book is "an attempt to plot the course of German history" that "shows that it was no more a mistake for the German people to end up with Hitler than it is an accident when a river flows into the sea."[1] Many historians would dissent from his conclusion, or at least modify it substantially, but none would take issue with his effort to see what the nineteenth century had in store for its successor.

As a result, apart from the panegyric nationalist histories written before World War I, no serious historians have failed to find considerable fault with the way Germany was united. Most German historians remain convinced that the unification was a good idea. They still evoke some of the excitement of the fulfillment of the nationalist dream and the powerful and successful state that, at least for a time, resulted. But they admit that serious structural flaws resulted as well. Non-Germans have an easier time condemning the process of unification. In any event, it is idle to question the desirability of viewing unification in such presentist terms, for no one has avoided it. No recent historian, either, has denied the importance of the links between Germany as it emerged in 1871 and the Germany of 1914 and 1933. But within this basic framework, there is much controversy. How inevitable was future disaster, in 1871? Were there not many alternate paths still available for Germany's future? What recent disaster, indeed, are we seeking to explain? It is worth noting the difference between historians writing soon after World War I, when Germany's defeat and/or her belligerence were the leading topics, and those writing at the high point of the Weimar Republic, when there was also some apparent political success to account for, and those who had the mournful duty of seeking the origins of nazism.

As with most questions that produce historical controversy, one must begin an evaluation with causation. For German unification, there are some classic issues, interesting in themselves as well as in the way they bear on the ultimate interpreta-

1. A. J. P. Taylor, *The Course of German History* (New York, 1961).

tion of the process. Was unification inevitable, given the pressure of German nationalism, the rise of the German economy, and the diplomatic situation of the period? Or was it, at least in the form it took, the doing of Bismarck alone? Nationalist historians long gave Bismarck the decisive credit for the achievement of unification; more recent students have assigned him equally decisive blame. Yet, without denying Bismarck's vital role, it is possible to see some supplementary factors, such as the pressure of popular opinion or the provocative quality of French diplomacy in 1870; to the extent these are stressed, unification can appear substantially justified and its authoritarian character can be at least modified. Further, what were the intentions of Bismarck himself? How fully did he control the events of unification and their outcome? And, if he wanted a Germany at all, what sort of political and diplomatic stance did he plan once it was achieved? Here again, there is much argument.

Closely related to the questions of causation is the issue of German liberalism in the unification process. Two key points arise here. First, to what extent did liberals deceive themselves or betray their purposes in coming to support Bismarck's unification of Germany? No one denies that they did support it. But should they be criticized or merely explained? The answer depends in part on one's view of liberalism in general and German liberalism earlier, particularly in 1848. But there is a newer issue as well: Did German liberalism, in accepting Bismarck's state, commit suicide? Here we go beyond the perhaps sterile effort to praise or blame, to a vital question of fact. There were people and parties who called themselves liberal after 1871, but were they really so? And had they enough power to be worth noting? There is outright disagreement here. Most recent non-German historians have seen the liberal compromises of 1867–71 as the essential end of German liberalism. But, as some German historians recall, the 1870's seemed to many a blossoming of liberal achievement. And de Ruggiero, writing before the rise of nazism, largely concurred, while noting some distinctive features of the German liberal attitude.

Was Germany really unified? Without denying unification in some senses, historians have raised two questions about its completeness. First, many German-speaking areas, particularly in the Hapsburg monarchy, were left out. The *grossdeutsch* leanings of many nationalists were ignored; yet the sentiment for a greater, all-inclusive Germany did not die. Second, particularism continued within the German state. Some historians have pointed to this as an explanation for an authoritarian political structure, which they believe was designed to keep the country together against the wishes of many citizens. Both of these issues raise again the problem of German nationalism—how powerful it was, how aggressive it was, and how widely it extended in the population.

Finally, what was the political and social structure of the new Empire? There are certain areas of definite agreement. The parliament was limited in its power. Prussia dominated many aspects of German politics. The aristocracy was given a new lease on life, with the apparent acquiescence of the middle class. Along with the military, which it controlled substantially, the aristocracy continued to influence all phases of politics. But there is wide disagreement on the causes and extent of these developments. Some historians see the importance of German militarism flowing inevitably from the imposition of Prussian institutions on Germany and the success of the military in the unification itself; others qualify the extent of militarism and attribute it to more specific factors in the situation after the war with France. The class analysis of unification is variously used and explained, and it is open to some challenge. Did the middle class abandon political pretensions completely and turn to compensatory (and dangerous) economic activity? Did the government remain in the hands of an unredeemed Junker class? On the whole, class terms have been used somewhat loosely by historians of unification (who are mainly attuned to political developments); they deserve careful scrutiny.

The questions about unification are, then, numerous and fundamental. Many of them involve issues of fact, but they are no easier to resolve because of this. Most involved, also, an orientation to modern Germany as a whole. Depending on the period in which the historian wrote, his nationality, and his emotions, Germany and its unification has been seen as glorious, evil, or something in between. And always there is the question of how much unification had to do with what Germany later became. Did it force an aggressive diplomacy, which only Bismarck's firm hand briefly moderated? Did it destroy healthy political life by its authoritarian character, or were there still opportunities for vitality? German unification dominates the diplomatic and political history of Europe in the nineteenth century. No event with such massive implications can be easily or calmly interpreted.

1. HEINRICH VON TREITSCHKE: Germany, France, Russia, and Islam*

To begin with a pre-World War I, nationalist history is not mere antiquarianism. Admittedly, such a history is in large part a document of the times; it cannot be taken fully seriously as an over-all interpretation. But one could argue that, precisely because of its bias, it conveys the contemporary atmosphere of unification more completely than any later interpretation does and that its bias is a useful counterweight to the distortions caused by subsequent German history. Heinrich von Treitschke (1834–1896) began his career as a liberal, but became an increasingly ardent and intolerant nationalist. A historian at the University of Berlin, his great work was the *History of Nineteenth Century Germany* (to 1848).

What we needed was a complete, incontestable victory, won solely by German strength, which would compel our neighbours to acknowledge at last respectfully that we, as a nation, had attained our majority. This was clearly understood by the Emperor William, who so often re-echoed his people's words, when he said in his address from the throne, "If Germany silently endured violations of her rights and of her honour in past centuries, that was only because she did not realize in her dismembered condition how strong she was." For a long time past we were no longer the poor, ill-treated nation of 1813, which had seen its colours disgraced, its lands laid desolate, prayed in holy wrath, "Save us from the yoke of slavery!" and then, quietly prepared for the worst, waged the unequal strife. On the contrary, at the King's summons, a free, strong, proud nation arose in radiant exultation; she knew her power, and from amid the confused tumult of public meetings and the din of the streets, of

* From Heinrich von Treitschke, *Germany, France, Russia, and Islam,* G. H. Putnam, tr. (New York: G. Putnam and Sons, 1915), pp. 203–204, 208–10, 211, 215–17, 218–20.

the newspapers and the pamphlets, one cry overpowered all other sounds, "We must, we will conquer." Poets have compared the grey-haired ruler as he rode majestically before his knights to the kings of armies in German antiquity. King William was more; he was a hero of our time, the dominating monarchic leader of an immense democratic mass-movement, which shook the nation from top to bottom, and, sure of its goal, stormily swept on, regardless of the caution of hesitating Courts.

France had already lost the leading position in Europe since the overthrow of the first Empire, and then apparently recovered it through the diplomatic skill of the third Napoleon. As soon as Prussia's victories in Bohemia threatened to restore a just balance of power, there took possession of those noisy Parisian circles, which had always dominated the wavering provinces, a fantastic intoxication of national pride. There reappeared the old delusion that France's greatness depended on the weakness of her neighbours. The public opinion of the agitators compelled the sick Emperor to declare war against his will; it arrogantly controlled and disturbed every movement of the enemy; it compelled the fatal march to Sedan. After the first defeats, the imperial throne, whose only support was good fortune, fell, and the party-rule of the new revolutionary government could neither exercise justice, nor command the general respect. The fact that a superior commands and a subordinate obeys was almost forgotten in the widespread and unnatural mistrust which prevailed. Every misfortune was regarded as a piece of treachery, even when the war had seasoned men, and the army of the Loire had found a commander in Chanzy. Finally, after the surrender of Paris, the conquered people, under the eyes of the conqueror, tore each other to pieces in a terrible civil war.

Seldom has it been so clearly demonstrated that it is the will which is the deciding factor in national struggles for existence, and in unity of will we were the stronger. France, which had so often fomented and misused our domestic quarrels, all at once found herself opposed by the vital union of the Germans; for a righteous war releases all the natural forces of character, and, side by side with hatred, the power of affection. Inviolable confidence bound the soldiers to their officers, and all of them to those in supreme command.

Those who remained at home also became more generous, broader-minded, and affectionate; the seriousness of the crisis lifted them above the selfishness of every-day life. Party strife disappeared, isolated, unpatriotic fools were quickly reduced to silence, and the longer the struggle lasted the more firmly did the whole nation unite in the resolve that this war should restore to us the German Empire and our old lost western provinces. One hundred and thirty thousand Germans fell a sacrifice to war's insatiable demands, but the lines of the old Landwehr's men which followed them appeared endless, till more than a million of our soldiers gradually crossed the French frontier. The war demanded all. When the reports of deaths arrived from the West, the fathers and brothers of those who had fallen said, "Much mourning, much honour," and even the mothers, wives, and sisters had in their heavy sorrow the consolation that their little house owned a leaf in the growing garland of German glory. . . .

At last came the time of harvest. Paris surrendered, and the last desperate attempt of the French against Southern Alsace came to a pitiable end. Four great armies were taken prisoners or disarmed, and all the German races had an equal and glorious share in the enormous success. In these last weeks of the war there stepped into the foreground of German history the strong man of whom the troops had so often spoken by their bivouac-fires. Ever since historical times began the masses of people have always rated character and energy above intellect and culture; the greatest and most boundless popularity was always only bestowed on the heroes of religion and of the sword. The one statesman who seems to be an exception only confirms the rule. In the popular mind Bismarck was never anything but the gigantic warrior with the bronze helmet and the yellow collar of the cuirassiers of Mars la Tour, as the painters depicted him riding down the avenue of poplars at Sedan. It was he who had once spoken the salutary word, "Get rid of Austria!" It was he who by treaties with the South German States had in his far-sighted way prepared for the inevitable war. And when twenty-five years ago he read to the Reichstag the French declaration of war, all felt as though he were the first to raise the cry, "All Germany on into France!" and it seemed to all as though he rode into the enemy's land like a herald in front of the German squadrons. Now when the war was over he summed up the net results of the great battles, and after troublesome negotiations settled the constitution of the new kingdom. This constitution seemed quite new, and yet it evoked the old sacred unforgettable emotions of German loyalty to the Kaiser. It appeared complicated even to formlessness, and yet it was fundamentally simple because it admitted of unlimited development. In her relations to foreign countries Germany was henceforth one, and in spite of much doubt all discerning people hoped that the Empire, possessing an imperial head, would now attain to its full growth.

This work of Bismarck's brought peace and reconcilation to nearly all the old factions which had hitherto struggled on our territory. They had all made mistakes, and almost all rediscovered in the constitution of the Empire some of their most deeply-cherished projects. Our princes especially had been in the wrong. In the course of an eventful history they had often been the protectors of German religious freedom and the rich many-sidedness of our civilization, but had been often misled by dynastic envy and pride, even to the point of committing treachery. At the middle of the century their pride was at its height, for what else was the object of the war of 1866 except to break in pieces the State of the great Frederick, and to degrade it to the wretched condition of the petty German princedoms? But the dethroning of the sovereigns of Hanover, Hesse, and Nassau was a tremendous warning to the princes. They recollected themselves and remembered the noble traditions of imperial sentiment in the old princely families; and as soon as the war began they gathered round their royal leader. Therefore they could, according to the old privileges of the German princes, themselves elect their emperor, and secure for themselves their proper share in the new imperial power. There in France was the first foundation laid for that invisible council of German princes, which is something else than the Council of the Confederation, which is not mentioned in any article of the imperial constitution, and yet always works perceptibly for the good of the Fatherland. Never yet at a critical time has the honest help of the princes failed the Hohenzollern Kaisers.

The heaviest blow befell the partisans of Austria, the "Great Germans." So severe was it that even their party-name entirely disappeared. But those who were sincere among them had only fought against the German "rival-Emperor" because they feared a Prussian imperial power would be too weak to sustain the position of the nation as one of the Great Powers. And how was it now? It was never doubtful whether a man was a German or not. We bore the mark of our good and evil qualities as distinctly impressed upon our brows as formerly did the Greeks, our kindred in temperament and destiny. But it was always a matter of dispute for centuries where Germany exactly was; its boundaries were constantly changing or disappearing in the fog of "rights of the Empire." Now for the first time there existed a German State whose frontiers were clearly defined. It had lost the frontier territories of the South-east, which for a long time past had only been loosely connected with the Empire, but as a compensation had finally recovered by conquest those on the Rhine and the Moselle, which had been torn away from the Empire. It had also, through the State of the Hohenzollerns, won wide territories in the East and North which had never or merely nominally belonged to the old Empire, *i.e.,* Silesia, Posen, Prussia, the land of the old Teutonic orders, and Schleswig. It was more powerful than the old Empire had been for six centuries. Who could now speak of it sneeringly as "Little Germany"? Out of the perpetual ebb and flow of races in Central Europe there had finally emerged two great Empires—one purely German with a mixture of religions, the other Catholic, and comprising a variety of races who yet could not dispense with the German language and culture. Such an outcome of the struggles of centuries could not fail to satisfy for a time even the imagination of the "Greater Germany" enthusiasts. The great majority of the nation joined in jubilantly when, in the Palace of Versailles, the acclamation of the princes and the army greeted the Emperor, who in his deep modesty accepted the new dignity only with hesitation.

2. ARTHUR ROSENBERG: Imperial Germany: The Birth of the German Republic*

Arthur Rosenberg (1889–1943) was a reporter for the Reichstag Commission which investigated the causes of Germany's defeat in World War I. A socialist,

* From Arthur Rosenberg, *Imperial Germany: The Birth of the German Republic,* pp. 1–8. Originally published in English by the Oxford University Press and reprinted with their permission.

he was concerned with showing what was wrong with German social as well as political structure under the Empire, and what had to be made right in the new Weimar Republic. His stress on the compromise of the middle class, which was caused in part because of a fear of socialism, deserves serious consideration, as does his belief in the instability of the empire from the first. Both themes have been taken up by more recent historians, but from a different perspective chronologically and with less explicit treatment of the social forces involved.

The Bismarckian Empire and the Prussian army formed an indissoluble entity. Bismarck himself thought his greatest achievement was his winning over of the King of Prussia and of the Prussian army for the ideal of a national unified Germany. He thought the failure of the Revolution of 1848 in Germany lay in the fact that the middle classes sought with their own strength to bring about the establishment of the Empire, regardless of the German dynasties and, above all, without regard to the historic evolution of Prussia. Bismarck chose another path. He united the military aristocracy of Prussia with the German middle class, placed the Hohenzollerns at the head of the whole edifice, and so gave the Empire its peculiar stamp. The history of the revived German Empire is made up of the reciprocal attraction and repulsion of the two elements which Bismarck thus brought together. The end came when the Prussian military caste collapsed in 1918 and the middle class took over the government.

Was Bismarck's conception of making Prussia serve the cause of German unity a false one? Was the situation in 1871 such that the German Empire could only be realized as a middle-class State based on liberal and parliamentary foundations—and in no other way? Did the Junkers and the middle class stand to one another as fire to water between whom no compromise is possible? Did Bismarck sacrifice his real convictions to a romantic dynastic ideal? It would be easy to answer these questions in the affirmative—and it would be exceedingly mistaken. The Revolution of 1848–9 showed that the German middle class was not capable of conquering by its own strength alone. The agrarian and military, the dynastic and bureaucratic, and even the clerical, elements in the old order in Germany were far stronger than at first appeared in the excitement of the March days of 1848. And, behind the middle class, the proletariate of the cities emerged as a new political entity ready to fight with the middle class against the governing aristocracy. But nevertheless it was possessed of ideals which were not those of the liberal middle class. The explosive force latent in the Labour movement was at that time far more apparent to impartial observers than to the workmen themselves.

It was in these circumstances that a realist politician of conservative-socialist tendencies as was Bismarck believed it possible to reconcile the middle class with the old ruling forces by means of a clever compromise, to achieve national unity through the co-operation of the two, and at the same time to raise a strong bulwark against the "red" revolution. Any one who occupied Bismarck's position in 1871, and who made such a calculation, was not overrating the existing forces in Germany. Even in the unprecedentedly favourable conditions of November 1918 the German working class itself was unable to seize the reins of power in the State. Far less could it have done so in the past. Moreover, until the outbreak of the Revolution in 1918, there was little sign in the German middle class of a Jacobin spirit seeking to sweep away the privileges of the Crown and the nobility. For the failure of Bismarck's ideal neither the opposition of the working class nor of the middle class was necessary. The Bismarckian Empire was mortally ill from the day of its birth. The glamour of military victories and commercial prosperity scarcely availed to conceal the political crisis existing from the *Kulturkampf* to the Chancellorship of Max of Baden: a crisis for which no solution was ever found, continually taking to itself new forms and dimensions, and which in the end destroyed the whole of Bismarck's work.

What caused this long-continuing political crisis? Bismarck was unable to weld together into an organic whole the various elements present in the German people: indeed he never once made a serious attempt to do so. The conflicting classes and forces in Germany were to be held together by the superimposed strength of the Empire. Up to 1890 Bismarck's power and the Imperial authority were synonymous. The personal dictatorship lived and died with the dictator himself. When in 1890 the old dictator was compelled to resign, when he saw in the weak and vacillating William II the thunderbolt that was to strike him down, the doom was sealed. Its coming became only a question of time and circumstance. Powerless to avert it, Bismarck from his retirement at Friedrichsruh beheld the storm that threatened to destroy his life-work. It is often said that Bismarck's successors ruined his creation. That is true in so far as the Bismarckian Empire could not exist without a Bismarck. But in that very fact lies the severest criticism of Bismarck himself.

The German Empire was not doomed to failure because it arose from a compromise between the German middle class and the Prussian military aristocracy, but because it embodied that compromise in the form of the Napoleonic autocracy. In order to avoid having to hand over his authority to the Imperial Chancellor, the King of Prussia had to be both by inclination and birth a Bonaparte. That Bismarck bound up the political life of the German nation with his own person, indeed with his own personal relation to William I, was an historical mistake of incalculable consequence. It must, nevertheless, be admitted that in the peculiar situation in Germany in 1871 Bismarck's mistake was a very natural one. At the time of the establishment of the Empire the liberal middle class was possessed of the intelligence, the commercial and industrial ability, of the Germany of that day. The vast masses of manual labourers and of the lower middle classes, the great majority of the factory workers, even a considerable part of the peasantry and a few of the nobility, adopted the nationalist and liberal ideals of the middle class and did service to its political mottoes. In opposition to this undoubtedly powerful force stood the Prussian army, the King, the corps of officers, the hierarchy of the Prussian bureaucracy, the great territorial magnates from east of the Elbe, a group of liberal nobles and the agrarian population dependent upon their landlords. How could a compromise be achieved between these two forces?

In Prussia the King and the military aristocracy wielded supreme power. Military discipline in the generation prior to 1871 had successfully emerged from the severest test; neither the Revolution of 1848 nor the wars of the sixties had seriously undermined the discipline of the Prussian army. The King chose his Ministers in accordance with his personal inclination. The Civil Service and the Police were firmly controlled by the Government. If a recalcitrant Parliament refused supplies, the King carried on the government without a parliamentary budget; and the wars of the sixties had clearly demonstrated his ability to do so. Confronted by the disciplined Prussian army, a popular rising was foredoomed to failure. Even the recruit inspired with subversive ideas submitted himself to the discipline of the army; and the iron institution of the Prussian corps of officers and non-commissioned officers displayed no cracks anywhere. Although here and there throughout the land a liberally-minded judge was to be found, nevertheless the machinery of the Law from the President of the Supreme Court to the last recruited policeman was entirely subservient to the Government.

Thus feudal and conservative Prussia held all the political trumps in its hand. A compromise was only conceivable if the military caste voluntarily surrendered an important part of its rights and privileges to the middle class, and this might be accomplished in two ways; either the middle class was given a share in the actual government in Prussia, or the middle class shared in the government of the Empire to such an extent that a counterpoise was thereby created to Prussia. At the establishment of the Empire, Bismarck avoided both these paths. He left Prussia untouched—that is to say, the King and the military aristocracy retained all authority—and he raised an Imperial constitutional edifice from which Prussia ruled the Empire, and not the Empire Prussia.

It would be erroneous to ascribe Bismarck's conduct to narrow pride of caste. Bismarck never entertained any special regard for the Prussian Junkers, and he never underrated the importance of the middle class. But he believed that in consequence of the perilous international situation in which it found itself the German Empire could not live without a powerful army. And an efficient German army, which would be able in case of need to defend the Empire on its eastern and western frontiers, could only be created with the help of Prussia. The destruction of the Prussian military system implied a defenceless Germany. But in a defenceless Germany it would be impossible to control the domestic political conflict. Bismarck therefore became a convinced supporter of the old Prussian military system. He championed the military dictatorship of the King of Prussia in Germany and the undisputed authority, free from all parliamentary control and interference, of the King over the army.

With Prussia as the military dictator of Germany, however, it was excessively difficult to induce the Prussian military caste to make concessions to other and unarmed sections of the nation. Even if Bismarck had ever desired to do so, it is improbable that he could have induced William I to renounce an important part of his prerogative. It was a misfortune for the subsequent evolution of Germany that the constitutional conflict in Prussia ended in so complete a victory for the Royal authority. Feudal Prussia hurled back the attack of middle-class liberalism along the entire front. The King of Prussia and his army were victorious in 1864, in 1866, and in 1870–1, and by their victories alone the German Empire was rendered possible. Was it conceivable that after such victories the King would renounce his prerogative in favour of a parliament? Hence Bismarck left Prussia untouched and entrusted it with the leadership of Germany.

The secret of the Imperial Constitution lay in the fact that in reality no Imperial Government was ever called into being. The place of an Imperial Government was taken by the Federal Council (*Bundesrat*), the organ of the individual State governments, with the Imperial Chancellor as its advisor and representative. From the very outset Bismarck must have known that the Federal Council, which was no more than a "Council of Ambassadors," was utterly incapable of governing. Thus the Federal Council became the constitutional camouflage for Prussia's governance of the Empire, while the Imperial Chancellor, who was also President of the Prussian Council of Ministers, formulated German policy. If a State, for example Bavaria, put forward definite demands, the matter had to be settled by diplomatic channels; and not once in the whole course of its history was the policy of the Empire determined by a collaboration between any of the component States. The corner-stone of Bismarck's edifice—the government of the Empire by the Federal Council—was from the outset an avowed fiction.

The Reichstag, indeed, could debate publicly all political questions. The army and foreign policy, however, were excluded from its sphere of influence. The Emperor—actually the Imperial Chancellor—formulated foreign policy without any regard for the speeches delivered in the Reichstag. Moreover, the right of voting army credits possessed by the Reichstag was in no circumstances permitted to infringe upon the Emperor's absolute authority over the armed forces of the Empire. In domestic affairs the Reichstag found its influence circumscribed by the special rights assured to the individual States as well as by its own complete lack of control over the actions of the Government. When the Reichstag, for example, found itself in disagreement with the Government's policy, the most that it could do was to refuse to pass the budget. But the struggle in Prussia between the King and the Parliament had shown plainly that the Government could continue to discharge its functions without the aid of supplies obtained in a constitutional manner. Hence the sole weapon in the possession of the Reichstag was from the very beginning useless.

Neither in the Prussian Parliament nor in the Reichstag were the middle classes able to exercise any real influence upon the course of German policy. Nevertheless, Bismarck knew very well that the German Empire could neither be established nor maintained against the will of the middle classes to whom, however, no constitutional rights were to be accorded at the expense of the Crown. Hence it was to be the duty of the executive power—theoretically the Emperor, actually the Imperial Chancellor—to ensure that the just demands of the liberal middle classes were fulfilled. The ideals of the middle-class patriots no less than the economic requirements of Industry and Commerce were to be realized in the nationalist character given to the German Empire. The demands of the Liberals for a modern, intelligent, and straightforward form of government were to be satisfied as far as possible. Bismarck himself was prepared to go even further by entrusting certain portfolios in the Prussian Cabinet and important administrative posts in the Empire to prominent Liberals; and by working in a sincere collaboration with the Liberal groups in parliament. In reality, however, all this was made to depend upon the arbitrary will of the Emperor, i.e. of his most influential advisers. Bismarck wished to retain for himself and his successors in office the possibility, if necessary, of being able to crush the Liberals as they had been crushed in the days of the struggle in Prussia.

From the middle class Bismarck demanded that it should be content with such concessions, and that it should realize the peculiar and exceptional nature of the situation in which Germany found herself in regard to politico-military and international affairs. The military power placed in the hands of the Emperor afforded the capitalist middle class the best defence against the danger of a proletarian socialist revolution. The Commune in Paris had made a profound impression upon Bismarck's mind. He was convinced that a middle-class parliamentary system—much less a republic—did not possess within itself sufficient powers of resistance to cope with the attack of the proletarian masses. For this reason alone the middle classes ought to rally round the existing conservative State, notwithstanding the fact that they might be dissatisfied with this or that detail in the Constitution of the German Empire.

At the same time Bismarck considered it to be no less essential that the old Prussian aristocracy should adapt itself to the new order. The Junker must learn that the German Empire could not be governed by the same methods that were employed in the working of an estate to the east of the Elbe. He must learn to reconcile himself to the existence of Liberal Ministers and to the growing wealth and power of the municipalities. He must be brought to recognize the power that lay in his hands through the undiminished prerogatives of the Prussian Crown. Finally, the Junker must be ready to support the Emperor and the Imperial Chancellor in all emergencies, even though at the moment he might not understand the meaning and purpose of this or that governmental action. In Bismarck's opinion the healthiest political situation would be that in which a large "Old Prussian" Conservative Party worked in collaboration with a large Liberal Party. It must, however, be left to the Government in each individual instance to decide how the balance of forces could best be maintained. If necessary, the Government must be prepared at one time to seek support from the Left and at another from the Right; but it should always bear in mind that its principal aim was the reconciliation and collaboration of the two fundamental forces in the Empire.

It is easy to see that the working of this system depended entirely upon the personality of the two Heads of the Executive. In order that the balance of forces should be maintained it would always be necessary to have a chancellor like Bismarck or a king like Frederick the Great. If the leadership were wanting, the whole system would dissolve in pieces. The balance of forces that had been achieved in England by the Revolution of 1689 depended upon the existence of a compromise between the landed aristocracy and the townsfolk. An organic collaboration and evolution of these two classes in the nation was attained in England. The two classes divided the task of governance between them; the squire exercised magisterial authority in the country districts as a Justice of the Peace, &c., while the mayors and aldermen ruled over the cities. In the House of Commons the two classes met as representatives of town and country boroughs. Each respected the privileges of the other because each recognized that the privileges of the one presupposed the privileges of the other. They watched in common over the integrity of the Constitution and they united to form the Government. The foundation-stone of the English system—autonomy—was wanting in Germany, where its place was taken by the all-powerful bureaucracy. The supreme power of the House of Commons resulted from the collaboration of all classes in the nation in the governance of the country. The impotence of the Reichstag forbade the conclusion of an effective compromise that would have resulted in a united governance of the Empire. In the Reichstag, as constituted by Bismarck, a parliamentary coalition could only achieve positive results for so long as it worked in collaboration with the Government. The most that could be achieved by a coalition of parties and classes inimical to the Government's policy was the annoyance of the Imperial Chancellor by the adoption of obstructionist and pin-pricking tactics.

3. GUIDO DE RUGGIERO: A History of European Liberalism*

De Ruggiero † does not pretend to offer a complete account of German unification; but given the importance usually attributed to the fate of liberalism in the unification process, his interpretation demands attention. He wrote before the Nazi takeover, when it was possible to believe in a renewed or enduring liberal tradition in Germany; this allowed him, if not greater objectivity, at least a different kind of bias. Even he finds German liberalism distinctive; his most important evidence of its continued vitality is in theory, not in political practice. Does he qualify or really confirm the more conventional picture of liberal decline?

Defeated in 1848 on the ground of politics, Liberalism as a party was unable to rally, and was only able to create unstable and ephemeral organizations, quickly dominated by stronger political forces. Yet the fundamental demands of the European consciousness have not been unfelt by the German people, but have found satisfaction in indirect ways. We can distinguish two groups of

* From Guido de Ruggiero, *A History of European Liberalism,* R. G. Collingwood, trans. (Boston: Beacon Press, 1959), pp. 251–56; 261–64. Reprinted by permission of the Clarendon Press, Oxford.

† See Chapter 7, on European liberalism.

these, the first consisting of political claims, the second of juridical. The defective development of German Liberalism concerns the first group only, and is compensated by the rapid progress of the second.

The political institutions of modern Germany, down to the European war, remained in the stage of pure constitutionalism, consisting in the spontaneous gift of a charter by the Crown creating a system of popular representation with a merely critical function and no active part in the government. The act of governing belonged to the Crown, and was exercised through its ministers, who were directly responsible to the Crown and independent of the vote of the chamber. Later, the creation of the Empire as a federal State brought into being a collegiate political organism formed by representatives of the various States, with governmental functions belonging to it in virtue of this State representation.

This political system remained intact and uninfluenced by any parliamentary ideas of French origin, not only through the constant desire of the imperial government, but also by the consent of the educated classes, which regarded it as a genuinely German form of State, and the parliamentary system as a feeble and inefficient government with a sham popular sovereignty paving the way to the indirect influence of amateur politicians. . . . The Germans regard a political power, out of proportion to the legal capacity and social activity of individuals, as an evil. They are content with a very narrow constitutionalism, so long as it is effectual. The true basis of any constitution lies, they believe, in the widespread legal feeling of the people, which forms a limit to the caprices not only of the government but of political parties. Their Liberalism consists not in an empty show of political forms, but in a firm consciousness of rights, which without identifying government and governed, the State and the people, determines their relations in such a way that no political encroachment, whether from above or from below, can disturb them.

The conception of the *Rechtsstaat* (the State according to rights) in which the essence of German Liberalism finds expression is not the creation of a single jurist; it is the legal tradition of the whole people, from Thomasius to Kant and Hegel; and in the second half of the nineteenth century it inspired the great scientific constructions of Mohl, Gerber, Gneist, Laband, Meyer, and Jellinek. Even in the court of Frederick William IV a politician, Stahl, found in it an insurmountable limit to any reactionary programme. . . .

The State is a civil juridical association. This does not mean that its only end is the declaration or sanction of rights, but only that the achievement of its ends, whatever they may be, must take place within the forms and limits of law. The merit of later writers, especially Gneist, is to have shown that this legal function of the State can only be effectively discharged when "through the intermediate organizations between the State and the social body there is promoted and maintained in society that sense of right and understanding of the law in which, under a constitutional government, all parties ought, in their political activity, to be indistinguishable."

The foundation-stone of the *Rechtsstaat* consisted in self-government, understood not as the participation of the people in a legislative and governing parliament, but as the possession by local bodies of governmental functions conferred upon them by the general judiciary, administrative, and financial laws of the State. "The complex organism of the English State is based not on a conventional division of powers, but on the unity of political power, which calls the social classes to take part no less in the autonomous execution of the laws than in their formation." Blackstone in his *Commentaries* confined himself to the external elements of the parliamentary constitution, ignoring the intermediate organism, the local judiciary and administrative power, which stands between parliament and the central government: thus the continent received a mutilated view of the system, giving the false impression that nothing was required except to represent the will of the nation through a political assembly. And England has in her turn been exposed to the effects of the continental democratic reaction.

This being so, the German rejection of parliamentary government did not mean a rejection of modern constitutionalism, but prepared the way for a deeper understanding of its real importance. Like England, Germany has an ancient tradition of self-government, marked by the autonomy of the three orders, the flourishing *Genossenschaften,* the independence of the courts, and a constant exercise of administrative functions by the aristocracy. . . .

It was natural that the German Empire, on emerging victorious from two wars, should reassert the *Rechtsstaat* in a form adapted to modern conditions. Bismarck brought about a great administrative reform based on self-government. Between the feudal party which wanted autonomous administration, but of a patrimonial type and in its own interest, and the Liberal *bourgeois* party, which meant by self-government a communal elective administration on the French model with a wide suffrage, Bismarck succeeded in finding a middle path, reconciling the old territorial interests with the new industrial and commercial interests of the *bourgeoisie*. His reform was based on the principle that the classes, in the modern sense of the term, must accept the task of personally discharging those public duties for which our times provide far more opportunity than any previous age. In modern conditions, it is impossible to get rid of the salaried State employee; but it is possible to supplement the rigid bureaucratic system at certain decisive points by calling in the help of the classes. Side by side with salaried officials, a system of unpaid officials can provide a juridical check on the administration, and at the same time train the educated classes in the practical exercise of political functions and so restore to them their lost legal consciousness. In this way Prussia effected a reconstruction of the political basis of the State which Gneist describes as unparalleled in Europe. On this foundation was rebuilt the whole structure of German juridical government, which, while recognizing the necessary rights of the State, draws an inviolable legal circle, unknown to antiquity, around the subject, with his family, his association, his commune, and his church. . . .

German thought has followed, from its own special point of view, the general evolution of the European public consciousness. The demands which we have seen put forward in France and England, on purely political grounds, for an introduction of the principles of the *Declaration of the Rights of Man* into a more modern conception of the State, for the addition of a system of self-government to a parliamentary régime, and so forth, appear no less in Germany, but formulated in the language of legal science. And from the point of view of European Liberalism, Jellinek's great work on *The General Theory of the State* is an important witness to the close bond between Germany and Western Europe, in spite of a difference of constitutional form. It contains an exposition of the concepts of sovereignty, representation, constitution, distinction of powers, and so forth, in a form entirely acceptable to Western and English Liberalism; indeed, in his lucid and penetrating historical introductions to his analyses of the various institutions of public law, the author abandons a strict legal formalism, and proceeds to sketch suggestive pictures of European political evolution in order to illustrate the relations and differences of the various nations. And it must not be forgotten that the *Declaration of the Rights of Man* has found its best interpreter in Jellinek, a student belonging to the nation which, according to a widespread but superficial view, has stood aloof from the Liberal movement of the nineteenth century.

It might, however, be suspected that in Germany the jurists have enjoyed a monopoloy of this enlightening grace, and that their work has met with no echo in the spirit of the nation and the minds of politicians. To convince onself that this suspicion is unjust, it is enough to examine the work of one of the political writers commonly regarded as most hostile to Liberalism, Treitschke. We shall there find, no doubt, many ironical or contemptuous references to Jacobinism, Liberal rhetoric, and the spirit of hostility to the State; but we shall also find, transformed into a new shape, the entire legal organization of the Liberal theory of the State. No one has criticized more keenly than Treitschke the monomania, ascribed to Hegel but in reality characteristic of the Hegelians, for making the State absorb into itself the entire life of the individual. Let the State content itself, says Treitschke, with external order, and not force its way into the intimacy of conscience. No Christian can live solely for the State, for he cannot renounce his eternal destiny. But if pan-Statism is false, no less false is the excessive individualism which would reduce the State to a night-watchman. There is a cultural end which the modern State must not neglect; but its activity in this expansion is "beneficent and wise when it promotes and strengthens the autonomy of the free and wise man; but it is an evil if it restricts and sterilizes the autonomy of the free man. People use mere words, when they speak of educational discipline as restriction of freedom; they ought to call it restriction *to* freedom."

On the other hand, to give the name of liberty to a denial of all authority, as the Poles did, is to ensure the complete dissolution of the State. An excess of liberty becomes slavery, because when all authority is suppressed the strong are unrestrained and the weak are exposed to the right of might. A fanatical attachment to liberty not only leads to slavery, but is itself slavery. It is a false conception of freedom which asks for freedom not *in* the State but *from* the

State: the power of the State and the freedom of the people are inseparably connected. It is not always that the true partisans of freedom are the so-called Liberals: it is undeniable that at the time of the Great Elector the real champion of liberty was absolutism; Leibniz, Pufendorf, and Thomasius, to whom we owe the reawakening of Germany, were all rigid absolutists. Who were the reactionaries of that time? The friends of so-called liberty, Conrad von Burgsdorff and General Kalkstein, the leaders of the noble party who wished to enslave the common man in the interests of a caste.

This is not an isolated case. To-day, asks Treitschke, who are the true Liberals? Are they the partisans of universal suffrage? It is quite untrue that the effect of universal suffrage is radical; the truth is that its effect is incalculable. The man who thinks that the external mechanism of the vote can create a true liberty is a mere radical doctrinaire. It leads visibly to a weakening of parliament. It is impossible out of this welter of clerical, political, and economic groups to form a majority capable of exercising a decisive influence upon the government. And that, quite apart from the true observation of a French historian that nothing can be less Liberal than the people.

Those who affirm that Germany is illiberal because she cannot establish party government overlook the peculiar character of the Imperial constitution. The Chancellor, the only responsible functionary, has the exclusive duty of obeying the orders of the Federal Council, whose members represent twenty-five governments. It is therefore his duty to represent opinions which in certain circumstances are not his own. Moreover, the constitution of the Empire lays down that a member of the Federal Council cannot be at the same time a member of the Reichstag, while the heads of the main branches of the Imperial administration must be *ipso facto* members of the Federal Council. Thus a parliamentary government is impossible by the terms of the constitution.

None the less, Treitschke adds, there is no State in Europe in which the parliamentary criticism of administration is so strict or so honest as in Germany; and this is because in Germany the government stands face to face with parliament as a real and genuine power. In England it is only the opposition that can criticize the acts of the administration. And the criticism is always moderate in tone, because it is a case of one hand washing the other: the opposition knows that it may very soon be itself in power and the butt of criticism. In Germany, on the other hand, the opposition can push its criticism to extremes because it knows that it will never be in power.

But liberty does not consist only in a central constitution. The constitutional life of the State, if it is to be healthy and active, presupposes a vigorous local self-government. It is of the essence of political freedom that the will of the State should be carried into effect not only by means of permanent officials, but by means of the administrative autonomy of communes and groups of communes. From this point of view the north of Germany is more free than the south, despite appearances to the contrary. There is no administrative autonomy in Bavaria; there is a system of prefectures, though in a tempered form, a thing absolutely foreign to the Prussian organization. In general, Northern Germany is far more careful than Southern to preserve the free movement of personality, habituated as the latter is to a Napoleonic régime.

As the reader can see, Treitschke's political conception harmonizes exactly with that of the jurists, and represents a form of Liberalism doubtless in many respects at variance with Western Liberalism, but at bottom inspired by the same motives, and equally tending to find in the autonomous personality the source of a rich and varied political life.

4. A. J. P. TAYLOR: The Course of German History*

A. J. P. Taylor finds the unification of Germany both a confirmation of and a major spur to the basic trends of German politics.† There is no doubt here about the death of liberalism, the aristocratic hold on the state, and the heavy weight of military compulsion. Interesting also is the decisive role attributed to Bismarck in creating the unification and the belittling of the importance of nationalism. One might note also a view of German character, or at least of the nature of German soldiers in 1870, which is not too different from that of the German nationalist historians of the time. In addition to the assessment of these major points, a further question might be raised: Does the distinctiveness of Professor Taylor's approach lie in important new views or information, or in the vigor of his style and the confidence of his often ironical generalizations?

One aim Bismarck never pursued: that of uniting all Germans in a single national state. Greater Germany would mean the end of Junker Prussia. The Junkers had neither the numbers nor the capacity to run all central Europe; instead German radicalism would run Prussia. A Prussian diplomat once said to Bismarck: "Our power must find its limits when the supply of Junker officers gives out." Bismarck replied: "I cannot say that in public, but it is the basis of my plans." Greater Germany, too, would be predominantly Roman Catholic: in 1855 52 per cent of the population of the German Confederation was Roman Catholic, as against 35 per cent if the Austrian lands were excluded. Above all, Greater Germany would mean a Greater German foreign policy, protection, that is, of the German communities in eastern and south-eastern Europe, conflict therefore with Russia to the ruin of the Junkers. For co-operation between Russia and Prussia was vital for the subjugation of Poland and so for the security of the Junker estates. Ultimately Greater Germany, with its programme of central Europe united under German authority, implied conflict not only with Russia, but with all the world; a conflict which Bismarck knew the Junkers were not powerful enough to sustain. Bismarck was ceaselessly active and his mind endlessly fertile in expedients, but in the last resort, his policy was, like Metternich's, negative: to bar the way to Greater Germany. Metternich and Bismarck both despaired of the old order for which

* From A. J. P. Taylor, *The Course of German History,* pp. 102, 107–20. Capricorn Edition.

† See Chapter 6, on the revolution of 1848.

alone they cared. Metternich defended the old order without hoping for success. Bismarck went with the new forces in order to draw their sting. He conjured up the phantom of unification in order to avoid the reality. . . .

To finish Austria off quickly, Bismarck made alliances with the three revolutionary "master" nations of 1848—with Italy, with the Magyars, and with German radicalism. With Italy, the alliance (made April 8th, 1866) was formal, an offensive alliance of two states. With Hungary, the alliance was implicit, but none the less real: the Magyars, still subjected to Vienna, hampered the Austrian defence, and Bismarck's victory gave them virtual independence. With the German radicals, the alliance was political, expressed in Bismarck's proposal of April 9th, 1866, for a German parliament elected by direct universal suffrage. This proposal marked the decisive breach with conservative Austria and the idea of the Holy Alliance; it marked equally the final breach with the Prussian liberals and with all those who hoped for reform in Germany by consent. Universal suffrage was not liberal, but revolutionary; and it had been persistently urged on Bismarck by the revolutionary Socialist, Lassalle, as a means of swamping the liberal lawyers of the Prussian parliament, with their middle-class constitutional principles. Bismarck stood Lassalle's idea on its head. Lassalle intended to enfranchise the industrial workers, trained by economic disputes to be the enemies of the liberal capitalists. Bismarck was concerned, in a Germany where two-thirds of the population lived on the land, to enfranchise the conservative peasantry. When later Germany became predominantly urban Bismarck's calculation seemed to have failed; and in his long struggle against the Social Democrats he himself confessed as much. Yet in an even longer run his calculation proved right. The masses, whether rural or urban, cared for material benefits, not for legal principles; and the revolutionary idea of the sovereignty of the people killed the liberal doctrines of respect for law and for established rights. Lassalle had already offered Bismarck his alliance to smash the Prussian constitution, if Bismarck in return would curb the economic absolutism of the capitalists and give the workers social security. Lassalle was a visionary, a general without an army—as Bismarck said: "What could the poor devil offer me?" He was repudiated by his fellow Socialists, Marx and Engels. But they too wrote triumphantly of Bismarck doing their work for them: the more centralized and powerful the German state, the easier it would be for them to take it over. Despite their theoretical enthusiasm for the great ideas of the French revolution, they saw in the Junker conquest of Germany and the Junker defeat of the German middle class nothing but gain. Thus the offer of universal suffrage completed the squaring of the circle by which Bismarck made the Junkers, the weakest and most reactionary social force in Germany, the welcome allies of all that was most progressive and powerful. The capitalists accepted Junker rule because it gave them prosperity and unification; the working classes accepted Junker rule because it gave them social security and the vote. The only loss was Freedom, and that is not an item which appears in a balance sheet or in a list of trade union benefits.

The proposal of universal suffrage shaped the future character of Germany. It miscarried in April 1866 as a practical manœuvre. The masses did not yet count as a political force; they could not be conjured into existence overnight by a Prussian manifesto. The few middle-class radicals, whether in Prussia or outside it, were not won over. For, despite their radicalism, they still attached importance to constitutional procedure, and could not so easily forget Bismarck's unconstitutional rule in Prussia. Moreover, universal suffrage estranged the moderate realist liberals of the National Union, who had hitherto favoured Prussian leadership in Germany, as the easier, more moderate way. As a result when, in June 1866, the dispute between Prussia and Austria broke out into war, all German opinion, except that of a few anti-Austrian irreconcilables, was on the Austrian side. Nothing could be more false than to suppose that the war of 1866 was, on the Prussian side, a people's war. In those parts of Prussia which were more German than Prussian, in the Rhineland in particular, there was considerable resistance to the call-up of reservists, and demonstrations against the war took place even in Berlin. At the Federal Diet, all the states not absolutely under Prussia's guns voted in condemnation of Prussia; and though this vote expressed primarily the opinion of the princes, it represented also the feeling of their liberal middle-class parliaments. The armies of the German states fought against Prussia willingly if not enthusiastically. None of the states except Saxony would agree, even at this crisis, to a common plan of defence or to make sacrifices for the common cause: this did not prove that they desired a Prussian victory, but merely demonstrated that a league of sovereign states is incapable even of self-preservation. In short, Germany was conquered not united. . . .

The Prussian parliament had been dissolved at the beginning of the war, and new elections were held on the day of the battle of Sadowa. The liberals, though reduced, were returned with a majority; but they realized that a new dissolution, after the news of victory, would ruin them. The moderates broke away from the Progressive party to form the National Liberal party, and on September 3rd, 1866, the Prussian parliament gave Bismarck by 230 votes to 75 an indemnity for the unconstitutional collection of taxes. The vote of September 3rd was as decisive a landmark in the history of Germany as was the Bill of Rights in the history of England or the oath of the tennis court in the history of France. In each case the struggle between crown and parliament reached its term; but in Prussia it was the crown which won. German liberalism, as expressed in the Frankfort assembly of 1848, had never fought a real enemy and therefore had no prospect of real success. Prussian liberalism had been fighting a real battle, however feebly, and would have won a real victory, if Bismarck had once lost his grasp on affairs. After September 3rd liberalism was dead in Prussia. The Prussian crown was a military monarchy and needed a parliament only to consent to its expenditure for military purposes; yet the liberals agreed that the King had done right to raise money for the army without the agreement of parliament. The liberals did not sacrifice their principles from fear or for material gain; they were bewitched by success, and success was the condition on which the Hohenzollern monarchy retained its power. The capitalist middle classes ceased on September 3rd to demand control of the state; they accepted Junker rule and confined their liberalism to hoping that this rule would be exercised in a liberal spirit—"liberal administration," not liberal government, became their aim.

The abdication of the Prussian liberals and the defeat of parliamentary government had a profound social result. Parliament did not control the state; therefore it could never be for the individual the path to power. Henceforth only men of the second rank went from the middle classes into politics. The intellectual ability of the politicians steadily, relentlessly, declined; all that survived was the gift of sterile negative criticism. Political parties became inevitably interest groups, solely concerned to win concessions from the state, but never supposing that they might have to accept responsibility themselves. The really able and ambitious members of the middle class shunned politics and turned exclusively to industry and finance. As Sombart, the great economic historian, wrote in 1903: "With us there is no diversion of talent into the field of politics, as in other countries. Neither the rich, nor what is more important, the gifted members of the middle class are withdrawn from economic life to devote themselves to politics." As a result the direction of German economic development was far more skilful, far more systematic than it was in other countries. German industry was directed by men of education and vision; no wonder it soon surpassed all the rest of the world. But there was something more. The leaders of industry were not primarily concerned with wealth nor with mere technical achievement. They were driven on by the same longing for power and the same desire to make their country great as in England and France led men to take up a political career. German industry therefore was a fighting, conquering industry, concentrating on the goods which make a state powerful, not on the goods which make a people prosperous. Germany predominated in heavy industry and in chemistry, in the weapons of war and in the scientific substitutes which lessened her dependence on supplies from overseas—again a preparation for war. All the talent of Germany sought a substitute in industry for the political power which they had renounced on September 3rd, 1866. They strengthened the military monarchy and urged it on to conquer others in order to console themselves for the fact that they had been themselves conquered. . . .

The success of Bismarck was so rapid and so perfect that many observers, both then and later, accepted it as inevitable. The development of German nationalism, and perhaps even the growth of German economic power, were inevitable: but there was nothing inevitable in the particular form they took. Without Bismarck the unification of Germany might have been accomplished against both the Prussian monarchy and the Prussian landowners; and without Bismarck's success German industrial development would certainly have taken other, less brutal, forms. To unite Germany under Prussia was to fly in the face of all the rules, a gigantic *tour de force,* and one which had later to be paid for by Germany, and still more by Europe, in many years of suffering. Still less inevitable was Bismarck's victory over the European powers who had for so long maintained German disunity. Bismarck owed his success to the disunion and lack of will of his opponents. A coalition, or even a prolonged war, would have ruined him. But all sense of European solidarity had vanished. Each Power pursued its own ends recklessly: Russia thinking only of the Black Sea, Napoleon III scheming for a stroke of prestige, and Austria conducting a series of contradictory policies, all of them selfish. The old community of aristocratic interests had broken down; a new community of interests between the peoples had not grown up. Bismarckian Germany was Europe's reward. The isolated combatants lacked all persistence. Neither Austria in 1866 nor France in 1870 would bid *va banque,* and that was the only call to make against a state and a class which had always lived on the margin of existence. After Sadowa the Habsburg monarchy thought only of preserving its dynastic position; after the fall of Paris the French peasantry and bourgeoisie thought only of preserving their comfortable economic position. The price of resistance which they then refused to pay was later charged a hundredfold against their descendants.

But it seems inadequate to explain Bismarck's success solely by the mistakes of his opponents. At the time, and for many years after, the Prussian victories were regarded as a proof of the strength of nationalism, and by a strange chain of reasoning Bismarck, thus supposed to owe his victory to nationalism, was himself decked out as a national enthusiast. In fact German nationalism had little more to do with the victories of 1866 and 1870 than with the victories of 1813. In 1866 German national feeling, so far as it existed, was almost united against Prussia; in 1870 nationalist professors killed Frenchmen from their university chairs, but the real war was fought by a Prussian officer class to whom national enthusiasm was altogether repugnant. William I represented the sentiments of his fellow officers when he tried to evade the Imperial Crown and when he refused to speak to Bismarck on the day that the Crown was forced upon him.

A later, more materialist generation found the explanation of Prussia's victory in her superiority in men and in material equipment. But this was to date back to 1866 and to 1870 the circumstances of 1914 or of 1940. In 1866 Prussia had a population of 18 million against Austria's population of 33 million. She added 3 million by the annexations of 1866 (a majority of them, however, unwilling and discontented subjects) and controlled a further 3 million through the North German Federation. Alliance with the south German states brought the total in 1870 to just under 40 million (annexation of Alsace and Lorraine carried the total to 41 million in 1871), but only the Prussian element in these was effectively organized for war. The French population was 37 million, and, as the birth-rate was lower, the proportion of men in the fighting years was higher than in Prussia. Equally mythical was Prussia's economic advantage. Her production of coal passed the French figure by about 1860, and by 1870 was about double; her production of iron and steel did not surpass that of France until after 1871. Moreover Prussia was actually inferior in the application of industry to war. In 1866 she possessed a rifle much superior to the Austrian musket; but Prussian artillery was inferior in number, calibre, and conduct to the Austrian. In 1870 not only was French artillery superior to Prussian, but the *chassepot,* the French rifle, was superior to the Prussian needle gun. In fact Prussia won despite the fact that Krupps were inferior to Skoda in 1866 and to Schneider-Creusot in 1870. Prussia had not even more railways than France: the difference was that she knew how to use them.

That was the core of the matter. Prussia's triumph was a triumph of will, not of material superiority, a triumph of planning, of forethought, of conscious direction. The Prussian generals were commonplace enough. Not only Bismarck, but Prince Frederick Charles, himself a distinguished general, spoke contemptuously of them. What was not commonplace was the Prussian General Staff, applying business methods to the conduct of an army. As always, "war was the national industry of Prussia," and the Prussian staff officers brought to war accuracy, precision, system. The basis of their success was the railway timetable. And behind that lay the sandy wastes of eastern Germany which had compelled their owners for long centuries to a ruthless relentless efficiency. But there was something more. Not all the planning of the general staff could have brought victory without the endurance of the Prussian soldier. He could march further, live on harder rations, stand heavier casualties than the soldiers of Austria or of France. Yet he was not, like the Austrian or French soldier, a long-term conscript, hardened by long years of military discipline. He was a citizen, recalled from civil life or soon to enter it. Therefore, added to his hardness, he possessed initiative, a civilian readiness to act for himself but in conformity to a military purpose. Against the well-drilled obedience of regular armies or even the patriotic enthusiasm of national levies, the Prussians brought the irresistible spirit of Crusaders. They were Ironsides like the men of Cromwell, inspired by belief in a cause. But in what cause? In nothing higher than the cause of conquest. German nationalists had long regarded the weakness of Germany as evidence of their lack of freedom; therefore, if Germany was powerful, Germans would automatically be free. Tamed by the Lutheran tradition, itself the product of the failures of the sixteenth century, and dispirited by the political failures of the nineteenth century, the Germans sought freedom in the conquest of others.

Convinced that they were fighting in a sacred cause, the Germans felt morally superior to their opponents as, centuries before, the Teutonic Knights had felt superior to the heathen of the Baltic, and introduced into the warfare of civilized nations the ruthless barbarity which they had inherited from their eastern borders. For long enough, and particularly since the time of the Enlightenment, the western world had seen only the western face of Germany—the Germany of literature and music, the Germany of liberalism and scholarship, the Germany of peaceful industry. In 1870 Germany first turned to the west her eastern face, the face which she wore towards the Slavs, the face of the intolerant exterminator and overlord. In England, and even in France, men of liberal mind refused to believe the record of German brutality or, at the most, expected the Germans to improve when they had had more experience of the ways of conquest. The Germans, it was argued, were merely conquering

France, as seventy years before Napoleon had conquered Germany. But Napoleon's armies marched under the banner of an idea, the German army under none. Prussia for the sake of Prussia; Germany for the sake of Germany; ultimately, world power for the sake of world power: such was the creed of the new Crusaders, a creed which could never win converts. The war of 1870 made Germany the strongest power in Europe, dominant as Spain had been in the sixteenth century and as France had been first under Louis XIV and then under Napoleon. Each of her predecessors had stood for something: Spain for the Counter-Reformation, Monarchist France for aristocratic civilization, Napoleonic France for equality and civil liberty. Germany stood for nothing, except German power. The organizing capacity, the selfless devotion, the critical intelligence, the scientific curiosity, which in western Europe were liberating men from the tyranny of others and, still more, from the tyranny of nature, were in Germany employed to liberate the German state from the control either of its neighbours or of its subjects. The highest faculties of the mind, and these the Germans possessed, were put to the service of a mindless cause.

The Reich which Bismarck established in 1871 is often spoken of as a compromise. But this is the wrong term. Compromise implies a mutual acceptance of the claims of opponents, an agreement to give way in the last resort. British history has been made by a series of true compromises. The landed classes compromised with the merchants at the beginning of the eighteenth century; this coalition compromised with the industrial capitalists in the time of Peel; and Peel's coalition has compromised with the industrial workers in our own day. Since the days of Cromwell there has never been in England a class or a party determined to force through its extreme claims, whatever the cost; the terrible exception was in the early months of 1914. No such compromise took place in Germany. The Bismarckian Reich was a dictatorship imposed on the conflicting forces, not an agreement between them. The parties did not compromise; they were manipulated by Bismarck—pushed down when they threatened to become strong, helped up when they appeared weak. Bismarck stood at the centre of a multiple seesaw, tilting it now this way, now that in order to keep his artificial creation in some sort of equilibrium; but the inevitable result was to give Germany ever more violent and uncontrollable oscillations. Bismarck's only asset was success. He had defeated liberalism; therefore the Junkers accepted him despite the national Germany he had forced on them. He had united Germany; therefore the middle classes accepted him despite the defeat of liberalism. But success is a wasting asset. It was effective in 1866 and in 1871; the memory of it was effective for the last time in 1887. In the long run Bismarck's system could not run on the reputation of the successes he had achieved twenty years before. A new justification had to be found—or else new successes had to be won against foreign powers. Bismarck's Reich was designed to give Germany stability and peace; but ultimately it doomed Germany to upheaval and war. Bismarck possessed political genius of the highest order; and he used that genius to prevent in Germany the liberal revolution which had transformed England in the seventeenth century and France in 1789. As a result nothing was solved. The disease was forced inward until it poisoned the body of Germany incurably, and the body of all Europe as well.

The Imperial constitution of 1871 was a hotch-potch, hastily put together by Bismarck to serve his own ends. Except for the change of name it was little more than an enlargement of the constitution of the North German Federation of 1867. Show-piece of the constitution was the Reichstag, elected by universal suffrage, the incorporation of German radical demands. The Reichstag could hold debates and could pass (though not initiate) laws; its consent was necessary to the expenditure of money. But it possessed no powers. The constitution laid down that the Imperial Chancellor was "responsible," but it did not say to whom—certainly not to the Reichstag. A majority in the Reichstag could do nothing against the Chancellor: if they voted against him, he did not resign, but dissolved the Reichstag. The Reichstag could certainly reject laws proposed by the Chancellor, but these laws contained reforms which the majority desired: their complaint was not against laws, but against a failure to legislate. The financial control was illusory. The revenue of the Reich was entirely derived from customs and excise, dues permanently fixed; and whenever these were changed the discussion usually turned on the economic policy involved, not on the way in which these dues would be spent. If the balance sheet of the Reich showed a deficit, the Reichstag was not asked to vote taxes to make up the balance: the states had to provide "matricular contributions" from their internal revenue, deficiency grants levied in proportion to the population of each state. When later the expenditure of the Reich increased, these matricular contributions became a regular annual item. The Reichstag which approved the expenditure did not have to provide the money; and the states which provided the money had no control over its expenditure. In any case much of the expenditure of the Reich—the Civil List, the administration, the diplomatic service—was included in the constitution and did not come up for annual review. Bismarck attempted to make the army grant permanent also, but in this he failed and had to be content with a grant for seven years at a time. Hence the crises which occurred at septennial intervals—in 1879, 1886, and 1893, when it was necessary to whip up enough enthusiasm to carry the army grant for a further seven years. Bismarck did not provide for a navy. Hence, in the twentieth century, another series of crises had to be manufactured first to establish a permanent naval grant, and then to increase it.

Bismarck's constitution was supposed to be federal, but its federalism was fraudulent, window dressing to make the dictatorship of Prussia more respectable. The few states which had been allowed to survive in 1866 were humble Prussian dependencies. The states south of the Main, Bavaria in particular, put on a brave appearance of independence and bargained obstinately before they accepted the Reich in 1871. But they too were unreal: they had owed their existence solely to the protection of Austria and of France, and this protection had ceased. Their military effort of 1866 had been contemptible, and Bismarck, if he wished, could have ordered them out of existence. Their survival suited

Bismarck's purpose. Their abolition would have put Bismarck too much in the hands of the radical nationalists and would have left the King of Prussia in undesired isolation. The sham existence of these kings and princes helped to cloak the very real existence of the Prussian monarchy and of Prussian military power. Bismarck played off the states against the Reichstag, as in his system of taxation; and the kings and princes kept their titles in return for acting as Prussia's agents in the government of Germany, much as they had acted as the agents of Napoleon at the beginning of the century.

It would be wrong to conclude from this that Germany was a completely unified state. What existed was not state patriotism but particularism, a feeling of local pride and loyalty which was especially strong in the former Free Cities. The citizen of Nuremberg still thought of himself as a citizen of Nuremberg, not as a Bavarian; and for that matter many Rhinelanders still thought of themselves as Rhinelanders, not as Prussians. As a result, the political energies of the best Germans went into local government and made of it a model to all the world. But this admirable development had no relevance to imperial affairs, or to the story of Germany as a great power.

The government of Germany in fact, was a dictatorship in the hands of the King of Prussia. He delegated his powers to two agencies: military matters to the general staff, civil matters to the Imperial Chancellor, and the two dealt with each other as independent, often hostile, authorities. The chief of the general staff was, in his sphere, absolute. He made his military plans and conducted his own foreign policy without consulting the Chancellor; and on each septennial interval issued orders to the Chancellor and the Reichstag as to his military needs. In Bismarck's time, the soldiers were kept in their place not by any constitutional provision, but through Bismarck's personal influence with William I; after Bismarck's time the situation was reversed and the Chancellor was kept in his place by the influence of the soldiers. On the Chancellor rested the conduct of all German affairs other than the army. . . .

The legislative system of Germany was outwardly democratic; the government of Germany was as autocratic as the government of Tsarist Russia, in flagrant contrast not only to the government of the countries of western Europe and of Hungary, but even of Austria, where, until the beginning of the twentieth century, the Prime Minister was supported or overthrown by a parliamentary majority. The fate of Germany was determined by the King-Emperor's absolute will, influenced in Bismarck's time by good advice, influenced after his time by bad advice or by none at all. The King-Emperor straddled between Prussia and Germany: kept Germany under Prussian control and, at the same time, tried to persuade the Junkers not to be too openly contemptuous of the German middle classes.

The essence of Bismarck's system was that he was saving the Junkers despite themselves. Bismarck recognized that the Junkers could survive only by putting themselves at the head of national Germany; and he put them there despite the Junker distaste, to call it no more, for nationalist enthusiasm. Most of the Junkers hated the German idea and hankered for the gentlemanly days of the

Holy Alliance. They were jealous of Bismarck—a landowner like themselves who had become a European statesman and a prince—and they resisted many of his administrative concessions to the liberal classes. Hence the period of Bismarck saw a paradoxical system of government in which the long-term interests of the Junkers were served against the wishes of the Junkers themselves. In fact, just as Bismarck gave national Germany the unity which it lacked the confidence to achieve for itself, so he tried to give the Junkers the vision and commonsense which they could not find in their own brains.

The most obvious side of the Bismarckian system was thus a balance between the landowners of eastern Germany and the liberal middle classes, military power in the hands of the Junkers, economic power in the hands of the capitalists, the power of the state in the hands of Bismarck. For each the bargain implied certain conditions. The Prussian nobles retained their social superiority and the monopoly of army commissions, on the condition of acquiescing in liberal reforms and nationalist claptrap. The liberals obtained all the classical liberal demands—modern administration, freedom of enterprise, secular education—on condition that they did not insist on office, still less power, in the state. Bismarck rode above both sides on the condition of success: his unrivalled ability foresaw and anticipated every danger.

5. FRIEDRICH MEINECKE: The German Catastrophe*

Friedrich Meinecke (1862–1954) was one of the outstanding German historians of this century, both as teacher and scholar. He edited the leading historical journal in Germany until 1936 and after World War II helped found the Free University of West Berlin. His political background was conservative, but World War I and Nazi rule weakened his belief in power politics and undemocratic rule. Soon after World War II he undertook an assessment of Germany's political tragedy, stressing the gulf between political and private ethics. He sees the role of unification in promoting political and diplomatic immorality, though he notes that Bismarck's methods were not unique; but he also believes that many hopeful elements persisted after unification and that Germany's fate was still open.

In the era when the Empire was founded, the aspects of Prussian militarism which were bad and dangerous for the general well-being were obscured by the imposing proof of its power and discipline in its service for national unity and in the construction of Bismarck's Empire. The military man now seemed to be a consecrated spirit—the lieutenant moved through the world as a young god and the civilian reserve lieutenant at least as a demigod. He had to rise to be reserve officer in order to exert his full influence in the upper-middle-class world and above all in the state administrtion. Thus militarism penetrated civilian life. Thus there developed a conventional Prussianism (*Borussismus*), a naïve self-admiration in Prussian character, and together with it a serious narrowing of intellectual and political outlook. Everything was dissolved into a rigid

* From Friedrich Meinecke, *The German Catastrophe,* Sidney B. Fay, trans. (Cambridge: Harvard University Press, 1950), pp. 12–15.

conventionalism. One must have observed this type in countless examples with one's own eyes in the course of a long life, one must have felt it in one's own self, struggled with it, and gradually liberated one's self from it, in order to understand its power over men's minds—in order to understand finally the effect of the touching comedy in the Potsdam church on March 21, 1933, which Hitler played with Hindenburg beside the tomb of Frederick the Great. For here National Socialism was expected to appear as the heir and propagator of all the great and beautiful Prussian traditions.

A man like Theodore Fontane, whose lifework represents as none other all that was great and beautiful in the Prussian tradition, could, in a letter written in 1897, near the end of his life when he had grown critical and keen of insight, utter words of displeasure about the Prussian world around him. His testimony is not to be rejected simply because it is sharply exaggerated in every direction. "Borussism," he wrote, "is the lowest form of culture that has ever existed. Only Puritanism is still worse, because it is completely given to lying." And another time he wrote: "What must be crushed first of all is militarism."

This evil Borussism and militarism was like a heavy mortgage imposed on Bismarck's work and inherited from him by his hybrid successor, Hitler. There was, however, also something in the immediate contribution of Bismarck himself which lay on the border between good and evil and which in its further development was to expand more on the side of evil. The truth of this criticism would never be readily conceded by those who grew great under Bismarck's work and richly enjoyed its blessings. We Germans often felt so free and proud, in contrast with the whole previous German past, in this mightily flourishing Empire of 1871 which gave living space to every one of us! But the staggering course of World War I and still more of World War II makes it impossible to pass over in silence the query whether the germs of the later evil were not really implanted in Bismarck's work from the outset. It is a query which courageous and unfettered historical thinking must pose in regard to every great and apparently beneficent historical phenomenon in which a degeneration takes place. One then breathes the atmosphere of the tragedy of history, of human and historical greatness, and also the problematical uncertainty which will ever hover around a Bismarck and his work—while Hitler's work must be reckoned as the eruption of the satanic principle in world history.

Consider now the year 1866 and Bismarck's blood and iron policy. Today we listen with more emotion to the voices which at that time expressed concern over the great evils of the future—voices of such important men as Jakob Burckhardt and Constantin Frantz, and one might add as a third the queer Swabian, Christian Planck. Bismarck's policy, according to them, was destroying certain foundations of Western culture and the community of states and was a really deep-reaching evolution which was opening the prospect of further revolutions and an era of wars. It meant, they said, the victory of Machiavellism over the principles of morality and justice in international relations and it let perish the finer and higher things of culture in a striving after power and pleasure.

Let us be honest. However one-sided these complaints may have been, there is a grain of truth in them. On the other hand, there are plenty of voices to defend Bismarck. They call attention to all the similar examples of Machiavellian practices in the rest of Europe of that day and especially to the fact that Bismarck himself recognized limits to his policy of force. These defenders likewise point out that in his peace policy after 1871 Bismarck did good service to the Western community of nations. "You know I cannot love Bismarck," a Danish historian friend said to me during the Third Reich, "but now I must say: Bismarck belongs to *our* world."

One must regard Bismarck as a borderline case. He still had in mind to some extent the conception of a synthesis of power and culture as it was understood by the leaders of the movement for German unity. These leaders themselves, with Treitschke at their head, originally were seriously offended by Bismarck's first steps in the period of the constitutional conflict, but became his defenders and admirers as a consequence of the war of 1866. The result was that in the synthesis of power and culture, of the things of the state and the things of the spirit, the preponderance slowly but steadily shifted further over to the side of power and its domain. From my own development I can bear witness to this—until, in the years before the First World War, a reaction of humanitarian feeling once more began to set in.

One can always object that the power-state and Machiavellism were not confined to Germany, that they were more often preached but not more strongly practiced by us Germans. This view is quite true. Specifically German, however, was the frankness and nakedness of the German power-state and Machiavellism, its hard and deliberate formulation as a principle of conduct, and the pleasure taken in its reckless consequences. Specifically German also was the tendency to elevate something primarily practical into a universal world-view theory. It was a serious thing for the future that these ideas about power-state and Machiavellism, at first expressed merely as theories, might become practical weapons in the hands of ruling authorities. The German power-state idea, whose history began with Hegel, was to find in Hitler its worst and most fatal application and extension.

The degeneration of the German people is what we are here trying, by groping and probing, to understand merely in its rough outlines. How difficult it is, however, to sketch a picture of the spiritual and cultural condition of Germany in the first decades after the founding of the Empire in 1871, of the good as well as the bad germs in it! The judgment commonly expressed today, often merely parroting Nietzsche, that liberalism had become flat and shallow, settles nothing. The silver age of classical liberalism, of which we spoke, still persisted and still produced in art and science much that was brilliant, while the average level and everyday taste remained decidedly low. But no one then would have thought possible the emergence in educated Germany of a phenomenon like National Socialism—only the uneducated, proletarian Germany of Social Democracy was feared as a serious menace to our culture in the future. We, especially we younger Germans, felt exceedingly safe, entirely too safe, in the possession of a high national and cultural heritage. Here and there, however, clouds began to appear in this bright sky.

6. ERICH EYCK: Bismarck and the German Empire*

Erich Eyck is a German historian who has written major works on the Weimar Republic as well as a three-volume study of Bismarck, from which a lecture series at Oxford was distilled. His account of unification is largely narrative, but an interpretive framework does emerge. Without denying the unfortunate results of unification, particularly a militarist spirit, he stops short of attributing them to any basic flaw in German character, seeing much more specific causes instead. And he retains some of the excitement about the achievement of unification which a non-German perhaps cannot share, but should understand.

It is not possible to tell here the story of the war and Bismarck's part in it. I propose to deal here only with the most important results of the victory: the unification of the German people in a great Reich, the head of which—the Prussian King—became Deutscher Kaiser (German Emperor).

The idea that this war had to bear fruit in German unity was, from the outset, strong in many minds. The overwhelming majority of the population in Northern Germany was in favour of it, and the same may be said of the majority in Baden and Hesse-Darmstadt. . . .

Nevertheless, in one point, and that perhaps is the most important of all, Bismarck's heritage has outlasted all the changes of the age. The militarism he impressed upon the German nation by his doctrine of "blood and iron" and its brilliant and triumphant realization remained overwhelmingly strong and proved stronger than the bitter disappointments of the first World War and the Weimar Republic, in which at least a part of the people tried to do without it.

One reason for the strength of German militarism is intimately connected with the peace which ended the war against France. As a result of this peace treaty two French provinces, Alsace and Lorraine, were torn from a defeated France and annexed to a victorious Germany. Bismarck's motive was not that historical romanticism which German historians professed, claiming that these two provinces had once, centuries ago, belonged to the Holy Roman Empire and should now return to a rejuvenated fatherland. All that he contemptuously termed a "Professor's idea." In a conversation during the war, in Vienna, Adolphe Thiers, the French statesman and historian, asked the great German historian, Leopold Ranke: "Whom are you fighting now after the downfall of the Napoleonic Empire?" Ranke answered: "Louis XIV." Bismarck would never have made a statement of this kind. As a practical statesman he knew that the historical process cannot be begun afresh after centuries during which populations have changed their feelings and interests. He knew that the population of Alsace and Lorraine felt French and would for a long time continue to be a very uncomfortable part of Germany. If he nevertheless insisted upon

* From Erich Eyck, *Bismarck and the German Empire* (London: George Allen & Unwin Ltd., 1958), pp. 174, 184–86. Reprinted by permission of George Allen & Unwin Ltd.

the annexation, it was for military reasons. He believed that the two provinces would be indispensable for the defence of Germany, especially South-western Germany, against a new French attack. Even so, he had doubts whether it would be advantageous to take Metz, the population of which was entirely French in feeling and language. But at last he gave way to the expostulations of the generals and the wishes of his King.

At this time Gladstone was Prime Minister of England. He was shocked when he heard of the German intention to annex the two provinces against the manifest wishes of their population. He deplored the relapse into "the old and cruel practice of treating the population of a civilized European country as mere chattels."

Here, he wrote to Queen Victoria, a general principle is involved whose violation "has caused much disturbance and much bloodshed in subsequent times to Europe." He wanted the neutral countries jointly to protest against the annexation, but was defeated in his cabinet. When it was apparent that the annexation would be carried out, he wrote to Granville: "I have an apprehension that this violent laceration and transfer is to lead us from bad to worse, and to the beginning of a new series of European complications."

How true Gladstone's prophecy was, everybody knows now. The annexations have made a real and lasting peace between Germany and France impossible. Bismarck's sleep at night was disturbed by the *Cauchemar des coalitions* (the nightmare of coalitions) against Germany. The whole European continent became an armed camp. Germany's first duty seemed to be to arm herself more and more strongly. Nobody seemed as important as the soldier and the officer, and militarism won a complete ascendancy.

But his criticism should not lead us to overlook Bismarck's enormous achievement, the fulfilment of the dream of the German nations, their unification in a powerful and glorious Empire. To understand what this meant for the generation which had longed for it and fought for it, we may read a letter which the historian Heinrich von Sybel wrote to his friend and colleague, Herman Baumgarten, when the Empire was proclaimed: "Tears run down my cheeks. By what have we deserved the grace of God, that we are allowed to live to see such great and mighty deeds. What for twenty years was the substance of all our wishes and efforts, is now fulfilled in such an immeasurably magnificent way." No doubt millions of the best Germans felt the same. It is not in every century that Fate allows a statesman to evoke feelings of this strength in a whole nation. And those statesmen who succeed in doing so are the heroes and the great men of history. Among these great men Bismarck will always be classed, and the critics of his methods and of his personality never can, nor will, doubt his singular greatness and his everlasting glory.

Chapter XI.

ANTI-SEMITISM

THE HISTORY of anti-Semitism in the nineteenth century has proved curiously hard to write. Aspects of it can be studied. Anti-Semitic writings are obviously open to interpretation; much of the research on anti-Semitism focuses on doctrines and constitutes an important part of the intellectual history of the period after 1870. Beyond this, it is possible to study anti-Semitic organizations, though less has been done here because the records are hard to get at, and many groups were too small and ephemeral to leave significant traces. Yet neither formal doctrines nor explicit organizations represented the whole of anti-Semitism in the period. Key questions about the extent and intensity of anti-Semitic feeling can be answered only through a broader approach. Historians are now beginning to work on the popularization of anti-Semitism, through newspapers and the like, on the signs of anti-Semitic attitudes in political and other organizations that were not solely or primarily anti-Semitic, and on the extent and basis for anti-Semitic agitation.

The crucial problem is that anti-Semitism was a mood, a state of mind, that was not necessarily articulated or even realized by every anti-Semite. Many historians recognize the need for some effort at psychological interpretation, but this is difficult and risky in retrospect. Possibly, direct and contemporary psychological work on prejudice can illuminate the historical phenomenon, but there will be an inevitable gap then between the theory and the available evidence. Most historians, however, rely primarily on more conventional explanations and approaches. Some look particularly to the social basis. It is possible to single out certain social classes (peasants, lower middle class, aristocracy, and so on) that were open to anti-Semitism and others that were not. But the number of classes that were is so great that one might ask if this approach provides sufficiently specific explanations; and there is the problem of knowing how large a portion of each class was in fact touched by the prejudice. Another approach is political, seeing anti-Semitism as a result of political competition and manipulation; still another is intellectual, looking to the doctrinal bases of the movement and, sometimes, to the biographies of major intellectual anti-Semites. With all these approaches, however, or with combinations of them, one must ask if the anti-Semitic frame of mind is adequately conveyed and explained. And each approach gives a distinctive impression of what the essence of the phenomenon was. The political approach, for example, leads to a natural concentration on the political features of anti-Semitism, but for this period particularly these were not necessarily the most widespread or significant aspects. Anti-Semitism as a whole remains elusive.

Some of the customary problems of historical interpretation do not apply to the divergent portrayals of anti-Semitism, at least not in the usual way. No historian of any note who has written on the subject has been sympathetic to it. Degrees of passion vary; some accounts are filled with the historian's moral revulsion against anti-Semitism; others seem somewhat calmer. But one can find no real partisans among historians for anti-Semitism, unlike almost any other subject in the century. This raises difficulties in itself, however. Without some defenders, can even the most repulsive movement be adequately understood? Hannah Arendt points out that almost all the historical approaches to anti-Semitism seek explanations that leave the Jews innocent victims of a vile prejudice. Some historians barely discuss the changing position of the Jews, believing that the sentiment against Jews referred to them only in the abstract, that without any real awareness of what they were actually like or were actually doing in business or politics. This may provide salutary moral lessons against the unreason of the prejudice for the present time, but it may not represent a complete historical picture.

The moral bias of historians of anti-Semitism leads to two specific difficulties. First, since the Germans were ultimately the most dreadful anti-Semites, there have been some tendencies not only to study German anti-Semitism particularly but also to seek peculiarly German explanations for it.[1] Yet anti-Semitism went well beyond Germany, and other historians accordingly look for far broader causes. The question of whether, before World War I, there was something special about German anti-Semitism, and why, remains perhaps to be fully answered. Second, since the most obvious motivation for the study of anti-Semitism is the explanation of what it was and what it caused in the twentieth century, one must ask whether any historical account puts it in proper focus for the late nineteenth-century period itself. In particular, is it given too much importance, is too much violence attributed to it because of the historian's knowledge of its violence and importance later? Again, questions of the extent and influence of the phenomenon are essential to its interpretation; it is not enough simply to know that it was there.

Most historians view the anti-Semitism of the later nineteenth century as something new. They differ on how much relationship it had to more traditional prejudice, and they differ also on how much anti-Semitism there was earlier in the century; but they see novelty in the causes, the forms of expression, and the extent of the feeling after about 1870. Most are inclined, though from quite different perspectives, to see in anti-Semitism a profound uneasiness with many basic tendencies in European society. This inclination itself must be assessed; if it is correct, it means that a historical understanding of the phenomenon has an importance far broader than the subject itself might first suggest. And it helps to account for the diversity of approaches to the subject, for the student of anti-Semitism must establish what the basic direction of European society and politics was.

1. JAMES PARKES: Anti-Semitism*

James Parkes, an Anglican minister active in international affairs, offers a distinctively political explanation of nineteenth-century anti-Semitism. In his view, the prejudice was a political tool, not connected with the Jews directly. The following selection brings out his general approach and presents his discussion of Germany, but it should be noted that he applies his approach to

1. See, for example, Eva G. Reichmann, *Hostages of Civilization: The Social Origins of National Socialist Anti-Semitism* (Boston, 1951), pp. 236–38.

* From James Parkes, *Anti-Semitism*, pp. 20–29.

other countries as well. His claim that Germany first developed modern anti-Semitism deserves attention, but he does not posit any exclusively German features for the phenomenon in this period. Is his political approach sufficient? Does it explain why anti-Semitism was used as an argument, or why the Jews seemed a logical target for so many grievances?

The political conflicts and opportunities of the 19th century are responsible for the particular form which antisemitism takes today. . . .

During this period the electorate was growing in numbers. But it was not necessarily growing equally in education; and political questions were becoming more and more complicated. These complications inevitably involved long and bitter conflict between rival groups with different interests; and in consequence new techniques had to be evolved for securing the favour and votes of the electorate. Governments likewise needed new techniques for winning popular support. For even if a Sovereign, a Chancellor, or the President of a Council of Ministers might not be constitutionally dependent on his Parliament, it was much easier for him to rule if he could carry a majority of them with him. The success of the techniques discovered was not always proportional to their honesty or their relevance. In fact forgery, deception and red-herrings were discovered to be as capable of winning enthusiastic support, and to have as great vote-catching value, as honest expositions of policy or the intellectual enlightenment of electors.

Even in France, the oldest representative democracy in Europe, the electors could be so completely misled that in 1851 they voted enthusiastically for the abolition of their own hard won rights. In that year Louis Napoleon, nephew of the great Emperor, secured from the eight million voters of the country a majority of nearly seven million for the abolition of the Constitution, the degradation of Parliament, and the vesting of all power personally in himself. The history of political democracy is shorter, more unstable and more embarrassed than people realise.

This book is concerned with an equally striking but more comprehensive example of the capacity of European electorates to be deceived. There is no better example of this capacity than the 19th-century emergence and use of antisemitism as a political weapon. There had, of course, been feeling against the Jews among particular classes, or generally among the populace, for many centuries of European history. . . . But it had tended to dwindle in the liberal and "modern" atmosphere of the 19th century, with its contempt for the superstitions of the past. Where it had survived it was either among the more ignorant of the peasants, or among the more obstinate of those who stood to lose from the developments of the century—the old landowning aristocrats, and the clericals anxious to retain the privileged position of the Churches. They hated the entry of the Jews into their "Christian" society; they hated the democratic, urban, commercial and secular civilisation in which the emancipated Jews found themselves at home. And they suddenly discovered that this feeling, rooted both in jealousy and in ancient prejudice, was a most convenient rallying point for those who, from the most diverse points of view, disliked the 19th century; and that it was a most versatile and effective stick wherewith the conservatives might beat the progressives.

Political antisemitism had extremely little to do with the Jews as such, just as it had extremely little to do with the real reform of the many evils of the untrammelled industrialism of the century which the Jews were supposed to control or exemplify. It is necessary to be clear on this point. There *were* serious moral and social problems created by the rapid progress of industry and commerce; there *were* many spiritual and cultural values which were lost, or gravely compromised, by the headlong rush after wealth and material comfort which characterised the period. In addition, the sudden emancipation of the Jews in western Europe, and the situation of those Jews who still lived a medieval life in eastern Europe, *did* create real problems. But the political antisemitic movement has not to its record a single example of a serious attack upon any of these real problems; in consequence, it has not to its credit any real analysis or understanding either of the Jewish position, or of the evils of the century. Of both it drew an imaginary picture for its own ends. In fact, just as the evils of the century were but a small part of its life, so the reference of the antisemites to actual and precise evils and their reform formed but a small part of their armoury; and just as the Jews formed but a minute fraction of the middle classes, so actual Jewish conduct formed but a tiny part of their onslaught on "the Jews." The enemy was "Liberalism," "industrialism," "secularism"—anything the reactionaries disliked; and they found by experience that there was no better way of persuading the electors to dislike these things also than to label them "Jewish."

There was also a particular advantage in possessing so comprehensive a weapon in circumstances where both sides of the conflict were made up of alliances and coalitions between various groups. It provided the attackers with a cement to bind them together, in spite of great diversity of interest; it enabled all the enemy to be lumped together under a single head, although they also, in fact, represented all sorts of groups and interests.

Finally a word should be said here about three of the four Jewries which form the background of this chapter. Russian Jewry needs special treatment, but in Germany and France were very small Jewish communities just over and just under one per cent of the general population respectively. In the old Austro-Hungarian empire the percentage was a little bigger, but the Jews were only one among many still larger minorities, Polish, Rumanian, southern Slav and so on. In France Jews had enjoyed citizenship since the French Revolution at the end of the eighteenth century. In Germany and Austria-Hungary it came later and more partially. But in all three countries the real problems, in which Jews were involved, were those of a new industrial and urban class coming into violent clash with the old landowning and peasant society which had prevailed for centuries, but which 19th-century developments shattered. In this new society Jews found every opportunity for advancement. It was urban, they were urban; it was speculative and adventurous, so were they; their concentration in the new fields was accentuated by the fact that many fields, open to others of a comparable standing in wealth or education, were closed to Jews in Germany and Austria-Hungary. Unless they were willing to be baptized, Jews were not welcome in the armed forces or the Civil Service. This meant that in the "free" professions of medicine and law, and the many branches of commerce, journalism and entertainment, Jews were numerous. But nowhere did statistics reveal that there was a special *Jewish* aspect of the problems involved in the new society thus created; and nowhere was there an exceptional Jewish delinquency, though there was often an exceptional Jewish participation.

Much influential as well as popular journalism, for example, was in Jewish hands, and so was much popular entertainment, so that it was natural, indeed inevitable, that anyone attacking the influence of these professions in Central Europe seemed to be attacking Jews. The trouble was that he usually assumed that he was attacking *the* Jews, whereas Jews were as frequent as Christians among those who disliked the brashness, speculation and materialism of the century. For a large proportion of them remained devoutly attached to traditional orthodoxy, and saw in the new society only temptations to apostasy.

IN GERMANY

The scene of the first successful political employment of 19th century anti-semitism was the new German Empire created by Bismarck. The year was 1879. Germany had only just realised her unity. It had taken three wars—against Denmark, Austria and France—and all the skill, strategy and lack of scruple of Bismarck, to win this unity out of the kingdoms, dukedoms, principalities, free cities, and what not into which Germany was still divided even after Napoleon had unified, modernised, and co-ordinated the nine hundred odd "states" which existed at the beginning of the century. The conservatives in Germany were those who, in various forms and from various motives, wanted to retain many of these old, almost independent societies resting on land ownership and ancient rights; and the progressives, of whom the most important section was the National Liberal Party, were the party of industry and the big cities, who saw no chance of development so long as the country was divided into so many separate units, each with its own legislation, its own control over expenditure, even its barriers against its neighbours. Industry required a larger field in which to manoeuvre; raw materials and man power were not conveniently divided according to the innumerable frontiers which broke up the country. The progressives desired unity largely for the purposes of trade and business development; but there was also a strong group of intellectuals who desired it in order that the German people might take its place among the peoples of Europe as a great cultural and political unit.

Bismarck also desired unity, but for the sake of the power of the House of Prussia. For many years the progressives and he worked amicably together. As Chancellor he was not dependent on a parliamentary majority, such as an English Prime Minister would need, for he held his power from above, from the German Emperor, not from below, from the elected representatives of the people; and he even ruled without any parliamentary sanction for his budget for a period of four years. But it was convenient, and on a long view necessary, that his policy should command the support of a majority of the Parliament, and up to 1879 the progressive group had provided this. The weakness of this support was that his motives were not theirs. Though the success of his policy, and the resounding *éclat* of his three successive military victories had roused a great deal of patriotic fervour, their effect was bound to wear off in time. The business element among the progressives was ultimately more concerned with the development of what was known as "Manchesterism," the free trade, *laissez-faire* policy under which England had become astoundingly wealthy and the factory of the world. The idealist element among the progressives desired to establish in Germany the responsible, representative, parliamentary government which they admired at Westminster. But Bismarck and his Sovereign, the aged William I, abhorred both Manchesterism and parliamentary democracy, and by 1879 the Chancellor felt strong enough to do without such dubious support. In consequence he set out to disrupt the progressives and destroy their influence.

Now that the Empire was unified and at peace, Bismarck had two immediate objectives. The first was to prevent the transfer of power from the Monarchy to the Parliament, and the second was to secure independent financial resources for the Imperial Chancery, which so far had been dependent on grants made by the separate states out of which the Empire was built up, or on allocations from the Parliament. The best source of this revenue he saw in the imposition of a tariff. In neither of these objects would the progressives help him, but both would be approved or, at least, accepted by two other groups, the various nationalist and conservative elements, and the Catholic elements grouped in the Centre Party. Unfortunately none of these were friendly to him.

Bismarck had demanded £200,000,000 from France after her defeat in 1870, and France had paid this huge indemnity—twice her total annual budget—in less than three years. This vast sum threw the German economy badly out of gear. There had been a short period of wild speculation, and then, in May 1873, an appalling crash. In this speculation many of the old landowning class had badly burnt their fingers, and naturally blamed the Government's alliance with the liberal industrialists and bankers for their own follies. And in addition they did not like the secularist, or idealist, or modernist atmosphere of the new Empire. More serious had been the conflict between Bismarck and the Catholics. In the German Empire which he had created Protestants outnumbered Catholics by about two to one. The centre of the Empire was Protestant Prussia, and the Catholic south and west were consequently inclined to foster separatist tendencies, and to regret the complete exclusion of Catholic Austria from German affairs. Fearing these inclinations, and disliking the political ferment among the Catholics which had followed the Vatican Council of 1870, Bismarck decided to call them to heel. In 1873 he launched a campaign of repressive legislation against them which had no parallel in a "modern" western European State. This attack—known as the *Kulturkampf*—lasted for several years, and brought the humiliating spectacle of a modern state persecuting and even imprisoning aged and respected bishops and priests for no more than loyalty to their religion. The Catholics were certainly not likely to be easily won to support the Chancellor.

Now it happened that, as one might expect since the Jews are largely occupied with commerce, there had been some spectacular Jewish bankruptcies in the crash of 1873; and it happened that among the prominent leaders of the National Liberal Party were two Jews, Eduard Lasker and Ludwig Bamberger; and it happened that an important Catholic newspaper of the Rhineland was in the hands of a fanatical priest of the name of Augustus Rohling, who was convinced that the Jews were at the back of everything which at any moment he disliked.

Although there was no notorious event in 1879 to draw any special attention to the National Liberal Party, all of a sudden a nation-wide campaign of extraordinary violence swept Germany of which the burden was the identification of the Jews with the National Liberals, and the National Liberals with everything any good German would avoid.

The actual origins of the campaign have never been fully explored but there is little doubt that the mind behind it was the mind of Bismarck. It was not due to any hostility to Jews on the Chancellor's part. He had been helped in the critical years of his policy by a section of the Parliament in which there were some prominent Jews, of whom Lasker and Bamberger were fairly intimate personal friends; and he had been able to finance the Austrian war by the aid of a Jewish banker, Bleichroder. But something had to be done to discredit the progressives and, as Bamberger himself says in his memories of Bismarck, "it was typical of his method that, when a weapon came along which others had forged for him, he should not let go of it, but keep it in his arsenal to make use of at a convenient moment for the discomfiture of his enemy." Bismarck himself is reported to have said: "I expressed my disapproval of it, but I did nothing more, as it was a most useful means of attacking the progressives," and this pleasant equivocation he communicated to those of his entourage who had relations with the press.

That the launching of an antisemitic campaign had in Bismarck's mind nothing to do with the Jews as such is shown by the facts that one of those whom he had invited to frame the imperial Constitution, which he was now determined to maintain against the progressives, was the converted Jew, Karl Rudolf Friedenthal; that the intellectual founder of the Conservative Party to which he proposed to turn for support was another Jewish convert, Friedrich Julius Stahl; and that the man whom he had chosen to be Minister of Justice in 1879 was a third, Emil von Friedberg. In fact nothing could more clearly show the nature of modern antisemitism than its first emergence. It was a political manoeuvre which found "the Jews" useful ammunition, but had no interest in them as Jews.

Having made this discovery, the German Conservatives proceeded to develop it vigorously. An Antisemitic League was founded, and the antisemites discovered a leader in a Lutheran Court Chaplain, Adolf Stoecker, creator of the

Christian Social Workingmen's Union. It mattered nothing to the Conservatives that the reason for Stoecker's semi-socialist antisemitism was that "the Jews" were capitalists, for Stoecker himself sat in Parliament with the Conservatives; and it did not disturb Stoecker that the Conservatives supported him because they felt that his tepid socialism would be an insurance against the more violent or "Jewish" form of the disease, represented by Marx and Lasalle. It was an adequate bond of union to regard "Jews" as the enemy. Antisemitism also helped to bring the second group whose support Bismarck desired to cultivate, the Roman Catholic Centre Party, into alliance with the Protestant Conservatives. For the *Kulturkampf* could now be represented as the work of Jewish-led Liberal secularists. Indeed Bismarck's lieutenant in executing his anti-Catholic decrees had been a Jewish lawyer, Heinrich von Friedberg. One could forget that he was the brother of the Minister of Justice, and that he had been converted many years previously to Christianity; or, perhaps one remembered that he had become a Protestant and not a Roman Catholic.

It was altogether a most curious alliance, and it is not surprising that the one thing which it never seriously attempted to do was to produce a policy on the Jewish question. For on this it could never have reached agreement, since its propaganda on the subject was quite incoherent. To Stoecker and the Christian Socialists Jews were an economic class; to Rohling and the Roman Catholics they were a religious group; and to the great historian, Heinrich von Treitschke, and the Conservative intellectuals they were a race. Its real point of union was hostility not to Jewry but to the progressive ideas of liberalism; it mattered little to Bismarck from which gun-site the enemy was discomfited.

If it did not produce a Jewish policy, the antisemitic movement certainly provided Germany politics during the fifteen years of its existence with an unexpected element of vulgarity, violence and vituperation, and in the dust storms it created the progressives disintegrated and their power disappeared. Germany had to wait until 1918 to make her first unsuccessful essays in parliamentary democracy and cabinet responsibility.

2. BOYD C. SHAFER: Nationalism: Myth and Reality*

Boyd Shafer, former editor of the *American Historical Review* and now professor of history at Macalester College, sees anti-Semitism as an outgrowth of the evolution and intensification of nationalism. His explanation is clear and simple. But he refers primarily to fairly formal ideological statements of integral nationalism. What were the connections between these and the sort of political anti-Semitism Parkes speaks of? What were the links with popular feeling? And did anti-Semitism spread as widely or as uniformly as integral nationalism did before World War I?

To the most ardent patriots, the nation had become the beginning, the way, and the end. In the nineteenth century the liberal patriot Michelet saw his

* From Boyd C. Shafer, *Nationalism: Myth and Reality,* pp. 205–207. Copyright, 1955, by Boyd C. Shafer. Reprinted by permission of Harcourt, Brace & World, Inc.

country "above everything, as dogma and principle." Before World War I the most passionate nationalists, the Frenchman Charles Maurras, the Englishman, L. J. Maxse, the Germany Heinrich Class, the leaders of the patriotic societies, and the professional patriots, had come to believe that everything should be integrated into the nation. All efforts were to be directed toward its defense, its power, its glory. All sacrifices were to be made in its name. Many men were coming to believe what a French schoolbook explained to French children, "The Fatherland is the nation which you should love, honor and serve with all the energy and all the devotion of your soul."

What the integral nationalists preached became most completely practiced in the totalitarian states that followed World War I, Fascist Italy and Nazi Germany. Though in these nations the nationalism was beclouded by individual ambitions, and in the case of Germany by racial nonsense, they became total states which totally represented the total nation and acted for the totality whether the people consented or not. The integral nationalists, the fascist totalitarians, went further, it is true, than did most patriots in peacetime. But in wartime, from 1914 to 1918, from 1939 to 1945, most other men followed the same fanatical faith. In peace and war, most Western men indeed came to regard their own nation as the greatest and best, the strongest bulwark against evil, the highest source of joy and happiness. In the words of Daniel Webster arguing against Hayne in the American Senate, the nation provided "safety at home," "consideration and dignity abroad," "a copious fountain of national, social, personal happiness," and "high, exciting and gratifying prospects." In addition, as Webster did not say, it offered the way to power, to dominion over other men. Patriotism toward the nation was thus both the expression of self-interest and in Hegel's prose, "the sentiment of regarding the weal of the community as the substantial basis and final end."

When men believed this, they could completely subordinate themselves to the nation. All their interests—economic, political, social—were swallowed up in it. They could apply, as Theodore Roosevelt told Americans and Maurice Barrès the French, the national solution to every problem; they could resolve every question by reference to the national interest. To them the truth itself became not universal but national. They now regarded their nation as a fit object of poetry and worship, something so wonderful that it was divine. The shibboleths by which they rationally and irrationally lived and perhaps died were no longer the Christian Trinity or the French Revolutionary "Liberty, Equality, and Fraternity," but embodied in the slogans, "My country, right or wrong," "America First," or "Deutschland über Alles." "The true nationalist," the French royalist newspaper *Action Française* correctly asserted, places "the fatherland above everything."

Since this was true, the best man, according to a true nationalist, was really a "chauvinist," a "jingo," a "one hundred percenter" who in his fervent, blind patriotism contributed his services, his money, his life to his country, its expansion, its power, its glory. The greatest reward such a man could win was the coveted and highest honor his country could bestow, the Congressional Medal, the Croix de Guerre, the Victoria Cross, and the Iron Cross. And these were won only in military action for his nation and most often awarded posthumously.

The true nationalist was also "anti" everything not of his nation. He was antiman, believing only in particular men. He was antiforeigner distrusting, disliking or hating men of other "breeds." He was anti-Semitic since the Jews represented an international tradition. He could be anti-Christian, as were the Nazis, because Christianity, no matter how practiced, stood for the brotherhood of man. He was antisocialist because socialism was international. He was anti-world government whether in a weak League of Nations or a stronger world federation. He could even deny the principle of nationality and urge his nation to conquer other nations.

Anyone who differed was "un," "uncivilized," "un-American," "un-German," that is, disloyal, subversive, a traitor. Once the words "heretic" and "sinner" were the worst epithets that could be applied to any man. With the nationalist it was "traitor." To be a traitor was to be the lowest and most despicable of criminals. A traitor committed "treason." Treason condemned a man to a fate worse than death, to being a man without a country.

3. PETER PULZER: The Rise of Political Anti-Semitism in Germany and Austria*

Peter Pulzer, of Oxford University, has undertaken one of the most recent historical studies of anti-Semitism. In it, he cites a large number of contributing factors, but he stresses the combined effect of the economic evolution of the Jewish community in central Europe and the reaction of key social groups to this. His explanation is not purely economic, however; he stresses the openness of certain social groups to ideological motivation.

The Jews establish themselves as an exclusively commercial class only when they enter a country less developed economically than they are themselves. When they crossed the Alps and the Rhine into Germany, they came into territory much more backward than the Mediterranean. Later, during the fourteenth and fifteenth centuries the kings of Poland invited them in order to supply their kingdom with a middle class. Similarly in nineteenth-century Hungary, where a rigid social structure prevented peasants and craftsmen from expanding in business and forbade aristocrats to soil themselves with money, Jews, experienced in seizing opportunities not already monopolized by Gentiles, inevitably rushed into the vacuum. They did the same, though to a lesser extent, in Germany and Austria.

No doubt, too, their natural concentration in commerce and towns sharpened those intellectual accomplishments which are generally said to accompany ur-

* From Peter J. Pulzer, *The Rise of Political Anti-Semitism in Germany and Austria* (New York: John Wiley & Sons, Inc., 1966), pp. 3–5, 11–12, 279–85. Reprinted by permission of John Wiley & Sons, Inc.

ban existence—greater perspicacity, the elaboration of theoretical thought, an inclination to radicalism—and sharpened also their alleged revulsion from agricultural work. A drift from country to town is observable at many periods of history; the opposite is rarer. Even highly organized "back to the land" movements in recent decades have met with little success. It is ironical, in fact, that one of the most spectacular voluntary enterprises of land reclamation in this century took place in Israel.

Jewish aversion to manual work was probably no greater than among the rest of mankind, but pressure to take it up could not always be resisted. Especially in the "Russian Pale"[1] Jews were too numerous and their freedom of movement too restricted to enable all of them to subsist in nonproductive occupations. They were forced to turn to handicraft and, later, industrial labor. Emaciated by having for generations lived in towns, they took, in the main, to industries and manufactures which required skill and concentration, in particular tailoring, rather than energy. According to the Russian census of 1897, more Jews than non-Jews in the Pale were engaged in the clothing industry, which occupied 16.5% of all gainfully employed Jews. Factory work was also inescapable for Jews who migrated from backward into highly developed countries, and most of the Jews who left Russia and Poland for the United States or Great Britain became wage earners.

Thus, for different reasons, absorption into the industrial proletariat became inescapable in both Russia and America; in Central Europe, and particularly in Germany and German Austria, Jews succeeded in staving off this fate. Their main motive was fear of becoming submerged in a mass-organized Gentile world. Often independence brought no economic benefit; shirt making or umbrella mending in a slum attic meant a low income and long hours, but it enabled the Jew to observe his religious festivals and dietary practices in peace, and to perpetuate voluntarily his own little ghetto.

It was the same tradition of being one's own master that led so many Jews into the liberal professions. The religious factor is less directly at work here, because most educated Jews broke with orthodoxy, but the long tradition of "being independent," ultimately traceable to religious causes, combined with the difficulties of entering the public service, were jointly responsible.

It is in the light of this exceptional Jewish concentration in the bourgeoisie of Germany and Austria that we must study the link between the fate of the Jews, and that of Liberalism. They contributed to its establishment, benefited from its institutions, and were under fire when it was attacked. It was not merely from legal emancipation that Jews hoped to gain. Their political ambitions went beyond the satisfaction of their own particular grievances and became those of the bourgeoisie in general: the abrogation of aristocratic privileges, the sweeping away of particularism, the repeal of paternalistic commercial legislation, and a unified legal system. Thus Gentiles could see their interests served by supporting Jewish emancipation. . . .

1. Those regions of the Russian Empire, comprising in the main Lithuania, Poland, White Russia, and the Western Ukraine, to which Jews were by law restricted.

Of Jewish predominance in finance much has been written and little need be added here. Since the eighteenth century the dynasty of Rothschild had risen to a pre-eminent place in four countries; the two leading banking houses of Berlin were Bleichröder and the *Disconto-Gesellschaft* of Hansemann—both Jewish. In Vienna all the major houses were Jewish except that of the Greek Sina. Beside them, were the numerous smaller bankers and brokers of Berlin, Frankfurt, Hamburg, and Vienna. A newer development, for the moneyed Jew was after all a familiar phenomenon, was the crowding of the liberal professions by Jews, especially in the capitals.

The first of these professions to attract Jews was medicine, which at one time was the only one open to them. The next profession to attract them was journalism, and finally the law and academic callings. What was particularly interesting was that the intelligentsia, which was ultimately the most hated section of the secularized Jewish bourgeoisie, was overwhelmingly recruited from those who had succeeded in business. This applied *a fortiori* to the great banking dynasties. In our day the Rothschilds, the Warburgs, the Sassoons, and the Cassirers are more famous for the books they write than the money they make. This recruitment of the intellectual professions from the sons of businessmen is not an exclusively Jewish phenomenon; it is common enough among Gentiles. In part it is a question of absorbing the surplus intelligence produced by the commercial classes; in part a question of social status. The businessman is never quite sure of being accepted, the professional man is safe from the suspicion of being a parvenu or a climber. We may spurn the millionaire for having once been a ragpicker, even while we drink his martinis. No one spurns the surgeon for being the son of a ragpicker. Thus stepping up socially might seem preferable, even at the expense of stepping down economically.

I do not suggest that this is the whole explanation for the Jewish quest of the intellectual; it is undoubtedly a trait which Jews betray more markedly than the average person, and one for the satisfaction of which a poor Jew will be prepared to make greater sacrifices than a non-Jew.

There is no doubt that Jews were "over-represented" (if one accepts such a concept) in the educated classes and the professions. The figures of children attending the grammar schools (*gymnasia*) of Berlin in 1887 were:

	Boys	*Girls*
Protestants	6904	3446
Catholics	278	63
Jews	1898	1693
Others	26	12

For every 100,000 males of each denomination in Prussia, there studied at Prussian universities (as an average for the period 1887–1897) 33 Catholics, 58 Protestants, and 519 Jews. Part of the explanation may be that the Jewish community as a whole was more prosperous than either of the other two; but that is unlikely to be the whole explanation. . . .

A great deal has already emerged in the preceding chapters about the social composition of the anti-Semitic movements in both countries; nevertheless a recapitulation and analysis would be useful here.

In general, anti-Semitism drew little strength from either the working class or the aristocracy. The industrial proletariat of Germany and Austria was well organized, well drilled, and politically conscious to a degree which was probably unequaled in any other country. The German party was the model child of the Second International and the Austrian party—or at least its German section—was its Siamese twin. Most of the worker's educational and cultural needs were met by party organizations, and he was proud of the understanding of history, economics, and politics he had gained from evening lectures, theoretical journals, and twenty-pfennig pamphlets. He knew that national and religious arguments were at best irrelevant to a solution of his problems and at worst a deliberate attempt to cloud his view of the "real issues."

Against such indoctrination by party educational machines, the Churches, Catholic and Protestant, could do little. As Bernanos puts it:

> It is merely comic for us to tremble with fervour and offer the encyclical *Rerum Novarum* to men who have read Marx and Lenin and have dreamt the great dream of proletarian revolution.

In Germany, it is true, the Centre Party continued to hold the loyalty of a substantial, though diminishing, proportion of Catholic workers, but they supported it less out of sympathy with its social program (which was not in any way remarkable) than out of traditional feelings, strengthened by the hard-pressed minority position of the German Church. Similarly, the Nationalist labor movement claimed some working men in Bohemia. But these two examples are worth mentioning as the only major exceptions.

The economic reform programs of the anti-Semitic parties did not hold out much attraction for industrial workers. Although some sort of factory legislation was generally urged, there were few proposals to remedy the even worse conditions of employees and apprentices employed in artisan businesses, where union organization was much more difficult, and an extension of the guild system would have threatened what little chance for betterment was open to the average working man.

The workers did not see the Jews with the same eyes as the upper or middle classes. If they were exploited by a Jewish employer, they generally knew that conditions in Gentile establishments were no better; and the financier and broker seemed a less immediate enemy than the capitalist. They did not fail to notice that there were many Jews—including some who could have led comfortable middle class existences had they chosen to—who had taken up their cause. They had no particular reason either to hate or to love Jews as a group. Certainly at a time when the working class as a whole felt discriminated against and without a stake in the country, they were not going to concern themselves too much with discrimination against Jews, some of whom, at any rate, seemed not to be doing too badly.

Similarly, the aristocracy did not associate itself in large numbers with political anti-Semitism, a fact which the handful of well-known anti-Semitic aristocrats should not allow us to overlook. Certainly there were social barriers which made it difficult for the moneyed Jew to mix on equal terms with the aristocracy, but these existed for the Gentile *parvenu* also. For Jews to be admitted in Vienna or Potsdam as freely as were the Sassoons, Cassels, or Rothschilds at the court of King Edward VII would have been unthinkable, but there was a fair amount of intermarriage, a tendency which the more radical, anti-Junker type of anti-Semites made much play of. (One anti-Semitic publication, the *Semi-Gotha,* listed over 1000 families whom penury had driven into *Verjudung.*)

The more hard-pressed *Krautjunker* might subscribe to the anti-Jewish clauses of the Tivoli Program, but neither they nor the Agrarian League can be considered the driving force of the anti-Semitic movement. The days of the Free Corps, the *Stahlhelm,* and the *Heimwehr* were not yet; the same snobbery which kept the aristocrat aloof from the Jewish bourgeoisie kept him also from demagogic anti-Semitism.

We are therefore driven to seek the bulk of anti-Semitic support in the middle class and above all in a particular section of it—the middle and lower professional grades and the middle and small businessmen. The large industrialists in general were not interested. There were few Jewish rivals at that level. Krupp, Stinnes, Thyssen, and Stumm had little to fear from Jew or fellow Gentile. This is borne out by such detailed analysis as is possible of the membership of anti-Semitic organizations. As good an example as any, because it was a nation-wide body, is the Pan-German League which was half-inside, half-outside the anti-Semitic camp.

The occupations of party leaders and members of parliament are a less re-

MEMBERSHIP OF PAN-GERMAN LEAGUE BY PROFESSIONS, 1901

	In Germany	*Outside Germany*
Professors, University Lecturers	5,339	560
Small Businessmen	4,905	383
Artists, Officials, Teachers	3,760	262
Artisans, Workers	2,673	186
Others	1,507	221
	18,184	1,612

PERCENTAGE OF TEACHING AND MEDICAL PROFESSIONS AMONG LOCAL OFFICERS OF THE PAN-GERMAN LEAGUE

	1896	*1906*	*1914*
Teaching Profession	25%	36%	24%
Medical Profession	8	10	8

liable guide, first because some professions, such as the law and journalism, are prominent in the parliamentary representation of all parties, second because many deputies describe themselves as "publicists" or "party secretaries," which gives no clue to their social origins. Summarizing the biographical information given about the German anti-Semitic deputies in the *Reichstaghandbücher*, "which is neither complete nor too specific," Massing observes:

> In terms of social background, three major groups were not, or hardly, represented. None of the members came from the ranks of industrial labour. With the exception of two, Liebermann von Sonnenberg and Count Ludwig von Reventlow, the aristocracy was ostensibly missing. . . . Although the group contained men who declared themselves to be merchants and the sons of merchants, not one of them came from, or represented, big industry, trade or finance. Next to small industrial and agricultural entrepreneurs, artisans and small merchants, the group counted among its members teachers, lawyers, civil servants and [white collar] employees.
>
> The group's educational level was above the average. Of the forty-three men for whom educational data are available, nineteen had a university background and only thirteen did not have more formal education than high school; the remainder had gone to college or its equivalent in special art schools, trade schools, etc. The proportion of men with academic background and holding public office increased somewhat in later years.

In Austria, as we have already noted, the German Nationalists were chiefly representative of the professional *Mittelstand*; indeed the *Volkspartei* came to be nicknamed *Professorenpartei*. Of its founders, Steinwender was a schoolmaster and Strohal a professor of law. The Nationalists, representing the literate—and therefore ultimately more dangerous—wing of anti-Semitism, could hardly feel at ease with Christian-Social fundamentalists like Hermann Bielohlawek who called Tolstoi an *"alter Tepp,"* and whose reactions to the mention of a book anticipated the more celebrated response of Baldur von Schirach on a similar topic.

The romantic nationalism imbibed during university days also influenced the politics of professional men in later life, again more decisively in Austria than in Germany, where the distinction between being "Christian" and "national" hardly existed. True, the wild enthusiasm of pan-German beer orgies gave way to the more staid and constitutional sentiments of, say, the *Volkspartei*, as the graduate began to taste Imperial patronage—and to take a pride in his part in the administration and maintenance of the Empire. Still, the nationalist sentiments of the older and younger generations sustained each other through the *Burschenschaften* where the *alte Herren* mixed with students; how decisively this cross-fertilization of ideas could act is shown by Professor Wandruszka who points out that in the 1930's in Austria it was in the main the younger generation of "national" opinion who persuaded their fathers that Nazism was merely the logical application of the slogans they had been mouthing since their *Burschenschaft* days—as indeed it was.

More significant than the parliamentary representation of a party is the social composition of its rank-and-file and subaltern leadership. Two undated manuscript registers of the Viennese executive committee of Schönerer's party indicate the fairly narrow range which formed the hard core of the movement. The first names forty professional and twenty-three businessmen: nine civil servants or clerks, seven lawyers, five doctors, five accountants, five property owners and three students are among those named. On the second there are twenty-three professional men, including seven officials, four lawyers, three teachers, three accountants, and two doctors; and fifteen businessmen, including a photographer, a dispensing chemist, and a coffee-roaster.

The pan-German movement, more active, as we have seen, outside the strictly political field than in it, also paid more attention to the economic needs of the *Mittelstand*. A party employment exchange, the *Deutschvölkische Stellen-*

PERCENTAGE INCREASE OF EMPLOYERS, INDUSTRIAL WORKERS, AND WHITECOLLAR WORKERS IN GERMANY

	1882–1907	*1895–1907*
Employers	—7.9	—2.52
Industrial Employees	109.78	44.28
Commercial Employees	592.40	160.10

vermittlung in Wien, a "nonpolitical association," existed for the purpose of "assisting unemployed Germans (of Aryan descent) to a livelihood" and in 1890 *Ostmark,* a co-operative society, savings bank, and low-interest loan institute for self-employed persons, was founded to shield prospective members "from the dangers of the international capitalist economy and exploitation by the ever-lusting workings of stock exchange speculation." The foundation appeal had ninety-four signatories—thirteen officials, six doctors, five teachers, three accountants, two architects, and altogether forty-three businessmen, including a soap-boiler, a decorator, a baker, a coppersmith, a glazier, an innkeeper, a cheese-monger, and Herr Josef Schneider, *Personaleinkommensteuerschätzungscommissionsmitgliedsersatzmann*. Other economic organizations in Vienna included a Register of German Tradespeople (1899) and a *Deutschvölkischer Gehülfenverein*.

The German *Handlungsgehilfenverband* had already shown what a fruitful field for anti-Semitic recruitment this was. The new class of white-collar workers, a natural result of the concentration and bureaucratization of industry and the expansion of the distributive trades, was in fact growing numerically more than any other section of society. In the great cities the percentage of inhabitants in commercial employment rose from 6.5 to 12.7.

Economically, the members of the "new *Mittelstand*" (as it was often called) were almost indistinguishable from the proletariat, since their essential function was to sell labor which was, at best, semi-skilled in exchange for wages. In social status, however, they were distinct from the working class and in a society as rigidly hierarchic as the German, they were strongly endowed with *Standesdünkel,* or "consciousness of class superiority." Their wages and conditions of work were generally far from good, and their aversion to cloth-cap methods like strikes and collective bargaining made their position even more precarious. They were therefore, despite the apparent increase of their economic importance, a classic example of a class constantly threatened with depression into the proletariat. Their two preoccupations were to keep their distance from those below and to secure from their employers—more likely to be Jewish in commerce than in industry—better conditions.

Some of the sources of political anti-Semitism, therefore, are self-evident. Among farmers and traders there was economic discontent; among aristocrats and climbers there was snobbery; among some of all classes there was religious prejudice, dating from a pre-Liberal, pre-capitalist era. But these did not provide the sole motivating force. The characteristic of twentieth-century politics has been the triumph of ideology over self-interest. The ideology which increasingly provided the impulse to political anti-Semitism toward the end of our period was common to both Germany and Austria—pan-Germanism.

4. BRUNO BETTELHEIM AND MORRIS JANOWITZ: Dynamics of Prejudice*

In this selection, a psychologist, Bruno Bettelheim, and a sociologist, Morris Janowitz, both of the University of Chicago, sum up the results of research on the bases for prejudice, both anti-Semitic and anti-Negro, in a group of American veterans of World War II. The advantages of direct and elaborate analysis of a diverse group of people are obvious. But can the conclusions be applied also to historical situations, different in place as well as time? This is an increasingly urgent problem for historians dealing with topics for which purely historical materials are inadequate. In the case of anti-Semitism, direct comparison is possible with historical treatments of the social and psychological bases of the phenomenon. Do the approaches contradict or supplement each other? Does one need to go beyond conventional historical methods?

The personality structures of the men in the sample were to a large degree formed under the impact of existing society. If ethnic intolerance is rooted in the intolerant individual's personality, then we must ask ourselves what in this society shapes personality in such a way that ethnic intolerance seems a frequent, if not a favorite outlet for hostility. While it is not true, as the Marxist maintains, that ethnic intolerance is a consequence of the capitalist system, ethnic intolerance occurring within a capitalist society will nevertheless be deeply influenced in character by that society.

It may once more be stressed that intolerance is always an outlet for hostility, but that it depends for its intensity on the degree of hostility accumulated, and on the strength of the controls which restrain it. While hostility against out-groups is probably as old as society, the particular form in which hostility

* From Bruno Bettelheim and Morris Janowitz, *Dynamics of Prejudice* (New York: Harper & Row, 1950), pp. 162–67, 169–71. Copyright American Jewish Committee. Reprinted by permission of the American Jewish Committee.

occurs is particular to the society in which it appears. Although anti-Semitism has been present in slave societies, feudal societies, capitalist societies, and recently too in communist society, it appears in each case to have been a different social phenomenon. What is historically permanent in anti-Semitism, for example, is only that members of a particular religious or ethnic group have been persecuted. The German-Jewish scientist, banker, physician, or laborer whom Hitler persecuted was as different from the medieval Jewish ghetto pawnbroker as was the German SS man from the German peasant or master craftsman who persecuted Jews in the Middle Ages. And as different as they were from one another, so also were their persecutions. Their differences originated in the different forms of society in which they lived—societies which shaped their personalities, outlooks, motives, and actions, which aroused their hostility, created frustration, and controlled its discharge. Hence their motives in persecuting the Jews were equally different, and equally rooted in the structure of their society.

In this book only that type of ethnic intolerance is analyzed which is prevalent in the urban centers of modern western society. Since the particular form in which it appears is an outgrowth of that society, it must be intimately connected with it, although it may still originate in each individual's personal frustrations, anxieties, hostilities, and so on. Two examples may serve to illustrate.

In a slave society in which one ethnic group rules another, the ruling group does more than simply tolerate the life—and even to some degree the well-being—of the discriminated group. The presence of this group is not only desired, it is vital to the working of society, and the latter, in case of need, must assure itself by warfare of securing new slaves. Some remnants of the attitudes originating in the needs of a slave society might account in part for observations made in the second chapter of this book. In that chapter it was mentioned that while the very intolerant men asked for the deportation of Jews, almost none of them requested deportation of Negroes, but requested instead that they be kept in their "place." The reason may well be that the Negro, although discriminated against, is nevertheless experienced as an important member of society, or at least as a person who serves a useful function. If the Negro were to leave, it would be left to the white man to perform those less desirable tasks which are now relegated to the Negro. Thus ethnic intolerance in its modern form was unthinkable in a society whose ethnic outgroups actually provided the economic base, as in a slave society. As a matter of fact, there are many ways in which modern ethnic intolerance tends to reestablish settings which were characteristic of slave society—the Negro must know and keep in his "place"; the Jew and members of other inferior races must labor in the concentration camp.

Ethnic intolerance as a social phenomenon takes on markedly different aspects depending on the social structure in which it occurs, and can be comprehended only when viewed in the context of that society. The example of medieval anti-Semitism may serve as an additional illustration. Jewish persecution in the Middle Ages charged the Jews with enjoying ill-begotten wealth —and the desire to gain, through plundering their riches, was an important incentive. But in medieval anti-Semitism these seemed only random phenomena. What seemed to excite real ire in the populace was that the Jews refused to be saved, thus reviving and enforcing in the Christians repressed doubts about their own salvation. (Without firsthand knowledge, all statements about the inner psychological processes of individuals who lived during the medieval period must remain conjecture. Still it might be reasonable to assume that his id, superego, and ego served similar functions in the psychological apparatus, but were differently constituted than those of modern man. Cleanliness was considered vain, if not unhealthy; the content of the superego was ordained by the Church; and the priest and the Church provided the most powerful superego representation. The superego had no need to evoke symbols of self-respect or individual conscience for restraining ego and id—the fear of hell and damnation were much more powerful incentives. Moreover, the ego was not confronted with an abundance of choices, and a relatively weak ego sufficed for mastering the tasks of life. Life activities were more rigidly organized and less subject to freedom of choice than they are today and the ego was less taxed in its need to synthesize opposing tendencies. Which of these tendencies, and in which ways they might be satisfied was more or less ordered by rules and tradition.)

It seems reasonable to assume that the ego of medieval man was at least as much concerned with saving his immortal soul as it was with making his temporal life successful. It is difficult to decide where his individual superego began, and where the Church and its teaching served him in its stead. Even the true medieval heretics (St. John of the Cross, etc.) bowed to the authority of popes, of whose individual shortcomings they were not unaware.[1]

What the individual during the Middle Ages appears to have feared most was not loss in status or economic security, but loss of grace. Much as he might have cherished the former, it was far more important, and a much greater threat, to fear damnation and the loss of eternal life. But it was not always easy to live by the rules of the superego-Church. (That the Church permitted considerable id gratification may be disregarded for the purpose of this discussion.) The id pressed for a gratification that was not always sanctioned by the Church, so that the ego and individualized superego may often have joined forces in doubting salvation through religious conformity. Such doubts had to be done away with, had to be persecuted and extinguished. They were the greatest threat to the individual's integration. One way to eliminate this threat was to project the conflict onto the Jews. In the Middle Ages, the most frequent accusation made against Jews, and the one which aroused the greatest hatred,

1. Thus the superego which forced them to take a stand against the temporary Church was not strong enough to assert its absolute independence. On the other hand, the Protestant reformers, and their forerunners from Wycliffe on, seem to have had more individualized superegos which permitted them to supplement faith with their own observations in taking a stand against Church and pope. But in this sense they were rather precursors of modern man than typically medieval and once the reforms they inaugurated were established, modern times had begun.

was that they had desecrated the host. Closely related was the other accusation that they had committed ritual murders, used children they had killed to say a black mass.

The example of the Marannos (Spanish Jews converted to Catholicism) shows that these accusations reflected a very probable origin of anti-Semitism at that time, namely the Christian's fear of being a bad Catholic (more so, at least, than modern accusations indicate the real reasons for modern anti-Semitism). These Spanish Jews were notoriously wealthy as well as culturally and politically influential, and aside from religious accusations, their wealth, too, was held against them.[2] Still a change of religion put an end to their persecution, provided they really meant it. As soon as Spanish Jews became Catholics, they were not only permitted to retain status and wealth, but were frequently known to increase in both.

In modern times when religious appeals have been introduced as a basis for the persecution of Jews, they have nearly always fallen flat.[3] Religious fear, or such inner conflicts as are based on it, is just no longer important enough to motivate large masses. Again and again ritual murder stories have been circulated, but have never been widely believed, or at least not in urban centers. The only places where they were lent some credence and led to persecutions were in eastern Europe, where economic, political, and religious organization was still very similar to that of the Middle Ages (the last time in the notorious Beilis case of 1911). Religious conversion which protected Spanish Jews was ultimately of little help to Jews in Germany. Thus although in the two examples, the German and the Spanish, both religious and economic accusations were used, the religious was more basic in the Middle Ages, while it is insignificant in modern times. On the other hand, the economic accusation seems all-important in modern times. The racial issue raised in National Socialist Germany seems but a return to the Middle Ages with racialism taking the place of religion. But into this new "religion" one cannot be "admitted"—the infidel, the man of a lower race, must be extinguished.

While the ethos of medieval society was largely religious, that of the men studied was largely economic. By and large, the latter considered income as the main status-providing factor. Security itself was experienced mainly as economic—as job or income security—and even those men who valued intellectual achievement viewed it chiefly as an economic asset.

The men strove little for religious salvation, but they certainly wished for economic security which was even more important to them than higher income, as some of them stated themselves. But economic security is not easily achieved in a competitive society. Moreover, the notion is widespread that in a competitive society everyone can better his status if he tries hard enough. This,

2. The modern accusation of clannishness (the one most frequently used by the men in the sample) was absent in medieval anti-Semitism, probably because the modern sense of isolation and the fear of alienation were not then prevalent.

3. Throughout the interviews when reasons for the dislike of Jews were mentioned, references to religion were almost totally absent.

of course, puts an added psychological burden on the man who does not even achieve an occupational position which he thinks will assure his economic well-being. In addition to not attaining needed security, he also experiences a blow to his self-esteem.

Thus the person who experiences a lowering of income is doubly deprived. He is dissatisfied with himself and in addition must fear for his economic welfare. Frustration therefore accumulates and presses for discharge in those men who experience downward mobility. To such men, ethnic discrimination offers a convenient outlet. But the fourth chapter has shown that it was not only those who experienced a lowering of economic status who were prejudiced, but also those who were stationary in that respect, although there was a significant difference in the intensity of intolerance between these two groups. In terms of existing society even the men whose status was unchanged had reason to be fearful, although they needed, in general, to be less anxious than those on the downgrade. The no-mobility group had failed to live up to the challenge that one better oneself which is inherent in competitive society. Although many social scientists would agree that to remain stationary in our society often indicates that a man has made good in competition, such an attitude is not yet part of the economic ethos. Therefore such men are not really at peace; their self-esteem, too, is threatened, though considerably less so than that of a member of the downwardly mobile group. Thus, among other reasons, even the stationary group took advantage of ethnic discrimination as a channel for the discharge of accumulated hostility. On the other hand, the upwardly mobile group, for their part, had gained enough courage from recent successes to feel they might weather a future depression which they, too, nevertheless feared.

Early in the book . . . it was mentioned that among the group studied there seemed to be a tendency to select the Jews as the group on whom to project those superego demands making for conflict within the individual, and that the character of anti-Semitism was strongly influenced by such projections. The intolerant men felt that the Jews were successful in those areas where they themselves had failed to make good. Their superegos—in line with the economic ethos of society—required that they increase their earnings and rise in the hierarchy of status. Against these demands, which they could not fulfill, the stationary and particularly the downwardly mobile group defended their egos by pointing to the Jews. It was the Jews, they claimed, who exercised undue control, possessed the money, and thus prevented their own success. . . .

After so much has been said about the economic concomitants of intolerance it should again be stressed that the comparison of objective army experiences and their subjective evaluation . . . has shown that objective reality seemed comparatively less important in shaping interethnic attitudes than the personal frame of reference within which objective reality is experienced. Despite the insecurities of the present day, quite a number of the veterans had egos which were adequate enough to master economic anxieties so that they were not forced to evaluate past, present, and future experiences as deprivational. They were relatively free of fear and found it possible to be optimistic even in adverse circumstances (combat, threat of depression, etc.). Such optimism and the self-confidence and self-respect which go with it, as well as the parallel ability to control hostility, all originate in fortunate childhood experiences. Positive relationships to parents and other members of the primary group and sufficient gratification of instinctual needs during childhood seem to equip a child with sufficient emotional strength to grow into an adult who feels able to master the difficulties of contemporary life.[4] Thus, in more than one way, anxiety about the future and the discharge of aggression in hostile action is a two-generation problem. The individual who has experienced even relative security in childhood will probably have acquired a personality structure which permits him to weather even relatively great frustrations and insecurities without experiencing them as a threat to his personal integration. He will not need to bolster his integration through the mechanism of projection, or the explosive and irrational discharge of hostility against members of an outgroup. On the other hand, a child born into a family which experiences actual deprivation during the child's most formative years will, in addition to actual deprivation, most probably be raised in an atmosphere of emotional insecurity. He will be unable to view his life experiences optimistically and thus every positive experience will lose much of its reassuring, ego-strengthening value. Conversely, every negative experience will seem according to expectation and thus even more deprivational and overpowering. . . .[5]

4. Clinical observations of severely disturbed children permit several interesting inferences on the consequences of actual and emotional deprivation during infancy and childhood. Children who on initial examination showed comparable degrees of disturbance, nevertheless showed marked differences in improvement during psychiatric treatment, depending chiefly on their past life experiences. Children who had suffered severe actual deprivation because they had been raised in submarginal families or in orphanages soon improved markedly. The abundant gratification of instinctual and interpersonal needs, as provided by the new environment, during treatment —they lived in a psychiatric institution—permitted them to modify their outlook on life quite rapidly. They learned soon enough that past deprivations were only one of many possible kinds of experiences and realized that life has more to offer than they had once thought. Hence, they did their best to adjust to it. On the other hand, children of well-to-do families who had always enjoyed abundance with regard to food and shelter—children who, as a matter of fact, had often been resentfully "overprotected" and in whose case "good" care covered up for intense rejection— these children took very much longer to conceive of the gratification offered at the treatment institution as anything desirable. Clinically speaking, their task was much more complex when compared to that of the "orphans." It was easier for the economically deprived children to change their outlook on life once—contrary to previous expectations—abundant gratification was regularly available. The same offer, and even its acceptance, remained ungratifying to the emotionally deprived children of well-to-do parents. Such offerings and whatever else was done for them were evaluated in terms of their old, pessimistic frame of reference and were, hence, of no positive value.

5. In Germany, it was not the middle-aged group of men who had served in the first World War, and many of whom had experienced great losses in the after-war years, who furnished Hitler with his most ardent followers, although the leader himself and his officers came from that group. The bulk of the middle-aged men, despite the downward mobility they had generally experienced, manned the *Reichsbanner* and the *Stahlhelm* (the liberal and the conservative military organizations) and not the SS. In part, this can be explained by the fact that they had, in their childhood, experienced the relative stability which characterized Germany at the turn of the century; most of their families had in fact improved in economic status during those years.

The sons of these men had been infants when their fathers were away at war. Their early

In this study an effort was made to establish the association between intolerance and isolated social, economic, and psychological factors; but the results should not be misconstrued as implying that these factors per se account for intolerance. On the contrary, they are only varying attributes of a total Gestalt, formed by the individual's total personality and the social structure in which he finds himself. The interplay between personality structure and those forces originating in the social field seemed to condition the presence, the absence, and the nature of intolerance.

Thus if the personality is very strong, or if, for particular personal reasons, the individual is strongly committed to tolerance or intolerance, the influence of the social field in respect to tolerance or intolerance is relatively small. The weaker the personality, the stronger becomes the influence of the social field.

5. FRITZ STERN: The Politics of Cultural Despair*

Fritz Stern's study of three anti-Semitic intellectuals (Paul de Lagarde, Julius Langbehn, and Moeller van der Bruck) in Germany, in the later nineteenth and early twentieth century, is a pioneering effort to study "second-level" intellectuals to see how the ideas of creative thinkers were filtering down to lower intellectual levels and to deal with the role of such intellectuals in spreading the ideas into society more generally. In his conclusion, he deals with the personal factors in the attitudes of the intellectuals. This demands comparison with a more formal psychological approach; and one must ask what connections the personalities of these anti-Semites have with anti-Semitism more generally. Note Stern's insistence on the Germanic nature of the prejudice and on its roots even in the nineteenth century. This is due to his search for the causes of anti-Semitism in formal culture, an approach that requires careful assessment. Professor Stern is a historian at Columbia University.

Lagarde, Langbehn, and Moeller belonged to different generations, but their style of thought and their aspirations were remarkably alike. The unity of their thought allows us to speak of the rise of the Germanic ideology; the similarities in their lives and the common psychological and intellectual roots of their struggle against modernity allow us to speak of them as a distinct cultural type, a new version of the alienated intellectual in the modern world. Once this type has been defined, it will be possible to assess the place of these writers in

---

childhood was often characterized by instability; food had been scarce, and their mothers, in addition to worrying about their husbands, had been working in war factories to keep the family going. They were still boys or had grown into early adolescence when their own and their parents' hopes for a better life after the war were terribly shattered by inflation, deflation, and unemployment. As young men in the Thirties, they could not believe they would ever be able to secure a decent life for themselves through their own efforts. Therefore they had to rely on a strong "leader," a father figure, to give them the emotional and economic security which their own fathers had been unable to provide. They had also to discharge the frustrations and hostility which had accumulated over a long period of insecurity and suffering, if they wished to retain their tenuous integration. Explosive action against minorities was then a convenient outlet.

* From Fritz Stern, *The Politics of Cultural Despair: A Study in the Rise of Germanic Ideology* (Berkeley: University of California Press, 1961), Anchor edition, 1965, pp. 326–41, 357–359. Reprinted by permission of the University of California Press.

German culture, and to analyze their relation to earlier intellectual traditions and to later political movements.

These three critics witnessed the gradual destruction of the old Germany and the emergence of a new, urban, secular country. They hated the temper and the institutions of this new Germany and decried the conditions of modernity. Their protests, as we have seen, were not unique. Others were dismayed as well: conservatives saw their beliefs and privileges challenged, Christians saw their faith attacked, and a new class, the urban proletariat, attacked the exploitative and inegalitarian character of modern industrial society. These groups and their spokesmen had a stake in the past or a tangible goal for the future. But Lagarde, Langbehn, and Moeller had no commitment to the past nor were they defending existing social privileges. Even their nationalism was an idealistic abstraction, a recollection of an ideal Germanic type that was supposed to have flourished once, but had since been betrayed. They had reluctantly repudiated the faith and the philosophical traditions of their ancestors. Dispossessed in a double sense, Lagarde, Langbehn, and Moeller cast their discontent into political visions which were as divorced from reality as their creators were from their society.

Our critics were simultaneously proud and resentful of their alienation. They were proud of the perspicacity which their "untimeliness" had granted them, but their deepest longing was for a new Germanic community in which they and all their countrymen would at last find the peace of complete unity. Because of this longing they made the leap from cultural criticism to politics, assuming that cultural evil could be dissolved by the establishment of the right kind of faith and community. However prescient their cultural criticism was, their political thought revealed the willful ignorance of political reality that often characterizes the alienated and unexperienced critic. Their political imagination grasped lifeless abstractions and the petty details of their proposed reforms. The middle range of practicality was foreign to them.

They knew that they were radically different from all those who had a real stake in society. To emphasize their apartness they called themselves conservative revolutionaries. They were conservative out of nostalgia and revolutionary out of despair. They were not concerned with compromise; they sought to destroy the present in order to usher in a future Reich—one which would realize on this earth some of the bliss that had once been promised for the hereafter. They exemplified in the realm of thought what the National Socialists were later to demonstrate with such practical thoroughness: that the annihilation of a culture can only be willed by the uprooted, the dispossessed.

These men, as I have said, have to be understood as a cultural type, a type moreover that made its simultaneous appearance in all Western countries.[1] The

1. The type clearly emerged in the 1880's, and ranged from Charles Maurras, Maurice Barrès, and Knut Hamsun to the poet Miguel de Unamuno. It thus included men of diverse interests and unequal talents who were linked by a feeling of alienation in the modern world and an attendant search for a new faith. The type was also depicted in a long line of fictional characters from *The Possessed* to D. H. Lawrence's James Sharpe in *Kangaroo* "who is half an artist, not more, and so can never get away from it or free himself from its dictates" (Penguin edition, London, p. 258).

distinctive qualities of these men are not to be found in their thought or their lives alone, but in the tension between their thought, their personalities and their culture, as well as in the form in which this tension was expressed. The conventional categories of social types have little relevance; for these three men were intellectuals *faute de mieux,* intellectuals whose work was emotional and seldom reflective; they were artists without talents of creative expression, prophets without a god. They exemplified and encouraged what they sought to combat and annihilate, the cultural disintegration and the collapse of order in modern Germany. They were the accusers, but also the unwitting proof of their charges. As a consequence, they were forever wrestling with themselves even as they were fighting others.

Their writings rang with the prophecy of impending doom, lightened only by an occasional note of hope that redemption might still be possible. It was as if their own Jeremiads on the real evils of the present so frightened them that they were forced to project a future or a regeneration beyond all historical possibility. Having abjured religious faith, they could not fall back on the promise of divine deliverance. Having abjured reason, they could not expect a natural human evolution toward the community they sought. The goal, consequently, was a mystique, and the means, though left obscure, suggested violence and coercion.

To speak of a cultural type requires us to show that these men had common personal and biographical characteristics, and that their lives and works described a similar and novel position in culture. This, I think, can be done, without violating the facts or reducing men to formulas; description will show these men to have been a complex instance of the search for salvation, by a type of mind that can neither endure nor overcome the conditions of modern life.

These men were born, or early in their lives became, urbanites, cut off from nature and the simple rural life that in their dreams they idealized. They were brought up in modest surroundings and challenged by the parental expectation that they should find for themselves a place in society, so as to live in comfortable distinction. Born into families with professional pretensions, they sought to attain status, to achieve recognition which would set them apart from other men. Was it an accident that two of our writers adopted new and more ornamental names, and that Langbehn sought to win fame from his elaborate mask of anonymity? They turned their backs on the abundant economic opportunities of business and finance. To live as free intellectuals was their ambition, but Moeller and Langbehn both spurned, or accepted only with reluctance, the customary employment of intellectuals. With neither secure employment nor sufficient independent means, they groped for something better, more rewarding than mere survival, always believing that others, usually the wicked men of power, owed them admiring deference and substantial help.

This type dominated the literature of the *fin de siècle* and of the German Expressionists. Philip Wylie's *Generation of Vipers* may be taken as a contemporary instance of the enduring quality of this genre. Note his bombast: "We have cancer—cancer of the soul. Religion has failed." This was already a commonplace among the Germanic critics. Philip Wylie, *Generation of Vipers,* New York, Farrar and Rinehart, 1942, p. 7.

Their intellectual ambition, first roused at home, was furthered by their education. All three attended the *Gymnasium,* though Moeller did not complete his studies. The German *Abiturient,* after his nine exacting years of Greek and Latin, acquired both an excellent education and the means for attaining greater prestige. He could, and often did, enter the university, or he could seek a managerial career in business. Lagarde and Langbehn proceeded to the university, earned their doctorates and thus won a certain kind of social distinction. But distinction often brings with it loneliness and, after their break with the academic world, they found it difficult to fit into any social group.

In the course of their formal education, notes of dissent and discord already began to appear. They experienced the inherent shortcomings of the nineteenth-century *Gymnasium,* its disdain for the natural sciences, and its carefully preserved isolation from the "real" world. Given its original impulse by Humboldt, the *Gymnasium* remained throughout a century of modernization the citadel of humanistic learning and of philosophical idealism. It was essentially a conservative force, controlled by anxious officials who feared that knowledge of social evils or of politics would breed corruption and radicalism. The role of the *Gymnasium* in German culture has yet to be assessed; its pedagogical excellence we are familiar with, but we have still to understand why so many young Germans felt such revulsion for it. The Youth Movement was only the most dramatic rebellion against what its members called the artificiality and pedantry of these schools. Much of the irrationalism and the hatred of "system" which characterized German youth sprang up in opposition to these schools. Even men who after graduation had themselves become teachers or academics remembered an ill-defined discontent with this prison-like ivory tower; it is a significant fact that most of the autobiographies of that age express simultaneous admiration and hatred of the *Gymnasium*.[2] Certainly Lagarde, Langbehn, and Moeller had loathed this kind of education. It had widened the gulf between them and society without giving them the training which would have enabled them to define logically or in historical perspective their opposition to modernity. Moreover, they spurned the positive values of the *Gymnasium*; they rejected the discipline of the mind which the less gifted student accepted as a matter of course, and they forsook the humanistic tradition which left its imprint on the better student. Lagarde's and Langbehn's writings bristled with scornful attacks on German schools and thus helped to unsettle the minds of countless other students.

Langbehn's and Moeller's years at school seem also to have reinforced their temperamental disinclination for rigorous thought and study. The customary pedantic instruction which completely starved the imagination confirmed them in their predilection for intuitive and nonsystematic knowledge. Langbehn's certainty, so proudly maintained in his mature years, that he had learned everything from his own travels found its counterpart in Moeller's cheerful courting

2. Friedrich Meinecke, for example, records with considerable puzzlement that even some sixty years after graduation, "The sudden sight of the red brick building of my old *Gymnasium* did not evoke any warm memories." *Erlebtes, 1862–1901,* Leipzig 1941, p. 63.

of expulsion from the *Gymnasium*. He, too, ridiculed the inadequacy of mere "bookish" learning and proceeded to educate himself—from books.

Langbehn, it will be remembered, had once begun to study chemistry but had quickly shifted to fine arts, before departing from the academic scene altogether. Lagarde and Moeller fared little better in their occasional studies of the sciences and were content with the conventional claptrap about the dangers of the age of science. In many ways, their lives, and Moeller's in particular, illustrate the shortcomings of the self-tutored man. Lagarde, it is true, had achieved great eminence in his field of scholarship, but he sought power and influence in areas that were removed from his training. In their political and social criticism they were all dilettantes who had not even mastered the art of acquiring knowledge. Moeller's perceptive understanding of contemporary literature was a measure of his ability, and yet in other fields, in his historical and political writings for example, he gained only a superficial breadth and uncritical knowledge. The political constructions of the Third Reich, like the antiscientific tirades of Langbehn, bore the stamp of an almost willful disregard of common knowledge. Their writings appealed not by their intellectual force but because they were suffused with passion, the passion of their indignation and their suffering.

Beyond their troubled education lay their individual unhappiness, already apparent in early childhood and perpetuated to the ends of their lives. Tragedy had touched each of them in his earliest years, depriving Lagarde of his mother and Langbehn of his father; of Moeller it is said that even as a child he had never been known to laugh. None of them had experienced a pleasant youth or even a moderately warm relationship with his parents. One further recalls Lagarde's numbness at his father's death, Langbehn's invariably disastrous attempts at friendship, or Moeller's long exile from Germany. Little is known of their marriages or their relationships with women, but Lagarde's and Moeller's silence about or indifference to their childless marriages and Langbehn's failure to convert his fitful attraction for women into abiding companionship deepens the impression of sadness, as do his obscure attempts at repressing what seem to have been strong sexual impulses. As a final element in their characters, one must remember that their achievements never measured up to their own extravagant images of themselves, largely because of the limitation of their talents but partly because of the stubborn opposition of society. Frustration forced them ever more inward, exaggerating Lagarde's crotchetiness and Langbehn's insane priggishness, and contributing to Moeller's breakdown, leading, perhaps, to his suicide. Their lives, one senses, lacked comforts or rewards; neither joy nor even self-acceptance made their journey easier. Only Langbehn found in the Catholic Church a release from himself.

Langbehn's conversion points to the fundamental unhappiness of their lives which was at once personal and cultural in origin; they had been born into an age of unbelief, an age when not only the overwhelming number of intellectuals but large parts of the public as well had withdrawn from organized religion into a personal, deistic religion, agnosticism, or atheism. The motives and conditions for this retreat were complex; they cannot be simply explained, as is often done, by referring to the rise of scientism or the pressures of the industrial society. Corresponding to the complexity of motives is the diversity of the manifestations of this break from Christianity, and neither can be dealt with here at any length. It suffices to say that in Germany the retreat was usually disguised, without the sharp struggle between believers and nonbelievers that characterized the same process in France. The educated German tended to glide into unbelief. For many Germans, Basil Willey's description of an English type applies: "The devout skeptic, the sage who rejects traditional religion not because he is shallow or immoral, but because he is too earnest to accept it—because he understands and tolerates all forms of religion too well to adopt any one of them." And, one might add among the younger generation another type, the suffering son who inherited his father's doubt but not the will to endure it. So it was with Lagarde, Langbehn, and Moeller, who were moved by strong religious compulsions.[3] They had from childhood been troubled by what they called the mystery of life and nature, and were never satisfied with the abstractions of "cold" science, longing for a more grandiose view of the world than that offered by atoms swirling endlessly and aimlessly in space. They felt and were awed by a mysterious power, inexplicable and yet immediately real to them, which they believed to rule the fate of man and the laws of nature. They avowed the existence of a supernatural order and of a deity and yearned to live in a community of dedicated believers.

But these sentiments did not lead them to the orthodoxy of the Christian faith; in fact, they broke with the Protestant faith into which they had been born, and heaped abuse upon its moral and political opportunism which sought to compromise with the modern world. Nor could Lagarde and Moeller accept the stricter Catholic religion, for their path was blocked by an inherited naturalism and agnosticism from which they could not escape. Like so many others, they were the victims of, not the participants in, the struggle over the validity of revealed religion; in the end, they hoped to invest their own beliefs with the passion of religion. They could neither banish the sense of awe and mystery nor could they submit to a faith whose dogmas had been riddled by generations of scientists and textual critics. Even the pantheistic love of Nature, which had inspired some of the great romantic writers, they rejected, largely because sci-

3. To define a person's religious consciousness is difficult at best, but is rendered more difficult here by the reluctance of Lagarde, Langbehn (except in the last years of his life), and Moeller to probe into their religious feelings and by the abstrusity of their scattered comments. Rudolf Otto, *The Idea of the Holy,* 2d ed., London 1950, in particular chapter 4, "Mysterium Tremendum," is perhaps the most penetrating insight into a similar state of mind. A recent definition of the religious view would certainly fit this type: "According to the religious view of the world there is a purpose in the scheme of things, into which human life must presumably in some way fit, so that human life is itself meaningful as being a part of the cosmic plan. The world is governed 'in the end' (whatever that phrase may mean) not by blind physical forces, but by spiritual forces which, in most actual religions, are conceived under the name God. Moreover, the world is a moral order in which, in spite of all appearances to the contrary, goodness must prevail and justice be done." W. T. Stace, *Religion and the Modern Mind,* Philadelphia, Lippincott, 1952, p. 179.

ence and scientism had in the interval pronounced that faith "unreal" and puerile. Only Langbehn succeeded in placing his faith in the Catholic Church, while Moeller and Lagarde cast about unable to join either the Church or the secular opposition. Moeller had avowed that God must exist even if we know that he is dead, and he proceeded to resolve the obstinate contradictions of mind and temper, culture and individuality, by fusing into art and politics the mystical impulses of his consciousness.

The portrait of this type emerges now with some clearness; certainly isolation, alienation, and self-hatred are the outstanding characteristics.[4] The Germanic critics had refused to accept society on any of its traditional terms; they had been hostile to its education and had accepted neither the formal beliefs of the majority nor the dogmas of the *avant-garde*. Equally, they brushed aside the possibilities of employment, even when this might have opened to them a career in harmonious relation with their professional peers. Langbehn and Moeller would have none of the hum-drum of daily work; only Lagarde continued to wrestle with the authorities for his rightful place in the academic world. Yet when his ambition had at last been amply satisfied and he had gained his well-deserved place of distinction, he quickly trained his guns on his new colleagues and after a while angrily complained that he was being snubbed. In fact all three were slighted upon occasion, though less often than they imagined. After all, they offended others with the abandon of men indifferent to civility, yet they resented and suffered from the slightest hint of criticism. One need only recall, for instance, Lagarde's egotism, or Langbehn's pose as the secret emperor, to realize that they were anything but independent of external recognition. They desperately wanted it, though on their own impractical terms. Perhaps no trait of the Germanic critics was more representative of a new type of discontent than this agonized search for status and prestige while denouncing the source of the honor sought and continuing to cling to isolation and self-inflicted cultural martyrdom. Among the leaders and the early followers of the National Socialist movement this conflict was often the mainspring of political action.

It is a truism that men can suffer from the burden of their time as easily as from their own failure; or they may, as did Lagarde, Langbehn, and Moeller, suffer from the convergence of the two. They had rejected the contemporary bourgeois world, partly following the dictates of their nature, partly because that society had made acceptance difficult and unrewarding. But how bitter that withdrawal made them! How they hated being monks without monasteries!

4. I note an interesting correspondence between my impression of these men and Eric Hoffer's description of the character of the true believer: "The most incurably frustrated—and, therefore, the most vehement—among the permanent misfits are those with an unfulfilled craving for creative work. . . . That hatred springs more from self-contempt than from a legitimate grievance is seen in the intimate connection between hatred and a guilty conscience." Eric Hoffer, *The True Believer. Thoughts on the Nature of Mass Movements,* New York 1951, pp. 46, 93. I should also mention the similarities between my views of these men and the authoritarian personality as defined by T. W. Adorno and his collaborators. I have purposely avoided the strictly psychological analysis which the authors of that book pressed. Cf. T. W. Adorno and others, *The Authoritarian Personality,* New York, Harper, 1950, esp. "Syndromes Found Among High Scorers," pp. 753–771.

As secular mendicants they preached the evils of this world, hoping still that their weariness and the weariness of all their fellow sufferers would some day be dispelled in a new Reich.

Lagarde, Langbehn, and Moeller thought of themselves as prophets, not as heirs. They were proud of their originality, proud of their intuitive sense of the crisis of their times. In fact, however, they had been much more influenced by past traditions than they realized, and without knowing it they served as cultural middlemen, transmitting old ideas in new combinations to later generations.

They acknowledged no intellectual masters and rarely mentioned earlier thinkers at all. Even in the realm of ideas, they felt lonely. But their silence attested also their distrust of the intellectual life, their unwillingness to wrestle with previous philosophers. They took seriously their own denigration of bookish learning, they were in truth "anti-intellectual intellectuals." What they read, they usually read uncritically, and what was said of one of them—"Lagarde was not a systematic thinker, but a rhapsodist"—was true of all of them. The irrationalism that they preached, they practiced as well.

Still, their thought contained many important themes from past traditions, and their influence was enhanced by the familiar ring of so much of their work. In dealing with their intellectual dependency, we must once more recall that they were essentially uninterested in abstract ideas, that they were more concerned with the moral tone or the idealistic commitment of an author. As a consequence, they were more attracted to men than to ideas, and especially to men whose fate resembled their own—to lonely, suffering, and unfulfilled geniuses. Langbehn, for example, felt an affinity for Novalis, Moeller for Nietzsche. Equally illuminating are their antipathies: they sneered at the "older," successful Goethe, they loathed Heine, and they were indifferent to Kant. From men they liked, they would appropriate certain "key ideas," or tags, which popular memory had fastened to these thinkers. These ideas reappeared in the works of the Germanic critics, as unidentified components of their own ideology. Their indebtedness to past thought was at once vast and insignificant. They were eclectics as well as *terribles simplificateurs*—those whom Burckhardt feared.[5]

They appropriated something from every intellectual tradition of modern Germany, except one. They consistently warred against the ideas of the Enlightenment and of the French Revolution—the so-called ideas of 1789—and hence they were most powerfully influenced by the men who shared this hostility, to wit, the romantics, the cultural nationalists of the late eighteenth century, and the more aggressive nationalists, like Jahn and Arndt, of the Napoleonic period. They illustrated what Nietzsche called "the hostility of the

5. In 1920, Moeller wrote about his political program: "At bottom it is all *very, very, very* simple: only by using concepts do we make everything complicated. What we seek is the *Word*." Letter to Ernst Krieck, quoted in Andreas Hohlfeld, *Unsere geschichtliche Verantwortung*, Leipzig 1933, p. 18. Italics in original.

Germans to the Enlightenment," this "obscurantist, enthusiastic, and atavistic spirit" which Nietzsche thought had been overcome, but which a half century later Thomas Mann noted was stronger than ever.[6]

The Germanic critics, following the accepted judgment of their time, condemned the romantics as ineffectual dreamers. Yet theirs was an essentially romantic temper: they exalted energy, will, passion, heroism—the demonic—and they despised the rational, contemplative, and conventional life. Hence they were particularly drawn to the *Stürmer und Dränger,* to the romantic genius as rebel.[7] They further exaggerated the already distorted notion of the romantics concerning the grayness of all theory and the emptiness of all "mechanistic" thought. They also shared the romantics' rejection of what they alleged was the eighteenth-century view of man as an essentially good and rational creature. They thought of man as a volitional and spiritual being, in need of a faith and a community, and they extolled the romantic sense of the tragic and the inexplicable in human fate. In much of this, unknown to themselves, they were remote Rousseauans, and like so many German conservatives they acknowledged their debt only by vilifying Rousseau's democratic thought.

Far greater and more direct, especially on Lagarde and Langbehn, was the impact of Herder. Lagarde's view of language, for example, and Langbehn's emphasis on the primitive, populistic quality of true art seem to be clear adaptations of certain aspects of Herder's cultural nationalism. Herder had been one of the first to associate nationalism with German folk traditions, with the primitive and spontaneous expression of the *Volksseele.* In 1773 appeared the original manifesto of this new nationalism, *Von deutscher Art und Kunst,* to which Goethe and Möser contributed as well. A few years later, Herder exclaimed: "Great Reich, Reich of ten peoples, Germany! You have no Shakespeare, but have you no ancient songs of which you can be proud? . . . Were the Germans from the beginning destined only to translate, only to imitate?" Herder's appeal to national self-consciousness was still subordinated to his cosmopolitan ideal of a common humanity, though he already believed that the German people had a unique calling for the realization of the goals of humanity. Under the impact of the revolutionary wars, later thinkers dissolved this association of nationalism and cosmopolitanism.

The Germanic critics were obviously influenced by the early nationalists, by

6. Nietzsche's aphorism is of particular relevance to the Germanic critics: "The whole tendency of the Germans ran counter to the Enlightenment, and to the revolution of society which, by a crude misunderstanding, was considered its result: piety toward everything still in existence sought to transform itself into piety toward everything that had ever existed, only to make heart and spirit full once again and to leave no room for future goals and innovations. The cult of feeling was erected in place of the cult of reason." *Morgenröte,* in *Friedrich Nietzsche, Werke in Drei Bänden,* ed. by Karl Schlechta, München 1954, I, 1145. Thomas Mann's remarks were contained in one of his attacks on the conservative revolution. "Die Stellung Freuds in der modernen Geistesgeschichte," *Gesammelte Werke,* East Berlin 1955, XI, 197–200.

7. In German usage, there is a sharp distinction between *Sturm und Drang* and *die Romantik,* the latter typically identified as "everything unreal and without substance, everything which is neither capable of life nor deserving of it." Rudolf Haym, *Die Romantische Schule,* 5th ed., Berlin 1928, p. 14. I am following the non-German usage of considering *Sturm und Drang* as the most vigorous expression of German romanticism.

the patriots who at the time of the French Revolution sought to liberate Germany from the tyranny of foreign rule and fashion. They were particularly attracted to Fichte, who at the moment of Germany's humiliation sought to exalt the cultural destiny of the nation. Moeller, we know, appeared to his contemporaries—and perhaps to himself—as a latter-day Fichte, who, at a time of still greater disaster, sought to save the nation.[8]

Certainly the "main ideas" of Fichte's *Addresses to the German Nation* reappeared in the works of the Germanic critics. Fichte's famous dictum "to have character and to be German [*Charakter haben und deutsch sein*] undoubtedly mean the same," became a principal tenet of later Germanic nationalism. Likewise his emphasis on *inner* freedom as the sufficient condition of human self-realization, his reconciliation of individualism and authority by means of a *Kulturstaat,* his appeal to youth because its "age lies nearer to the years of childlike innocence and of nature," and his projection of a great future for Germany, his echo of Schiller's "each people has its day in history, but the day of the Germans is the harvest of all times"—all of these were themes of the later ideology as well. The Germanic critics were still moved by the same faith that Fichte expounded at the end of his *Addresses:* "You are of all modern peoples the one in whom the seed of human perfection most unmistakably lies, and to whom the lead in its development is committed. If you perish in this your essential nature, then there perishes together with you every hope of the whole human race for salvation from the depths of its miseries."

Lagarde, Langbehn, and Moeller shared more with Fichte than the ideas they snatched from his much subtler and more complex philosophic thought. Fichte had inaugurated a new genre of political thinking; as Meinecke said, "among pure thinkers there is no more important example of the invasion of unpolitical ideas into Germany's political life than Fichte's." This metaphysical, moralistic, and thoroughly unempirical manner of dealing with political questions characterized other German romantics as well. Consider, for example, Novalis's poetic approach to politics, his lyrical evocation of a Christian empire, his vision of a Germany reborn, whose faith and spirit would lead and reconcile the warring parties of Europe. Langbehn thought himself inspired by Novalis, as did so many of the neo-romantics of the early twentieth century—and yet how remote Langbehn and his followers were from the Novalis who in his *Christendom or Europe* glorified not only the sublimity of the past but also the promise of the new world, which he saw in the "delightful feeling of freedom, the unqualified expectation of vast domains, pleasure in what is new and young, informal contact with all fellow citizens, pride in man's universality and joy in personal rights and in the property of the whole, and strong civic sense"!

The Germanic critics quarried many ideas from the romantics—the organis-

8. Max Hildebert Boehm, Moeller's friend and associate, wrote in his article on Moeller in the *Encyclopedia of the Social Sciences,* New York, Macmillan, 1948, X, 569: "His [Moeller's] thought was intuitive in character and his influence on the younger generation in post-war Germany might be compared to that of Fichte's *Reden an die Deutsche Nation* during the War of Liberation."

mic view of the state, the idealization of a corporatist and religious organization of society, and finally Schelling's belief in the resolution [*Aufhebung*] of opposites in "higher thirds." More importantly, they emulated the German romantics' esthetic and spiritual interpretation of politics and history, and their disdain for the empirical and material fact. Because of these similarities, Lagarde, Langbehn, and Moeller have often been called romantics, but such a designation overlooks the fact that they were indiscriminate and partial borrowers, who appropriated from incompatible traditions only the elements they happened to know about and that corresponded to their own prejudices.

Lagarde's and Langbehn's primitivist and anti-Semitic notions were foreshadowed by the works of Arndt and Jahn, by their glorification of the German folk, and by the xenophobic spirit of the *Burschenschaften*. Throughout the restoration period, this kind of folk ideology and *Germanomanie* was kept alive by journalists like W. Menzel, and by various artisan groups that blamed their decline on the Jewish exploitation of liberal free-trade principles. We saw that Lagarde's father was close to these groups. . . .

The National Socialist ideology, in motive, form, and content, resembles the Germanic ideology. Their negative views were indistinguishable. For both, liberalism was the chief enemy, an alien and corrosive force that was devouring the true Germanic spirit and destroying the German Reich. Both demanded the unity and aggrandizement of a folkish Reich, and both insisted that only a *Führer* could establish and rule such a Reich. Both were embittered critics of the bourgeois way of life, of the spirit of capitalism, and Moeller anticipated the National Socialist belief in a Germanic socialism. Lagarde and Langbehn had emphasized the central place of anti-Semitism in such an ideology, and the Germanic critics as well as the National Socialists believed—with more or less literal-mindedness—in the racial determination of character and history. Lastly, their common thoughts sprang from a common hatred and alienation. We may conclude from this resemblance that the National Socialist leaders were not creating a false ideology with which to manipulate the political will of the masses. The example of the Germanic critics demonstrates that such an ideology has a great intrinsic appeal, and the success of national socialism convinces us that this particular translation of resentment and discontent into political myth offered hope to those who, caught in the throes of economic disaster and social disintegration, craved the certainty of a spiritual redemption.

The two movements then sprang from similar psychological conditions and professed similar ideologies. More, their lines of march often crossed. Abundant evidence attests the direct influence of Lagarde and Langbehn on the most important National Socialist ideologists. Alfred Rosenberg, the chief ideologist of the Hitler movement, considered himself Lagarde's disciple. Ernst Krieck, the National Socialist theorist of education, freely borrowed from and acknowledged the works of Lagarde and Langbehn. The several founders of the Germanic religion based themselves on Lagarde's work. The young idol of National Socialist historians, Christoph Steding, attempted a metahistorical critique of European civilization and placed Langbehn's thought at the center of his own work. The National Socialists celebrated the older pair as their forebears and, although at one time or another repudiating every other influence, never wavered in their loyalty to these two.

Still more clearly is the junction seen in the person and the work of Moeller. He was the dominant figure of the conservative revolution in the Weimar Republic, and his idea of the Third Reich constituted the most powerful myth of the antirepublican forces. His direct influence on the National Socialists was not very great: when *Das Dritte Reich* appeared, Hitler was already concerned with disengaging himself from the National Socialist program, rather than elaborating it. Goebbels, on the other hand, had been immensely impressed by the book in 1925, and seven years later, on the occasion of a new edition of *Das Dritte Reich,* he enthusiastically endorsed it: "I welcome the dissemination of Moeller's work which is so very important for the history of National Socialist political ideas."

6. HANNAH ARENDT: The Origins of Totalitarianism*

Like Fritz Stern but on an even more sweeping basis, Hannah Arendt, the noted German-born political scientist, sees direct links between late nineteenth-century anti-Semitism and twentieth-century totalitarian structures. But her views on the causes and nature of anti-Semitism are quite distinctive, as her criticisms of some traditional approaches indicate. She uses both economic and political factors in her own explanation, but in an unusually generalized manner; for example, political anti-Semitism for her is no simple matter of manipulation, but a basic reaction to the modern state itself. Her view of the role of Jews in the development of anti-Semitism is also worth special note. Here is a case of a use of history, not in the cautious manner of most historians but with the certainty of one who has discovered the basic forces of the modern world. The scope and vigor of the presentation excite admiration, but do they lend themselves to careful empirical assessment?

Many still consider it an accident that Nazi ideology centered around antisemitism and that Nazi policy, consistently and uncompromisingly, aimed at the persecution and finally the extermination of the Jews. Only the horror of the final catastrophe, and even more the homelessness and uprootedness of the survivors, made the "Jewish question" so prominent in our everyday political life. What the Nazis themselves claimed to be their chief discovery—the role of the Jewish people in world politics—and their chief interest—persecution of Jews all over the world—have been regarded by public opinion as a pretext for winning the masses or an interesting device of demagogy.

The failure to take seriously what the Nazis themselves said is comprehensible enough. There is hardly an aspect of contemporary history more irritating and mystifying than the fact that of all the great unsolved political questions of our century, it should have been this seemingly small and unimportant Jewish

* From Hannah Arendt, *The Origins of Totalitarianism,* New Edition (New York: Harcourt, Brace & World, Inc., 1966), pp. 3–10, 14–15, 23–25. Reprinted by permission of Harcourt, Brace & World, Inc.

problem that had the dubious honor of setting the whole infernal machine in motion. Such discrepancies between cause and effect outrage our common sense, to say nothing of the historian's sense of balance and harmony. Compared with the events themselves, all explanations of antisemitism look as if they had been hastily and hazardously contrived, to cover up an issue which so gravely threatens our sense of proportion and our hope for sanity.

One of these hasty explanations has been the identification of antisemitism with rampant nationalism and its xenophobic outbursts. Unfortunately, the fact is that modern antisemitism grew in proportion as traditional nationalism declined, and reached its climax at the exact moment when the European system of nation-states and its precarious balance of power crashed.

It has already been noticed that the Nazis were not simple nationalists. Their nationalist propaganda was directed toward their fellow-travelers and not their convinced members; the latter, on the contrary, were never allowed to lose sight of a consistently supranational approach to politics. Nazi "nationalism" had more than one aspect in common with the recent nationalistic propaganda in the Soviet Union, which is also used only to feed the prejudices of the masses. The Nazis had a genuine and never revoked contempt for the narrowness of nationalism, the provincialism of the nation-state, and they repeated time and again that their "movement," international in scope like the Bolshevik movement, was more important to them than any state, which would necessarily be bound to a specific territory. And not only the Nazis, but fifty years of antisemitic history, stand as evidence against the identification of antisemitism with nationalism. The first antisemitic parties in the last decades of the nineteenth century were also among the first that banded together internationally. From the very beginning, they called international congresses and were concerned with a co-ordination of international, or at least inter-European, activities.

General trends, like the coincident decline of the nation-state and the growth of antisemitism, can hardly ever be explained satisfactorily by one reason or by one cause alone. The historian is in most such cases confronted with a very complex historical situation where he is almost at liberty, and that means at a loss, to isolate one factor as the "spirit of the time." There are, however, a few helpful general rules. Foremost among them for our purpose is Tocqueville's great discovery (in *L'Ancien Régime et la Révolution,* Book II, chap. 1) of the motives for the violent hatred felt by the French masses for the aristocracy at the outbreak of the Revolution—a hatred which stimulated Burke to remark that the revolution was more concerned with "the condition of a gentleman" than with the institution of a king. According to Tocqueville, the French people hated aristocrats about to lose their power more than it had ever hated them before, precisely because their rapid loss of real power was not accompanied by any considerable decline in their fortunes. As long as the aristocracy held vast powers of jurisdiction, they were not only tolerated but respected. When noblemen lost their privileges, among others the privilege to exploit and oppress, the people felt them to be parasites, without any real function in the rule of the country. In other words, neither oppression nor exploitation as such is ever the main cause for resentment; wealth without visible function is much more intolerable because nobody can understand why it should be tolerated.

Antisemitism reached its climax when Jews had similarly lost their public functions and their influence, and were left with nothing but their wealth. When Hitler came to power, the German banks were already almost *judenrein* (and it was here that Jews had held key positions for more than a hundred years) and German Jewry as a whole, after a long steady growth in social status and numbers, was declining so rapidly that statisticians predicted its disappearance in a few decades. Statistics, it is true, do not necessarily point to real historical processes; yet it is noteworthy that to a statistician Nazi persecution and extermination could look like a senseless acceleration of a process which would probably have come about in any case.

The same holds true for nearly all Western European countries. The Dreyfus Affair exploded not under the Second Empire, when French Jewry was at the height of its prosperity and influence, but under the Third Republic when Jews had all but vanished from important positions (though not from the political scene). Austrian antisemitism became violent not under the reign of Metternich and Franz Joseph, but in the postwar Austrian Republic when it was perfectly obvious that hardly any other group had suffered the same loss of influence and prestige through the disappearance of the Hapsburg monarchy.

Persecution of powerless or power-losing groups may not be a very pleasant spectacle, but it does not spring from human meanness alone. What makes men obey or tolerate real power and, on the other hand, hate people who have wealth without power, is the rational instinct that power has a certain function and is of some general use. Even exploitation and oppression still make society work and establish some kind of order. Only wealth without power or aloofness without a policy are felt to be parasitical, useless, revolting, because such conditions cut all the threads which tie men together. Wealth which does not exploit lacks even the relationship which exists between exploiter and exploited; aloofness without policy does not imply even the minimum concern of the oppressor for the oppressed.

The general decline of Western and Central European Jewry, however, constitutes merely the atmosphere in which the subsequent events took place. The decline itself explains them as little as the mere loss of power by the aristocracy would explain the French Revolution. To be aware of such general rules is important only in order to refute those recommendations of common sense which lead us to believe that violent hatred or sudden rebellion springs necessarily from great power and great abuses, and that consequently organized hatred of the Jews cannot but be a reaction to their importance and power.

More serious, because it appeals to much better people, is another commonsense fallacy: the Jews, because they were an entirely powerless group caught up in the general and insoluble conflicts of the time, could be blamed for them and finally be made to appear the hidden authors of all evil. The best illustration—and the best refutation—of this explanation, dear to the hearts of many liberals, is in a joke which was told after the first World War. An antisemite claimed that the Jews had caused the war; the reply was: Yes, the Jews and the bicyclists. Why the bicyclists? asks the one. Why the Jews? asks the other.

The theory that the Jews are always the scapegoat implies that the scapegoat might have been anyone else as well. It upholds the perfect innocence of the victim, an innocence which insinuates not only that no evil was done but that nothing at all was done which might possibly have a connection with the issue at stake. It is true that the scapegoat theory in its purely arbitary form never appears in print. Whenever, however, its adherents painstakingly try to explain why a specific scapegoat was so well suited to his role, they show that they have left the theory behind them and have got themselves involved in the usual historical research—where nothing is ever discovered except that history is made by many groups and that for certain reasons one group was singled out. The so-called scapegoat necessarily ceases to be the innocent victim whom the world blames for all its sins and through whom it wishes to escape punishment; it becomes one group of people among other groups, all of which are involved in the business of this world. And it does not simply cease to be coresponsible because it became the victim of the world's injustice and cruelty.

Until recently the inner inconsistency of the scapegoat theory was sufficient reason to discard it as one of many theories which are motivated by escapism. But the rise of terror as a major weapon of government has lent it a credibility greater than it ever had before.

A fundamental difference between modern dictatorships and all other tyrannies of the past is that terror is no longer used as a means to exterminate and frighten opponents, but as an instrument to rule masses of people who are perfectly obedient. Terror as we know it today strikes without any preliminary provocation, its victims are innocent even from the point of view of the persecutor. This was the case in Nazi Germany when full terror was directed against Jews, *i.e.,* against people with certain common characteristics which were independent of their specific behavior. In Soviet Russia the situation is more confused, but the facts, unfortunately, are only too obvious. On the one hand, the Bolshevik system, unlike the Nazi, never admitted theoretically that it could practice terror against innocent people, and though in view of certain practices this may look like hypocrisy, it makes quite a difference. Russian practice, on the other hand, is even more "advanced" than the German in one respect: arbitrariness of terror is not even limited by racial differentiation, while the old class categories have long since been discarded, so that anybody in Russia may suddenly become a victim of the police terror. We are not concerned here with the ultimate consequence of rule by terror—namely, that nobody, not even the executors, can ever be free of fear; in our context we are dealing merely with the arbitrariness by which victims are chosen, and for this it is decisive that they are objectively innocent, that they are chosen regardless of what they may or may not have done.

At first glance this may look like a belated confirmation of the old scapegoat theory, and it is true that the victim of modern terror does show all the characteristics of the scapegoat: he is objectively and absolutely innocent because nothing he did or omitted to do matters or has any connection with his fate.

There is, therefore, a temptation to return to an explanation which automatically discharges the victim of responsibility: it seems quite adequate to a reality in which nothing strikes us more forcefully than the utter innocence of the individual caught in the horror machine and his utter inability to change his fate. Terror, however, is only in the last instance of its development a mere form of government. In order to establish a totalitarian regime, terror must be presented as an instrument for carrying out a specific ideology; and that ideology must have won the adherence of many, and even a majority, before terror can be stabilized. The point for the historian is that the Jews, before becoming the main victims of modern terror, were the center of Nazi ideology. And an ideology which has to persuade and mobilize people cannot choose its victim arbitrarily. In other words, if a patent forgery like the "Protocols of the Elders of Zion" is believed by so many people that it can become the text of a whole political movement, the task of the historian is no longer to discover a forgery. Certainly it is not to invent explanations which dismiss the chief political and historical fact of the matter: that the forgery is being believed. This fact is more important than the (historically speaking, secondary) circumstance that it is forgery.

The scapegoat explanation therefore remains one of the principal attempts to escape the seriousness of antisemitism and the significance of the fact that the Jews were driven into the storm center of events. Equally widespread is the opposite doctrine of an "eternal antisemitism" in which Jew-hatred is a normal and natural reaction to which history gives only more or less opportunity. Outbursts need no special explanation because they are natural consequences of an eternal problem. That this doctrine was adopted by professional antisemites is a matter of course; it gives the best possible alibi for all horrors. If it is true that mankind has insisted on murdering Jews for more than two thousand years, then Jew-killing is a normal, and even human, occupation and Jew-hatred is justified beyond the need of argument.

The more surprising aspect of this explanation, the assumption of an eternal antisemitism, is that it has been adopted by a great many unbiased historians and by an even greater number of Jews. It is this odd coincidence which makes the theory so very dangerous and confusing. Its escapist basis is in both instances the same: just as antisemites understandably desire to escape responsibility for their deeds, so Jews, attacked and on the defensive, even more understandably do not wish under any circumstances to discuss their share of responsibility. In the case of Jewish, and frequently of Christian, adherents of this doctrine, however, the escapist tendencies of official apologetics are based upon more important and less rational motives.

The birth and growth of modern antisemitism has been accompanied by and interconnected with Jewish assimilation, the secularization and withering away of the old religious and spiritual values of Judaism. What actually happened was that great parts of the Jewish people were at the same time threatened by physical extinction from without and dissolution from within. In this situation, Jews concerned with the survival of their people would, in a curious desperate misinterpretation, hit on the consoling idea that antisemitism, after all, might be an excellent means for keeping the people together, so that the assumption of eternal antisemitism would even imply an eternal guarantee of Jewish existence. This superstition, a secularized travesty of the idea of eternity inherent in a faith in chosenness and a Messianic hope, has been strengthened through the fact that for many centuries the Jews experienced the Christian brand of hostility which was indeed a powerful agent of preservation, spiritually as well as politically. The Jews mistook modern anti-Christian antisemitism for the old religious Jew-hatred—and this all the more innocently because their assimilation had by-passed Christianity in its religious and cultural aspect. Confronted with an obvious symptom of the decline of Christianity, they could therefore imagine in all ignorance that this was some revival of the so-called "Dark Ages." Ignorance or misunderstanding of their own past were partly responsible for their fatal underestimation of the actual and unprecedented dangers which lay ahead. But one should also bear in mind that lack of political ability and judgment have been caused by the very nature of Jewish history, the history of a people without a government, without a country, and without a language. Jewish history offers the extraordinary spectacle of a people, unique in this respect, which began its history with a well-defined concept of history and an almost conscious resolution to achieve a well-circumscribed plan on earth and then, without giving up this concept, avoided all political action for two thousand years. The result was that the political history of the Jewish people became even more dependent upon unforeseen, accidental factors than the history of other nations, so that the Jews stumbled from one role to the other and accepted responsibility for none.

In view of the final catastrophe, which brought the Jews so near to complete annihilation, the thesis of eternal antisemitism has become more dangerous than ever. Today it would absolve Jew-haters of crimes greater than anybody had ever believed possible. Antisemitism, far from being a mysterious guarantee of the survival of the Jewish people, has been clearly revealed as a threat of its extermination. Yet this explanation of antisemitism, like the scapegoat theory and for similar reasons, has outlived its refutation by reality. It stresses, after all, with different arguments but equal stubbornness, that complete and inhuman innocence which so strikingly characterizes victims of modern terror, and therefore seems confirmed by the events. It even has the advantage over the scapegoat theory that somehow it answers the uncomfortable question: Why the Jews of all people?—if only with the question begging reply: Eternal hostility.

It is quite remarkable that the only two doctrines which at least attempt to explain the political significance of the antisemitic movement deny all specific Jewish responsibility and refuse to discuss matters in specific historical terms. In this inherent negation of the significance of human behavior, they bear a terrible resemblance to those modern practices and forms of government which, by means of arbitrary terror, liquidate the very possibility of human activity. Somehow in the extermination camps Jews were murdered as if in accordance with the explanation these doctrines had given of why they were hated: regardless of what they had done or omitted to do, regardless of vice or virtue. Moreover, the murderers themselves, only obeying orders and proud of their passionless efficiency, uncannily resembled the "innocent" instruments of an inhuman impersonal course of events which the doctrine of eternal antisemitism had considered them to be.

Such common denominators between theory and practice are by themselves no indication of historical truth, although they are an indication of the "timely" character of such opinions and explain why they sound so plausible to the multitude. The historian is concerned with them only insofar as they are themselves part of his history and because they stand in the way of his search for truth. Being a contemporary, he is as likely to succumb to their persuasive force as anybody else. Caution in handling generally accepted opinions that claim to explain whole trends of history is especially important for the historian of modern times, because the last century has produced an abundance of ideologies that pretend to be keys to history but are actually nothing but desperate efforts to escape responsibility. . . .

The simultaneous decline of the European nation-state and growth of antisemitic movements, the coincident downfall of nationally organized Europe and the extermination of Jews, which was prepared for by the victory of antisemitism over all competing isms in the preceding struggle for persuasion of public opinion, have to be taken as a serious indication of the source of antisemitism. Modern antisemitism must be seen in the more general framework of the development of the nation-state, and at the same time its source must be found in certain aspects of Jewish history and specifically Jewish functions during the last centuries. If, in the final stage of disintegration, antisemitic slogans proved the most effective means of inspiring and organizing great masses of people for imperialist expansion and destruction of the old forms of government, then the previous history of the relationship between Jews and the state must contain elementary clues to the growing hostility between certain groups of society and the Jews. We shall show this development in the next chapter.

If, furthermore, the steady growth of the modern mob—that is, of the *déclassés* of all classes—produced leaders who, undisturbed by the question of whether the Jews were sufficiently important to be made the focus of a political ideology, repeatedly saw in them the "key to history" and the central cause of all evils, then the previous history of the relationship between Jews and society must contain the elementary indications of the hostile relationship between the mob and the Jews. We shall deal with the relationship between Jews and society in the third chapter.

The fourth chapter deals with the Dreyfus Affair, a kind of dress rehearsal for the performance of our own time. Because of the peculiar opportunity it offers of seeing, in a brief historical moment, the otherwise hidden potentialities of antisemitism as a major political weapon within the framework of nineteenth-century politics and its relatively well-balanced sanity, this case has been treated in full detail.

The following three chapters, to be sure, analyze only the preparatory elements, which were not fully realized until the decay of the nation-state and the development of imperialism reached the foreground of the political scene. . . .

The schematic outline of the simultaneous rise and decline of the European nation-state system and European Jewry unfolds roughly in the following stages:

1. The seventeenth and eighteenth centuries witnessed the slow development of nation-states under the tutelage of absolute monarchs. Individual Jews everywhere rose out of deep obscurity into the sometimes glamorous, and always influential, position of court Jews who financed state affairs and handled the financial transactions of their princes. This development affected the masses who continued to live in a more or less feudal order as little as it affected the Jewish people as a whole.

2. After the French Revolution, which abruptly changed political conditions on the whole European continent, nation-states in the modern sense emerged whose business transactions required a considerably larger amount of capital and credit than the court Jews had ever been asked to place at a prince's disposal. Only the combined wealth of the wealthier strata of Western and Central European Jewry, which they entrusted to some prominent Jewish bankers for such purposes, could suffice to meet the new enlarged governmental needs. This period brought with it the granting of privileges, which up to then had been necessary only for court Jews, to the larger wealthy class, which had managed to settle in the more important urban and financial centers in the eighteenth century. Finally emancipation was granted in all full-fledged nation-states and withheld only in those countries where Jews, because of their numbers and the general backwardness of these regions, had not been able to organize themselves into a special separate group whose economic function was financial support of their government.

3. Since this intimate relationship between national government and Jews had rested on the indifference of the bourgeoisie to politics in general and state finance in particular, this period came to an end with the rise of imperialism at the end of the nineteenth century when capitalist business in the form of expansion could no longer be carried out without active political help and intervention by the state. Imperialism, on the other hand, undermined the very foundations of the nation-state and introduced into the European comity of nations the competitive spirit of business concerns. In the early decades of this development, Jews lost their exclusive position in state business to imperialistically minded businessmen; they declined in importance as a group, although individual Jews kept their influence as financial advisers and as inter-European middlemen. These Jews, however—in contrast to the nineteenth-century state bankers—had even less need of the Jewish community at large, notwithstanding its wealth, than the court Jews of the seventeenth and eighteenth

centuries, and therefore they frequently cut themselves off completely from the Jewish community. The Jewish communities were no longer financially organized, and although individual Jews in high positions remained representative of Jewry as a whole in the eyes of the Gentile world, there was little if any material reality behind this.

4. As a group, Western Jewry disintegrated together with the nation-state during the decades preceding the outbreak of the first World War. The rapid decline of Europe after the war found them already deprived of their former power, atomized into a herd of wealthy individuals. In an imperialist age, Jewish wealth had become insignificant; to a Europe with no sense of balance of power between its nations and of inter-European solidarity, the non-national, inter-European Jewish element became an object of universal hatred because of its useless wealth, and of contempt because of its lack of power. . . .

Of all European peoples, the Jews had been the only one without a state of their own and had been, precisely for this reason, so eager and so suitable for alliances with governments and states as such, no matter what these governments or states might represent. On the other hand, the Jews had no political tradition or experience, and were as little aware of the tension between society and state as they were of the obvious risks and power-possibilities of their new role. What little knowledge or traditional practice they brought to politics had its source first in the Roman Empire, where they had been protected, so to speak, by the Roman soldier, and later, in the Middle Ages, when they sought and received protection against the population and the local rulers from remote monarchical and Church authorities. From these experiences, they had somehow drawn the conclusion that authority, and especially high authority, was favorable to them and that lower officials, and especially the common people, were dangerous. This prejudice, which expressed a definite historical truth but no longer corresponded to new circumstances, was as deeply rooted in and as unconsciously shared by the vast majority of Jews as corresponding prejudices about Jews were commonly accepted by Gentiles.

The history of the relationship between Jews and governments is rich in examples of how quickly Jewish bankers switched their allegiance from one government to the next even after revolutionary changes. It took the French Rothschilds in 1848 hardly twenty-four hours to transfer their services from the government of Louis Philippe to the new short-lived French Republic and again to Napoleon III. The same process repeated itself, at a slightly slower pace, after the downfall of the Second Empire and the establishment of the Third Republic. In Germany this sudden and easy change was symbolized, after the revolution of 1918, in the financial policies of the Warburgs on one hand and the shifting political ambitions of Walter Rathenau on the other.

More is involved in this type of behavior than the simple bourgeois pattern which always assumes that nothing succeeds like success. Had the Jews been bourgeois in the ordinary sense of the word, they might have gauged correctly the tremendous power-possibilities of their new functions, and at least have tried to play that fictitious role of a secret world power which makes and unmakes governments, which antisemites assigned to them anyway. Nothing, however, could be farther from the truth. The Jews, without knowledge of or interest in power, never thought of exercising more than mild pressure for minor purposes of self-defense. This lack of ambition was later sharply resented by the more assimilated sons of Jewish bankers and businessmen. While some of them dreamed, like Disraeli, of a secret Jewish society to which they might belong and which never existed, others, like Rathenau, who happened to be better informed, indulged in half-antisemitic tirades against the wealthy traders who had neither power nor social status.

This innocence has never been quite understood by non-Jewish statesmen or historians. On the other hand, their detachment from power was so much taken for granted by Jewish representatives or writers that they hardly ever mentioned it except to express their surprise at the absurd suspicions leveled against them. In the memoirs of statesmen of the last century many remarks occur to the effect that there won't be a war because Rothschild in London or Paris or Vienna does not want it. Even so sober and reliable a historian as J. A. Hobson could state as late as 1905: "Does any one seriously suppose that a great war could be undertaken by any European state, or a great state loan subscribed, if the House of Rothschild and its connexions set their face against it?" This misjudgment is as amusing in its naïve assumption that everyone is like oneself, as Metternich's sincere belief that "the house of Rothschild played a greater role in France than any foreign government," or his confident prediction to the Viennese Rothschilds shortly before the Austrian revolution in 1848: "If I should go to the dogs, you would go with me." The truth of that matter was that the Rothschilds had as little political idea as other Jewish bankers of what they wanted to carry out in France, to say nothing of a well-defined purpose which would even remotely suggest a war. On the contrary, like their fellow Jews they never allied themselves with any specific government, but rather with governments, with authority as such. If at this time and later they showed a marked preference for monarchical governments as against republics, it was only because they rightly suspected that republics were based to a greater extent on the will of the people, which they instinctively mistrusted.

How deep the Jews' faith in the state was, and how fantastic their ignorance of actual conditions in Europe, came to light in the last years of the Weimar Republic when, already reasonably frightened about the future, the Jews for once tried their hand in politics. With the help of a few non-Jews, they then founded that middle-class party which they called "State-party" (*Staatspartei*), the very name a contradiction in terms. They were so naïvely convinced that their "party," supposedly representing them in political and social struggle, ought to be the state itself, that the whole relationship of the party to the state never dawned upon them. If anybody had bothered to take seriously this party of respectable and bewildered gentlemen, he could only have concluded that loyalty at any price was a façade behind which sinister forces plotted to take over the state.

Just as the Jews ignored completely the growing tension between state and society, they were also the last to be aware that circumstances had forced them into the center of the conflict. They therefore never knew how to evaluate antisemitism, or rather never recognized the moment when social discrimination changed into a political argument. For more than a hundred years, antisemitism had slowly and gradually made its way into almost all social strata in almost all European countries until it emerged suddenly as the one issue upon which an almost unified opinion could be achieved. The law according to which this process developed was simple: each class of society which came into a conflict with the state as such became antisemitic because the only social group which seemed to represent the state were the Jews. And the only class which proved almost immune from antisemitic propaganda were the workers who, absorbed in the class struggle and equipped with a Marxist explanation of history, never came into direct conflict with the state but only with another class of society, the bourgeoisie, which the Jews certainly did not represent, and of which they were never a significant part.

Chapter XII.

IMPERIALISM

NO ISSUE in nineteenth-century history has given rise to so clear or varied a controversy as has the nature and causes of imperialism. The phenomenon itself was massive, more than justifying the diverse efforts to comprehend it. In a few decades, largely between 1870 and 1900, Europe, with the United States, took over most of the world. At the same time the number of imperial powers increased, with the addition of Germany, Italy, and Belgium to the older roster of Britain, France, Russia, and others. Popular interest, not especially aroused by earlier colonial development, was now greatly stirred; imperialism, then, was closely connected with political and other attitudes.

The magnitude of the topic is one of the causes of the diversity of interpretation surrounding imperialism. The most important aspect of imperialism was, in the long run, its impact on the territories acquired. But even in limiting one's view to the European base, to the causes and results of imperialism in Europe, the standpoints are numerous. A study of imperialism is in part a study of biography, for the initiators of imperial advance in many areas were individual men whose motives must be assessed in any final evaluation of the phenomenon. Imperialism is a leading topic in European diplomatic history and can be quite plausibly treated from this viewpoint alone. Imperialism can be seen as a major ingredient in European political development, largely serving to reinforce conservative political movements, though some historians dispute the importance of this link. It can be related to European intellectual history, in its connections with social Darwinism and Christianity. Certainly, the values and mood of the supporters of imperialism, as well as the importance of these supporters to the imperialist advance, must be considered. Can imperialism be usefully explained by some effort to grasp the collective psychology of the period?

Finally, the relationship between imperialism and economics must be examined. Here the debate began, first with J. A. Hobson and then with Marxist historians. The economic explanation of imperialism can be challenged on many points, but it has not been decisively defeated. In part, at least, this is because precise facts are hard to come by in the discussion of causes. We may know fairly well whether the acquisition of a particular colony led to increased trade with the mother country and increased capital investment by the mother country, though there might be great disagreement even about this. But to provide such facts for imperialism in general is extraordinarily difficult. And to go from such facts to a statement of causes is more difficult yet. Say, for example, that a historian conclusively proves that the cost of imperialism was more than the profit; has he therefore eliminated economic motives as a cause? Few would claim so, for the profits of individual imperialists might still have been compelling, and even mistaken notions about the economic benefits of imperialism could have been sufficient causes. This is why, despite all the attacks on the economic explanation of imperialism, the issue remains alive.

Many students, of course, will shy away from any one approach to the phenomenon, believing that a combination of major factors was involved. This is certainly defensible, but for the study of imperialism it is probably unwise to be too eclectic. Among other things, there are so many possible explanations that to accept them all as equally important would be quite confusing. One must, then, try to set some sort of order of priorities among contributing factors. This involves, first of all, a definition of what imperialism is in essence. Possibly it should be broken down chronologically. There is a tendency to assume that imperialism is an entity, a constant. But one could argue that it changed even within a few decades, in terms of the political support it received, the arguments used to justify it, and so on. Similarly, might geographical distinctions be useful in breaking down the problem of causation? Imperialism was not necessarily the same in Russia as in England.

Throughout the history of the debate, of course, imperialism has been both attacked and praised by its students. Attack is the more common approach, and not only recently. Many interpreters of the causes of imperialism are not merely trying to explain what happened, but to explain how something so monstrous happened. This approach, needless to say, may well color the assessment of causes; among other things, it might be tempting to explain one monstrous development by another, assuming that their common monstrosity helps prove the linkage.

Most historians agree that some aspects of imperialism were deeply rooted in late nineteenth-century Europe. This is why the discussion of causes is no idle exercise; it may say something quite basic about European history. Did imperialism result from a strong, confident, and assertive Europe? Or did it stem from growing weakness and insecurity? Both positions have been taken, on various grounds. This is the essence of the debate.

One final complication: What are the historical limits of imperialism? The above remarks, and most of the following selections, focus on a few decades. Obviously, the term can be used much more broadly than this and is constantly employed to describe contemporary events. Some also find cases of imperialism throughout human history. Obviously, positions on this question of boundaries affect discussions of causation. If imperialism is limited in time, the search for causes can be relatively precise. If not, one must look for more persistent or recurrent factors, even perhaps to human nature itself; and this approach, while quite possibly correct, is hard to assess in the usual terms of the historian.

1. J. A. HOBSON: Imperialism: A Study*

John Atkinson Hobson (1858–1940) was one of the first serious students of imperialism. He was an economist hostile to classical economics and to a capitalism unfettered by a concern for social welfare. He saw imperialism as a grotesque extension of capitalism and condemned it as such. But his economic explanation of imperialism, though the most famous, was not his only approach; many other theories of imperial expansion can be traced to his work.

* From J. A. Hobson, *Imperialism: A Study* (London: George Allen & Unwin Ltd., 1938; 1st printed 1905), pp. 80–81, 130, 150–52, 196–98, 204–205, 214, 217–22. Reprinted by permission of George Allen & Unwin Ltd.

Hobson's solution to the problems that engendered imperialism was primarily economic, however; a liberal socialist, he urged internal redistribution of income, to provide new markets, and a liberalization of international trade.

Over-production in the sense of an excessive manufacturing plant, and surplus capital which could not find sound investments within the country, forced Great Britain, Germany, Holland, France to place larger and larger portions of their economic resources outside the area of their present political domain, and then stimulate a policy of political expansion so as to take in the new areas. The economic sources of this movement are laid bare by periodic trade-depressions due to an inability of producers to find adequate and profitable markets for what they can produce. The Majority Report of the Commission upon the Depression of Trade in 1885 put the matter in a nutshell. "That, owing to the nature of the times, the demand for our commodities does not increase at the same rate as formerly; that our capacity for production is consequently in excess of our requirements, and could be considerably increased at short notice; that this is due partly to the competition of the capital which is being steadily accumulated in the country." The Minority Report straightly imputed the condition of affairs to "over-production." Germany was in the early 1900's suffering severely from what is called a glut of capital and of manufacturing power: she had to have new markets; her Consuls all over the world were "hustling" for trade; trading settlements were forced upon Asia Minor; in East and West Africa, in China and elsewhere the German Empire was impelled to a policy of colonization and protectorates as outlets for German commercial energy.

Every improvement of methods of production, every concentration of ownership and control, seems to accentuate the tendency. As one nation after another enters the machine economy and adopts advanced industrial methods, it becomes more difficult for its manufacturers, merchants, and financiers to dispose profitably of their economic resources, and they are tempted more and more to use their Governments in order to secure for their particular use some distant undeveloped country by annexation and protection.

The process, we may be told, is inevitable, and so it seems upon a superficial inspection. Everywhere appear excessive powers of production, excessive capital in search of investment. It is admitted by all business men that the growth of the powers of production in their country exceeds the growth in consumption, that more goods can be produced than can be sold at a profit, and that more capital exists than can find remunerative investment.

It is this economic condition of affairs that forms the taproot of Imperialism. . . .

Imperialism—whether it consists in a further policy of expansion or in the rigorous maintenance of all those vast tropical lands which have been earmarked as British spheres of influence—implies militarism now and ruinous wars in the future. This truth is now for the first time brought sharply and nakedly before the mind of the nation. The kingdoms of the earth are to be ours on condition that we fall down and worship Moloch. . . .

It remains to point out how the spirit of Imperialism poisons the springs of democracy in the mind and character of the people. As our free self-governing colonies have furnished hope, encouragement, and leading to the popular aspirations in Great Britain, not merely by practical successes in the arts of popular government, but by the wafting of a spirit of freedom and equality, so our despotically ruled dependencies have ever served to damage the character of our people by feeding the habits of snobbish subservience, the admiration of wealth and rank, the corrupt survivals of the inequalities of feudalism. This process began with the advent of the East Indian nabob and the West Indian planter into English society and politics, bringing back with his plunders of the slave trade and the gains of corrupt and extortionate officialism the acts of vulgar ostentation, domineering demeanour and corrupting largesse to dazzle and degrade the life of our people. Cobden, writing in 1860 of our Indian Empire, put this pithy question: "Is it not just possible that we may become corrupted at home by the reaction of arbitrary political maxims in the East upon our domestic politics, just as Greece and Rome were demoralised by their contact with Asia?"

Not merely is the reaction possible, it is inevitable. As the despotic portion of our Empire has grown in area, a larger and larger number of men, trained in the temper and methods of autocracy as soldiers and civil officials in our Crown colonies, protectorates and Indian Empire, reinforced by numbers of merchants, planters, engineers, and overseers, whose lives have been those of a superior caste living an artificial life removed from all the healthy restraints of ordinary European society, have returned to this country, bringing back the characters, sentiments, and ideas imposed by this foreign environment. The South and South-West of England is richly sprinkled with these men, many of them wealthy, most of them endowed with leisure, men openly contemptuous of democracy, devoted to material luxury, social display, and the shallower arts of intellectual life. The wealthier among them discover political ambitions, introducing into our Houses of Parliament the coarsest and most selfish spirit of "Imperialism," using their imperial experience and connexions to push profitable companies and concessions for their private benefits, and posing as authorities so as to keep the yoke of Imperialism firmly fixed upon the shoulders of the "nigger." The South African millionaire is the brand most in evidence: his methods are the most barefaced, and his success, social and political, the most redoubtable. But the practices which are writ large in Rhodes, Beit, and their parliamentary confederates are widespread on a smaller scale; the South of England is full of men of local influence in politics and society whose character has been formed in our despotic Empire, and whose incomes are chiefly derived from the maintenance and furtherance of this despotic rule. Not a few enter our local councils, or take posts in our constabulary or our prisons: everywhere they stand for coercion and for resistance to reform. Could the incomes expended in the Home Countries and other large districts of Southern Britain be traced to their sources, it would be found that they were in large measure wrung from the enforced toil of vast multitudes of black, brown, or yellow natives, by arts not differing essentially from those which supported in idleness and luxury imperial Rome.

It is, indeed, a nemesis of Imperialism that the arts and crafts of tyranny, acquired and exercised in our unfree Empire, should be turned against our liberties at home. Those who have felt surprise at the total disregard or the open contempt displayed by the aristocracy and the plutocracy of this land for infringements of the liberties of the subject and for the abrogation of constitutional rights and usages have not taken sufficiently into account the steady reflux of this poison of irresponsible autocracy from our "unfree, intolerant, aggressive" Empire.

The political effects, actual and necessary, of the new Imperialism, as illustrated in the case of the greatest of imperialist Powers, may be thus summarised. It is a constant menace to peace, by furnishing continual temptations to further aggression upon lands occupied by lower races and by embroiling our nation with other nations of rival imperial ambitions; to the sharp peril of war it adds the chronic danger and degradation of militarism, which not merely wastes the current physical and moral resources of the nations, but checks the very course of civilization. It consumes to an illimitable and incalculable extent the financial resources of a nation by military preparation, stopping the expenditure of the current income of the State upon productive public projects and burdening posterity with heavy loads of debt. Absorbing the public money, time, interest and energy on costly and unprofitable work of territorial aggrandisement, it thus wastes those energies of public life in the governing classes and the nations which are needed for internal reforms and for the cultivation of the arts of material and intellectual progress at home. Finally, the spirit, the policy, and the methods of Imperialism are hostile to the institutions of popular self-government, favouring forms of political tyranny and social authority which are the deadly enemies of effective liberty and equality. . . .

There exists in a considerable though not a large proportion of the British nation a genuine desire to spread Christianity among the heathen, to diminish the cruelty and other sufferings which they believe exist in countries less fortunate than their own, and to do good work about the world in the cause of humanity. Most of the churches contain a small body of men and women deeply, even passionately, interested in such work, and a much larger number whose sympathy, though weaker, is quite genuine. Ill-trained for the most part in psychology and history, these people believe that religion and other arts of civilization are portable commodities which it is our duty to convey to the backward nations, and that a certain amount of compulsion is justified in pressing their benefits upon people too ignorant at once to recognize them.

Is it surprising that the selfish forces which direct Imperialism should utilize the protective colours of these disinterested movements? . . .

So Leopold, King of the Belgians, claimed for his government of the Congo —"Our only programme is that of the moral and material regeneration of the country." It is difficult to set any limit upon the capacity of men to deceive themselves as to the relative strength and worth of the motives which affect them: politicians, in particular, acquire so strong a habit of setting their projects in the most favourable light that they soon convince themselves that the finest result which they think may conceivably accrue from any policy is the actual motive of that policy. As for the public, it is only natural that it should be deceived. All the purer and more elevated adjuncts of Imperialism are kept to the fore by religious and philanthropic agencies: patriotism appeals to the general lust of power within a people by suggestions of nobler uses, adopting the forms of self-sacrifice to cover domination and the love of adventure. So Christianity becomes "imperialist" to the Archbishop of Canterbury, a "going out to all the world to preach the gospel"; trade becomes "imperialist" in the eyes of merchants seeking a world market.

It is precisely in this falsification of the real import of motives that the gravest vice and the most signal peril of Imperialism reside. . . .

Yet it is quite evident that sincere men are prepared to support the use of political and military force in order to open fields for missionary enterprise, and that the missionary, who is by turns trader, soldier, and politician, seems a most desirable instrument of civilization.

How close in motive and in conduct this combination really is may be thus illustrated from the history of the Soudan.

> Detachments of officers and men from every regiment, British and Egyptian, were conveyed across the Nile in the gunboats to take part in the Gordon memorial service, and to witness the hoisting of the British flag on the ruins of Khartoum. . . . Surrounded by the soldiers he had directed with terrible and glorious effect, the successful general ordered the flags to be hoisted. . . . The officers saluted, the men presented arms, and the band played the Egyptian National Anthem and our own. Then the Sirdar called for three cheers for Her Majesty. . . . The memorial service followed, and the solemn words of the English Prayer Book were read in that distant garden. . . . The bands played their dirge and Gordon's favourite hymn, "Abide With Me"; a gunboat on the river crashed out the salute. . . . The Highlanders played a long lament, and thus the ceremony was duly fulfilled. Nine thousand of those who would have prevented it lay dead on the plain of Omdurman. Other thousands were scattered in the wilderness, or crawled wounded to the river for water.

While the writer of this passage [Winston Churchill] omits the final touch, the deliberate shooting of wounded crawlers by troops under British commanders, the picture is profoundly suggestive, with its strange amalgam of the British flag, "Abide with Me," and the avenging of Gordon. . . .

The sporting and military aspects of Imperialism form, therefore, a very powerful basis of popular appeal. The desire to pursue and kill either big game or other men can only be satisfied by expansion and militarism. . . .

Most serious of all is the persistent attempt to seize the school system for Imperialism masquerading as patriotism. To capture the childhood of the country, to mechanize its free play into the routine of military drill, to cultivate the savage survivals of combativeness, to poison its early understanding of history by false ideals and pseudo-heroes, and by a consequent disparagement and neglect of the really vital and elevating lessons of the past, to establish a "geocentric" view of the moral universe in which the interests of humanity are subordinated to that of the "country" (and so, by easy, early, natural inference, that of the "country" to that of the "self"), to feed the always overweening pride of race at an age when self-confidence most commonly prevails, and by necessary implication to disparage other nations, so starting children in the world with false measures of value and an unwillingness to learn from foreign sources—to fasten this base insularity of mind and morals upon the little children of a nation and to call it patriotism is as foul an abuse of education as it is possible to conceive. Yet the power of Church and State over primary education is being bent consistently to this purpose, while the blend of clericalism and autocratic academicism which dominates the secondary education of this country pours its enthusiasm into the same evil channel. Finally, our centres of highest culture, the universities, are in peril of a new perversion from the path of free inquiry and expression, which is the true path of intellectual life. . . .

The interference with intellectual liberty is seldom direct, seldom personal, though both in the United States and Canada some instances of the crudest heresy-hunting have occurred. The real danger consists in the appointment rather than in the dismissal of teachers, in the determination of what subjects shall be taught, what relative attention shall be given to each subject, and what text-books and other apparatus of instruction shall be used. The subservience to rank and money, even in our older English universities, has been evinced so nakedly, and the demands for monetary aid in developing new faculties necessarily looms so large in academic eyes, that the danger here indicated is an ever-growing one. It is not so much the weight of the "dead hand" that is to be feared as that of the living: a college so unfortunate as to harbour teachers who, in handling vital issues of politics or economics, teach truths deeply and obviously antagonistic to the interests of the classes from whom financial aid was sought, would be committing suicide. . . .

The area of danger is, of course, far wider than Imperialism, covering the whole field of vested interests. But, if the analysis of previous chapters is correct, Imperialism stands as a first defence of these interests: for the financial and speculative classes it means a pushing of their private businesses at the public expense, for the export manufacturers and merchants a forcible enlargement of foreign markets and a related policy of Protection, for the official and professional classes large openings of honourable and lucrative employment, for the Church it represents the temper and practice of authority and the assertion of spiritual control over vast multitudes of lower people, for the political oligarchy it means the only effective diversion of the forces of democracy and the opening of great public careers in the showy work of empire-making. . . .

For these business politicians biology and sociology weave thin convenient theories of a race struggle for the subjugation of the inferior peoples, in order that we, the Anglo-Saxon, may take their lands and live upon their labours; while economics buttresses the argument by representing our work in conquering and ruling them as our share in the division of labour among nations, and history devises reasons why the lessons of past empires do not apply to ours while social ethics paints the motive of "Imperialism" as the desire to bear the "burden" of educating and elevating races of "children." Thus are the "cultured" or semi-cultured classes indoctrinated with the intellectual and moral grandeur of Imperialism. For the masses there is a cruder appeal to hero-worship and sensational glory, adventure and the sporting spirit: current history falsified in coarse flaring colours, for the direct stimulation of the combative instincts. But while various methods are employed, some delicate and indirect, others coarse and flamboyant, the operation everywhere resolves itself into an incitation and direction of the brute lusts of human domination which are everywhere latent in civilized humanity, for the pursuance of a policy fraught with material gain to a minority of co-operative vested interests which usurp the title of the commonwealth.

2. V. I. LENIN: Imperialism: The Highest Stage of Capitalism*

V. I. Lenin's (1870–1924) *Imperialism,* written in 1916, became the classic Marxist statement of the nature and causes of imperial expansion. It was one of his most important additions to Marxist theory generally, for by claiming that imperialism was capitalism run wild, he could justify the possibility of communist revolution in any colonial area, for even if the area itself was not yet capitalist in structure, it was part of the capitalist world and could rebel against it. Lenin's explanation of imperialism was rigidly economic; the conditions of monopoly capitalism compelled the division of the world. That his argument is dogmatic, or that it can easily be used for propaganda, should not preclude a serious effort to evaluate it historically and to compare it with other explanations, both economic and noneconomic.

Imperialism emerged as the development and direct continuation of the fundamental attributes of capitalism in general. But capitalism only became capitalist imperialism at a definite and very high stage of its development, when certain of its fundamental attributes began to be transformed into their opposites, when the features of a period of transition from capitalism to a higher social and economic system began to take shape and reveal themselves all along the line. Economically, the main thing in this process is the substitution of capitalist monopolies for capitalist free competition. Free competition is the fundamental attribute of capitalism, and of commodity production generally. Monopoly is exactly the opposite of free competition; but we have seen the latter being transformed into monopoly before our very eyes, creating large-scale industry and eliminating small industry, replacing large-scale industry by still larger-scale industry, finally leading to such a concentration of production and capital that monopoly has been and is the result: cartels, syndicates and trusts, and merging with them, the capital of a dozen or so banks manipulating thousands of millions. At the same time monopoly, which has grown out of free competition, does not abolish the latter, but exists over it and alongside of

* From V. I. Lenin, *Imperialism: The Highest Stage of Capitalism* (New York: International Publishers Co., Inc., 1939), pp. 88–9, 123–25, 126. Reprinted by permission of the International Publishers Co., Inc.

it, and thereby gives rise to a number of very acute, intense antagonisms, friction and conflicts. Monopoly is the transition from capitalism to a higher system.

If it were necessary to give the briefest possible definition of imperialism we should have to say that imperialism is the monopoly stage of capitalism. Such a definition would include what is most important, for, on the one hand, finance capital is the bank capital of a few big monopolist banks, merged with the capital of the monopolist combines of manufacturers; and, on the other hand, the division of the world is the transition from a colonial policy which has extended without hindrance to territories unoccupied by any capitalist power, to a colonial policy of monopolistic possession of the territory of the world which has been completely divided up.

But very brief definitions, although convenient, for they sum up the main points, are nevertheless inadequate, because very important features of the phenomenon that has to be defined have to be especially deduced. And so, without forgetting the conditional and relative value of all definitions, which can never include all the concatenations of a phenomenon in its complete development, we must give a definition of imperialism that will embrace the following five essential features:

1) The concentration of production and capital developed to such a high stage that it created monopolies which play a decisive role in economic life.

2) The merging of bank capital with industrial capital, and the creation, on the basis of this "finance capital," of a "financial oligarchy."

3) The export of capital, which has become extremely important, as distinguished from the export of commodities.

4) The formation of international capitalist monopolies which share the world among themselves.

5) The territorial division of the whole world among the greatest capitalist powers is completed.

Imperialism is capitalism in that stage of development in which the dominance of monopolies and finance capital has established itself; in which the export of capital has acquired pronounced importance; in which the division of the world among the international trusts has begun; in which the division of all territories of the globe among the great capitalist powers has been completed. . . .

[Therefore] the economic quintessence of imperialism is monopoly capitalism. This very fact determines its place in history, for monopoly that grew up on the basis of free competition, and precisely out of free competition, is the transition from the capitalist system to a higher social-economic order. We must take special note of the four principal forms of monopoly, or the four principal manifestations of monopoly capitalism, which are characteristic of the epoch under review.

Firstly, monopoly arose out of the concentration of production at a very advanced stage of development. This refers to the monopolist-capitalist combines, cartels, syndicates and trusts. We have seen the important part that these play in modern economic life. At the beginning of the twentieth century, monopolies acquired complete supremacy in the advanced countries. And although the first steps towards the formation of the cartels were first taken by countries enjoying the protection of high tariffs (Germany, America), Great Britain, with her system of free trade, was not far behind in revealing the same basic phenomenon, namely, the birth of monopoly out of the concentration of production.

Secondly, monopolies have accelerated the capture of the most important sources of raw materials, especially for the coal and iron industries, which are the basic and most highly cartelised industries in capitalist society. The monopoly of the most important sources of raw materials has enormously increased the power of big capital, and has sharpened the antagonism between cartelised and non-cartelised industry.

Thirdly, monopoly has sprung from the banks. The banks have developed from modest intermediary enterprises into the monopolists of finance capital. Some three or five of the biggest banks in each of the foremost capitalist countries have achieved the "personal union" of industrial and bank capital, and have concentrated in their hands the disposal of thousands upon thousands of millions which form the greater part of the capital and income of entire countries. A financial oligarchy, which throws a close net of relations of dependence over all the economic and political institutions of contemporary bourgeois society without exception—such is the most striking manifestation of this monopoly.

Fourthly, monopoly has grown out of colonial policy. To the numerous "old" motives of colonial policy, finance capital has added the struggle for the sources of raw materials, for the export of capital, for "spheres of influence," *i.e.,* for spheres for profitable deals, concessions, monopolist profits and so on; in fine, for economic territory in general. When the colonies of the European powers in Africa, for instance, comprised only one-tenth of that territory (as was the case in 1876), colonial policy was able to develop by methods other than those of monopoly—by the "free grabbing" of territories, so to speak. But when nine-tenths of Africa had been seized (approximately by 1900), when the whole world had been divided up, there was inevitably ushered in a period of colonial monopoly and, consequently, a period of particularly intense struggle for the division and the redivision of the world.

The extent to which monopolist capital has intensified all the contradictions of capitalism is generally known. It is sufficient to mention the high cost of living and the oppression of the cartels. This intensification of contradictions constitutes the most powerful driving force of the transitional period of history, which began from the time of the definite victory of world finance capital.

Monopolies, oligarchy, the striving for domination instead of the striving for liberty, the exploitation of an increasing number of small or weak nations by an extremely small group of the richest or most powerful nations—all these have given birth to those distinctive characteristics of imperialism which compel us to define it as parasitic or decaying capitalism. More and more prominently there emerges, as one of the tendencies of imperialism, the creation of the "bondholding" (rentier) state, the usurer state, in which the bourgeoisie lives on the proceeds of capital exports and by "clipping coupons." It would be a mistake to believe that this tendency to decay precludes the possibility of rapid growth of capitalism. It does not. In the epoch of imperialism, certain branches of industry, certain strata of the bourgeoisie and certain countries betray, to a more or less degree, one or other of these tendencies. On the whole, capitalism is growing far more rapidly than before. But this growth is not only becoming more and more uneven in general; its unevenness also manifests itself, in particular, in the decay of the countries which are richest in capital (such as England). . . .

The receipt of high monopoly profits by the capitalists in one of the numerous branches of industry, in one of numerous countries, etc., makes it economically possible for them to corrupt certain sections of the working class, and for a time a fairly considerable minority, and win them to the side of the bourgeoisie of a given industry or nation against all the others. The intensification of antagonisms between imperialist nations for the division of the world increases this striving. And so there is created that bond between imperialism and opportunism, which revealed itself first and most clearly in England, owing to the fact that certain features of imperialist development were observable there much earlier than in other countries. . . .

From all that has been said in this book on the economic nature of imperialism, it follows that we must define it as capitalism in transition, or, more precisely, as moribund capitalism. . . .

3. NICHOLAS MANSERGH: The Coming of the First World War*

Nicholas Mansergh is a historian of the British Commonwealth at Cambridge University. His book, *The Coming of the First World War,* was a general effort at reinterpretation of the prewar period, particularly in diplomacy. He argues that, aside from some early efforts by individuals, imperialism resulted primarily from efforts at political and diplomatic advantage, rather than economic gain. In a calm and carefully documented way, he is as wedded to an explanation by a single primary cause as are the economic determinists.

The opening up of Africa was the work not of governments but of individuals possessed of great courage and remarkable powers of endurance. There is something very revealing in that description by a companion, of Livingstone "tramping along with the steady, heavy tread which kept one in mind that he had walked across Africa." But where individuals had pioneered, governments soon intervened, and it is only with the motives that prompted their intervention that this book is concerned. The political and economic importance of Africa

* From Nicholas Mansergh, *The Coming of the First World War* (London: Longmans, Green & Co. Ltd., 1949), pp. 43–45, 46–51, 61–62. Reprinted by permission of Longmans, Green & Co. Ltd.

was popularly overestimated. In Western Europe it was commonly believed that the acquisition of colonies was the high road to rapid economic development. Many writers, principally, though not only, German, failed, as Mr. Taylor has written, "to grasp the truth about the British Empire—that it had come into being as the result of British commercial enterprise and industrial success; and they asserted the reverse, that the prosperity and wealth of Great Britain were due to the existence of her Empire. The German campaign for colonies rested on the simple dogma—give Germany colonies and the Germans will then be as prosperous as the English." Such popular beliefs may have influenced the minds even of autocratic governments, but they were not the directing force in overseas colonial expansion. The rulers of Europe thought primarily in terms of political not economic advantage and it was on the struggle for power in Europe that their eyes were always fixed. Expansion overseas was for the Continental States, not an end, but a means to an end.

Bismarck was a late and always a sceptical convert to "colonialism." His indifference was a source of strength. In the colonial field he could play the hand that best suited his purpose in Europe. For it was on the European scene that his eye was always riveted. And not his alone. "If you were to bring me all the empires of Asia and Africa . . . ," said General Garnier des Garets, "they wouldn't in my eyes be worth an acre of the earth where I fought in 1870, and where the *Cuirassiers* of Reichshoffen and the Zouaves of Froeschwiller lie." But the balance of forces in Europe left France after 1870 with the alternatives of enlarging her Empire overseas or a policy of resignation. Alsace-Lorraine could only be a question "reserved for the future." In the meantime, was it not folly to sit by idly nursing wrongs while other Powers extended their control over large parts of Africa and Asia? "Au nom d'un chauvinisme exalté et à courtes vues," exclaimed Jules Ferry, the protagonist of Republican imperialism, "devrions-nous acculer la politique française dans une impasse et, les yeux fixés sur la ligne bleue des Vosges, laisser tout faire, tout s'engager, tout se résourdre, sans nous, autour de nous, contre nous?"[1] This was the reasoning produced by the psychological reaction to defeat and reinforced by a revival of France's traditional belief in mercantilist economics that led her, a country with a declining population, to embark, with direct encouragement from Bismarck, on an active policy of colonial expansion in North and Central Africa, in Madagascar and in Indo-China.

Bismarck's sympathetic interest in French imperialism was an experiment on his side, in the possibilities of Franco-German reconciliation. That France should remain ostracized in Europe was his settled policy, but clearly it was not in the interests of Germany that she should be driven to despair. An outlet for her energies, preoccupation in colonial fields in which Germany had no interest,

1. "Must we, for the sake of an excessive and shortsighted chauvinism, drive French policy into a blind alley and, with our eyes fixed on the blue line of the Vosges, let everything be done, everything be undertaken, everything be decided—without us, around us, against us?" [Editor's note]

except for bargaining purposes, had everything to recommend it. The fact that, incidentally, French expansion in North Africa, and particularly in Tunis, would bring her into conflict with Italy, enhanced the attractions of this policy, even if it were not its primary purpose. To the French Ambassador, in January 1879, the Chancellor gave effusive encouragement. "Now indeed, I believe," observed Bismarck, "that the Tunisian pear is ripe and that the time has come for you to pluck it. The effrontery of the Bey has been like the August sun for this African fruit, which might very well have been spoilt or stolen by somebody else if you had let it remain too long on the bough. I don't know what you intend to do or whether it tempts you, but I take the opportunity of repeating . . . my desire to give you proofs of my good will on questions which concern you and in which there are no German interests in opposition to yours." That Italy had already received German encouragement to seize Tunis must have heightened the Chancellor's satisfaction with French reactions. For his advice was heeded, and by the end of 1881 this former province of the Turkish Empire was securely French and Italy estranged.

Not only France and Italy but also England had traditional interests in North Africa. If it was the anxiety of the Third Republic to restore French self-respect after 1870; of a united Italy to raise herself to the level of a first-class Power by the acquisition of colonies on the southern shore of the Mediterranean; it was England's concern for imperial communications that led her with some reluctance to intervene in Egypt and so come into conflict with France. The Suez Canal of which control had been dramatically acquired by Disraeli was, as Bismarck admitted, "of vital importance" to her Empire, being "like the spinal cord which connects the backbone with the brain." It was that fact that left England no freedom of choice. After "Dual Control" had been established in Egypt in the interests of British and French bond-holders in 1876, Lord Salisbury summed up the alternatives before his country. "You may," he said, "renounce, or monopolize or share. Renouncing would have been to place France across our road to India. Monopolizing would have been very near the risk of war. So we resolved to share." . . .

England's task in Egypt was undertaken with German goodwill, which soon evaporated. Where Bismarck had once acknowledged comparative German indifference in the affairs of Egypt, he felt by the end of 1883 that the time had come when a less passive attitude would better serve his ends. "We are uncommonly grateful to Prince Bismarck," Lord Granville had said to Count Herbert Bismarck in January 1883, "for the friendly attitude of German policy this summer was of great service to us. Our being left with a free hand in Egypt we owe, when all is said, to Germany's goodwill. We are all aware that at a particular moment Prince Bismarck could have upset the coach if he had chosen to, and we realize with much thankfulness that he refrained from doing so." The price however had still to be paid, and in Egypt pressure was easy to apply. For the Gladstone Government, reluctant to contemplate annexation on principle, were left with no practicable alternative to acting as the nominal mandatory of the Powers. That left Britain in a weak and vulnerable position, for, of the Powers, France burned with resentment at her exclusion from Egypt, and Russia, without any direct interest in the Nile Valley, was hostile to the consolidation of Britain's position in the Eastern Mediterranean. This was a situation from which Bismarck was not slow to profit. The situation in Egypt made England, as Baring frankly recognized, dependent on German goodwill.

It seems clear now that Bismarck's colonial policy was more the incidental offshoot of tactical moves in Europe than a departure undertaken on its own merits. The price that Bismarck was most concerned to exact from England in return for German goodwill in Egypt, was some form of guarantee in Europe which would reinsure Germany in the West against French aggression. When it was made plain that this was a price that England was not prepared to pay he decided to explore again the possibility of friendship with France, founded on Franco-German hostility to England in the colonial field. That he was also influenced by internal political considerations is hardly to be denied. A forward colonial policy was well calculated to enhance the Chancellor's popularity at home.

While early in 1884 the German Ambassador in London, Count Münster, was happily contemplating the friendly acquisition of Heligoland, encouraged at once by the Chancellor's interest, and the remark of the Colonial Secretary, Lord Derby, who said "this perfectly useless piece of rock in the North Sea, the smallest of our Colonies, gives me the most trouble of any," a far-ranging area of Anglo-German colonial friction loomed on the horizon. The Chancellor took up the grievances of German traders in Fiji; he then turned a more formidable gaze on South-West Africa. The Ambassador was instructed "to cease to mention the question of Heligoland" because it might make German colonial claims seem of secondary importance. If Germany failed to obtain satisfaction for her claims overseas, the Chancellor declared that "she must try to gain closer touch with seafaring Powers, France included." But in actual fact the colonial grievances had been put forward largely because they might make closer co-operation with France possible. It was on the foundation of joint hostility to Great Britain overseas that Bismarck hoped to build up friendship with France.

From 1883 to 1885 the new policy was put into practice. The weak but well-meaning Foreign Secretary, Lord Granville, noticed with dismay the abrupt change in the temper of Anglo-German relations. An atmosphere of friendly co-operation was transformed by a recital of German grievances in many parts of the world, which lost nothing in the telling by the Chancellor's arrogant son, Count Herbert Bismarck. Of all the disputes which followed, the most protracted was concerned with the fate of Angra Pequeña on the west coast of Africa some 200 miles north of the frontier of the Cape Province. There a German trader, named Lüderitz, established himself and asked for protection. Could the British Government give protection? inquired Herbert Bismarck, for "if not, the German Government will do their best to extend to it the same measure of protection which they could give to their subjects in remote parts of the world—but without having the least desire to establish any footing in South Africa." In replying to his inquiry there was unpardonable delay due partly, as Lord Granville explained, to the need of consulting the Cape. "We cannot," he observed, "act except in agreement with the Government of the Colony which has an independent Ministry and Parliament." To Bismarck this sounded singularly unconvincing. But there was a difference of view between London and the Cape. To a German settlement in South-West Africa, London might be comparatively indifferent, but the Cape was resolutely opposed. And in the event, what began as an inquiry about protection at Angra Pequeña developed, against their wishes, into German South-West Africa. The reasons are to be found in the weakness of the British position in Egypt, which made dependence on German goodwill inevitable, and strained relations with Russia which made the more desirable friendly co-operation with the Triple Alliance.

By the end of 1855 Bismarck's new policy had laid the foundation of the German Colonial Empire, for by then she had secured her position in the Cameroons and in New Guinea as well as in South-West Africa together with a foothold in East Africa. Where the British Colonial Empire had been founded largely by the private enterprise of the chartered companies, Germany's was created through the impetus of a deliberate policy of state. If that policy met a weak and dilatory response in London, that was due to misunderstanding of its aim and not to unfriendliness. For it was generally accepted that it was right and just that Germany should have her "place in the Sun." Owing to earlier indifference and her late start, her African territories compared unfavourably with those of France or of the Belgians in the Congo Basin, or of the British. But, judged by her subsequent policy, her interest in colonial expansion remained very secondary to her interests in Europe. By 1914 the total number of German colonial settlers was no more than 23,000. While the number of European emigrants is in itself no criterion of the quality of colonial government, these trifling numbers are at least an indication that colonies did not serve as an outlet for surplus population in Germany.

While Germany was acquiring a Colonial Empire in Africa and the Pacific, France, assured of German goodwill, extended her empire chiefly in North and West Africa but also by the acquisition of Madagascar, a convenient stepping-stone to Indo-China, between 1883 and 1885, and after a protracted struggle in Tonkin and Annam. It was the losses and set-backs in Tonkin that brought about the fall of the second Ferry Ministry, and with it the end of an active imperialist policy leaning on German goodwill. "The patronage of Bismarck," noted Lord Lyons, British Ambassador in Paris, "overthrew the Freycinet Cabinet; it is not strengthening Jules Ferry. . . . The *revanche* is still at the bottom of every French heart." With the fall of Ferry, that was no longer to be disguised. Bismarck's colonial policy, in so far as it was an experiment in Franco-German reconciliation, had failed.

The years 1885–89 witnessed the height of the scramble for Africa. But unlike the preceding years they were marked by a revival of Anglo-German co-operation under the aegis of Bismarck and Salisbury. If Bismarck, in laying the foundations of a German Colonial Empire, had not effected a reconciliation with France, he had at least succeeded in his other objectives. France and Italy were estranged over Tunis and Italy was compelled to seek alliance with the Central Powers: England and France were divided by Egypt; and England, partly because of her concern for the security of the Nile Valley, which was the cardinal consideration in determining her colonial policy in Africa, and partly because of the advance of Russia to the Afghan frontier, was also impelled towards more friendly relations with the Central Powers. This had two consequences. The first was the Mediterranean Agreement of 1887 by which England reached an understanding, first with Italy, later extended to Austria, to preserve the *status quo* in the Mediterranean. Highly satisfying to Bismarck, under whose auspices it was negotiated, the agreement brought England, even if loosely, into the orbit of the Triple Alliance Powers. The other consequence was to be found in the general Anglo-German colonial settlement in Africa, concluded in 1890 after Bismarck's fall, and made possible by the cession of Heligoland. In the first instance it was hoped by the Germans that South-West Africa might be surrendered for Heligoland. Count Herbert Bismarck, very unfavourably impressed by a visit to South-West Africa, sponsored this proposal. "I think," he wrote on 27th March 1889, "the deal would be very advantageous to us and enormously popular in Germany. Our South-West African Company is stagnant, bankrupt and hopeless. . . . In the colonial area we have not in fact a single soul who would qualify as a German citizen." But the negotiations proceeded slowly, largely because Bismarck was once more concerned with the possibility of negotiating a wider agreement with England which would carry European commitments, and partly because he felt it was the course of prudence to go slow lest it might be suspected in London how much importance Germany attached to an island which commanded the entrance to the Kiel Canal, then being built. When agreement was finally reached, the *quid pro quo* for England was not in South-West but mainly in East Africa. The Sultanate of Zanzibar became a British Protectorate and German penetration in East Africa was barred by the delineation of the boundaries of British East Africa. . . .

Though on more than one occasion colonial rivalries brought the Great Powers within sight of war, it is not for that reason to be concluded that colonial rivalry was a fundamental cause of war. On the contrary the colonial policies of the Continental states were formulated in the light of the European balance of power and designed to serve European ends. When they no longer served those ends the colonial scene slips unobtrusively into the background. From 1900 onwards there were no important colonial disputes between Germany and England because of the preoccupation of the Powers in the Far East between 1900–1904; and after 1904 because the Anglo-French Entente had removed the possibility of attaining the political ends which German colonial policy in the 'eighties had been designed to promote. . . .

4. JOSEPH A. SCHUMPETER: Imperialism and Social Classes*

Joseph A. Schumpeter (1883–1950) was born and educated in the Hapsburg monarchy; he taught economics in Austria and Germany until 1932; in 1919–20 he served as Austrian Minister of Finance. He taught at Harvard University from 1932 until his death. He published many noted works in economics, such as *The Theory of Economic Development,* but his interests ranged widely in history and philosophy as well. He was, broadly speaking, a conservative in economic matters and a vigorous defender of capitalism. His interpretation of imperialism specifically exculpates capitalism and relies on psychological and institutional factors. He extends the notion of imperialism well beyond the late nineteenth century, judging it in that period to be the product of anachronistic remnants of an older order.

Our analysis of the historical evidence has shown, first, the unquestionable fact that "objectless" tendencies toward forcible expansion, without definite, utilitarian limits—that is, non-rational and irrational, purely instinctual inclinations toward war and conquest—play a very large role in the history of mankind. It may sound paradoxical, but numberless wars—perhaps the majority of all wars—have been waged without adequate "reason"—not so much from the moral viewpoint as from that of reasoned and reasonable interest. The most herculean efforts of the nations, in other words, have faded into the empty air. Our analysis, in the second place, provides an explanation for this drive to action, this will to war—a theory by no means exhausted by mere references to an "urge" or an "instinct." The explanation lies, instead, in the vital needs of situations that molded peoples and classes into warriors—if they wanted to avoid extinction—and in the fact that psychological dispositions and social structures acquired in the dim past in such situations, once firmly established, tend to maintain themselves and to continue in effect long after they have lost their meaning and their life-preserving function. Our analysis, in the third place, has shown the existence of subsidiary factors that facilitate the survival of such dispositions and structures—factors that may be divided into two groups. The orientation toward war is mainly fostered by the domestic interests of ruling classes, but also by the influence of all those who stand to gain individually from a war policy, whether economically or socially. Both groups of factors are generally overgrown by elements of an altogether different character, not only in terms of political phraseology, but also of psychological motivation. Imperialisms differ greatly in detail, but they all have at least these traits in common, turning them into a single phenomenon in the field of sociology, as we noted in the introduction.

Imperialism thus is atavistic in character. It falls into that large group of

* From Joseph A. Schumpeter, *Imperialism and Social Classes* (New York: Augustus M. Kelley), pp. 83–96, 117–18, 120–22.

surviving features from earlier ages that play such an important part in every concrete social situation. In other words, it is an element that stems from the living conditions, not of the present, but of the past—or, put in terms of the economic interpretation of history, from past rather than present relations of production. It is an atavism in the social structure, in individual, psychological habits of emotional reaction. Since the vital needs that created it have passed away for good, it too must gradually disappear, even though every warlike involvement, no matter how non-imperialist in character, tends to revive it. It tends to disappear as a structural element because the structure that brought it to the fore goes into a decline, giving way, in the course of social development, to other structures that have no room for it and eliminate the power factors that supported it. It tends to dissappear as an element of habitual emotional reaction, because of the progressive rationalization of life and mind, a process in which old functional needs are absorbed by new tasks, in which heretofore military energies are functionally modified. If our theory is correct, cases of imperialism should decline in intensity the later they occur in the history of a people and of a culture. Our most recent examples of unmistakable, clear-cut imperialism are the absolute monarchies of the eighteenth century. They are unmistakably "more civilized" than their predecessors.

It is from absolute autocracy that the present age has taken over what imperialist tendencies it displays. And the imperialism of absolute autocracy flourished before the Industrial Revolution that created the modern world, or rather, before the consequences of that revolution began to be felt in all their aspects. These two statements are primarily meant in a historical sense, and as such they are no more than self-evident. We shall nevertheless try, within the framework of our theory, to define the significance of capitalism for our phenomenon and to examine the relationship between present-day imperialist tendencies and the autocratic imperialism of the eighteenth century.

The floodtide that burst the dams in the Industrial Revolution had its sources, of course, back in the Middle Ages. But capitalism began to shape society and impress its stamp on every page of social history only with the second half of the eighteenth century. Before that time there had been only islands of capitalist economy imbedded in an ocean of village and urban economy. True, certain political influences emanated from these islands, but they were able to assert themselves only indirectly. Not until the process we term the Industrial Revolution did the working masses, led by the entrepreneur, overcome the bonds of older life-forms—the environment of peasantry, guild, and aristocracy. The causal connection was this: A transformation in the basic economic factors (which need not detain us here) created the objective opportunity for the production of commodities, for large-scale industry, working for a market of customers whose individual identities were unknown, operating solely with a view to maximum financial profit. It was this opportunity that created an economically oriented leadership—personalities whose field of achievement was the organization of such commodity production in the form of capitalist enterprise. Successful enterprises in large numbers represented something new in the economic and social sense. They fought for and won freedom of action. They compelled state policy to adapt itself to their needs. More and more they attracted the most vigorous leaders from other spheres, as well as the manpower of those spheres, causing them and the social strata they represented to languish. Capitalist entrepreneurs fought the former ruling circles for a share in state control, for leadership in the state. The very fact of their success, their position, their resources, their power, raised them in the political and social scale. Their mode of life, their cast of mind became increasingly important elements on the social scene. Their actions, desires, needs, and beliefs emerged more and more sharply within the total picture of the social community. In a historical sense, this applied primarily to the industrial and financial leaders of the movement—the bourgeoisie. But soon it applied also to the working masses which this movement created and placed in an altogether new class situation. This situation was governed by new forms of the working day, of family life, of interests—and these, in turn, corresponded to new orientations toward the social structure as a whole. More and more, in the course of the nineteenth century, the typical modern worker came to determine the overall aspect of society; for competitive capitalism, by its inherent logic, kept on raising the demand for labor and thus the economic level and social power of the workers, until this class too was able to assert itself in a political sense. The working class and its mode of life provided the type from which the intellectual developed. Capitalism did not create the intellectuals—the "new middle class." But in earlier times only the legal scholar, the cleric, and the physician had formed a special intellectual class, and even they had enjoyed but little scope for playing an independent role. Such opportunities were provided only by capitalist society, which created the industrial and financial bureaucrat, the journalist, and so on, and which opened up new vistas to the jurist and physician. The "professional" of capitalist society arose as a class type. Finally, as a class type, the rentier, the beneficiary of industrial loan capital, is also a creature of capitalism. All these types are shaped by the capitalist mode of production, and they tend for this reason to bring other types—even the peasant —into conformity with themselves.

These new types were now cast adrift from the fixed order of earlier times, from the environment that had shackled and protected people for centuries, from the old associations of village, manor house, clan fellowship, often even from families in the broader sense. They were severed from the things that had been constant year after year, from cradle to grave—tools, homes, the countryside, especially the soil. They were on their own, enmeshed in the pitiless logic of gainful employment, mere drops in the vast ocean of industrial life, exposed to the inexorable pressures of competition. They were freed from the control of ancient patterns of thought, of the grip of institutions and organs that taught and represented these outlooks in village, manor, and guild. They were removed from the old world, engaged in building a new one for themselves—a specialized, mechanized world. Thus they were all inevitably democratized, individualized, and rationalized. They were democratized, because the picture of time-honored power and privilege gave way to one of continual change, set in motion by industrial life. They were individualized, because subjective opportunities to shape their lives took the place of immutable objective factors. They were rationalized, because the instability of economic position made their survival hinge on continual, deliberately rationalistic decisions—a dependence that emerged with great sharpness. Trained to economic rationalism, these people left no sphere of life unrationalized, questioning everything about themselves, the social structure, the state, the ruling class. The marks of this process are engraved on every aspect of modern culture. It is this process that explains the basic features of that culture.

These are things that are well known today, recognized in their full significance—indeed, often exaggerated. Their application to our subject is plain. Everything that is purely instinctual, everything insofar as it is purely instinctual, is driven into the background by this development. It creates a social and psychological atmosphere in keeping with modern economic forms, where traditional habits, merely because they were traditional, could no more survive than obsolete economic forms. Just as the latter can survive only if they are continually "adapted," so instinctual tendencies can survive only when the conditions that gave rise to them continue to apply, or when the "instinct" in question derives a new purpose from new conditions. The "instinct" that is *only* "instinct," that has lost its purpose, languishes relatively quickly in the capitalist world, just as does an inefficient economic practice. We see this process of rationalization at work even in the case of the strongest impulses. We observe it, for example, in the facts of procreation. We must therefore anticipate finding it in the case of the imperialist impulse as well; we must expect to see this impulse, which rests on the primitive contingencies of physical combat, gradually disappear, washed away by new exigencies of daily life. There is another factor too. The competitive system absorbs the full energies of most of the people at all economic levels. Constant application, attention, and concentration of energy are the conditions of survival within it, primarily in the specifically economic professions, but also in other activities organized on their model. There is much less excess energy to be vented in war and conquest than in any precapitalist society. What excess energy there is flows largely into industry itself, accounts for its shining figures—the type of the captain of industry—and for the rest is applied to art, science, and the social struggle. In a purely capitalist world, what was once energy for war becomes simply energy for labor of every kind. Wars of conquest and adventurism in foreign policy in general are bound to be regarded as troublesome distractions, destructive of life's meaning, a diversion from the accustomed and therefore "true" task.

A purely capitalist world therefore can offer no fertile soil to imperialist impulses. That does not mean that it cannot still maintain an interest in imperialist expansion. We shall discuss this immediately. The point is that its people are likely to be essentially of an unwarlike disposition. Hence we must expect that anti-imperialist tendencies will show themselves wherever capitalism penetrates the economy and, through the economy, the mind of modern nations—

most strongly, of course, where capitalism itself is strongest, where it has advanced furthest, encountered the least resistance, and preeminently where its types and hence democracy—in the "bourgeois" sense—come closest to political dominion. We must further expect that the types formed by capitalism will actually be the carriers of these tendencies. Is such the case? The facts that follow are cited to show that this expectation, which flows from our theory, is in fact justified.

1. Throughout the world of capitalism, and specifically among the elements formed by capitalism in modern social life, there has arisen a fundamental opposition to war, expansion, cabinet diplomacy, armaments, and socially-entrenched professional armies. This opposition had its origin in the country that first turned capitalist—England—and arose coincidentally with that country's capitalist development. "Philosophical radicalism" was the first politically influential intellectual movement to represent this trend successfully, linking it up, as was to be expected, with economic freedom in general and free trade in particular. Molesworth became a cabinet member, even though he had publicly declared—on the occasion of the Canadian revolution—that he prayed for the defeat of his country's arms. In step with the advance of capitalism, the movement also gained adherents elsewhere—though at first only adherents without influence. It found support in Paris—indeed, in a circle oriented toward capitalist enterprise (for example, Frédéric Passy). True, pacifism as a matter of principle had existed before, though only among a few small religious sects. But modern pacifism, in its political foundations if not its derivation, is unquestionably a phenomenon of the capitalist world.

2. Wherever capitalism penetrated, peace parties of such strength arose that virtually every war meant a political struggle on the domestic scene. The exceptions are rare—Germany in the Franco-Prussian war of 1870–1871, both belligerents in the Russo-Turkish war of 1877–1878. That is why every war is carefully justified as a defensive war by the governments involved, and by all the political parties, in their official utterances—indicating a realization that a war of a different nature would scarcely be tenable in a political sense. (Here too the Russo-Turkish war is an exception, but a significant one.) In former times this would not have been necessary. Reference to an interest or pretense at moral justification was customary as early as the eighteenth century, but only in the nineteenth century did the assertion of attack, or the threat of attack, become the only avowed occasion for war. In the distant past, imperialism had needed no disguise whatever, and in the absolute autocracies only a very transparent one; but today imperialism is carefully hidden from public view—even though there may still be an unofficial appeal to warlike instincts. No people and no ruling class today can openly afford to regard war as a normal state of affairs or a normal element in the life of nations. No one doubts that today it must be characterized as an abnormality and a disaster. True, war is still glorified. But glorification in the style of King Tuglâtî-palisharra is rare and unleashes such a storm of indignation that every practical politician carefully dissociates himself from such things. Everywhere there is official acknowledge-

ment that peace is an end in itself—though not necessarily an end overshadowing all purposes that can be realized by means of war. Every expansionist urge must be carefully related to a concrete goal. All this is primarily a matter of political phraseology, to be sure. But the necessity for this phraseology is a symptom of the popular attitude. And that attitude makes a policy of imperialism more and more difficult—indeed, the very word imperialism is applied only to the enemy, in a reproachful sense, being carefully avoided with reference to the speaker's own policies.

3. The type of industrial worker created by capitalism is always vigorously anti-imperialist. In the individual case, skillful agitation may persuade the working masses to approve or remain neutral—a concrete goal or interest in self-defense always playing the main part—but no initiative for a forcible policy of expansion ever emanates from this quarter. On this point official socialism unquestionably formulates not merely the interests but also the conscious will of the workers. Even less than peasant imperialism is there any such thing as socialist or other working-class imperialism.

4. Despite manifest resistance on the part of powerful elements, the capitalist age has seen the development of methods for preventing war, for the peaceful settlement of disputes among the states. The very fact of resistance means that the trend can be explained only from the mentality of capitalism as a mode of life. It definitely limits the opportunities imperialism needs if it is to be a powerful force. True, the methods in question often fail, but even more often they are successful. I am thinking not merely of the Hague Court of Arbitration but of the practice of submitting controversial issues to conferences of the major powers or at least those powers directly concerned—a course of action that has become less and less avoidable. True, here too the individual case may become a farce. But the serious setbacks of today must not blind us to the real importance or sociological significance of these things.

5. Among all capitalist economies, that of the United States is least burdened with precapitalist elements, survivals, reminiscences, and power factors. Certainly we cannot expect to find imperialist tendencies altogether lacking even in the United States, for the immigrants came from Europe with their convictions fully formed, and the environment certainly favored the revival of instincts of pugnacity. But we can conjecture that among all countries the United States is likely to exhibit the weakest imperialist trend. This turns out to be the truth. . . .

The character of capitalism leads to large-scale production, but with few exceptions large-scale production does *not* lead to the kind of unlimited concentration that would leave but one or only a few firms in each industry. On the contrary, any plant runs up against limits to its growth in a given location; and the growth of combinations which would make sense under a system of free trade encounters limits of organizational efficiency. Beyond these limits there is no tendency toward combination inherent in the competitive system. In particular, the rise of trusts and cartels—a phenomenon quite different from the trend to large-scale production with which it is often confused—can never be explained by the automatism of the competitive system. This follows from the very fact that trusts and cartels can attain their primary purpose—to pursue a monopoly policy—only behind protective tariffs, without which they would lose their essential significance. But protective tariffs do not automatically grow from the competitive system. They are the fruit of political action—*a type of action that by no means reflects the objective interests of all those concerned* but that, on the contrary, becomes impossible as soon as the majority of those whose consent is necessary realize their true interests. To some extent it is obvious, and for the rest it will be presently shown, that the interests of the minority, quite appropriately expressed in support of a protective tariff, do not stem from capitalism as such. It follows that *it is a basic fallacy to describe imperialism as a necessary phase of capitalism, or even to speak of the development of capitalism into imperialism.* We have seen before that the mode of life of the capitalist world does not favor imperialist attitudes. We now see that the alignment of interests in a capitalist economy—even the interests of its upper strata—by no means points unequivocally in the direction of imperialism. We now come to the final step in our line of reasoning. . . .

Trade and industry of the early capitalist period thus remained strongly pervaded with precapitalist methods, bore the stamp of autocracy and served its interests either willingly or by force. With its traditional habit of feeling, thinking, and acting molded along such lines, the bourgeoisie entered the Industrial Revolution. It was shaped, in other words, by the needs and interests of an environment that was essentially noncapitalist, or at least precapitalist—needs stemming not from the nature of the capitalist economy as such but from the fact of the coexistence of early capitalism with another and at first overwhelmingly powerful mode of life and business. Established habits of thought and action tend to persist, and hence the spirit of guild and monopoly at first maintained itself, and was only slowly undermined, even where capitalism was in sole possession of the field. Actually capitalism did not fully prevail *anywhere* on the Continent. Existing economic interests, "artificially" shaped by the autocratic state, remained dependent on the "protection" of the state. The individual organism, such as it was, would not have been able to withstand free competition. Even where the old barriers crumbled in the autocratic state, the people did not all at once flock to the clear track. They were creatures of mercantilism and even earlier periods, and many of them huddled together and protested against the affront of being forced to depend on their own ability. They cried for paternalism, for protection, for forcible restraint of strangers, and above all for tariffs. They met with partial success, particularly because capitalism failed to take radical action in the agrarian field. Capitalism did bring about many changes on the land, springing in part from its automatic mechanisms, in part from the political trends it engendered—abolition of serfdom, freeing the soil from feudal entanglements, and so on—but initially it did not alter the basic outlines of the social structure of the countryside. Even less did it affect the spirit of the people, and least of all their political goals. This explains why the features and trends of autocracy—including imperialism—proved so resistant, why they exerted such a powerful influence on capitalist development, why the old export monopolism could live on and merge into the new.

5. WILLIAM L. LANGER: A Critique of Imperialism*

William L. Langer was a professor of history at Harvard University for over thirty years; he is a past president of the American Historical Association and served in the United States government during and after World War II. His work on *The Diplomacy of Imperialism* was one of two massive studies of the diplomatic history of Europe in the late nineteenth century. Though largely a narrative drawn from diplomatic archives, it includes an assessment of the popular and intellectual mood in which imperialism developed. This selection is drawn from a related essay that evaluates the various approaches to imperialism. Langer clearly attempts to find some balance among the various interpretations, but he is drawn to the popular-psychological base particularly, while keeping this much more strictly defined in time and cause than Schumpeter did. One can, of course, accept his doubts about other interpretations without embracing his own approach. For the latter, the chief questions arise from his reliance on purely British examples of imperialism and from a possible failure directly to connect the popular mood to actual decisions about imperial acquisition.

It is now roughly fifty years since the beginning of that great outburst of expansive activity on the part of the Great Powers of Europe which we have come to call "imperialism." And it is about a generation since J. A. Hobson published his "Imperialism: a Study," a book which has served as the starting point for most later discussions and which has proved a perennial inspiration for writers of the most diverse schools. A reappraisal of it is therefore decidedly in order. The wonder is that it has not been undertaken sooner.

Since before the outbreak of the World War the theoretical writing on imperialism has been very largely monopolized by the so-called Neo-Marxians, that is, by those who, following in the footsteps of the master, have carried on his historical analysis from the critique of capitalism to the study of this further phase, imperialism, the significance of which Marx himself did not appreciate and the very existence of which he barely adumbrated. The Neo-Marxians, beginning with Rudolf Hilferding and Rosa Luxemburg, have by this time elaborated a complete theory, which has recently been expounded in several ponderous German works. The theory hinges upon the idea of the accumulation of capital, its adherents holding that imperialism is nothing more nor less than the last stage in the development of capitalism—the stage in which the surplus capital resulting from the system of production is obliged by ever diminishing returns at home to seek new fields for investment abroad. When this surplus capital has transformed the whole world and remade even the most

* From William L. Langer, "A Critique of Imperialism," *Foreign Affairs* (October, 1935), pp. 102–115. Reprinted by permission of *Foreign Affairs*.

backward areas in the image of capitalism, the whole economic-social system will inevitably die of congestion.

That the classical writers of the socialistic school derived this basic idea from Hobson's book there can be no doubt. Lenin himself admitted, in his "Imperialism, the Latest Stage of Capitalism," that Hobson gave "a very good and accurate description of the fundamental economic and political traits of imperialism," and that Hobson and Hilferding had said the essentials on the subject. This, then, has been the most fruitful contribution of Hobson's essay. When we examine his ideas on this subject we refer indirectly to the larger part of the writing on imperialism since this day.

As a matter of pure economic theory it is most difficult to break down the logic of the accumulation theory. It is a fact that since the middle of the last century certain countries—first England, then France, Germany and the United States—have exported large amounts of capital, and that the financial returns from these investments in many instances came to overshadow completely the income derived by the lending countries from foreign trade. It is also indisputable that industry embarked upon the road to concentration and monopoly, that increased efficiency in production led to larger profits and to the amassing of ever greater surpluses of capital. We must recognize further that, as a general rule, the return from investments abroad was distinctly above the return on reinvestment in home industry. In other words, the postulates of the socialist theory undoubtedly existed. There is no mentionable reason why the development of the capitalist system should not have had the results attributed to it.

But, as it happens, the actual course of history refutes the thesis. The course of British investment abroad shows that there was a very considerable export of capital before 1875, that is, during the climax of anti-imperialism in England. Between 1875 and 1895, while the tide of imperialism was coming to the full, there was a marked falling off of foreign investment. Capital export was then resumed on a large scale in the years before the war, though England was, in this period, already somewhat disillusioned by the outcome of the South African adventure and rather inclined to be skeptical about imperialism. Similar observations hold true of the United States. If the promulgation of the Monroe Doctrine was an act of imperialism, where was the export of capital which ought to have been its condition? Let us concede that the war with Spain was an imperialist episode. At that time the United States was still a debtor nation, importing rather that exporting capital. In Russia, too, the heyday of imperialism coincided with a period of heavy borrowing rather than of lending.

There is this further objection to be raised against the view of Hobson and his Neo-Marxian followers, that the export of capital seems to have little direct connection with territorial expansion. France, before the war, had plenty of capital to export, and some of her earliest and most vigorous imperialists, like Jules Ferry, declared that she required colonies in order to have adequate fields for the placement of this capital. But when France had secured colonies, she did not send her capital to them. By far the larger part of her exported funds went to Russia, Rumania, Spain and Portugal, Egypt and the Ottoman Empire. In 1902 only two or two and a half billion francs out of a total foreign investment of some 30 or 35 billion francs was placed in the colonies. In 1913 Britain had more money invested in the United States than in any colony or other foreign country. Less than half of her total export of capital had been to other parts of the Empire. The United States put more capital into the development of Canada than did England; and when, after the war, the United States became a great creditor nation, 43 percent of her investment was in Latin America, 27 percent in Canada and Newfoundland, and 22 percent in European countries. What she sent to her colonies was insignificant. Or let us take Germany, which in 1914 had about 25 billion marks placed abroad. Of this total only three percent was invested in Asia and Africa, and of that three percent only a small part in her colonies. Pre-war Russia was a great imperialist power, but Russia had to borrow from France the money invested in her Far Eastern projects. In our own day two of the most outspokenly imperialist powers, Japan and Italy, are both nations poor in capital. Whatever the urge that drives them to expansion, it cannot be the need for the export of capital.

At the height of the imperialist tide, let us say from 1885 to 1914, there was much less talk among the advocates of expansion about the need for foreign investment fields than about the need for new markets and for the safeguarding of markets from the tariff restrictions of competitors. It is certain that in the opinion of contemporaries that was the mainspring of the whole movement. But this economic explanation, like the other, has not been borne out by the actual developments. Very few colonies have done even half of their trading with the mother country and many have done less. Taken in the large it can be proved statistically that the colonial trade has always played a relatively unimportant part in the total foreign commerce of the great industrial nations. These nations have always been each other's best customers and no amount of rivalry and competition has prevented their trade from following, not the flag, but the price-list. The position of Canada within the British Empire did not prevent her from levying tariffs against British goods, nor from developing exceedingly close economic relations with the United States. In the pre-war period German commerce with the British possessions was expanding at a relatively higher rate than was Britain's.

If one must have an economic interpretation of imperialism, one will probably find its historical evolution to have been something like this: In the days of England's industrial preëminence she was, by the very nature of the case, interested in free trade. In the palmiest days of Cobdenism she exported manufactured goods to the four corners of the earth, but she exported also machinery and other producers' goods, thereby preparing the way for the industrialization of the continental nations and latterly of other regions of the world. In order to protect their infant industries from British competition, these new industrial Powers threw over the teachings of the Manchester school and began to set up tariffs. The result was that the national markets were set aside, to a large extent, for home industry. British trade was driven to seek new markets, where the process was repeated. But the introduction of protective tariffs had this further effect, that it made possible the organization of cartels and trusts, that is, the concentration of industry, the increase of production and the lowering of costs. Surplus goods and low prices caused the other industrial Powers likewise to look abroad for additional markets, and, while this development was taking place, technological improvements were making transportation and communication safer and more expeditious. The exploration of Africa at that time was probably a pure coincidence, but it contributed to the movement toward trade and expansion and the growth of a world market. Fear that the newly opened areas of the world might be taken over by others and then enclosed in tariff walls led directly to the scramble for territory in Asia and Africa.

The socialist writers would have us believe that concentration in industry made for monopoly and that the banks, undergoing the same process of evolution, were, through their connection with industry, enabled to take over control of the whole capitalist system. They were the repositories of the surplus capital accumulated by a monopolistic system and they were therefore the prime movers in the drive for imperial expansion, their problem being to find fields for the investment of capital. This is an argument which does violence to the facts as they appear historically. The socialist writers almost to a man argue chiefly from the example of Germany, where cartelization came early and where the concentration of banking and the control of industry by the banks went further than in most countries. But even in Germany the movement towards overseas expansion came before the growth of monopoly and the amalgamation of the banks. In England, the imperialist country *par excellence,* there was no obvious connection between the two phenomena. The trust movement came late and never went as far as in Germany. The same was true of the consolidation of the banking system. One of the perennial complaints in England was the lack of proper coördination between the banks and industry. To a certain extent the English exported capital because the machinery for foreign investment was better than the organization for home investment. In the United States, to be sure, there was already a pronounced concentration of industry when the great outburst of imperialism came in the last years of the past century, but in general the trust movement ran parallel to the movement for territorial expansion. In any event, it would be hard to disprove the contention that the growth of world trade and the world market brought on the tendency toward better organization and concentration in industry, rather than the reverse. It is obvious not only that one large unit can manufacture more cheaply than many small ones, but that it can act more efficiently in competition with others in the world market.

But this much is clear—that territorial control of extra-European territory solved neither the trade problem nor the question of surplus capital. The white colonies, which were the best customers, followed their own economic interests and not even tariff restrictions could prevent them from doing so. In the backward, colored, tropical colonies, which could be more easily controlled and exploited, it proved difficult to develop a market, because of the low purchasing power of the natives. The question of raw materials, of which so much has always been made, also remained open. The great industrial countries got but a fraction of their raw materials from the colonies, and the colonies themselves continued to show a tendency to sell their products in the best market. As for the export of capital, that continued to flow in an ever broader stream, not because the opportunities for investment at home were exhausted, but because the return from foreign investment was apt to be better and because, in many cases, foreign investment was the easier course. Capital flowed from the great industrial countries of Europe, but it did not flow to their colonies. The United States and Canada, Latin America (especially the Argentine) and even old countries like Austria, Hungary and Russia, got the bulk of it. The export of capital necessarily took the form of the extension of credit, which in turn implied the transfer of goods. Not infrequently the granting of loans was made conditional on trade concessions by the borrowing country. So we come back to the question of trade and tariffs. In a sense the export of capital was nothing but a device to stimulate trade and to circumvent tariff barriers, which brings us back to the coincidence of the movement for protection and the movement toward imperialism.

This may seem like an oversimplified explanation and it probably is. Some may argue that imperialism is more than a movement toward territorial expansion and that financial imperialism in particular lays the iron hand of control on many countries supposedly independent. But if you try to divorce imperialism from territorial control you will get nowhere. Practically all writers on the subject have been driven to the conclusion that the problem cannot be handled at all unless you restrict it in this way. When Hobson wrote on imperialism, he had reference to the great spectacle of a few Powers taking over tremendous areas in Africa and Asia. Imperialism is, in a sense, synonymous with the appropriation by the western nations of the largest part of the rest of the world. If you take it to be anything else, you will soon be lost in nebulous concepts and bloodless abstractions. If imperialism is to mean any vague interference of traders and bankers in the affairs of other countries, you may as well extend it to cover any form of influence. You will have to admit cultural imperialism, religious imperialism, and what not. Personally I prefer to stick by a measurable, manageable concept.

But even though Hobson's idea, that imperialism "is the endeavor of the great controllers of industry to broaden the channel for the flow of their surplus wealth by seeking foreign markets and foreign investments to take off the goods and capital they cannot sell or use at home," proved to be the most stimulating and fertile of his arguments, he had the very correct idea that imperialism was also a "medley of aims and feelings." He had many other contributory explanations of the phenomenon. For example, he was keenly aware of the relationship between democracy and imperialism. The enfranchisement of the working classes and the introduction of free education had brought the rank and file of the population into the political arena. One result of this epoch-making change was the rise of the so-called yellow press, which catered to the common man's love of excitement and sensationalism. Northcliffe was one of the first to sense the value of imperialism as a "talking point." Colonial adventure and far-away conflict satisfied the craving for excitement of the industrial and white-collar classes which had to find some outlet for their "spectatorial lust." The upper crust of the working class, as Lenin admitted, was easily converted to the teaching of imperialism and took pride in the extension of empire.

No doubt this aspect of the problem is important. The mechanization of humanity in an industrial society is a phenomenon with which we have become all too familiar, and every thoughtful person now recognizes the tremendous dangers inherent in the powers which the demagogue can exercise through the press, the motion picture and the radio. In Hobson's day propaganda was still carried on primarily through the press, but later developments were already foreshadowed in the activities of a Northcliffe or a Hearst. Hobson himself was able to show how, during the war in South Africa, the English press took its information from the South African press, which had been brought very largely under the control of Rhodes and his associates. Even at that time Hobson and others were pointing out how imperialistic capital was influencing not only the press, but the pulpit and the universities. Indeed, Hobson went so far as to claim that the great inert mass of the population, who saw the tangled maze of world movements through dim and bewildered eyes, were the inevitable dupes of able, organized interests who could lure or scare or drive them into any convenient course.

Recognizing as we do that control of the public mind involves the most urgent political problems of the day, it is nevertheless important to point out that there is nothing inexorable about the connection of propaganda and imperialism. Even if you admit that a generation ago moneyed interests believed that imperialism was to their advantage, that these interests exercised a far-reaching control over public opinion, and that they used this control to dupe the common man into support of imperial ventures, it is obvious that at some other time these same interests might have different ideas with regard to their own welfare, just as it is evident that public opinion may be controlled by some other agency—the modern dictator, for example.

But the same thing is not true of another influence upon which Hobson laid great stress, namely the biological conception of politics and international relations. During the last years of the nineteenth century the ideas of "social Darwinism," as it was called, carried everything before them. Darwin's catchwords—the struggle for existence and the survival of the fittest—which he himself always refused to apply to the social organism, were snapped up by others who were less scrupulous, and soon became an integral part of popular and even official thought on foreign affairs. It not only served to justify the ruthless treatment of the "backward" races and the carving up *in spe* of the Portuguese, Spanish, Ottoman and Chinese Empires and of other "dying nations," as Lord Salisbury called them, but it put the necessary imprimatur on the ideas of conflict between the great imperialistic Powers themselves, and supplied a divine sanction for expansion. It was currently believed, in the days of exuberant imperialism, that the world would soon be the preserve of the great states—the British, the American and the Russian—and it was deduced from this belief that survival in the struggle for existence was in itself adequate evidence of superiority and supernatural appointment. The British therefore looked upon their empire as a work of the divine will, while the Americans and Russians were filled with the idea of a manifest destiny. It will be at once apparent that glorification of war and joy in the conflict was intimately connected with the evolutionary mentality. Hobson, the most determined of anti-imperialists, was finally driven to define the whole movement as "a depraved choice of national life, imposed by self-seeking interests which appeal to the lusts of quantitative acquisitiveness and of forceful domination surviving in a nation from early centuries of animal struggle for existence."

The last phrases of this quotation will serve to lead us to the consideration of what has proved to be another fruitful thought of Hobson. He speaks, in one place, of imperialism as a sociological atavism, a remnant of the roving instinct, just as hunting and sport are left-overs of the physical struggle for existence. This idea of the roving instinct has made but little appeal to later writers, but the basic interpretation of imperialism as an atavism underlies the ingenious and highly intelligent essay of Joseph Schumpeter, "Zur Soziologie der Imperialismen," the only work from the bourgeois side which has had anything like the influence exerted by the writers of the socialist school. Schumpeter, who is an eminent economist, worked out a most convincing argument to prove that imperialism has nothing to do with capitalism, and that it is certainly not a development of capitalism. Capitalism, he holds, is by nature opposed to expansion, war, armaments and professional militarism, and imperialism is nothing but an atavism, one of those elements of the social structure which cannot be explained from existing conditions, but only from the conditions of the past. It is, in other words, a hangover from a preceding economic order. Imperialism antedates capitalism, going back at least to the time of the Assyrians and Egyptians. It is, according to Schumpeter, the disposition of a state to forceful expansion without any special object and without a definable limit. Conquests are desired not so much because of their advantages, which are often questionable, but merely for the sake of conquest, success and activity.

Schumpeter's theory is in some ways extravagant, but it has served as the starting point for some very interesting speculation, especially among German scholars of the liberal persuasion. It is now fairly clear, I think, that the Neo-Marxian critics have paid far too little attention to the imponderable, psychological ingredients of imperialism. The movement may, without much exaggeration, be interpreted not only as an atavism, as a remnant of the days of absolute monarchy and mercantilism, when it was to the interest of the prince to increase his territory and the number of his subjects, but also as an aberration, to be classed with the extravagances of nationalism. Just as nationalism can drive individuals to the point of sacrificing their very lives for the purposes of the state, so imperialism has driven them to the utmost exertions and the extreme sacrifice, even though the stake might be only some little known and at bottom valueless part of Africa or Asia. In the days when communication and economic interdependence have made the world one in so many ways, men still interpret international relations in terms of the old cabinet policies, they are still swayed by out-moded, feudalistic ideas of honor and prestige.

In a sense, then, you can say that there is, in every people, a certain indefinable national energy, which may find expression in a variety of ways.

As a general rule great domestic crises and outbursts of expansion follow each other in the history of the world. In many of the continental countries of Europe, and for that matter in our own country, great internal problems were fought out in the period before 1870. The energies which, in Germany and Italy, went into the victory of the national cause, soon began to project themselves beyond the frontiers. While the continental nations were settling great issues between them, England sat "like a bloated Quaker, rubbing his hands at the roaring trade" he was carrying on. In those days the British cared very little for their empire. Many of them would have felt relieved if the colonies had broken away without a fuss. But, says Egerton, the best-known historian of British colonial policy, when the Germans and the French began to show an interest in colonial expansion, then the British began to think that there must be some value as yet undiscovered in the colonies. They not only started a movement to bind the colonies and the mother country more closely together, but they stretched out their hands for more. In the end they, who had the largest empire to begin with, got easily the lion's share of the yet unappropriated parts of the world. Some thought they were engaged in the fulfilment of a divine mission to abolish slavery, to spread the gospel, to clothe and educate the heathen. Others thought they were protecting the new markets from dangerous competitors, securing their supply of raw materials, or finding new fields for investment. But underlying the whole imperial outlook there was certainly more than a little misapprehension of economics, much self-delusion and self-righteousness, much misapplication of evolutionary teaching and above all much of the hoary tradition of honor, prestige, power and even plain combativeness. Imperialism always carries with it the connotation of the *Imperator* and of the tradition of rule. It is bound up with conscious or subconscious ideas of force, of brutality, of ruthlessness. It was these traits and tendencies that were so vividly expressed in the poetry and stories of Kipling, and it was his almost uncanny ability to sense the emotions of his time and people that made him the greatest apostle of imperialism.

We shall not go far wrong, then, if we stress the psychological and political factors in imperialism as well as its economic and intellectual elements. It was, of course, connected closely with the great changes in the social structure of the western world, but it was also a projection of nationalism beyond the boundaries of Europe, a projection on a world scale of the time-honored struggle for power and for a balance of power as it had existed on the Continent for centuries. The most casual perusal of the literature of imperialism will reveal the continued potency of these atavistic motives. In a recent number of this very journal a leading Italian diplomat, explaining the policy of the Duce, recurred again and again to the failure of the other countries to appreciate the fact that Italy is a young and active country "animated by new spiritual values." By the much-decried Corfu episode of 1923, Mussolini, to give a concrete example, "called Europe's attention to the respect due to the new Italy and to the reawakened energies of the Italian people." In the present Ethiopian crisis there is not very much suggestion of economic or civilizing motives on the part of the Italians; rather the Duce holds before his followers the prospect of revenge for the defeat at Adua (reminiscent of Britain's thirst to avenge Gordon) and promises them a glorious future. Not long ago he spoke to a group of veterans among the ruins of ancient Rome and told them that every stone surrounding them should remind them that Rome once dominated the world by the wisdom of her rule and the might of her arms and that "nothing forbids us to believe that what was our destiny yesterday may again become our destiny tomorrow." In much the same spirit an eminent Japanese statesman expressed himself recently in *Foreign Affairs:* "As soon as the Meiji Restoration lifted the ban on foreign intercourse, the long-pent-up energy of our race was released, and with fresh outlook and enthusiasm the nation has made swift progress. When you know this historical background and understand this overflowing vitality of our race, you will see the impossibility of compelling us to stay still within the confines of our little island home. We are destined to grow and expand overseas." It is the same emphasis given by the Italian diplomat to the need for an outlet for surplus energies.

It is, of course, true that both Italy and Japan have a serious population problem and that Japan, at any rate, has an economic argument to back her imperialistic enterprises in Manchuria and China. But it has been shown long ago that the acquisition of new territory has no direct bearing on the population problem and that emigrants go where their interest calls them, not where their governments would like to have them go. As for Japan's economic needs, it may at least be questioned whether she would not be better off if she avoided political and military commitments in China. Her cheap goods have made very extensive inroads in all the markets of the world, and her eventual conquest of the whole Chinese market is perhaps inevitable. Far from having gained much from her recent policy, she has had to face boycotts and other forms of hostility. In this case, certainly, one might debate whether the game is worth the candle.

Baron Wakatsuki, whose statement is quoted above, was careful to avoid mention of a factor in Japanese imperialism which, as every well-informed person knows, is probably the real explanation of Japanese policy. After the Meiji Restoration it was more the exuberance and bellicosity of the military caste in Japan than the enthusiasm of the country at large which determined the policy of the government. If one reads modern Japanese history aright one will find that from 1870 onward the military classes were constantly pressing upon the government for action in Korea. Only with the greatest difficulty did the civil authorities stave off this pressure. In 1894 the Tokyo government more or less rushed into the war with China in order to avoid a dangerous domestic crisis. In other words, the ideas of honor and patriotism were appealed to in order to divert attention from the parliamentary conflict which was then raging. After the Japanese victory it was the military men who, against the better judgment of men like Count Ito and Baron Mutsu, insisted on the cession of the Liaotung Peninsula, which netted Japan nothing but the intervention of Russia, Germany, and France. We need not pursue this subject in all its minute details. The point I want to make is that in the case of Japan, as in the case of many other countries, it is easier to show that the military and official classes are a driving force behind the movement for expansion than to show that a clique of nefarious bankers or industrialists is the determining factor. Business interests may have an interest in the acquisition of territory, or they may not. But military and official classes almost always have. War is, for the soldiers, a profession, and it is no mere chance that war and imperialism are so commonly lumped together. For officials, expansion means new territories to govern and new jobs to be filled.

Hobson, with his pronouncedly economic approach to the problem, held that "the struggle for markets, the greater eagerness of producers to sell than of consumers to buy, is the crowning proof of a false economy of distribution," of which imperialism is the fruit. The remedy, he thought, lay in "social reform." "There is no necessity to open up new foreign markets," he maintained; "the home markets are capable of indefinite expansion." These contentions sound familiar enough in this day of world depression. Whether the home markets are capable of indefinite expansion is a question on which the economic internationalists and the advocates of autarchy hold different opinions. The interesting thing for us to consider, however, is the fact that movements towards autarchy should have developed at all and that so much stress should now be laid upon the problems of redistribution of wealth, of building up purchasing power, and, in general, of domestic social reform. The current of activity has shifted distinctly from expansion to revolution, peaceful or violent. Perhaps it may be argued from this that the socialist thesis regarding imperialism is now being proved; that capitalism has already transformed the backward areas to such an extent that the markets are ruined, and that the capitalist system is rapidly choking. This view might be acceptable if it were not for the fact that the colonies and backward areas are still very far from developed and if it were not for the further fact that before the depression the colonial trade with the older countries was steadily increasing. In the last five years, to be sure, international commerce has sunk to an unbelievably low point, but the difficulty has been chiefly with the trade between the great industrial Powers themselves. It is quite conceivable that the crisis is primarily due to the special situation arising from the World War and that the root of the trouble lies in the impossibility of fitting tremendous international payments into the existing framework of trade relations. The fantastic tariff barriers which have been set up on all sides have simply aggravated a situation which has been developing since the teachings of Cobdenism first began to fall into disrepute.

But whatever the true explanation of our present difficulties, very few voices are raised in favor of a solution by the methods of imperialism. Indeed, the movement toward autarchy is in a way a negation of imperialism. Economically we have been disillusioned about imperialism. We have learned that colonies do not pay. Britain's expenditure for the defense of the empire alone is enormous, yet she has never yet devised a method by which anything like a commensurate return could be secured. The French military outlay on the colonies in 1913 was more than five hundred million francs, at a time when the entire trade of France with her colonies came to hardly three times that figure. Similar statistics could be quoted for Germany, and it is a well-known fact that the colonies of both Spain and Portugal were much more of a liability than an asset.

In the same way it has turned out that foreign investments of capital are not all that they were expected to be. The higher returns from colonial investments have often been counterbalanced by the greater insecurity that went with them. European countries had more than one opportunity to learn the lesson even before the war. We need only recall the Argentine fiasco of 1890 and the wildcat Kaffir Boom in South African securities in 1895 as classical examples of what might happen. But of course all these instances are completely dwarfed by the experiences of the postwar—or perhaps better, the pre-depression decade. Foreign investments have caused acute international tensions and have resulted in phenomena like American dollar diplomacy in Latin America. The expenditure has been immense and what has been salvaged has been unimpressive enough. The nations of the world are still on the lookout for markets, as they have been for centuries, but the peoples of the world have become more or less convinced that the markets, if they can be got at all, can be got only by the offering of better and cheaper goods and not by occupation, political control or forceful exploitation. As for foreign investments, no one has any stomach for them and most of those fortunate enough to have money to invest would be glad to learn of a safe investment at home. The assurance of needed sources for raw materials is as much if not more of a problem today than it was a generation ago, but there is little sense in taking over the expensive administration of tropical or other territory to guarantee a source of raw materials, because somehow or other it usually turns out that the other fellow has the materials that you want, and it has long since become obvious that the idea of controlling sources of all the materials you may need is a snare and a delusion.

6. D. K. FIELDHOUSE: The Colonial Empires*

The debate over the nature and causes of imperialism has continued in recent studies. D. K. Fieldhouse, Beit lecturer in the History of the Commonwealth, at Oxford University, offers two approaches to the subject in his general survey of modern empires. First, he evaluates several previous interpre-

* From D. K. Fieldhouse, *The Colonial Empires*, pp. 207–212, 373. Copyright © Fischer Bucherei KG, Frankfurt am Main; copyright © Dell Publishing Co., Inc., and George Weidenfeld & Nicolson Ltd. Reprinted by permission of Delacorte Press, publisher.

tations and selects a primarily diplomatic one, though with a distinctive stress on Germany that invites comparison with Mansergh. Both his criticisms and his ultimate choice must be assessed with care. Is it enough, for example, to point to the later and fuller development of capitalistic big business, to dispose of the economic explanation? Even the earlier stages of mature capitalism could have had a great effect. Does the stress on Germany fit the dates of the new imperialist surge? Does it explain its extent? Fieldhouse's second approach seems quite different; it certainly reflects a larger view, drawing on a comparison with earlier European colonial efforts. How can one evaluate this sort of generalization—not uncommon in diplomatic history—about the inevitable workings of the balance of power, of vacuums that have to be filled? If late nineteenth-century imperialism was inevitable in this sense, what need is there to look for more precise and proximate causes?

Three features distinguish the thirty years between 1883 and the outbreak of the First World War. The rate of imperial expansion increased considerably: more colonial territory was acquired than during the previous three-quarters of a century. Annexation was no longer usually or necessarily the outcome of strong pressures from the circumference on reluctant European governments. The number of European powers concerned was multiplied by the revival of Spanish and Portuguese interest and by the intervention of states with no previous colonial tradition—Germany, Italy, the United States and King Leopold II of the Belgians. These facts were of sufficient importance to distinguish the period of partition from that of expansion: yet by no means all was new. There was no break in the continuity of European expansion, and the forces already making for imperial growth continued. The fundamental question after 1883 is why selective acquisition by a few states as a response to problems on the periphery became headlong partition of the world among so many.

Four basic interpretations have been provided: two assign one overriding cause for the new imperialism. The first alleges that partition was due to economic necessity. The industrialization of continental Europe and the revived protectionism of the last quarter of the century made tropical colonies necessary as never before to provide markets for manufactures, fields for the investment of surplus capital, and an assured source of raw materials. Colonies were deliberately acquired to fill these needs, and were circumscribed by tariffs and monopolies to ensure the advantage of the metropolis. This economic approach was given a specialized form by liberal-socialist writers like J. A. Hobson and by Marxists such as V. I. Lenin. Lenin emphasized the need of industrial capitalism in Europe to invest overseas, on the principle that the growth of "finance capital" and monopoly within Europe resulted in ever-declining profit margins for new investment. Thus tropical colonization was a means of staving off the eventual sterility of European capitalism and the coming of the socialist revolution.

Another single-cause explanation regards imperialism as an expression of European nationalism. By the 1870s the unification of Germany and Italy, the defeat of France in 1870–71, and the growth of jingoism in all countries generated a degree of international rivalry unknown since 1815. Colonies became sources of national power and symbols of prestige. Pressure of the uneducated mass vote in this first phase of European democracy forced aristocratic statesmen to acquire colonies; competition produced partition.

The weak points of these explanations cannot be examined in detail. Basically, both fall down on chronology. The phenomena on which they concentrate existed at one time or another, but developed too late to have been critical in the vital period before 1900. The great age of "finance capital," international cartels, banking trusts, etc., was after 1900 and still more after 1920. Britain, Russia, Germany, Italy, Spain, Portugal, and France were not seriously affected by them during the period of partition. Jingoistic imperialism also came late, reaching its peak in the 1920s: certainly there is little evidence that European statesmen were acting under such pressures in the 1880s and 1890s; more usually they had to stimulate public enthusiasm for acquisitions they had already made. In short, the colonial partition cannot be explained as the result of any one novel phenomenon within Europe.

A third approach assumes that partition was no more than a continuation of trends evident in the past half-century. Europe still did not hunger for new colonies; but the option was no longer open. Growing pressures on non-European societies now produced crises, similar to those in Tunisia or Fiji, in which indigenous governments cracked up or local nationalism reacted against "informal" alien interference. Thereafter "informal" control was no longer feasible: annexation became the alternative to evacuation. General partition was necessary both because older imperialisms had reached points of collision in West Africa, the Pacific and South-East Asia; and because more European states now had commercial or other interests in the colonial world which had to be accommodated. There are elements of truth in this theory: it rightly stresses that many new acquisitions can be explained in terms equally applicable to the previous half-century and were the result of pre-existing situations. Yet it is not a full explanation of the partition. It is satisfactory only in certain cases. It cannot explain the new speed or extent of European expansion, for there were no irresistible local stimuli to European action in many places made colonies in the twenty years after 1882.

The fourth interpretation denies that Europe needed tropical colonies for economic reasons or that there was a great public demand for them. It recognizes that previous trends were accelerating, and were likely to generate full occupation and partition of certain regions. But it maintains that the suddenness and speed with which Africa and the Pacific were divided after 1882 were not fully explicable in these terms, and looks for new influences. It sees the answer in new diplomatic patterns within Europe, and pinpoints Bismarck's sudden claim for German colonies in 1884–5 as the genesis of the new situation. Bismarck treated colonies as undifferentiated diplomatic pawns which any great power could claim and use as bargaining counters. By staking large claims in Africa and the Pacific, and by bringing colonial disputes in West

Africa to an international conference table, he created a stock-market in colonial properties which none could thereafter ignore. Any power which failed to make its own claims, however unsubstantiated, was liable to find itself ultimately barred from further expansion. Thus the essence of the partition was that a central-European statesman imposed continental methods of procedure on maritime powers who had hitherto treated colonies as their special preserve. Only along these lines is it possible to explain the sudden partition of Africa and the Pacific, or contemporary events in South-East Asia after 1882.

This last interpretation seems to fit the known facts most closely, and will be adopted in this survey of events between 1883 and 1914.

The eight years after 1883 were the most important in the second expansion of Europe. By 1890 the greater part of Africa and the Pacific had been claimed by one power or another as spheres of influence or full possessions; the partition of South-East Asia was almost complete; and it was predictable that the rest of the independent world would soon come under European rule.

The crisis which led to partition had its roots in the Congo situation and Anglo-French disagreement over Egypt; but it was made explosive by Bismarck. Leopold's Congolese claims could have been dealt with as a local issue. French resentment at British occupation of Egypt in 1882 was likely to stimulate French activity wherever she already had points of contact with Britain—in West Africa, South-East Asia and the Pacific. But it takes more than friction between two powers, who had no intention of fighting over such marginal issues, to generate a partition of the world. Partition could have come only if other major European powers entered the field. The entry of Germany as a claimant for colonies in 1884–5 was the cause of the new phase of European expansion.

The motives which led Otto von Bismarck, the German Chancellor, to claim colonies remain a matter of debate. It seems unlikely that he was convinced by the propaganda of theoretical German imperialists, or by German commercial groups with interests in Africa and the Pacific, that Germany needed colonies for economic reasons. He recognized that Germans needed protection in these places, and suffered from the absence of German bases; but it seems unlikely that Bismarck ever thought colonies intrinsically worth while. He remained a central European: security against Russia and France was infinitely more important than the dubious commercial advantage of possessing colonies. On the other hand by claiming colonies he might achieve strictly tactical political objectives on two fronts. Probably the more immediately important of these was to win the support of the National Liberals in the 1884 Reichstag elections by contriving a demonstration of national power in the colonial field. Certainly this policy succeeded, leading first to National Liberal support in 1884 and then to their coalition with the Conservatives in 1887. But the new colonial policy can also be linked closely with Bismarck's international calculations. His specific aim in 1884–5 was to mollify France by supporting her over Egypt and in West Africa. At the same time he wished to demonstrate to Britain the desirability of her working with rather than against Germany. He could achieve both objects by claiming colonies in areas which would not outrage France but would inconvenience Britain; claims which would, in fact, constitute weapons like the existing "Egyptian baton" which he could wield to bring Britain into line. Probably Bismarck had no long-term plan for using such colonies as diplomatic counters, though his successors in fact later did so. Devious though such motives may appear, it remains likely that the entry of Germany into colonial politics was in part the result of domestic political needs, in part, as has been said "the accidental by-product of an abortive Franco-German entente."

Bismarck's action in 1884–5 blew up half a century of imperial arrangements like a land-mine. In May 1884 he declared a protectorate over Angra Pequena, in South-West Africa, where there was already a private German claim to land. By July the German explorer Gustav Nachtigal had obeyed Bismarck's instructions to declare protectorates over Togoland, west of Lagos, and the Cameroons. In December Bismarck imposed a protectorate over the northern coast of New Guinea, on the basis of treaties made by a new German plantation company. Earlier a German warship had forced King Malietoa of Samoa to sign a new treaty giving Germany predominance in the Samoan group. Finally, in February 1885 Bismarck accepted treaties made by the German explorer, Carl Peters, imposing German protection on part of the East African coast opposite Zanzibar.

Tentative though these claims were—none amounting to more than a protectorate which could later be denounced—they set the tone for European expansion for the next quarter-century. Bismarck had demonstrated that any power strong enough to support its claims with authority could acquire colonies without occupying them: a few ambiguous treaties with native chiefs were all that was required. Once such lines had been drawn on the map they had considerable importance, for they could be erased by rivals only if they made counter-concessions to Germany. This demonstration had two consequences. It induced other states to make counter-claims for fear of losing their chances for good, or having later to pay too high a price for territory reserved by someone else; and it freed them from the need actually to occupy their claims. The first partition was, therefore, only an exercise in cartography by the chancelleries of Europe, who were often hard put to find in the gazetteers the more remote places they now possessed. Yet it had serious consequences. The first claims could be relatively uncontroversial; there was still much to choose from. Taste grew with indulgence: by the 1890s the instinct to partition was stronger, yet had to be satisfied from a much reduced supply. The growing international bellicosity of the later 1890s and 1900s was a product of the bloodless partition of the 1880s. . . .

The earlier empires were in no sense inevitable, for Europe had no power advantage over many civilized and well-organized non-European states. The modern empires, however, probably were inevitable. At some point between 1700 and the mid-nineteenth century the balance of power between the western nations and the rest of the world shifted decisively. The west became absolutely stronger as a result of industrial mechanization, improved military techniques and equipment, modern communications, sophisticated finance, scientific medicine and surplus capital. The trend was shown by the British conquest of India, the decline of Ottoman power in the Balkans and Mediterranean, the growth of a favourable trade balance with the advanced economies of the east, the spread of Christian missions, and the universal infiltration of European adventurers and traders. European power remained overwhelming until others adopted the skills which generated it: nothing could have prevented her from dominating the rest of the world. The only question was the particular form this predominance would take. "Informal empire"—political or economic—was for long its main expression; but, for reasons already considered, "informal empire" ultimately grew into "formal empire" almost everywhere. This was not invariably a matter of choice, for Europe did not need new formal empires. Her power was such that she could not escape them.

7. RONALD ROBINSON AND JOHN GALLAGHER: Africa and the Victorians*

In another recent study of imperialism—specifically, of one of the major centers of imperialist interest—two Cambridge historians, Ronald Robinson and John Gallagher, seek to point out the complexity and variability of the causes of imperialism. Though their approach is worded quite differently, it deserves comparison with Schumpeter's in stressing the role of governmental policy and official thinking. Like Fieldhouse, Robinson and Gallagher largely reject public opinion or economic pressure as major factors, but their reliance on a diplomatic framework is more diffuse and less tied to developments in the era of imperialism alone. Their claim that the policies and attitudes behind imperialism were rather traditional is highly interesting, but can it account for such a novel development? Note, too, that their focus is on England. Here, as so often, one must evaluate an approach in terms of both the area to which it is applied and the broader phenomenon it touches. Can one explain German or French actions in the same way? If not, is imperialism a definable entity at all? Finally, the suggestion that developments in Africa actually triggered imperialist advance deserves comparison with interpretations more exclusively focused on Europe and, perhaps, with Fieldhouse's notion of vacuums of power.

The Victorians after 1882 saw an almost unbelievable revolution in their political relations with Africa, as if their former calm and rational courses had run into some freakish whirlwind in the dark. As Lord Salisbury observed: "I do not exactly know the cause of this sudden revolution. But there it is." Against all precept and prejudice, against the experience and trends of previous expansion, the British occupied Egypt and staked out a huge tropical African empire. What was more, they were ready by the end of the century to fight

* From Ronald Robinson and John Gallagher, *Africa and the Victorians* (London, 1961), pp. 17–25, 462–65. Reprinted by permission of the authors and of Macmillan and Co., Ltd.; The Macmillan Company of Canada Ltd.; and St. Martin's Press, Inc.

major wars for Sudanese deserts and south African *Kopjes*. Why, after centuries of neglect, the British and other European governments should have scrambled to appropriate nine-tenths of the African continent within sixteen years, is an old problem, still awaiting an answer.

At the centre of late-Victorian imperialism in Africa lies an apparent paradox. The main streams of British trade, investment and migration continued to leave tropical Africa practically untouched; and yet it was tropical Africa that was now bundled into the empire. There is a striking discrepancy of direction here between the economic and imperial aims. The flag was not following trade and capital; nor were trade and capital as yet following the flag. The late-Victorians seemed to be concentrating their imperial effort in the continent of least importance to their prosperity.

What were the causes and incentives? Which of them were merely contributory and which decisive? The question of the motives for African empire may be opened afresh. There are several well-known elements in the problem. Perhaps the late-Victorians were more enthusiastic imperialists than their fathers. Possibly business men were driven to bring the unopened continent into production and so relieve surfeit and depression. The custom was once to account for the partition in such terms. Or it may be that heightened rivalries between the Powers in Europe made them seek relief in Africa from their tensions nearer home. For any or all of these reasons, the forces of imperialism in Britain and in Europe may have intensified dramatically in the last quarter of the century and caught up all Africa as they did so.

But in the British case at least, there are other possible elements which have sometimes been neglected. It cannot be taken for granted that positive impulses from European society or the European economy were alone in starting up imperial rivalries. The collapse of African governments under the strain of previous Western influences may have played a part, even a predominant part in the process. The British advances may have been the culmination of the destructive workings of earlier exercises of informal empire over the coastal *régimes*. Hence crises in Africa, no less than imperial ambitions and international rivalries in Europe, have to be taken into account. Allowance has also to be made for the diversity of interest and circumstance in the different regions of Africa. It seems unlikely that the motives in regions as dissimilar as Egypt, the Niger and south Africa can be fitted easily into a single, simple formula of "imperialism."

Another factor must be included. Victorian expansion by the Eighteen eighties had long historical roots and world-wide ramifications. Its manifold workings tended sometimes to build up, and sometimes to break down the societies drawn under its influence. While in some countries, British agencies helped to create vortices of disorder and nationalist reaction, in others they helped local communities to grow until they became expansive in their own right. In these ways the processes of expansion were soon receding out of metropolitan control. Some satellites tended to break up; others were beginning to throw off galaxies of their own. It is not unlikely that both these tendencies helped to drag British ministries into African empire. Lastly, it is quite possible that they did not acquire a new empire for its intrinsic value, but because Africa's relationship to their total strategy in Europe, the Mediterranean, or the East had altered.

The elements in the problem might seem so numerous and disparate as to make it insoluble. Some unified field of study has to be found where all possible incentives to African empire may be assembled without becoming indistinguishable in their several effects. Historically, only the government in London registered and balanced all the contingencies making for British expansion in Africa. In following the occasions and motives, all roads lead ineluctably to Downing Street. The files and red boxes which passed between ministers and officials at the time contain the problem in its contemporary proportions.

The collective mind of government assembled and weighed all the factors making for and against advances. Party leaders and Whips anxiously consulted the tone of the Commons and the trend of the by-elections. Secretaries for India, the Colonies and Foreign Affairs, along with the Chancellor of the Exchequer and the Service ministers, gauged the pressures: the condition of domestic and European politics, the state of the economy, the expansive demands from India and the white colonies, the risks and crises in Africa and in the whole world. Furnished with intelligences from distant ambassadors, governors and consuls, they took the rival theses of their departments to the Cabinet; and there, the Prime Minister and his colleagues argued out the differences and balanced the considerations of profit and power.

A first task in analysing the late-Victorians' share in the partition is to understand the motives of the ministers who directed it, and the study of official thinking is indispensable to this. Policy-making was a flow of deliberation and argument, of calculation and mediation between differing impulses. Secondly, it was a reading of the long-run national interest which stayed much the same from ministry to ministry, regardless of the ideological stock in trade of the Party in power. Ministers in their private calculations used a complex political arithmetic to decide whether to advance or not. Their thinking included analogues for the expansive pressures coming from business enterprise and Home politics, from foreign rivals and British agents on the spot.

By trying to reconstruct the calculations behind the higher decisions, the interplay of these elements as they worked at different levels may begin to emerge. The study of government's own reasoning is the obvious yardstick for measuring the urgency of incentives and contingencies at the point of action. Policy-making, in other words, is the unified historical field in which all the conditions for expansion were brought together.

This is not to say that ministers and their advisers were fully aware of the forces at work, or that they knew to a nicety where they were going. Neither is it to say that they were in control of the process of expansion and could start and stop it at will. Again, their recorded arguments for this course or for that did not always bring out fully their unconscious assumptions. What is more, there are many things too well understood between colleagues to be written down. There is no denying these limitations to the study of policy. But for all its shortcomings, official calculations throw most light on the deeper reasons for imperial expansion into Africa. They offer the unique method for making a first approximation to the relative strength of the different drives.

But the study of policy-making may not only advance the subject of motives, it may in addition help toward a break-through into the crucial problem—the objective causes of the partition of Africa. Once the weights in the balance of decision have been recorded, it may still be necessary to check the scales themselves. The official mind has to be taken along with the other elements in the problem as a possible cause in its own right.

Statesmen did more than respond to pressures and calculate interests; their decisions were not mere mechanical choices of expedients. Judgements and actions in fact were heavily prejudiced by their beliefs about morals and politics, about the duties of government, the ordering of society and international relations. And their attitudes to such questions tended to be specialised and idiosyncratic because they felt that their unique function and responsibility set them apart. If official thinking was in one sense a microcosm of past and present experience of expansion, in another sense it was consciously above and outside those processes. The aristocrat by right, the official by *expertise,* both felt socially superior and functionally detached from those who pushed trade and built empires. It was their high calling to mediate between jarring and selfish interests and to keep the state from being used as the tool of any of them. As governors, their profession was to take the long and the broad, not the short and narrow view, to reconcile one principle with another in action—and, in a hard-headed way, even to do right and eschew wrong. Whether a man entered the ruling circle through patronage, which was still usual, or through examination, which was becoming less rare, aristocratic traditions of duty to the whole nation and disdain for its parts persisted, as did the legalism with which they approached their problems. Those who governed still thought of themselves as arbiters above the tumult, slightly contemptuous of the shortsighted business man, the impractical philanthropist and the ignorant populace alike.

But the London policy-makers' detachment from their problems overseas was physical as well as professional. In Africa they were usually dealing with countries which they had never seen, with questions apprehended intellectually from reports and recommendations on paper. Their solutions and purposes on the other hand, were charged with the experience and beliefs of the society in which they lived and worked. Inevitably, the official idea and the African reality, the analysis of Whitehall and the local significance of Arabi or Kruger, or Goldie or Rhodes, were worlds apart. Yet in the end it was the idea and the analysis of African situations in Whitehall, and not the realities in Africa as such which moved Victorian statesmen to act or not to act. The working of their minds is therefore of the utmost importance in establishing the motives of imperialism. Because those who finally decided the issue of African empire were partly insulated from pressures at Home, and remote from reality in Africa, their historical notions, their ideas of international legality and the codes of honour shared by the aristocratic castes of Europe had unusually wide scope in their decisions.

The possibility that official thinking in itself was a cause of late-Victorian imperialism, although once brilliantly suggested by an economist, [Joseph Schumpeter] has usually been neglected by historians. England's rulers had inherited not only a world empire but the experience gained in bringing it together, and the assumptions and prejudices accumulated from past successes and failures inevitably influenced their behaviour in the partition. In the course of events, the great Departments of State and the Indian Service had compiled special historiographies of their own. Time and practice had ingrained upon the minds of the oligarchy who still controlled policy abroad special notions of the national interest, and of supremacy and security in the world. England's rulers shared an esoteric view of desirable and undesirable trends stretching from the past and present to the future. And they had evolved well-tried techniques for dealing with certain situations and swinging the issue in Britain's favour.

The tradition of policy had come down unbroken from Pitt and Canning to Palmerston and Clarendon. And in the great country houses of the land, their apothegms had been passed on to the descendants of the favoured few. The continuity of Victorian leadership was remarkable. New faces were few and far between. Almost all of Gladstone's colleagues of 1868–74 served with him again between 1880 and 1885; while most of Disraeli's second ministry returned to office under Salisbury in 1886. The homogeneity of leadership was equally striking, for all its hardy individualism. Most ministers had been born in the Eighteen twenties and thirties, read classics or mathematics at Oxford or Cambridge and served their political apprenticeships in junior posts under Palmerston or Disraeli in the late Fifties and Sixties. Their cast of mind had been fixed by the personalities and experiences of their mid-Victorian prime. As Colonial Secretary under Peel, the young Mr. Gladstone's mind had been formed upon the confident assumptions of early Victorian expansiveness, and they still inspired the ageing Prime Minister of the Eighteen eighties. As Secretary for India in the Sixties, the youthful Lord Cranborne had formed that high view of its worth which resolved the later Lord Salisbury to protect it at any cost. And the lesser officials in Whitehall, Calcutta, Cape Town and Cairo shared the tradition. It was a tradition in which the Indian, the Colonial, the Palmerstonian and the Cobdenite views of expansion commingled. Hence situations were reported from abroad and judged at Home through the distorting glass of inherited prejudice and preconception. The policy-makers' choices may have been fuddled by the distortions of this special historiography, or indeed by sheer ignorance of Africa; but their peculiar angle of vision made them take decisions which might not have been made for any other reasons in any other circumstances.

How far this official mind in all its different facets was itself a cause of partition partly depends on the relation of government to society at the time. It was a relation in which a mature élite of birth and talent continued to lead, provided that it respected popular sentiments and to some extent responded when they could no longer be denied. The coming of the mass-vote, the redistribution of seats, and the rise of the modern party all set narrowing limits to the independent action of the Whig and Tory dynasts. But if the control was tightening in some fields, it remained slack in others. Ministers of both parties were careful to court the new voter in domestic affairs. They entreated his opinion about the schooling of children or the limiting of drink. But the higher statecraft of empire and world security they usually managed to seal off from his ignorant enthusiasms. Throughout the partition of Africa, the Foreign Secretaries were all peers and great landowners. Foreign policy, of which African policy was part, was still made at house parties, not by the man in the street or the man in the Stock Exchange. But this freedom abroad had its conditions, and the party leaders were careful to observe them. They had to respect the public's thirst for peace, economy and prestige, its traditional shibboleths of trusteeship and antislavery. No powerful business interests must be offended or jettisoned. Disasters in Britain's foreign ventures had to be avoided.

The mass voter was still an enigma to England's governors. Fearing that *demos* was a Radical, they presumed that he was also an anti-imperialist. Gladstone, it seemed, had roused him for peace and against extensions of empire, and had thereby won an overwhelming victory in the "Midlothian Election" of 1880. The risks of another Midlothian haunted ministers throughout the partition. They feared that the country was turning against imperial expansion, and they knew that it was set against expense. Since such imperial enthusiasm as there was in the Eighties was directed to consolidating the white empire and not to extending tropical dependencies, leaders of the day might well wonder with the fifteenth Earl of Derby whether the democracy would tolerate for long the burdens of defence and empire; several of them prophesied that to annex more provinces would over-tax the nation's financial strength and open the way to bankruptcy and class war.

Altogether the Eighties were years of harrowing uncertainty rather than ebullient confidence in British politics. It was the Irish, not the African question which held the stage, and old party loyalties, shaken already by the reforms of Gladstonian Liberalism, were being dislodged by the struggle over Irish Home Rule. Amid this confusion no ministry commanded more than a composite and conditional majority between 1881 and 1895. As to affairs abroad, Salisbury could complain in 1888 that:

> The misfortune—the root difficulty—we have in dealing with [such] questions . . . is that public opinion in its largest sense takes no note of them. . . . The Members of the House of Commons are each like a ship without an anchor.

To ministers pondering the dangers of democracy, the Irish rifts, the ingrained dislike of expenditure and tropical dependencies, there seemed to be no clear call in British politics for imperial expansion in Africa. When it came to acting there they did so more in fear of the nation's criticism than in hope of its approval.

Although there was little instructed public interest in Africa during the Eighteen eighties, some of the vague benevolence released by Wilberforce and Livingstone still persisted. Most Britons still agreed on the need for preaching the Gospel of Christ in the Dark Continent, if few regarded it as a duty of the state. That is why the lonely end of Livingstone and Gordon's martyrdom on the steps of the palace at Khartum haunted the imaginations of their fellow-countrymen. But these archetypal figures were but the heroes of an hour. Popular attention was never directed toward Africa for long. Ministers too approached their African problems with minds deeply influenced by feelings of ethical and religious obligation. All this was common doctrine, whether in Downing Street or in Exeter Hall. The official mind took pleasure in supposing that in the pursuit of the national interest it was also putting down the slave trade and spreading sweetness and light. Hence it was natural rather than hypocritical for government to clothe its African actions in the public garb of philanthropy. But since public interest in Africa was vague and intermittent, ministers feared to rely on it for support of vigorous intervention.

In business no more than in political opinion did party leaders perceive any strong incentives to African empire. Industrial growth might be slowing down after the Eighteen seventies; but as the official inquiry into the so-called depression found, it was to the established markets of America, Australasia, India and China that nearly all chambers of commerce were looking for relief. The hazardous speculations of northern and tropical Africa did not attract them. Throughout the partition, only the southern sub-continent, its prospects newly gilded with gold, was to draw British commercial enterprise powerfully into Africa.

All these considerations stress once again the paradoxical nature of late-Victorian imperial expansion in Africa. Not only was it unaccompanied by any corresponding thrust of the expanding economy, except in the south, but in the Eighteen eighties at least, strong social impulses toward a new African empire do not appear on the surface of British opinion or politics. Yet it was in this decade that the ground plan of African dominion was truly laid. If the impulses from the British Isles were as weak and sporadic as they seem at first sight, then the contribution of the official mind is even more in need of investigation. For its role must have been correspondingly greater.

Naturally, government's ability to intervene would have been stronger if it had been backed by a deep social impetus. But as things stood, its powers of action were restricted. On the other hand, if ministers could evade the electorate's indifference and zeal for retrenchment, they would be that much freer to follow their traditional canons of policy. Whether confronted with European rivals or African crises, they would be guided by their own esoteric concepts. But they would have to find African governments or private agents to act on their behalf; or—and this they much preferred—they would have to ward off foreign action with diplomatic bargains. All this strengthens the possibility that the inherited notions and biases of official thinking may have been a significant cause of this imperialism without impetus. . . .

Did new, sustained or compelling impulses towards African empire arise in British politics or business during the Eighteen eighties? The evidence seems unconvincing. The late-Victorians seem to have been no keener to rule and develop Africa than their fathers. The business man saw no greater future there, except in the south; the politician was as reluctant to expand and administer a tropical African empire as the mid-Victorians had been; and plainly Parliament was no more eager to pay for it. British opinion restrained rather than prompted ministers to act in Africa. Hence they had to rely on private companies or colonial governments to act for them. It is true that African lobbies and a minority of imperialists did what they could to persuade government to advance. Yet they were usually too weak to be decisive. Measured by the yardstick of official thinking, there was no strong political or commercial movement in Britain in favour of African acquisitions.

The priorities of policy in tropical Africa confirm this impression. West Africa seemed to offer better prospects of markets and raw materials than east Africa and the Upper Nile; yet it was upon these poorer countries that the British government concentrated its efforts. These regions of Africa which interested the British investor and merchant least, concerned ministers the most. No expansion of commerce prompted the territorial claims to Uganda, the east coast and the Nile Valley. As Mackinnon's failure showed, private enterprise was not moving in to develop them; and they were no more useful or necessary to the British industrial economy between 1880 and 1900 than they had been earlier in the century. Territorial claims here reached out far in advance of the expanding economy. Notions of pegging out colonial estates for posterity hardly entered into British calculations until the late Eighteen nineties, when it was almost too late to affect the outcome. Nor were ministers gulled by the romantic glories of ruling desert and bush. Imperialism in the wide sense of empire for empire's sake was not their motive. Their territorial claims were not made for the sake of African empire or commerce as such. They were little more than by-products of an enforced search for better security in the Mediterranean and the East. It was not the pomps or profits of governing Africa which moved the ruling *élite,* but the cold rules for national safety handed on from Pitt, Palmerston and Disraeli.

According to the grammar of the policy-makers, their advances in Africa were prompted by different interests and circumstances in different regions. Egypt was occupied because of the collapse of the Khedivial *régime*. The occupation went on because the internal crisis remained unsolved and because of French hostility which the occupation itself provoked. Britain's insistent claims in east Africa and the Nile Valley and her yielding of so much in west Africa were largely contingent upon the Egyptian occupation and the way it affected European relations. In southern Africa, imperial intervention against the Transvaal was designed above all to uphold and restore the imperial influence which economic growth, Afrikaner nationalism and the Jameson fiasco had overthrown. Imperial claims in the Rhodesias, and to a lesser extent in Nyasaland, were contingent in turn upon Cape colonial expansion and imperial attempts to offset the rise of the Transvaal. The times and circumstances in which almost all these claims and occupations were made suggest strongly that they were called forth by crises in Egypt and south Africa, rather than by positive impulses to African empire arising in Europe.

To be sure, a variety of different interests in London—some religious and humanitarian, others strictly commerical or financial, and yet others imperialist—pressed for territorial advances and were sometimes used as their agents. In west Africa, the traders called for government protection; in Uganda and Nyasaland, the missionaries and the anti-slavery groups called for annexation; in Egypt, the bondholders asked government to rescue their investments; in south Africa, philanthropists and imperialists called for more government from Whitehall, while British traders and investors were divided about the best way of looking after their interests. Ministers usually listened to their pleas only when it suited their purpose; but commercial and philanthropic agitation seldom decided which territories should be claimed or occupied or when this should be done, although their slogans were frequently used by government in its public justifications.

It is the private calculations and actions of ministers far more than their speeches which reveal the primary motives behind their advances. For all the different situations in which territory was claimed, and all the different reasons which were given to justify it, one consideration, and one alone entered into all the major decisions. In all regions north of Rhodesia, the broad imperative which decided which territory to reserve and which to renounce, was the safety of the routes to the East. It did not, of course, prompt the claiming of Nyasaland or the lower Niger. Here a reluctant government acted to protect existing fields of trading and missionary enterprise from foreign annexations. In southern Africa the extension of empire seems to have been dictated by a somewhat different imperative. Here the London government felt bound as a rule to satisfy the demands for more territory which their self-governing colonials pressed on them. Ministers did this in the hope of conserving imperial influence. Nevertheless, the safety of the routes to India also figured prominently in the decision to uphold British supremacy in south Africa. It was the same imperative which after impelling the occupation of Egypt, prolonged it, and forced Britain to go into east Africa and the Upper Nile, while yielding in most of west Africa. As soon as territory anywhere in Africa became involved, however indirectly, in this cardinal interest, ministries passed swiftly from inaction to intervention. If the papers left by the policy-makers are to be believed, they moved into Africa, not to build a new African empire, but to protect the old empire in India. What decided when and where they would go forward was their traditional conception of world strategy.

Its principles had been distilled from a century and more of accumulated experience, from far-reaching and varied experiments in the uses of power to promote trade and in the uses of trade to promote power. Much of this experience confirmed one precept: that Britain's strength depended upon the possession of India and preponderance in the East, almost as much as it did upon the

British Isles. Therefore, her position in the world hung above all upon safe communications between the two. This was a supreme interest of Victorian policy; it set the order of priorities in the Middle East and Asia, no less than in Africa, and when African situations interlocked with it, they engaged the serious and urgent attention of the British government. At the first level of analysis, the decisive motive behind late-Victorian strategy in Africa was to protect the all-important stakes in India and the East.

An essentially negative objective, it had been attained hitherto without large African possessions. Mere influence and co-operation with other Powers had been enough to safeguard strategic points in north Africa; while in south Africa control of coastal regions had sufficed. The ambition of late-Victorian ministers reached no higher than to uphold these mid-Victorian systems of security in Egypt and south Africa. They were distinguished from their predecessors only in this: that their security by influence was breaking down. In attempting to restore it by intervention and diplomacy, they incidentally marked out the ground on which a vastly extended African empire was later to arise. Nearly all the interventions appear to have been consequences, direct or indirect, of internal Egyptian or south African crises which endangered British influence and security in the world. Such an interpretation alone seems to fit the actual calculations of policy. Ministers felt frankly that they were making the best of a bad job. They were doing no more than protecting old interests in worsening circumstances. To many, the flare-up of European rivalry in Africa seemed unreasonable and even absurd; yet most of them felt driven to take part because of tantalising circumstances beyond their control. They went forward as a measure of precaution, or as a way back to the saner mid-Victorian systems of informal influence. Gloomily, they were fumbling to adjust their old strategy to a changing Africa. And the necessity arose much more from altered circumstances in Africa than from any revolution in the nature, strength or direction of British expansion.

Hence the question of motive should be formulated afresh. It is no longer the winning of a new empire in Africa which has to be explained. The question is simpler: Why could the late-Victorians after 1880 no longer rely upon influence to protect traditional interests? What forced them in the end into imperial solutions? The answer is to be found first in the nationalist crises in Africa itself, which were the work of intensifying European influences during previous decades; and only secondarily in the interlocking of these crises in Africa with rivalries in Europe. Together the two drove Britain step by step to regain by territorial claims and occupation that security which could no longer be had by influence alone. The compelling conditions for British advances in tropical Africa were first called into being, not by the German victory of 1871, nor by Leopold's interest in the Congo, nor by the petty rivalry of missionaries and merchants, nor by a rising imperialist spirit, nor even by the French occupation of Tunis in 1881—but by the collapse of the Khedivial *régime* in Egypt.

Chapter XIII.

REVISIONISM AND THE CRISIS OF GERMAN SOCIAL DEMOCRACY

THE REVISIONIST movement which began in the 1890's was the most important challenge to Marxism after the rise of socialism as a major political force. Formal revisionism was a German development, and this alone gave it importance, for the German Socialist party was the largest in the world. But theories akin to revisionism arose elsewhere. Eduard Bernstein himself was strongly influenced by British Fabianism, which began as a theoretical challenge to Marxism; and reformist socialist groups in France antedated their German counterparts. Moreover, the questions that revisionism raised persisted long after the formal movement ended. The use of the term revisionist, as a grave condemnation, by revolutionary Marxists in our own day is one indication of the continuing passion surrounding the movement. And in a broad sense, many of the choices that socialists and communists still have to make, in theory and in political practice, reflect the problems with which revisionism tried to deal and are influenced by some of the historical interpretations of the movement.

There is relatively little disagreement about what formal revisionism was, in a purely descriptive sense. It was a conscious attack on major aspects of Marxist theory, stressing the continued vitality of capitalism and the middle class and urging an accommodation of tactics to these facts. This meant, in turn, that revolution was both impossible and unnecessary and that socialists should work to build reforms gradually, and with the cooperation of all sympathetic parties and groups. Historians have, implicitly, differed over how widely to use the term. Some, particularly those who have studied Bernstein directly and who pay primary attention to socialist theory, prefer to confine the term to Bernstein's ideas and the socialists who adopted them. They specifically disavow the extension of the term to reformist socialists in general. But other historians, particularly the Marxists, believe that other types of reformists can be usefully described as revisionists too, and not only in Germany or in this period.

The causes of revisionism are open to considerably more debate. Most non-Marxist historians would agree on a list of causes including the prosperity of the late nineteenth century, the tactical opportunities and problems of the German party once it attained mass support, Bernstein's own personality, and pressures from ordinary members of the party and of socialist unions to achieve concrete results from their activity. The balance among these factors differs considerably, however, and can reveal much about the historian's conception of what socialism is. The revolutionary Marxist approach to causation is most obviously distinctive. Here, broad problems of causation are played down, for there is, after all, no desire to find justification for revisionism in the situation of the times, so that personal factors are stressed—the errors and betrayals of Bernstein and his followers. The personal failings, in turn, relate to class differences—hence the applicability of terms like "petty bourgeois" to distinguish revisionists from true, and therefore proletarian, socialists—and to the lure of rewards in capitalist society. This approach, though probably incomplete, is not necessarily inaccurate. If it seems unfair to someone like Bernstein, it can be seen as a useful interpretation of the motives of many revisionists and, particularly, of the results of the revisionist effort.

There are several key differences of orientation toward the evaluation of revisionism as a whole. One is obvious: whether revisionism is regarded as a beneficial or harmful development in socialism. Another stems from real disagreements about what socialism is. For some historians, socialism is first and foremost a set of doctrines. Revisionism is therefore interpreted as an alteration of socialist ideology; and because it was less rigorous and thorough than Marxist ideology it is often found wanting. Other historians view socialism above all as a political movement and see the importance of revisionism in its suggestions for changes in tactics and in its divisive effects on socialist parties. Still others add trade unionism to pure politics in their formula for judging socialism; this can lead to yet another viewpoint for the interpretation of revisionism. Finally, some historians try to get beyond the organizations of socialism to their constituencies, primarily the working class, and assess the causes and effects of revisionism in terms of the interests and gains of ordinary socialist voters and union members. Most historians combine these viewpoints to some degree, differing mainly in the stress placed on each. But real distinctions remain. As a result, interpretations can agree on what Bernstein intended and even on whether revisionism was good or bad for socialism, but still convey radically different pictures of what the movement was.

Most American students of revisionism have been sympathetic to it. The revisionists' impatience with abstraction, their desire to do justice to what was actually happening in society, and their devotion to gradualism and democratic parliamentarism—all these correspond substantially to what most Americans deem appropriate in a political movement. At the other extreme, revolutionary Marxists have not reduced their original hostility to revisionism, and they are not alone in their condemnations. Many observers have seen revisionism as a weakening of socialist purity and vigor in a society that demanded strength. Revisionist politicians were more likely to be opportunistic and to make concessions than their orthodox opponents. The question is whether socialism and society as a whole would have been better served by a firmer stance, a stance that would have resisted war in 1914, for example, or one that would have led to a thorough attack on the social and military hierarchy in Germany after 1918.

There is, of course, a serious risk of distortion in debates of this sort. Many of the subsequent weaknesses and failures of socialism were beyond the socialists' control; many were due to socialists who were not formal revisionists. And there is always danger in applying judgments of responsibility for later developments to an interpretation of a group or a set of ideas in a given period. Still, both the revisionists and their opponents claimed greater realism in tactics and in goals. It is probably impossible for the historian to separate his own sympathy for or dislike of the goals and his own judgment of the ultimate efficacy of the tactics from his interpretation.

Finally, what was the fate of revisionism? All historians agree that the Social Democratic Party formally disavowed it and yet in effect turned increasingly more reformist. But did its evolution go as far as the revisionists wished? Was the ideological rejection of revisionism meaningless? The range of opinion here is considerable. Vigorous partisans and vigorous opponents of revisionism may both tend to see it effectively victorious; at the other extreme, some historians view its defeat as a very real and tragic development in German socialism.[1]

1. PETER GAY: The Dilemma of Democratic Socialism*

Peter Gay, an intellectual historian at Columbia University, offers a sympathetic treatment of Bernstein's motives, stressing his ethical concern. He is troubled, however, by Bernstein's ideological shallowness and admits that, in prewar Germany, revisionist tactics were not necessarily realistic.

Critics have succeeded in showing that Revisionism lacked profundity and originality—that, as a matter of fact, some of its assumptions rested on misunderstandings. Bernstein, as we noted, did not fully grasp the significance of the dialectic to Marxism, and he wrongly took Kant's separation of the natural sciences from the rational study of ethics for a denial that ethics could be a rational discipline. But it must be said that he had absorbed far more of the Marxist view of history than these criticisms would indicate. To Bernstein, Marx's interpretation was a living thing, not a stereotyped model. It was "above all a method of *understanding* history," as he once wrote to Kautsky, and he objected, rightly, to a rigid application of Marxian terminology and categories. This procedure, he felt, put historical truth in a straitjacket in order to fit the infinite variety of life to a single scheme. Bernstein's own use of Marx's historical materialism—in *Cromwell and Communism*—had resulted in a brilliant study which was free from the flaws of a narrow orthodoxy and which did not do violence to facts for the sake of a theory.

The core of Revisionist philosophy has now begun to emerge. We know that Bernstein abandoned dialectical materialism and approached, but did not adopt, neo-Kantianism. He stood between these two major schools and really belongs to a third: Naturalism. Two elements gave Revisionism its particular form: one was its empiricism, the other its keen interest in naturalist ethics.

Bernstein's empiricism is apparent everywhere. His philosophical case against Marxism was really an afterthought; it was appended to his attempt to refute Marxist conclusions on empirical grounds. He distrusted metaphysical structures as Utopian constructions and suspected abstract thought of leading to unwarranted results. The world to him was "a complex of ready-made objects and processes." True, his empiricism was not identical with the extreme anti-

1. For an over-all account of the Social Democratic Party in the period, see Carl E. Schorske, *German Social Democracy, 1905–1915* (New York, 1965).

* From Peter Gay, *The Dilemma of Democratic Socialism* (New York: Collier Books, 1962), pp. 161–65, 298–303.

philosophical attitude of the Fabians, whom he condemned for reducing Socialism to "a series of sociopolitical measures, without any connecting element that could express the unity of their fundamental thought and action." But his kinship to the Fabians was closer than he cared to admit.

Siegfried Marck has compared the period of Revisionism to a kind of Enlightenment epoch, that is, an era of doubt which usually follows on the heels of a time of dogmatic creativity. Revisionism, according to this theory, represents the application of the acid of skepticism to a theoretical structure; it is "the attempt to corrode dogmatic incrustations and to test the apparently eternal truths of orthodoxy in an empirical fashion." Revisionism came, of course, at a time which was favorable to just such an enterprise. Further, Marck says that this empiricism is at once the strength and weakness of Revisionism. Strength, because the danger of drawing arbitrary conclusions from dialectical materialism was growing ever greater and needed the cool shower of empirical investigation supplied by the Revisionists. Weakness, because it gave up the very real advantages of the dialectical method and tended to pay too much attention to short-run developments. "Even the unjustified anticipations (*Vorwegnahme*), the false time estimates in the system of a genius have a peculiar endurance and force. Often, they are apparently contradicted by the happenings of the day, but they are then confirmed in the long run in the most striking fashion."

Bernstein's strong concern with ethical problems forced him to qualify his empiricism. His training—both the earlier influences of Marx and Engels and the later one of Kant—was far too strong to permit him to range himself along the side of the Positivists. The latter, in their infatuation with "facts" and with the methods of the natural sciences, reduced all investigations of human problems to ethically neutral pursuits. In any event, Bernstein's "Positivism" must be sharply differentiated from twentieth-century Logical Positivism, for which ethical speculation is the remnant of outmoded metaphysical thinking and ethical issues are pseudo problems.

Marxist Socialism, following Hegel, had no distinct ethical theory. The work of Revisionism resulted in nothing less than the reintroduction of ethics into Socialism. Marxism, Bernstein argued, is partly an analysis of existing conditions and current developments. To that extent it is free from bias; that is, scientific. But Socialism is also a pattern of demands. True, in Marxism these demands are clothed in terms of predictions based upon the tendencies previously examined in scientific fashion, but this is merely a scientific cover disguising desires for a just society. These desires are not scientific, since they exhibit an orderly system of preferences—in other words, they are ethical judgments. A Socialist theory without these ethical elements would be sterile.

Equally sterile, Bernstein continues, would be a Socialist *movement* without ethics, and, in fact, the movement is shot through with moral preferences. The workers *want* a new world order. To the extent that this wish is more than self-interest grandiloquently expressed, it is a genuine ethical impulse. Thus the Socialist movement, side by side with the theory that animates it, is largely ethical in character.

Bernstein distinguishes two kinds of Utopianism. The first sort, championed by the great Utopian Socialists, set a goal apart from an investigation of the possibilities of its realization. The second, which Bernstein advocates, sets itself the task of studying present-day society without fear or favor. It then establishes its aims realistically; it goes beyond ascertained fact, making an imaginative leap into the future, but it is careful to curb its imagination. To Bernstein, the goal of Socialism appears as a never-ending task. The world is never finished, never perfect; the reformer's work, like the housewife's, is never done. This is one sense in which his remark, "The goal is nothing, the movement everything," may be understood. Bernstein's concept of never-ceasing effort was derived from Fichte, who had posited the Self (*Ich*) as incomplete, and as constantly striving to transcend its limitations. Fichte, like Bernstein after him, saw the eternal striving of the Self as the response to resistance and the overcoming of obstacles.

This ethical theory of Revisionism, which allied Bernstein with Marx's predecessors, has been variously evaluated. Orthodox Marxists called it "a throwback to the most primitive level of the labor movement." They regarded the revival of ethics as a paralyzing element which deprived the Socialist movement of its dialectical certainty of victory and of its "scientific" character. The unity of thought and action, of dynamic interpenetration of tactics and final goal, so highly prized by the orthodoxy, was destroyed by Revisionism.

More friendly critics, on the other hand, pointed out that the separation of theory from practice was necessary for the clarification of either. If we pretend to see the final goal in every move of the working class, if we put the proletariat in place of the Hegelian Absolute Spirit, these critics reasoned, the dialectic finally becomes the snare that Bernstein had thought it to be; anything and everything can be deduced from such speculative constructions. What is more, it is not true to say that the positing of ethical goals weakens the proletariat. Quite on the contrary, this would strengthen it by placing a value on the moral will of the participant in the struggle. Marxist neutral determinism had acted to cripple just that moral will. The loss of the certainty of victory is small compared to the gain that lies in the recognition of the ethical worth of the struggle and the moral character of the hoped-for goal.

Philosophical questions were not as significant for Revisionism as the analysis of economic and political developments. But whatever the impact of philosophy on the movement, its stress was on ethics and the striving for limited, attainable goals. It strongly supported the other Revisionist arguments against revolution and in favor of parliamentary gradualism. . . .

Eduard Bernstein was one of the most attractive personalities produced by German Social Democracy. If he is remembered less vividly today than, say, Bebel, this is due largely to his lack of spectacular qualities upon which the popular imagination could fasten. Bernstein was the opposite of the demagogue or the charismatic leader. He was a scholar—intelligent, widely read, patient, and above all, honest. His concern with the truth had an almost obsessive quality: it drove him into abandoning theories in which he had found security, giving up friends with whom he had found happiness, turning his back on a party which had filled his life. He was nervous and easily wounded by criticism, but when he felt that the truth demanded it, he spoke fearlessly before hostile groups and willingly made enemies.

Whatever the psychological mainsprings of his drive for truth, it made him the great figure he was: it allowed him to submit Marxist dogma to searching examination while not surrendering the Socialist standpoint.

It must be said, however, that his doctrine made only a negligible *theoretical* contribution to Socialist thought. Revisionism was not sufficiently clear on its underlying philosophy; its rationalist optimism was derived from common sense and empirical observations of immediate facts. This had certain advantages: Revisionism was not shackled by dogma; it could allow considerable flexibility in its description of the development of capitalism. That is what gave Revisionism its timeliness. While orthodox Marxists were offering tortured explanations of the prosperity of the 1890s and beyond, the Revisionists blithely admitted the general upswing and incorporated it into their theory.

On the other hand, Bernstein's optimism was not well founded; it took a short-run prosperity and converted it into the law of capitalist development. True, Marxism had underrated the true expansive powers of late capitalism and had not appreciated its capacity for distributing the growing national product even among the workers. Nor was Marxism later able to offer more than a crudely mechanistic explanation of the rise of Fascism. But Revisionism, too, was to run afoul of the developments of history: World War I severely shook its optimistic foundations, and the great depression disproved its hopeful assumption that the period of great crises was over. He who would revise Revisionism, therefore, ought to begin with its philosophic basis.

The contribution of Revisionism to Socialist tactics was equally problematic. As we have seen, Bernstein's whole position was predicated on the possibility of parliamentary action and peaceful transition to Socialism. Yet he realized—not always clearly—that the political structure of the German Empire would frustrate such tactics.

Nevertheless, the Revisionist position on tactics was of great value. It served as an antidote against the Leninists on the one hand and the Syndicalists on the other. It emphasized the *possibility* of parliamentary action and called attention to the value of democratic processes even in crisis situations. It was one of Bernstein's fundamental convictions that violence for its own sake was barbarian; his bitter and unremitting campaign against Bolshevism testifies to his devotion to liberal parliamentarism. Bernstein was the antithesis of the dogmatic revolutionists; he would have refused to impose the will of his party upon a hostile country, and he was anxious to arrive at the desired end—Socialism—only with the proper means—democracy. In other words, he was unwilling to kill for the sake of logic.

This emphasis on parliamentary democratic Socialism, which is the keystone of Revisionism, is of the greatest significance. Of course, Bernstein was not alone in connecting these strands of thought—the Fabians had done the same.

But Bernstein belongs in the very foreground of those who believed that it was possible to combine socialized means of production with parliamentary democracy, nationalized banks and transportation systems with civil liberties. In our time, in which the uninformed and the biased like to tax Socialists with lack of devotion to freedom, Bernstein's writings deserve much greater attention than they have hitherto received.

It will be admitted, then, that Bernstein's general political position is of great relevance to countries with genuine parliamentary institutions. What of his views on Germany? Here, as we have emphasized, Bernstein himself frequently doubted that an alliance with the more radical sections of the bourgeoisie would work. His theory, however, required such collaboration, and to this end Bernstein called upon his party to change its programmatic stand on tactics, to "appear what it really is today: a democratic-Socialist reform party." This standpoint has been criticized as unrealistic. These critics hold that an open admission of its nonrevolutionary nature would not have won for the SPD any better treatment at the hands of the German government and would, in the bargain, have forced the radical left wing to break away from the party. This estimate appears to be valid for the short run: the Luxemburgs would no doubt have had to form their own party, and Germany would certainly *not* have become a parliamentary monarchy of the English type if the Erfurt Program had been rewritten in the manner Bernstein had demanded. But for the long run the split between revolutionary declarations and reformist practices served the party ill: the revolutionary goals were never reached anyway, and the liberal segments of the bourgeoisie, which wanted nothing more than leadership into a democratic republic, could never bring themselves to support a party that marched under the revolutionary banner of the Erfurt Program. When the SPD switched to the reformist Görlitz Program in 1921, it was too late.

Another charge against Revisionist tactics that has frequently been leveled is that Bernstein's activities "emancipated the right wing of the party," which strengthened the conservatives in the SPD and developed the philosophy which led to the party split during the war. However, as this study has tried to show, the reformists gained power in the party quite independently of the Revisionist theorists. No doubt, the *Voraussetzungen* hastened and rationalized the process, but it would have gone on anyway. The trade unionists, the party bureaucrats, for the most part did not bother with theory. Nor can it be demonstrated that the Revisionist philosophy drove the party into voting for the war credits—the act which really caused the party split. The motives were mixed: the SPD had accepted the German state almost completely—an acceptance doubtless strengthened by the Revisionist theoreticians but caused chiefly by the needs of the trade unions and of the legal, parliamentary party. Further, we must list fear of bloody retribution, hatred of Russia, and the sudden discovery of patriotic sentiments. While many of the Revisionists were in the forefront of the patriotic tide among the Socialists, the orthodox Marxists contributed their share. If the Revisionist Heine's outpourings outdid the effusions of many bourgeois journalists, they were no more unfortunate than the chauvinistic publications of the ex-radicals Lensch and Haenisch. That the support of the war cannot be charged to Bernstein's Revisionism is best seen in Bernstein's own behavior during the conflict. His courageous stand has been underestimated and, instead, Revisionism has been judged by the attitudes of a David or a Heine. It is certainly true that Bernstein was unfortunate in his supporters—not one of them understood his democratic Socialism sufficiently to develop it further. Instead, they converted it into a fundamentally conservative concept which understood gradualism to be an admonition to do little and to do that slowly.

Bernstein's Revisionism was the child of its time: the logical expression of the belief in progress which motivated wide circles in Europe before it was destroyed by the war. Its advent, as has been shown, was inevitable: the Revisionists did not create the Reformist mood, but the mood, instead, called forth the theory.

From the outset, Revisionism faced a dilemma that confronts all democratic movements intent on radical social change: What methods shall be used to gain the desired end? The use of violence may overthrow the ruling class that bars the way—but is it not likely that the exigencies of the revolution will transform the movement into a repressive tyranny? Can the rule of terror not be established in the sacred name of the general will? On the other hand, if the parliamentary path is followed and the use of force eschewed, will the reformers ever gain the power they must have to put their theories into practice?

These questions allow of no dogmatic answer. In Germany, contrary to Revisionist expectations, a revolution was needed to dislodge the powers in control; however, that revolution was not prompted by any consciously revolutionary party. It was, instead, the by-product of defeat in the field and starvation at home. The Socialists who benefited from the revolution were far from initiating a tyranny; indeed, an excellent case can be made out for the contention that they failed precisely because they refused to crush the old centers of power and thus permitted the enemies of the Republic to gather strength.

In any event, Revisionist theory and practice form a chapter in the never-ending debate on political methods. It is a debate that cannot be easily resolved: how can a party safely navigate between the Scylla of impotence before the adversary and the Charybdis of betrayal of its cause? We know—as did Bernstein—that means and ends are intimately related and that rotten means may permanently disfigure a movement that uses them, no matter how dedicated it may be in theory to humane ends. But we know, too—and Bernstein had some idea of this—that a determined and ruthless opponent will not be cowed into surrender by speeches. A fanatic revolutionary movement does not face this problem, but a democratic theoretician must conscientiously grapple with it, patiently judging each great occasion by its peculiar and unique circumstances.

This political dilemma of means and ends is heartbreakingly difficult, but Eduard Bernstein never wavered in his conviction: "Democracy is at the same time means and end. It is the means of the struggle for Socialism and it is the form Socialism will take once it has been realized."

2. HERBERT MARCUSE: Reason and Revolution: Hegel and the Rise of Social Theory*

Herbert Marcuse, another intellectual historian, views revisionism here within an ideological context alone. His approach contrasts with Gay's in its implications of a serious intellectual content in revisionism. Relatedly, Marcuse portrays the opponents of revisionism as upholders of an ideology vital to their revolutionary purpose, not merely as defenders of unnecessary theory. Professor Marcuse teaches philosophy at the University of California, La Jolla.

The Marxian theory, however, had itself begun to undergo fundamental changes. The history of Marxism has confirmed the affinity between Hegel's motives and the critical interest of the materialist dialectic as applied to society. The schools of Marxism that abandoned the revolutionary foundations of the Marxian theory were the same that outspokenly repudiated the Hegelian aspects of the Marxian theory, especially the dialectic. Revisionist writing and thought, which expressed the growing faith of large socialist groups in a peaceful evolution from capitalism to socialism, attempted to change socialism from a theoretical and practical antithesis to the capitalist system into a parliamentary movement within this system. The philosophy and politics of opportunism, represented by this movement, took the form of a struggle against what it termed "the remnants of Utopian thinking in Marx." The result was that revisionism replaced the critical dialectic conception with the conformist attitudes of naturalism. Bowing to the authority of the facts, which indeed justified the hopes of a legal parliamentary opposition, revisionism diverted revolutionary action into the channel of a faith in the "necessary natural evolution" to socialism. The dialectic, in consequence, was termed "the treacherous element in the Marxian doctrine, the trap that is laid for all consistent thinking." Bernstein declared that the "snare" of dialectic consists in its inappropriate "abstraction from the specific particularities of things." He defended the matter-of-fact quality of fixed and stable objects as against any notion of their dialectical negation. "If we wish to comprehend the world, we have to conceive it as a complex of ready-made objects and processes."

This amounted to the revival of common sense as the organon of knowledge. The dialectical overthrow of the "fixed and stable" had been undertaken in the interest of a higher truth that might dissolve the negative totality of "ready-made" objects and processes. This revolutionary interest was now renounced in favor of the secure and stable given state of affairs that, according to revisionism, slowly evolves towards a rational society. "The class interest recedes, the common interest grows in power. At the same time, legislation becomes increasingly more powerful and regulates the struggle of economic forces, governing increasingly more realms which were previously left to the blind war of particular interests."

With the repudiation of the dialetic, the revisionists falsified the nature of the

* From Herbert Marcuse, *Reason and Revolution: Hegel and the Rise of Social Theory*, pp. 398–401. Copyright Humanities Press, 1954. Reprinted by permission of the Humanities Press.

laws that Marx saw ruling society. We recall Marx's view that the natural laws of society gave expression to the blind and irrational processes of capitalist reproduction, and that the socialist revolution was to bring emancipation from these laws. In contrast to this, the revisionists argued that the social laws are "natural" laws that guarantee the inevitable development towards socialism. "The great achievement of Marx and Engels lay in the fact that they had better success than their predecessors in weaving the realm of history into the realm of necessity and thus elevating history to the rank of a science." The critical Marxist theory the revisionists thus tested by the standards of positivist sociology and transformed into natural science. In line with the inner tendencies of the positivist reaction against "negative philosophy," the objective conditions that prevail were hypostatized, and human practice was rendered subordinate to their authority.

Those anxious to preserve the critical import of the Marxian doctrine saw in the anti-dialectical trends not only a theoretical deviation, but a serious political danger that threatened the success of socialist action at every turn. To them the dialectical method, with its uncompromising "spirit of contradiction," was the essential without which the critical theory of society would of necessity become a neutral or positivist sociology. And since there existed an intrinsic connection between Marxian theory and practice, the transformation of the theory would result in a neutral or positivist attitude to the existing societal form. Plekhanov emphatically announced that "without dialectic, the materialist theory of knowledge and practice is incomplete, one sided; nay more, it is impossible." The method of dialectic is a totality wherein "the negation and destruction of the existing" appears in every concept, thus furnishing the full conceptual framework for understanding the entirety of the existing order in accordance with the interest of freedom. Dialectical analysis alone can provide an adequate orientation for revolutionary practice, for it prevents this practice from being overwhelmed by the interests and aims of an opportunist philosophy. Lenin insisted on dialectical method to such an extent that he considered it the hallmark of revolutionary Marxism. While discussing the most urgent practical political matters, he indulged in analyses of the significance of the dialectic. The most striking example is to be found in his examination of Trotsky's and Bukharin's theses for the trade union conference, written on January 25, 1921. In this tract Lenin shows how a poverty of dialectical thinking may lead to grave political errors, and he links his defense of dialectic to an attack on the "naturalist" misinterpretation of Marxian theory. The dialectical conception, he shows, is incompatible with any reliance upon the natural necessity of economic laws. It is furthermore incompatible with the exclusive orientation of the revolutionary movement to economic ends, because all economic ends receive their meaning and content only from the totality of the new social order to which this movement is directed. Lenin regarded those who subordinated political aims and spontaneity to the purely economic struggle to be among the most dangerous falsifiers of Marxian theory. He held against these Marxists the absolute predominance of politics over economics: "Politics cannot but have precedence over economics. To argue differently, means forgetting the ABC of Marxism."

3. W. A. MC CONAGHA: Development of the Labor Movement in Great Britain, France, and Germany*

W. A. McConagha has sketched the history of European labor mainly in terms of the development of trade unions. He believes that unions have a natural tendency toward pragmatism which coincides with both the wishes and the interests of workers. With this approach, he finds revisionism a natural and healthy development in German socialism. It was caused by facts rather than ideas and reflected not only the position of the party but also the positive realism of German workers. Since it opened the way to immediate gains from union activity, revisionism was undeniably a good thing. McConagha's approach conveys the standards of the American labor movement; but are these appropriate to the German situation? And were German workers so uniformly pragmatic, especially before the transformation of their party?

It must not be assumed that with [the] declaration of independence and the recognition of trade union autonomy there came about, as time passed, an increasing divergence between the union and the Party point of view or that there was a growing lack of sympathy between the two organizations. For, quite to the contrary, this clarification of limits of authority and nature of function had a wholesome pacifying influence on both groups. "After Mannheim," as Professor Perlman expresses it, "harmony reigned."

While union membership was no longer held as a prerequisite to membership in the Party, nevertheless the Party was still largely made up of members of trade unions, and, conversely, unionists were for the most part still allied to the Party. Furthermore the very interesting fact is that the unions in deciding to try to fit their program into a world of tangible realities rather than into a world of philosophical concepts were merely taking a direction in which, as we shall now see, the Party itself was turning and was destined soon openly to follow.

So long as the socialists had been all aglow with their impressive triumph over Bismarck's schemes for their extermination and were waiting breathlessly for the breakdown of the existing order, orthodoxy was easy and unity prevailed. Even those variations in the conception of tactics which were the natural product of the extremity of their situation during the period of anti-socialist legislation now melted away, and the platform adopted at Erfurt in 1891, as they prepared once more to live openly, represented a rededication to a creed so thoroughly Marxian as to seem in part like a restatement of the Communist Manifesto.

Victory, however, did not continue to be added to victory with the ease and

* From W. A. McConagha, *Development of the Labor Movement in Great Britain, France and Germany* (Chapel Hill: University of North Carolina Press, 1942), pp. 179–85. Reprinted by permission of the University of North Carolina Press.

rapidity that past experience seemed to promise. The conviction so confidently expressed by Bebel at the Erfurt convention that "bourgeois society is working so mightily towards its own downfall that we need only to wait for the moment when we shall have to take up the power falling from its hands . . . there are few in this hall who will not live to see the day" began more and more to have the air of a wishful prophecy rather than that of a tangible fact.

While the voting strength of the Party did indeed continue to increase with gratifying rapidity and parliamentary representation at a corresponding pace, these gains brought no practical political advantage. The increasing demonstration of power on the part of the socialists had brought with it an increasing tendency to coalition on the part of the opposition; so that in spite of seeming progress the ultimate goal—socialist domination—remained as distant as ever. Furthermore the fall of profits, the increase of misery, the intensification of crises, the sharpening of the class struggle—in short the whole Marxian category of fatal diseases undermining, presumably, the capitalist order—as time passed showed no alarming tendency either to appear or to increase in their intensity. On the contrary the phenomenal expansion of German industry which now began to get under way brought with it a perversely increasing prosperity, which seemed, for the time being at least, to belie the whole doleful socialist prophecy and to drive the expected social revolution farther and farther into the realms of speculation and unreality.

The logic of this trend of events was inescapable. Evidently the capitalistic system was endowed with a vitality which Marx in the wishfulness of his thinking had never been willing to grant it. The kingdom of heaven was not yet at hand.

This fact, borne in upon the minds of Party leaders, seemed now to necessitate a reappraisal of tactics. The original attitude of "mere inactive waiting," which conforms so perfectly with the fatalistic qualities of Marxism and the general illusion of socialism's imminence, now began to appear much less satisfactory. Moreover, while the spectacular successes of Social Democracy had drawn into its ranks a mass of mere camp-followers, mercenaries, and malcontents of all kinds, it was perfectly clear that as a party it was still a proletarian institution and that whatever endangered the loyalty or confidence of its working-class members endangered likewise its very existence as well. Since it is recognized that workers are essentially realists with a keen sense of "time preference," obviously it would grow increasingly difficult either to placate or inspire them with checks on the bank of the coming socialist state as that state faded farther and farther into the future. Thus Social Democracy, it began to appear, was more and more to be called upon to forsake the future and to justify itself to its constituents in terms of the affairs of the moment.

It is not to be supposed, of course, that there was complete unanimity in the socialist reaction to this situation. Theories tend always to a hardy existence and to survive the conditions which justified their birth. Then, too, Marxism was a religion, and the most conclusive evidence penetrates with difficulty minds already fortified by contrary emotions. Thus the Party found itself once again divided into two factions. One was determined to observe to the utmost the letter of the original Marxian revelation, particularly as it was interpreted in the Erfurt program; the other, convinced that faith in dogma must give way to some very solid works in behalf of labor now struggling to cope with the conditions immediately surrounding it, argued for a more realistic program.

This latter, the Revisionist point of view, found in Eduard Bernstein a very able exponent. Under the mellowing influence of long association with the English Fabians during his years of exile in London Bernstein's original Marxian orthodoxy had yielded perceptibly. The point of view to which he and his fellow Revisionists now adhered was that in view of the Marxian error concerning the speed of social evolution it became necessary for the Social Democratic Party to devote itself more to the problems of reform and less to those of revolution. To do this it must forsake its old pose of abstraction and cynical aloofness, as in fancy it witnessed the existing bourgeois society moving head on to its inevitable destruction, and must devote every effort to the determination of the policy of the existing state where that policy affected the day-by-day problems of proletarian welfare.

This controversy, which had been smoldering for years, particularly in the more democratic South Germany, was actively precipitated by Bernstein's letter to the Congress of the Party at Stuttgart in 1898 and came to a climax in the Congress at Dresden in 1903. At this latter meeting Revisionism was defeated by an overwhelming vote, and thus, officially at least, the Party washed its hands, presumably for all time, of all responsibility for interfering with immediate social issues in the interests of reform.

This repudiation, however, may be interpreted as more in the nature of a refusal to publicly acknowledge and sanction a shift in Party attitude than as a denial of all interest in current reforms or in the means of their achievement. Little by little within the Party the demands of orthodoxy were yielding steadily before the demands of expedience. So, while the creed, indeed, remained the same, devotion to it was being noticeably altered.

This change, occurring as it did gradually, almost imperceptibly, was hastened, by some events of particular significance. One of these, surely, was the necessity itself for the acknowledgment of trade union independence at Mannheim. There, perhaps for the first time, Party members were shocked out of their complacency concerning the "manifest destiny" of the socialist movement in Germany and the comfortable conviction that the very stars in their courses fought to bring them victory.

Close upon the heels of Mannheim came the so-called "Hottentot" election of 1907. The issue was the Kaiser's program of imperialism and colonial expansion. Nothing, it is obvious, could represent much more completely a flouting of the socialist point of view. Accordingly the Party girt itself to lead the opposition. In this election, fought as it was in an atmosphere of emotionalism and in the face of a rising tide of nationalist and pan-Germanic sentiment, the socialists found themselves supporting a hopelessly unpopular issue and were swept back with the loss of almost half of their seats in the Reichstag. This reverse had a tremendously sobering effect and brought in its wake a marked softening in the tone of the internationalist and anti-militaristic utterances of Party members.

The coming of the World War, however, was the climactic event contributing to this steady "degeneration." With its outbreak almost the last vestige of the old revolutionary philosophy of the seventies vanished. Internationalism and loyalty to class were swallowed up in a surging loyalty to country. In spite of previous stout utterances and some internal dissensions, in its historic "fourth of August" decision the Social Democratic Party voted solidly for war credits, and thenceforth, instead of posing as an enemy of the existing "class" state, waiting only for a favorable opportunity for its destruction, it became that state's strong and open supporter, asking in return only some modifications in the interests of democracy and social reform.

With this return of German workers, first the trade unionists and now their intellectual sponsors and leaders, from the realms of the abstract and the speculative to a world of realities, where human welfare is demonstrably, at least in part, a matter of one's own achievement, there is added another impressive increment to the mass of evidence that workers are not social philosophers. Neither are they an "abstract mass" willing to face years of misery for which there is a possible alternative in order that some prophecy of ultimate historic destiny may be fulfilled.

Because of this abandonment by the Social Democratic Party of its historic revolutionary point of view and its corresponding change of front, the line of demarcation between German socialism and German trade unionism once again sank into obscurity. Fundamentally their attitudes toward the existing order were now identical; neither demanded its destruction; both sought its reform. The difference became thus primarily one of choice of technique. In this respect old distinctions persisted, for, while the socialists strove along the political front, the trade unionists still placed their faith in a more direct economic action.

So far as prestige was concerned, this shift in relationships favored the unions. Since both groups were now opportunistic, relative advantage lay with whichever one demonstrably was most likely to "bring home the bacon." In this respect the trade union program with its greater objectivity and precision was able to present the more effective appeal.

4. ADOLF STURMTHAL: The Tragedy of European Labor, 1918–1939*

Adolf Sturmthal, a prominent German socialist, taught in the United States after the Nazi takeover. He was profoundly convinced that socialism wasted great opportunities to use its increased power after World War I. He believes

*From Adolf Sturmthal, *The Tragedy of European Labor, 1918–1939* (New York: Columbia University Press, 1943), pp. 22–25. Reprinted by permission of Columbia University Press.

that the defeat of revisionism played a major role in this failure, for it left socialism with an unrealistic philosophy in theory, and a piece-by-piece reformism in practice. He accepts the same sorts of facts as McConagha uses, but puts them in a different perspective.

The suppression of Socialist activity by many of the European governments and the difficult economic situation following the great crisis of the early seventies greatly contributed to the maintenance of the revolutionary temper of the movement. Towards the end of the century the political and economic situation changed favourably for the working class. Economic conditions improved, allowing for great advances in working-class conditions and rapid progress of social insurance systems. Government pressure ceased, or at least diminished considerably, except in czarist Russia. The early radicalism of the Socialists began to give way to new ideas. The end of capitalism seemed farther away than it had seemed when the movement sprang up. The development of military techniques—in particular the invention of the machine-gun—as Friedrich Engels pointed out, made revolutionary upheavals against well-armed troops seem increasingly difficult. Reforms of a social and even political nature, on the other hand, appeared much more probable than in the seventies. Rising national wealth enabled the working class to obtain important concessions. In the semi-feudal Central European countries liberal middle-class groups strongly advocated democratic reforms, and an alliance between them and the Socialists seemed to promise a democratization of Germany and Austria in the near future. Would it not be better, the Reformists or Revisionists asked, to postpone or abandon the hopeless revolutionary dreams and to concentrate upon the prospects of immediate advantage to the movement?

The struggle between Radical revolutionaries and Reformists reached a climax in the strongest and most successful Socialist party of the world, that of the German Social Democrats. In the "battle of the Titans" at the German party conference in Dresden in 1903, August Bebel and Karl Kautsky, the Radical leaders, defeated the right-wingers, and shortly afterwards the International—the alliance of all Socialist parties of the world—endorsed the Radical victory at the Congress in Amsterdam in 1904.

This was perhaps the most fateful event of pre-World War socialism. Out of the Reformist defeat emerged the pressure-group mentality of European labour. The two possible ways for labour to take political action were lost at that time. One of these would have been co-operation with progressive middle-class groups for democratic aims. This was prevented by the Radical victory. The alternative was to strike a revolutionary blow for democracy or for socialism; this was impossible not only because of the military strength of the governments, but also because even under Radical leaders the Socialist parties were developing into great electoral machines rather than into revolutionary shock troops. Thus, no serious activity for political objectives was possible. The main attention of the labour movement was focused upon trade-union problems, to the neglect of basic political and even economic issues. It would be interesting to speculate as to what might have happened if the Reformists had carried the day in the 1903 conference.

The British Labour party came into being during the same period that saw the rise of the Reformist tendencies on the Continent, and was completely lacking in the radical spirit of the early Continental movement. The party was founded and controlled by trade unions, and was intended from the beginning to be an instrument for pressing most effectively their demands in Parliament. The Socialist groups within the movement were small minorities eager to please the unions and to win them over for political action and for socialism by showing the effectiveness of parliamentary activities for the achievement of trade-unionist aims. Trade unionism thus formed the core of the party.

From the turn of the century until the end of the First World War, the European Socialist movement, under its cloak of a revolutionary party, was thus a mere parliamentary instrument of trade unionism. Its real activity was restricted to trade-unionist problems, its constructive action to questions of wages and hours, social insurance, tariff problems, and, at the most, suffrage reform. The struggle against militarism, for a democratic foreign policy, and for the prevention of war, important as it was, was "incidental" to the main work of the party.

The revolutionary struggle for socialism was abandoned by all but a few Socialists on the extreme left. But the great majority did not seriously inquire how its Socialist aims could be reached by non-revolutionary methods. The Reformists felt that the everyday activity of the movement would slowly change the character of the social system so that it would somehow gradually be transformed into a Socialist order. By concentrating upon its immediate tasks the party would thus, in a distant future, attain its major objectives. With this forecast the Radicals were in profound disagreement. They were convinced that at some crucial stage the bourgeois classes would resist further Socialist advances and that the decisive battle would probably have to be fought with revolutionary means. But the question of how the party, now organized as a tremendous vote-getting machine and led by parliamentary and trade-unionist experts rather than by military men or revolutionary adventurers, could effectively engage in an armed revolt, remained unanswered. The Radicals felt that the future would provide the answer. In the meantime, the movement would go ahead in its daily work of attracting the entire working class, and of creating a situation in which the overwhelming majority of the population would oppose the small capitalist minority.

Thus, no programme for the transformation of society by non-violent democratic means was ever thought out or adopted by the Socialist movement. Deeply engrossed in its pressure-group activity, the party "wasted" little time on theoretical problems of this type. It kept intact its old programme of a full-fledged Socialist society next to its statement of immediate aims, but no bridge joined them. The Socialist movement had a philosophy, but no policy to implement its basic creed. Its real trade-unionist activity, it was believed, would eventually lead into socialism. . . .

In 1914 the Socialist parties were minority groups with little influence upon the real major decisions. In 1918 labour was on the threshold of power. An evolution which might have taken a quarter of a century had been telescoped into a few years by the war. But the mental growth of the movement had not kept step with its rise in influence. German labour was still primarily a pressure group when the breakdown of the Hohenzollern empire forced political control upon the Socialists. . . .

The lack of a constructive Socialist programme on issues outside the realm of labour's traditional pressure-group activity became painfully patent once labour was in political control, as a few examples above have shown. . . .

This is the essence of the history of the German revolution of 1918–19 and of the German Republic's congenital weakness.

5. JOSEPH A. SCHUMPETER: Capitalism, Socialism, and Democracy*

Joseph Schumpeter (1883–1950), the famous Austrian economist who was generally conservative in his views and certainly no partisan of Marxist socialism, here carries further the sorts of criticisms of the revisionists that Peter Gay mentioned in the first selection; he says firmly that the Party was right in rejecting the revisionist argument, given the traditions of German socialism and the political conditions of the time. Yet Schumpeter also implies an essentially reformist attitude among the adherents of socialism.

But why was it that the English methods and tactics did not prevail in Germany? Why that Marxist success which accentuated antagonisms and split the nation into two hostile camps? This would be easy to understand if there had been no extra-socialist groups to work for social reconstruction or if the ruling stratum had turned a deaf ear to their proposals. It becomes a riddle as soon as we realize that German public authority was not less but more alive to the social exigencies of the time than was English political society and that the work of the Fabians was being done not less but more effectively by a very similar group.

Germany did not lag behind but, until the passing of the security legislation primarily associated with the name of Lloyd George, led in matters of "social policy." Also, it was the government's initiative that placed those measures for social betterment on the statute book, and not pressure from below asserting itself by exasperating struggles. Bismarck initiated social insurance legislation. The men who developed it and added other lines of social improvement were conservative civil servants (von Berlepsch, Count Posadowsky) carrying out the directions of William II. The institutions created were truly admirable achievements and they were so considered all over the world. Simultaneously, trade-union activity was unfettered and a significant change occurred in the attitude of public authority toward strikes.

The monarchist garb in which all this appeared no doubt constitutes a differ-

* From Joseph A. Schumpeter, *Capitalism, Socialism and Democracy,* pp. 341–42, 343–48.

ence as against the English procedure. But this difference made for more and not less success. The monarchy, after having for a time given in to economic liberalism ("Manchesterism" as its critics called it), simply returned to its old traditions by doing—*mutatis mutandis*—for the workmen what it had previously done for the peasants. The civil service, much more developed and much more powerful than in England, provided excellent administrative machinery as well as the ideas and the drafting skill for legislation. And this civil service was at least as amenable to proposals of social reform as was the English one. Largely consisting of impecunious Junkers—many of whom had no other means of subsistence than their truly Spartan salaries—entirely devoted to its duty, well educated and informed, highly critical of the capitalist bourgeoisie, it took to the task as a fish takes to water.

Ideas and proposals normally came to the bureaucracy from its teachers at the universities, the "socialists of the chair." Whatever we may think of the scientific achievements of the professors who organized themselves into the *Verein für Sozialpolitik* and whose work often lacked scientific refinement, they were aglow with a genuine ardor for social reform and entirely successful in spreading it. They resolutely faced bourgeois displeasure not only in framing individual measures of practical reform but also in propagating the spirit of reform. Like the Fabians, they were primarily interested in the work at hand and they deprecated class war and revolution. But, also like the Fabians, they knew where they were going—they knew and did not mind that socialism loomed at the end of their way. Of course, the state socialism they envisaged was national and conservative. But it was neither a fake nor utopian.

The world at large never understood this social pattern and the nature of the constitutional monarchy it produced. At any rate, it has forgotten whatever it may have once known. But as soon as we get a glimpse of the truth, we find it still more difficult to understand how in that unplutocratic environment it was possible for the greatest of all socialist parties to grow up on a purely Marxist program and on a Marxist phraseology of unsurpassed virulence, pretending to fight ruthless exploitation and a state that was the slave of slave drivers. Surely this cannot be explained by the "logic of the objective social situation." . . .

The fatal mistake was really Bismarck's. It consisted in the attempt, explicable only on the hypothesis that he completely misconceived the nature of the problem, at suppressing socialist activities by coercion culminating in a special enactment (*Sozialistengesetz*) which he carried in 1878 and which remained in force until 1890 (when William II insisted on its repeal), that is to say, long enough to educate the party and to subject it for the rest of the prewar period to the leadership of men who had known prison and exile and had acquired much of the prisoner's and exile's mentality. Through an unfortunate combination of circumstances, it so happened that this vitiated the whole course of subsequent events. For the one thing those exile-shaped men could not stand was militarism and the ideology of military glory. And the one thing which the monarchy—otherwise in sympathy with a large part of what reasonable socialists considered as immediately practical aims—could not stand was sneers at the army and at the glories of 1870. More than anything else, this was for both what defined the enemy as distinguished from the mere opponent. Add Marxian phraseology—however obviously academic—at the party conventions on the one hand and the aforesaid blustering on the other, and you have the picture. No amount of fruitful social legislation and no amount of law-abiding behavior availed against that reciprocal *non possumus,* that cardboard barrier across which the two hosts reviled each other, made the most terrible faces at each other, devoured each other in principle—all without really meaning any serious harm.

From this state of things a situation developed that no doubt had its dangers—great power without responsibility is always dangerous—but was not anything like as uncomfortable as it might seem. The federal and state governments—or the old civil servants promoted to cabinet rank who formed those governments—cared primarily for honest and efficient administration, for beneficial and on the whole progressive legislation, and for the army and navy estimates. None of these objects was seriously jeopardized by the adverse votes of the socialists, the passing of the army and navy estimates in particular being assured most of the time by the support of a large majority of the population. The Social Democratic party in turn, well organized and brilliantly led by August Bebel, was absorbed in consolidating and expanding its vote which in fact increased by leaps and bounds. This was not seriously interfered with by the governments, the bureaucracy scrupulously observing the letter of the law which gave all the freedom of action really necessary for partisan activity. And both the managing bureaucracy and the party had reason to be grateful to each other, especially during Bülow's tenure of power, for providing outlets for oratorical excess capacity of which both of them stood in need.

Thus the party not only developed satisfactorily but also settled down. A party bureaucracy, a party press, a staff of elder statesmen developed, all adequately financed, as a rule secure in their positions and, on the whole, highly respectable in every—and also in the bourgeois—sense of the word. A nucleus of working-class members grew up for whom membership was no longer a question of choice but a matter of course. More and more people were "born into the party" and educated to unquestioning acceptance of its leadership and catechism which then, for some of them, meant as much and no more than religious catechisms mean to the average man or woman of today.

All this was greatly facilitated by the inability of the non-socialist parties to compete effectively for the labor vote. There was an exception to this. The Centrist (Catholic) party, on the one hand, commanded all the talent required because it had the support of a priesthood of quite exceptionally high quality and, on the other hand, was prepared to make a bid for the labor vote by going as far in the direction of social reform as it felt itself able to do without affronting its right wing, and by taking its stand on the doctrines of the encyclicals *Immortale Dei* (1885) and *Rerum Novarum* (1891). But all the other parties, though for different reasons and in different degrees, stood on a footing of mutual distrust, if not of hostility, with the industrial proletariat and never so much as attempted to sell themselves to any significant number of labor voters. These, unless they were active Catholics, accordingly had hardly any party to turn to other than the Social Democratic party. Unbelievable as such ineptitude seems in the light of English and American experience, it is yet a fact that the socialist army was allowed, amid all the clamor about the horrible dangers threatening from it, to march into politically unguarded territory.

We are now in a position to understand what, on the face of it, seems so incomprehensible, viz., why German socialists so tenaciously clung to the Marxian creed. For a powerful party that could afford a distinctive creed yet was completely excluded not only from political responsibility but from any immediate prospect of it, it was natural to conserve the purity of the Marxian faith once it had been embraced. That purely negative attitude toward non-socialist reform and all the doings of the bourgeois state—which as we have seen above was the tactical principle Marx recommended for all save exceptional cases—was really thrust upon it. The leaders were not irresponsible nor were they desperadoes. But they realized that in the given situation there was not much for the party to do except to criticize and to keep the banner flying. Any sacrifice of revolutionary principle would have been perfectly gratuitous. It would have only disorganized their following without giving to the proletariat much more than it got in any case, not on the initiative of the other parties but on that of the monarchist bureaucracy. Such small additional successes as might have been attained hardly warranted the party risk. Thus, serious, patriotic and law-abiding men continued to repeat the irresponsible slogans of revolution and treason—the sanguinary implications of which came so strangely from many a pacific and bespectacled countenance—blissfully conscious of the fact that there was little likelihood of their having to act upon them.

Before long however the suspicion began to dawn upon a few of them that some day or other the revolutionary talk might meet the most deadly weapon of political controversy—smiles. Perhaps it was an apprehension of this kind or simply the perception of the almost ludicrous discrepancy between Marxian phraseology and the social reality of those times that eventually prompted no less a personage than old Engels to pronounce *ex cathedra*—that is to say, in a preface he wrote to a new edition of Marx's *Class Struggles in France*—that street fighting presented certain inconveniences after all and that the faithful need not necessarily feel committed to it (1895).

This timely and modest adjustment roused the wrath of a small minority of thoroughgoing hotspurs, Mrs. Rosa Luxemburg in particular surpassing herself in fiery denunciations of the old man. But it was acquiesced in by the party—possibly with a sigh of relief—and further cautious steps in the same direction might perhaps have been tactfully made. When however Eduard Bernstein coolly proceeded to "revise" the whole structure of the party creed, there was a major row. After what I have said about the situation this should not be surprising.

Even the most worldly party is aware of the dangers involved in altering any of its more important planks. In the case of a party whose program and whose very existence were based on a creed every detail of which had been worked out with theological fervor, root-and-branch reform was bound to mean a terrific shock. That creed was the object of quasi-religious reverence. It had been upheld for a quarter of a century. Under its flag the party had marched to success. It was all the party had to show. And now the beloved revolution—that was to them what the Second Coming of the Lord was to the early Christians—was to be unceremoniously called off. No class war any more. No thrilling war cries. Cooperation with bourgeois parties instead. All this from a member of the old guard, a former exile, and, as it happened, one of the most lovable members of the party!

But Bernstein went further still. He laid sacrilegious hands on the hallowed foundations of the doctrine. He attacked the Hegelian background. The labor theory of value and the exploitation theory came in for stricture. He doubted the inevitability of socialism and reduced it to tame "desirability." He looked askance at the economic interpretation of history. Crises would not kill the capitalist dragon; on the contrary, with time capitalism would gain in stability. Growing misery was nonsense of course. Bourgeois liberalism had produced lasting values which it was worth while trying to conserve. He even said that the proletariat was not everything. Think of that!

This of course was more than the party could stand. It would have been unbearable even if Bernstein had been incontestably right on every point, for creeds embodied in an organization cannot be reformed by means of holocausts. But he was not. He was an excellent man but he was not Marx's intellectual peer. We have seen . . . that he went too far in the matter of the economic interpretation of history which he can hardly have fully understood. He also went too far in his assertion that developments in the agrarian sector refute Marx's theory of the concentration of economic control. And there were other points inviting effective reply so that the champion of orthodoxy, Karl Kautsky, found it not too difficult to hold his ground—or some of it. Nor is it so clear that it would have been to the advantage of the party had Bernstein's tactical recommendations prevailed. A wing would certainly have broken away. The prestige of the party would have suffered greatly. And, as has been stated before, no immediate gain would have accrued. There was hence a lot to be said for the "conservative" view.

Under the circumstances, the course which Bebel took was neither so obviously unwise nor so obviously tyrannical as fellow travelers and other critics made out at the time. He denounced Revisionism vigorously, so vigorously as to keep his hold on his leftists. He had it anathematized at the conventions in Hanover (1899) and Dresden (1903). But he saw to it that the resolutions reaffirming class war and other articles of faith were so framed as to make it possible for "revisionists" to submit. They did, and no further measures were taken against them though there was, I believe, some cracking of the whip. Bernstein himself was allowed to enter the Reichstag with the support of the party. Von Vollmar remained in the fold.

Trade-union leaders shrugged their shoulders and murmured about the chewing of doctrinal cud. They had been revisionists all along. But so long as the party did not interfere in their immediate concerns and so long as it did not call upon them to do anything they really disliked, they did not much care. They extended protection to some revisionists and also to some of their literary organs. They made it quite clear that, whatever the party's philosophy, business was business. But that was all.

The intellectual revisionists for whom doctrine was not a matter of indifference, and the non-socialist sympathizers some of whom would have liked to join a socialist party that did not stress class war and revolution, thought differently of course. It was they who talked about a party crisis and shook their heads about the future of the party. They had every reason to do so. For *their* future in and around the party was indeed jeopardized. In fact Bebel, himself no intellectual and no friend to parlor pinks, lost no time in warning them off the premises. The rank and file of the party however were but little disturbed about all this. They followed their leaders and repeated their slogans until, without any compunction about what Marx or, for that matter, Bebel would have said, they rushed to arms in order to defend their country.

6. HARRY J. MARKS: The Sources of Reformism in the Social Democratic Party of Germany*

Without dealing directly with the question of whether revisionism was a good thing, Harry J. Marks, who now teaches at the University of Connecticut, here undertakes a social analysis of the causes of reformist socialism, which he believes took control of the Social Democratic Party. He specifically disavows some of the conventional explanations, particularly that which states that reformism flowed naturally from rising worker prosperity; and he shows little interest in purely ideological factors. Divisions in the social constituency of the party and related changes in the bureaucracy are the key elements in this account, which draws heavily on the analysis of the Marxist Zinoviev.†

Although socialism has been a factor in European history since 1848, its importance has varied greatly. Just prior to the outbreak of the Great War, the Social Democratic party of Germany, with its million members the largest political party in the country and the largest socialist party in the world, enjoyed all the prestige attaching to a leading position in a leading world-power. According to its program and the repeated pronouncements of its outstanding spokesmen, it was an anticapitalist revolutionary organization, among whose chief objectives was the preservation of world-peace. By accepting the policy of the German government on August 4, 1914, as fundamentally its own, the role of this enormous organization as an independent factor in world-

* From Harry J. Marks, "The Sources of Reformism in the Social Democratic Party of Germany," *Journal of Modern History,* XI, No. 3 (Sept., 1939), pp. 334–35, 338–43, 345–50. Reprinted by permission of the *Journal of Modern History* and the author.

† G. Sinowjew, *Der Krieg und die Krise des Sozialismus* (Vienna, 1924); first published in Russia, in 1917.

history sank to insignificance and became no more than that of a cog to gear the labor movement into the German war machine.

Revolutionary movements have been the subject of innumerable inquiries. Far fewer have been the efforts to investigate the reasons why an avowedly revolutionary party should become essentially a liberal reformist organization. In the case of the Social Democratic party of Germany, the very existence of this problem has scarcely been acknowledged. Friedrich Stampfer, the former Social Democratic deputy in the Reichstag and editor of *Vorwärts,* the official organ of the party, in reviewing the past from the distance of exile, wrote: "The Social Democratic party long before August 4, 1914, had chosen its path, the path of reformism." The question seems to be natural (although Stampfer does not ask it, let alone attempt an answer): Why did Social Democracy choose the path of reformism? . . .

If the general treatments of economic conditions in Germany in the pre-war quarter of a century are consulted with a view to discovering the concrete conditions of the working class, it will be found that almost all authors fail to discuss the question with any discrimination. Even those writers directly concerning themselves with the status of labor frequently treat the subject with a crudity defying analysis. It is common, for example, for skilled and unskilled workers to be lumped together; wages of highly skilled workers are assumed to be typical; and almost universally no consideration is taken of the increase in the intensity of labor, i.e., the increase in actual energy expended. As a matter of fact, the money wages of skilled workers in the first decade of the twentieth century reached levels considerably above those prevailing two or three decades earlier in the building trades, woodworking industries, machine industry, and printing trades. But the cost of living was also rising. According to Carl von Tyszka's calculations, the expenditure of an average German worker's family for the most important foods increased about one-third in the period from 1886–95 to 1911–12. In his chart of the comparative costs of living of English and German workers' families, the German curve rises steadily from 1896–1900 on, rising more sharply than the English curve after 1901–5.

From such statistics it was not difficult for the reformists to select evidence to prove indubitably that wages were rising more rapidly than the cost of living; that consequently real wages were increasing; and that *ergo* the condition of the German working class was improving. In this they were in agreement with the contemporary academic economists. Bernstein and other Social Democrats who wished to revise the party program along liberal lines and away from revolution advocated pure and simple trade-unionism, placing their hopes in the possibility of economic organization to improve the conditions of the working class and to lead to socialism. Apart from the theoreticians, there were union leaders like Hué, Timm, Legien, and Boemelburg. The trade-unions were coming to regard the party as a rival organization rather than as the leader of the labor movement. Both wings of the reformist trend—the intellectuals and the union leaders—based their views on the proposition that the well-being of the working class was improving. Together, they rejected the Marxist theory that the "absolute misery" of the proletariat was increasing. "The intellectual transformation of Social Democracy," wrote W. J. Ashley, "is simply the outcome of an improvement in the condition of the German people—explain it how one may—which cannot be gainsaid."

This interpretation is invalidated by its excessive simplicity. In the first place, real wages form but one factor affecting the physical welfare of the wage-earners. Unemployment, illness, industrial accidents and diseases cannot be ignored. Real wages measure only what a worker receives, not what he produces. At this point it is necessary to introduce the concept of intensity of work. By this is meant the rate of expenditure of physical energy by the worker. If the source of increased production is the increased expenditure of energy by the worker and not technical improvements in the process of production, his work is said to have been intensified. Intensity of work can be measured in the laboratory, but at present it is impossible to offer any quantitative estimates of the intensification of the work of German labor from 1890 to 1914. Measurement, nevertheless, is not the only instrument of social historiography, and in the absence of statistics it will be enough here to sketch the problem.

The principle of intensification of labor, as set forth by students of fatigue, has been formulated as follows:

> Supposing it needs 1 unit of energy to produce 1 article in an hour, it does not need only 2 units of energy to produce two articles in the hour, but distinctly *more* than two units. The greater the speed of production, the relatively greater the call upon the physical energies of the body.

It is evident in this illustration that doubling the real wages would not suffice to compensate the worker for the additional energy he must put forth. While the principle is clear, the difficulty is to disentangle the intensification of labor from the genuine increase in productivity due to improved technique and equipment. As illustrative of this difficulty Sombart cites the fifteen-fold increase in the iron smelted per worker in Germany from 1860 to 1913, the doubling of iron cast per foundry worker in the period from 1860 to 1910, etc. These figures are valueless because no account is taken of changes in machinery and tools. On the other hand, Sombart offers two genuine examples of intensification of labor. In a large Augsburg cotton mill there were thirteen workers per thousand spindles in 1865, and slightly more than six workers serving the same number of spindles in 1912. In the weaving-room in the 1870's a worker tended but one loom, but by 1900 he had to operate from two to four looms. In the period from 1895 to 1907 the production of the average German worker increased 95 per cent, and the average wage rose 53 per cent.

> How much of this increase is to be attributed to the increasing employment of capital goods, and how much to the increasing amount of work performed by the individual workers, cannot, of course, be determined on the basis of the available data.

In considering the stratification of the working class it is useful to distinguish between the mass of the proletariat and its upper section. "In all high-capitalist economies of the present day, besides entrepreneur aristocracies there are labor aristocracies." To the best of my knowledge, only one of the younger German economists, Jürgen Kuczynski, has made the effort to get to the bottom of the wage statistics. He establishes approximate index numbers of the real wages of "the great mass of the workers," on the one hand, and of the labor aristocracy, on the other. To avoid misleading comparisons between single years, he groups his data according to economic cycles. Table 1 presents his results, re-reckoned

TABLE 1. REAL WAGES IN GERMANY, 1887–1914

Years	*Mass of Workers*	*Labor Aristocracy*
1887–94	100	100
1894–1902	102.0	111.1
1903–9	106.1	116.6
1909 to 1913–14	105.1	113.2

to a base of 1887–94 equal to 100. From this table it is clear that the upper stratum of the working class won a much greater increase in real wages than did the mass of the proletariat. But by omitting factors other than wages and cost of living, the table fails to present a complete picture of the conditions of labor. Kuczynski attempts to take the other elements into consideration (intensity of labor, unemployment and part-time employment, increase in accidents, etc.) and summarizes his calculations in Table 2, which is offered for what it may be worth.

TABLE 2. RELATIVE CONDITIONS OF WORKERS IN GERMANY, 1887–1914

Years	*Mass of Workers*	*Labor Aristocracy*
1887–94	100	100
1894–1902	77	83
1903–9	65	71
1909 to 1913–14	60	64

Without affirming the exactness of these figures, we may accept the general conclusion that the actual condition of the working class at least failed to improve as much as the rise of real wages would suggest, and even possibly declined. In short, the picture was far from obvious and gave rise to a questionable optimism which encouraged the right wing of the labor movement. There is no doubt that German economy, rising to leadership in Europe, was able to grant substantial gains in purchasing-power to the upper sections of the working class, tending to give them the sensation of belonging to the middle class. In fact, in 1907 Waltershausen wrote:

> The present age of social politics, which operates toward favoring the mass of the people and burdening the well-situated minority by means of direct taxes, contributions to workers' insurance, legal regulations, and administrative measures, is particularly suited to rear a middle class out of the lower class.

Representing the point of view of these "middle-class" workers, reformism repudiated the theory and practice of revolution. On the other hand, Arthur Dix in 1898 predicted a new stage of development: when the social elevation of the fourth estate approached the limits of an "embourgeoisement" (*Verbürgerlichung*) of the upper strata of the working class, then a new radicalism of the fifth estate, the lowest strata of workers, with a strong admixture of Slavic workers from the east, would rise up against the moderation of the labor aristocracy. In this, Dix not only expressed the division of interest between the labor aristocracy and the bulk of the working class but also tried to foresee the social base upon which a new revolutionary left wing would have to be reared. . . .

That only a small proportion of the voters of the Socialist ticket were members of the party was shown in a tabulation of membership and votes in thirty election districts in 1903 made by Robert Michels. His conclusion awarded the party membership only 15.9 per cent of the total vote. In the judgment of R. Blank the nonproletarian portion (*bürgerlicher Teil*) of the vote approximated one-quarter of the total, or three-quarters of a million votes in 1903. Schmoller estimated the sources of the four and a quarter million Social Democratic votes in 1912 as follows: not quite a million came from party members, a million and a half came from the trade-unions, while the rest, one to two million, were sympathizers. "The latter consist of small impoverished artisans, home workers, peddlers, unorganized workers, dissatisfied petty state and business employees." In Zinoviev's opinion, the masses of sympathizers were "one of the main causes of opportunism." They were

> the strata of the electorate recruited mainly from the petty bourgeoisie who do not belong to the Social Democratic party, are not convinced socialists, but who, under the influence of this or that accidental circumstance, adhere for the time being to the Social Democracy and in the elections give it their vote.

Zinoviev attributed the attractive power of Social Democracy over the petty bourgeoisie to the absence of genuine liberal parties. The party drew all the insulted and the injured. The influence of this strong sector of nonsocialist supporters of Social Democracy was effective within the party:

> The world of the sympathizers floated its own leaders to the surface. Heine [lawyer], Südekum [a man of independent wealth], Landsberg [lawyer], David [Gymnasium teacher and editor], these are the typical representatives and leaders of these strata. . . . . Dependent on backward strata of the workers, the idealist political leaders of the sympathizers create an entire faction within Social Democracy. A state within a state is formed. Petty bourgeois influences become stronger and stronger. Social Democracy itself becomes a campfollower of the campfollowers, the sympathizers do not adapt themselves to it, but it adapts itself to the sympathizers.

In no instance was this statement more strikingly corroborated than in the elections of 1912, when political principles were thrown overboard in order to gain seats. It was significant, in view of the character of the electorate, that the party failed to draw any sharp distinction between its members and its voters.

The form of organization, based on election districts, itself tended to identify voters and members of the party.

Factual data on the officialdom of the labor movement were not broadcast to the eyes and ears of labor. In the privately printed *Handbuch des Vereins Arbeiterpresse* (1914), however, there was an index of the paid functionaries of the party and "free" trade-unions, occupying twenty-six pages of three columns each in small print and containing approximately 4,100 names. In each great metropolitan center there clustered hundreds of these officials, in Greater Berlin 751 of them, in Hamburg 351, etc. This immense bureaucracy was of comparatively late growth. "The party officials who joined their General Benevolent Society grew in the years 1902 to 1911 from 433 to 2,948. Among them are many trade-union leaders, but the majority of them did not join this society," for they had their own association. While the majority of these officials were working-men by origin, "in reality they are no longer workers, they have an income which is greater than that of a middle bourgeois, and they have long given up their occupations as workers." They were drawn, moreover, from the better-paid ranks of the working class, with whom they had common interests. These paid functionaries constituted an independent body. "The four thousand officials form a special corporation having a variety of its own purely professional interests. For the protection of their corporative interests they established their special professional associations of party and trade-union officials." This functionaries' trade-union had 3,617 members in 1913 and collected 252,372 marks in dues. The functionaries of the co-operatives had their own organization, numbering 7,194 members, with a treasury of 2,919,191.20 marks in 1912.

Such considerable sums could only have been raised by fairly well-paid people. According to Zinoviev's reckoning, each official on the average held three different posts, a practice which allowed salaries to accumulate and also centralized power. "Many of the officials of the labor movement earn 10,000 marks and more a year." When von Elm died, it was learned that he had been holding eighteen offices, nor was this considered exceptional. The leading party functionaries "drew increasing salaries of 2,000 to 8,000 marks." In the metal-workers' union a membership of from 400,000 to 500,000 (1909) supported 409 full-time, paid officials, whose salaries ranged as follows: 117 received 2,000 marks or less, 163 got between 2,000 and 2,400, 100 got from 2,400 to 2,800, 15 got 2,800 to 3,000, while there were seven officials drawing salaries of more than 3,000 marks a year. If each of these men held one or two other positions, it is easy to see how a relatively tidy income was insured.

The effect of relative affluence upon the outlook of one who came from simple stock is illustrated by an anecdote told by Bülow. Bülow, in private appears to have regarded the reformists sympathetically as people one might work with, although in public he railed against the party as a whole without distinguishing factions within it. Of Ignaz Auer, the bland mainstay of the reformists in the executive committee of the party until his death in 1907, Bülow wrote respectfully, expressing his admiration of the enormous knowledge Auer had gathered:

The representative in Berlin of the *Kölnische Zeitung,* Herr von Huhn, once told me that, while lunching together, he expressed his astonishment to representative Auer at his intimate knowledge not only of our legislation but also of our entire domestic politics. With a melancholy smile Auer replied, half joking, half in earnest: "I would give all my knowledge to know exactly whether you eat fish and asparagus only with a fork, or whether you can also use a knife."

With clear insight, Max Weber revealed the significance of the bureaucracy at the Magdeburg congress of the Verein für Sozialpolitik in 1907:

The Social Democracy today is manifestly in the process of turning into a powerful bureaucratic machine employing an immense army of officials, turning into a state within a state. . . . Above all, like the state, it has an increasing army of people who, beyond all else, have an "interest in getting ahead." Don't take that merely in the bad sense; there is also the question of purely ideal interests, of getting one's own philosophy accepted in the party—but this army of officials and those maintained in dependence on the party *in addition* also has a highly material interest *in being taken care of*. This interest group includes not only the official employees of the party but also the restaurateurs who rent their halls, the editors of socialist papers, etc.

Weber saw "the antagonism between the material interest, on the one hand, of the professional politician in being provided for and revolutionary ideology, on the other." It is easy to understand how the bureaucracy came to regard "organization," the apparatus which furnished their livelihood, as an end in itself. Jeopardizing the organization by rash acts would jeopardize their own existence; and rash acts meant revolutionaries, who would invite the wrath of the state. It is not surprising that nearly all the well-known reformists were functionaries of the labor movement. "In their professional activity they learned to prize positive day-to-day work. Daily they saw the labor organizations flourish and observed the successes of the inevitable compromise policies." The function of trade-union officials became in part that of acting as a brake upon the "undisciplined" workers who wanted more militant action:

Occasionally the aversion of the workers to their leaders in such cases goes so far that they dismiss them from their positions, as was the case with the shipyard workers in Hamburg. Nevertheless, the official concerned is usually not wholly sacrificed to the displeasure of the masses, since the administration, in such cases where he acted in the interest of the union, assigns him to another post in the administration.

In this way the community of interest of the officials became a factor antagonistic to the demonstrated wishes of the workers they were supposed to represent.

The employment of thousands of full-time functionaries was expensive, and the possibility of losing these people to private employment led the party to raise salaries. These and other expenses could not be met by the low and irregular dues payments alone. As early as 1890 Auer observed: "Our newspapers in the future will have to serve essentially in pecuniary respects to form the backbone of the party. The party can no longer exist on dues; we need the profits of the press." It is easy to recognize here an additional factor furthering the legality-at-any-price policy that sprang from a fear of provoking the state to reprisals against the press of the party, unions, and co-operatives.

The new party officials who moved to the forefront in the decade before the outbreak of the war were men of a different stripe from the veterans of the antisocialist law such as Bebel, Singer, Wilhelm Liebknecht, and even Auer. The new leaders were more distinguished as organizers and administrators in a narrow sense than as political generals. Such, for example, were Friedrich Ebert, elected to the party executive committee in 1905, and Otto Braun, who became a member of the committee in 1911. They were solid and dependable officials, skilful drivers of the party machine. They were opportunists and fearful especially lest untoward policies upset the functioning of the vast apparatus that supported them. Politically, their horizon was bounded by the walls of the Reichstag.

7. GERHARD A. RITTER: The Labor Movement in the Wilhelmian Empire*

The most important recent German study of socialism at the turn of the century, originally a doctoral thesis for the Free University of Berlin, stresses the political causes of revisionism. For Ritter, German socialism cannot be equated with the working class in general—with the economic pressures and opportunities that bore on the class—or with formal Socialist ideology, though all had important influence. Relatedly, the role of Bernstein is less central here. Revisionism resulted above all from political choices and possibilities, on the local as much as on the national level. Ritter's study adds much useful detail about the working of the Social Democratic Party. His definition of revisionism could be criticized by those who prefer a precise statement—which might differentiate between revisionism, which had an ideology behind it—and a more general reformism; or by those who seek broader explanations of the decisions of political leaders, explanations at least partly outside the immediate political situation. Finally, as with many close, scholarly studies of a subject, one must distinguish between new and important facts and really new approaches; it may be the rare historian who can provide both at the same time. Does Ritter's interpretation displace basic definitions of revisionism established by other historians of the subject, or does it largely illustrate these in new ways?

The Social Democratic rejection of the demand for a flexible accommodation of Party tactics to the problems of the day, that became overwhelmingly clear in the position of the Party on the agrarian question, had its roots in the growing, doctrinaire rigidity of traditional Party outlook. Amid the basic pressures of some Party members for specialization and modification of tactics and the insistence on an urgent broadening of the framework of Party activity, great

* From Gerhard A. Ritter, *Die Arbeiterbewegung im Wilhelminischen Reich* (Berlin, 1959), pp. 176, 177–79, 182–85, 186–87, 208–209, 216–17. Reprinted by permission of Colloquium Verlag, Berlin 45.

clashes arose within Social Democracy in the final years of the nineteenth century.

The summary of many criticisms in the catchword "Revisionism" assumes a unity of opposition groups which did not exist in actual opinions. "Revisionism" in Social Democracy was not a unitary view but rather the designation of a critical position toward the traditional concepts of the Party. Aside from this comprehensive impulse in general approach, "Revisionism" degenerated into an abundance of different currents and groups, which mostly subjected certain points of Social Democratic theory and tactics to critical consideration as a result of work in definite and narrow areas of practical activity.

The slow crumbling of the final structure of the Social Democratic Party's ideology by the operation of these criticisms could scarcely be concealed by the weak attempts at transformation of the theoretical foundation of Party activity.

The tendencies in this direction were nothing more than a multiplication of inadequate substitutes for the splintering parts of the total structure, which, existing without relationship one to the other, could have no effect on the various special areas of activity. The gradual emergence of Social Democracy from its ivory tower of Party opinions delivered from above improved its capacity for accommodation to changing political situations and also gradually removed the isolation of the Social Democratic Party, which only furthered the process of merging the working class with existing political and social systems. . . .

Due to the lack of a Prussian State organization of the Party, questions of Prussian politics and thereby also the question of participation in elections to the Prussian Parliament became questions for the whole party. Here was a real dilemma for Social Democracy. Because of the Prussian three-class voting system, the Party had no prospect of practical success unless it agreed to compromises with bourgeois parties. On the other hand, to ignore the Prussian Parliament—one of the prime units of political decision-making in Germany— . . . could only harm the Party itself.

Eduard Bernstein first proposed Social Democratic participation in Prussian parliamentary elections, in an article in *Neue Zeit* which already suggested the huge complexity of the issues involved. Convinced that abstention from voting was "the weakest and most impotent form of protest imaginable" against the three-class voting system in Prussia, Bernstein pleaded for compromises with the bourgeois parties, pointing to the significance of the Prussian Parliament and the possibility of influencing the composition of the lower house by Social Democratic participation in the elections.

Bernstein's belatedly published proposal, coming a few weeks before the end of the Prussian parliamentary elections, was modified further in detail by the university lecturer Dr. Leo Arons and was supported by "Parvus," the "enfant terrible" of the Social Democratic Party. This Russian emigrant, one of the most versatile and clever leaders of the international labor movement, who until shortly before the World War belonged to the radical, revolutionary wing of German Social Democracy, had in spite of or indeed because of his revolutionary tendencies a great sensitivity to the demands of practical politics and even in 1893 explained to the left wing of the Party the necessity of Social Democratic participation in the Prussian elections, because of the significance of the elections for the "agitation among the peasants." "The enlightenment of the masses occurs through practice, through political activity, through the social battle." One of the most interesting moments in the later discussion of this question was the collaboration of radical and reformist circles, who in the common desire for a revival of practical politics through the acquisition of a new approach to the masses directed their attacks against a limitation of the Party's possibilities of action which was, in turn, based on pseudo-radical arguments.

On the whole, however, the reactions of the Party press to Bernstein's initiative were limited to an emphasis on the practical difficulties and an energetic suggestion of the corrupting effect of electoral negotiations with the bourgeois parties. As a result also of the hope that a powerful wave of agitation, after the pattern of Austrian and Belgian socialist efforts, could compel the government to change the Prussian election law, the Party Conference in Cologne unanimously declined to participate in the Prussian elections.

After the view that the Prussian three-class suffrage law would perish by the simple lack of participation of the people was at last abandoned, a further development of tactics could not be prevented. In 1895 Bebel had to argue to the Party Conference in Breslau that the agitation on the electoral law issue, demanded in Cologne, had failed to materialize. It was becoming increasingly clear that any agitation not linked to definite questions of Prussian politics and any agitation that did not guide the attention of the proletariat to the injustices of the Prussian three-class system by the participation of Social Democracy in the elections, would remain ineffective.

In addition to the demands for successful agitation, the attempt of the government to attack Social Democracy through the Prussian legislation on associations . . . was a decisive reason for the strong support that Kautsky's revival of Bernstein's idea, in 1897, found in the Party. The Party's interest in sheer survival also demanded an active battle against the one-sided domination by Junkers of the Prussian parliament, by strengthening the bourgeois influence with the help of Social Democracy; for the uncertain, bare majority of four votes against the "Prussian anti-Socialist law" could naturally be no guarantee against a renewed effort to suppress Social Democracy in the Prussian territory. . . .

The reluctance to compromise with bourgeois parties which emerged so clearly in the discussions about participation in the Prussian parliamentary elections, which was also displayed in the question of Social Democratic behavior in the second-round ballots, was not a sign of Marxist thinking. Rather, it was a legacy of the Lassallean phrase, sharply criticized by Marx, about "a reactionary mass," which was really opposed to the Marxist conception in which the bourgeoisie was seen "as the bearer of big industry, opposite feudal and middle classes," as a "revolutionary class." In a letter to Bernstein of May 23, 1884, which must be seen as a key document in Engels' tactical ideas, Engels stated that he felt it nonsensical to establish a single rule on second-round ballots, to be valid in all cases:

"We possess a great strength which would remain completely unused if electoral behavior is proclaimed for all cases in which none of our people is in the second-round ballot. . . . For example in places like Berlin, when the electoral battle lies between us and the Progressives, agreements for even the main ballot are not out of the question: you yield this electoral district to us, in return for which we yield that one to you—naturally only when we can be sure the agreement will be kept."

Kautsky was also an opponent of the notion of "a reactionary mass" and pronounced expressly for a policy of compromise in a letter to Victor Adler of May 5, 1894. These views about the possibility of compromise with bourgeois parties were rejected by the majority of the Party as an opportunistic betrayal of principle. The question of second-ballot support for candidates of other parties was one of the most contentious issues in Social Democracy. After it had been vehemently discussed in the Party Conference in Copenhagen in 1883, the Conference in St. Gall unanimously recommended Social Democratic abstention in all second-round ballots in which no Social Democratic candidate was involved, on grounds of the bad experiences in the previous national parliamentary elections in 1887. The special political situation of 1890 caused the Party leadership to disregard this resolution. Two years later a renewed proposal for a general non-participation in second-round ballots was rejected by only a bare majority, and the same majority sharply condemned direct or indirect compromises with bourgeois parties.

The Party Conference of 1897 set forth a comprehensive catalogue of conditions (reduced only in the Party Conference of 1911) which bourgeois candidates had to accept if they wished to obtain Social Democratic support in second-round ballots.

In all these cases the support envisaged was unilateral, not reciprocal. There were isolated proposals for agreements between Social Democracy and other parties over reciprocal support in second-round elections for the national parliament in the 1890's, on the regional level, but these proposals were not generally known. Even the second-round ballot agreement of 1912, so sharply attacked by the radical wing of the party, in which the Social Democrats, in return for the second-round electoral help of the Progressives in 31 electoral districts, pledged support for Progressive candidates in conflict with candidates of other parties in 16 electoral districts, did not go as far as Engels' proposals of 1884, which suggested renouncing the presentation of some of the Party's own candidates, even in the first round of an election.

The questions of principle involved in concluding electoral agreements with bourgeois parties had been positively decided earlier by the Social Democratic state parties in the South German States, for their own region. As Vollmar alleged in the Dresden Party Conference of 1903, the (Bavarian) Party was ready in principle even in 1886 to negotiate over an offer by the Liberals, issued in a democratic newspaper in Hamburg, to set up a common procedure for the election of candidates. Only the fact that the Party did not receive enough votes in the original elections to be decisive between the Center Party and the National Liberals prevented the question from becoming acute. In the Bavarian parliamentary elections of 1899 the Center and the Social Democrats concluded an electoral pact against the National Liberals in the districts of Munich I, Speyer-Ludwigshafen, and Pirmaseus-Zweibrucken, that specified independent procedure in the original elections and combinations of lists in the later (second-round) election of deputies. Through this agreement the strength of the Party's representation in the Bavarian parliament was raised from five to eleven. . . .

If the questions about party tactics were discussed even among the mass adherents of the Party, the debates over the various charges of Revisionism were limited to a thin layer of the Party leaders; only slowly and in coarser and distorted form did they reach the broad masses of Party members.

The conflicts in the '90's between the orthodox Party majority, hardened in the old Party concepts, and the advocates of an up-to-date practical politics and broadening of Party activities, through the formation and accentuation of the tactical procedures of Social Democracy, had scarcely touched the central concepts of the Party. In the newly opened and constantly extended areas of Party activity the previously reformist views were preponderant, and with the growth of the Party they increasingly overran the old way of thinking. A new world of reformist worker politics developed, whose importance for the party constantly grew, amid a number of quarrels over competence and areas of friction but without a decisive break, next to the very limited sections of Party activity that were not capable of further development. Meanwhile, first with Schippel and Bernstein in 1897, the attack began on the central concepts of the Party, which previously, in the process of expansion, had been avoided. The decisive importance for the development of German Social Democracy, however, lay clearly in the thousands of individual involvements of workers in new areas of practical activity. "Revisionism" was only a weak reflection of the many-sided reformist activity. Not men like Schippel, Bernstein, Heine, Calwer, and Hildenbrand, but men like Vollmar, Grillenberger, Auer, Kloss, v. Elm, Legien, Leipart, Hué, Dr. Südekum, Ebert, Scheidemann, Keil and Löbe; not the revisionist academics of the *Socialist Monthly Review* (*Sozialistische Monatshefte*), but the worker secretaries and union leaders, the municipal politicians and the state parliamentary deputies, finally the unassailable because inevitable agents of day-to-day political effort—these defined the character of the Party, which already by 1900 had changed into a practical labor party with some revolutionary phrases that were not taken seriously. . . .

In political practice, amid almost unashamed retention of the old radical catchwords and in spite of the opposition of scruples of principle, the Social Democratic Party extended increasingly in the direction, already suggested, of a reformist Emancipation Party of the working class. The gradual transformation of Social Democracy from a party of agitation with definite, firmly established lines of theoretical direction, to a practically active Reform party with a disjointed combination of changeable views shaded according to the concrete circumstance, was the final cause of all the partial manifestations of revisionism. In the steadily-growing relative importance of individual issues that could not be disposed of summarily, compared to expectations in principle, lay also the strength of revisionism, which like the legendary Hydra constantly grew new heads. The revision of basic concepts was not bound to the fate of a theoretical view, but as a consideration from the practical political standpoint depended on a host of changeable factors; though difficult to grasp as a total view and therefore not the equivalent of a firmly established, rigid doctrine in particular matters, it was on the whole infinitely superior. Hence the victories over revisionism in the Party inevitably remained Pyrrhic. The change of concrete conceptions was the unavoidable fate of the Party, as the result of reformist politics that grew ever more dominant in Party life.

The revolutionary phrases and radical axioms were the characteristic signs of a party that depended for decades on the national parliament as the only tribune for its ideas but remained without sufficient influence over concrete, day-to-day politics. While in the parliament itself the summary treatment of current questions yielded, with the growing number of Social Democratic deputies, to a serious examination and objective assessment, an expanding field of activity developed for Social Democracy in the administrative bodies of the social insurance system, as well as in the state parliaments and community governments. These new activities, unsuitable for propaganda purposes, required growing measures of objective judgments and practical abilities. This path from national parliament to state and communal governments, from firmly established theory to practical politics, from the general to the particular, was typical of the German labor party, in contrast to the development of the English labor movement, which was oriented toward concrete questions, scarcely to be distinguished from middle-class reform movements, and which from a whole range of local tendencies slowly and belatedly formed into a parliamentary party.

Around the turn of the century, Social Democracy was represented in the majority of the parliaments of the individual German states. While in the national parliament the sharp conflicts over questions of military policy, foreign policy, colonial policy as well as over tax and tariff policy set narrow limits to the cooperation of Social Democracy in the government, there were, in general, in questions falling within the competence of the state parliaments, in social, church, and educational policies, no unbridgeable differences in principle between the government and the bourgeois parties and Social Democracy. By clever exploitation of the conflicts among the other parties—the Center and the Liberals above all—in states like Bavaria, Baden, Württemberg, Gotha, and above all Bremen, Social Democracy succeeded in invigorating state politics and in carrying through some essential reform measures. . . .

The whole extent of Social Democratic work in community government and its effect on the character of local party groups can only be revealed by special studies for the individual cities. Since questions of principle played little role on the communal level, participation in community governments—in 1913 there were 10,981 Social Democrats in local assemblies and 320 in magistracies and community executives—was a first lesson for local party leaders in the understanding of complex problems of modern administration and a chance to experiment with cooperation with adherents of different political opinions. The experiences in this work inevitably had great impact. It was difficult to speak of class war and revolution in a Party meeting on Sunday when one had agreed the day before with one's liberal colleagues about the need for lighting in some of the dark streets of the city.

Besides the state parliaments and the communes, another fruitful field for practical work was the representative and administrative bodies for worker insurance, the trade and merchant courts, as well as the communal labor exchanges, in all of which, by Bernstein's estimate in 1910, almost 100,000 Social Democrats were active.

Taking steadily deeper roots in existing systems, Social Democracy did not organize the workers in the sense of its theory, as a special, hostile class against the existing order. Rather, it became the lever, along with the economic organizations of the labor movement, through which the working class joined the structures of social life as a contributing element and through which earlier hostilities were bridged and reconciled.

Chapter XIV.

THE DECLINE OF THE HAPSBURG MONARCHY

THE HISTORY of the Hapsburg monarchy in the later nineteenth century poses for the historian, once again, the dilemma of knowing all too clearly how his story has to end. The Hapsburg monarchy was no more after 1918, though whether it collapsed or was dismembered is a key issue in its history. There is no question that it was seriously unstable for decades before this, nor that the instability primarily consisted of the diverse and intense nationalist agitation within its borders. But was it irreversibly doomed? Words like inevitable permeate many of the histories of the period; and historians who dissent from the fatalistic approach must spend much of their time specifically refuting it.

The main issue, then, is neatly posed, and a number of subsidiary problems flow from it. If the monarchy was irremediably sick, when was its fate sealed? Some historians view its whole nineteenth-century history as an inevitable progression toward an inevitable end. Others focus on later developments, such as the *Ausgleich* of 1867, which excluded Slavic peoples from a share in power. Again, what created the inevitability? Some historians see a role for diplomatic errors, ranging from the break with Russia in the 1850's to the annexation of Bosnia in 1908; others stress internal factors alone. How important was the ineptitude of the Hapsburgs themselves? Would more alert leadership have saved the monarchy? Or must the process of decay be seen as a cosmic conflict between national and supranational principles, with the latter doomed to defeat?

Seldom has the account of the inexorable decline of the Hapsburg monarchy been written without some passion. The fervor of Slavic or Hungarian nationalism (which often infects even English or French students of the area) can easily infuse a history and add to a vigorous statement of the inevitability of collapse a clear belief that it came none too soon.

The crucial problem, for the advocate of inevitability, is the evaluation of the role of World War I in the dismemberment of the monarchy. He must prove that collapse would have come without the war or that the war itself resulted from the decay of the monarchy, or both; and he will normally try to show that the monarchy split from within well before intervention by the Western powers in the peace negotiations. The partisan of the continued vitality of Austria-Hungary, on the other hand, must show that the war alone destroyed the monarchy and that Allied intervention, not internal strife, played a key role.

There are, then, two issues in evaluating the two principal strands of interpretation. First, there is the question of fact: What happened in World War I? Ideally, this question ought to be susceptible of solution, but it has not been. The other issue can probably never be fully resolved, for it is of necessity speculative. The advocate of inevitability can amass all sorts of evidence to show the low state of the monarchy by 1914, but he cannot prove that collapse would have come without the war, for the war happened. His opponent can point to signs of vitality in the same period and assert that, without the war, the monarchy might have survived, but again, the war did come. The debate goes around and around. In the process, a great deal of information has been discovered about the monarchy; but one may legitimately ask whether such research could not be as well conducted without the speculations about what might have been.

Several recent treatments of the Hapsburg monarchy have turned away from a belief in inevitability and have pointed to some strengths of the monarchy as late as 1914. This view may simply reflect increasing knowledge, plus perhaps the sympathy that many historians involved in elaborate research often gain for their subject. The passage of time has blunted some of the nationalist sentiment associated with studies of the area before World War II, particularly for some English and American writers; and, like some of the nationalists themselves around World War I, one can now wonder if the monarchy for all its faults was not preferable to the divided and often bickering states that succeeded it.

One merit of the opponents of fatalism has been to point to major aspects of Austrian history in the late nineteenth century that do not fit into a study confined to an obituary alone. The cultural vitality of the period, the advance of the economy and social welfare programs, the new political movements—all these deserve historical attention and are now beginning to receive it. To discuss them in no sense necessarily disproves the theory of inevitable collapse; one could even view some of the cultural creativity as a symptom of decay; but it does fill out the picture of the period.

No matter what position is taken on the inevitability question, the central topic of the period is the role and intensity of the nationalisms within the monarchy. Historians have differed widely on the nature of the Hapsburgs' policies toward minority nationalisms and the degree of flexibility possible to them; on the goals of the nationalists themselves and the extent to which they explicitly sought the destruction of the monarchy; and on the role of conflicts among the various national groups in modifying the ultimate pressure of any one nationalism on the government. Beyond this, the historian must ask how widespread nationalist sentiment was and how intensely it was felt, both questions that are extremely difficult to examine empirically. Some historians (usually in the ranks of the fatalists) tend to assume that pointing out the existence of a national group, for this period, is almost equivalent to stating a vigorous and widespread national feeling. Others note great differences in the types of nationalism current in the monarchy. No one contests the importance of nationalism in the history of the monarchy in the period; precisely for this reason, the varied approaches to the subject are fundamental to the whole historical debate.

1. OSCAR JASZI: The Dissolution of the Habsburg Monarchy*

Oscar Jaszi (1875–1957) was a Hungarian leader during World War I, who later taught for many years in the United States at Oberlin College. He was not opposed to the principle of the Hapsburg monarchy, but in retrospect believes that it was doomed by its own coercive policies and the universal hostility of its subjects. This hostility was primarily nationalistic but also had roots in grave social injustice. Here is a clear statement of an inevitability thesis, citing developments long before the war, which also conveys something of the intensity of political passions of the period.

Before proceeding to examine the causes which made the attempt at consolidation of the Habsburg empire a failure, a word may be said in anticipation of objections that may be taken to my viewpoint. There will be those who will resolve this whole problem into a sham by asserting that the dissolution of the monarchy was not the result of inner forces, but that it was due exclusively to external factors which had nothing to do with the psychic and political structure of the empire. This point of view, which in a former book I termed the "Habsburg legend" and which is disseminated by the propaganda of very influential dynastic and feudal groups, represents the Habsburg monarchy as an innocent lamb, a victim of the antagonism of German and English imperialism which, arousing the World War, buried under its ruins the free and happy Danubian League of Nations.

This historical materialism *à la Habsburg* has been recently advanced by a naïve and superficial historical and sociological literature which, investigating the responsibility for the World War, looks only on the diplomatic side of the problem, its chief interest consisting in the inquiry whether the world-catastrophe was actuated by the diplomatic maneuvers of Berchtold, Poincaré, Izvolsky, or Grey, or whether the Serb government did or did not have a previous knowledge of the murderous attack at Sarajevo. Such a point of view, which sees in the world-catastrophe exclusive personal intrigues and responsibilities, makes the real problem appear both shallow and obscure. For however great may be the crime of the individual politicians and statesmen in setting the date of the world-catastrophe, it is sufficiently clear that these men did not do more than detonate that mass of dynamite which the social and national unrest of Central Europe had piled up during the last hundred years.

Therefore, if we wish to understand history more clearly both from the point of view of the present and the future, and if we really try to follow a constructive policy of peace, we must have an end of that sentimental pacifism which considers all wars simply as the private affairs of criminal kings and diplomats or of capitalistic interests, and does not understand that the real causes of modern conflicts lie far deeper in the impeded evolutionary processes of the

* From Oscar Jaszi, *The Dissolution of the Habsburg Monarchy,* pp. 6–13, 98–99, 448–49.

masses checked by stupid or criminal internal policies. I have no place here to amplify this point of view; I wish only to say that the warlike liquidation of the former Habsburg monarchy is no sane argument for the assertion that its collapse was purely a mechanical process and not the end of an organic development of almost two hundred years. We know not a single national or social crisis on a large scale in world-history which could have created a radical new equilibrium without awakening a series of international and warlike complications. This concatenation of the inner evolution and of outer warlike complications is also clearly demonstrated by the genesis of the other national states; and it is not a sane argument against the organic nature of English and French national unity to say that the movement toward unity of the moral and economic forces was very often protected in both countries by the militaristic and political centralization of the respective dynasties.

The dissolution of the Habsburg monarchy and the establishment of new national states on its ruins was, in its essence, the same process which in many other states of Europe led to the state integration of those peoples having a common language and culture. The same fundamental causes working for unity in the nationally homogeneous states worked toward dissolution in the ethnographical mosaic of the Habsburg empire. Even the World War can only be fully understood from this historical perspective. The detonator of the European explosion was perhaps a capitalistic one, but its violence would have been unimaginable without the powder magazine formed by the unsolved and accumulating national and social problems of Central and Eastern Europe.

In whatever manner we may regard the Habsburg problem—whether we analyze its historical atmosphere, the mass psychology of its people, or the international complications arising from its national and economic conditions—from all these points of view we must come to the same conclusion, namely, that this vast historical drama was not the result of diplomatic quarrels, but grew out of the inevitable logic of a long series of social causes.

This conception is not merely an *a posteriori* assertion, but it was already alive many years, even decades before in the consciousness of all those who were capable of regarding the problems of the Danubian monarchy with sufficient intellectual force. Many of the best statesmen, poets, scholars, and publicists were unanimous in the understanding that the empire of the Habsburgs had become an anachronistic impossibility, that it was doomed to death or at least could have been saved only by a major operation. Such and similar declarations, even well-founded sociological analyses, are so abundant that I must limit myself to the most characteristic and conspicuous ones.

Mickiewicz, the great Polish poet, almost a hundred years ago wrote the following startlingly clear-sighted description of the Habsburg empire:

> This Empire counts thirty-four million inhabitants, but in reality it has no more than six million people; namely six million Germans keeping twenty-eight millions of other stocks in bondage. If one subtracts from these six millions the numbers of peasants, artisans, merchants, etc., who have no share at all in the government,

there remain at most two million Austrians who rule all these masses. These two millions or rather their interests and opinions are represented approximately by a hundred families which are German, Hungarian, Polish, or Italian but which commonly speak French and have their capital largely outside the country. Using in their service two million bureaucrats and soldiers they rule through them the other thirty-two millions. That is a society modelled on the pattern of the English East Indian Company. . . . . Ordinarily, people have a false idea of this Austrian Empire which never was a German, Hungarian or Slavish empire, but a kinship of all those who aim at drawing out the marrow of so many extensive countries rich in population.

Even more striking than this were the diagnoses and prognostications several times expressed by the great apostle and theoretical founder of the national idea, Giuseppe Mazzini. He clearly described the irresistible movement both of the Northern Slavs and the Southern Slavs toward unification. He prophesied that this movement, combined with the struggles for emancipation of the Greeks and the Rumanians, would inevitably destroy both the Austrian and the Turkish empires, "these two serpents which paralyze the heart of Europe." Already in 1843 he wrote that "in the Austrian Empire a movement of the Slav population is progressing" (he even foresaw the unification of Bohemia and Moravia with the Slovak tribes of Hungary) "for which nobody cares and which one day, united with our own efforts, will cancel Austria from the map of Europe. . . . ."

In another direction, but scarcely less pessimistically, the situation of the monarchy was elucidated in 1822 by Charles Sealsfield, a brilliant German-American who fled before Austrian absolutism into the New World where he later wrote his powerful denunciation of the system of Metternich, an arraignment which is one of the most direct and penetrating documents of the empire of Emperor Francis. Sealsfield characterizes Austria as a "big agglomeration of provinces," and describes with vivid colors the exasperated public mind of the Slav majority against the German absolutist rule. He writes:

One can even hear the Bohemians gnash their teeth if one begins to praise English liberty. They are filled with unspeakable sorrow if their own country is mentioned, the battles which they were obliged to fight for a strange cause, the armies for which they furnish the soldiers and bear the costs and which in reality serve for their oppression. They feel depressed that they exist for a dynasty which remained foreign to them and their wishes in spite of a rule of several hundred years, and which in its incapacity cares only how to subdue Bohemia and how to kill its national aims.

This system, according to the opinion of Sealsfield, is untenable. The country as a unified whole is very near a crisis. Though it will not come to a general upheaval since the provinces are too sharply watched and the inner antagonisms are too great (the Bohemians would march against Hungary, the Poles against the Italians, and the Germans against both), the inner immorality of the system and its disregard for all loyal principles will ultimately destroy itself.

About ten years later the same *facies hippocratica* of the monarchy was seen by a Russian observer, by the Pan-Slav historian, Pogodin, who made several trips of investigation in Central Europe and gave an account of them to his government. He wrote:

> The Slavs seem to be on the eve of a renaissance, the empire of the Danube must tremble even more than the Turkish empire in the face of twenty millions of a hostile race in its interior. Austria is a white sepulchre, an old tree which is rotten within, though it still bears leaves on the outside, but which the first blast of wind will uproot.

Again, ten years later, quite similar was the diagnosis of Charles Montalembert, the eminent French conservative statesman who spoke the following words (1846) on the tribune of the French Parliament: "The Austrian monarchy is a bizarre composition of twenty nations which justice could have maintained but which injustice will push into dissolution."

The same mood is reflected in the opinions of many other foreign observers. Napoleon III called Austria a corpse with which nobody can make a contract. At the other pole of social life Karl Marx fixed the death-sentence of the Habsburg empire: "The only circumstance," he wrote in 1860, "which legitimates the existence of Austria since the middle of the eighteenth century is its resistance to the advances of Russia in eastern Europe . . . . a resistance helpless, inconsequent, cowardly, but tough." And, following the trend of thought of his master, Frederick Engels in 1888 made the assertion that the destruction of Austria would have been a misfortune for European civilization before the approaching triumph of the Russian Revolution; after which its annihilation becomes unnecessary, for Austria, becoming superfluous, will go asunder by itself.

Similar considerations were expressed from a quite different angle by the noted French historian, Louis Leger, who on a pamphlet published in 1866 and treating the problem of Austria, alluding to the oppressed nationalities, put the following significative motto: *Ave Caesar resurrecturi te salutant!* And in a more comprehensive work, in 1879, he wrote this judgment: "Abandoned to the blind egotism of the Germans and the Magyars the Habsburg Monarchy could not solve the problem of the East. She will witness its solution against its own interests."

It may be objected that the assertions quoted above emanate from strangers and from the enemies of the monarchy, but we shall soon see that the friends of the empire did not think otherwise than its enemies. Let us continue our survey with the opinion of two Hungarian statesmen of whom the first cannot be counted among the enemies of the dynasty. Count Stephen Széchenyi, the conservative promoter of the Hungarian renaissance, whom his noted political antagonist, Louis Kossuth, called the greatest Hungarian, prophesied as early as 1813 the dissolution of the monarchy. When, after the battle of Dresden, he was convalescing in a Prague hospital, he exposed before his officer colleagues the probable future of the monarchy. Of this conversation, a court spy (these men of Metternich filled even the hospitals) reported to Vienna that the count before an audience consisting chiefly of Prussian officers made the declaration that in spite of its victories, Austria would go asunder "within a century because its parts are unequal and they separate more and more from each other."

Louis Kossuth, in 1881, was naturally more capable of describing accurately the pathology of the monarchy. The Viennese secret police sent an able *agent provocateur* to Turin in order to extract from the great man in exile his point of view concerning the international situation. The maneuver succeeded, and Kossuth, knowing not to whom he was speaking, gave his unveiled opinion concerning the future of Austria, which was later reported to the Viennese commissioner by the spy. According to this report, Kossuth predicted the approach of the Russian Revolution which he thought would be a deathknell for Austria. As Augustulus was the last Roman emperor, so Rudolphulus would be the last Habsburg. That was an allusion to Crown Prince Rudolph who died in 1889. It can scarcely be doubted that if the catastrophe of Meierling of which Rudolph became a victim had not happened and Rudolph had remained alive, the prophecy of Kossuth would have been literally realized.

But even the guiding spirits of Austria were not more optimistic over the situation of the monarchy. One may say, in terms of recent psychology, that the whole policy of Metternich stood under a "dissolution complex," and this attitude fomented his almost monomaniacal struggle against democracy and liberalism. His wife, the princess Melanie, called him often the "Cassandra of the monarchy," for he was saturated with alarming news about the collapse of the empire. It is quite natural that in such a milieu the judgment of the more liberal and freer spirits was even more emphatically unfavorable to the reigning system and its consequences. So in 1830, after the revolution of July, Grillparzer, the greatest poet of Austria, wrote the following really visionary lines:

> The whole world will be strengthened by the unexpected change, only Austria will go to pieces by it. The shameless Machiavellism of the leaders who, in order that the reigning dynasty should remain the only connecting tie of the state, have fomented and nourished the reciprocal national antipathies of the separate provinces, is responsible for it. The Hungarian hates the Bohemian, the Bohemian hates the German, and the Italian hates them all, and as horses absurdly harnessed together, they will scatter in all directions as soon as the advancing spirit of the times will weaken and break the bonds.

This conviction of the grave danger facing the monarchy gained a deep statesman-like elucidation ten years later in a book anonymously published at Hamburg in 1842, which, under the title *Austria and Its Future,* gave a pitiless analysis of the formidable inner antagonisms of the monarchy. The author of this book was Baron Victor Andrian von Werburg, a chamberlain and a high official in the court administration, and later vice-president of the National Assembly. As one of the most cultivated aristocrats of his time, his opinion may be regarded as representative. Andrian was of the opinion that "Austria is a purely imaginary name which does not signify any compact people, any country, any nation . . . . a conventional term of several nationalities sharply distinct each from the other." There are Italians, Germans, Slavs, Magyars, but there is no Austrian national consciousness. The idea of the state is annihilated by the principle of nationality. There arose a Slav, a Hungarian, and an Italian national feeling which consolidated itself more from day to day, rejected all foreign elements, and expanded with a prophetic vehemence. The system of these particularistic consciousnesses menaces the very existence of Austria. Only inertia succeeds in holding the monarchy together. "This state of mind is like the buried corpses in Pompeii which, preserved during many centuries, fall into dust and ashes as soon as a beam of God's free sun or a blast of wind touches them." How could such a state resist the growing consciousness of unity of the Slavs which begins to form a compact phalanx from Troppau to Cattaro?

Thoughtful men of later generations judged the future of the monarchy with the same pessimism. Ferdinand Kürnberger, the greatest Austrian publicist of the second half of the nineteenth century, agreed with these opinions, and he always regarded Austria as an anachronistic country and contrary to the spirit of Europe. He repeatedly emphasized the essentially Asiatic nature of Austria.

And lest these remarks be regarded as the impressionist utterances of exacerbated poets and publicists, I would call attention to the diagnosis of Ottokar Lorenz, the distinguished historian who, though a native Austrian, did not hide his deeply pessimistic opinions. He too talked of the second "sick man of Europe," and he never took the so-called new constitutional era of Francis Joseph seriously. On the contrary, he considered the various constitutional experiments to be like the experiments of England to remold the Turkish empire, because he was of the opinion that the old Austria had died as a consequence of the Revolution of 1848.

This pessimistic attitude also gradually took possession of the leaders of practical politics, and Count Taaffe, prime minister of Austria during two decades, called his own policy, with crude honesty, the policy of *Fortwursteln* ("to go on in the old groove"). That this policy would earlier or later demoralize the national forces was clearly understood by the enlightened elements of the state. Professor Masaryk, now president of Czecho-Slovakia, disgusted by the petty compromises without principle, called the Austrian parliament a *Tandelmarkt* (a "junk market"). And Ernest Körber, one of the last premiers of the monarchy "saw the situation of the monarchy as darkly as Metternich did after 1848."

This pessimistic public opinion penetrated even the circles of the Viennese court itself. General von Margutti, one of the leaders of the chief military bureau, narrates in his memoirs that beginning with his earliest youth he heard that the monarchy was not an up-to-date state, that it had no right to existence, and that it was only upheld by the personality of the old Emperor after whose death it would fall asunder "like an old barrel robbed of its hoops." This conviction exasperated and perhaps drove to death Crown Prince Rudolph himself. "I am only anxious to know as a silent observer," he once wrote to a friend, "how much time such an old and tough edifice as this Austria takes before it cracks in all its joints and falls asunder." The successor of Rudolph, Archduke Francis Ferdinand, heir apparent, was even more impressed by the approaching catastrophe, and endeavored in vain to avoid the fate which menaced not only the state but his own life. This feeling of an approaching disaster dominated the more clear-sighted elements of the army also. Conrad von Hötzendorf, later the chief of general staff during the war, emphasized for many years in his memoranda to the Emperor that the Italian and Jugo-Slav *irredenta* threatened the monarchy with collapse. Similarly, General Auffenberg as minister of war judged the situation in 1912. At the time of the Balkan crisis he uttered the following prophetic words to the German ambassador:

> We need at least a half century of peace in the Monarchy to put the southern Slavs in order and this quietness can be maintained only by eliminating all the hopes of the southern Slavs for Russian protection, otherwise the Monarchy goes to pieces.

This insecurity of the future oppressed even the old Emperor in spite of the fact that those around him tried carefully to keep all alarming news from him. A documentary witness of this pessimistic mood is a testamentary provision of the Emperor of 1901 in which Francis Joseph established a family property in trust of sixty-million gold crowns the purpose of which was determined by the following words:

> If in the course of events and in the historical evolution, the form of government of the Austro-Hungarian Monarchy should suffer a change and, what God may prevent, the crown should not remain in our house, the order of succession for the family property in trust established by me should be determined by those principles of common right which are in existence in the ordinary code of law from June first, 1811.

The chief ally of the Dual Monarchy, the German government itself, was also haunted by the ghost of the approaching dissolution of the Danube empire. The German chancellor, Prince Bülow, in order to avoid possible dangerous conflicts in the case of the disaster of Austria, suggested in 1905 through his ambassador in St. Petersburg, a plan of a "Treaty of Disinterestedness" according to which both Germany and Russia would declare not to make an annexation in the case of collapse of the Danube monarchy.

These many and various declarations and utterances, which all denounce the extreme uncertainty of the existence of the monarchy, cannot be a pure accident, but are a symptom and almost a symbol of a deeply rooted organic crisis. There can be no doubt that many of the better intellects clearly saw or felt that the monarchy was being pushed toward disaster by irresistible historical forces. . . .

[The suppression of the 1848 Revolution]. According to Hungarian tradition, which was held three generations, the various terror tribunals handed down 114 death sentences and imprisonment was resorted to in 1,765 cases. The later official historians have tried to mitigate the poignant memory of these horrors by affirming that the young emperor had no knowledge of these judicial murders but later investigations demonstrated that Francis Joseph had previous information of the execution of the Hungarian generals.

But the revenging arm of Haynau and his men struck not only the rebels of the army but all those who were in contact with political life in that stormy period. Bishops and ministers encountered harsh imprisonment and several leaders of the Hungarian revolution were hung in effigy. And on the same day when the martyrs of Arad ended their lives, there was executed in Pest one of the most excellent and most moderate Hungarian statesmen, the premier of the first Hungarian constitutional government, Count Louis Batthyány. Thus the whole monarchy was pacified by the old Spanish methods of blood and iron. The jovial people of Vienna, the successors of the Hussites in Prague, the Italian patriots, and the Magyar "rebels," all succumbed to the bloody arms of the Habsburgs. No wonder that these events profoundly impressed the public opinion of all those peoples who suffered by these terrible methods. That is the reason why I try the patience of the reader with an enumeration of all these details. *For these facts are not only facts of the past in the Habsburg drama but they were direct causes of the process of dissolution*. These bloody facts created such a psychological state among the masses, for instance, in Hungary, that it influenced most powerfully the whole political life of the country. The slogan of the *accursed Austria-Vienna* remained always a kindling symbol in the imagination of the masses. "Vienna" remained always equivalent to the wailings of the Protestant galley slaves, to the insurrections choked in blood, and above all to the constitution stolen by the help of the Russian bayonets. In the face of this emotional complex all rational argumentation broke down. Habsburg remained hated and abhorred even when he tried to give rights and liberties to the people. *Timeo Danaos* . . . . "We accept nothing from the *Viennese camarilla,* not even the good." That feeling was so intense that ten years after the catastrophe when Count Stephen Széchenyi, the great conservative statesman, was placed with broken spirit in a Viennese asylum shortly before his tragic suicide, he gave in his diary to Francis Joseph the epithet of "the apostolic usurper" and he called the gallows the "pillars of Francis Joseph." And even in the last decade of the monarchy when attending public meetings, I often observed that the memory of "the thirteen of Arad" swayed the masses as the wind does the standing grain. That is what many Austrian and Hungarian statesmen never realized. They did not understand how insignificant demagogues could excite the feeling of the masses into paroxysms against institutions which, as the free-trade policy or the Austro-Hungarian bank, could serve the very interests of the Hungarian majority too. They did not understand because they always used rationalistic methods and they did not know that the masses are led more by old memories and semiconscious ancestral sentiments than by the rational calculations of economic motives. All political dissatisfaction and all social discontent could be easily directed against Vienna in such manner. And I think I am quite safe in believing that the same mental processes were going on in the soul of the Czech, of the Polish, and of the Italian masses. What Arad was to the Hungarian, the scaffold of Prague was to the Czech, the jail of Spielberg was to the Italian, and the bloody parade of Tarnow was to the Pole. . . .

It is highly characteristic that the only nation of the monarchy which did not produce a national hymn in the proper sense was the first leading nation of the monarchy, the German. Why? Because the center of gravity of the German national consciousness, even for the Germans of the monarchy, was not the anational Austria but the German empire as a nation state. At the same time the German leading nation in Austria was so intimately connected with the Habsburg dynasty that the glory of the monarchy as a whole held back the expressions of a special German patriotism within the empire.

No wonder that the intensity of all these national feelings was stronger than the artificial suggestions of a receding dynastic patriotism. And this growing trend of national feeling and consciousness was neither checked nor coordinated by any other moral synthesis. The Habsburg empire became more and more a conglomerate of various nationalistic feelings among peoples which did not know each other but which hated each other bitterly. The dynastic patriotism, the faith of some ten thousand officers, aristocrats, priests, bureaucrats, and industrial magnates was powerless against the popular enthusiasm of the exuberant national individualities. The state of the Habsburgs collapsed, in the final analysis, because it was unable to offer a real solidarity to its various nations by the help of a system of serious civic education. The more enlightened Habsburgs knew very well the fatal importance of this problem but they could not solve it. The means which were employed were far too mechanical and incoherent. Outside the army we have not a single example of a real type of civic education. . . .

The collapse of the Habsburg empire was not anything surprising but rather the long continuance of this amalgamation of peoples without a common state idea, based on the mutual hatred and distrust of the various nations. Manifestly their inner revolutionary forces were not sufficient, in time of peace, to get rid of the Habsburg yoke. Regarding the process as a whole, the most outstanding groups of causes which undermined the cohesion of the old patrimonial state were threefold:

1. The growing national consciousness of the various nations which could not find place for a true consolidation and adequate self-expression in the rigidity of the absolutistic structure, later not changed but only modified by the semi-absolutism of the Dualistic System under which neither a confederated constitution nor even a sound local national autonomy could be achieved.

2. The economic and social pressure of the feudal class rule, allied with a usurious kind of capitalism, which did not allow the productive forces of the various nations to be developed. Vienna was not only a natural economic leader but at the same time an economic exploiter of the weaker nations through her financial and administrative monopolies. The national exasperation of the peoples was strengthened by the feeling of being a kind of a colony for German capitalism. At the same time the hunger-belt of the latifundist system paralyzed

to a large extent the beneficent influences of a united customs territory. A true division of labor among the various territories remained rudimentary whereas a new national middle class arose everywhere which felt its economic interests incompatible with the supremacy of big Viennese finance.

3. The lack of any serious kind of civic education. All the nations lived as moral and intellectual strangers to one another. Both the dynastic epic in Austria and the feudal in Hungary were incapable of creating a sufficiently strong and cohesive state idea. Finally these two fallacies pushed the two hegemonic nations into a fatal conflict, even more pernicious than that in which they were engaged with their lesser nationalities.

This growing dissolution and final collapse of the Habsburg empire was mainly the work of three factors:

1. The continuous growth of the various nations which realized more and more clearly that their hope for the rebuilding of the Habsburg empire and for their reasonable national independence was a fallacious one. The ideas of separation or secession became stronger.

2. The irredentistic propaganda of those surrounding countries which harbored a claim for their co-nationals living under Habsburg "oppression," partly from sentimental reasons, partly animated by the imperialistic conceptions of the respective war parties.

3. The disintegrating influence of the World War which made the latent hatred of the nations burst into flame and gave opportunity to the dissatisfied intelligentsias to form fighting diplomatic and military organizations against the empire. This internal dissension and antagonism gradually paralyzed the moral and economic forces of the monarchy.

2. A. J. P. TAYLOR: The Habsburg Monarchy, 1809–1918*

A. J. P. Taylor † offers another statement of irremediable decay. Like Jaszi, he believes that the national principle had to triumph, but he differs in his evaluation of the nature of nationalism, and he does not view the collapse of the monarchy in terms of internal developments alone. Diplomatic errors contributed, and well before the war the monarchy was maintained by diplomatic support alone.

The other principal change is in treatment. Despite efforts to face reality, [my] earlier book was still dominated by the "liberal illusion"; many passages talked of "lost opportunities" and suggested that the Habsburg Monarchy might have survived if only this or that statesman or people had been more sensible. It was difficult to escape from this approach after reading the works of innumerable contemporary writers of good-will, who either wrote before the fall of the Monarchy or still could not believe that it had vanished. These regrets are no part of the duty of a historian, especially when the story which he tells makes it

* From A. J. P. Taylor, *The Habsburg Monarchy, 1809–1918* (London: Hamish Hamilton Ltd., 1948), pp. 7–8, 225–26, 228–30, 233–34. Reprinted by permission of Hamish Hamilton Ltd.

† See chapters 6 and 10, on 1848 and German unification.

clear, time after time, that there were no opportunities to be lost. The conflict between a super-national dynastic state and the national principle had to be fought to the finish; and so, too, had the conflict between the master and subject nations. Inevitably, any concession came too late and was too little; and equally inevitably every concession produced more violent discontent. The national principle, once launched, had to work itself out to its conclusion. My earlier version had also perhaps a "national illusion": it tended to suggest that the national movements were, by the twentieth century, movements of "the people." I have tried here to modify this view and to make it clear that mass-nationalism, where it existed, was very different from the nationalism of the intellectuals. . . .

The fate of the Habsburg Monarchy had been decided by the war of 1866; it owed its further independence to the grace of Bismarck and must lose it as soon as Bismarck's successors abandoned his moderate course. Men thought to alter the European position of the Habsburg Monarchy by changing its internal structure; in reality a change in its internal structure could come only after a change, or rather catastrophe, in its European position.

Thus, all the schemes of the pre-war era postulated the impossible. If only the Monarchy had not been defeated in 1866; if only the Magyars would accept the Slavs as equals; if only the Germans would not look to the German Empire; if only the peoples of the Empire would become again illiterate peasants and return to the unquestioning dynastic loyalty of the days of the Counter-Reformation; if only the Habsburgs would promote trade unions and agrarian reform; then the problem would be solved, for, indeed, it would not exist. So, standing round a deathbed, the mourners might say: "If only the dead man would breathe, he would be quite all right." This medley of wishes turned into a uniform chorus: if only Francis Joseph would die and be succeeded by Francis Ferdinand, then all the various "solutions" would come true. Those who looked to Francis Ferdinand knew little of his character: he represented change, and they foolishly supposed that any change would be a change for the better. Francis Ferdinand was one of the worst products of the Habsburg House: reactionary, clerical, brutal and overbearing, he was also often insane. He lacked even the pessimism and hesitation which had made Francis Joseph a tolerable ruler. The only constant element in Francis Ferdinand's political outlook was hostility to Dualism: without sympathy for the peoples oppressed by Magyar nationalism, he had a dynastic jealousy of Hungarian freedom and wished to reduce Hungary to a common subordination. For he was equally hostile to the Czechs and even to German liberals, though not to German nationalism. His ideal was the absolutist militarism created by Schwarzenberg in 1849; this had been the ideal also of Francis Joseph until he had been taught better by events.

Much was written of the constructive plans which Francis Ferdinand would carry out when he came to the throne. He would refuse to be crowned King of Hungary until the settlement of 1867 had been undone; this much was clear, thereafter his plans turned to smoke. He encouraged clerical nationalism among the Slovaks, sympathised with the Roumanians, and welcomed, most of all, the dynastic nationalism of the Croat Party of Pure Right. He, too, was a "federalist." This meant no more than the restoration of a Kingdom of Croatia severed from Hungary and directly dependent on the Emperor. He dared not propose even the union of the Serb lands of Hungary with Croatia, for this would admit the South Slav idea; and his "trialist" scheme was designed to disrupt the South Slav peoples, as Napoleon's Confederation of the Rhine disrupted the Germans. "Trialism," in fact, would have provoked South Slav discontent more than ever, would have driven the Magyars into opposition to the Monarchy, and yet have done nothing to settle the conflict between Czechs and Germans in Bohemia. Moreover, the schemes of Francis Ferdinand did not envisage the co-operation of the peoples or advance beyond the "historico-political individualities" of Old Conservative clap-trap. Francis Ferdinand might break with the Magyar gentry and the German bureaucracy, on whom the Empire rested; he would still be faced with the question which had baffled every reformer from Joseph II to Badeni—how could a Habsburg become a Bonaparte, Emperor of peasant peoples? The associates of Francis Ferdinand were professional soldiers and sham-feudal nobles, the Old Conservative bloc of Windischgrätz and Belcredi; only a few clericalist politicians had been added, evidence of the political immaturity of the peoples whom they claimed to represent. The October Diploma represented the utmost of Francis Ferdinand's vision, and the Diploma, two hundred years out of date in 1860, had not been made more modern by the passage of fifty years.

To place hope in any Habsburg was to fail to understand the nature of the Habsburg Monarchy. Kossuth atoned for all his shortcomings by recognizing that the overthrow of the Habsburg dynasty was the first condition for a reconstruction of central Europe; Michael Károlyi was the only Hungarian to see, and to accept, the consequences of this doctrine. In Austria men were too awed by the physical presence of the Emperor to imagine central Europe without the dynasty: even the most advanced Socialists dreamt of a democratic Socialism imposed by dynastic initiative, and those Germans who hated Habsburg rule desired instead the rule of the Hohenzollerns. Only the solitary Czech professor Masaryk had confidence in the peoples and wished them to learn reality by the exercise of responsibility. . . .

The ossified carcass of the Habsburg Monarchy kept a balance from its own dead weight. The impulse which brought the gigantic structure down had to come from without; though it could never have achieved its tremendous effect had not all been rotten within. The Habsburg Monarchy could survive internal discontent and even foreign rivalry; both flattered its importance and treated it as a European necessity. What the Habsburgs could not survive was a denial of the need for them. To such a denial force seemed the only answer; yet the more it was threatened the more useless it proved. Italian nationalism had been the David which brought down old Austria; Serb nationalism was the David of Austria-Hungary. The mistakes of Metternich and Buol in Italy were repeated now against the Serbs. Driven wild by the challenge to their existence, Habsburg statesmen lost their skill in balancing and manœuvre: Serbia became an obsession with them, as Italy had been, and every step they took increased their difficulties. The Bosnian crisis created the Serb peril; the campaign against the Serbo-Croat leaders presented Serbia with a powerful weapon. Independent Serbia, Orthodox in religion and for long a Turkish province, had little interest in the Habsburg lands. The Serbs aspired to liberate their brothers still under Turkish rule and to recover all the territory once historically Serb; this ambition extended to Bosnia and Hercegovina, not beyond. The Serbs had certainly no reason to feel affection for the Croats, Roman Catholic, pro-Habsburg, and "western" in culture; they had little sympathy even with the Serbs of Hungary, also too "western" for the taste of Belgrade. The Great Serb programme was adopted by the Serbs only on Habsburg insistence; the South Slav programme was never more than an auxiliary weapon.

Maintenance of the Ottoman Empire in Europe had been the essential element in Habsburg foreign policy from Metternich to Aehrenthal. In 1912 for the last time, Austria-Hungary tried to impose peace on the Balkans by a coalition of the Great Powers; this move was supported by Russia, alarmed at the approach of the Balkan avalanche, which she had herself helped to prepare. Metternich's conservative alliance made a final appearance, ghostly and ineffective. The Balkan states knew that Russia would not use force against them and were confident that they could defeat Turkey without Russian assistance. In October, 1912, the Ottoman Empire in Europe, last fragile prop of the old order, was broken in pieces; and the Habsburg Monarchy stood helplessly by, although its own fall was also being prepared. Berchtold, who had become Foreign Minister on the death of Aehrenthal, saved only the fragment of Albania from the wreck of a century-old policy. Albania, denied to Serbia, was evidence that Austria-Hungary could still exert her will as a Great Power. Yet it was degrading that the sham independence of Albanian brigand chiefs should be treated as essential to the existence of a great Monarchy. Even the creation of Albania was achieved only by repeated mobilisations, expensive demonstrations which lost force with every repetition. And, despite Albania, the Turks had vanished. The national principle had triumphed on every frontier of the Habsburg Monarchy, and the prophecy of Gentz, of Albert Sorel, and of Andrássy, proved true: Austria-Hungary now became the sick man of Europe.

The Balkan Wars marked the virtual end of the Habsburg Monarchy as a Great Power. The Balkans had been Austria-Hungary's "sphere of influence"; yet, in the crisis, her influence achieved nothing—even Albania was saved only with Italian assistance. Berchtold tried to hold Serbia in check by encouraging Bulgaria against her; this, too, was a failure, with Bulgaria defeated in a few days. Even had it been more successful, the Bulgarian alliance was evidence of Habsburg weakness: it placed Austria-Hungary on the level of a Balkan state. In armaments, as in policy, Austria-Hungary had fallen out of the ranks of the Great Powers. Fifty years before, in the days of Schwarzenberg and Radetzky, old Austria had carried an armaments bill of the same size as France or Russia; in 1914, though ranking only after Russia and Germany in population, Austria-Hungary spent less on armaments than any Great Power—a quarter of Russian or German expenditure, a third of British or French, and less even than Italian. The "military monarchy" of the Habsburgs was, in fact, the least militarised state in Europe. It possessed military tastes and industrial resources; it lacked the national unity and enthusiasm for a great patriotic effort.

The Habsburg Monarchy was kept in being by German support; even this support had its dangers. Germany, a dynamic Great Power, could not be content with the Habsburg policy of resistance, particularly when this proved unsuccessful. The Germans saw dimly the vision of a new Europe, with Berlin as its centre; in this Europe Vienna had no great place. The Austro-German alliance had been a partnership to preserve the old Europe, and in essence an exclusive partnership of Germany with the Habsburg dynasty and the "Hungarian nation." Once the Germans abandoned Bismarck's conservative line, this exclusive partnership was inadequate for them. After all, the Balkan Wars, though a disaster for the Habsburg Monarchy, were not necessarily a disaster for Germany: they were a triumph for the national states, and therefore an incentive to Germany, the greatest of national states. After the Balkan Wars, the Germans urged a conciliatory policy towards Serbia and Roumania, even if this involved an amputation of Hungary. Such a policy, carried to its logical conclusion, would have strengthened Germany: Hungary would have been reduced to its true national size, and the rest of the Habsburg Monarchy incorporated in the German Reich. The Germans followed this line consciously in their second bid for the domination of Europe; before 1914, they were still restrained by dynastic scruples and even by twinges of Bismarck's caution. In this sense, the Habsburg dynasty represented a genuine barrier against German domination—though only so long as it assisted German expansion by peaceful means. . . .

The declaration of war against Serbia was intended to reassert the position of Austria-Hungary as an independent Great Power; instead, it ended both greatness and independence. The strength of the Habsburgs lay in suppleness and manœuvre: faced with danger, from the Ottoman Turks to Napoleon, they could "give." What they could not risk was a life-and-death struggle, with no prospect of a compromise at the end; for, in this struggle, the less sophisticated combatant would survive. In 1859 the Habsburgs had set out to "destroy" Italian nationalism; in 1914 they set out to "destroy" Serbia—both impossibilities, even if the Habsburg armies had been victorious, still more so when in 1914, as in 1859, the appeal to force was a failure. The Austro-Hungarian army, invading Serbia, was driven out, and instead the Serbs invaded Hungary; for the Serbs, unlike the Italians of 1859, were a real people with a real fighting force. The greater part of the Austrian army was sent to meet the Russian attack; it also failed. The Russians overran most of Galicia and reached the passes of the Carpathians, only deterred from penetrating into Hungary by the great German victory further north at Tannenberg. By every analogy of Habsburg history, this would have been the moment to make peace: there would have been some concessions to Russia, perhaps even to Serbia, but the Habsburg Monarchy would have remained in existence.

Instead Austria-Hungary was "saved" by Germany; this "saving" marked the real end of the Habsburgs. They had offered a tolerable alternative to German rule; the alternative ceased to exist when the Germans took over the military and political direction of Austria-Hungary. Early in 1915 German troops and German generals drove the Russians out of Galicia; late in 1915 German generals directed the campaign which destroyed independent Serbia and carried the Central Powers to the gates of Salonica. Germany was now committed to a bid for the mastery of Europe; and the Habsburgs were no more than German auxiliaries.

3. EDWARD CRANKSHAW: The Fall of the House of Habsburg*

Edward Crankshaw, long the Russian correspondent for the *London Observer,* has written widely on contemporary European affairs; this is his first major historical work. He writes from the standpoint of the dynasty, which is the focus of his book. He may be too attached to his subject, but by conveying the viewpoint of the rulers of Austria he adds an important element to the evaluation of the state of the monarchy by 1914. His opinion is clear: that dissolution was not inevitable and that it came about only because of a long, burdensome war and the diplomatic maneuvers of Austria's enemies.

It is commonly believed that the Monarchy found itself in a state of suspended dissolution from the very outbreak of the war and that the end from that moment was inevitable. In the light of what happened it is impossible to sustain this view. The worst has been presented in previous chapters. If the worst had been the whole truth the Empire could not have held together for a month under the impact of the violence now let loose upon it. In fact it held together for four years, surviving by nearly two years the death of Franz Josef and the end of the mystique attached uniquely to his person.

To begin with, the obvious contradictions were scarcely felt at all. Even in the most disaffected provinces there was no attempt at revolt. The army was at first wholly loyal, and the greater part of it was to remain loyal, in the teeth of fearful punishment, for the next four years, justifying all the claims that had been made for its supranational quality. Even the Czechs, who were later to go over in large numbers to the Russians, were for a long time staunch. The famous demonstration of two Prague regiments in 1915 was not a signal for revolt. They marched off to the front with banners saying: "We march against Russia, but we don't know why!" The military authorities and the Vienna

* From Edward Crankshaw, *The Fall of the House of Habsburg* (London: Longmans, Green & Co. Ltd., 1963), pp. 411–19.

government regarded this as an anti-Habsburg demonstration, and treated it accordingly. But the civilian Governor of Bohemia, Count Thun, saw deeper. He insisted that this was no political demonstration but, rather, a failure of discipline within the army, for which the officers, not the troops, must be blamed. It was, in fact, an early manifestation of war-weariness, that same war-weariness that was soon to be made articulate by the English poet, Siegfried Sassoon, and, much later, celebrated in innumerable books about the war. It was to produce the French army mutiny in 1917, to trigger off the Russian Revolution, and, in the end, to infect the armies of the Central Powers, so that—but only at the end—they got out of control. It arose in the field from the bombardment of too many ordinary human beings dressed in uniform by too much metal and high explosive as they struggled for too long in too much mud; it arose at home from hunger and privation. It was a revolt against the politicians who had started the war without knowing what they were doing and to no obvious end, and against the generals for not knowing how to win it quickly. Even so, until 1918 the only serious defections were among the Czechs; and the Czechs defected because they felt they had somewhere to go, being closer to their Slav brothers of Muscovy than to the Germans, who, as the war went on, gained more and more the upper hand.

Masaryk, the university professor of genius, once he had decided that the Monarchy must be broken, had a hard row to hoe; but, unlike the extremists, represented by Kramář and Klofáč, who had clamoured for the destruction of the Habsburgs while Masaryk still saw them as a shield, once he had made his decision he knew what to do. He had to get America on his side.

Already in the spring of 1915 the Croat, Trumbić, had been able to set up a Yugoslav Council in London, dedicated to the liberation of the Southern Slavs of the Empire and their unification with those outside it. The sculptor Mestrović, from Dalmatia, was one of his right-hand men. But in fact he did not get far: his fellow-countrymen in the Imperial and Royal Army were, as good Catholics, not at all interested in uniting with the Orthodox Serbs: indeed, they were using the Habsburg war as a heaven-sent opportunity for punishing the "barbarians" in Belgrade: Stepan Tisza in Budapest gave them their heads. Masaryk went more slowly; but, in the end, it was he, the father of Czechoslovakia, who was also the real creator of the Yugoslav State, mobilizing the whole weight of Slav *émigré* opinion, above all in America, and gaining the ear of President Wilson.

It was not until May 1916 that the Czech National Council was set up in Paris, and even then Masaryk received little support from Prague and Bratislava. Apart from Kramář and his friends (who were sentenced to death in June 1916, but never executed), the Czechs went very carefully while the war hung in the balance. Until 1917 every anti-Habsburg gesture was regularly condemned by the local Czech authorities and countered by formal declarations of solidarity with the Monarchy and loyalty to the throne. The conduct of the military gave every cause for resentment, but what finally swung the Czechs was, at home, fear of Budapest, and, abroad, the gradual emergence of Allied war aims, which involved the dismemberment of the Monarchy. As Vienna fell increasingly under the dominion of Berlin, so Czech disaffection grew: the Czechs knew very well that Berlin would be a tougher nut to crack than Vienna had ever been. And in this connection it is sometimes forgotten that the Germans of the Sudetenland, whose incorporation into Hitler's Germany of 1938 was to be the occasion of Munich, had never been citizens of the Reich: until 1918 they had been subjects of the Habsburgs.

The attitude of the Entente was for a long time ambiguous. Certainly in 1914 there was no thought at all in Paris, London or Petersburg of the destruction of the Habsburg Monarchy. As we have seen, as late as the early spring of 1917 the French, through Prince Sixtus, were assuring the new Emperor Karl that they had no desire for any such consummation. But already by then there were new influences at work. Taking advantage of the peace feelers of the Central Powers put out in the autumn of 1916, President Wilson had invited all the belligerents to make formal statements of their war aims. The reply of the Entente was delivered in Washington on 10 January 1917, at the very time when Poincaré and Briand were engaged in their tortuous discussions with Vienna. The reply started, as was to be expected, with demands for the restoration of Montenegro, Serbia and Belgium and the evacuation of all those parts of France, Russia and Rumania occupied by the Central Powers. It then, however, proceeded, almost as an afterthought, to develop a new and fateful theme by insisting on "the liberation of Italians, of Slavs, of Rumanians and Czecho-Slovaks from foreign domination." This, if it meant anything at all, meant the dismemberment of the Empire, which would have been left with the Austrian hereditary lands, less parts of Styria and Carinthia, and the rump of Hungary. It made nonsense in advance of the French avowals to the Emperor Karl. It meant the end of the dynasty.

But it seems that these far-reaching demands were not very seriously intended at the time, or even understood by the men who put them forward. The Entente, having rejected the peace offer of the Central Powers, were now concerned with impressing the democratic Americans with the purity of their cause. With this in mind they sought to emphasize their interest in the sacred concept of self-determination, without properly understanding what lay behind that all too facile phrase: certainly the British Prime Minister of the day, David Lloyd George, whose defeat of Mr Asquith at the end of 1916 reflected the new spirit calling for total victory and unconditional surrender, knew nothing of most of the minority races of the Empire. No less certainly the Russian Tsar had no intention of applying the principle of self-determination to his own subject-peoples. The use of the term Czecho-Slovaks in that document is interesting in itself: Czechs and Slovaks were not natural collaborators, and the concept of a new State of Czechoslovakia was Masaryk's own.

The important thing however was that this set of war aims, compiled in a hurry and for an *ad hoc* purpose, from now on began to assume a life of its own. The political exiles from the Habsburg lands, who had lately been thrown into despair by the fear that the fighting might be brought to an end before the old order had been irretrievably shattered, were strengthened; and the idea of self-determination, as well as sentiments of an anti-dynastic kind, increasingly coloured the thinking of the Entente.

The more so when, in March 1917, the Russian Monarchy was overthrown. So long as the Entente included among them an absolutist autocracy, the Russia of Nicholas II, it was difficult for Lloyd George and Briand, though not impossible (such is the stuff that politicians are made of), to pretend that they were fighting a war for democracy against autocracy. But with the disappearance of Nicholas from the scene, all that was changed. The British and the French did not at first perceive their great good fortune: they were perturbed by the vacuum in the East and the prospect of the collapse of Russia as a fighting Power. But the Americans were farther away and not fighting for their lives: they saw it at once. On 20 March the American Secretary of State, Robert Lansing, was able to inform the Cabinet in Washington that the Russian Revolution "had removed the one objection to affirming that the European war was a war between Democracy and Absolutism." America could now join in with a clear conscience. And this, three weeks later, she did, her passage being greatly eased by Germany's announcement of her new policy of unrestricted submarine warfare.

Germany, now dragging Austria in her train, had made one gratuitous blunder in the overbearing tone of her peace overtures in the autumn of 1916; she made a second with the launching of her submarine campaign; she made a third by failing to perceive that the Russian Revolution, allowed to proceed unchecked, must strike a death-blow to the principle of legitimacy which was the main prop of the Hohenzollerns, no less than of the Habsburgs. Instead of recognizing the nature of the avalanche that had been started she proceeded to aggravate it by introducing Lenin, like a bacillus, into Petersburg—all in the short-term interests of a quick victory on the Eastern front (but a victory for what?) and the conquest of the granary of the Ukraine. The war continued. When Lenin and his Bolsheviks seized power in November 1917 his immediate appeal for an end to the fighting went unregarded. At the same time, and for very different reasons, Lord Lansdowne, whom nobody could accuse of being less than patriotic, was launching his own appeal in London for a compromise peace on rational lines. The Third Battle of Ypres had been in progress during all the late summer and autumn. The French army had mutinied. In the atrocious mud of Passchendaele 400,000 men had fallen, without, apparently, achieving anything. Russia, under Lenin, was about to get out of the war. It seemed a sensible moment to talk peace; but things had gone too far: the Germans were already planning their great offensive for the spring of 1918; the Entente, disembarrassed of Russia and reinforced by the great transatlantic democracy, were engaged in a struggle to the finish with the forces of evil. Only the Habsburg Monarchy was interested in peace without outright victory.

Austria was now hungry. She was dominated by Germany and blackmailed by Budapest. From the very beginning Stepan Tisza had made his own arrangements for the war, which involved sacrificing Cisleithnia for the greater glory of St Stephen. He had fought intelligently and stubbornly to keep the destinies of his own minorities in the hands of Budapest. Above all he had contrived to keep Croatia out of the hands of the military government. The lands of St Stephen were to be held intact, come what might, let the Monarchy be shattered and the King of Hungary thrown to the wolves. In so doing he assisted the doom of his own country as well as of the Empire as a whole. Now he was virtual master of the Empire, using the immense reserves of Hungarian grain to put pressure on a Vienna which had nowhere to turn. Germany could have fed Vienna from the newly acquired resources of the Ukraine, and, indeed, had promised to do so. But Germany was selfish too. The Peace of Brest-Litovsk, known as the "Bread Peace," brought no relief. Germany ate the bread. This was Germany's fourth great blunder. For the time was close when, with the launching of Ludendorff's great March offensive, Germany would badly need a restored, unified and revitalized Austria-Hungary at her side. Instead, the Monarchy was riven by strikes and threats of revolution. The immediate danger now was less the defection of the nationalities—though the Czechs had gone over in large numbers to the Russians, and the Budapest politicians, with the splendid and courageous exception of Count Karolyi, were now actively working against Vienna—than a working-class revolt, stimulated by the Russian Revolution.

The remarkable thing was that the Habsburgs had held on for so long and that their army had proved so loyal. The deeds of that great army remain unsung. For four years it fought, always with amazing tenacity, sometimes with great skill, first against the Russians and the Serbs, then, as well, against the Italians and the Rumanians, on a front that ran from the Adriatic to Central Poland, and then along the terrible Alpine barrier. From the beginning Conrad's dream of a swift conquest of Serbia had had to be abandoned—and with it the only meaning of the war. Instead of crushing the Serbs according to plan with a massive deployment, he had to move against the Russians advancing into Galicia. He relied on swift German assistance; but the Germans were otherwise engaged. They also were fighting an action the failure of which deprived the war of its whole meaning for them too. To sweep France from the board before turning to smash Russia they threw their weight into the execution of the Schlieffen Plan, the great turning movement, via Belgium, which was to envelop Paris. But the young Moltke lacked both the genius and the nerve of his uncle: he wrecked the plan and finished up in front of Paris on the Marne—so that the Germans were indeed faced with their familiar spectre of a war on two fronts—the endless war of attrition on the Western Front, and the war of immense slogging battles, finally turning also into one of attrition, on the Eastern Front. Further, by invading Belgium, they had brought England into the war against them: Aehrenthal's dying prophecy had come true.

It was not until 1915 that Germany could go to the help of the Austrians. Meanwhile vast numbers of the Habsburg army had been engaged in a losing campaign against superior Russian forces, which, with climax on climax, lasted without interruption for four months on end. Two million men were locked together in those battles, of which nobody has ever heard. On both sides there were tremendous strategic deployments and dramatic advances, stormings and retreats. By the time the Italians came in, the Imperial and Royal army had already fought the greatest, bloodiest and most exhausting battles in the history of the dynasty, and the war was only beginning. It managed, nevertheless, to keep the fighting on Italian soil.

We have heard a great deal about the mud of Flanders and the torturing heat of Gallipoli; but we have heard little or nothing about the mud of the great Polish plain and the Serbian river valleys; the bitter and terrible fighting in the Carpathians, the Bosnian hills, the Karst of Istria—where the totally barren limestone rock, splintering under shellfire, magnified a thousand times the effect of every burst; in the high Dolomites, where Austrians and Italians in sub-zero temperatures and eternal snow tunnelled and counter-tunnelled through ice and living rock to emerge facing each other at point-blank range thousands of feet above the valley floor: the relics of that mountain war still, half a century later, clutter the sheer precipices of Monte Marmolata, so that it is possible to be freshly amazed and incredulous that ordinary men, Italians and Austrians alike, managed to exist at all, let alone fight, in such conditions—and to marvel at historians and military critics who generalize comfortably about the poor fighting qualities of both armies.

As for the great Galician deployments: who remembers the battles of the San, of Lutsk, of Lemberg? Some of the great moments of human courage and endurance have fallen into oblivion for no other reason than that both the winners and the losers were in the end defeated. It was not for Lenin to glorify the epic of the San. As for the Austrians, they lost the war and their Empire: it was not for the victors to celebrate the four battles of the Karst, the storming of Belgrade, the twelve battles of the Isonzo. In the end the whole terrible story was reduced to the horizon of "the good soldier Schweik." That, perhaps, could have been endured if only the good soldier Schweik had been determined to defend his birthright, instead of surrendering it to the first plausible rabble-rouser.

In Cisleithnia it was not until the beginning of 1918 that affairs got quite out of hand. Parliament had been recalled at last in May 1917; but it was too late. While academic politicians who had helped to drive Berchtold to the brink in 1914 now wrestled with liberal solutions, the nationalities, at last, backed by Allied promises, now entered the game in earnest. There were demands in the new Parliament for a federation of free and equal demands in the new Parliament for a federation of free and equal national States, for a union of all the Slavs under the Habsburgs, for sovereign constitutional national assemblies for every individual people. Budapest watched aloofly. This state of affairs did not prevent the army from breaking the Italian front in October 1917 in the Twelfth Battle of the Isonzo, better known as Caporetto. But the check after Caporetto, when Italy's allies stopped the gap, was too much. And then, on 8 January 1918, came the Fourteen Points of President Wilson. Lloyd George could still declare that "the dissolution of the Monarchy is not one of our war aims"; but the Fourteen Points spoke differently: autonomy for all the peoples of Austro-Hungary, the rectification of the frontier with Italy "on clearly recognizable national lines," the creation of an independent Poland with access to the sea. . . . "Our programme is justice for all peoples and nationalities, be they strong or weak. . . ."

Kramář, amnestied, proclaimed the foundation of the State of Czechoslovakia. The Poles went over to active opposition. The Czech legion in Russia, which had fought for the Tsar but held aloof from the Bolsheviks, made it their business to obstruct the return of Austrian and Hungarian prisoners of war to the Habsburg army. In June 1918 the Czech National Council in Paris was formally recognized as the provisional government of a Czechoslovak State. The South Slav rebels, still a minority of the Croats and Slovenes of the Monarchy, proclaimed in Lubliana a new nationalist organization conceived as "part of the general South Slav National Council in Zagreb, which will shortly assemble to prepare for the assumption of all rights of State sovereignty."

On the Western Front the great March offensive had shot its bolt. On the new Eastern Front Franchet d'Esperey, based on Salonika, had broken the Bulgarians, who asked for an armistice. In Vienna harassed intellectuals clutched at straws in a starving, mutinous city incapable of facing another winter of war. At what they took to be the eleventh hour they persuaded the Monarchy to offer to transform itself into a federation of democratic States; but they had misread the time. It was long past the hour. The Hungarians, clinging to their dreams with characteristic single-mindedness, regarded these manoeuvres with contempt. As the army prepared itself for a last stand against the threat from Italy, and while the Allies mopped up the Germans in the West, Budapest demanded the immediate return of all Hungarian units: they were needed at home by Tisza to preserve the integrity of St Stephen and the estates of the great magnates.

This was the end. While Karl still wrestled with the politicians in Vienna, seeking through expedient after desperate expedient to hold the Habsburg inheritance together, somehow, anyhow, round the unifying symbol of the Crown, the army at last began to break and the break became a rout. On 24 October the Allies mounted a great offensive against what was left of the army in Italy. It was a superfluous operation. The Monarchy existed no longer. There was only a monarch. The troops who tried to stem the attack belonged now to half a dozen countries, some of them already bound to the Entente. But the troops did not know this: they thought they were still Austrians, and they tried to fight back. There was nobody to tell them when to stop. In the end they simply broke away, not knowing where to go, or indeed where they belonged. Karl waited a little at Schönbrunn, while the German liberals and socialists wrangled endlessly about the exact shape their new State was to take. It turned out to be a socialist republic. On 11 November 1918, poor Karl, who was a peace Emperor or nothing, at last got the peace for which he had striven so long; but he was no longer Emperor. His formal abdication (from what?) he proclaimed in a note which he signed with a pencil; quite soon, after some absurd adventures, he died in Madeira. The peoples had taken over; but they were not ready. The stage was set for the dictators.

4. ARTHUR J. MAY: The Hapsburg Monarchy, 1867–1914*

Professor Arthur J. May, of the University of Rochester, has written two major studies of Austria in the late nineteenth century. Here, he presents a statement of the continuing strengths of the monarchy that differs from Crankshaw's without necessarily contradicting it. For May, one does not need to rely merely on the pragmatic test of Austria's performance in the first years of the war; there were clear bonds within the Empire in the prewar economy and political structure. May also re-evaluates the strength of nationalist opposition to confirm his picture of a monarchy that was by no means healthy, but that was some distance from a deathbed as well.

From the birth of the dualistic compromise until the resounding downfall of the ramified Hapsburg structure in 1918, the impending dissolution of the realm was freely and frequently predicted in responsible quarters and others. Naturally the intensity of the belief that the Monarchy was doomed to destruction varied, but from 1895 on, as the feud between German and Czech waxed hotter, as the struggle between the crown and the Magyars attained dangerous dimensions—developments that stimulated nationalistic agitation among other groups in the realm—and as the Hapsburg quarrel with Serbia was only superficially adjusted, the conviction deepened that the Monarchy had taken a bed alongside Turkey in the hospital of the dying. Diplomatic reports that emanated from Vienna just before 1914 were peppered with prognostications of the imminent disruption of the Monarchy and with speculations on the political and strategic changes that would follow.

In an epoch of emergent and jealous nationalisms it seemed hard to believe that the multinationality Hapsburg realm could much longer endure. Yet, as has earlier been explained, the potency of the nationalisms within the Monarchy in so far as they had separatist, secessionist implications may easily be exaggerated. Among wide masses of the rural minority populations, national consciousness was only feebly awakened, and even among those elements of the citizenry in which nationalism was mature, among the intelligentsia and other sections of the bourgeoisie, advocacy of independence and the disruption of the venerable Monarchy was exceptional rather than representative.

It must be said, and said again, that nowhere in continental Europe, except in Switzerland, were the peculiar interests of national minorities given more protection and consideration, unsatisfactory though they were, than in the Austrian half of the Dual Monarchy. It was possible for a Rumanian to write with perfect candor that Austria had "organized and civilized, rather than

* From Arthur J. May, *The Hapsburg Monarchy, 1867–1914* (Cambridge: Harvard University Press, 1951), pp. 476–77; 484–92.

Germanized, her peoples." And nowhere as much as in the Austrian empire were the tangled problems of national minorities subjected to more thorough or competent analysis; literally scores of studies on the subject, learned and polemical, were published. It was, however, another story in Hungary where, in striking contrast, the settled policy of Magyarizing minorities was sedulously, and to a remarkable extent successfully, pursued.

Plans were not wanting for the abandonment of the dualistic regime, considered by a host of thoughtful observers as the largest source of political evil in the Hapsburg state, and for the constitutional reordering of the dominions. Indeed, attached to the office of the Austrian prime minister was a special department for the revision of the constitution, presided over by a Professor von Hold, which reviewed various proposals for the transformation of the monarchy and prepared patterns of its own.

Public men, scholars, and publicists at home and abroad concerned themselves in the main with two broad types of program for reconstruction. One called for the organization of a third unit of the realm containing the Yugoslav subjects of the Hapsburgs; the other, more far-reaching, the conversion of the Monarchy into a "monarchical Switzerland," in which each nationality would have considerable control over local affairs but the economic solidarity of the realm would be preserved and the federalized state would present a united front in its dealing with foreign powers. . . .

Whether without the intervention of World War I the Hapsburg Monarchy would have endured much longer must always remain, as it has already been, a subject of lively academic speculation. The Hapsburg institution, like others, carried within it the seeds of its own destruction. Nonetheless, four terribly wasting years of war, crowned by catastrophic military defeat and accompanied by cruel human suffering and militant separatist propaganda, were required to bring about the actual dissolution of the realm. That record in itself proves that the seemingly "unworkable anachronism" of the Hapsburgs possessed elements of toughness and vitality which the clashing national disharmonies tended to conceal or smother. What indeed were the sources of strength of the venerable Hapsburg state, what the forces that combined to hold the congeries of Irelands which was Austria-Hungary together?

Palacký's oft-quoted utterance that if Austria had not existed it would have been necessary to create her applied with peculiar force in the economic sphere. In greater or lesser degree, all Hapsburg citizens benefited from living in the largest free-trade area in Europe outside of Russia, and tariff protection shielded manufacturers from the superior industrial establishments of Germany and Britain and guarded agricultural producers from transatlantic, Russian, and Balkan competition. The maintenance of economic unity under dualism was possible because when the customs union was from time to time prolonged Austria almost invariably made concessions to Hungary—concessions which tended to work to the injury of Austrian manufactures and were of advantage to Hungarian agriculture and industry. At the renewal in 1907, the customs union was for the first time defined as a treaty, an arrangement which underscored the fact that the economic partnership was wearing thin and suggested that when the treaty expired in 1917 the Magyars might be content with nothing short of full economic independence. Roseate Hungarian plans for industrial progress looked, in fact, to the time when the kingdom would be essentially self-sufficient in manufactured goods.

Across the generations of political unity the economy of the Hapsburg peoples and provinces had become integrated, though huge disparities existed between west and east in material development and standards of comfort. A kind of rudimentary division of labor had evolved, with the productions of one region complementing those of another. Greater specialization was handicapped by traditional differences in customs and costumes, in the methods of farming, by the hindrance which linguistic differences imposed, and by the low purchasing ability of the mass of the population. But with the passing of time a delicate economic balance had emerged, production and consumption within the borders of the Monarchy were fairly matched, and, except for rubber, cotton, nickel, copper, and wool, the Hapsburg dominions were virtually self-sustaining.

Surpluses of wheat and corn and livestock raised on the plains of Hungary and Galicia were advantageously marketed in the industrialized areas of Austria. And Italian winegrowers had more profitable outlets than would have been theirs if they had been citizens of the kingdom of Italy. The timber of the Alpine provinces and of the northern reaches of Hungary, the coal of Bohemia and Moravia, the iron ore and magnesite of Styria, the oil of Galicia—these resources met the requirements of other sections of the sprawling realm remarkably well. Moreover, large-scale industries in Bohemia, in the Vienna area, in Styria, in parts of Hungary, all of which expanded phenomenally in the decade before 1914, went far to satisfy the rising though still relatively limited demands for finished textiles and other manufactures; and Vienna was the financial and commercial heart of the realm, with arteries running off in every direction.

True, competitive nationalism generated friction in the economic sphere in the form of local boycotts and the like. Yet the material advantages of the Hapsburg union were pretty generally recognized, save in extreme secessionist circles. Representative Czech, Magyar, Slovak, and Slovene spokesmen acknowledged that their nationalities were too small to form viable independent states in an age of mass production demanding broad markets.

Integration of trade and exchange was matched and promoted by the transportation facilities of the Dual Monarchy. The great Danube and her tributaries tied the realm together except for the provinces of Galicia, the Bucovina, Dalmatia, and Vorarlberg. The Danube was the natural highway for internal commerce, though as a means of world trade the river had two major drawbacks: the haul to the principal markets of western Europe was circuitous and long; and traders had always to reckon with possible political complications at the lower end of the river and in the Turkish-ruled zone of the Straits.

Railways that discharged their burdens at Trieste or Fiume afforded better communication to the west than the Danube, and trackage into the Balkans facilitated business to the southeast. After 1890, the international trade of the Monarchy actually advanced more rapidly than exchange between Austria and Hungary. Internal commerce profited enormously from the network of railways; as a rule, lines followed historic trade routes linking the different sections of the Monarchy in economic interdependence to a degree that had not been true when the Danube and roads had been the sole ways of travel. Uniformity of gauge prevailed on the principal railways, though there was no uniformity in rates, since both Austria and Hungary—the latter more energetically than her partner—manipulated charges so as to foster their respective economies rather than to promote the common welfare of the realm.

So long as the Monarchy remained intact, it would confer material blessings on all national groupings; in union there was economic strength. Dissolution, likely enough, would bring lowered standards of comfort, already exceedingly low in the more backward and unprogressive sections. Logic of this order (or something like this) proved a potent force in holding the supranational state together.

The heritage of political traditions and of a common dynasty was another substantial unifying bond in the Dual Monarchy. For many generations the Hapsburg family had been the connecting link between the motley complex of peoples and provinces of the realm. Conservatism, the force of inertia, the dead hand of the past were themselves subtle bonds of solidarity.

Through the churches, particularly the Roman Catholic, through the fighting services, and partly through the press and schools loyalty to the ruling house was inculcated. Roman Catholic clergymen, conservative for the most part, were notably *Hapsburgtreue,* allied with the dynasty for mutual self-perpetuation, and their sway over parishioners, carried all the weight of centuries of hallowed acceptance. Some divines, to be sure, enlisted in national movements with centrifugal tendencies, but they were distinctly in a minority, and seldom were national patriots found in the higher, more influential offices of the Church. Of the value of Catholicism as an agency in holding the disparate peoples together, Hapsburg statesmen were fully aware; and in different ways and words many a leader gave voice to the conviction ascribed to Bach in the fifties: "The only sound internal policy for Austria is one which is favorable to Catholicism. The Monarchy has really only two sound bases for its unity: the dynasty and religion."

It was the considered judgment of the distinguished British Catholic historian, Lord Acton, that the Dual Monarchy was the perfect exemplar of Christian polity because it bound together a large number of distinctive nationalities by common attachment to Church and Crown.

In the rural districts especially, the sentiment of dynastic patriotism was strong and real, and the circumstance that Francis Joseph had reigned so long and refused to die tightened that sentimental and moral bond. No other monarch of Europe in all probability was so popular nor so beloved by his subjects as the old Hapsburger, who posed as mediator, as it were, between the jarring sections and nationalities, the guardian of monarchical unity. It was often prophesied that his departure would remove one of the stoutest pillars of the state, unless his successor possessed personal qualities and a political outlook that were almost universally appealing.

A consideration of a negative sort that contributed to the perdurance of the Dual Monarchy was the inability or unwillingness of the politicians of the lesser nationalities to join forces for simultaneous or sustained action against the *status quo*. Austrian Slavs, despite the untiring efforts of men like Masaryk, were more generally at odds with one another than coöperative for common ends; seldom did Poles in particular see eye to eye with Czechs and Yugoslavs. And rarely was coöperation among the chiefs of the Hungarian minorities anything more than sporadic or halfhearted; and, of course, Magyar policies were emphatically calculated to prevent the formation of a united front.

Moreover, the government at Vienna had traditionally fostered ill will between the various nationalities on the assumption that if they fought with one another they could the more readily be governed. Shrewd observations of Emperor Francis I to the French ambassador at his court possessed a certain enduring validity. "My peoples," he said, "are strangers to one another; so much the better. They do not take the same diseases at the same time. In France, when the fever comes, it seizes you all on the same day. I place Hungarians in Italy, Italians in Hungary, each guards his neighbor. They do not understand each other and they detest each other. From antipathies is born order and from their reciprocal hates general peace." Count Taaffe, we are told, boasted that as prime minister he contrived to govern Austria "by keeping all the nationalities in a state of uniform, nicely tempered discontent."

And yet it is defiance of fact to accept without reservation the assertion sometimes met with that in the dualistic era the ruling class elevated the principle of "divide and rule" into a deliberate and consistent doctrine of public policy. In many parts of the dominions it was unnecessary indeed for the Hapsburg to stir up national discontents, for local political and social differences, fostered by intensifying nationalisms, taught Croats and Slovenes to hate Italians, Poles to despise Ruthenians and vice versa, the Magyars to look down upon all Hungarian minorities, Czechs and Germans to engage in mutual recriminations, and so forth. National prejudices and jealousies required no subtle stimulation from on high and got relatively little in the age of dualism. The aphorism that "the Hapsburgs ruled their dominions by a judicious distribution of discontent," like many another clever epigram, carries more journalistic color than historical validity.

Historically, the Hapsburg official world, the bureaucracy, both civilian and military, had been a unifying and consolidating institution of considerable significance, and that continued to be true in large measure to the very end of the life of the Dual Monarchy. Bureaucratic conventions reaching back to the eighteenth century and reinforced in the age of Metternich lingered on without radical modification, though, in consequence of the rapid expansion of the bureaucracy in the dualistic period, *esprit* appears to have deteriorated; new recruits failed to measure up to traditional standards of diligence and service. Civil servants were greatly increased as social-welfare legislation was extended and government took over the management of railways and other services. It was frequently charged, in Hungary especially but in Austria as well, that there were altogether too many officials for the work that had to be done.

Public servants were modestly compensated, assured of pensions in the eventide of life, and enjoyed a certain social prestige. Many of the lower positions were filled by former noncommissioned officers in the army while the more responsible offices were reserved for technically trained experts or the socially accomplished. The various grades of the bureaucracy formed almost exclusive castes and it was not easy to attain a higher rank, unless one were the favorite of an official well up in the hierarchy. Though the real makers of policy were drawn heavily from the German and Magyar nationalities, the central administration was a supranational body, with a growing representation of Slavs after, say, 1880. Mutual "racial" antagonisms in Austria made it impolitic to transfer local officials from one area to another. Rigorous, almost military, discipline prevailed in the bureaus, with their heads exercising tyrannical authority over their subordinates. Ministries rose and ministries fell but the bureaucracy plodded on with dogged persistency. . . .

Loyalty to the Monarchy and the established order were surely traits of the Hapsburg bureaucracy. Among lesser officials in Austria, evidence of separatist feeling was not unknown, but it was never pronounced, while in Hungary civil servants were uniformly Magyar or Magyarone. Men drawn into the joint ministries seldom showed national sentiments. Officials in the foreign office were exceptionally harmonious; one who served there for fourteen years knew of only a single dispute caused by differences in nationality.

As a rule, the higher Hapsburg officials were recruited from families in which service to the dynasty was a settled tradition. For them devotion to monarchical interests transcended all considerations of nationality. Officers in the fighting services, too, displayed that sense of loyalty which was characteristic of their profession the world around. Aristocratic and well-to-do elements of the Monarchy, more so perhaps in Austria than in Hungary, were, speaking generally, *Hapsburgtreue,* if for no other reason because they feared that radical political change would be accompanied by social upheaval. These classes constituted a mighty pillar of the *status quo*.

And dread of the consequences of disintegration effectively operated to keep Hungary and Austria from flying apart. "Nothing holds Austria and Hungary together," wrote the American minister to Vienna in 1895, "but the fear of the result of separation and the great personal influence of Francis Joseph. Separation means disintegration; it means the creation of two or more smaller states, the loss of prestige which the nation has held so long in the affairs of Europe: its erasure from the list of the Great Powers and the degradation of each to the place occupied by the smaller and dependent nations. It means more, it means subjection to the great nations which make and unmake the map of Europe as well as shape the policy of other continents. Hungary would at once become the prey of the Slavs by which she is surrounded, while Austria would become bound to Germany."

Common international interests and mutual concern for the security and integrity of their respective states helped to keep the dominant Austro-Germans and the Magyars together; for defense, as in trade, they realized their interdependence. Overriding the endless bickerings and dissensions between these two groups was the conviction that unless they presented a common front in foreign affairs both would go down in common ruin. Only the more extreme and turbulent of the Magyar chauvinists ignored this truth.

Austro-German, Magyar, and Pole distrusted the ambitions and power of Russia, real or fancied, and feared the spread of corrosive Pan-Slav propaganda and the vaunted aspirations of the Great Serb propaganda. Mistrust and hatred of Italy were almost universal in the Monarchy; even dissidents among the Yugoslavs cherished that emotion. By reason of their apprehensions, Austro-German and Magyar at least looked upon the alliance with Germany as their shield and buckler; and the influence of Germany upon the Monarchy was in itself a not inconsiderable unifying force.

The fighting services, finally, raised on the principle of manhood liability, infused vitality into the monarchical regime. However deficient the army may have been in capacity for war as compared with the great German or French military machines, it was at once a visible symbol of the unity of the Monarchy, and an earnest of the intention to perpetuate the state. Until the very smash-up of the realm the paean of Grillparzer to the Hapsburg army, "In deinem Lager ist Osterreich [Austria is in your camp]," rang true. Francis Joseph, it has already been emphasized, would brook no compromise on any proposal that threatened to impair the solidarity of the armed forces; he never forgot that the sword had saved the dynasty in 1848 and he consistently balked Magyar pressures for an independent Hungarian army. . . .

Owing to the polyglot composition of the army it is not surprising that there was lively skepticism, both within the Monarchy and outside, as to the fighting and staying qualities of the forces in the event of war. To cite but a single illustration, Governor Casimir Badeni of Galicia, who had won the plaudits of the authorities in Vienna for the manner in which he had kept the province steady during the grave Russian war scares of 1886–87, remarked in 1895, "Every war [is] an impossibility for Austria. Should we be attacked, we must accept the situation with God's help . . . A State of nationalities can make no war without danger to itself. Among a conglomeration of nations victory or defeat causes almost equal difficulty."

Nonetheless, out of the babel of tongues a manageable army was fashioned by the professional officers' corps, who were recruited largely from the German and Magyar elements in the Monarchy. In their first lessons these professional soldiers were indoctrinated with the idea that they formed a military brotherhood with the sacrosanct monarch as their grand master and all were obliged to swear personal fealty to the crown. Within the officers' corps a spirit of camaraderie tended to blot out national heritages and distinctions. Bismarck's reflection that "in Bohemia the antagonism between Germans and Czechs has in some places penetrated so deeply into the army that the officers of the two nationalities in certain regiments hold aloof from one another even to the degree that they will not eat at mess," contains more than a kernel of truth, but gives a somewhat distorted impression of the general situation in the Hapsburg officers' corps.

Raw conscripts drawn into the military service were inculcated with some kind of dynastic sentiment and discipline which counteracted, or tended to counteract, the particular national patriotism that had touched them in their boyhood environments. The Hapsburg army was, in fact, a veritable monarchical melting pot, a school of the civic virtues of devotion and discipline. At induction, soldiers swore a "solemn oath to God Almighty, of loyalty and obedience to His Majesty, our exalted Prince and Master, Francis Joseph, Emperor of Austria, King of Hungary . . . Also to obey his generals, to follow their orders against every enemy whatever . . . at all times, in all places, and on all occasions, to fight manfully and bravely, and in this way to live and die in honor. So help us God! Amen!" Aside from dynastic feelings, the great majority of the soldiers were united by their common Catholicism, of which the troops were constantly reminded by the image of the Madonna that figured on the Hapsburg banners and the mass celebrated by the chaplain.

Disaffection and discontent among the rank and file, inspired by considerations of nationality, were by no means unheard of, and that was unquestionably a weak link in the monarchical armor. And yet, except among some of the Slav soldiers, Czechs notably, who threw down their arms when ordered against Russia, months elapsed after the cannon began to boom in 1914 before national antagonisms or ideological cleavages seriously affected the prosecution of the war. And the spirit of monarchical patriotism was conspicuously fervent in the naval services of the House of Hapsburg.

Once upon a time the Hapsburg mission in central Europe had been to stem and then to hurl back the onrushing forces of the Turk and to preserve and extend western European civilization along the great Danube reaching from the Black Forest to the Black Sea. In very modern times the task of the Dual Monarchy was to maintain in a single political community an array of discordant, more or less nationalistically intoxicated peoples. Economic traditions and conditions, the historical and dynastic heritage, the wide popularity of Francis Joseph, the absence of concord among the smaller national groupings, the monarchical patriotism of the official, conservative, aristocratic, and well-to-do classes, and the menace of external dangers—these circumstances enabled the ancient realm of the Hapsburgs to maintain its standing as one of Europe's great powers.

And many months of extraordinary strain and war stress were required to bring the old structure tumbling to the ground. After the collapse, a wise wit likened the Danube Monarchy to a beautiful old vase whose value was depreciated until it fell to the floor and shivered into fragments.

5. PETER F. SUGAR: The Nature of the Non-Germanic Societies Under Habsburg Rule*

The debate continues. Peter F. Sugar, a historian at the University of Washington, recently contributed to the thesis of inevitable collapse by noting social as well as national factors that led to dissolution.

The "special something which characterizes most of the history of the [Habsburg] monarchy compared with the history of other states is the fact that we do not find a single common ideal or sentiment which could have united the peoples and nations of the monarchy in any political solidarity whatsoever." This was the judgment of one of the best known historians of the Habsburg state, Oszkár Jászi. This statement directs our attention to the central issue of the history of the Habsburg state and of the peoples who lived in it. They had very little in common. Robert A. Kann considered the multinational character of the Habsburg empire the chief problem of the many it faced and devoted his very able study to the conflict of nationalities within the Habsburg state.

Jászi, Kann, and other scholars believed that the monarchy's ills could have been cured by its reorganization into a democratic federation along ethnic lines. Most of those who wrote after 1920 were somewhat regretful that this reorganization never took place, seeming to rephrase Francis Palacky's famous dictum to read: "If the Austrian Empire had to disappear after an existence of many centuries, it ought to be recreated in the very interest of Europe and of humanity." Given the events that have occurred since the end of the First World War in the lands once ruled by the Habsburgs, one can certainly understand their view.

However, concentration on the problem of nationalities, though fully justified, has left certain other questions inadequately explored. My view is that even the timely introduction of democratic federalism based either on ethnic or individual "sovereignty" would not have prevented the disintegration of the Habsburg state complex. The reasons lie in the manner in which the Habsburgs built their state, and in the socioeconomic organization of each "nation and nationality."

The Habsburgs, like other successful dynasties in history, followed a purely dynastic policy of protecting their Hausmacht (patrimonial rights), emphasizing *Kaisertreue* (loyalty to the emperor and his family), and promoting a sort of dynastic patriotism. They followed this policy to the very end, while other ruling families slowly adjusted to the various changes that occurred in their realms. These adjustments were possible in states which were practically homogeneous ethnically or linguistically or in those which had succeeded in

* From Peter F. Sugar, "The Nature of the Non-Germanic Societies Under Habsburg Rule," *Slavic Review*, XXII, No. 1 (March, 1963), pp. 1–2, 28–30. Copyright American Association for the Advancement of Slavic Studies. Reprinted by permission of the *Slavic Review* and the author.

creating a strong centralized government before the middle of the eighteenth century, when modern nationalism began to appear. The Habsburg state was neither, and therefore the rulers clung, as much from necessity as from stubbornness, to their family policy, which they considered the only force unifying their lands. In the event, the diverse peoples of the empire never developed any common loyalties which could have sustained a Central European and larger-scale Belgium or Switzerland; but the Habsburgs' dynastic policy was amazingly effective for centuries. . . .

In attempting to analyze the societies of the numerous non-German people of the Habsburg Empire, we have used their potential abilities to manage their own affairs within the framework of a democratic federation as a means of bringing into focus a great variety of historical factors and social structures. Before drawing our conclusions we must, by cutting across linguistic, ethnic, and political borders, endeavor to establish whether the population of the monarchy could have found a basis for cooperation if it had disregarded "nationalistic" considerations.

Such a supranational principle might be found in socio-economic classes or in religions. By the end of the eighteenth century, when the various peoples of the Habsburg monarchy were reaching national consciousness, religion could hardly compete with nationalism for the masses' allegiance, as proven by the fantastic plan of the exiled Louis Kossuth. The old estates system, rule by large landed interests, or a state based on the cooperation of the various aristocracies (although this was attempted) had even less appeal after 1815 than the Habsburgs' family policy. But a few other possibilities still remain, in theory at least.

Since the days of Maria Theresa the economy of the empire was changing with great if not equal speed in all parts of the empire. Industries, railroads, and banks appeared, and with them a middle and a working class. The middle class had many interests and goals irrespective of where it developed or what the nationality of its members was. Political and social equality with the aristocracy, tariff and custom legislation, adequate communications, and industrial legislation are only the most important of a middle class's desiderata. As its numbers, financial power, and international connections steadily grew, a real, united middle class could possibly have transformed Austria-Hungary into a "July Monarchy." But we really do not have to look closely to discover that the Habsburg monarchy did not have such a class.

The Viennese bourgeoisie had real financial power, education, and connections but practically refused to use them. They were the captives of the *fin de siècle* spirit of their city, proud yet somewhat ashamed of its imperial glory, addicted to its pleasures, financing the social life of which they were a tolerated part, and proud of the titles of Hofrat, Geheimrat, and those of minor nobility which they were able to purchase. They knew that they lived in a dying world, yet did not have the determination and courage to save it by substituting their own values for those which were strangling the state they sincerely loved.

Without the cooperation of the Germans of Vienna, the middle class of the rest of the empire was impotent.

In any event, across the Leitha even a politically active German middle class could have found allies only with great difficulty. The Magyar middle class grew with amazing speed in the nineteenth century and especially after the *Ausgleich*. They spoke Hungarian, even at home, and signed their private and business mail with Magyar names. Under the Magyar veneer were mainly Germans and Jews, but they were ardent Magyars in spirit nonetheless. The Magyar nobility, as "liberals," liked to point to "my Jewish friend" and had no objection to the income which they earned as the *Parade Gojim* of Jewish or as the Magyar presidents of German enterprises. Cover men were needed by these companies to get their licenses, to act as contact men in the ministries, and so forth. This curious relationship created an alliance between aristocracy and middle class and facilitated the magyarization of the latter which, for obvious reasons, pleased the former very much.

Like all converts, these new Magyars embraced their new nationality with extreme passion. A minor title, admission to the exclusive clubs, the right to wear the uniform known as *Diszmagyar*, to save and buy a little estate, in short to become members of the aristocracy, real Magyars, became as important for these people as the success of their business ventures. In short, the Magyar middle class earned its living in business and the professions, but tried hard to live as and to become aristocrats. They did not want any changes except to be admitted into the circles where everybody called everybody "thou."

The Czechs were the only other national group in which a large and strong middle class had real significance. Here there was a real middle class, living and acting like one. But even with the leadership of those elsewhere in the monarchy who shared their professional interests, they probably would have been Czechs first.

The lack of a middle-class policy is not surprising; there was no political theory that claimed the exclusive loyalty of such a class. The socialists claimed to speak for such a supranational policy, demanding and to a considerable extent receiving the backing of the workers. The Austrian Socialist Party was a well-organized political organization, led by such able men as Victor Adler, Karl Renner, and Otto Bauer. It was a parliamentarian, democratic party, deeply interested in welfare legislation, universal suffrage, the maintenance of the monarchy, and its federative reorganization. But it was basically a German party, and when the Czechs and Slovenes formed their own socialist movements, which included in their programs the national aspirations of these people, the unity of the Austrian socialist movement was destroyed. The Hungarian party never achieved the stature of the Austrian, did not produce leaders of similar stature, and never was a real political force, because the Hungarian workers—only 2 per cent of whom had the right to vote—retained their connections with the village and were basically only homesick, displaced peasants with little understanding of, and even less sympathy with, socialist theories and aims.

We have considered federalism in relation to nationalism and the Habsburgs' dynastic policy. Though federalism may not be the best possible key to understanding the problems of the Habsburg minórities, it is not the worst either. We know much more about the political, cultural, and economic activities of the peoples of the Habsburg monarchy than we do about the social stratification and dynamics of these people. The approach which was used revealed some aspects of the various social structures, though suggesting the need for more studies dealing with this least-known side of the life of these peoples. However, the main conclusion is that the growth of nationalism had proceeded far enough to make it doubtful that the Habsburg realm could have been saved, even by the most democratic kind of reorganization.

Today nobody would seriously assert that the breaking up of the empire after World War I created an ideal situation in Central Europe. On the contrary, some kind of federation seems more essential than ever if political and economic stability are to be restored in this part of Europe. Western Europe, whose peoples have at least as much diversity of institutions and traditions as the former Habsburg realm, is right now solving its old problems quite successfully. But even Western Europe could not have done this before 1914. It had to learn the lessons taught by two great wars, the instability of the interwar years, American strength, and the Soviet menace before the first steps toward a West European Union could be taken. Central Europe had to learn the same lessons. There may be some hope that when the peoples of that region are again masters in their own houses they may attempt to create a similar union, which in territorial extent and ethnic composition would be not unlike the old Austro-Hungarian monarchy.

6. HANS KOHN: The Viability of the Habsburg Monarchy*

Hans Kohn, professor of history emeritus at the City College of the City University of New York, has written widely on the history of central Europe, with particular attention to the forces of nationalism. His comment on Professor Sugar's article focuses on the national problem, but stresses possibilities of reform that existed throughout much of the nineteenth century.

I find myself in general agreement with the main thesis and observations of Professor Peter Sugar's thoughtful and thought-provoking essay. Thus I have to confine myself to some reflections that may throw additional light on a complex problem, on the solution of which the fate of central and central-eastern Europe depended and the nonsolution of which was mainly responsible for bringing about the two great European wars of the twentieth century.

(1) I believe Professor Sugar is too pessimistic about the possibility of transforming the Habsburg Empire in the nineteenth century in a way that would have satisfied, more or less (and the emphasis is on "more or less") the nationalities of the multinational empire. Such a transformation would have

* From Hans Kohn, "The Viability of the Habsburg Monarchy," *Slavic Review,* XXII, No. 1 (March, 1963), pp. 37–42.

brought the eighteenth-century dynastic state (the state of the *Hausmacht*) into line with the growth of nationalism, and it would have pointed the way toward the emergence of supranational forms of political integration, which the need for economic cooperation and the requirements of security render essential in the second half of the twentieth century.

That no such attempt was made in the eighteenth century does not speak against the statesmanship of the Habsburgs. The problem did not arise before the French Revolution. In fact, the Austrian lands and Tuscany were (for that time!) relatively well ruled by the Habsburgs. Even Switzerland found it possible to create a modern state—and to use for the first time officially the name "Swiss nation"—only in 1848. Until then, certainly until the Helvetic Republic imposed by France, Switzerland resembled the ramshackle Holy Roman Empire much more than a modern state and accepted as "natural" the subjection of some of its territorial components to others (*Untertanenländer*) within the very loose confederation. The concept of equality of language, ethnic group, and class was introduced into Switzerland forcibly by the French Revolution.

The opportunity for a timely transformation of the Habsburg Empire came, as it did for Switzerland, in 1848. It came in both cases after a civil war or a sequence of revolutions and counterrevolutions, of ideological conflicts, which threatened to destroy the framework of the *ancien régime* state. The Swiss, who among the continental peoples most resemble the English in statesmanship (and that means in a happy mixture of adherence to tradition and realistic accommodation to changing circumstances, in a nonmetaphysical pragmatism which avoids all extremes and satisfies itself with a "more or less"), seized the opportunity and succeeded in creating a Swiss idea bridging the often very deep cleavages caused by geography, by differences of language, religion, ethnic origin, and political ideology, and by the memories of past oppression and arrogant master attitudes. They did it by the willing application of two fundamental principles—equality, which came to Switzerland through the French Revolution, and federalism, which the Swiss adapted after the model of the United States.

Switzerland was—except for Scandinavia—the only country on the European continent where in 1848 the liberal ideas triumphed. Everywhere else absolutism, whether in a traditional or in a plebiscitary form, reasserted itself. In Austria, Francis Joseph, then an inexperienced youth, poorly prepared for the throne and under the influence of the haughty and energetic aristocrat Prince Schwarzenberg, followed the general trend. The great opportunity, offered by the Kremsier Constitution, based on equality and federalism, which would have established a new Austria and an Austrian idea, was allowed to pass, a mere episode; in that respect the fate of the Kremsier Constitution was very different from that of the Swiss Constitution of 1848.

But more disastrous for the possibility of a supranational Austrian structure, which Lord Acton had foreseen in 1862, was that when the empire turned toward constitutionalism in the 1860's—a turn then common to the whole of

Europe in one or the other form—it abandoned the idea of federalism. In the Compromise with the Hungarian nobility in 1867, the aspirations of the Czechs, Slovaks, Serbs, Croatians, and Rumanians, who in a large majority were then still loyal to the dynasty, were sacrificed for the purpose of winning the assent of the Magyars to a common foreign and military policy on the part of what now became the Dual Monarchy, a policy to which Francis Joseph's real interest throughout his life belonged. The prenationalist concept of the unity of the lands of the Crown of St. Stephen was made the foundation of a Magyar nationalist state. The ruling Magyar oligarchy became predominant in its position vis-à-vis the non-Magyar peoples, not only in the Hungarian kingdom but throughout the Dual Monarchy. The Compromise was a blow not only to federalism but to equality and democracy. Until 1918 (and beyond) Hungary and her peoples remained a semifeudal, underdeveloped society. This was not true, by 1910, of the Austrian half of the Dual Monarchy (perhaps with the exception of Galicia, where the dynasty arrived at a similar "compromise" with the Polish nobility at the expense of the native peasantry and of the non-Polish population).

The years 1866–67 marked a disastrous turn not only in the Austrian monarchy but in the history of all Central Europe. In Prussia Bismarckism triumphed over liberalism and turned it into a national liberalism which differed from Western liberalism as later national socialism differed from Western socialism. Thoughout Central Europe the bright hopes of 1848–49 were frustrated and the catastrophes of 1914 and 1938–39—both of which involved the end of Austria in its then prevailing form—were in the making.

(2) Professor Sugar perhaps overstresses the division between the German and the non-German subjects of the Habsburg Empire. Such a division was certainly valid in the absolutist centralizing decade of the 1850's. It lost in significance after 1867. The really dominant element in the Dual Monarchy, the pressure group most successful in increasing its share in the communality, was then no longer the Germans but the Magyars. Austria-Hungary lost more and more the character of a predominantly German state. The spread of democracy, literacy, and economic well-being in the western half of the monarchy after 1867 strengthened the non-Germanic nationalities there at the expense of the former political, cultural, and economic predominance of the Germans. The result was that many Germans in the monarchy lost their faith in an Austrian idea as much as many Slavs or other non-Germanic peoples did. In my youth in Bohemia at the beginning of the century I found at the German Charles-Ferdinand University a deeper loyalty to the dynasty, to *náš císař pan,* among the Czech peasants than among the students, who came mostly from what became later known as the Sudetenland.

By the end of the nineteenth century many Austrian Germans looked to the Prussian German Reich as their real home and venerated Bismarck. It was not only German nationalism which brought them to abandon Austrian patriotism —or to indulge in a kind of amalgam of the two attitudes, made possible by Austria-Hungary's close alliance with the German Reich—it was also the feeling that the Habsburg monarchy was slow-moving, less efficient, less "modern" than the briskly expanding Wilhelminian Reich. Pan-Germanism had its origin largely among Austrian Germans, as Pan-Slavism had its origin among Austrian Slavs. But whereas the Russian government frequently favored Pan-Slavism and tried to use it for its purposes, the government of the German Reich under Bismarck and under William II did not support Pan-Germanism in Austria. After 1879 Francis Joseph was in his foreign policy a loyal ally of Germany, but neither Crown Prince Rudolph nor Archduke Francis Ferdinand were, to use an understatement, enthusiastic about the alliance. German circles in Austria were widely suspicious of Francis Ferdinand and regarded him as "pro-Slav."

The position of many Germans in Austria could be compared with that of the Austrian Poles or Italians. They felt part of a larger national entity the majority of whose people lived outside the Habsburg monarchy. The Austrian Germans had more recent memories of community with the Germans beyond the border, whereas the Italians of Trieste or of Trentino had never formed part of any Italian state, and Polish statehood (with the exception of the Republic of Krakow) had gone out of existence by the end of the eighteenth century. But the Austrian Germans had been part of the German Bund until 1866 and participated actively in the National Assembly at Frankfurt am Main. Thus the situation of the Germans in the Habsburg monarchy was in the age of nationalism not so fundamentally different from that of the non-Germanic elements.

(3) Perhaps the possibility of overcoming the narrow concept of an ethnic or linguistic nation-state can be illustrated by recalling the different attitudes of the Italians in the Habsburg monarchy and of those in Switzerland. Though geography, economics, and reason favored the lasting connection of the Italians in Trieste with Austria, they did not wish to remain in the Habsburg Empire, and their irredentism was of the most violent and extremist kind. Yet their connection with the Habsburgs was ancient. To secure independence from Venetian rule, the city had placed itself under Habsburg protection in 1382. In the later part of the nineteenth century the city grew most prosperous as the natural port of the vast Austrian hinterland. However, the Italian-speaking middle class, which was a socially and culturally favored class, showed itself bitterly hostile to the Austrian government, a hostility which was also directed against the numerous Slavs in and around Trieste and against the Socialist Party in the city. When Francis Joseph visited Trieste in 1882, a young man from that city, Guglielmo Oberdan (1858–82), tried to kill the emperor, was consequently executed, and among Italians extolled as a martyr in the nationalist cause.

On the other hand, the Swiss Italian-speaking canton of Ticino decided in 1798, when asked by Napoleon to join the Cisalpine Republic, to remain Swiss, although geography, the international situation, and reason seemed to dictate the opposite course. The population of the Ticino was neither economically nor culturally prosperous. The canton is geographically separated from the rest of

Switzerland by high mountain ranges, and its riverways and all its natural connections lead to the Lombardian plain. Nevertheless, the large majority of the Swiss Italians have faithfully adhered to Switzerland. Since 1848 Switzerland has formed a federal democracy in which the federal administration identified itself with none of the ethnic, linguistic, or religious groups, so that no feeling of majority or minority relationship could powerfully assert itself.

(4) But the final disintegration of Austria was not only due to the rejection of federalism in 1867 but—a point which Professor Sugar does not sufficiently stress—to its foreign policy. In the Europe of the age of nationalism a multinational or a supranational state was most desirable in the interest of peace, and since 1918 many people have for that reason and to a growing degree regretted the disappearance of the Austro-Hungarian monarchy. But to have been able to fufill this function, the monarchy would have had to follow, as Switzerland did, a policy of neutrality. Without such a policy, Switzerland, in spite of its democracy and federalism, might have distintegrated in 1870 or in 1914. Even in neutral Switzerland the tensions between the German-speaking and the French-speaking population were then running high.

Austria unfortunately did not understand the need for a policy of neutrality. Francis Joseph concluded the unfortunate Compromise of 1867 because he wished to gain Magyar cooperation in order to be able to resume competition with Prussia for German leadership. When this question was finally settled in 1871 by Bismarck's triumph over France, Francis Joseph accepted this outcome loyally but did not renounce an active foreign policy. He turned his attention toward the Balkans, claiming a share in the heritage of the disintegrating Ottoman Empire and came there into conflict with similar aspirations of the Russian Empire and of the Christian Balkan nations, each of which followed its own aggressive nationalist policy. The occupation of Bosnia-Hercegovina was a step in the wrong direction, and the war which Austria did not survive was sparked by an incident stemming directly from the action of 1878.

The occupation of Bosnia-Hercegovina brought the threat of conflict with Russia and the Balkan Slavs nearer and drove the Dual Monarchy, under Count Gyula Andrássy, into an alliance with Germany. Through this alliance, which was favored by the Magyars and Germans in the monarchy but bitterly resented by the Slavs, Austria-Hungary became the chief battleground of Pan-German and Pan-Slav aspirations. Even before the war of 1914 broke out, the German Chancellor, Bethmann Hollweg, in a speech on April 7, 1913, characterized the coming struggle as a conflict between the Germans and the Slavs. When the war came, many Slavs, even moderate leaders such as Thomas Masaryk, feared that a German-Magyar victory over the Serbs and Russians might bring about a general deterioration of the position of the non-Germanic and non-Magyar peoples under Habsburg rule.

Before 1914 Masaryk, as a disciple of Palacký, believed in an Austrian federation as a bulwark against Pan-Germanism and Pan-Russianism. In his most important programmatic book *The Czech Question: Efforts and Longings of the National Rebirth,* which was first published in 1895 and in a second edition in 1908, Masaryk wrote: "As regards the relation of the Czech lands to the Austrian state, I regard [Palacký's] idea of the Austrian state, in spite of all constitutional changes, as a still reliable guide: it is regrettable, that Palacký . . . himself abandoned to a certain degree his idea and recommended a more exclusively Slav national program; . . . I express my political experiences in the words that our policy cannot be successful if it is not supported by a true and strong interest in the fate of Austria, . . . by the cultural and political effort to work in harmony with the needs of our people for the advancement of the whole of Austria and its political administration."

The War of 1914 changed Masaryk's outlook. But the possibility cannot be rejected that had Austria established a federal regime in 1849 and followed a policy of neutrality, the crown could have become a symbol of the common interests of the various peoples who in isolation were threatened by Russian or German expansionism. The disintegration of the Habsburg monarchy not only offered the opportunity for such expansionism; it proved also that the hostility among the various peoples of the monarchy was not primarily created by the monarchy according to the famous rule of *divide et impera* but was deeply rooted in that extreme nationalism which animated the various peoples before and even more after 1914–18 and which the monarchy, alas with little success, tried to moderate.

Chapter XV.

THE NATURE OF THE NINETEENTH CENTURY

WHAT WAS the nineteenth century in Europe? For the historian, does it represent anything more than a chronological unit? To what extent was there a nineteenth-century civilization?

Surprisingly few historians have dealt with this issue. Yet in teaching and in the writing of textbooks, many use the nineteenth century as a major unit, beginning either with 1789 or with 1815 and ending or at least breaking sharply at 1914. The resultant unit is manageable and has the merit of being bounded on either side by a huge event. Perhaps one need ask for no more. Still, after dealing with several of the major problems and tendencies of the extended nineteenth century, it seems useful to ask if it has any further meaning.

The following selections do not exactly conform to the previous chapters of this collection. The problem they treat is too broad, too diffuse and, again, insufficiently examined to allow a full sense of argument to arise, though there are differences of view. It is hoped that enough possible lines of interpretation are suggested to stimulate the reader to an effort of his own; for there is no more basic task in historical study than the determination of periods and their significance.

Any attempt to assess the coherence of the nineteenth century in Europe raises a number of problems. What was Europe? This is a question often treated for earlier centuries, when identity might be determined by a common Christendom or its heritage, but it is relatively rarely raised for the nineteenth. The geographical boundaries are clear enough, and within them there was a real diplomatic community. But for discussions of values, politics, or social structure the historical coherence of such a large Europe may be questioned. Certainly, a statement of a common nineteenth-century culture must be tested in terms of geography. We are inclined to take developments in England or in England and France as the norm, in terms of liberalism, industrialization, and even in terms of a "Victorian" mentality—but does this approach in fact tell us about anyplace else in Europe?

Next, and more obviously, what about the starting point? Aside from choosing a date (whether 1789 or 1815), one must ask how significant a break it represents. There were changes, of course, and rather dramatic ones, but were they opening up a radically new era in European history or a new period that would dominate only one or two generations? One can return to an evaluation of the French Revolution for part of the answer, but other factors must be adduced to support a claim of a really new age. Relatedly, what factors are most important in shaping a new age, at least in modern history?

Following this question, one must ask if there is a more decisive break than 1914 which ended the period opened at the beginning of the century. One might argue for 1848 or, more defensibly, for 1870 as such a break. No essays are included specifically on this problem, but again, it requires assessment.

Finally, how decisive was 1914? On this question there is some important controversy. Without doubt, many in the generation of the war itself felt that an age, perhaps a civilization, had ended; this belief put some of them to arguing, interestingly, about what this civilization had consisted of and why it had failed. Further away from the event, many historians have questioned the extent of the break created by the war, both by noting important continuities between our own age and the nineteenth century as a whole and by noting the many challenges to nineteenth-century virtues and institutions that were developing before the war.

It is still hard to place so recent a period into clear perspective, and historians must constantly re-evaluate periodization of any sort. Yet questions about the basic nature and distinctiveness of the nineteenth century must be asked. They underlie any historical approach to modern times, and they underlie any historical identification of our own times. For despite all the controversies we do know some of the basic dynamics of nineteenth-century history. If we also know our own links to the century, we are close to the sort of heightened understanding that history, at its best, can provide.

1. FRANKLIN L. FORD: The Revolutionary-Napoleonic Era: How Much of a Watershed?*

Franklin L. Ford is professor of history and Dean of the Faculty of Arts and Sciences at Harvard University. He has worked in seventeenth- and eighteenth-century French history and in modern German history, which contributes to his attempt to discern differences between the two periods of his interest. His article clearly lists the criteria that in his opinion worked to create modern Europe around 1815; they should be assessed in themselves, and compared with those used in a retrospective view.

Every student of history, regardless of his special field, faces a problem of choice, endlessly recurring but constantly recast. Put in terms that seem to us worn only because none of us can wholly avoid using them, the choice is between emphasis on continuity and emphasis on change. No matter how he may hedge or qualify, the historian, before he completes an investigation, must respond to the question Carl Becker used to ask his seminar at Cornell: "Should we finally insist that while the world may change, it changes slowly—or that while the world may change slowly, it does change?" Everything in our professional training supports the first proposition, yet our fascination with historical process would forsake us if we did not also believe the second.

Actually, of course, real sophistication implies an ability to keep both tendencies in view, to exploit within our own minds the dialectic between solid

* From Franklin L. Ford, "The Revolutionary-Napoleonic Era: How Much of a Watershed?", *American Historical Review*, LXIX, No. 1 (Oct., 1963), pp. 18–30. Copyright Franklin L. Ford. Reprinted by permission of the *American Historical Review* and the author.

evidence of continuity and unblinkable signs of change. It is equally clear that one may tip the balance this way or that in his analysis of a particular situation without thereby assuming a rigid posture in defense either of change or of continuity as the key to all understanding of the past. Hence, I assume that I may express some views on the European record from 1789 to 1815 and yet not be classified hereafter, forever, and in all things as "either a little Liberal, or else a little Conservative."

A number of powerful arguments have been leveled against the view, early expressed, though for very different reasons, by both Leopold von Ranke and Alexis de Tocqueville, to the effect that in the years after 1789 an older Europe collapsed and that a new one, ominous in its strangeness, came into being. Various scholars have warned us that to interpret the revolutionary-Napoleonic era as a chasm over which no one could cross from the eighteenth century into the nineteenth, or as a wall of flame through which nothing could pass intact, would be to distort reality beyond recognition.

Against even the more modest image of a revolutionary "watershed" the arguments are impressive. They are also, in my view, an essential antidote to the kind of oversimplification to which such an image may lend itself. It should be noted, however, that not all of these arguments go to the question of continuity, strictly defined. Some of them attempt only to show that particular characteristics often assigned to the nineteenth century were anticipated in at least the later decades of the eighteenth. Conversely, some others refer to instances of reaction toward pre-1789 conditions in the years after 1815, when they do not center on the reign of Napoleon I, himself. In both clusters of interpretation, what is involved is not really a demonstration of statics, but rather a series of disputes over the timing and the direction of particular changes in the European scene. I do not suggest that one kind of emphasis, whether it be on long-term continuity, on eighteenth-century anticipation of the nineteenth century, or on nineteenth-century reversions toward the past, is necessarily the most significant. I only suggest that they *are* different kinds of emphasis. All three have tended, nevertheless, to merge into a formidable case against any theory that stresses the cleavage between the political forms, the diplomatic patterns, the social structure, the economic conditions, the influential ideas of Europe before 1789, on the one hand, and those of Europe after 1815 on the other.

As most commonly formulated, this case rests on the assertion that it was the seventeenth century, sometimes extended to include the first years of the eighteenth, which saw the fundamental break between an old and a "modern" Europe. Once this great change in both ideas and institutions had occurred, so runs the argument, there ensued a period extending into the early twentieth century, a period best envisaged as a plateau, marked by hummocks and creek beds, but never divided by a major watershed. Specifically, the revolutionary-Napoleonic interlude appears to shrink to the dimensions of an overrated episode the dust from which, once it settled, proved to have been just that—dust, having no deep significance for the substratum of continuity in human affairs.

The image of a "modern plateau" is nowhere more gracefully suggested than in Paul Hazard's *Crise de la conscience européenne* (Paris, 1935). This brilliant synthesis of the intellectual ferment between 1680 and 1715 incorporates several different levels of interpretation, the most obvious of which has to do with the period's own singular importance in the odyssey of European thought. More immediately relevant here, however, is Hazard's implicit conviction that with Locke, Newton, and Bayle, to name only three protagonists, Western civilization embarked upon two centuries of discussion, acrimonious and often divergent to be sure, but confined within a shared system of rational assumptions, mechanical models, and empirical-analytic methods. Not until the antirationalistic revolt of the early twentieth century would this system be attacked at its foundations.

Now, given this general conception, what special importance in the history of ideas can be assigned the noisy crisis midway through those two hundred or more years? What point is there in denying that both Marx and Darwin were in their time just as recognizable philosophes as Voltaire and Gotthold Lessing had been in theirs? Frank Manuel, in the *The Prophets of Paris,* has recently spelled out the striking similarities, if not in character or rhetoric, at least in social concern and a certain urgency, at once chiliastic and self-important, that connect a series of eighteenth- and nineteenth-century French thinkers, from Turgot through Condorcet, Saint-Simon, and Fourier to Comte. Neither Hazard nor Manuel would deny, of course, that the revolutionary crisis constituted a major chapter in the history of modern intellectual traditions, but both, if I understand them, would stress the solidity of those traditions in the face of numberless shocks and challenges. To many other historians of ideas, it has seemed increasingly difficult to take very seriously any departure from the basic premises bequeathed by the giants Hazard treats until, at the turn of our own century, Einstein repudiated Newton, while Locke's ideas were assaulted on the political front by Vilfredo Pareto and Nikolai Lenin, allies in nothing else, and on the psychological, by Sigmund Freud.

If the argument ended here, we might conclude that what confronts us is only an interesting example of continuity at the level of ideas, cutting across the political, social, and economic changes of the late eighteenth and early nineteenth centuries. But the case against the watershed metaphor, as applied to that period, is much broader, too broad in fact to be assigned to the history of abstract thought and thus fitted into a neat jurisdictional compromise. Perhaps the earliest argument for continuity was published by Albert Sorel almost eighty years ago in the first volume of his *L'Europe et la Révolution française,* which stressed the tenacious ambitions governing the intercourse of sovereign states from the eighteenth century through the revolutionary age. Readers of John U. Nef's *War and Human Progress* will recall his rejection of the older, more cataclysmic vision of an "Industrial Revolution." According to Nef, the crucial economic changes by which Europe and the rest of the world have indeed been revolutionized cannot be assigned to the years 1760–1832, mentioned in the titles or prefaces of countless books on the subject. Rather, those changes may be seen in the offing by the mid-seventeenth century, accelerating unevenly both in England and in France during the eighteenth, reaching literally earth-shaking intensity in Germany and the United States by the mid-nineteenth. We should add Russia and Japan in the first half of the twentieth century, and presumably China and India in its second half.

It seems to me to have been demonstrated beyond question that the development both of ideas and of institutions from what most of us still call early modern into modern times must today be discussed, if not in terms of flat continuity, at least in terms of complex, irregular, and in some areas exceedingly slow change. The influence of this demonstration on historical thinking has been reinforced, as earlier noted, by examples of both the eighteenth century's foreshadowing the nineteenth, and the latter's turning backward toward the former. We have been warned, for instance, that the preconditions for an outburst of popular nationalism existed long before that force was unleashed by revolutionary France. We have been reminded that Rousseau, Diderot, and the young Germans of the *Sturm und Drang* in the 1770's adumbrated many of the characteristics of later romanticism. Looking in the opposite direction, we have had to examine the revival of ecclesiastical power after the long humiliation of the papacy, a revival symbolized in 1814 by the rehabilitation of the Society of Jesus. In a different quarter, we have been shown how many of the administrative and social changes launched by the Prussian reformers of Baron von Stein's era had been undone by 1819 at the latest. Finally, we reflect that the dynastic principle, challenged by mobs and by political theorists, perverted by a Corsican family's willingness to serve, was in 1815 firmly reasserted in France, Spain, and the Italian principalities, extended to the Netherlands, and given new scope in the kingdoms and grand duchies of southern Germany.

Taken by themselves, all these affirmations and reminders seem to leave us no choice but to abandon the conception of a revolutionary-Napoleonic "watershed," advising Tocqueville and Ranke that they were standing too close to what they thought was the beginning of a new age—and that hence they quite naturally exaggerated its significance. It is just at this point, however, that I must define a view which will be developed in the remainder of these remarks, for I believe that it is not enough simply to recognize important strands of continuity linking the eighteenth century to the period that followed. When all due attention has been paid to those strands—and surely the continuity of human life, the overlapping of generations, was the most important of all—it still is not clear that we must slide into suggesting to ourselves, our readers, or our students that the revolutionary-Napoleonic era really did not make much difference. On the contrary, it is time again to emphasize certain changes witnessed by that era, changes so fundamental that no historian can move from eighteenth- to nineteenth-century subject matter without major adjustments in his conception of Europe and in the terms he must use. It is time to say, if I may in a sense use Alfred Cobban's phrase against him, that the Revolution was no "myth." [1]

1. In fairness to Alfred Cobban, whose inaugural lecture as Professor of French History in the University of London was entitled *The Myth of the French Revolution* (London, 1955), it should

Enough authorities, be it said at once, have lent support to this view so that no one, in adopting it, should pose as a lonely dissenter. My own thinking has benefited greatly from recent works by R. R. Palmer and Richard Herr. The British author of a new volume on the eighteenth century, M. S. Anderson, concludes his work: "By the 1780's modern history in the genuine as opposed to the textbook sense of the term was beginning." All I can hope to add to these and other studies is my own way of dissecting the process of change and of estimating its importance in the period under discussion.

There are several quite different types of evidence to which we might usefully address ourselves. Who can deny, for example, that nearly every major European government came out of the revolutionary-Napoleonic crisis with its administrative organization profoundly and, as time was to show, irreversibly altered? After 1815 France retained a set of budgetary procedures, a network of departmental prefects, and a system of centrally appointed judges in place of the deficit financing ex post facto, the quaint chaos of provincial powers, and the court system based on ownership of office with which the old monarchy had lived for centuries. But it was not only the brilliant and terrible homeland of the Revolution that changed its methods of conducting governmental business. The administrations of other states, hostile to France but stunned by its success in mobilizing national resources, moved toward lasting reforms through what might be termed "defensive modernization." I shall here mention just three imposing examples: the British income tax, begun by William Pitt in 1799, revamped by Henry Addington in 1803; the establishment of the Prussian Ministry of War, the Great General Staff, and the Military Academy by Gerhard von Scharnhorst and his collaborators after 1807; and the creation in 1802 of central ministries even for stubborn Russia. However the governments of Europe may be characterized after the Congress of Vienna, they cannot be dismissed as mere survivals of the *ancien régime*.

A second set of changes took place in the nature of warfare, going far beyond the reorganization of military command functions and training, just mentioned in the case of Prussia. What happened over the twenty-three years between Valmy and Waterloo, the years of Marengo and Trafalgar, Austerlitz and Borodino, was a revolution in the demands, the implications, the very sociology of war. Nef, cited earlier as skeptical about a sharp and dramatic "Industrial Revolution," has no such misgivings about the explosive effect of combining the technological advances already achieved by the 1790's with the *levée en masse,* the harnessing of hordes of citizen-soldiers and their patriotic sentiments in the service of national aims. Here again, the continental enemies of France had to imitate or perish. By the time Napoleon was at last defeated, Europeans had

---

be said that one of several "myths" he attacks in that paper is the simplistic notion that there was *a* French Revolution. Instead, as he says quite rightly, the historian must deal with a whole generation of turmoil involving disparate, or in some instances conflicting, elements and directions. Cobban's much-discussed essay, nevertheless, by emphasizing the extent to which the Revolution was "the child of the eighteenth century" (p. 21) and by casting doubt on the reality of fundamental, especially institutional changes resulting from it, appears to support the general line of interpretation I am here attempting to counterbalance.

experienced, if not total war, at least their first taste of what total war, including economic warfare, might be like under modern conditions.

The broadening and intensification of conflict were only the most obvious symptoms of a third type of change. This was the increased public involvement in politics. It was not just a matter of patriotism. Behind the sharp call of duty to the fatherland in danger, to the *patrie* as it was coming to be understood, could be heard a rising chorus of insistence on political rights for more citizens, though nowhere yet for all citizens. Palmer, in the study already noted, has shown that even before 1789 this insistence had been so clearly heard, and so strongly resisted by privileged groups, that the great crisis both inside and outside France was in part a "reaction against reaction." It was the Revolution itself, nevertheless, which mounted the most sweeping demands that, somehow, the people's representatives must be heard. Napoleon, while he subverted that demand, paid it lip service. After his fall, the restored dynasties compromised with it where necessary and condemned it where possible. If, however, it had subsided after 1815 like the winds of a passing storm, historians would not speak of the era of repression as essentially an episode. Instead, they could describe a lasting resumption or aristocratic "normalcy" drawn to the specifications of Friedrich von Gentz and Prince Metternich.

Still a fourth level of revolutionary change belongs to the realm of literature, music, and the visual arts. When dealing with the communication of sentiments, of course, we can scarcely expect to emerge with anything more tangible than an awareness of altered tone, an impression of changed intensity. It was just such an awareness, in this case one of lowered intensity, that struck R. H. Tawney some forty years ago, as his historical imagination moved out of the seventeenth century and its thunderous debates to contemplate their sequel. "In the great silence which fell when the Titans had turned to dust," he wrote, "in the Augustan calm of the eighteenth century, a voice was heard to observe that religious liberty was a considerable advantage, regarded 'merely in a commercial view.' " How can we in turn, considering a later epoch, escape a powerful sense of change in just the opposite direction, of heightened emotional temperature, of art struggling to express newly unleashed passions when we contrast Pope with Shelley, Mozart with Berlioz (or even the Beethoven of the later symphonies), Goya of the court portraits and the tapestry cartoons with him of the "Horrors of War"? Must we not acknowledge that the differences represent long strides away from the sometimes cold confidence of the eighteenth century in *la raison raisonnate*? "And furthermore," as an elderly scholar of my acquaintance would say, with more petulance than precision, "things have never really calmed down since!"

Having said this much, let me now state my own conviction that nowhere—neither in administrative innovations, nor in the altered conditions of war, nor in the first uneven surge toward political democracy, nor in the highly charged cultural atmosphere—do we perceive at its clearest the fundamental shift that makes the last years of the eighteenth century and the first of the nineteenth a historical watershed too imposing to be disregarded. The most important change of all occurred in social structure and, equally important, in the way men conceived of social structure. We need above all to consider what it meant for European society to lose the appearance of a hierarchy of legally defined orders of men. By the same token, we must consider what it meant to have nakedly revealed the social subdivisions identified by Max Weber in a famous and by no means outdated essay: classes, as economic groupings; status groups, reflecting degrees of honorific recognition; and parties, organized around shared political aspirations, if not always ideals or principles.

It is worth noting in this connection that before 1789 social and political commentators labored under a double handicap in seeking to analyze the realities confronting them. In the first place, the cherished medieval vision of orders —noblemen, clergymen, burghers, peasants—seemed less and less meaningful, even when applied to Europeans who quite clearly, in a technical sense, did belong to nobility or clergy, bourgeoisie or peasantry. What real use, one might ask, was a category that covered English dukes, French lawyers, and the *glota,* the "barefoot gentry" of Poland, or Italian cardinals, Spanish friars, and poor German schoolmasters in clerical garb? What was the bourgeois brotherhood that united town patricians with the poor cobbler who stared hopefully at their shoes? What good did it do to call "peasants" both the independent *laboureur* on his French farm and the miserable worker on a Bohemian estate?

A second, still more serious trouble with the language of corps and orders was that it did not apply at all to large numbers of people who nonetheless deserved to be taken very seriously. The new Manchester textile manufacturer, the Genevan watch exporter only lately arrived from Basel or Lausanne, the immigrant Dutch wine merchant in Bordeaux were not legally "bourgeois" of their cities, but they most assuredly were businessmen. And what of the growing army of workers not accommodated by the guild system—to what order did they belong?

Let us not oversimplify. If it would be wrong to assume that European society before 1789 was in fact a tightly knit system of orders, it would be just as great an error to suppose that classes, status groups, and parties were as yet completely invisible. Quite the reverse was true, as we realize when we read bitter strictures concerning "the rich"—English nabobs back from India, French tax contractors, German speculators in grains. There was an old awareness too of "the poor" as a polyglot, urban-rural mass, an awareness born of countless seventeenth-century upheavals and of eighteenth-century troubles as recent as E. I. Pugachev's vast rebellion in Russia. If there were emergent classes, there were also eighteenth-century social elements whose honorific status escaped the traditional definition in terms of orders. We need here mention only the place occupied in most countries by the higher civil service, the major bureaucrats, often humbly born and only moderately wealthy, whose power nevertheless excited both respect and animosity. And political parties, as Palmer has shown, can be identified with relative ease by the 1780's: "Patriots" and "Orangists" in the United Provinces, "Vonckists" and the "Estates Party" in the Austrian Netherlands, "Republicans," "Moderates," and "Patriots" in beleaguered Poland.

Yet the language of orders hung on until the Great Revolution, and in so far as that language expressed the accepted, the respectable way of describing human relationships, it was itself a conditioning factor in the situation. For while Europe's population was not, in fact had never been, neatly subdivided into nobility, clergy, bourgeoisie, peasantry, and certain less general orders, a conventional terminology suggesting that those were the only meaningful rubrics still helped to shape men's reactions to developments. Edmund Burke, like Montesquieu before him, both pleaded for reform and denounced revolution in the name of healthy relations among stable ranks of men. Gaspar Melchor de Jovellanos, gifted and enlightened though he was, saw fit to dramatize Spain's ills in 1787 by composing a poem on the sad decline of the ancient nobility. In Württemberg and in other German states, the critics of princely absolutism scarcely went beyond a reassertion of the rights of the legal orders, the *Stände*. Even in the early polemical writings of the French Revolution, notably including those of the Abbé Sieyès, we perceive the hold that old terms and categories had maintained on the political imagination of the day. The confused vehemence of the 1780's, the impression of issues badly joined, not only in France but in other countries as well, seems to me to testify to the inadequacy of an inherited conceptual scheme when applied to recalcitrant circumstances.

It was the pitiless test of power imposed upon most of Europe by the revolutionary-Napoleonic crisis that killed the old image of society—not completely nor all at once, to be sure. Vestiges of archaic language and values have survived to the present day, sometimes twisted to more modern polemical uses. (Incidentally, when we label "bourgeois" a suburban ranch house, with a television antenna above and a two-car garage on the side, do we speak with the scorn of noblemen, the pride of burghers, the envy of peasants, or the righteous wrath of proletarians?) In any case, the false symmetry of a single hierarchy of orders never recovered from the shock it received in the quarter century that opened in 1789.

That the Revolution contained elements of class conflict, in its most precise, economic sense, was apparent even before the Estates-General came together at Versailles. The *Affaire Reveillon* of April 1789, for instance, was a bloody riot touched off by the efforts of two wealthy Parisian manufacturers (members of the Third Estate) to impose lower wage scales. It is my own belief that Marxist historians, from Albert Mathiez to Albert Soboul, have sought to make class conflict explain more facets of the French Revolution than it can in fact account for. It would be foolish, however, to deny that the struggle between poor men and those more comfortable runs back and forth through the historical fabric of the period, from the Faubourg Saint-Antoine to German cities on the Rhine, from the streets of Amsterdam to the shimmering water front of Naples.

At the same time, we also encounter intensified party strife, the competition of political groups for power as an end in itself. The succession of such groups in the French assemblies—Feuillants, Girondists, *Montagnards, Hébertistes*—is so familiar that it can easily be underrated as a new chapter in parliamentary history. No less significant, however, was the effect of events in France on other countries, the tendency in one government after another for "anti-" and "pro-French" parties to appear under such conditions as the local situation offered. In England, for example, war fever and the dread of Jacobin excesses combined to discredit Charles James Fox in the 1790's, but not before his collision with Pitt had given a new sharpness to the struggle between Whigs and Tories.

Gradations of social status, no less than economic and political alignments, were deeply affected by the upheaval. In France, and in other lands that experienced even a forced transplantation of the Revolution, a decade-long assault both on ecclesiastical independence and on the privileges of birth left the honorific position of clergy and nobility—not to mention their physical base of power, especially in land—damaged beyond hope of complete repair. Admittedly, neither order was destroyed, but henceforth neither could look down with secure disdain on the rest of society. The revolutionaries' glorification of "citizen" as the proudest of all titles, like their insistence that love of country outweighed humble birth, struck at the very roots of inherited rank and at the mystical awe surrounding prelates.

In place of the old determinants of status, certain others gained a degree of general acceptance that they have commanded ever since. I refer to wealth, special abilities, and service to the community (especially if recognized by the bestowal of public office or military rank). Questions might still be asked about an individual's family tree and his way of life, but they seemed less and less relevant when compared with other, more urgent queries: Is he rich or poor? What can he do? What is his present position? The modern status system may seem no more attractive than that of the *ancien régime,* but the differences between the two are unmistakable.

The Imperial Nobility established by Napoleon in 1808 provides, somewhat surprisingly, an excellent example of basic change. To a superficial observer it might appear that the Emperor was simply resurrecting aristocratic privilege, as underpinning for his dynasty. But let us not overlook two features of this new hierarchy. First, its titles were assigned on the basis of military services rendered or public offices already held by the recipients. Ministers and senators became counts; presidents of departmental electoral colleges, higher judges, mayors of the larger cities became barons; members of the Legion of Honor became chevaliers. Second, such a title, even after having been conferred on an individual, could pass to his descendants only if accompanied by a fortune sufficient to support it. To meet this requirement, a prince of the Empire would have to bequeath an estate yielding at least 200,000 francs per year, while the corresponding figure for a count was 30,000, for a baron 15,000, and for a chevalier 3,000. Napoleon visualized not only a nobility of service, but also one that would remain an "upper class" in specifically economic terms. In his shrewd, cynical mind and in the minds of many of his contemporaries there remained no room for arguments about the virtues of aristocratic birth or leisured refinement or genteel poverty.

I have asked for due consideration of a series of institutional, military, political, and aesthetic changes and, in slightly more detail, a set of complex but crucial changes in social structure. Any one of these factors might in itself be dismissed as unrepresentative, or at most a matter only of degree. Taken together, however, they reveal a revolution in the fullest sense, a fundamental departure from some of the most important conditions of human life before 1789. The magnitude and the nature of this phenomenon will surely escape the historian whose gaze is riveted on just one country or on only one type of evidence, be it diplomatic correspondence, official enactments, personal reminiscences, or belles-lettres. But the historian who is willing to look up, however briefly, from his specialized labors and to indulge in a panoramic view can scarcely avoid the impression of looking back toward a massive divide, a true watershed.

To recognize such a divide is not to ignore all the important threads of continuity mentioned at this essay's beginning. I do not, for example, support the claim that the men of the old regime are more remote from us than St. Thomas Aquinas was from them. On the other hand, there is little to be gained and much to be lost by overlooking the watershed of the Revolution or by underestimating the effort required for us to think our way back across it into the eighteenth century. In 1789, after long, confused preliminaries, the old Europe began a transformation, convulsive, bewildering, to some of the participants wildly exhilarating, to others bitterly tragic. In 1914 another convulsion began. Its successive spasms were destined to last even longer than those of its predecessor. Its human cost was far more terrible, and it contained much less that was either generous or hopeful. Perhaps the greatest tribute that can now be paid to European civilization, to its vitality, its adaptability, and its tenacity, lies in the observation that through two such cataclysms we can still trace so many familiar lines, truly uniting the centuries. Fully aware of those lines, historians should not shrink from marking the changes along the way.

2. GILBERT MURRAY: The Ordeal of This Generation*

Gilbert Murray (1866–1957) was one of the most distinguished classical scholars of our time, serving as regius professor of Greek at Oxford University from 1908 to 1936. He was very active in the interest of international understanding, acting several times as a delegate to the League of Nations Assembly. His book on the broad effects of World War I clearly reflects some of the nostalgia for the nineteenth century common among many people in the 1920's. The fact that he was not a specialist in modern history may allow a clearer view of the import of the century as a whole, or it may render his generalizations too facile. Obviously, his view is seriously colored by his own times and his focus on Britain.

As we get farther away from the England of the nineteenth century, and see it separated from us by the great gulf of the war, we shall perhaps be better able

* From Gilbert Murray, *The Ordeal of This Generation*, pp. 36–56. Reprinted by permission of George Allen & Unwin Ltd., London.

to see it as it really was, to appreciate its extraordinary greatness, its peculiar faults and flaws, and to a remarkable degree its unity.

Beyond question it was a very great age indeed. For Great Britain especially it marked the zenith of national success, the widest expansion over the world of British government, British commerce, British political thought, British morals, philosophy, science, poetry, and prose literature. It was a time when Indian rajahs and Chinese mandarins learnt to play cricket and read Macaulay, as now they are learning baseball and frequenting the movies. The material advance in population, wealth, shipping, commerce, etc., is simply overwhelming, and needs no illustration. The advance in scientific discovery, first in mechanics and physics, later in biology, is probably without a parallel in the history of the world. The advance of humanity and care for the alleviation of suffering is also, so far as I know, without a parallel: in England alone in this period we find the abolition of slavery—at the cost of £20,000,000 of public money willingly given; the sweeping reform of the old criminal law and the barbarous penal system which accompanied it. In 1818 about 1 in every 200 of the population was in prison; a hundred years later, with a far more efficient police, it was about 1 in 2,000. We find the reform in the treatment of lunatics; the laws against cruelty to children and to animals; the Factory Acts; the Married Women's Property Acts; the immense spread of education in all its stages, both by public authority and by private experiment; the beginnings of the care for public health; the greatly increased consumption of coffee, tea, fruit, and light viands, along with a greatly decreased consumption of alcohol. An interesting study might be made of the effects on society of the discovery of safe anaesthetics. The use of anaesthetics has doubtless made men in general more sensitive to pain in themselves and others; but one must also realize that the determination of doctors to find and to use some safe anaesthetic was more directly the result of an increasing reluctance to inflict pain on their patients than of any inability to bear it themselves when they happened to be patients. The discovery was quite as much due to the increase of humanity as a cause of that increase afterwards. In poetry the nineteenth century from Wordsworth and Shelley to Tennyson, Browning and Swinburne, must, I think, fairly be recognized as either the greatest or the second greatest age in the history of English literature; in prose it was indisputably the time in which the English novel, from Scott and Jane Austen to Dickens, Thackeray and Meredith, burst into bloom at home and sallied forth successfully to conquer Europe. In painting, opinions will be divided: much may be said from the strictly technical side against the great Victorian painters, but it probably remains true that such artists as Watts and Millais and Burne-Jones did somehow interpret in a very rare degree the higher imagination of their time.

What reason, then, what strange reason, is it that fills the pages of our minor contemporary writers with an open contempt for the Victorian Era or the whole nineteenth century? It is worth discussing, though I doubt if I can find any complete answer. One contributing cause may be the wish of rebels to find some name for the thing they want to rebel against; and the word "Victorian," with its suggestion of a repressive and somewhat reactionary lady in her declining years, has for the purpose many advantages. There are certain obvious political prejudices: for it was, of course, the great age of Liberalism. There is also the natural opposition felt at the time of any change of fashion between the old and the new. It is perhaps difficult for people who are not acutely conscious of their own clothes or furniture to understand the strength of feeling with which a young man, full of excitement over his wide pink flannel trousers, may regard those who have not taken the same plunge, or with which young householders, flushed with pride over a drawing-room with black walls and one picture, may look upon a Morris pomegranate paper and a crowd of watercolours. But these are trivialities.

A more serious cause can be seen in the reaction against Victorian earnestness. In Bernard Shaw's *Quintessence of Ibsenism* it is remarked that there are two kinds of moral reformers. One discovers that something which most people do is wrong and must not be done. He, says Mr. Shaw, is publicly praised and secretly hated. The other proclaims that something hitherto condemned and forbidden is really harmless, and there is no reason why you should not do it if you like. This man is publicly condemned and reprobated; in secret he is adored by all the people whom he has, so to speak, set free. Now the Victorian Age, or the nineteenth century as a whole, was a great moral reformer of the first type. It proclaimed that men, even courtiers and noblemen, ought not to be drunken or dissolute or even corrupt, that politics were really concerned with the welfare of the people, and that the rich had duties towards the poor. The transition from George IV and his unpleasing brothers to the young Queen and the Prince Consort was typical of a much wider change. When Lord Palmerston was caught chasing a maid of honour into her bedroom, the excuse made for him was: "Your Majesty should remember that he is a very old gentleman and accustomed to the manners of the late Court." And it would be a complete mistake to suppose that the change was a mere increase in decorum. There was a re-birth of public spirit. Gentlemen ceased to take bribes. Justice became incorruptible. Literature not only observed a reticence in language and subject which had already begun in the late eighteenth century, but was inspired by the spirit that we rather vaguely term "idealism." It has been observed that up to about 1820 the laws passed by Parliament had almost all been for the protection of the privileged few against the many; after that time they are predominantly for the protection of the nation as a whole against abuse and privilege. Instead of the ferocious defence of property, a spirit of sympathy and help to the oppressed begins to inspire legislation. The old revolutionary doctrine of the infinite perfectibility of mankind, which had set on fire the enthusiasm of Godwin, Shelley and Condorcet, passed in a milder and more reasonable form into the general imagination of the age. Whether or no man might be made perfect, he certainly might be made better and happier than he is; and the conscious pursuit of that object became an accepted source of inspiration to politics and literature. With it went the conception that the necessary condition of the pursuit was freedom: set man free, let him have room to move and external conditions which do not starve or cramp him, and human nature of itself will strive to rise higher. This spirit shows itself in almost all the best English fiction of the period, from romantics like the Brontës, and realists, like George Eliot, to satirists, like Dickens and Thackeray. It had been utterly lacking in Fielding and Smollett, and even in Jane Austen. It shows itself in the immense increase of charitable institutions, of religious missions, of societies for the education of the people. There is no question of hypocrisy. To suppose there is, is the mere petulance of jealousy. Shelley's or Gladstone's love of moral improvement was just as genuine as Falstaff's love of sack. But an age of moral earnestness seems in our own day to have been succeeded by an age of relaxation; and one can see in, for instance, such a book as Mr. Strachey's *Eminent Victorians* that the moral earnestness of Gladstone or Dr. Arnold is felt by the author to be a hateful quality and not easily forgiven. One seems to see the resentment of an over-tired man against a muscular and energetic walking companion.

That, I think, is an element to be borne in mind and liberally discounted, because, after all, it is the resentment of the inferior against the superior for being superior. But none the less there is in the criticism that is now launched against the Victorian Age one element which is perfectly sound and valid, though it detracts but little from the real greatness of that time. In almost every department of human activity we feel that the nineteenth century, for all its magnificent achievement, does not quite satisfy us. After all, how could it, unless we were all dead or asleep? We have gone on practising the same arts, studying the same problems; and of course we have in most cases discovered some new facts or thought out some new piece of technique. Thousands of people have been working at Darwin's subject, and naturally they have found some things to correct in him, though none of them may be as great a discoverer as Darwin. A modern novelist can show many tiresome tricks of style, superficialities of observation, or defects of analysis in Dickens or Thackeray, Meredith or Hardy, but would not therefore pretend to be able to write better novels. Every honours student of philosophy at any British university has learnt to summarize the inconsistencies of John Stuart Mill; most art students can point out the improvements in technique made by Sargent as compared with Turner or Millais, though he may be less convincing when he expounds the further immense improvement made on Sargent by some more recent idol. I am not clear that any recent poet can claim to surpass Tennyson, or even Browning, in sheer mastery of technique, but he can at any rate demand some change of subjects or some less old-fashioned ideas. This is all true. To some extent one may say it is really a matter of course. In every society that has any life in it, each succeeding age must be able to show some points of advance upon the last. The age of Dryden was in literary power far inferior to that of Shakespeare, but it could point out convincingly the faults of Elizabethan prose and poetry. None the less, when all these allowances are made, I think that in the Victorian Age, or the nineteenth century as a whole, there is one real weakness on which later criticism has seized quite justly and correctly. It is the defect that belongs naturally to its great virtue. It was so creative that it forgot to criticize. It was so sanguine that it overlooked flaws and dangers; so confident in its achievements that it preferred to acquiesce in a comfortable faith rather than vex its spirit with the search for a strictly consistent philosophy.

The sort of optimist view of the world which runs through most of the great Victorian writers and statesmen seems to me to be based on the ideal dreams of the Revolution modified, not by any philosophical analysis, but by an instinct of moderation and common sense. Godwin and Condorcet had real philosophies, which ended either in smoke or in disasters. Macaulay and Sidney Smith had in their hearts much the same philosophy; but they never believed in it enough to do anything really foolish. They did on the whole think it likely that if you were virtuous you would be happy; that education would remove most moral evils; that the voice of the people was likely to be right; that an increase of freedom would bring about probably an increase of virtue and almost certainly an improvement in government. But they did not trust theory when it conflicted with experience, and they would always sooner be inconsistent than obviously wrong. "I have a passionate love," said Sidney Smith, "for common justice and common sense." You cannot make a philosophy out of that, but you can make a most excellent rule of conduct. Macaulay and Hallam conceived of English history as a logical development of constitutional freedom up to the principles of the Revolution of 1689; such a view is philosophically almost grotesque, since the Revolution of 1689 was a complicated compromise dependent on very peculiar circumstances. It was not the expression of an eternal principle. Yet for practical purposes it was probably the best conception of English history that had yet been struck out, the wisest, the most practical, the most full of hope for the future. Hegel had given a far more profound interpretation of human history, but it has never been of use, as far as I know, to anyone. Nietzsche had given one far more consistent and subtle, but it was mad. The English nineteenth-century view of the world was apt to be shallow, apt to be inconsistent, but it worked. It was true to "common justice" and "common sense." It seldom or never did harm; in almost all great crises it was—to use a golfing metaphor—"as good as a better."

To take one signal instance: the religious teaching established in state schools by the Act of 1870. There were two or three possible views which might claim to be logical. If Parliament knew what religious doctrine was true, it should have that doctrine taught in the schools; presumably it would be that of the Church of England. If Parliament did not know what religion was true, it could either abstain from religious teaching altogether and have lay schools, as in France, or it could allow all sects to have a right of entry to the schools in order to inculcate their particular preferences. Parliament did none of these things. It accepted a motion from a private member, Mr. Cowper Temple, authorizing the teaching of Christianity, but ordaining that "no religious catechism or religious formulary distinctive of any particular denomination shall be taught in the schools." Disraeli, out for mischief as usual, riddled the clause with hostile criticism. It was unintelligible; it founded, on the spur of the moment, a new religion; it made the teachers into a new sacerdotal class. Yet, as a matter of fact, the clause expressed the real fundamental wish of the best minds of the nineteenth century, it stood the test of experience, it enabled religious teaching to move as men's aspirations moved, and it did in a rough-and-ready way separate the kernel of religion from the husk of dogmatic theology. Established religions do not cut a very distinguished figure in the history of human thought, but that unconsciously created by Mr. Cowper Temple is perhaps, for practical purposes, about the best there has ever been.

Do not suppose that I am praising the lack of logic in itself, or that the statesmen and others whom I am praising actually prided themselves on lack of logic. Quite the contrary. They tried hard to be as logical as they could. Every reasonably intelligent person does. The difference between what is called the "practical Anglo-Saxon mind" and the "logical Latin mind" is that the Latin sometimes tends to take one single line of thought and follow it to its logical result, whereas the Englishman, at his best, takes into consideration a great many lines of thought, covering as far as possible all the relevant facts, and, since some point one way and some another, does not attempt to follow any one of them to the bitter end. He tries to give due weight to all factors, and to act in such a way that one mistake will not be fatal. But he is not absolved from the duty of thinking as closely and logically as he can about each element of the problem.

This was, I would suggest, what the Victorian Age characteristically did. It cared more for life than for thought; consequently it produced abundant and fine life, while its thought was comparatively unambitious and aimed mainly at serving the practical purposes of life. It cared intensely for morals and little for metaphysics; a good deal for religion and scarcely at all for theology; and since morals depend ultimately on metaphysics and religion on theology, it left always a large extent of vague and misty margin in the beliefs which it held most firmly. It had an immense faith, a faith in goodness, in duty, in the future of mankind. It believed with a certain passion in the maxims of the copybook or even the nursery, and where these led to awkward or puzzling consequences it took refuge in a masterly reticence. It realized especially the immense value of reticence in art. In its imaginative literature it almost ignored dirt, it ignored obscenity, it ignored all the multitudinous vibrations of meanness, spite, and sensuality below the threshold which so enchain and almost monopolize the attention of many modern writers. And, since its creative power was gigantic, it created a world of imaginative literature in which these things were practically non-existent. Or perhaps I am wrong in saying that the nineteenth-century artists ignored these things; they knew them, probably, well enough; but at least they were reticent about them. Shelley knew all about the suppressed horrors under the threshold of consciousness;[1] Dickens and Thackeray knew well the seamy sides of life. They could even produce, for artistic purposes, the full effect of it with extreme economy of means. In the midst of so much habitual reticence every word told.

1. See *Prometheus,* Act I, 483–91, and the whole scene.

In politics there was the same reticence, the same idealism. Where a social evil could be dealt with they talked about it; otherwise not. It is curious how little Peel or Gladstone or Lord Salisbury, from their public utterances, would seem ever to have realized the deeper horrors and cruelties of the *res publica.* A friend of mine who proposed standing as a Labour candidate in 1918 was, after a speech full of eloquence and sympathy, told to stand down: the audience did not want "any of that damned middle-class idealism." It was the Victorian Age condemned by that which came after: the "middle-class idealism" of people who did not suffer, but sympathized with suffering and wished to be good, condemned by people who themselves suffered and hated those who did not suffer, and did not in the least care to be good. One can see the same uncritical idealism in the painting of the Victorians. It is literary, emotional, imaginative, at times even intentionally edifying. Thousands of people loved Watts's *Hope* or Burne-Jones's *Merciful Knight,* but more for their poetry than for their painting. Science itself was humane and sanguine. So strong was the spirit of the age, that science swallowed its great new discovery of the struggle for life and the survival of the fittest with hardly a shudder, hardly a moment's interruption in its vision of universal benevolence. The struggle merely led to "scientific meliorism," with George Eliot as its imaginative prophet. Business was optimistic, adventurous, full of self-congratulation—much as it is now in America. A later time found it full of weaknesses, ignorant of foreign languages and foreign customs, unwilling to take intellectual trouble or even to believe that intellect in any form was much good; but in its day, by its very faith and confidence and cheerful enterprise, it attained a degree of prosperity never before known in the world.

The point I wish to bring out is this: One finds in the history of human civilization a constant alternation between two processes—first organization and then disorganization; in the language of biology, first anabolism and then katabolism; first the slow building up of an ordered social structure or cosmos, then the reduction of that cosmos into chaos. No human cosmos endures very long. If it is not shattered by invasion or civil war or external disaster, it is undermined by the advance of knowledge, by the growth of social elements hitherto neglected and making for confusion, by some inherent contradiction in its own basis, or the like. The Chinese philosophers, I find, have a conception that is similar, though not quite the same. They say that a period of *Yin,* the female principle, peaceful, continuous, anabolic, is regularly followed by one of *Yang,* the male principle, violent, shattering and katabolic, but creative. *Yin* is very pleasant, but if it lasts too long it means stagnation and decay.

The conception is not an unfamiliar one. The Greek City State was a cosmos; it produced a world in which the good citizen knew exactly how to behave; it was overthrown by a chaos of military conquests, in which no one felt clear what to think or what to do. The Roman Empire was a cosmos; its break-up a chaos. The mediaeval conception of the unity of Christendom under the Pope and the Emperor was, in conception, a cosmos, though one that failed before it was realized. In our own day, travellers often tell us of a Polynesian or African tribe, living in good order, with a fixed social system and a code of conduct which is duly respected: that is cosmos. Then they tell how the same tribe is plunged into dissolution by the advent of the White Man. It is not merely the introduction of drink and Western vices that does the destruction; it is the bewildering contact with a stronger and more complex civilization. To take a very simple example, a certain tribe of Eskimo in Alaska lived till lately a peaceful, orderly and contented life, hunting the seal and dependent on it for almost everything. The seal gave them their food, their light, their fuel, their clothes, their houses, and many of their tools. Then American traders came to them. They did nothing obviously bad. They did not plunder them or teach them to drink; they merely offered a good price for sealskins. The Eskimo proceeded to kill more seals in order to sell the skins; they bought guns in order to kill them faster; they have by now nearly exterminated the animal on which they depend and are living in a state of extreme misery and distraction. Cosmos has, by the introduction of one new factor, been reduced to chaos.

Now I wish to suggest that the Victorian Era was in the main a cosmos, an ordered unity, and that we have witnessed its breakdown. In a later chapter I will develop the idea further. I do not, of course, suggest that the cosmos was complete. There were all sorts of flaws and excrescences in it. For one thing, as Mr. and Mrs. Hammond have shown in a striking book, the Industrial Revolution, which began at the end of the eighteenth century, was itself a dissolvent force, breaking up the order of country life, with its mutual ties and duties, as it had existed for many generations, and substituting a life of mere economic struggle. That is true; and the nineteenth century, though it grappled hard with the chaos of the industrial revolution, never quite conquered or assimilated it. No political or social cosmos is ever complete. If it were, I presume we should have that condition of stable equilibrium which is fatal to further progress, and "one good custom would corrupt the world." There were obviously great social inequalities in the Victorian Age, but the general will was steadily working to remove them. The power of wealth was too great, but was being steadily reduced. The state of public education and intelligence was rather low, but was constantly and vigorously rising. The representation of the people, on which so much depended, was still imperfect. The system of parliamentary government was, though much the best system yet invented for governing a state, in its essence far from ideal. (I sometimes think of it as rather like a parody of trial by jury, with no rules of evidence, no judge to guide the contest, any number of self-appointed advocates, and a jury wandering in and out of court at will, mostly attending to other things but listening to the evidence when it sounds spicy.) The actual rapidity of progress during most of the century makes it more difficult to speak of a fixed order, and if we speak of a spirit instead of an order, as constituting the cosmos, we must remember that it was a spirit of great freedom, admitting and encouraging the expression of most diverse opinions.

But it was not for any of these reasons that the Victorian Cosmos actually failed. True, the vices of the industrial revolution were not worked out of its blood, and might in the course of time have proved fatal. Other causes, such as the advance of knowledge, and the industrialization of the East, were at work, and we are feeling their effects now. But none of these imperfections was the cause of the Great War. The Great War was due to another flaw in the political and social organization of Europe, a flaw perfectly definite and easily distinguishable: the belief in the independent sovereign state.

3. JOHN MAYNARD KEYNES: The Economic Consequences of the Peace*

John Maynard Keynes (1883–1946), one of the most eminent economists of the twentieth century, started his career as an official in the British Treasury and attended the Peace Conference in Paris in 1919 as its representative. His book on *The Economic Consequences of the Peace* resulted from his great disgust with the terms of the peace settlement, and it had a significant part in shaping subsequent British attitudes. His view of the nineteenth century, though stressing economic characteristics, agrees with Murray's in seeing an essential unity, broken by developments before and during the war.

Before 1870 different parts of the small continent of Europe had specialized in their own products; but, taken as a whole, it was substantially self-subsistent. And its population was adjusted to this state of affairs.

After 1870 there was developed on a large scale an unprecedented situation, and the economic condition of Europe became during the next fifty years unstable and peculiar. The pressure of population on food, which had already been balanced by the accessibility of supplies from America, became for the first time in recorded history definitely reversed. As numbers increased, food was actually easier to secure. Larger porportional returns from an increasing scale of production became true of agriculture as well as industry. With the growth of the European population there were more emigrants on the one hand to till the soil of the new countries, and, on the other, more workmen were available in Europe to prepare the industrial products and capital goods which were to maintain the emigrant populations in their new homes, and to build the railways and ships which were to make accessible to Europe food and raw products from distant sources. Up to about 1900 a unit of labor applied to industry yielded year by year a purchasing power over an increasing quantity of food. It is possible that about the year 1900 this process began to be reversed, and a diminishing yield of Nature to man's effort was beginning to reassert itself. But the tendency of cereals to rise in real cost was balanced by other improvements; and—one of many novelties—the resources of tropical Africa then for the first time came into large employ, and a great traffic in oil-seeds began to bring to the table of Europe in a new and cheaper form one of the essential foodstuffs of mankind. In this economic Eldorado, in this economic Utopia, as the earlier economists would have deemed it, most of us were brought up.

* From John Maynard Keynes, *The Economic Consequences of the Peace,* pp. 9–25. Copyright, 1920, by Harcourt, Brace & World, Inc.; renewed, 1948, by Lydia Lopokova Keynes. Reprinted by permission of Harcourt, Brace & World, Inc.

That happy age lost sight of a view of the world which filled with deep-seated melancholy the founders of our Political Economy. Before the eighteenth century mankind entertained no false hopes. To lay the illusions which grew popular at that age's latter end, Malthus disclosed a Devil. For half a century all serious economical writings held that Devil in clear prospect. For the next half century he was chained up and out of sight. Now perhaps we have loosed him again.

What an extraordinary episode in the economic progress of man that age was which came to an end in August, 1914! The greater part of the population, it is true, worked hard and lived at a low standard of comfort, yet were, to all appearances, reasonably contented with this lot. But escape was possible, for any man of capacity or character at all exceeding the average, into the middle and upper classes, for whom life offered, at a low cost and with the least trouble, conveniences, comforts, and amenities beyond the compass of the richest and most powerful monarchs of other ages. The inhabitant of London could order by telephone, sipping his morning tea in bed, the various products of the whole earth, in such quantity as he might see fit, and reasonably expect their early delivery upon his doorstep; he could at the same moment and by the same means adventure his wealth in the natural resources and new enterprises of any quarter of the world, and share, without exertion or even trouble, in their prospective fruits and advantages; or he could decide to couple the security of his fortunes with the good faith of the townspeople of any substantial municipality in any continent that fancy or information might recommend. He could secure forthwith, if he wished it, cheap and comfortable means of transit to any country or climate without passport or other formality, could despatch his servant to the neighboring office of a bank for such supply of the precious metals as might seem convenient, and could then proceed abroad to foreign quarters, without knowledge of their religion, language, or customs, bearing coined wealth upon his person, and would consider himself greatly aggrieved and much surprised at the least interference. But, most important of all, he regarded this state of affairs as normal, certain, and permanent, except in the direction of further improvement, and any deviation from it as aberrant, scandalous, and avoidable. The projects and politics of militarism and imperialism, of racial and cultural rivalries, of monopolies, restrictions, and exclusion, which were to play the serpent to this paradise, were little more than the amusements of his daily newspaper, and appeared to exercise almost no influence at all on the ordinary course of social and economic life, the internationalization of which was nearly complete in practice.

It will assist us to appreciate the character and consequences of the Peace which we have imposed on our enemies, if I elucidate a little further some of the chief unstable elements, already present when war broke out, in the economic life of Europe.

I. POPULATION

In 1870 Germany had a population of about 40,000,000. By 1892 this figure had risen to 50,000,000, and by June 30, 1914, to about 68,000,000. In the years immediately preceding the war the annual increase was about 850,000, of whom an insignificant proportion emigrated.[1] This great increase was only rendered possible by a far-reaching transformation of the economic structure of the country. From being agricultural and mainly self-supporting, Germany transformed herself into a vast and complicated industrial machine, dependent for its working on the equipoise of many factors outside Germany as well as within. Only by operating this machine, continuously and at full blast, could she find occupation at home for her increasing population and the means of purchasing their subsistence from abroad. The German machine was like a top which to maintain its equilibrium must spin ever faster and faster.

In the Austro-Hungarian Empire, which grew from about 40,000,000 in 1890 to at least 50,000,000 at the outbreak of war, the same tendency was present in a less degree, the annual excess of births over deaths being about half a million, out of which, however, there was an annual emigration of some quarter of a million persons.

To understand the present situation, we must apprehend with vividness what an extraordinary center of population the development of the Germanic system had enabled Central Europe to become. Before the war the population of Germany and Austria-Hungary together not only substantially exceeded that of the United States, but was about equal to that of the whole of North America. In these numbers, situated within a compact territory, lay the military strength of the Central Powers. But these same numbers—for even the war has not appreciably diminished them [2]—if deprived of the means of life, remain a hardly less danger to European order.

European Russia increased her population in a degree even greater than Germany—from less than 100,000,000 in 1890 to about 150,000,000 at the outbreak of war,[3] and in the year immediately preceding 1914 the excess of births over deaths in Russia as a whole was at the prodigious rate of two millions per annum. This inordinate growth in the population of Russia, which has not been widely noticed in England, has been nevertheless one of the most significant facts of recent years.

The great events of history are often due to secular changes in the growth of population and other fundamental economic causes, which, escaping by their gradual character the notice of contemporary observers, are attributed to the follies of statesmen or the fanaticism of atheists. Thus the extraordinary occurrences of the past two years in Russia, that vast upheaval of Society, which has overturned what seemed most stable—religion, the basis of property, the ownership of land, as well as forms of government and the hierarchy of classes—may owe more to the deep influences of expanding numbers than to Lenin or to Nicholas; and the disruptive powers of excessive national fecundity may have

1. In 1913 there were 25,843 emigrants from Germany, of whom 19,124 went to the United States.

2. The net decrease of the German population at the end of 1918 by decline of births and excess of deaths as compared with the beginning of 1914, is estimated at about 2,700,000.

3. Including Poland and Finland, but excluding Siberia, Central Asia, and the Caucasus.

played a greater part in bursting the bonds of convention than either the power of ideas or the errors of autocracy.

II. ORGANIZATION

The delicate organization by which these peoples lived depended partly on factors internal to the system.

The interference of frontiers and of tariffs was reduced to a minimum, and not far short of three hundred millions of people lived within the three Empires of Russia, Germany, and Austria-Hungary. The various currencies, which were all maintained on a stable basis in relation to gold and to one another, facilitated the easy flow of capital and of trade to an extent the full value of which we only realize now, when we are deprived of its advantages. Over this great area there was an almost absolute security of property and of person.

These factors of order, security, and uniformity, which Europe had never before enjoyed over so wide and populous a territory or for so long a period, prepared the way for the organization of that vast mechanism of transport, coal distribution, and foreign trade which made possible an industrial order of life in the dense urban centers of new population. This is too well known to require detailed substantiation with figures. But it may be illustrated by the figures for coal, which has been the key to the industrial growth of Central Europe hardly less than of England; the output of German coal grew from 30,000,000 tons in 1871 to 70,000,000 tons in 1890, 110,000,000 tons in 1900, and 190,000,000 tons in 1913.

Round Germany as a central support the rest of the European economic system grouped itself, and on the prosperity and enterprise of Germany the prosperity of the rest of the Continent mainly depended. The increasing pace of Germany gave her neighbors an outlet for their products, in exchange for which the enterprise of the German merchant supplied them with their chief requirements at a low price.

The statistics of the economic interdependence of Germany and her neighbors are overwhelming. Germany was the best customer of Russia, Norway, Holland, Belgium, Switzerland, Italy, and Austria-Hungary; she was the second best customer of Great Britain, Sweden, and Denmark; and the third best customer of France. She was the largest source of supply to Russia, Norway, Sweden, Denmark, Holland, Switzerland, Italy, Austria-Hungary, Roumania, and Bulgaria; and the second largest source of supply to Great Britain, Belgium, and France.

In our own case we sent more exports to Germany than to any other country in the world except India, and we bought more from her than from any other country in the world except the United States.

There was no European country except those west of Germany which did not do more than a quarter of their total trade with her; and in the case of Russia, Austria-Hungary, and Holland the proportion was far greater.

Germany not only furnished these countries with trade, but, in the case of some of them, supplied a great part of the capital needed for their own development. Of Germany's pre-war foreign investments, amounting in all to about $6,250,000,000, not far short of $2,500,000,000 was invested in Russia, Austria-Hungary, Bulgaria, Roumania, and Turkey. And by the system of "peaceful penetration" she gave these countries not only capital, but, what they needed hardly less, organization. The whole of Europe east of the Rhine thus fell into the German industrial orbit, and its economic life was adjusted accordingly.

But these internal factors would not have been sufficient to enable the population to support itself without the co-operation of external factors also and of certain general dispositions common to the whole of Europe. Many of the circumstances already treated were true of Europe as a whole, and were not peculiar to the Central Empires. But all of what follows was common to the whole European system.

III. THE PSYCHOLOGY OF SOCIETY

Europe was so organized socially and economically as to secure the maximum accumulation of capital. While there was some continuous improvement in the daily conditions of life of the mass of the population, Society was so framed as to throw a great part of the increased income into the control of the class least likely to consume it. The new rich of the nineteenth century were not brought up to large expenditures, and preferred the power which investment gave them to the pleasures of immediate consumption. In fact, it was precisely the *inequality* of the distribution of wealth which made possible those vast accumulations of fixed wealth and of capital improvements which distinguished that age from all others. Herein lay, in fact, the main justification of the Capitalist System. If the rich had spent their new wealth on their own enjoyments, the world would long ago have found such a regime intolerable. But like bees they saved and accumulated, not less to the advantage of the whole community because they themselves held narrower ends in prospect.

The immense accumulations of fixed capital which, to the great benefit of mankind, were built up during the half century before the war, could never have come about in a Society where wealth was divided equitably. The railways of the world, which that age built as a monument to posterity were, not less than the Pyramids of Egypt, the work of labor which was not free to consume in immediate enjoyment the full equivalent of its efforts.

Thus this remarkable system depended for its growth on a double bluff or deception. On the one hand the laboring classes accepted from ignorance or powerlessness, or were compelled, persuaded, or cajoled by custom, convention, authority, and the well-established order of Society into accepting, a situation in which they could call their own very little of the cake that they and Nature and the capitalists were co-operating to produce. And on the other hand the capitalist classes were allowed to call the best part of the cake theirs and were theoretically free to consume it, on the tacit underlying condition that they consumed very little of it in practice. The duty of "saving" became nine-tenths of virtue and the growth of the cake the object of true religion. There grew round the non-consumption of the cake all those instincts of puritanism which in other ages has withdrawn itself from the world and has neglected the arts of production as well as those of enjoyment. And so the cake increased; but to what end was not clearly contemplated. Individuals would be exhorted not so much to abstain as to defer, and to cultivate the pleasures of security and anticipation. Saving was for old age or for your children; but this was only in theory,—the virtue of the cake was that it was never to be consumed, neither by you nor by your children after you.

In writing thus I do not necessarily disparage the practices of that generation. In the unconscious recesses of its being Society knew what it was about. The cake was really very small in proportion to the appetites of consumption, and no one, if it were shared all round, would be much the better off by the cutting of it. Society was working not for the small pleasures of today but for the future security and improvement of the race,—in fact for "progress." If only the cake were not cut but was allowed to grow in the geometrical proportion predicted by Malthus of population, but not less true of compound interest, perhaps a day might come when there would at last be enough to go round, and when posterity could enter into the enjoyment of *our* labors. In that day overwork, overcrowding, and underfeeding would have come to an end, and men, secure of the comforts and necessities of the body, could proceed to the nobler exercises of their faculties. One geometrical ratio might cancel another, and the nineteenth century was able to forget the fertility of the species in a contemplation of the dizzy virtues of compound interest.

There were two pitfalls in this prospect: lest, population still outstripping accumulation, our self-denials promote not happiness but numbers; and lest the cake be after all consumed, prematurely, in war, the consumer of all such hopes.

But these thoughts lead too far from my present purpose. I seek only to point out that the principle of accumulation based on inequality was a vital part of the pre-war order of Society and of progress as we then understood it, and to emphasize that this principle depended on unstable psychological conditions, which it may be impossible to recreate. It was not natural for a population, of whom so few enjoyed the comforts of life, to accumulate so hugely. The war has disclosed the possibility of consumption to all and the vanity of abstinence to many. Thus the bluff is discovered; the laboring classes may be no longer willing to forego so largely, and the capitalist classes, no longer confident of the future, may seek to enjoy more fully their liberties of consumption so long as they last, and thus precipitate the hour of their confiscation.

IV. THE RELATION OF THE OLD WORLD TO THE NEW

The accumulative habits of Europe before the war were the necessary condition of the greatest of the external factors which maintained the European equipoise.

Of the surplus capital goods accumulated by Europe a substantial part was exported abroad, where its investment made possible the development of the new resources of food, materials, and transport, and at the same time enabled the Old World to stake out a claim in the natural wealth and virgin potentialities of the New. This last factor came to be of the vastest importance. The Old World employed with an immense prudence the annual tribute it was thus entitled to draw. The benefit of cheap and abundant supplies, resulting from the new developments which its surplus capital had made possible was, it is true, enjoyed and not postponed. But the greater part of the money interest accruing on these foreign investments was reinvested and allowed to accumulate, as a reserve (it was then hoped) against the less happy day when the industrial labor of Europe could no longer purchase on such easy terms the produce of other continents, and when the due balance would be threatened between its historical civilizations and the multiplying races of other climates and environments. Thus the whole of the European races tended to benefit alike from the development of new resources whether they pursued their culture at home or adventured it abroad.

Even before the war, however, the equilibrium thus established between old civilizations and new resources was being threatened. The prosperity of Europe was based on the facts that, owing to the large exportable surplus of foodstuffs in America, she was able to purchase food at a cheap rate measured in terms of the labor required to produce her own exports, and that, as a result of her previous investments of capital, she was entitled to a substantial amount annually without any payment in return at all. The second of these factors then seemed out of danger, but, as a result of the growth of population overseas, chiefly in the United States, the first was not so secure.

When first the virgin soils of America came into bearing, the proportions of the population of those continents themselves, and consequently of their own local requirements, to those of Europe were very small. As lately as 1890 Europe had a population three times that of North and South America added together. But by 1914 the domestic requirements of the United States for wheat were approaching their production, and the date was evidently near when there would be an exportable surplus only in years of exceptionally favorable harvest. Indeed, the present domestic requirements of the United States are estimated at more than ninety per cent of the average yield of the five years 1909–1913.[4] At that time, however, the tendency towards stringency was showing itself, not so much in a lack of abundance as in a steady increase of real cost. That is to say, taking the world as a whole, there was no deficiency of wheat, but in order to call forth an adequate supply it was necessary to offer a higher real price. The most favorable factor in the situation was to be found in the extent to which Central and Western Europe was being fed from the exportable surplus of Russia and Roumania.

4. Even since 1914 the population of the United States has increased by seven or eight millions. As their annual consumption of wheat per head is not less than 6 bushels, the pre-war scale of production in the United States would only show a substantial surplus over present domestic requirements in about one year out of five. We have been saved for the moment by the great harvests of 1918 and 1919, which have been called forth by Mr. Hoover's guaranteed price. But the United States can hardly be expected to continue indefinitely to raise by a substantial figure the cost of living in its own country, in order to provide wheat for a Europe which cannot pay for it.

In short, Europe's claim on the resources of the New World was becoming precarious; the law of diminishing returns was at last reasserting itself, and was making it necessary year by year for Europe to offer a greater quantity of other commodities to obtain the same amount of bread; and Europe, therefore, could by no means afford the disorganization of any of her principal sources of supply.

Much else might be said in an attempt to portray the economic peculiarities of the Europe of 1914. I have selected for emphasis the three or four greatest factors of instability,—the instability of an excessive population dependent for its livelihood on a complicated and artificial organization, the psychological instability of the laboring and capitalist classes, and the instability of Europe's claim, coupled with the completeness of her dependence, on the food supplies of the New World.

4. BENEDETTO CROCE: History of Europe in the Nineteenth Century*

Benedetto Croce (1866–1952),† writing in the same period as Gilbert Murray, admits many of the apparent differences between the nineteenth and twentieth centuries, but is nonetheless more impressed by the continuity. Is he referring to the character of the nineteenth century as such, or to movements that began then but only flourished later? Perhaps he implies a sort of ongoing conflict, with liberalism one constant protagonist, that precludes any statement of the dominant values of either century.

Whoever compares the political geography of before and after the World War, and sees the German Republic in the place of the Germany of the Hohenzollerns, the Austrian Empire disintegrated and in its place the new or enlarged national states with German Austria and Magyar Hungary restricted to narrow frontiers, and France with her provinces lost in 1870 restored to her, and Italy, who has gathered in her *irredente* lands and stretches out her frontiers to the Brenner, and Poland reconstructed, and Russia no longer Czarist but Soviet, and the United States of America risen to be one of the greatest factors in European politics, and so on through all the other great changes worked in territories and relationships of power; and whoever, on the other hand, remembers the orderly, rich Europe of other days, flourishing in commerce, full of comfort, with her agreeable life, bold and sure of herself, and considers her now, impoverished, troubled, mournful, all divided by customs barriers, the gay international society that used to gather in her capitals dispersed, each nation busied with its own cares and with the fear of worse, and therefore distracted from spiritual things, and the common life of thought, and art, and civilization extinguished—he is induced to see a profound difference between the two Europes and to mark the separation with the line, or rather

* From Benedetto Croce, *History of Europe in the Nineteenth Century* (New York: Harcourt, Brace & World, Inc., 1963), pp. 351–53. Reprinted by permission of Agenzia Litteraria Internazionale, Milan, Italy.

† See Chapters 2 and 7, on romanticism and liberalism.

with the abyss, of the war of 1914–18. But he who instead passes from what is external and secondary to what is intrinsic, and seeks for the passions and acts of the European soul, at once mentally sets up the continuity and homogeneity between the two Europes so diverse in appearance, and if he looks closely, without letting himself be put off by these superficial impressions, he finds in the two aspects the same features, even if after the war and what has followed it they are somewhat sharpened. In the altered political conditions he finds the same dispositions and the same spiritual conflicts, however aggravated by that heaviness and obtuseness that the war, killing millions of lives, creating the habit of violence and destroying the habit of the eager critical and constructive labour of the mind, was bound to produce along with the severer effects of its lofty tragedy.

Activism is developing with the same impulsiveness, and even with greater vehemence. The nationalist and imperialist outbursts inflame the victorious nations because they are victorious and the vanquished nations because they are vanquished. The new states that have arisen add new nationalisms and new imperialisms. The impatience for liberal institutions has given rise to open or masked dictatorships, and to the desire for dictatorships everywhere. Liberty, which before the war was a static faith or a practice with scant faith, has fallen from the minds of men even where it has not fallen from their institutions, and has been replaced by activistic libertarianism, which more than ever dreams of wars and upheavals and destruction, and bursts out into disordered movements and plans showy and arid works. It cares nothing for or despises such works as are built with meditation and love, with the pious sentiment of the past and with the ardent force that opens up the future: actions that come from the heart and speak to hearts; the speculations that speak words of truth; the histories that supply a knowledge of all that man has laboriously created by working and struggling; the poetry that is poetry and, as such, a thing of beauty.

Communism, which under the name of socialism had been inoculated into the life of politics and the state and into the course of history, has appeared once more in its scission and crudity, another bitter enemy of liberalism, which it derides and ingenuously calls moralistic. On a par with activism, with which it is often merged, this communism is sterile, and it suffocates all thought, religion, art, all these and other things that it would like to enslave and can only destroy. And once more we behold on the scene, almost as though they were ideas freshly born of youthful truth, all the distortions and decrepit sophisms of historical materialism, of which every man with a little knowledge of criticism and of the history of ideas well knows what to think, but which, none the less, have once more taken on an air of novelty and modernity simply because, transported from Europe to Russia, they have returned thence more simplified and more gross than they were before, and are successful once more in times of grossness, simplification, and credulity. On the other hand, Catholicism, which had attempted to regather strength from irrationalism and mysticism, has received and continues to receive, in great numbers, feeble or enfeebled souls and confused or turbid adventurers of the spirit. Even pessimism and the voices of decadence, which were heard in pre-war literature, are now heard once more, and are preaching the downfall of the West or even of the human race, which, after trying to rise from the animal to man, is about to relapse (according to the new philosophers and prophets) into the life of the beast.

5. CARLTON J. H. HAYES: A Generation of Materialism, 1871–1900*

Carlton J. H. Hayes here assesses not the whole nineteenth century, but the mood at its close. The common values—the belief in progress and the criteria used to measure it—resemble those cited by Gilbert Murray. Indeed, the obvious result of the war was to disillusion many of the buoyant optimists of the previous decade. Two questions, however: How widely was the cult of progress disseminated by 1900; in what areas and among what groups? And how fully and permanently was the cult interrupted by the war? The latter question cannot be answered without an examination of the twentieth century, but it must be raised if we are to know how far we have departed from nineteenth-century values.

In the correspondence columns of popular journals, a desultory, though occasionally heated, debate was carried on in 1899 as to whether this year or the next would bring the nineteenth century to a close. Ecclesiastical authority at Rome, appealed to by an enterprising American daily, confirmed the seemingly odd judgment of historians and mathematicians that the year 1900 belonged to the 1800's and that not until January 1, 1901, would a new century dawn.

The passing of the nineteenth century, its posterity can now see, had significance beyond the merely arbitrary timekeeping of calendars and almanacs. Whether its actual demise be dated from 1899 or 1900 doesn't matter, but it does matter that about this time the generation which had come into the European limelight in the days of the Franco-Prussian War of 1870 was fast disappearing. The generation had been preponderantly materialist. That is, it had been especially devoted to, and proud of, material achievements, and it had been imbued, in so far as it had a philosophy, with simply material and mechanical conceptions and a frankly this-worldly pragmatism.

The materialism of this generation must not obscure, however, its intimate relationship to, and its apostolic succession from, those eighteenth-century generations which gave birth and mission to the most distinctive intellectual movement of modern times—the so-called Enlightenment. The Enlightenment did not end, as one might gather from textbooks, with Voltaire, Gibbon, or Beccaria, with Hume, Adam Smith, or the French Encyclopedists. It extended to a climax in the final decades of the nineteenth century. The Generation of Materialism was the supreme one of Enlightenment.

* From Carlton J. H. Hayes, *A Generation of Materialism, 1871–1900*, pp. 328–36.

Of abiding features of the Enlightenment, probably the most characteristic and most cherished was the belief in progress, and in a progress which proceeded not along a jagged line of ups and downs, with the ups only slightly exceeding the downs, but rather along a straight line steeply ascending. Such progress had originally been posited for science, education, and reform; and after two centuries it was most strikingly evident in precisely these three domains.

There had certainly been steady and glorious progress in science. Crowning the pioneer labors of Galileo and Newton were such ultimate physicists as Helmholtz and James Thomson and Röntgen; and the fruitful method of the physical sciences was now being applied with ever greater fruitfulness to the chemical and biological sciences, to the social sciences, to psychology and sociology. All phenomena, it seemed, were explicable in terms of matter and force; all were governed by mathematical and mechanical laws; and matter was so simple and so real. Science, moreover, was so practical and beneficent. Its continually multiplying applications were enabling men to converse with one another wherever they might be, to escape physical pain, to lengthen their span of life, and to possess knowledge and enjoy creature comforts beyond the experience of any philosopher or prince of previous ages.

Progress in education was quite as clear. The generation of materialism was finally realizing the hopes of eighteenth-century *philosophes* and the *projets* of French Revolutionaries; it was putting the youth of entire nations into school and teaching them to read and write and to aspire to fuller knowledge. Thereby, with increasing leisure for self-improvement and greater opportunities for higher technical education, the masses no less than the classes bade fair to assure the continuity of progress.

There was palpable progress in the reforming of government and society. Throughout central as well as western Europe, both constitutional government and personal liberty, which had once been deemed wildly revolutionary, were now usually regarded as respectably evolutionary and quite normal. Not merely Jacobins and Liberals accepted them, but likewise most Conservatives and most Marxians. Indeed, reforms were now being wrought, not violently or dictatorially in the perverse manner of a Robespierre or a Bonaparte, but intelligently by a process of enlightened free consent. Liberty was being supplemented by democracy, and the abuses of economic liberalism by a socializing state solicitude for the health and material well-being of the whole citizenry.

Progress in these and all other respects depended, the eighteenth-century champions of Enlightenment had believed, on man's proper use of his own reasoning powers, which were then assumed to be very real and very great. To the later materialistic generation of the Enlightenment, however, such confidence in rationalism might have seemed a bit naïve. In the light of the newer evolutionary conceptions of Darwinian biology and physiological psychology, one could well question whether man's "animal mind" was capable of independent direction or truly rational functioning. Yet perhaps because the men of the 1880's and 1890's were more inclined to the practical than to the theoretical, few pushed the lessons of biology and psychology to upsetting conclusions. Most of them talked and acted as if they shared the full rational faith of the men of the 1770's. But if peradventure one seriously doubted the efficacy of "pure reason" in a being akin to cave men and gorillas, and ultimately maybe to carbon compounds, one could now repose a new and livelier faith in the efficacy of the evolutionary process itself. To this, Herbert Spencer pointed the way, and Francis Galton landmarked it with eugenics, and Nietzsche with supermen. Individual men might not be so reasonable as had been imagined in the eighteenth century, but the race was evolving upward and could be assisted by science or "will" to evolve faster. In fine, evolution bolstered the generation's optimism by rendering progress automatic.

The Enlightenment from its inception had been associated not only with humanitarianism, which found progressive expression in social reform, in emancipation of slaves and serfs, in ameliorative penal and labor and health legislation. It had been associated also with the humanism of still earlier modern times—the neo-paganism of a Boccaccio, for example; the delighting in man as man, and in man's body as well as in his mind. There had been, of course, an interregnum in the sway of this humanism in the nineteenth century, especially in "mid-Victorian" England. But prudery and smug respectability proved transitory. By the 1890's a complete restoration of humanism impended. The English word "sport" passed into every other European language. Outdoor games and athletic contests multiplied and spread. Women everywhere took to bicycling. Circumlocution gave place to startling paradox, and this in turn to stark frankness. And while such literary artists as Anatole France, George Moore, and Samuel Butler inveighed against hypocrisy, the nude became once more a favorite subject of pictorial art. Here, too, one detected vitalizing progress.

To be sure, the climax of the Enlightenment was attended, as had been its initial stages, by some curious anomalies which smacked of credulity and even superstition. Just as Voltaire and Hume had had to divide popularity back in the 1770's with Mesmer and Cagliostro, so in the 1880's and 1890's multitudes of Europeans (and Americans) were not sufficiently scientific to be deterred from patronizing astrologers, palmists, or phrenologists, who still plied their lucrative professions in every sizeable town. Besides, since the astonishing exploits of the Fox sisters in America in the late 1840's, there had been a constant crescendo of spiritist séances, with mysterious mediums and strange rappings and tumultuous table-turnings. Even scientists as distinguished as Alfred Russel Wallace and Sir Oliver Lodge insisted that there must be something in all this spiritism, and in 1882 was founded at London a *Society for Psychical Research,* which over succeeding years and in voluminous reports recorded its testing of various hypotheses—"telepathy," "suggestion," "psychical radiation," "disembodied spirits." It was queer business for a generation of materialism, but in justice to the generation it should be said that the chief concern was with material manifestations (and explanations) of the "spirits."

Another and allied curiosity of the era was hypnotism. It was eighteenth-century mesmerism with Mesmer's "animal magnetism" expurgated. One no longer stroked the patient with magnets. One merely fixed him with a look. Yet there was a progressive popularity about it. It provided entertainment alike for the masses and for persons of fashion; and by many contemporary medical men and psychologists it was regarded as a phenomenon of the highest importance. One of the most popular stories of the 1890's was George Du Maurier's about Svengali's hypnotic power over Trilby.

Curious also was the attraction of would-be intellectuals to semiesoteric cults imported into Europe from the Orient or from America. Some found a kind of escape from materialism in the gospel of Mary Baker G. Eddy and dismissed physicians to call in Christian Science "readers." Others discovered in a Syrian mystic, Abdul Baha, an up-to-date prophet, a new incarnation of the divine. Still others, following the lead of that much-traveled Russian lady, Helena Blavatsky, joined the *Theosophical Society* which she founded at New York in 1875 to propagate "the occult wisdom of the East," and which ushered in a vogue of quaintly garbed mahatmas and yogis. Despite numerous "exposures" of Madame Blavatsky and her cult, the professed Theosophists in Europe numbered over 100,000 at the time of her death in 1891. Apparently there were many different ways of being enlightened and progressive.

The Enlightenment, since its beginnings in the seventeenth and eighteenth centuries, had been essentially an intellectual movement, and for long its progress had been measured chiefly by the advance of experimental science, of education and literacy, and of individual liberties and constitutional government. In the latter part of the nineteenth century, however, a new and more material measuring rod was applied—that of the machine production of goods. The Generation of Materialism saw industrial machinery on all sides, doing all sorts of work and doing it ever faster and more efficiently. Machinery was indeed dynamic, not static. By a kind of parthenogenesis, it multiplied itself; so that everybody was now minded to talk, in the manner of the enlightened Englishman described by Chesterton, "as if clocks produced clocks, or guns had families of little pistols, or a penknife littered like a pig." And the resulting output of manufactured commodities must continue to grow, it seemed fair to expect, as by a geometric progression approaching infinity.

Increase of mechanical production was tangible and statistically measurable proof of progress—and of progress in which everyone could share and from which were derivable the greatest expectations for the future. By the aid of machinery, the time should soon come, it was reasoned, when nobody need fear famine or inclement weather, when more food would be provided than could be consumed, more clothing made than could be worn, more houses built than could be inhabited. Not just the bare necessities of life would be available, but an abundance and range of luxuries, and withal a leisure and a physical health, beyond the ken of any lord of previous ages. Europe, once reputed a poor and sparse continent, was already rich and populous. The prediction did not seem too sanguine that by the turn of another century at least eight hundred million persons would be living quite comfortably and happily in Europe.

At the turn of the nineteenth century there appeared to be no serious problem about the production of wealth. Machinery was solving it. There were, admittedly, some new-found paradoxes about capitalism and some stubborn problems about the distribution of wealth. But these, too, it was confidently believed, would in time be solved. The Enlightenment had led to machinery and physical health and material wealth, and these things must inevitably lead to still greater and more diffused enlightenment, through which some sort of utopia was sure to be achieved for everybody. Not Marxians alone expected it, but the general run of intellectuals and also industrialists and statesmen. One had only to follow the latest trends of corporate enterprise and social legislation.

Material progress was spatial, as well as temporal. As it had already spread from England to the Continent, so now from Europe it was spreading fanlike to the whole world. This was, after all, the role of the newest imperialism, to Europeanize all the other continents in the sense of superimposing on their several traditional cultures the material civilization of Europe—the same science and technology, the same mechanical modes of production, the same ways of working, traveling, and living. And with common civilization over the entire globe, where could barbarians come from to destroy, or even threaten, the civilization of Europe?

An interesting index to the advancing international character of material civilization was furnished by the series of industrial expositions which had begun with the one in the Crystal Palace at Hyde Park, London, in 1851. None of those held down to and including the Vienna Exposition of 1873 was really "universal" or attended by any extraordinary number of visitors. But then, with the expansion of industry and education and the greater facilities for transport and travel brought about by the extension of railways and steamship lines, a change occurred. At the Philadelphia Exposition of 1876 the display of machinery was the largest and finest yet seen, and the visitors numbered close to ten million.

The Paris Exposition of 1878 covered sixty-six acres of the Champ de Mars, with an Avenue des Nations devoted to specimens of domestic architecture and products of almost every country in Europe (except Germany) and of several in Asia, Africa, and America, and with capstone, on the right bank of the Seine, in the bizarre Palace of the Trocadero. The visitors totaled thirteen million. Still more impressive was the Paris Exposition of 1889. This, covering seventy-two acres, drew its thirty-two million visitors to the latest miracle of steel construction, the Eiffel Tower, a thousand feet high, and especially diverted them with a faithful reproduction of a street in Cairo. Industrial America was host to the next great universal exposition, that of Chicago in 1893, with most countries represented and with plethora of side shows along a "Midway Plaisance."

Then came the Paris Exposition of 1900. It was the climax of one cycle and harbinger of another. It brought to the French capital mountains of marvelous exhibits and multitudes of awe-struck tourists from practically every country of the world, this time including Germany. It was high-lighted with magnificent electrical displays, and graced with two exquisite palaces of the fine arts and a beautiful new bridge named in honor of the Tsar Alexander III. The grounds embraced five hundred and fifty acres, and the attendance reached the amazing figure of thirty-nine million.

As civilization was becoming worldwide, why shouldn't the world have a common language? And if everything else could be manufactured, why not language? Very progressive people were as expectant of synthetic philology as of synthetic rubber, and inventors of either were not lacking. A German priest, Johann Schleyer, invented the odd-looking language of "Volapük" in 1879–1880. A first congress of its devotees was held on Lake Constance in 1884, a second at Munich in 1887, a third at the Paris Exposition of 1889. By this date there were 316 textbooks in the new language.

But in the 1890's Volapük was largely supplanted by a still newer language, the invention of a Polish Jew, Louis Lazarus Zamenhof. He published in 1887 a pamphlet entitled "La Lingvo Internacia de la Doktoro Esperanto," meaning, of course, to English-speaking people, "The International Language of Dr. Hopeful"; and Esperanto was created. It was subsequently improved and perfected, like any industrial product, and in 1898 it began to be advertised by a *French Society for the Propagation of Esperanto.* It was the subject of a paper read before the French Academy in 1889; and at the Paris Exposition of 1900 it was, so to speak, placed upon the world market. Great expectations were attached to the future of Esperanto.

At least to many optimists in the year 1900, a made-to-order world language was but the natural accompaniment of a trend toward a new world order which would be not only mechanically productive but spiritually pacific. One felt pretty sure of this trend as one looked back from 1900 over the preceding quarter-century. One beheld so many ripening fruits of international co-operation—the Universal Postal Union of 1875, the convention of 1883 for the standardization of patent laws and that of 1887 for uniform copyright laws, the succession of world's fairs from the Viennese of 1873 to the Parisian of 1900. What was still more reassuring, one failed to descry latterly within Europe any bloody revolution or deadly civil war or any large-scale international war. Armed conflict was now confined to "backward" areas, principally outside Europe, and was incidental to the imperialism which was Europeanizing and civilizing the world. It appeared reasonable to expect that the trend would continue, that just as the duel and the blood feud had disappeared, just as interurban and internecine warfare had ceased, so in another generation even imperialistic wars would not have to be waged. At any rate, the great civilized powers must already be too intelligent and too humane to resort to war among themselves; and besides, in the face of constantly expanding industrialization, any struggle between huge national armies equipped with the latest mechanical implements of destruction must be quite too costly and too risky. It seemed not inappropriate that the nineteenth century—and the Generation of Materialism—should culminate in the Hague Conference which discussed the limitation of armaments and established the Permanent Court of International Justice.

6. GEORGE L. MOSSE: The Culture of Western Europe*

Professor Mosse † suggests quite a different picture of Europe's mood at the end of the century from that painted by Hayes. Are the views in full contradiction, or do they refer to different sources of opinion? Professor Mosse deals primarily with intellectuals and artists. Did their views coincide with changing values in a broader public, as has been asserted, or, as has also been claimed, was there a growing gulf between them and the leading values of the day? Either view would lead to a more complex evaluation of the late nineteenth century than that suggested by Hayes; and here, the suggestion that the coherent nineteenth century ended more significantly in 1870 than in 1914 is worth noting.

Benedetto Croce (1866–1952) saw in the years after 1870 a change in the public spirit of Europe which ended the nineteenth century and began the twentieth. In politics such a change was clear enough—the two nations of Germany and Italy were now unified, and within each nation, a strong and politically conscious labor movement arose. The decades after 1870 saw the founding of most modern fortunes and, in spite of some crises, a remarkable wave of prosperity engulfed society. The upper-middle classes, which benefited most by these good times, felt secure, and this smugness seemed, at least to the critics of bourgeois society, to climax the *embourgeoisement* of Europe. Though today we know that these decades spelled the end of this kind of security even as it reached its climax, many of these critics, who could not foresee the total destruction the First World War would bring, felt that these years were the beginning of a dreary prospect (bourgeois society) that stretched endlessly into the future.

National pride and bourgeois security went hand in hand during these years. They, in fact, urged on the drive for a positivist, scientific explanation of the world. Here reality was identified with matter. Materialism as discussed in the last chapter was used not only to give meaning to the aspirations of the working classes, but also to explain and support the acquisitive society. It is small wonder, therefore, that as man passed from the nineteenth to the twentieth century he was met by a variety of movements which attempted to revolt against this state of affairs. Some Marxists sought to temper their materialism through an infusion of idealism. In like manner, others, working from a bourgeois context, found their way back to a revived romanticism and attempted to find in the search for beauty a consolation for the drabness of their age. Chateaubriand, Matthew Arnold, and others had taken this road during the height of romanticism; Stefan George and many others would do so again in the new century. Young people tried to escape the prison of bourgeois convention by fleeing to the countryside and, with the *Wandervoegel* (Roamers),

* From George L. Mosse, *The Culture of Western Europe* (Chicago: Rand McNally & Co., 1961), pp. 213–15; 224–30. Reprinted by permission of Rand McNally & Company.

† See Chapter 2, on romanticism.

began the history of the modern youth movements. Though much of this repudiation of the material world was of an antibourgeois nature, middle-class society itself was not wholly materialistic and given over totally to books like Haeckel's *Riddle of the Universe* (1899). For here, too, there was an escapism from the drabness of everyday existence, an escapism which manifested itself in the popularity of Wagner's operas or the acceptance of racial ideas and ideals. The bourgeoisie tended to fasten onto national themes and aspirations. Not in a cult of beauty or nature but in an emotional nationalism did the middle classes seek escape from a material society to which they paid apparent outward allegiance.

This change of public spirit after 1870 tended toward a recapturing of the irrational—a revolt against positivism which was later to form part of the totalitarian movements of our century. Many people accepted the positivist definition of the universe, to be sure, but the dominant modes of thought tended to become increasingly antipositivistic. This has led Stuart Hughes to write about an "intellectual revolution" as a number of thinkers, independently of one another, proposed views quite different from those society accepted. They all tried to penetrate behind the façade of the material world, to return to a preoccupation with man's consciousness of himself, placing a renewed stress upon the role of the unconscious in the formation of man and his society. Small wonder that this period not only saw a revival of romanticism and idealism but was also the age in which Sigmund Freud (1856–1939) did his most important work. As André Gide was to write, looking back over his life, "how much stronger are innate values than acquired ones." For him, "in spite of every kind of starching, dressing, pressing and folding, the natural stuff persists and remains unchanged—stiff or limp as it was originally woven." It was the changeless substratum of man which was important; his environment changed man in only a superficial way. It became the task of writers and artists to capture this base of human nature while political theorists like Vilfredo Pareto (1848–1933) attempted to manipulate it for the sake of strong government and Georges Sorel for the sake of revolution. Reality, material reality, was the "myth" beneath which man's irrational impulses worked.

The change from impressionism to expressionism in art provides a good example of this new definition of reality. The impressionist artist grasped reality's movement and color with his eye. What he painted was, to him, an actual representation of reality. The artist's form of expression was subjective, personal, but what he expressed about the world was what he could obtain through visual impression. The Expressionists did not want to picture the world as it seemed to the human eye; they wanted to penetrate beneath any visual reality to those forces which they believed to be behind reality. Real art was not the formal reproduction of visual experiences, but instead a projection of those basic urges, those soul experiences which underlay reality. Traditional form and beauty must be sacrificed for the expression of the tormented soul of the artist. . . .

The frustration and conflicts which engulfed this group of writers is important beyond the kind of literary merit it gave to their works. This product of the revolt against a positivistic society became the distinguishing feature of a whole class of intellectuals who were the best minds of their respective nations. Concretely, it meant a withdrawal from participation in the concerns of their society. When later in life Gide wrote his *Journals* he expunged from them any reference to contemporary affairs lest they interfere with aesthetic judgments and form. What these intellectuals denied was the importance of drab, everyday political life. Though most despaired of ever attaining it, many idealistically held to a vision of a new society. This idealism was divorced from parliamentary democracy, however. The squabbles of political parties and their humdrum personalities seemed dreary, "external," and conventional. This attitude led such intellectuals into sympathy with totalitarian, if idealistic, concepts of society. Gide, for a time, joined the Communist party, and Benedetto Croce held the Italian Parliament contemptible—he fought fascism only at that moment when it seemed opposed to artistic creativity. Many others, despairing that man's internal conflicts would ever be resolved, doubted that society could be improved or, indeed, that it was worth improving.

The political attitude of these intellectuals was paralleled by a growing realization, on a more popular level, that there were human longings which established society did not satisfy. The feeling, especially strong in Germany, that romanticism had a greater validity than positivism has already been mentioned. Moreover, the racial movements which were gathering strength toward the end of the century symbolized an emotionally-directed undercurrent in much of Europe. The political successes of the Prussian Stoeckers' and the Austrian Luegers' combination of Christianity and race testifies to the growing strength of these tendencies among popular aspirations. Though only the First World War brought these trends into prominence, their organization as political faiths, and their survival as such, took place during this period. Haeckel was read side by side with Houston Stewart Chamberlain or De Lagarde. On the nonpolitical level, popular taste had never accepted a positivistic explanation of life and of man's emotions. The penny novel in England or the works of Courths-Mahler in Germany provided escape through romantic love, stimulating the heartfelt tears of many a servant girl.

This intellectual atmosphere had another consequence, though its true importance was only revealed after the First World War. A group of men attempted to find the reality behind the myth of the material world in a purely emotional and mystical direction. Where men like Pareto tried to harness man's emotion for the purposes of government, and all the men discussed saw a conflict between society and sincerity, this group turned to a kind of mysticism. They rejected existent society because it represented progress and therefore a material orientation. Instead they looked back to a past which had not been materialistic, a past whose reality they felt "intuitively." In Munich, Alfred Schuler (1865–1923) thought that conventional progress had led to a dark and evil goal; its course through history had obliterated those antique "times of light" which he himself still felt, and which in his own mind he relived so vividly. As early as

1895 he saw in the swastika a symbol of an era unstained by modern rationality and which, as the ancient sign of the wheel, signified the "open life" recalling a harmonious past. Concentrating around Schuler in Munich and in another group in Vienna, these men rejected modern intellectualism, reason, and progress for an intuitively-felt past. They combined this with anti-Christian ideas, for they felt Christianity had smashed this past in constructing the modern world. Moreover, Christianity sprang from Judaism which, in the name of progress, conspired to defeat the intuitive and harmonious life. Schuler believed himself to be the new embodiment of a never-extinguished ideal of the primitive and Roman past. In Austria, Lanz von Liebenfels founded a new order of Templars to keep the flame alight. He also proclaimed Judaism the enemy, and in his case the Germanic and Aryan past represented true, intuitive reality.

We may smile at Liebenfels' or at Schuler's symbolic mysticism, but these movements, though small and unimportant at the end of the century, had a double significance for the future. They supplied one element of the national socialist ideology. Second, they exhibited in an exaggerated fashion the lengths to which the revolt against positivism would go.

These men believed that their ideals possessed a tremendous magnetism for the hopeless, rationalistic world of the present, but pessimism seen in men of far greater intellectual stature also contributed to their ideology. Some took to the spiritualism of Madame Blavatsky or to the fad for Oriental sects which promised nirvana from the present. Only one thinker of great importance attempted to break through this pessimistic retreat into mysticism. Friedrich Nietzsche tried to extract from the intellectual atmosphere something positive: to affirm where others had merely despaired, to transform human values where others had either thought this transformation impossible or had looked for it in a revival of a mystical past. While the men already discussed searched for truth, Nietzsche rejected truth itself as a constant: ". . . *fiat veritas, pereat vita.*"

Man was constantly modifying his values. In place of truth he has images only, according to Nietzsche. Therefore man abandoning himself to the forces of life must be shocked into a conscious self-awareness. "God is dead," and the human situation will not be helped by creating gods in a vain search for security which, because no truth exists, must be artificial. Nietzsche's target was contemporary society. Despite what society believed, "happiness and virtue are no arguments"; they were self-deceptions, for there were also in society "the wicked who are happy and about those the moralists are silent." Many of Nietzsche's writings were given over to the destruction of this false security and its attendant self-deceptions. In reality chaotic man lived in a chaotic universe, and to master this reality man must detach himself from the preconceptions of society, indeed from society itself.

Society was, for Nietzsche, inimical to man; therefore any idea that man must lead a socially useful life was also misleading. Above all Christianity, with its tendency toward slave morality, was the enemy. To Nietzsche, slave morality was the idea of service to society and, beyond that, the concept of the equality of man. Christianity was the forerunner of democracy and thus, by burying man within the group, had defeated man's attempt to deal with the chaos of life. Christianity was the morality of the Old Testament in decay, a morality which Nietzsche saw symbolized in the old patriarchs—autonomous man, wicked and sensual. They were not inhibited and limited by the devouring urge for security. For Nietzsche, however, true man was embodied not so much in the Old Testament as in the classical tradition. He did not want to revive the past as did Schuler and his group; instead Nietzsche chose one part of the classical tradition as the true path for modern man's salvation. The barbarian was the crux of this tradition, for to Nietzsche, he was the true transformer of values.

The phrase "transformation of values" can, however, be misleading, for the barbarian totally discarded the values of society and created his own. Man was, after all, as Nietzsche put it, "suspended in a void." If this were true how could man cope with his chaotic world? Nietzsche's answer was that man must live both in conflict and in harmony with this world. He must live "cosmically," revering life and life alone, but he must also master the chaos of life. Man could only master the chaos of the world by resisting it. His enemy was the maelstrom into which man was born in hate and violence. But this resistance could only be successful if man accepted life in a void and faced his own nature. Such a new barbarian was beyond good and evil as society had understood them since the victory of Christianity. For resisting meant abandoning yourself to the world, taking risks and making sacrifices. Nietzsche believed, with Darwin, that life was a universal and invisible force. Man must give way to this force if he were to cope with the world. This life force was a positive thing, and to give oneself to it meant the release of all positive passions—"pride, joy, health, sexual love, enmity and war." To accomplish this man needed what Nietzsche called the will to power, for the will to power reinforced man's will to life. Such a man Nietzsche characterized with the Greek term of "Dionysian man," a barbarian who created his own values, since, through his will to power, he entered fully into the force of life, mastering the chaos of the world by affirming it.

Man was at war, perpetually at war, but this war was won through the will for power and through becoming a Dionysian man rather than a bourgeois man. Nietzsche's individualism meant complete alienation from the mass of men. In Zarathustra he portrayed a man determined to convert the world to these ideas. He fails to influence the common people; he fails to form a coterie—only when he goes out into the world alone, by himself, is he the true superman. Nietzsche did come to believe in an elite of supermen, but they were all individuals suspended in the void. At the end of his life, just prior to his insanity, he discovered the incarnation of his barbarian in the Germanic sagas, but nationalism was as foreign to his thought as racism. Anti-Semitism was a feeble expression of the mass instinct for security, and in man's eternal struggle for mastery over chaos nationalism could play no part. Indeed one of his heroes was the Italian Cesare Borgia, not because Borgia unified central Italy, but because he seemed to create his own values.

Nietzsche's rejection of positivism led to an affirmation of life. From this vantage point Nietzsche called upon youth to rid itself of the burden of conventional learning. In his attack upon the German educational system he was at one with the Expressionists and the youth movement. The rote learning of factual knowledge, the idea of knowledge for the sake of knowledge, was sharply rejected. For Nietzsche such education was a part of that fear of life which led to a search for security, part of the instinct of a people whose "nature is still feeble and uncertain." How different this is from Schopenhauer's concept of nirvana or his retreat into scholarship! The will of man which Schopenhauer exalted and feared Nietzsche accepted unquestionably as the true expression of man. His attack on contemporary education inspired the revolt already mentioned, as did his rejection of the bourgeois age in general.

Nietzsche's influence was furthered by another facet of his work. His thought was never entirely clearly stated, for he wrote as if in ecstasy, especially in those passages which described life and its affirmation. As a result later movements tried to capitalize on his name. His sister gave Hitler his walking stick as a symbolic gesture of succession. Yet how Nietzsche would have despised a movement like national socialism, a movement founded on the manipulation of the "herd" which he despised! Others tried to use his ideas for national or racial purposes, emphasizing Nietzsche's stress upon ancient times in an attempt to play off the past against the present. But again, Nietzsche's individualism would have been appalled by such a misuse of his ideas. Above all, one group of men saw in him their founder, and this, once more, with only partial justification. These were nihilists who called themselves "revolutionaries without banners," those who despised all ideologies in the name of an undisciplined attempt to fulfill themselves. They will be met after the First World War in the German Free Corps, but, unlike their supposed master, they banded together in groups stressing a leadership principle quite foreign to Nietzsche's thought.

Nietzsche's greatest influence as a catalyst of revolt against the present was a vague one. Reading his ecstatic prose, generations longed somehow to free themselves of conventions and affirm life, to live it at the fullest. He sounded a much clearer call to arms than the tortured Gide or the other groups discussed. Nietzsche had grasped the illness of the times when he wrote that "the inhabitants of this Europe live in the midst of countless uncertainties and contradictions." But his solution was too extreme to produce a school of thought, though it did serve as an inspiration for other revolts against society.

It is useful at this point to contrast Nietzsche with that man who in France came to stand for the change in the spirit of European philosophy, Henri Bergson (1859–1944). The differences between the two men seem to summarize a difference between the temper of this thought in Germany and France. Bergson also believed in the primacy of intuition, and in his *Creative Evolution* (1907) he equated this with an *élan vital*. This *élan* was close to the instinct of the animal world; it was a tremendous drive inherent in man which could enable him to overcome all resistance, perhaps even death itself.

Bergson's *élan vital* seems to run parallel to Nietzsche's lust for life. But this is not so, for the French philosopher did not negate the intellect. It led not to a denial but to a deepening of the life spirit. Only through his mental faculties can man comprehend the irrational stream of life. Intuition was redefined as "intellectual sympathy" through which man's mind must learn to grasp fluid concepts—the constantly changing reality as the *élan vital* drives man forward. The faculties of the mind were important to the Frenchman, and he called his ideas "not anti-intellectual but supra-intellectual"; they completed but did not destroy the intellect. Their result was to be a reinvigorating of the human spirit. At the close of his life Bergson intended to join the Catholic faith which seemed to penetrate the deeper layer of consciousness with a similar emphasis upon reason (the intellect), as well as upon the spiritualization of man. The exuberance of the *élan vital* was drowned in both spiritualization and the stress upon the intellect.

This is quite different from Nietzsche. Bergson, for all his drives of the mystical unconscious, could not shake and did not want to shake the strong tradition of rationalism in France, a tradition which hardly existed in Germany and which had, in that country, been almost obliterated by romanticism. Bergson also shows the strength of Catholic thought in France which retained intellectual vitality despite the rightist stances of the hierarchy. Bergson with his *élan vital* is a part of the changed European intellectual atmosphere, yet in France this change was never to lead to the excesses of a sheer ecstatic or mystical irrationalism like that of Schuler or of Nietzsche himself.

The last years of the century saw a change in the ideological climate of Europe. We have called it the revolt against positivism which became a dissatisfaction with society, an attempt at disassociating reality and materialism. Men tried to look beneath the externals into the depths of their own immaterial and irrational natures. In all of this there was something reminiscent of romanticism which, in reaction to the materialism of the eighteenth century, had attempted to do something of the same sort. In fact, did the specifically romantic impetus extend from the nineteenth into the twentieth century?